Massachusetts Historical Society

Founded 1791

WINTHROP

PAPERS

VOLUME IV

1638-1644

The Massachusetts Historical Society

1944

Published at the Charge of the Robert Winthrop Fund

THE MERRYMOUNT PRESS, BOSTON, MASS., U. S. A.

PREFACE

THE fourth volume of the *Winthrop Papers* covers a span of seven years, 1638–1644. Using it as a vantage point, one can trace, with varying degrees of completeness, all the major threads in the increasingly complex web of New England history as it was spun out during those years.

There is a note of optimism at the beginning and again at the conclusion of these pages. Early in 1638 the leaders of Puritan orthodoxy sealed their triumph over the Antinomian heresy by the banishment of the leading schismatics. By 1644 there was good reason to believe that the economic foundations of the new colonies had been soundly laid.

The intervening period, however, witnessed difficulties in full store. Each expansion of English settlement not only created new possibilities of conflict with the Indian population but also gave rise to new political strains and jealousies to disturb the relations between the various colonial jurisdictions. At the same time, as though troubles of purely local origin were not enough, the Puritans in New England discovered to their dismay that they had to pay heavily for political victories won by their sympathizers at home over their common enemy, Charles I. Early in 1640 Governor Winthrop's correspondents in England began to send warnings that the improvement in political conditions there would result in a sharp decline in the volume of emigration to New England, with consequent harmful repercussions on the local economy. Events speedily proved the correctness of these gloomy prognostications. Not only did the boom of the first decade quickly vanish; it was even discovered that it required the most vigorous sort of leadership to scotch a movement for the abandonment of the whole New England enterprise. It is regrettable that the Winthrops' correspondence for the years that saw

the beginning of economic recovery has not survived in greater full-
ness. But a fair sample of the ingenuity by which the threats of disaster were overcome can be found in these pages in the beginning of
the story of the younger John Winthrop's mining and ironworks
enterprises, significant details about which are now made available
for the first time.

The documents presented here illuminate the characters of all the
leading New England personages of the day, none more completely
than that of Governor Winthrop. These were for him years of great
and trying contrasts, for in the course of them he was both at the
peak of his personal powers and influence and at the lowest ebb of
his material fortunes. The character that emerges from these pages is
a noble tribute to the faith to which he was dedicated.

ARTHUR MEIER SCHLESINGER
For the Committee of Publication

JULY 1, 1944

CONTENTS

Papers designated by an asterisk are now printed for the first time.

1642

1643

ADDENDA

ILLUSTRATIONS

LIST OF ABBREVIATIONS

Collections   Massachusetts Historical Society, *Collections* (Boston, 1792–   ).

D.A.B.   *Dictionary of American Biography*, Allen Johnson and Dumas Malone, Editors, 20 vols. (New York, 1928–1936).

D.N.B.   *Dictionary of National Biography*, Leslie Stephen et al., Editors, 63 vols. (London, 1885–1900).

G.S.   Gorges Society, *George Cleeve of Casco Bay, 1630–1667, with Collateral Documents*, James Phinney Baxter, Editor, II (Portland, Maine, 1885).

L. and L.   *Life and Letters of John Winthrop*, Robert C. Winthrop, Editor, 2 vols. (2nd ed., Boston, 1869).

N.C.   "The Letters of Roger Williams," John R. Bartlett, Editor, *Publications of the Narragansett Club*, First Series, VI (Providence, 1874).

Proceedings   Massachusetts Historical Society, *Proceedings* (Boston, 1859–   ).

Savage, 1825   John Winthrop, *The History of New England from 1630 to 1649*, James Savage, Editor, I (Boston, 1825).

Savage, 1826   The same. II (Boston, 1826).

Savage, 1853   The same. 2 vols. (Boston, 1853).

Twichell   *Some Old Puritan Love-Letters: John and Margaret Winthrop, 1618–1638*, J. H. Twichell, Editor (New York, 1893).

W. Au., W. Deeds, W. 1, 1B., 2, 3, 4, 5, 7A., 10, 11, 12, 14, 15, 18, 19   Manuscript volumes of Winthrop Papers in the Library of the Massachusetts Historical Society.

WINTHROP PAPERS

Volume IV

1638–1644

WINTHROP PAPERS

ROGER WILLIAMS TO JOHN WINTHROP[1]

For his much honoured Mr. Governour these

SIR, Having vsed many meanes and many Atturnies (in my absence) to recover a debt of Mr. George Ludlow, and fayled by all, and now last of all by Richard Collicut[2] who vndertooke seriously, but comes of weakly in it: let me humbly beg what helpe in a righteous way may be affoorded (now in his departure) to cause him to deale honestly with me who haue many yeares and in many wants bene patient toward him. The debt was for mine owne and wiues better apparell put of to him at Plymmouth. My bills are lost, but his owne hand which the bearer will deliver is testimony sufficient. He hath vsed so many slights and told so many false hoods that sir, if you believe more then you see, I must patiently giue my debt for desperate: howeuer with my best respects to your kind selfe and Mrs. Wintrop, and sighes to heaven for you, I rest Your Worships vnfaignedly faythfull till death

ROGER WILLIAMS

[*Ca.* 1638]

ROGER WILLIAMS TO JOHN WINTHROP[3]

For his much honoured Mr. Governour of the Massachusets these

MUCH HONOURED SIR, I was bould to present you with 2 letters by Thomas Holyway, some weekes since. I am occasioned againe at present to write a word by this bearer Wequash: whome (being a Pequt himselfe) I commended for a guide in the Pequt Expedition.

I presume he may say something to your selfe or to such other of my loving friends as may report vnto your Wo[rshi]p what befell him at Cowesett.

He hath bene 5 or 6 dayes now at my howse in which time I haue had much opportunitie to search into Particulars, and am able to present you with naked Truth.

He came from Monahiganick to Coweeset within night and lodged with his friend called Pananawokshin. At Cowweesit an old man (Weeokamin) hath made great Lamentation for the death of 2 Sons in the Pequt Warrs.

---

[1] Original not located; 4 *Collections,* VI. 212; *N.C.,* VI. 65. For Williams, see *D.A.B.*
[2] See Roger Williams to Richard Collicott, September 12, 1637, *Winthrop Papers,* III. 496–497.
[3] W. 2. 108; 4 *Collections,* VI. 242–244; *N.C.,* VI. 242–244.

This Weeokamun with divers of his Consorts in the night time layd hold vpon Wequash intending to bind him, charging him with the death of his 2 Sonns: Much bickring there was betweene them, but no hurt done only Weeokamun strugling with one of Wequash his Company was sore bitten on his hand and also bit the young mans fingers which are well againe. So that their Host kept peace in Caunounicus his name and brought them safe to me the next day: Yet in the Fray they lost a Coate and other small things, which (comming forth before day) they left behind them.

I sent vp a Messenger to the Sachims to demaund a reason of such vsage and their goods: Caunounicus sent his Sonn and Miantunnomu his brother (Yotaash) who went to Cowweeset and demaunded the reason of such vsage and the goods and so came to my howse causing the goods to be restored, professing the Sachims Ignorance and Sorrow for such passages, and giving charge to all Natiues for their safe travell.

Having those Messengers and Wequash at my howse I caused them sollemnly to parley of what I knew was grievance betwixt them, and what els I could any way pick out from either of them concerning our selues the English, or the Pequts, or themselues. All which I carefully writt downe the particulars, and shall readily at your Wo[rshi]ps pleasure acquaint you with them: either concerning some Squaws which Wequash acknowledgeth he parted with (and iustly) to Caunounicus and Miantunnomu, or other brablings which I thought not fit to trouble your Wo[rshi]p with, without Commission.

Deare Sir (notwithstanding our differences concerning the Worship of God and the Ordinances ministred by Antichrists power) you haue bene always pleased lovingly to answer my boldnes in civill things: let me once more find favour in your Eyes to gratifie my selfe Mr. James and many or most of the Townesmen combined, in advising what to say or doe to one vnruly Person who openly in Towne meeting more then once, professeth to hope for and long for a better Government then the Countrey hath yet, and lets not to particularize, by a generall Governour, etc. The white which such a Speech or Person levells at can be no other then the Rasing of the Fundamentall Liberties of the Countrey, which ought to be dearer to vs then our Right Eyes. But I am allwayes too bold in prolixitie, etc. therefore at present with humble respect remembred and Cries to Heaven for Mercy to you and yours Roote and Branches and the whole Countrey by your Blessing I rest Your Wo[rshi]ps most vnworthy

ROGER WILLIAMS

[Ca. 1638]

Sir, Mr. James and his, my wife and selfe respectiuely salute your honoured selfe and Mrs. Wintrop.

Wequash intends to beg of you and requested me to specify his desire of a Coate, Wastcote and shirt etc. which I could not deny though your wisedome may doe as seemes good.

JOHN WINTHROP TO JOHN WINTHROP, JR.[1]

To my loving sonne mr. John Winthrop at Ipswich

Sonne, I received your lettre and doe blesse the Lorde for your recovery and the wellfare of your family. you must be very carefull of taking colde about your loynes: and when the grounde is open I will send you some pepper-worte roots. for the fluxe there is no better medicine then the Cuppe vsed 2 or 3 times: and in case of suddain torments a Clyster of a quart of water boyled to a pint which with the quantity of 2 or 3 nuttmeggs of Salt-peeter boiled in it will give present ease.

for the pilles they are made of grated peper made vp with turpentine, very stiff, and some flouer withall: and 4 or 5 taken fasting and fast 2 howers after but if ther be any feauer with the flux: this must not be vsed till the feauer be removed by the Cupp. this bearer is in great hast and so am I so with our blessing to you and yours and salutations to all etc. I rest your loving father

Jo. Winthrop

[*Ca.* 1638]

this bearer can tell you all the newes, which is come from England by the fishing shipps etc.

[*Written below the superscription:*] Salutem tibi Tuæque plurimam in Christo Jesu.

Joh: Wilson

HUGH PETER TO JOHN WINTHROP, JR.[2]

NEWES

Deerest Sir, We haue a fishing ship come in hither of 200 tuns the M[aste]r Mr. King shee belongs to Mr. Hooke of Bristoll whose son dwells

---

[1] W. 7A. 62; Savage (1825), 394; (1853), I. 474; *L. and L.*, II. 265–266.
[2] W. 2. 50; 4 *Collections*, VI. 94–95. For Peter, see *D.A.B.*

at Agamenticus and marryed Capt: Nortons widdow, to whom his father hath sent 10 cowes and not lost one by the way, lesse then 10 weekes coming from Bristoll. All they say is That Capt: Raynsborough is come from Sally, brough[t] 140 slaues English made a peace with the K[ing] of Morocco, who beleaguered it by land whilst ours did it by sea, and it was deliuerd by accord. 20 Morocco gallants came home to our K[ing] with presents a great fleet goes for Angier. Not a Turke about our Coasts. some ships are making ready this way. Corne cheaper here then in England.

INVOYCE

Butter at 7d per li.	Mascadine 6d 6s
Cheese at 7d per li.	Irish beefe the hun: 50s
Sack the gal. 6s	Irish rugs 14s

they are so deere wee shall not deale with them. Another ship is gone into Pascataway; they had the cold storme at sea.[1] Boston-men are thinking of Delaware Bay. Mr. Prudden goes to Quinipiak, Mr. Dauenport may sit down at Cha[rles]towne. Mr. Eaton very ill of the skurvey. An eele py. Angells appeare at Boston. be secret. Your sister Symonds recouering. Bendall hath buryed his wife.[2]

Another eele py. Wee haue tomorrow morning Jiggells going to your Governour laden with wood; some died of the frost at Boston. I wish you were here to goe with vs to Boston 2d day. Salute your wife from vs. I am you know

H: P.

[*Ca.* January, 1637/38]

I pray pay Samuel Greenfield 10s for mee he is of your towne and will come to you.

HUGH PETER TO JOHN WINTHROP[3]

To our noble Gouernor these deliver Boston

SIR, I humbly thanke you for your tender care of vs to let vs to vnderstand how the lord hath honored himselfe vpon these heathen; I am afrayd that

---

[1] Cf. *Winthrop's Journal*, "*History of New England*," *1630–1649*, James K. Hosmer, Editor (New York, 1908), I. 258. Subsequent references to the Journal are to this edition unless otherwise indicated.

[2] Ann Bendall, wife of Edward Bendall, died December 25, 1637.

[3] W. 2. 55; 4 *Collections*, VI. 102–103.

these women and children are not where they should bee, nor can I foresee euents.

For this woman that troubles you thus: indeed shee should haue any thing from mee were fit, but shee hath already bin very chargeable, and in conscience I cannot answer her desire. Shee hath 4 spoones, six slighter I sold Mr. Endecot which are euen broken with thinnes and for lynnen it is most disposed of: but I haue striuen to giue her satisfaction by a letter to Mrs. Wilson. I desire my cossen Stephen should pay her passage, and 4*li* out of my beuer; and that shee may haue all conuenient content; I think a few words of your selfe would doe it.

I was at Ipswich where the towne haue dealt very nobly with your son, and giuen him another farme neere the towne called Castle-hill,[1] where hee hath 100 akers of medow, and all intire to himselfe: but of this hee hath written to you. I intend to bee with you on Monday   still remembring you all to him in whom I am Yours if any thing

H: PETER

SALEM 5 day [*ca.* January, 1637/38]

Mr. Endecot and Ancient Reade wonder at your bounty in your Graynes sent etc.

RICHARD SALTONSTALL, JR., TO JOHN WINTHROP[2]

To our worthy honoured Governour John Winthrop Esqr. deliver Boston

HONOURED SIR, I had not any oportunitie (before this) that I was aware of, to lett you know, that vppon my comming hoame I agreed with goodman Medcalfe to bring aboute the boate; (shee was then frozen in) but there beeing possibilitie to gett her out, wee intended to procure the helpe of many of the towne the next day; and that very night it did freeze soe bitterly that wee sawe, it would bee in vayne to endeauour it, if wee could have had all the hands in the towne. It would very much have contented mee if by any means I could have procured you the vse of her this winter. And for the boate itselfe I must crave leave to sett my owne prise (which shall bee much more then shee is worth) and that is, your acceptance, without any further troble

---

[1] According to the Ipswich town records, Castle Hill was granted to John Winthrop, Jr., on January 13, 1637/38. Thomas F. Waters, *A Sketch of the Life of John Winthrop the Younger* (Cambridge, 1899), 23.

[2] W. 3. 68; 4 *Collections*, VII. 254. For Saltonstall, see 4 *Collections*, VII. 251n.

to your selfe, or thought aboute it (directly, or indirectly). If you deale otherwise with mee, truly, I shall count it an abatement of the prise I have sett
vppon her. It is but a meane testimony of my duty, and thankfullnesse,
where soe much, (and indeede my selfe toe) is more then due. I have very
good cause to make such accompt in regard of your greate love and favour
to mee; although you have seene my vnworthynesse therof. Thus with my
humble duty and sarvice to yourselfe, besceeching the lord that (in much
marcy to vs all) your life and health may bee prætious in his eyes, I take my
leave and shall ever rest, yours vnfaynedly

RICHARD SALTONSTALL

[*Ca.* January, 1637/38]

EDWARD RAINSFORD'S BILL OF EXCHANGE[1]

*To his Louinge Master: Mr. Owen Rowe at the signe of the three golden Keyes
in Cheape Syde*

BOSTONNE January the [*torn*] 1637[/38]

SIR, This is to intreat you to p[ay] [at] 20 dayes sight to pay to the Assignes
of Mr. John Winthorpe the some of Fowreteene poundes for soe muche
Receaued for your vse heere, this beinge my first bille the second not beinge
payde I say the some of 14*li*

per me EDWARD RAYNSFORD

ROGER WILLIAMS TO JOHN WINTHROP[2]

PROVIDENCE 10th of the 11th mon: [1637/38]

MUCH HONOURED SIR, It having pleased the most high to besiege vs all with
his white Legions[3] I reioice at this occasion from Qunnihticut (these letters
sent to me by Mr. Hooker) that I may here of your wellfare and health,
which I wish and beg vnfaignedly of the Lord.

Mr. Hooker intimates a report to me that they heare from the Monahiganeucks that Miantunnomu intends Tho: Stantons death: I haue taken
some paines in it and other passages sent me finding them slanders: and since

---

[1] W. 1. 122. For Rainsford, see James Savage, *A Genealogical Dictionary of the First Settlers of New
England*, III (Boston, 1861), 502.

[2] W. 2. 104; 4 *Collections*, VI. 221–223; *N.C.*, VI. 84–85.

[3] In the margin: "Job 38. 23."

(for many good ends and) for keeping a passage open betweene yourselues and Qunnihticut by natiues Summer and winter a peace is much to be desired betweene the Monahig: and Nanhiggon I have proffered my paines in procuring a meeting of the Averse Sachims if it please the Magistrates of Qunnihticut to order Wokace (the Monahig Sachim) to touch in at the Nanhiggonset mouth where I hope to get the Nanhiggonset Sachims aboord, and it may please the God of Peace to saue much blood and evill, etc.

Only it behooues our friends of Qunnihticut as I haue writ to them to looke to the 2 or 300 Pequts harboured by Wocase the Monahiggen as allso Wm. Baker of Plymmouth (of whome formerly I wrote) who is there hid, is turned Indian in nakednes and cutting of haire, and after many whoredomes, is there maried: this fire brand with those Pequts may fire whole Townes: I haue intimated how they may with ease take him.

Sir, let me [be] humbly bold to request a favour of you: I am at present destitute of a Man Servant, and much desire if you light on one that desires to feare the Lord remember me: I haue a lustie Canow and shall haue occasion to runn downe often to the Iland (neere 20 mile from vs) both with mine owne, and (I desire allso freely) your wo[rshi]ps swine, so that my want is greatt; I would spare no charge, either out of those beads and Coate in your owne hand: the Tobacco from Mr. Ludlow, and 8 or 10*li* in James and Tho: Hawkins hand of which I heare not yet.

Sir If any letters from your selfe or other friends are for Qunnihticut I entreate you make hast and speede by this messenger for I cause 4 natiues who came from Qunnihticut to stay his Comming: I haue allready paid him so that his expectation is not great. Thus longing to heare of your healths and with earnest and dayly wishes for that peace which this world cannot giue nor take from you and my poore wiues and mine owne best Salutes to your dearest Companion I rest Your Wo[rshi]ps to my power faythfull

ROGER WILLIAMS

My due respects to Mr. Deputie Mr. Bellingham theirs, and other lo[ving] friends etc.

ANN HOSKINS TO JOHN WINTHROP, JR.[1]

DEERE COSEN, my best respets remembred unto you and my son if he be liveing I am very mush trobled that I could never here from my son nor

[1] W. Au. 70. Ann Hoskins, wife of Henry Hoskins, was a daughter of John Winthrop, Governor Winthrop's uncle, by his second wife.

from you sense hee left me   i should be very glad if i did but know wher my son were liveing or dead   my hosband hath ben dead this three eare and there is none of us alive but I and my dafter   I have wished myselfes with you many times   I have ben here in iarland ever sens you left me but I can get nothing of my land and i have mush adoo to live here   you bromised me to send mee word as sune as you ware ouer but i doe mush admire that i colde neuer here from you all this wile   I pray if my son be living let him riht me a letter and send word how hee is as sune as he can   I hope you have don the part of a kinsman for him as you promised mee   I shoold be very glad if pleas god i could see my child again   if he were with me againe i should never part with him for he hath put me to mush sorow and greue for him ever sens he left.

this praying to god bles my son and to make him his sarand and so I giveing you many thankes for your last kindnes my dafter and i both re-member our serves to you and her love to her brother willum Hoskins and so i rest your ever loving kinswoman

ANN HOSKINS

ienuary the 13, [1637/38]

[*Endorsed by John Winthrop, Jr.:*] Cos: An: Hoskins from Ireland.

JOHN WINTHROP TO WILLIAM
CODDINGTON, JOHN COGGESHALL, AND WILLIAM COLBURN[1]

*To my worthy friends and beloued breth[ren] mr. Coddington, mr. Coxall
and mr. Colburn*

BEL[OVED] BR[ETHREN], I mett lately with the Remo[nstrance] subscribed by yourselves with others   I must confess I saw it once before, but had not then tyme to reade it advisedly, as now I have. I hope soon (by Gods assist-ance) to make it appear, what wrong hath been done to the Court yea and to the truth it self, by that rashe, unwarranted and seditious enterprise: In the mean tyme I thought fitt, to advertise you of some miscarriages therein: and though your Countenancing of others in the like practice leaves me small hope, that you will hearken to my counsel in this, yet in disch[arge] of

[1] W. I. 120; Savage (1825), 403–404; (1853), I. 483–484; *L. and L.*, II. 214–215. For Codding-ton, see *D.A.B.*; Emily Coddington Williams, *William Coddington of Rhode Island* (Newport, R. I., 1941). For Coggeshall, see Savage, *Genealogical Dictionary*, I. 421. For Colburn, see *ibid.*, 423.

my duty and broth[erly] respect towards you, I have given this attempt, and shall leave the success to God.

1: In this you have broke the bounds of your calling, that you did publish such a writinge, when you were no members of the Court.

2: In that you tax the Court with iniustice.

3: In that you affirm that all the Acts of that mai[or] part of that C[our]t are voide, whereby you goe about, to overthrow the foundation of our Com-[mon]w[ealth] and the peace thereof: by turning all our magistrates out of Office, and by nullifying all our Laws.

4. In that you invite the bodye of the people, to ioyn with you in your seditious attempt against the Court, and the Aut[horit]y here estab[lished] against the rule of the Ap[ost]le, who requires every soule to be subiect to the higher powers and every Ch[ristia]n man, to studye to be quiet, and to meddle with his own business.

I earnestly desire you, to consider seriously of these things: and if it pl[ease] the Lo[rd] to open your eyes, to see your failings, it wilbe much ioy to me, and (I doubt not but) the C[our]t wilbe very redy to pass them by, and accept of your submission. and it may be a meanes of a further and firmer reconciliation, which the L[or]d grant, and in his good tyme effect, so I rest your loving broth[er]

J:W:

xith 15: 1637[/38][1]

JOHN WINTHROP TO JOHN WINTHROP, JR.[2]

To his verye lovinge sonne Mr. John Winthrop at Ipswich deliver

MY GOOD SONNE, I received your Lettre, and doe heartyly reioyce and blesse the Lord for his mercifull providence towards vs all in deliuering your wife

---

[1] The date of this letter arouses doubt as to whether Charles Francis Adams was correct in say-ing that it relates to the Remonstrance submitted to the Massachusetts General Court on behalf of John Wheelwright in March, 1636/37. Charles Francis Adams, *Antinomianism in the Colony of Massa-chusetts Bay, 1636-1638* (Prince Society, Boston, 1894), 135n.-136n. Winthrop invariably used the old-style calendar. This date, therefore, is January 15, 1637/38. It indeed seems strange that Winthrop, writing ten months after the appearance of the Remonstrance, could, in view of all that had tran-spired during that period, say that he had only recently had time to read the document carefully. This difficulty would not be wholly avoided if it were to be assumed that Winthrop had dated this letter according to the new-style calendar; but certainly the date November 15, 1637, is more plausible because of its proximity to the date of the trial of Mrs. Hutchinson. If one accepts an old-style date for the letter, it seems more reasonable to assume that Winthrop was referring to some document, now lost, occasioned by some later phase of the Antinomian controversy, during all of which all three addressees were openly aligned on the side of Wheelwright and Mrs. Hutchinson.

[2] W. 7A. 60; Savage (1825), 393-394; (1853), I. 472-473; *L. and L.*, II. 217-218.

from so greate a danger. the Lord make us truly thankfull: and I hope it will teach my daughter and other woemen to take heed of puttinge pinnes in the mouth, which was never seasonable to be fedd with such morsells: I can write you no newes onely we had letters from Conectecott, where they were shutt vp with snowe aboue a month since: and we at Boston were almost readye to breake vp for want of wood, but that it pleased the Lorde to open the Bay (which was so frozen as men went ouer it in all places) and mitigate the rigor of the season blessed be his name: on fryday was fortnight a pinnace was cast away vpon Longe Iland by Natascott, and mr. Babbe and others which were in her came home upon the Ice: we have had one man frozen to death: and some others have lost their fingers and toes: 7 men were carried out to sea in a little rotten skiffe and kept there 24 houers without foode or fire, and at last gat to pullen point.

we have appointed the general Court the 12 of the 1 month. we shall expect you heere before the Court of Assistants. so with all hearty salutations from my self and your mother to your self and wife and little Betty and all our good friends with you I commende you to the blessing of the Lord and rest Your loving father

Jo: W:

I send you herein the warrants for Ipswich and Newbury. commend me to your brother and sister Dudly.

xith 22: 1637[/38]

JOHN WINTHROP TO JOHN WINTHROP, JR.[1]

To my lovinge sonne Mr. Jo: Winthrop at his howse in Ipswich deliver

DEARE [SONNE], I wrote to you last weeke by Robert [*torn*] and therewith sent you 2 warrants for the [general] Court the 12 of the first month, one for your Towne and the other for Newberye. I desire to knowe whether they came to you, because otherwise, I would sende newe. Mr. Endecott and my brother Peter are now with vs. we are all in health, I prayse God, and hope to hear the like of you and yours: and shall long to heare of our good daughters safe delivery which we seriously commende to the Lord. Salute all our good friends with you, and particularly your Reverend min[iste]rs, and desire them all from me, to be verye carefull in admission of members, for there be

[1] Essex Institute; *L. and L.*, II. 418.

some of these newe opinions, that will simulare and dissimulare beyond expectation, to gett into our churches: and when they are once in, then will
they goe to worke, thoughe they never stirred before: I hope the sad experience of the effects of such spiritts in other churches wilbe caution enoughe
to them and others, to beware and knowe men well ere they admitt them;
but enough of this. we salute you and yours and your brother D[eane] and
sister are well. Your loving father

Jo: Winthop

I sende you [*torn*].

xiith 31: 1637[/38]

SAMUEL SYMONDS TO JOHN WINTHROP, JR.[1]

To the Right Wo[rshipfu]ll his much honored Brother John Wenthrop
of Ipswich Esqr: speed this I pray

Good Sir, I have received your lettre I thanke you for it; it hath bin my
earnest desire to have had an oportunity longe 'ere this to have bene with
you againe But was hindered by the weather, and still my desire lasts but
now I cannot by reason that my wife her tyme draweth very neare. Concerneinge the Bargaine that I have made with you for Argilla,[2] my wife is
well content, and it seemes that my father Peter hath imparted it to the
Governer who (he tells me) approoves of it very well alsoe. Soe I hope I
shall now meete with noe rub in that businesse; but goe on comfortablely
accordeing as I have and daily doe dispose my affaires for Ipswich. Concerneinge the frame of the howse I thanke you kindely for your love and care
to further my busines. I could be well content to leave much of the contriv-
ance to your owne liberty vpon what we have talked together about it
already. I am indiferent whether it be 30 foote or 35 foote longe 16 or 18
foote broade. I would have wood chimnyes at each end, the frames of the
chimnyes to be stronger then ordinary to beare good heavy load of clay for
security against fire. you may let the chimnyes be all the breadth of the
howse, if you thinke good, the 2 lower dores to be in the middle of the howse
one opposite to the other. be sure that all the dorewaies in every place be
soe high that any man may goe vpright vnder. the staiers I thinke had best

---

[1] Essex Institute; 4 *Collections*, vii. 118–121. For Symonds, see 4 *Collections*, vii. 118n.
[2] Symonds bought Argilla Farm from John Winthrop, Jr., February 8, 1637/38. Thomas F.
Waters, *Ipswich in the Massachusetts Bay Colony*, 1 (Ipswich, 1905), 19.

be placed close by the dore. it makes noe great matter though there be noe particion vpon the first flore   if there be, make one biger then the other. for windowes let them not be over large in any roome, and as few as conveniently may be. let all have current shutting draw-windowes, haveing respect both to present and future vse. I thinke to make it a girt howse will make it more chargeable then neede. however, the side bearers for the second story being to be loaden with corne etc. must not be pinned on but rather eyther lett in to the studds, or borne vp with false studds and soe tenented in at the ends; I leave it to you, and the Carpenters. In this story over the first, I would have a particion, whether in the middest or over the particion vnder I leave it; In the garrett noe particion, but let there be one or two lucome windowes, if two, both on one side. I desire to have the sparrs reach downe pritty deep at the eves to preserve the walls the better from the wether. I would have it Sellered all over, and soe the frame of the howse accordengly from the bottom. I would have the howse stronge in timber though plaine and well brased. I would have it covered with very good oake-hart inch board *for the present*, to be tacked on onely for the present as you tould me; let the frame begin from the bottom of the Seller, and soe in the ordinary way vpright for I can hereafter (to save the timber within grounde) run vp a thin brickworke without. I thinke it best to have the walls without to be all clapboarded besides the clay walls. It were not amisse to leave a dore-way or two within the Seller that soe hereafter one may make comings in from without, and let them be both vpon that side which the lucome window or windowes be.

I desire to have the howse in your bargaineing to be as compleatly mentioned in particulars as may be, at least soe far as you bargaine for, and as speedily done alsoe as you can. I thinke it not best to have too much timber felled neare the howse place westward, etc. Here are as many remembrances as come to minde. I desire you to be in my stead herein, and what ever you doe shall please me.

I desire you would talke with Mr. Boreman and with his helpe, buy for me a matter of 40 bushells of good indian corne of him or of some honest man to be paidd for now in ready mony, and to be delivered at any tyme in the sumer as I please to vse it. I would deale with such a man as will not repent if corne rise, as I will not if it fall. Thus acknowledging my bouldnes I desire to present our respectfull love to you my sister and your litle one, not forgetting my daughter. I cease committing you to him that is mercy and wisdome it selfe, and soe rest Yours ever

S. Symonds

[*Ca.* February, 1637/38]

My wife desires her speciall love to be remembered to you both and to let you vnderstand that she is very glad that she shalbe your neighbour at Ipswich.

I have herewith sent you inclosed 50*li* for yourselfe in part of payment as my father Peter willed me from you to doe, and twenty pounds more to be disposed in Corne, and to workemen as you please   and for the payment for the rest as you are willing to let my father Peter set downe the tyme soe am I.

My wife and I desire to be kindely remembered to your good neighbours Mr. Boreman and his wife and the rest of our frends. I could have wished he had written one word by Mr. Tuttell how those 3 bullocks be disposed of. our desire now is to hasten to Ipswich as fast as we can, at least our servants.

I heare that your Church hath setled the choyce of your ministers in their offices and that now things are likely to goe on very well and comfortablely, which ministers matter of great ioy to all that love Jesus Christ.[1] And truely the peace of any Church (because pretious) is soe difficult to preserve in respect of the subtilty and mallice of the Common enymy that it requires answerable cautelousnes on all hands, every one waighing well that one sentence of the Apostle let every one esteeme an other better then him selfe, and studdy the vally-way to rise to true honour.

HUGH PETER TO JOHN WINTHROP, JR.[2]

For the Wor[shipfu]ll John Winthrop Esqr. Ipswich

DEERE SIR, Wee are glad to heare of you, and my wife intends to bee with you per first.

Your sister Symonds is deliverd last weeke of a dead child, and is in much weaknes, it came by a fall, let your wife looke to herselfe. John Baker will tell you abondance of newes from the bay. For Ipswich it will never bee well till the Church goe on, aduise them to that if you meane to save them. Wee are in good order here, blessed bee the lord, continue your affection to him who is Yours or nothing

H. PETER

SALEM 2d day [*ca.* February, 1637/38]

I must earnestly intreat you to give Mr. Broadstreet 40*s* in corne for mee,

---

[1] Nathaniel Rogers was ordained as pastor and John Norton as teacher of the church in Ipswich on February 20, 1637/38.

[2] Essex Institute; 4 *Collections*, VI. 105–106.

or mony, it is for one goodman Tompson of your towne. I will make the mony good here, or any where. Salute your Betty and little Betty from vs all. I have sent you the booke of the proceedings at the Court, which when it is coppyed out for your towne I must have agayne.

THOMAS DUDLEY TO JOHN WINTHROP[1]

To the R[igh]t Wor[shipfu]ll John Winthrop esqr. Gov[ernou]r

Sir, In answeare to yours, and to what Mr. Coddington hath by word motioned I say as followeth that I am content himselfe, Mr. Wildboare, Mr. Coggeshall, Goodman Freeborne and Richard Carder shall haue lycence to departe out of this Patent within a moneth from hence following, and after to retourne at their pleasures to remoove their famyles, soe it be with in halfe a yeare from this day, onely Mr. Coddington and Mr. Wildboare are to come and goe and trade and comerce and take their owne tyme for remoovall of their famylyes. likewise for Serieant Hutchinson and Serieant Boston and for John Porter, I consent to their departure and the release of their Fynes, provyded that they shall departe before the thirteenth day of the next moneth and not retourne any more, which if they doe they are to be lyable to the payement of their fynes and all three to such further censure as the Court shall thinck meete. Thus with my service remembred I take leave and rest Yours at command

THO: DUDLEY

19 of the 12, 1637[/38]

[*The following order, in the handwriting of Governor Winthrop, appears, in rough draft, on the next leaf of this letter.*][2]

Mr. Wm. Coddington Mr. Jo: Coggeshall and Mr. [*blank*] Wildbore are licenced to depart out of this Jurisdiction and they haue liberty to remove their famylyes and dispose of their estates heere in convenient tyme at their owne liberty and to goe and come at their liberty except they or any of them shalbe otherwise limited by the gen[eral] Court.

---

[1] W. 3. 28; 4 *Collections*, VII. 110–111. For Dudley, see *D.A.B.* The persons named in this letter had all been supporters of Wheelwright and Mrs. Hutchinson during the controversies of the previous year.

[2] Cf. *Records of the Governor and Company of the Massachusetts Bay in New England*, Nathaniel B. Shurtleff, Editor, 1 (Boston, 1853), 223.

Wm: Baulston and Edw: Hutchinson have license to depart out of this Jurisdiction, provided that they submitt to the Order of the Gen[era]ll Court in regarde of the Censure they lye vnder.

JOHN WINTHROP TO WILLIAM STEVENS AND TO EDWARD GIBBONS[1]

MR. STEPHENS, If you will vse meanes that the Bark may be brought to Boston forthwith, we will take Order, vpon the sale of her, that you shalbe payd the money due to you for your work vpon her: so we rest your loving friends

Jo: WINTHOP
JNO. JOLLIFE

xijth 20th 1637[/38]

MR. GIBBONS, We desire you to paye mr. Stephens out of the money due for mr. Lovells Barke fifteen pounds due to him for work vpon her, and take at this [*illegible*] and another Bill from mr. Lovell for the same summe.

Jo: WINTHOP

xii: 29: 1638[/39][2]

[*Endorsed:*] Mr. Stephens for the Bark Lovells paid 17*li* 13*s* 6*d*.

ROGER WILLIAMS TO JOHN WINTHROP[3]

For his much honoured and beloved Mr. Gov[ernou]r these

PROVIDENCE 28th of the 12th [1637/38]

SIR, Some few dayes since I receaved letters from Mr. Hooker who had safely receaved your packet with thancks etc.

He intimated that according to Miantunnomues informacion by my selfe: Wm. Baker was hid at Monahigganick but they had made Okace and Wequash to bring him in, since which time (Seargeant Homes baling him) he is againe escaped.

---

[1] W. I. 121. The recipient of this letter was undoubtedly William Stevens of Marblehead, a shipbuilder. For Gibbons, see Savage, *Genealogical Dictionary*, II. 245.

[2] Since Winthrop invariably used the old-style calendar, this has been dated a year later than the letter to William Stevens, although a date nine days later seems more plausible.

[3] W. 2. 104; 4 *Collections*, VI. 223–226; *N.C.*, VI. 86–89.

He allso signified the desire of the Magistrates at Qunnticut that there the meeting should be:[1] as allso that in the meane season they had charged the Monahiganeucks not to molest any natiues in their passage and travell etc. requiring the same of the Nanhiggonsicks towards the Monahiganeucks.

Accordingly I haue bene since at Nanhigonsick and find Miantunnomu willing to goe to Qunnticut by the time limited the end of the next month: only first he desired to know Mr. Governours mind: 2ndly in case his Father in Law, Caunounicus his brother, (whome I saw neere death with aboue a thoughsand men mourning and praying about him) in case he recover, otherwise it is vnlawfull for them (as they conceaue) to goe farr from home till toward mid sommer. 3rdly, he desires earnestly my Companie, as being not so confident of the English at Qunnticut who haue bene (I feare) to full of threatnings: 2ndly he can not be confident of Tho: Stantons faythfullnes in point of Interpretation These things make me much desire (as I have written back) that you would both please by some deputed to make my poore howse the Center where seemes to be the fairest offer of Convenience, and I hope no Question of wellcome.

Visiting Caunounicus lately recovered from the pits brinck this winter, he asked how Mr. Governour and the English did, requesting me to send him 2 words: 1st that he would be thanckfull to Mr. Governour for some sugar (for I had sent him mine owne in the depth of the winter and his sicknes) 2ndly he calld for his Sword which said he Mr. Governour did send me by you and others of the English, saying Mr. Governour protested he would not put vp his Sword, nor would he haue vs put vp ours, till the Pequt were subdued, and yet sayth he at Monahiganick there are neere 300, who haue bound and robd our men (euen of the very covering of their Secret Parts) as they haue past from Qunnticut hether: after much more to this purpose, I told him that Mr. Governour had promised him to sett all in order this Spring.

Sir I vnderstand that Okace the Monahigon hath Sasacous his sister to wife and one of the wiues of Sasacous his father Tattaopaine, and thats one reason beside his ambition and neerenes that he hath drawne all the scattered Pequts to himselfe and drawn much wealth from them: more I could trouble you with etc.

Caunounicus and Miantunnomu both desired that there might be a division made of these surviving Pequots (except the Sachims and murtherers) and let their share be at your owne Wisedome.

[1] I.e., the meeting between the Narragansetts and the Mohegans which was the subject of a letter from Williams to Winthrop on January 10, 1637/38 (see pages 6–7, above).

I shall be humbly bold to present mine owne thoughts concerning a division and disposall of them: Since the most high delights in mercy, and great Revenge hath bene allready taken what if (the murtherers being executed) the rest be divided and dispersed, (according as their numbers shall arise and division be thought fit) to become subiect to your selues in the Bay and at Qunnticut which they will more easily doe in case they may be suffred to incorporate with the natiues in either places: as allso that, as once Edgar the Peaceable did with the Welsh in North Wales, a tribute of wolues heads be imposed on them etc. which (with submission) I conceaue an incomparable way to saue much Cattell aliue in the land.

Sir I hope shortly to send you good newes of great hopes the Lord hath sprung vp in mine Eye of many a poore Indian soule enquiring after God. I haue convinced hundreths at home and abroad that in point of Religion they are all wandring etc. I find what I could never heare before, that they haue plenty of Gods or divine powers: the Sunn, Moone, Fire, Water, Snow, Earth, the Deere, the Beare etc. are divine powers. I brought home lately from the Nanhiggonsicks the names of 38 of their Gods all they could remember and had I not with feare and caution withdrew they would haue fallen to worship O God (as they speake) one day in 7, but I hope the time is not long that some shall truely blesse the God of Heaven that euer they saw the face of English men. So waiting for your pleasure and advice to our neighbours concerning this intended meeting for the establishing of Peace through all the bowells of the Countrey and beseeching the most high to vouchsafe his peace and truth through all your Quarters, with my due respects to Mrs. Wintrop, Mr. Deputie Mr. Bellingham etc. I rest Your Wo[r-shi]ps in all true respect and affection

ROGER WILLIAMS

Sir I heard no more as yet from Charlstowne men comming this way   Mr. Coxall and Mr. Aspinwall haue sent to me about some of these parts, and in case for shelter for their wiues and children.

[*Endorsed by Governor Winthrop:*] Provisions to be sent by the Salem Bark to Mr. Williams and Mr. Throckmorton, Mr. Harlackenden knowes more.

JOAN WINTHROP TO JOHN WINTHROP[1]

*To her loving and aproued good frend and Kinseman Mr. John Winthrop
theis be deliuered in new Ingland*

LOVING COSEN, My comendations remembred vnto you your bedfellow
and to all the rest of my cosens in generall hoping in God that you with all
the rest be in good health as I myself with the rest of our freinds that are
living here God be praise att the writing hereof Theis are to certife vnto
you that my husband is deade three years agoe and I am left destitute without
any freinds that are able to affoard any of there Comforts to helpe me, soe
that now pouerty Constrayneth me att this time being in want and pouerty
Earenesly to desire and intreat you to extend and shewe you frendly and
naturall loue towards me in this my great want and nececissitie imbolding my
self to troub[l]e you with theis few lynnes, which I haue sent vnto you by mr.
Georg Sheppard and his sonne by whom I did vnderstand that he knoweth
you very well and that you live richly and very well which I desire my lord
god you may soe still continewe to his will and pleasure in this world and in
the world to Come life eternall. soe this are my last desire that you will
rememeber in this my necessitie and pouerty And I shall rest my selfe very
thankefull vnto and greatly bound to pray for you and yours Thus expecting you Charitable loue and affection and letter either by mr. Sheppard
or by some other sufficient and trustie messinger, craving pardon for my
boldnes I rest and Comitt you to the protection of god almightie Your poore
and loving Cosen

JOANE WINTHORP
daughter to Willyam Hills

From BANDON BRIDG in Ireland the 5th Day of March 1637[/38]

JOHN DAVENPORT AND THEOPHILUS EATON TO THE MASSACHUSETTS GENERAL COURT[2]

To the much honored the Governor, Deputy and Assistants, etc.

It may please the worthy and much Honored Governour, Deputy, and
Assistants, and with them, the present Courte, to take knowledge that our

---

[1] W. Au. 71; 5 *Collections*, I. 86–87. Joan Winthrop was the widow of Adam Winthrop, a cousin
of Governor Winthrop.

[2] New York Public Library; Savage (1825), 404–405; (1853), I. 484–486; 3 *Collections*, III. 165–

Desire of staying within this patent was Reall and Strong, if the eye of Gods providence (to whom we have committed our Waies especially in so important an enterprise as this, which, we confess, is farr above our Capacityes) had guided us to a place convenient for our familyes, and for our freinds. Which as our words have often expressed, so, we hope, the trueth thereof is sufficiently declared by our almost nine moneths patient wayting in expectacion of some opportunity to be offered us, for that end, to our great charge and hindrance, many waies.

In all which time we have, in many prayers commended the guidance of our apprehensions, judgments, spirits, resolucions and wayes into the good hand of the onely wise God, whose prærogative it is to determine the bounds of our habitacions according to the ends for which he hath brought us into these Countryes, and we have considered, as we were able, by his helpe, whatsoever place hath bene propounded to us, being ready to have, with contentment, accepted (if by our stay any publick good might be promoved) smaller Accommodacions, and upon dearer termes (if they might be moderatly commodious) then, we beleive, most men, in the same Case with us, in all respects, would have done. And, whereas a place for an Inland plantacion beyond Watertowne, was propounded to us, and pressed with much importunity by some, whose words have the power of a law with us, in any way of God, we did speedily, and seriously deliberate thereupon, it being the subject of the greatest part of a Dayes discourse: The conclusion was, that, if the upland should answer the meddow ground in goodnes and desirablenes (whereof yet there is some ground of doubting) yet, considering that a Boate cannot pass from the Bay thither, nearer then 8 or 10 miles distance, and that it is so remote from the Bay, and from any towne, we could not see how our dwelling there would be advantagious to these plantacions, or compatible with our conditions, or commodious for our familyes, or for our freinds:

Nor can we satisfye our selves that it is expedient, for our selves, or for our freinds, that we chuse such a condition, wherein we must be compelled to have our dwelling houses so farr distant from our Farmes, as Boston, or Charlestowne is from that place, few of our freinds being able to beare the charge thereof (whose Cases nevertheles we are bound to consider) and some of them that are able not being persuaded that it is lawfull for them to live continually from the greatest part of theyre familyes, as, in this Case, they

167. For Davenport, see Samuel E. Morison, *The Founding of Harvard College* (Cambridge, 1935), 374–375, and *D.A.B.*; for Eaton, see *D.A.B.* The body of this letter is in the handwriting of Davenport, and the superscription is in the handwriting of Eaton.

would be necessitated to doe. The Season of the yeare, and other weighty Consideracions, compelled us to hasten to a full and finall Conclusion which we are, at last, come unto, by Gods appointment and direction, we hope, in mercy, and have sent letters to Connectacutt for a speedy transacting the purchase of the parts about Quillypieck from the Natives which may pretend title thereunto. By which Act we are Absolutely, and irrevocably ingaged that way, and we are persuaded that God will order it for good unto these plantations, whose love so abundantly, above our desarts, or expectacions, expressed, in your desire of our abode in these parts, as we shall ever retaine in thanckfull memory, so we shall account ourselves thereby obliged to be any way instrumentall, and serviceable for the common good of these plantacions as well as of those; which the Divine providence hath combined together in as strong a bond of Brotherly affection, by the sameness of theyre condition, as Joab and Abishai were, whose severall armyes did mutually strengthen them boath against severall enimyes, 2 Sam. 10. 9. 10. 11. or rather they are joyned together, as Hippocrates his Twinnes, to stand, and fall, to growe and decay, to flourish, and wither, to live and dye together. In witnes of the premises we subscribe our names

JOHN DAVENPORTE
THEOPH: EATON

The 12th day of the first moneth Anno 1638[1]

EMMANUEL DOWNING TO JOHN WINTHROP, JR.[2]

[*Mutilated*] I haue spoken with the lord Brooke and the rest of that Companie for your allowance. I haue cleared your reputation and fidelity with them all. after some discourse for your recompence they haue [*torn*] read your lettre. Mr. Fenick said that you gave him an account, which after 2 or 3 dayes you desired of him againe, which he forgott to call for back, soe they all agreed yt fitt to see some account, though not strictly for euerie penny, and then they said they would deall freely with you to content.

I write you noe newes, because God willing I hope to be with you verie shortly. All things stand well in the Eye of our State concerning your plantation; noe word of any Murmuring against yt. your new vpstart opinions

---

[1] This letter is either dated according to the new-style calendar or else is misdated for March 12, 1637/38. Cf. *Journal* (1. 265), under date March 30, 1638.

[2] W. 4. 91; 5 *Collections*, 1. 256. For Downing, see 4 *Collections*, VI. 33*n*.

are here generally cryed downe. soe with my love to yourselfe your wife etc. I
leave you and yours to the blessing of God.

[EMMANUEL DOWNING]

13 Martij 1637[/38]

[*Endorsed by John Winthrop, Jr.:*] Letter about Seabrooke company.

STEPHEN WINTHROP TO MARGARET WINTHROP[1]

To my much honered mother Mrs. Winthrope at hir howse in Boston these
present new England

DEARE MOTHER, My humble duty Remembered vnto yow with my harty
love to My brothers: havinge this ocation to wright by this first shipe I
thowght it my duty to sende you word of my wealfeare: althowghe I shall
Not be longe behinde them: My vnckles and aintes are all very well. I have
A letter for yow but shall Not sende it Now. Mones is very scarce here: Yow
were willing that I showld have had 100*li* for my owne vse which I did
Reseve: but I am forced to laie out againe to pay for somme thinges you sent
for which are bought and will coume ouer with vs. I have browght your
thinges from Chence howse and put them In a Chest: Your feather bed is
left behinde. I know not the Reason. If had pleased to acquaint me with
thoese thinges I would have shewed my willingenes to doe yow serves. I have
noe newse to wright. I Rest your Dewtifull sonne

STEPHEN WINTH.

March 20, 1637[/38]

EDWARD HOWES TO JOHN WINTHROP, JR.[2]

21⁰ March: 1637[/38]

MY FRIND ETC., Yours of the 1st of August last I received, and alsoe the
Mapp of the Coast about Pequot for which and former kindnes I thanke you.
the relation of your fight with the Indians I haue read in print, but of the
fight amonge yourselues Bellum linguarum, the strife of tongues, I haue
heard much, but little to the purpose. I wonder your people that pretend to

---

[1] W. I. 122; 5 *Collections*, VIII. 199–200. For Stephen Winthrop, first son of the Governor by his
third wife, Margaret Tyndal, see 5 *Collections*, VIII. 199*n*.

[2] W. 2. 169; 4 *Collections*, VI. 504–505. For Howes, see *Winthrop Papers*, II. 226*n*.

knowe soe much, doe not knowe that Loue is the fulfilling of the Lawe, and
that against Loue there is noe Lawe. but noe marvell: when many haue not
the begining (the feare of the Lord) of wisdom in them; and howe can they
that feare not God, keepe his Commandements or fulfill them: but I hope
when I come to find more vnitie, peace, and Loue. The terra incognita cog-
nita est paucis, arcanum Jehouæ adest reuerentibus ipsum; to tell you my
thoughts or knowledge of it, its neither earth, water, aire, nor fire, nor Æther,
soe that its beyond sence, or my expression, but to giue you an intelligible
taste, its lesser then the least, it cannot be diuided nor comunicated, its bigger
then the bigest, for its perfect its beyond the highest, and below the lowest, for
thought cannot reach it, if you knowe it I need not tell you it, if I speake in
an vnknowne tongue, I doe but beate the Aire. Your Aunt D[owning] can
informe you of my dwellinge where I shalbe glad to heare from you that I
may continue to be as I desire Tuus vt possim

                                                                    E. H.

[Endorsed by John Winthrop, Jr.:] Mr. Ed. Howes with a parable.

JOHN WINTHROP TO LORD ———[1]

R[IGH]T H[ONORA]BLE, Your lettres on the behalf of Jo: Th: I have received and Communicated with those of our Councell, and we doe with all
thankfullnesse acknowledge your wisdome and integrity, that you are pleased
to call for no other at our hands, then right and Justice shall require, which
thoughe (we trust) we shall allwayes have respect vnto, yet our care and
endeavour herin shalbe the more quickned vpon your Lo[rdshi]pps gentle
remindinge vs of that which duty binds vs to in this behalf. and more (I perceive) your Lo[rdshi]pp expects not from vs in this Case: which makes vs
the more forward to tender our selues to your Command in whatsoever we
may be serviceable to your Lo[rdshi]pp. so I humbly take leave and shall
ever desire to be your Lo[rdshi]pps servant

                                                                    J: W:

B: in N: E: Apr: 6: 1638

---

[1] Suffolk County Court Files, No. 21. The text printed here is from Winthrop's rough draft.

WILLIAM BRADFORD TO JOHN WINTHROP[1]

To the Right Wor[shipfu]ll Mr. John Winthrope Gouernour of the Massachusets
these be delivered

BELOUED SIR, I thanke you for your letter touching Mrs. Huchingson; I heard since of a monsterous, and prodigious birth which she should discouer amongst you; as also that she should retracte her conffession of acknowledgmente of those errours, before she wente away; of which I haue heard many various reports. If your leasure would permite, I should be much behoulden vnto you, to certiffie me in a word or tow, of the trueth and forme of that monster, etc. Vpon the Information and Complainte of our neigbours at Sityate, I am requested by our assistants to write vnto you, touching a late parttition, or limiting of confines, betweene you and vs;[2] of which we heard nothing of late. Wherin we vnderstand you haue Intrenched farr vpon those lands, which we haue conceiued to belong to vs by right diuerce waies; as first by composision, and anciente compacte with the natiues to whom the right and souerainite of them did belonge, which did extend as farr as Conahasete, which was the bounds between the Sachimes of the Massachusets, and those of these parts; 2ly. It since hath been confirmed vnto vs by patente from his Majesties authoritie. 3ly. herevpon we haue posest it, and planted it some years agoe. We desire you will giue vs a reason of your proceedings herein; as also that ther may be a faire, and freindly desission of the controuercie; that we may preserue peace and brotherly loue amongst our selues, that haue so many enimies abroad. Ther was not long since hear with vs Mr. Cottington and some other of your people, who brought Mr. Williams with them and prest vs hard for a place at, or near Sowames, the which we denid them; Then Mr. Williams Informed them of a spatious Iland caled Monachunte,[3] touching which they solisited our good will, to which we yeelded (so they would compound with Ossamequine) the which we heard was Ill taken by you, but you may please to vnderstand that it is not In our Pattente (though we tould them not so) for It only was excepted out of it. And we thought (If they likte it) It were better to haue them, (though they differ in oppinions) then (hapily) worse neigbours, both for vs, and you. We thinke it is also better for vs both to haue some strength in that bay. Thus

---

[1] W. I. 195; 4 *Collections*, VI. 156–158. For Bradford, see *D.A.B.*
[2] Cf. *Journal*, I. 287; William Bradford, *History of Plymouth Plantation, 1620–1647* (Boston, 1912), II. 277.
[3] Aquidneck, or Rhode Island.

comending you, and your affairs to the Lord; with my loue remembred to your selfe, and the rest of my worthy friends with you, I take leaue and rest Your vnworthy freind

WILLIAM BRADFORD

Aprill 11, 1638

Memorandum by Governor Winthrop on the Superscription Leaf of the Above Letter

My Answere to this Lettre (which I shewed to the Deputy) was to this effect: that before we did any thing we acquainted mr. Hatherly and had men of either parte to sett out the bounds, but they not agreeinge etc., I tould mr. Winslow, and wished there might be some friendly course for setlinge the same, so as might neither strengthen Scituate nor Hingham   he answered, that what our Patent gave us we must have, and it was all one to them whither Sc[ituate] fell to them or to vs etc: and advised vs to sett out our bounds etc: which we did accordingly etc, but have [nede?] to Acte upon it, nor disposed anythinge to Hingham etc: ergo we see not why we should be called to give a Reason of: etc; that this was vpon some misinformation, or want of information; that we would be sorye that matter of jurisdiction should bringe our peace and loue into question: that if we had come hither for lande or if we had feared that our friends of Pl[ymouth] would have bounded vs to 3 or 4 miles of Natanscott, we could have more easily have enlarged our Grant than theirs. for the kings Confirmacion I supposed it a mistake, the k[ing] dothe not use to confirme Indians grants   for their purchase of the Indians, it was the 1st I heard of it, and it would be hard to make their title good, and as hard to proue their grant to them. For Mr. Hatherlys company, we thought it were better for us both if they were further off: we had not to doe with it but we were persuaded they would not haue furthered them etc: before they had advised with vs; and they might have expected the like Correspondency from vs. conclusion for a friendly devision etc.

(2) 16, 1638

ROGER WILLIAMS TO JOHN WINTHROP[1]

For his much honoured and beloved Mr. Governour at Boston these

PROVIDENCE 16th of this 2nd [1638]

MUCH HONOURED SIR, I kindly thanck you for your loving inclination to receaue my late protestation concerning my selfe ignorant of Mr. Greenes letter etc.[2] I desire vnfeignedly to rest in my Appeale to the most high in what we differ as I dare not but hope you doe: it is no small griefe that I am otherwise perswaded, and that some times you say (and I can say no lesse) that we differ: the fire will try your workes and mine, the Lord Jesus helpe vs to make sure of our persons that we seeke Jesus that was crucifyed: howeuer It is and euer shall be (the Lord assisting) my Endeavour to pacifie and allay where I meete with rigid and censorious spirits who not only blame your actions butt doome your Persons: and indeede it was one of the first grounds of my dislike of John Smith the miller especially of his wife viz: their iudging of your persons as [Divells][3] etc.

I allso humbly thanck you for that sad relation of the monster etc. The Lord speakes once and twice: he be pleased to open all our Eares to his Discipline.

Mrs. Hutchinson (with whome and others of them I haue had much discourse) makes her Apologie for her Concealement of the monster, that she did nothing in it without Mr. Cottons advice, though I can not belieue that he subscribes to her Applications of the Parts of it. The Lord mercifully redeeme them, and all of vs from all our delusions and pitie the desolations of Zion and the Stones thereof.

I find their longings great after Mr. Vane although they thinck he can not returne this yeare: the Eyes of some are so earnestly fixt vpon him that Mrs. Hutchinson professeth if he come not to New she must to Old Engl.

I haue endeavoured by many Arguments to beate of their desires of Mr. Vane as G[eneral] G[overnor][4] and the chiefe are satisfied vnles he

---

[1] W. 2. 105; 4 *Collections*, VI. 226–228; *N.C.*, VI. 89–94.

[2] "While the general court sate, there came a letter, directed to the court, from John Greene of Providence, who, not long before, had been imprisoned and fined, for saying that the magistrates had usurped upon the power of Christ in his church, and had persecuted Mr. Williams and another, whom they had banished for disturbing the peace by divulging their opinions against the authority of the magistrates, etc.; but upon his submission, etc. his fine was remitted; and now, by his letter, he retracted his former submission, and charged the court as he had done before." *Journal*, I. 261–262. See also *Records of Massachusetts* under date of March 12, 1637/38 (I. 224).

[3] The word in brackets has been crossed out in the original.

[4] One of the purposes of the Fast Day observed in Massachusetts on April 12, 1638, was "for

come so for his Life but I haue endeavoured to discover the Snare in that allso.

Sir concerning your intended meeting for reconciling of these Natiues our friends and dividing of the Pequts our Enemies I haue ingaged your name, and mine owne; and if no Course be taken the name of that God of Truth whome we all profess to honour will suffer not a little, it being an ordinary and common thing with our neighbours if they apprehend any shew of breach of promise in my selfe thus to obiect: doe you know God and will you lye? etc.

The Pequts are gathered into one, and plant their old fields: Wequash and Okace carying away the people and their treasure which belong to your selues: I should be bold to presse my former Motion or else that with the next Convenience they might be sent for other parts etc.

I hope it will never be interpreted that I press this out of feare of any revenge vpon my selfe by any of them: I euer yet (in point of reason to say no more) conceaved this place the safest of the land, and can make it appeare etc. but out of desire to cleare your names and the name of the most High which will be ill reported of in case (according to so many Promises) an honourable and peaceable Issue of the Pequt warr be not established.

Sir the bearer hereof (not daring either to bring my letter or attend for an Answere) I must request you to send your letter to Rich: Collicuts that so a natiue may convey it or els to Nicholas Vpshalls: and I should be bold humbly to propound to the Countrey whether in case there be a necessitie of keeping leauge with the Natiues and so consequently many occasions incident, (and some which I will not write of) as allso a Conveniencie of Informacion this way how matters may stand with you on the sea shoare, as I say whither it be not requisite so farr to dispence with the late Order of Restraint as to permit a messenger freely.[1]

Tis true I may hire an Indian: yet not alwayes, nor sure, for these 2 things I haue found in them: sometimes long keeping of a letter: 2ndly if a feare take them that the Letter concernes themselues they suppresse it, as they did with one of special Informacion which I sent to Mr. Vane.

---

seeking the Lord to prevent evil, that we feared to be intended against us from England by a general governor." *Journal*, I. 269.

[1] "Now because the court knew, that divers other of Providence were of the same ill affection to the court, and were probably suspected to be confederate in the same letter, the court ordered, that, if any of that plantation were found within our jurisdiction, he should be brought before one of the magistrates, and if he would not disclaim the charge in the said letter, he should be sent home, and charged to come no more into this jurisdiction, upon pain of imprisonment and further censure." *Journal*, I. 262.

Sir there will be new Heavens and a new Earth shortly but no more Sea (Revel. 21.2.)   The most holy God be pleased to make vs willing now to beare the Tossings Dangers and Calamities of this Sea and to seale vp to vs upon his owne grounds, a great Lot in the glorious State aproaching   So craving Pardon for Prolixitie, with mine and wiues due respect to Mrs. Wintrop Mr. Deputie Mr. Bellingham etc. I rest Your Wo[rshi]ps desirous to be ever yours vnfeigned

ROGER WILLIAMS

JOHN SANDBROOKE TO JOHN WINTHROP[1]

For the Right Wor[shi]p[fu]ll Mr. Winthrop Gouernour dwellinge at Boston these present New England per a freind whome god preserue

RIGHT WORSHIPFULL AND MUCH HONOURED MASTER, my humble service presented vnto yow etc.; these are to let your worship vnderstand how it hath pleased god wonderfully to provide for vs and to preserve and keepe vs all alive, and in good health vntill this present, blessed bee his name for it, but how long it may be thus continued I know not, but this I am sure our sinns have long agoe cried lowd, for bitternes woe and desolation, but he who is pleased many tymes to be found of those which seeke him not, and made manifest vnto those which never enquired after him, may of his grace be pleased through his grace in his owne good time, to exspell those clowdy mists of gloomy darkenes; and let in the soonne shine of his love vpon the soules of all his elect in Christ, and that in his owne good time, and at his owne good will and pleasure. It hath pleased god of his owne free grace, in some measure to make mee the vnworthiest of all creatures less then the least of all his mercyes (sensible) not only of the want which wee are now in for provisions and sustenance for the outward man, but also of the want, yea and inevidable and irrecoverable pitt which euery soule is ready euery moment to fall into, that hath not their sines pardoned their persons accepted and freely iustefied and that in and through and by the blood of the lord Jesus, who will have mercy on whom he will have mercy, and whome he will he hardens,[2] so that it is out of thes riches of his free grace, and out [of] the abundant compassion pitty and good will vnto any pore soule that he is pleased to call whome vnto himselfe acording to that in the 16 of Ezekell,

    [1] W. 4. 92; 5 *Collections*, I. 256–259. For Sandbrooke, see Edward Howes to John Winthrop, Jr., June 22, 1633 (*Winthrop Papers*, III. 132).
    [2] In the margin: "Rom. 8" (Romans 9:18).

behold whilest thow wast in thy blood and no eye pitied (I said) vnto thy sowle live, which as it hath pleased the lord to give mee some poore weake vnderstanding I conceive it thus. If there is nothing in heaven nor nothing on earth that can speake lyfe vnto any poore soule who lyes wallowing in the blood and mire and clay of his sinns and corruptions, but only the lord Jesus Christ takeing of the soule vnto him selfe, and that while it is in its blood when no eye pittyes it, then he out of the riches of his free grace towards the soules of his elect, is pleased to redeme them from death to lyfe and that by the shedding of his pretious blood vpon the Cross once shed for all his elect, and so by his stripes wee are healed, yea even by the death of him who came not to call the righteous but sinners to repentance; As for this Iland vpon which wee are; as I conceiue it may in some measure be compared to Philadelphia; though it is not subiect to earthquakes, yet it is somtimes so shaken with stormes of wind and seas that one would wonder, and so various for alterations and changes of winds and weather that I stand amazed somtimes to see it. I will not troble your worship with any further intelligence of the Iland, because our Comander Lieftenant Morris can certefie your worshipp of all things how they stand, and in what a condition we are now in, and what short allowance wee are brought too, our provisions being almost spent, and had not god wonderfully provided for us above and beyond our exspectations for ought I know, wee might have bin many of us dead ere now, for want of food. Sir I should request your worshipp yf yow thinke meete, after the 10 monthes are exspired, for to give me that remainder of my time that I am to serve your worship which is till michalmes day it being the 29th as I take it of September. I should be very thankefull to your worship for it; I should likewise desire your worship to send mee some shirts and some other cloathes   I have a desire to stay a while longer vpon the Iland yf there bee any probability of doeing good vpon the horse,[1] which I question it not, only I desire to have your worships advise in the thinge and yf I have any letters come from any of my freinds I should desire your worship would be pleased to send them mee   James Yelke remembers his humble service to your worship, and Daniell Hendrick. James is vnwilling to stay any longer then till the 10 months be exspired. thus with our harty prayers to the lord for yow and yours I rest Your humble servant to his power

JOHN SANDBROOKE

---

[1] "Twentymen went in a pinnace to kill sea horse at the Isle of Sable. . . ." *Journal* (August 31, 1636), I. 231.

From WINTERTOWNE vpon the Ile of Sables the 30th of the 2d month caled Aprill [1638]

blessed be god for it our stomacks can disgest seales gulls foxes owle, and such meate as the lord is pleased to provide for us.

I have sent your worship a Catalouge of the winds and weather which wee have had since our comming from boston to this present.

Our Comander will acquaint your worship what cloathing is best for to weare.

I should request your worship to send mee a bible a quire of paper and some sealeing wax.

And for the choyce of a Comander over vs for the time to come, I haveing not my vote with the rest of the company because I am a servant, I desire to acquaint your worship whome I conceive is fittest for a Commander and whome I most desire, namely, Leiftenant Morris, whome is a man as I conceive most fitt and one who is so sensible of wants and knows so well how to order and affaires, and one whome the company so affects, that the maior part yf not allmost all have and doe desire to have him come our Commander againe.

JOHN ENDECOTT TO JOHN WINTHROP[1]

DEAREST SIR, The severall reports of your sick condition since I came home have bene so divers that I cannot tell wether my feares or my hopes of your recovery have been the greatest.[2] Though when I came from you, your phisick had wrought so kindly made mee scarce to doubt of the best effects. My truest love makes mee feare what my best hopes would willinglye carry mee through, especially when I consider the further imployment the Lord hath yet for you heere amongst his people. When the worst tidings come I am yet comforted in this that hee that giveth both health and salvation to his people, heareth in heaven, and is overcome by his poore wrestlers here on Earth. Such thoughts I have had of Gods dealings with you, and with us all in visiting you at present, and what his meaning might be therein; But his thoughts are aboue our thoughts, and hee is onely wise. Sure I am he will doe that which shall be for the glory of his owne name, the true comfort

---

[1] W. 2. 70 (copy); 4 *Collections*, VI. 133-134. For Endecott, see Lawrence S. Mayo, *John Endecott, A Biography* (Cambridge, 1936); *D.A.B.*

[2] "The same day [May 2, 1638], at night, he [Winthrop] was taken with a sharp fever which brought him near death; but many prayers were put up to the Lord for him, and he was restored again after one month." *Journal*, I. 270.

and the good of his people. We have had many former experiences of Gods great mercies unto us in divers great deliverances since we came over, and why might we not expect that mercy also, even your deliverance from death. Surely it was not our worthynes that procured the former, and I still hope that our unworthiness (though it might Justly) shall not bereaue us of this latter: Hee that raised up Lazarus can (why shall I not say will?) also restore you unto us: Meethincks when I loock upon all things as they now are amongst us, I might be confident herein, witch the Lord in mercie graunt if it stand with his good pleasure.

I longe to see you, and would 'er this have bene with you, could I have conceaved myself to be any way usefull to you, and would how ever had not Mr. Peters illness onely detayned mee, for hee hath bene very ill. But I hope the worst is past, though hee be as sick in his thoughts as ever. We both resolve the begininge of the weeke to visitt you. In the meane while I commend and commit you into the armes of our deare and loving father the God of all our consolation, health and salvation beseeching him to make your Bed for you in your sickness, to comfort you in your greatest trialls and anguishes, to strengthen you in your greatest weakenesses; to stand by you as longe as you live, that you may live longe amongst us, if it be his bleassed will, to his praise, and at length to rest with him for ever in glorie, for the Lord Jesus Christ his sake amen amen. Yours truelie whiles I live

JO: ENDECOTT

SALEM the 13 of the 3d moneth 1638

ROGER WILLIAMS TO JOHN WINTHROP[1]

PROVIDENCE the 22 of 3rd mon. [1638]

SIR, Blessed be the Father of Spirits in whose hand our breath and wayes are that once more I may be bold to salute you and congratulate your returne from the brinck of the pit of Rottennes! What is man that thou shouldest visit him and trie him etc. Job 7th: You are put of to this tempestuous Sea againe, more stormes await you, the good Lord repaire our leakes, fresh vp the gales of his blessed Spirit steadie our Course by the Compasse of his owne Truth reskue vs from all our spirituall Adversaries not only men, but fiends of warr and assure vs of an harbour at last, euen the bozome of the Lord Jesus.

[1] W. 2. 109; 4 *Collections*, VI. 244–245; *N.C.*, VI. 94–96.

Sir you haue many an Eye (I presume) lift vp to the hills of mercy for you: mine might seeme superfluous: yet privately and publikely you haue not bene forgotten and I hope shall not while these Eyes haue sight.

Sir This last night Mr. Allen of Hartford and Lieftenant Holmes lodgd with me, and relate that Mr. Heynes or some chiefe resolved to be with you this weeke So that you may please a litle to stop till their Comming. Lieftenant Homes relates that William Baker who lay hid so long among the Monahiggens and Pequts, for whome he gave bale etc. was hid againe the second time among the same by Okace, but the Lieftenant by a Providence heard of him and returnd him to Hartford where he hath suffred for his much vncleanenes 2 severall whippings. This fellow notorious in villany and strongly affected by those wretches, both studying Revenge, is worthy to be watcht euen by the whole Countrey and to be dispersed from the Pequts, and they each from other according as I haue bene bold to motion formerly.

Sir, we haue bene long aflicted by a young man, boysterous and desperate, Philip Verins Sonn of Salem, who, as he hath refused to heare the word with vs (which we molested him not for) this twelue month, so because he could not draw his wife a gracious and modest woman to the same vngodlines with him, he hath troden her vnder foote tyrannically and brutishly: which she and we long bearing though with his furious blowes she went in danger of life at the last the maior vote of vs discard him from our Civill Freedome, or disfranchize etc. he will haue Justice (as he clamours) at other Courts: I wish he might for a fowle and slanderous and brutish Cariage, which God hath delivered him vp vnto: he will hale his wife with ropes to Salem, where she must needes be troubled and troublesome as differences yet stand. She is willing to stay and live with him or else where, where she may not offend etc. I shall humbly request that this Item be accepted, and he no way countenanced vntill (if need be) I further trouble you: So with due respects to Mrs. Wintrop Mr. Deputie Mr. Belingham etc. I rest Your Wo[rshi]ps vnfaigned

ROGER WILLIAMS

WILLIAM TOMPSON TO JOHN WINTHROP[1]

To the noble governor of Metachasets Baye Mr. John Winthroppe theis bee delivered

I know not (worthie Sir) how it hath beene put of and protracted that you haue beene all together neglected of vs, that liue at Accomenticus, and what

---

[1] W. I. 142. For Tompson, see Morison, *Founding of Harvard College*, 402. In 1642–1643 Tompson

hath beene the cause, whether it was bashfulnesse, as some of vs truly are
affrayd to presente a letter into the hande, of so noble and wyse a governor:
or whether it was the minister expected the people should wryte, or that
the people thought it most fitte the minister should wryte. thus noble Mr.
Winthroppes loue, and deare respecte is neglected of vs, and not so much as
one of Accomenticus sends him a paper schroule, in waye of acknowledgmente of his faithfulnesse, or in the waye of regratulation or thankfulnesse.
yet lest you, in the least measure mighte seeme to bee neglected, whom wee
(I speake the truth I lye not, I flatter not) so much honor, and if it mighte
stande with gods will, could wish, might still bee governor, I am bolde to
wryte theis two or three fewe rude lynes vnto you: for my selfe I cannot but
thanke you noble Sir, for your good conceites of mee, a meere straunger to
you, and for your testimoniall written to the people in my behalfe. your good
conceites were stronge of mee, that carried you to wryte so farre in the behalf
of a poore ignorante, stonieharted, faithlesse almost, fruitlesse creature, vnfitte for anie thinge almost, especially vnfitte for so great a busienesse as to
carrie Chrysts name, to a sorte of poore creatures, that haue a longe tyme
sette in darkenesse and in the region and shaddowe of death: yet if you haue
sayd anie thinge of mee, I hope you neede not bee ashamed: and though I
bee in my selfe most ignorante, and most vnfitte, yet hath the lord by his
grace in some measure fitted mee for my hearers, and his grace, as I hope
hath not beene altogether in vaine, for I am persuaded (let god haue the
prayse) hee hath wroughte some good by his grace, through my poore en-
deavors. some grace I saye in some of their soules: some haue prettie knowledge, crye out that they canne gette their harts no more humbled Though
cannot refraine teares in the pub[lic] assembly, carrye themselues honestly
circumspectly: all the plantation is convinced, that their is neede of an alteration: most of the families vse prayer as well as they are able: wee haue a
lecture everie thursdaye they neglecte worldly occasions to come to it: on
the sabboth sometyme I goe to blesse my parrishioners. some I fynd searchinge the scriptures and comparinge place with place, others singeinge, others
conferringe, so that they stoope to the ordinances, and giue mee hope, that
they are a people, out of whom hee intends to gather stones to make a spirituall
temple, where hee will dwell and sette his name their: their loue and respecte
to mee is not little, neither haue I founde small loue or respecte amongst.
the lord [grant] that it maye bee reckoned vpon their score at that daye:

preached in Virginia, being one of the clergy sent from Massachusetts in response to the request of
"some godly people" there "to be helpfull to them in instructing them in the truth. . . ." *Johnson's
Wonder-Working Providence*, J. Franklin Jameson, Editor (New York, 1910), 265.

because their are some, as my landlord, whom with others theis things concerne fully as much as my selfe, and for the presente are vnsettled, till your
answere come in. I would wish you to consider their condition and to giue
them present satisfaction that they may knowe how to determine and resolue.
noble Sir I praye you, let vs haue your prayers, as wee haue heard by your
man that wee haue: and doe you speake for vs, for the prayers of the elders,
if not in publicke, (though wee lifte vp you in publicke) yet in private, that
the poore english blood, the poore ignorante soules eastwarde maye bee
converted, churches maye bee gathered, his name maye bee sette their, his
maiestie walke their, and that soules maye bee saved. oh praye for vs. maye
their not bee manie soules that sette by our rivers sydes, that you thinke not
of, that maye belonge to the election of grace, for whom Chryst hath shedde
his blood? are not our soules capeable of the knowledge of god, the mysterie
of Chryst: as well as others? oh then, let vs haue your prayers: the churches,
the elders faine if out of contempte, or out of desperie, they praye not for vs,
for god manie tymes is founde of those that seeke him not, hee sends to those
in the highe wayes: noble Sir, their is a little matter, I must bee bolde with
you in. it concernes my poore landlord, who hath shewed mee no small
kyndnesse, as his kynde wyeffe lykewyse. they both to meewarde haue beene
verie fait[h]full. I know you heare that hee is lyke to come in some trouble
in regarde of some debts: that you would shewe him what mercie you canne
lawfully: Another thinge, if I durst bee so bolde, I would intreate. it is for the
whole plantation: that you would conferre with kynde Mr. Mavericke, about
our Lotts what assurance hee could make vs, or by what meanes our Lotts,
or the lotts of our Frends could bee assured if they come to vs: and further,
that noble Mr. Winthroppe would speake a worde or two to him, concerninge
discipline: for I came not out of England, for loue of discipline, that I mighte
liue in churches, rightly gathered and instituted; to liue out of the churches:
or to liue longe where their must not bee church discipline: Though I loue
Accomenticus dearely, and hope well of divers of them, and I perceiue god
is goinge on, yet I will not staye amongst them, without wee maye haue
libertie to all gods ordinances: Though wee bee lyke the men of Gilead, on
the other syde Jordan, yet wee will either haue a patterne of your altars, and
your churches, or truly wee will god willinge come over Jordan againe: for
your god shall bee our god, and your meanes and manner of worshippe will
wee vse. it is not twentie leagues of by water shall hinder vs god willinge,
from you: oh blesse god for his goodnesse to you, reioyce in your priviliges.
oh what people lyke vnto you, to whom the lord is so neere, that hath such
blessed conduite pypes? ordinances? wee mourne for our absence from the

house of god: Though as Nehemiah about the buildinge of the wall: wee
about buildinge god a house, wee though poore brethren lyke them that
wente as farre as [*illegible*] in the meane tyme, wee are gladde to heare god
is with you: to heare how god goes in his house: Noble Sir, Remember mee
I praye you to Reverend Mr. Cotton though of little acq[uaintance] and I
confesse my faulte, that I asked not his iudgmente, and tooke no more solemne
leaue when I wente to Acc[omenticus]   Noble Sir remember mee I praye
you to kynde and Rev: mr. Wilson: to kynde Mr. Mav[erick] to whom I am
so much indebted for his kynde respectfull letter, besydes kynde intertein-
mente with him by the waye: I know Mr. Hooke Mr. Broadburie Mr. Johnson
with others would willingly haue remembred their duties to you: but they
knew not I writte: The god of heaven continue to you the spirit of govermente
wisdome and courage: blesse your assistants: blesse the churches, keep them
in vnitie, builde them vp further, that now in dayes of peace they maye
treasure vp peace against harde tymes: that they maye walke in the comforts
of the holy ghost, and in the feare of god and bee edifyed: so prayes a poore
brother that loues the churches, honors the elders, and wisheth all grace
truth, lighte, happinessie to you all.

WM. TOMPSON

The 25 of Maye [1638]

ROGER WILLIAMS TO JOHN WINTHROP[1]

PROVIDENCE, 27 of 3rd [1638]

MUCH HONOURED SIR, I haue presumed to send this Nahigonsick man, to
attend your pleasure concerning the Pequts, and Caunounicus and Miantunnomues Complaint against them and their protectours.

The Summe of their desire I lately acquainted you with viz: that you
would please (euen all the English) to sit still and let themselues alone with
them according to Consent when Miantunnomu was last with you, who
comming home fell vpon Nayantaquit men who sheltred the Pequts but was
stopt by our friends of Qunnihticut.

Or 2ndly that some other Course (in Consultation) might be taken for
dispersion of them: euen as farr as Old England or elswhere, as they speake.

Sir I doe conceaue either Course will be difficult because our Friends at
Qunnihticut are strangely bewitched with the Subiection of these Pequots

[1] W. 2. 109; 4 *Collections*, VI. 246–247; *N.C.*, VI. 96–98.

to themselues, and are allso as strangely resolued vpon fighting and violent Courses (as I vnderstand by letters and otherwise by speech) vnles Miantunnomu come over personally to them to answer for proud Speeches which they heare of.

Miantunnomu hath long since promised and still waites to goe any whither you shall please to make answer, to meete etc.

Some from Qunnihticut write me word, that Indians will testifie such speeches to Miantunnomues teeth: and it may be so, whether true or false.

I allso in case I should listen to Indian Reports shall bring many who will affirme that Tho: Stanton hath receaved mighty Bribes (whence origo mali) that Okace the Monahiggon hath receaved litle less then a thoughsand fathom of beades whence he caries out some present to our friends at Qunnihticut, but I say I will not belieue it.

But this I know, that according to Leauge in 2 Articles that the Pequts shall not be sheltred nor disposed of without mutuall Consent of the English and the 2 Nahiggonsick Sachims.

2ndly that if the Pequts be suffred in the land to congregate and vnite into 4 or 500 togeather (as Lieftenant Howe confest to me) it will cost more bloud on all sides then yet hath bene spilt: for one the one part the Nanhiggonsicks can no more forbeare them then a wolfe his pray and on the other side for the Pequts vpon all Advantages the English shall find that *Vindicta levis vitâ iucundior ipsâ est.*

3rdly that our friends at Qunnihticut are marveilously deluded by the Monahiggons, as to be so confident of them, that Mr. Hooker writes no Proofe can be brought against them for word or deede: when it is cleare they were Pequts, and lately hid (once and the second time) hid William Baker from the English and that vpon paine of death to any that should reveale him as Lieftenant Homes tould me: Sir my desire is that it would therefore please the Lord to guide you all to make a prudent disposall and dispersion of the Pequts, which the Nanhiggonsick will further by peace or warr: So with all due Salutacions I humbly rest, vnfaigned in all desire of your present and eternall peace.

Roger Williams

Mr. Allen tould me that there were numbers of the Pequts at Narrigonset, but I satisfied him that they were at Nayantaquit whence (if themselues had not stopt) they had long since bene remooved.

ROGER LUDLOW, IN BEHALF OF
THE GENERAL ASSEMBLY OF CONNECTICUT,
TO THE GOVERNOR AND ASSISTANTS OF MASSACHUSETTS[1]

To our much ho[noured] frends the Gouernour and brethren of the Masachusetts Baye

HONOURED SIR, There beinge of late a Generall assembly of these plantacions in this River and fallinge into consideracion of divers particulers that
might or may concerne the generall good of these parts, as alsoe our eyes
reflectinge toward your selues from whence most of vs haue of late yssued into
these quarters And beinge desirous to reteine that old loue and familiarity
which formerly wee enioyed, And beinge confidently perswaded that your
endes of Comminge into these westerne partes were and soe remaine the
same with our selues, Which was to establish the lord Jesus in his Kingly
Throne as much as in vs lies here in his churches and to maynteine the
Common Cause of his gospell with our liues and estates, And whereas wee
knowe that our profession will finde fewe frends vppon the face of the earth
if occasion serue and therefore vnlikely to haue any ayde or succour from
Forraine parts if our neede should soe require, It is our wisdom therefore to
ymprove what wee haue to walke close with our God and to combine and
vnite our selues to walke and liue peaceably and lovingly togeather that
soe if there be Cause wee may joine hartes and hands to maynteine the
Common Cause aforesaide and to defend our priviledges and freedomes
wee nowe enioye against all opposers. And although our Beginnings be but
smale yet gods power is most seene in weakenes and as you knowe Con-
cordia parv[a]e res crescunt discordia magna[e] dilabuntur. And wee make
noe doubt but your wisdomes will easilie conceiue that the way to continue our loue each to other and to liue in peace is to bringe our selues to
some Rules Articles and agreements by which wee may be regulated and
to which wee may haue recourse as the bottom vppon which our Peace and
loue may be anchored and may be as evidence to each in case either should
goe aboute through any Corrupcion to make a breach And for this wee
haue an example in Davide and Jonathan although their loue was greate
each to other yet they made a Covenante to perpetuate the same Wee
therefore presuminge of your readines this waye as hath beene heretofore
manifested haue thought meete to request our Beloued John Haines esq.
William Pyncheon esqr. and Mr. John Steele to treate with your selues con-

---

[1] W. 4. 92; 5 *Collections*, I. 260–261. For Ludlow, see *D.N.B.*; *D.A.B.*

cerninge the premisses accordinge to such instruccions as they haue received from vs And wee haue authorized them with Comission to conclude in wrytinge of such thinges as are agreed on by both sides. some particulers they will ympart vnto you and therefore wee shall desire they may haue speedy Audience and may haue full aunsweres from your selues that there may bee noe longer delayes but that there may bee certeine Conclusions betweene vs to which wee may haue recourse as aboue said as occasion serue. And soe with our loue wee commend you and your proceedinges to the Almighty and rest Your lovinge frend

Ro. Ludlowe in the name of the whole

Conectecott Windsor May 29th 1638

ROGER WILLIAMS TO JOHN WINTHROP[1]

Providence [ca. June, 1638]

Sir, I sometimes feare that my lines are as thick and over busie as the Muskeetoes etc. but your wisedome will conniue, and your Loue will cover etc.

2 things at present for Informacion.

First in the affaires of the most High; his late dreadfull voice and hand: that audible and sensible Voice the Earthquake.[2]

All these parts felt it, (whether beyond the Nanhiggonsick I yet learne not) for my selfe I scarce perceaved ought but a kind of Thunder and a gentle mooving etc. and it was no more this way to many of our owne and the Natiues apprehensions, and but one sudden short motion.

The younger Natiues are ignorant of the like: but the Ellder informe me that this is the 5th within these 4 score yeare in the Land: the first about 3 score and 10 yeare since: the second some 3 score and 4 yeare since the third some 54 yeare since the 4th some 46 since: and they allwayes observed either plauge or pox or some other epidemicall disease followed: 3 4 or 5 yeare after the Earthquake, (or Naunaumemoauke, as they speake).

He be mercifully pleased himselfe to interprete and open his owne Ridles and graunt (if it be pleasing in his Eyes) it may not be for Destruction but (as the Earthquake before the Gaolors Conversion) a meanes of shaking and turning of all hearts (which are his) English or Indian, to him: to further

---

[1] W. 2. 105; 4 *Collections*, vi. 229–230; *N.C.*, vi. 99–100.

[2] For Winthrop's account of the earthquake, see the entry in his Journal under date June 1, 1638 (1. 270).

this (if the Lord please) the Earthquake sensibly tooke about a thoughsand of the natiues in a most sollemne meeting for play etc.

2ndly a word in mine owne particular, only for Informacion I owe betweene 50 and 60*li* to Mr. Cradock for Commodities receaued from Mr. Mayhew: Mr. Mayhew will testifie that (being Mr. Cradocks agent) he was content to take payment, what (and when) my howse at Salem yealded: accordingly I long since put it into his hand, and he into Mr. Jollies, who beside my voluntarie Act and his Attachment since, sues as I heare for dammages, which I question: since I haue not failed against Contract and Content of the first Agent but the holy pleasure of the Lord be done: vnto whose mercifull Armes (with all due respects) I leaue you, wishing heartily that mercie and goodnes may euer follow you and yours

ROGER WILLIAMS

Sir to your deare companion Mr. Deputie Mr. Bellingham and theirs all respectiue Salutes etc.

ROGER WILLIAMS TO JOHN WINTHROP[1]

For his much honoured and [belo]ved Mr. Governour of Massachusets these in hast

PROVIDENCE this 5t of present weeke [*ca.* June 7, 1638]

MUCH HONOURED SIR, Blessed be the Father of mercies that once againe I receaued your hand the last night by the Messengers by whome I sent.

By them I vnderstand that according as you please to intimate your expectation, Mr. Heynes is come: with Okace 34 Monahiggins and 6 Pequts.[2]

One of the 6 Pequts is Pametesick which was one of the Murtherers who cut of the 3 English going in a boate for clay vpon Qunnihticut river after the Fort was cut of: They not only spilt their bloud, but exercised inhumane and tormenting revenge vpon 2 of them, which cries for Vengeance to heaven.

So that I refer it humbly to your wisedome whether (although I desire not the destruction of the surviving Pequts but a safe dispersion of them yet) the actuall murtherers be not to be surrendred vp and this Pametesick (I am partly confident this is he) at present apprehended.

Our lo[ving] friends of Quinnihticut reported that some Monahigganie

---

[1] New York Public Library; 4 *Collections*, VI. 230–231; *N.C.*, VI. 106–107.
[2] Winthrop records Uncas's arrival in Boston under date June 5, 1638 (I. 271).

women were wronged (as their hair cut of etc.) by the Nanhiggonsicks: but Okace knowes it was done by Wequashcuck of Nayantuquit to whom Okace sent for a Pequt Queene: they 2 haue got in the Pequts (though Okace haue the Harvest). Against Wequashcuck Caunounicus and Miantunnomu had long since proceeded, but our lo[ving] friends of Qunnihticut interposed: I hope for the best to saue blood: So beseeching the great Councellour and Prince of Peace to guide your Councels I rest Your Wo[rshi]ps most vn-worthy yet vnfaigned

ROGER WILLIAMS

All respectiue Salutes etc.

ROGER WILLIAMS TO JOHN WINTHROP[1]

For his much honoured and beloved Mr. Governour of Massachusetts, these

SIR, I perceive by these your last thoughts, that you have received many accusations and hard conceits of this poor native Miantunnomu, wherein I see the vain and empty puff of all terrene promotions, his barbarous birth or greatness being much honoured, confirmed and augmented (in his own conceit) by the solemnity of his league with the English and his more than ordinary entertainment, etc. now all dashed in a moment in the frowns of such in whose friendship and love lay his chief advancement.

Sir, of the particulars, some concern him only, some Caunounicus and the rest of the sachims, some all the natives, some myself.

For the sachims, I shall go over speedily, and acquaint them with particulars. At present, let me still find this favour in your eyes, as to obtain an hearing, for that your love hath never denied me, which way soever your judgment hath been (I hope and I know you will one day see it) and been carried.

Sir, let this barbarian be proud and angry and covetous and filthy, hating and hateful, (as we ourselves have been till kindness from heaven pitied us, etc.) yet let me humbly beg relief, that for myself, I am not yet turned Indian, to believe all barbarians tell me, nor so basely presumptuous as to trouble the eyes and hands of such (and so honoured and dear) with shadows and fables. I commonly guess shrewdly at what a native utters, and, to my remembrance, never wrote particular, but either I know the bottom of it, or else I am bold to give a hint of my suspense.

[1] Original not located (see *Winthrop Papers*, III. 412, *n.* 1); 3 *Collections*, I. 166–169; *N.C.*, VI. 101–106.

Sir, therefore in some things at present (begging your wonted gentleness toward my folly) give me leave to show you how I clear myself from such a lightness.

I wrote lately (for that you please to begin with) that some Pequts, (and some of them actual murderers of the English, and that also after the fort cut off) were now in your hands. Not only love, but conscience, forced me to send, and speedily, on purpose, by a native, mine own servant. I saw not, spake not with Miantunnomu, nor any from him. I write before the All-seeing Eye. But thus it was. A Nanhiggontick man (Awetipimo) coming from the bay with cloth, turned in (as they use to do) to me for lodging. I questioned of Indian passages, etc. He tells me Okace was come with near upon forty natives. I asked what present he brought. He told me, that Cutshamoquene had four fathom and odd of him, and forty was for Mr. Governour. I asked him, how many Pequts. He told me six. I asked him, if they were known. He said Okace denied that there were any Pequts, and said they were Monahiggens all. I asked, if himself knew any of them. He answered, he did, and so did other Indians of Nanhiggontick. I asked, if the murderer of whom I wrote, Pametesick, were there. He answered, he was, and (I further inquiring) he was confident it was he, for he knew him as well as me, etc.

All this news (by this providence) I knew before ever it came to Nanhiggontick. Upon this I sent, indeed fearing guilt to mine own soul, both against the Lord and my countrymen. But see a stranger hand of the Most and Only Wise. Two days after, Okace passeth by within a mile of me (though he should have been kindly welcome.) One of his company (Wequaumugs) having hurt his foot, and disabled from travel, turns in to me; whom lodging, I question, and find him by father a Nanhiggontick, by mother a Monahiggon, and so freely entertained by both. I further inquiring, he told me he went from Monahiggon to the bay with Okace. He told me how he had presented forty fathom (to my remembrance) to Mr. Governour, (four and upwards to Cutshamoquene,) who would not receive them, but asked twice for Pequts. At last, at Newtown, M. Governour received them, and was willing that the Pequts should live, such as were at Monahiggon, subject to the English sachims at Qunnihticut, to whom they should carry tribute, and such Pequts as were at Nanhiggontick to Mr. Governour, and all the runaways at Monahigganick to be sent back. I asked him, how many Pequts were at Nanhiggontick. He said, but two, who were Miantunnomue's captives, and that at Nayantaquit with Wequash Cook were about three score. I asked, why he said the Indians at Nanhiggontick were to be the governour's subjects. He said, because Nayantaquit was sometimes so called, although there hath been of late no coming of Nanhiggontick men thither. I asked him, if he heard all this. He said, that himself and the body of the company staid about Cutshamoquene's. I asked, how many Pequts were amongst them. He said six. I desired him to name them, which he did thus: Pametesick, Weeaugon-hick, (another of those murderers) Makunnete, Kishkontuckqua, Sausaw-pona, Qussaumpowan, which names I presently wrote down, and (pace vestra dixerim) I am as confident of the truth, as that I breathe. Again, (not to be too bold in all the particulars at this time,) what a gross and monstrous untruth is that concerning myself, which your love and wisdom to myself a little espy, and I hope see malice and falsehood (far from the fear of God) whispering together? I have long held it will-worship to doff and don to the Most High in worship; and I wish also that, in civil worship, others were as far from such a vanity, though I hold it not utterly unlawful in some places. Yet surely, amongst the barbarians, (the highest in the world,) I would rather lose my head than so practise, because I judge it my duty to set them better copies, and should sin against mine own persuasions and resolutions.

Sir, concerning the islands Prudence and (Patmos, if some had not hindered) Aquedenick, be pleased to understand your great mistake: neither of them were sold properly, for a thousand fathom would not have bought either, by strangers. The truth is, not a penny was demanded for either, and what was paid was only gratuity, though I chose, for better assurance and form, to call it sale.

And, alas! (though I cannot conceive you can aim at the sachims) they have ever conceived, that myself and Mr. Coddington (whom they knew so many years a sachim at Boston) were far from being rejected by yourselves, as you please to write, for if the Lord had not hid it from their eyes, I am sure you had not been thus troubled by myself at present. Yet the earth is the Lord's and the fulness thereof. His infinite wisdom and pity be pleased to help you all, and all that desire to fear his name and tremble at his word in this country, to remember that we all are rejected of our native soil, and more to mind the many strong bands, with which we are all tied, than any particular distastes each against other, and to remember that excellent precept, Prov. 25, If thine enemy hunger, feed him, etc.; for thou shalt heap coals of fire upon his head, and Jehovah shall reward thee; unto whose mercy and tender compassions I daily commend you, desirous to be more and ever Your worship's unfeigned and faithful

ROGER WILLIAMS

[*Ca.* June 14, 1638]

Sir, mine own and wife's respective salutes to your dear companion and all yours; as also to Mr. Deputy, Mr. Bellingham, and other loving friends.

I am bold to enclose this paper, although the passages may not be new, yet they may refresh your memories in these English-Scotch distractions, etc.

DEED OF MASCONOMET TO JOHN WINTHROP, JR.[1]

I Musconominet Sagamore of Agawam, doe by these presents acknoledge to haue Receiued of Mr. John Wintrop the Some of Twenty poundes, in full satisfacion of all the Right property and Cleame, I haue or ought to haue, vnto all the lands lying and being in the Bay of Agawam, alls. Ipswich being so Called now by the English, as well alsuch land as I formerly reserued vnto my owne vse at Chibocco as alsoe all other lands belonging vnto me in those parts Mr. Dummers farme excepted only, And I herby relinquish all the Right and Interest I haue vnto all the Hauens Rivers Creekes Ilands, huntings and fishings with all the woodes Swampes Timber and whatsoever ells is or may be in or vpon the said ground to me belongeing, and I doe hereby acknoledge to haue receiued full Satisfacion from the said Jno. Wintropp for all former agreements touching the premises or any part of them, And I doe hereby bind my selfe, to make good the foresaid bargaine and Saile vnto the said John Wintrop his heires and assignes foreuer, and to secure him against the tytle and Cleame of all other Indians and Natiues whatsoeuer. Witnesse my hand this 28 June 1638.

MUSCONOMINET his X marke

Witnesses herevnto
    THOMAS COYTMORE
    JAMES DOWNINGE
    ROBART HARDINGE
    JNO. JOLLIFE

This deed aboue written so signed and witnessed being Compared with the originall 4 B. p. 381:2 word for word stands thus entred and Recorded at the request of Captaine Wayte Winthrop this 15th of february 1682 as Attests

EDWARD RAWSON *Secret.*

[1] Essex Institute; Waters, *Ipswich in the Massachusetts Bay Colony*, I. 9. For the acknowledgment of Masconomet, Sagamore of Agawam, see pages 104–105, below.

SAMUEL SHARPE TO JOHN WINTHROP[1]

To the Right Wor[shi]p[fu]ll Jno. Winthop Esquire Gouernour

RIGHT WOR[SHI]P[FU]LL, I receiued a note from yow lately concerning your servants Walters time he spent at Salem for which I hoped yow had receiued satisfaction before this: my bargaine with his M[aste]r Wilks was To giue him 10*li* for his Terme if he would serve my turne if not To returne him backe againe within 14 dayes which I did after Eight dayes tryall, but he as it seemes not willing to returne to his M[aste]r, hired himselfe with Georg Norton a carpenter and our pastor (in whose worke Georg Norton then was) vndertooke to giue satisfaction to his M[aste]r Wilkes, but this was done without my priuity. when your first note came to pay it to our pastor, Georg Norton was willing to giue satisfaction to him which I supposed had beene accounted for betwixt them. I am sorry things haue thus beene deferred. I suppose I was free from him yet if any thing seeme due I thinke it must be after 50*li* per annum acording to our baygaine but in nothing would I bee contentious but willing to giue satisfaction as yow thinke meete. Your wor[ships] in all humble service

SAM: SHARPE

[*Ca.* July, 1638]

ROGER LUDLOW TO JOHN WINTHROP[2]

To the right wo[rshi]pp[ful] Jo: Wenthropp, esqr. the Gouernor of the Masachusetts Bay be these delivered

RIGHT WO[RSHI]PP[FUL] SIR, I am to relate vnto you some passages that are befallen the Indians att longe Iland by Aonemo the Sachem of Naanticke neer to the naragancetts within the Jurisdiccion of Maantonemo the Sachem of Naragancett. the saide Indians of longe Iland are Tributaries to your selues and vs by agreement vnder hand made by Captaine Stoughton the last Summer they are to paye twoe parts to you one part to vs. It was aboute eight dayes since, And the Sachem himself with divers of his men are here to complain and I will verbatim declare the matter of their Complaint. Aonemo with some 80 men whereof 20 of them were a kinde of Pequoitt

---

[1] W. I. 141. Samuel Sharpe was one of the group who came to Salem in 1629 in the fleet which brought the Reverend Francis Higginson and the Reverend Samuel Skelton.

[2] W. 4. 93; 5 *Collections*, I. 261–264.

Captaines came to the saide long Iland and divers att first came into the Sachems wigwam But Aonemo was not with them and the Sachem asked them whether they were goeinge, and they said they were come to see fashions, and after a while one of them sawe the Sachems Quiver of Arrowes and would haue him giue it vnto them. he aunswered noe But if trucke it they might. nay say they but Aonemo will come by and by and then they would haue it and wampam to. Then the saide Sachem beinge aduised by a frend amonge them that the saide Aonemo intended to take him the saide Sachem and his bretheren beinge 5 prisoners and carry them away wherevppon he fledd into the woodes. presently the saide Aonemo came and inquired for the saide Sachem and seinge he could not come by him he told them he must haue some wampom and if deny it he would kill them, wherevppon for feare of their liues the old men and Squas gaue him some 60 fathom of wampom. Soe they went from thence and went vpp and downe the Iland robbinge and pillaginge and gott more aboute some 30 fathom of wampom and tooke away their shoes stockins deare Skinnes and burnt their wigwams, as alsoe in a base part after hee had ronged a Sachem and robbed him tooke away his breeches and left him naked, which is accounted amongest them the greatest disgrace that may be and deserues death amongest them and the Sachem told them he had rather die then haue such a disgrace putt vppon him. And after these outrages comitted the old men did somwhat capitulate with the saide Aonemo and demanded of him whether he would come and rifell them that are frends to the [E]nglish and asked him howe he thought the [E]nglish would take it espicially they of Conectecott. he aunswered it noe matter for the english of Conectecott they will speake much but doe little. But what say you of the [E]nglish in the Bay   he saies he would doe well enough with them   The Gouernor was a great man and his frend and he could with half the wampam goe to the saide Gouernor and he should say wereagea. And he did purpose to goe to him and buy them all of him, therefore saies he plant your corne and weede it well and I will come att haruest and eate it. The old men likewise saide that the [E]nglish had promised them they should not be soe vsed   Aonemo replied the [E]nglish men are liars they doe it but onely to gett your wampom. As soone as they had done this the saide Sachem comes to vs and relates as aforesaide, and tells vs plainely that if this be suffered hee cannott be able to paye their Tribute for when it is prouided they will come and take it awaye and besides wishes vs to consider what the yssue will be that noe Indians will trust vs and claimes a promise of vs that they should be righted. wherevppon haveinge aduised togeather wee cannot see but wee are bounde to see them righted and therefore haue concluded and doe purpose god willinge within these 8 dayes to send 8 men by water to the saide Aonemo to demand satisfaccion of these Iniuries, and if he doth refuse it is purposed by vs to make warr against him. Captaine Mason goes with the saide 8 men and thinges preparing to send. The Indians are soe earnest vppon vs and tell vs they will not goe awaye vntill they see some thinge done, for say they there be 100 Sachems greate and smale amonge the Naragancetts and if they shall all haue liberty thus to ransacke them they must desert the place and goe to the Southward and that hath inforced vs to be soe speedy in this execucion, makeinge little question you will doe the like with speede least by degrees they come to the same height the Pequoitts did. wee shall alsoe desire your aduise concerninge the remander of the Pequoitts, For there were in this designe 20 of them, and Aonemo gaue them 30 fathom of the wampom they tooke away as aboue saide for their valour, and if they be soe forward against the Indians our frends whoe knowes howe soone they may doe the like against our selues. I will alsoe relate howe farr Maantonemo hath an hande in it as the Sachem tells vs. the Sachem saies a frend of his tould them that Canonicos Sonne was willing either to haue gone with the Aonemo in this designe or to haue followed shortelie after   But Maantonemo told him he should not for hee were as good goe against the [E]nglish them-selues for these Indians were as it were their men, and this might be a meanes to procure warr against the saide Aonemo and then he must be gladd to fight against him. soe he knewe of it and yet notwithstanding hindered it not. Sir wee should desire you not to take it amisse wee haue written backe no thinge aboute your propositions sent by Mr. Haines   our imployments are soe many att this tyme wee cannot drawe our people togeather. But as soone as conveniently wee cann wee intend to consider of it. I should wright some other thinges vnto you But our neighbour goeinge soe suddenly inforces mee to [be] breife and somewhat rude hopeinge you will not curiously obserue the confusednes of these lines. And therefore with my seruice remembred I desire the almighty to giue you aduise and assistance in the thinge in hand and rest Your lovinge frend

                                        Ro: Ludlowe

Windsor July 3d 1638

ABRAHAM SHURT TO JOHN WINTHROP[1]

*To the Right Wor[shipfu]ll John Winthrop Gouernour of the Baye
of Messthusett deliver*

PEMAQUID the 16th of Julye 1638

WOR[SHIPFU]LL, My dutye remembred ettc. Att my cominge from the Baye to Richmonds Iland I sent the first bill of exc[h]a[nge] for the 100*s* and the 2d by the waye of Bristoll, and arrivinge hither I received a lettre from Mr. Elbridge in which he writes that he had received 100*s* of Sir Rich: Saltonstall in part of the bill of exc[h]a[nge] and dammadge, and now I haue written vnto him to retourne the bills agayne, beinge confident that he will without presentinge them: and to that ende I haue sent vnto Mr. Mayhew that he may forbeare the payment of it to Mr. Ballard. Had I knowne of the receipt of the 100*s* I would not haue sent the bills for England not presentinge elce at present, I take leaue and rest ever Your Wor[shi]ps to command

ABRAHAM SHURT

ROGER WILLIAMS TO JOHN WINTHROP[2]

For his much honoured and beloued Mr. John Wintrop at his howse in Boston these

PROUIDENCE 23 5th [1638]

2 dayes since I was bold to present you with a line, and still (so it pleaseth the most High) I am occasioned againe to be a constant trouble etc.

These your Wo[rshi]ps Servants visiting me in their Travell, I enquire after your Runnawayes: The man sayth he hath much to relate to your selfe, and wanting vtterance desires me to write. He sayth he hath enquired much after the Runnawayes and vnderstands for certaine that they are all at Monhiggin.

That the Flight was long since plotted, for he hath now heard by a Pequot that came from Monhiggin, that the 10 Monhiggins which came to your Wo[rshi]p in the Spring to buy one of the maidens and offered 10 fathom of Beades, came from Onkas who intended that maide for his wife.

That he gaue order to those 10 men, that (in case they could not buy her)

---

[1] W. 2. 182; 4 *Collections*, VI. 572. For Shurt, see 4 *Collections*, VI. 570n.
[2] W. 2. 106; 4 *Collections*, VI. 231–233; *N.C.*, VI. 108–109.

they should leaue one man there at your Howse to perswade and worck their Escape.

That man was the Pequt Robin (Causa Senamut) who hath effected his busines for which (as he heares) Onkas promised him and hath giuen him the 10 fathom of wompam.

Onkas hath taken the 2 daughters Marie and Jane both to wife and sayth that now he hath done sending of presents to Massachuset.

Repriue was promised Joane by the Old Squaw for the futherance of the busines and hath her   He advised their Escape by Neepmuck, because once before, escaping through the Narigansett Countrey, himselfe was sent back, by the Nariganset Sachims.

This man thincks allso that no Indian meanes will be able to effect their Returne, but that the English must fetch them: It will be your Wo[rshi]ps wisedome to forecast so much and to prepare (Captaine Patrick and many more may be occasioned to fetch theirs allso) yet I request your Wo[rshi]ps patience a few dayes.

Sir this young man who comes along is this Womans Nephew an ingenuous sober fellow, one of my long acquaintance (whome I called Oldway as his Indian name (Necawnimeyat) signifies)   he tells me he hath a good mind to abide one yeare with these his Friends in your Wo[rshi]ps Service   I incourage him and present him to your Wisedome and pity, not knowing but that the purpose of the only wise and most pitifull God may be toward him for good. Vnto the euerflowing streames of the most holy fountaine of Living Waters (whose Drops are able to refresh and saue worlds of wandring Soules) I heartily recommend your Wo[rshi]p, your dearest Companion, and all yours, Grieuing That I dare be no more Your Wo[rshi]ps

R: WILLIAMS

GEORGE NORTON TO JOHN WINTHROP[1]

This is to certifie your Worship that your man water after that he Cam from mr. sharpe his seruis with me was About thre wekes   the other part of his time was spent in goinge and Cuming from the bay   alsoe he had of me mony to beare his Charges Cuming and going and I paid for the bringine his Chist to salem which all the Charg I haue bine at: Com nere to 5s   soe Considering the time he was with me and the Charge I was at for what more

---

[1] W. 1. 124. George Norton was a carpenter who came to Salem in the fleet with the Reverend John Higginson and the Reverend Samuel Skelton in 1629.

your worship shall require I am willing to make you payment to home you please soe in hast I Rest Yours in any seruis to Comand

GEORGE NORTON

SALEM this Last of July 1638

ROGER WILLIAMS TO JOHN WINTHROP[1]

MUCH HONOURED SIR, The bearer lodging with me, I am bold to write an hasty advertisement concerning late passages. For himself, it seems he was fearful to go farther than forty miles about us, especially considering that no natives are willing to accompany him to Pequat or Monahiganick, being told by two Pequots (the all of Miantunnomue's captives which are not run from him) what he might expect, etc.

Sir, Capt. Mason and Thomas Stanton landing at Nanhiggontick, and at Miantunnomue's denouncing war within six days against Juanemo, for they say that Miantunnomu hath been fair in all the passages with them, Juanemo sent two messengers to myself, requesting counsel. I advised him to go over with beads to satisfy, etc.

He sent four Indians. By them Mr. Haynes writes me, that they confest fifteen fathom there received at Long Island. Thereabout they confest to me, (four being taken of Pequts by force, and restored again,) as also that the islanders say fifty-one fathom, which sum he demanded, as also that the Nayantaquit messengers laid down twenty-six fathom and a half, which was received in part, with declaration that Juanemo should within ten days bring the rest himself, or else they were resolved for war, etc. I have therefore sent once and again to Janemo, to persuade himself to venture, etc. Caunounicus sent a principal man last night to me, in haste and secrecy, relating that Wequash had sent word that, if Juanemo went over, he should be killed, but I assure them the contrary, and persuade Caunounicus to importune and hasten Juanemo within his time, ten days, withal hoping and writing back persuasions of better things to Mr. Haynes, proffering myself (in case that Juanemo through fear or folly fail) to take a journey and negotiate their business, and save blood, whether the natives' or my countrymen's.

Sir, there hath been great hubbub in all these parts, as a general persuasion that the time was come of a general slaughter of natives, by reason of a murther committed upon a native within twelve miles of us, four days since, by

[1] Original not located (see *Winthrop Papers*, III. 412, n. 1); 3 *Collections*, I. 170–173; *N.C.*, VI. 110–114.

four desperate English.[1] I presume particulars have scarce as yet been presented to your hand. The last 5th day, toward evening, a native, passing through us, brought me word, that at Pawatuckqut, a river four miles from us toward the bay, four Englishmen were almost famished. I sent instantly provisions and strong water, with invitation, etc. The messengers brought word, that they were one Arthur Peach of Plymouth, an Irishman, John Barnes, his man, and two others come from Pascataquack, travelling to Qunnihticut; that they had been lost five days, and fell into our path but six miles. Whereas they were importuned to come home, etc. they pleaded soreness in travelling, and therefore their desire to rest there.

The next morning they came to me by break of day, relating that the old man at Pawatuckqut had put them forth the last night, because that some Indians said, that they had hurt an Englishman, and therefore that they lay between us and Pawatuckqut.

I was busy in writing letters and getting them a guide to Qunnihticut, and inquired no more, they having told me, that they came from Plymouth on the last of the week in the evening, and lay still in the woods the Lord's day, and then lost their way to Weymouth, from whence they lost their way again towards us, and came in again six miles off Pawatuckqut.

After they were gone, an old native comes to me, and tells me; that the natives round about us were fled, relating that those four had slain a native, who had carried three beaver skins and beads for Caunounicus' son, and came home with five fathom and three coats; that three natives which came after him found him groaning in the path; that he told them that four Englishmen had slain him. They came to Pawatuckqut, and inquired after the English, which when Arthur and his company heard, they got on hose and shoes and departed in the night.

I sent after them to Nanhiggantick, and went myself with two or three more to the wounded in the woods. The natives at first were shy of us, conceiving a general slaughter, but (through the Lord's mercy) I assured them that Mr. Governour knew nothing, etc. and that I had sent to apprehend the men. So we found that he had been run through the leg and the belly with one thrust. We drest him and got him to town next day, where Mr. James and Mr. Greene endeavoured, all they could, his life; but his wound in the belly, and blood lost, and fever following, cut his life's thread.

Before he died, he told me that the four English had slain him, and that

---

[1] For Winthrop's account of this episode, see *Journal*, i. 273, 274; for Bradford's account, see *History of Plymouth*, ii. 263–268; for the account of the Englishmen's trial, see *Records of the Colony of New Plymouth in New England*, Nathaniel B. Shurtleff, Editor, i (Boston, 1855), 96, 97.

(being faint and not able to speak) he had related the truth to the natives who first came to him, viz. that they, viz. the English, saw him in the bay and his beads; that sitting in the side of a swamp a little way out of the path, (I went to see the place, fit for an evil purpose,) Arthur called him to drink tobacco, who coming and taking the pipe of Arthur, Arthur run him through the leg into the belly, when, springing back, he Arthur, made the second thrust, but mist him; that another of them struck at him, but mist him, and his weapon run into the ground; that getting from them a little way into the swamp, they pursued him, till he fell down, when they mist him, and getting up again, when he heard them close by him, he run to and again in the swamp, till he fell down again, when they lost him quite; afterwards, towards night, he came and lay in the path, that some passenger might help him as aforesaid.

Whereas they said, they wandered Plymouth way, Arthur knew the path, having gone it twice; and beside, Mr. Throckmorton met them about Naponset River in the path, who, riding roundly upon a sudden by them, was glad he had past them, suspecting them. They denied that they met Mr. Throckmorton.

The messenger that I sent to Nanhiggontick, pursuing after them, returned the next day, declaring that they showed Miantunnomu letters to Aquedenick, (which were mine to Qunnihtiqut,) and so to Aquedenick they past, whither I sent information of them, and so they were taken. Their sudden examination they sent me, a copy of which I am bold to send your worship enclosed.

The islanders (Mr. Coddington being absent) resolved to send them to us, some thought, by us to Plymouth, from whence they came. Sir, I shall humbly crave your judgment, whether they ought not to be tried where they are taken. If they be sent any way, whether not to Plymouth. In case Plymouth refuse, and the islanders send them to us, what answers we may give, if others unjustly shift them unto us. I know that every man, quatenus man, and son of Adam, is his brother's keeper or avenger; but I desire to do bonum bene, etc.

Thus, beseeching the God of heaven, most holy and only wise, to make the interpretation of his own holy meaning in all occurrences, to bring us all by these bloody passages to an higher price of the blood of the Son of God, yea of God, by which the chosen are redeemed, with all due respects to your dear self and dear companion, I cease. Your worship's most unworthy

ROGER WILLIAMS

[*Ca.* August 1, 1638]

This native, Will, my servant, shall attend your worship for answer.
My due respect to Mr. Deputy, Mr. Bellingham, etc.

RECEIPT OF THEOPHILUS EATON[1]

Received the 3d of August 1638 of the wor[shipfu]ll John Wynthropp the Somme of Eight pownds two shillings and nine pence } 8*li* 2*s* 9*d*
in full of all reconings to this day I say Received per

THEOPH: EATON

[*Memorandum by Governor Winthrop:*] Robt. Griffin complaines.

HUGH PETER TO JOHN WINTHROP[2]

RIGHT DEERE AND HONORD, These are not only to salute you and your
good gentlwoman, cum cæteris; but earnestly to intreat you to let mee haue
a word from you about Mrs. Beggerly's, or rather Mr. Skeltons house,[3] which
is now falling to the ground, if some thing bee not done: we haue referd it,
and would earnestly intreate you for a writing (they say) you haue about it,
which you promised her, and shee sayes will lende to the busines for light:
and thus wayting for that writing, and wishing you the fullnes of all good,
as to myne owne soule, I rest Yours euer and euer

HUGH PETER

SALEM, 8th of the (6) [1638]

[*Endorsed by Governor Winthrop:*] Mr. Petter; Salem, 8 (10).

---

[1] W. I. 124.

[2] Original not located; 4 *Collections*, VII. 201–202. Due to the loss of the original manuscript, it is impossible to clear up the uncertainty about the date of this letter which arises from the fact that in the earlier printed version the date as given by Peter himself is said to have been August 8, while that of Winthrop's endorsement is given as December 8.

[3] See *New England Historical and Genealogical Register*, XXXV. 318–320.

ROGER WILLIAMS TO JOHN WINTHROP[1]

For his much honoured and beloved Mr. Gov[ernou]r of Massachusets

PROVIDENCE 14th of the 6th [1638]

SIR, Since my last (vnto which you were pleased to giue answere with kind advice concerning the murther of the natiue) I have receaued divers letters from Qunnihticut. the Summ of all is this, that it hath pleased the Lord to encline all hearts to peace. Juanemo was perswaded to goe over in person and to giue that Satisfaction which was demaunded: Only concerning a Mare killd by some Nayanticks, (others say by Pequts) but as yet no proofe: Our friends haue taken his promise to enquire and informe, and so they dismist him.

It hath pleased the Magistrates at Qunticut to envite Miantunnomu over to them to discover some Pequt passages and Murtherers, which are denied, and to enter vpon some Articles with themselues: denying themselues to be obliged in the Articles of the Bay.[2]

I haue conceaved that all the English in the Land were wrapt vp in that Agreement (a Copie of which you were pleased Sir to send me): nevertheles I perswade him to goe over: His desire was (which Agowaun Sachim Masquanominity had in charge to expresse to you) that Mr. Go[vernour] would please to spare 4 English from himselfe as witnesses of Passages: as allso my selfe with Cutshamoquene and Masquanominit.

I haue formerly engaged my Promise to Miantunnomu: and resolue to take 2 or 3 English from hence, and hope (through the Lords mercy) that the iourney may be for peace.

Sir vnles any passe by accident to Qunnihticut (if so you shall see good) that desire of 3 or 4 English may be denied and yet graunted in effect by the going of some freely with my selfe.

Only Sir, be pleased to giue an hint of your pleasure in any matter considerable which we shall endeavour to effect.

The natiues, friends of the slaine had Consultacion to kill an English man in revenge: Miantunnomu heard of it and desired that the English would be carefull on the high wayes, and sent himselfe expresse threatnings to them etc. and informed them that Mr. Governour would see Justice done. Ousamequin, comming from Plymmouth told me that the 4 men were all guiltie: I answered but one: he replied true one wounded him, but all lay in wait 2

[1] W. 2. 110; 4 *Collections*, VI. 248–249; *N.C.*, VI. 115–116.
[2] I.e., the treaty negotiated with the Narragansetts in 1636. Cf. *Journal*, I. 193–194.

dayes and assisted   in Conclusion: he tould me that the Principall must
not dye for he was Mr. Winslowes man: and allso that the man was by birth
a Neepmuck man: and so not worthy an other man should die for him: I
answered what I thought fit but conceaue there will be neede of Wisedome
and Zeale in some and remembrance of that Vox Cœli: He that doth Violence to the blood of any Person let him flee to the Pit, let none deliver
him. The Lord mercifully cleanse the Land from bloud, and make the bloud
of his sonn Jesus more precious in all our eyes. So prayes Your Wo[rshi]ps
most vnworthy

ROGER WILLIAMS

To Mrs. Wintrop Mr. Deputie and his all yours best respects etc.

JOHN WINTHROP'S SUMMARY
OF HIS LETTER TO THOMAS HOOKER[1]

1638. 6. 28. In my letter to Mr. Hooker, I complain of three things:

1. That they told the Narragansetts, that they were not tied to the agreement[2] we made with the Indians; and that they did this, to advance their
own reputation with the Indians, and to abase ours; that it was a point of
state policy in them not to dissent, while the war was at their doors, for they
had need of our help etc. that it was done without any pressing occasion;
that it was done unseasonably, after their own commissioners had propounded that before the Indians we should in all things appear as one.

2. That they altered the articles of confederation in the most material
point, and all because some preeminence was therein yielded to the Massachusetts, and being again agreed, (only referred to consent etc.) in three
months we had no answer from them; that the way which they would have
taken, of referring differences to the churches, would occasion infinite trouble
and expense, and yet leave the issue to the sword.

I expostulated about the unwarrantableness and unsafeness of referring

---

[1] Original lost; Savage (1826), 349–350. This summary was among various memoranda written
by Governor Winthrop at the end of the second volume of his Journal. This volume was destroyed
by fire in Savage's Boston office on November 10, 1825.

J. Hammond Trumbull, in editing Hooker's answer to the letter here abstracted by Winthrop,
has, in his introduction and notes, supplied the background and explanations necessary for the
understanding of Winthrop's summary. *Collections of the Connecticut Historical Society*, 1 (1863), 1–3,
15–18. Hooker's answer is printed in this volume (pages 75–84, below). See also the rough draft of
Winthrop's rejoinder (pages 99–100, below).

[2] See note 2, page 52, above.

matter of counsel or judicature to the body of the people, quia the best part is always the least, and of that best part the wiser part is always the lesser. The old law was, choose ye out judges etc. and thou shalt bring the matter to the judge etc.

3. That they did still exercise jurisdiction at Agawam, though one of their commissioners disclaimed to intermeddle in our line, and thither we challenged our right, and it was agreed so, and I had wrote to them to desire them to forbear until etc. that Mr. Pincheon had small encouragement to be under them; that if his relation were true, I could not see the justice of their proceeding against him etc.

That the end of my writing to him was, that he might help quench these sparks of contention; that I did open our grievances to him in their most true and reasonable intendment; that though I be strict for our right in public, quia their magistrates are so, yet I am willing to listen to advice, and my aim is the common good.

PETITION OF JOHN UNDERHILL
TO THE MASSACHUSETTS GENERAL COURT[1]

Wheare as itt is somewhatt questionable whether the three Moneths I was Absentt, as well in the service off the Contrie, as otherr perticular persons: My request therefore is, thatt this honoured Corte would be pleased to disside this controvercie, my selfe Alledgeing itt to be the custome off Nations: Thatt if A Commander be lentt to another State, by thatt state to whome he is a servantt, booth his place and meanes is nott detayned from him, soe longe as he dooth nott refuse the call of his owne state, to which he is a servantt, In case they shall call him home, Butt I leave itt to your Wisdomes. And further thatt this honoured Corte would be pleased to answer my antyentt Suite thatt 250 acres off land promissed me in my first Covenants which some of our honoured Magistrats vndertooke to performe in the name of the whole, And if the honoured Corte shall vouchsafe to make some addition, thatt which hath nott bene deserved: by the same power of god may be in due season: Thus leaving my request to your wise Consideracions I rest: Yours in all service whatt I may to be commanded:

JOHN VNDERHILL

[*Ca.* September, 1638]

---

[1] W. 3. 44; 4 *Collections*, VII. 177–178. This document is not in Underhill's handwriting. For Underhill, see L. Effingham de Forest and Anne L. de Forest, *Captain John Underhill, Gentleman,*

[*Memorandum on verso:*] The tyme was when a little went far, then much was not knowne nor desired: now the tyme is that a great deale goeth but a little way; the reason of the difference lyeth only in the error of Judgment, for nature requires no more to vpholde it now then when it was satisfied with lesse.

EDWARD COOKE TO JOHN WINTHROP[1]

To the right wor[shipfu]ll my most Honoured friend Mr. John Winterop Governour in New Englande present these

NOBLE SIR, I conceive I am not out of your remembrance, and being confident of your goodness, have presumed to intreate your favour in the behalfe of the Bearer hereof, my sonn. it hath pleased the wise disposer of all things to affect his heart for New England, and nothing could please him but my consent to that affection. I haue bredd him vpp vnder my selfe in my profession of an Apothecarie 5 yeares. hee hath proffited in that way reasonable well, and had his affection stood constant to continue with mee, I should have made him a compleate Artist. hee is honest and religiouse, and I doubt not but hee will soe approve himselfe, and may proove a vsefull man in that place. I was the more willinge to condescend to this his desire in respect of your selfe, and my reverend friend Mr. Hooker, Mr. Theophilus Eaton, Mr. Hopkins, and divers others of my good friends in that place, and now Noble Sir, my Suite to your selfe is this, that yow willbe pleased to countenance him, and advise him. hee shall not bee chargable to yow, for I intend God willing to supply him in all respects, with whatsoever hee shall wante, and if hee take liking to the Cuntrey (as I suppose hee will), then God willing I will sett him vpp in that profession hee hath exercised. yow may please to remember I am an adventurer one of the first, when Mr. Cradock my Loveing Cousin was Governour and payde to the Tresurer Mr. Harwood at two payments 100*li* as these notes acquittances vnder his hand will shew, and to what end. besides I lent the Company 50*li* vppon there seale, as my sonn will make knowne. I hope by your good favour and furtherance my sonn may enjoye those priviledges due in Compensation of these sommes of money so longe agoe disbursed by mee in that action, which profitts or assignements from the worthy Company in New England I have given to my sonn Robert

Soldier of Fortune (New York, 1934); Henry C. Shelley, *John Underhill, Captain of New England and New Netherland* (New York, 1932); *D.A.B.* Cf. *Records of Massachusetts*, I. 237, under date September 6, 1638; *Journal*, I. 275, under date September 7, 1638.

[1] W. 3. 103; 4 *Collections*, VII. 381–382. For Cooke, see 4 *Collections*, VII. 381*n*.

Cooke,[1] beseeching yow to stand his friend, and I shall bee much obleiged to yow for your favour and will bee ready to serve yow in any thinge in this kingdom to my power. thuss nothing doubting of your kinde acceptance of this my Suite, and of your favour to this poore stranger who hath forsaken all his friends, I take my leave, and commend yow to the divine providence, and will ever rest, Your assured loveinge friend to serve yow

EDWARD COOKE

LONDON the 10 Septembris 1638

PETITION OF HUGH PETER
TO THE MASSACHUSETTS GENERAL COURT[2]

To the Honored Court now set at Boston

Whereas it pleased the Lord by diuers occasions to exercise our honored brother Mr. Humfrey so as his condition is generally taken notice of in the Country to bee such that without some helpe his frends feare the Gospell may suffer by his sufferings.

By the aduice of frends I am bold to desire the Counsell, fauor, and assistance of the Court now assembled in his behalfe, and finding the Country so charged already by necessary rates I haue only this way of some succor to present to your wisedomes viz: that wheras hee hath some mony in his hands intended to some publike vse, if that may bee remitted to his owne being one hundred and odde pounds; and if therunto you shall aduise I shall pay him what Mr. Geere left to some of vs to dispose of for the Country, I suppose it may answer good part of his necessity, thoughe I perceiue lesse then 700*li* besides the sale of much of his estate will not cleere him.

Herin I shall wayt your pleasure and shall euer bee (as I am bound) Yours

HUGH PETER

SALEM, 10 (7) [1638]

[*Endorsed by Governor Winthrop:*] The Court vpon hearinge this Petition, and muche argument and consideration thereof did declare their tender regard of the gentleman and his condition, and their readynesse to helpe to supporte

---

[1] In Octòber, 1640, Robert Cooke, then of Charlestown, was granted eight hundred acres of land "in regard of his fathers 100*li* aduentured in the ioynt stock." *Records of Massachusetts*, I. 307.
[2] W. 2. 51; 4 *Collections*, VI. 96–97.

him: but they are not satisfied that his estate is so lowe as it should call for any such publ[ic] helpe: and if it should appeare so, they would then see a faire waye how such helpe may be vsefull to him for the intended ende.[1]

ROGER WILLIAMS TO JOHN WINTHROP[2]

For the right Wo[rshi]pfull and his much honoured friend Mr. Gov[ernou]r of the Massachusetts these

At NARIGANSETT the 10th of the 7th: early [1638]

MUCH HONOURED SIR, These Sachims with myself consulting the last Lords day as soone as I here arrived: I dispatched a letter to meete our Qunnihticut friends at Monahiggin: desiring a speedie word from Capt: Mason (according as he found the busines Easie or Difficult) to giue direction for the Course of the Narigansetts, either to Monahiggin or Pequt. With all the Messenger had charge to deale with Onkas, from vs all Caunounicus Miantunnomu etc. to be wise and faythfull to vs in what we should propose to him.

The Messenger returned the last night (and being a discreete man to obserue passages) he related that comming neere the towne viz. to wit Monahiggin he heard 6 guns, which perswaded him that English were come but drawing neerer he found they were the Guns which formerly the Pequts had got from the English. Entring the Court he found the House mingled full of Monahiggins and Pequts, who desired his newes, but he silent: They told him that they heard that the English were comming against them, and they had sent vp 2 chiefe men who found the English trayning: They were examined of 2 things viz: why they had lately let goe 2 of the murtherers at Nayantaquit whom they had bound and why they had seazed vpon all the Corne at Pequt, belonging to hiether Nayantaquit Pequts: so they were ymprisoned and bound: word whereof comming to Onkace 40 men were sent vp with their Bead girdles to redeeme them: The Messenger got Onkace private, who would not be drawne to yeald vp any of his Pequts, but alleadging that he had bought them with his money of the English (as the Nayantaquit Sachims said, for which purpose I am bold to inclose Mr. Heynes his answere) he said they found the English so false that the last night in a generall meeting they were resolved to fight it out, and for himselfe although the

---

[1] This answer by the Court to Peter's petition does not appear in the records of the General Court.

[2] W. 2. 110; 4 *Collections*, VI. 250–252; *N.C.*, VI. 117–119.

English bound him and killd him he would not yeald: He related that Mr. Heynes had given him a letter of Securitie to lye by him, in case that any English should iniure him, but in this pursuing his Pequts and binding his men he had throwen away his letter etc. Sir your wisedome (I know) catcheth at my request before I make it viz: that in case I am directed from our Friends of Qunnihticut, to send for aide, you would please to cause a readines at litle warning. I could make true Relacion of the brags of the chiefe of these wretches viz: that the Massachusett English did but gleane after the Qunnihticut men etc. in the wars: but I am confident you desire their good, with the safetie of your owne state: therefore I rest with a Description briefe of the Pequt Townes now againe vnder Okace and the Nayantaquit Sachims established: At Pequt Nayantaquit are vpward of 20 howses, vp the river at Mangunckakuck 8, vp still at Sauquonckackock 10, vp still at Paupattok-shick 15, vp still at Tatuppequauog 20, 3 or [4] mile further with Onkace at his towne Monahiggin a great number mingled, which are all vnder Onkas, beside those at Qunnipiuck and others of Long Iland and Sasacous his Con-federates. At Nayantaquit the hither vpwards of 20 howses all vnder the Nayantaquit Sachims, except 6 or 7 men vnto whome your Wo[rshi]p was pleased to giue life vpon Miantunnomues motion by my letter vpon their submission. these are still Miantunnomues Subiects, yet refusing to liue with him at Narigansett, he disclaimes them, in case according to promise they assist not in this busines. The most High graciously sanctifie all his holy pleasure to vs, prosper these our present Enterprises to his prayse, but es-pecially against those Enemies (1 Pet. 2. 11.) Lusts which fight against our Soules: in him I desire to be Your Wo[rshi]ps more and to Eternitie

ROGER WILLIAMS

ROGER WILLIAMS TO JOHN WINTHROP[1]

MUCH HONOURED SIR, Through the mercy of the Most High, I am newly returned from a double journey to Qunnihticut and Plymouth. I shall pre-sume on your wonted love and gentleness to present you with a short relation of what issue it pleased the Lord to produce out of them, especially since your worship's name was some way engaged in both.

I went up to Qunnihticut with Miantunnomu,[2] who had a guard of up-

[1] Original not located (see *Winthrop Papers*, III. 412, *n.* 1); 3 *Collections*, I. 173–177; *N.C.*, VI. 120–125.

[2] The negotiations between the Connecticut authorities, Miantunnomoh, and Uncas, the pre-

wards of 150 men, and many sachims, and his wife and children, with him. By the way (lodging from his house three nights in the woods) we met divers Nanhiggontick men complaining of robbery and violence, which they had sustained from the Pequts and Monahiggins in their travel from Qunnihticut; as also some of the Wunnashowatuckoogs (subject to Canounicus) came to us and advertised, that two days before, about 600 and 60 Pequts, Monahiggins and their confederates, had robbed them, and spoiled about twenty-three fields of corn, and rifled four Nanhiggontick men amongst them; as also that they lay in way and wait to stop Miantunnomue's passage to Qunnihticut, and divers of them threatened to boil him in the kettle.

This tidings being many ways confirmed, my company, Mr. Scott (a Suffolk man) and Mr. Cope, advised our stop and return back; unto which I also advised the whole company, to prevent bloodshed, resolving to get up to Qunnihticut by water, hoping there to stop such courses. But Miantunnomu and his council resolved (being then about fifty miles, half way, on our journey) that not a man should turn back, resolving rather all to die, keeping strict watch by night, and in dangerous places a guard by day about the sachims, Miantunnomu and his wife, who kept the path, myself and company always first, and on either side of the path forty or fifty men to prevent sudden surprisals. This was their Indian march.

But it pleased the Father of mercies, that (as we since heard) we came not by till two days after the time given out by Miantunnomu, (by reason of staying for me until the Lord's day was over,) as also the Lord sent a rumour of great numbers of the English, in company with the Nanhiggonticks, so that we came safe to Qunnihticut.

Being arrived, Okace had sent messengers that he was lame, and could not come. Mr. Haynes said, it was a lame excuse, and sent earnestly for him, who at last came, and being charged by Mr. Haynes with the late outrages, one of his company said, they were but an 100 men. He said, he was with them, but did not see all was done, and that they did but roast corn, etc. So there being affirmations and negations concerning the numbers of men and the spoil, not having eye-witnesses of our own, that fell, as also many other mutual complaints of rifling each other, which were heard at large to give vent and breathing to both parts.

At last we drew them to shake hands, Miantunnomu and Okace; and Miantunnomu invited (twice earnestly) Okace to sup and dine with him,

liminaries of which are the subject of the first part of this letter, resulted on September 21, 1638, in a formal treaty between the English and the Indians.

he and all his company (his men having killed some venison;) but he would not yield, although the magistrates persuaded him also to it.

In a private conference, Miantunnomu, from Caunounicus and himself, gave in the names of all the Pequts sachims and murderers of the English. The names of the sachims were acknowledged by Okace, as also the places, which only I shall be bold to set down:

Nausipouck, Puttaquappuonckquame his son, now on Long Island.

Nanasquiouwut, Puttaquappuonckquame his brother, at Monahiganick.

Puppompogs, Sasacous his brother, at Monahiganick.

Mausaumpous, at Nayantaquit.

Kithansh, at Monahiganick.

Attayakitch, at Pequat or Monahiganick.

These, with the murderers, the magistrates desired to cut off, the rest to divide, and to abolish their names. An inquisition was made; and it was affirmed from Caunounicus, that he had not one. Miantunnomu gave in the names of ten or eleven, which were the remainders of near seventy, which at the first subjected themselves, of which I advertised your worship, but all again departed, or never came to him; so that two or three of these he had with him; the rest were at Monahiganick and Pequt.

Okace was desired to give in the names of his. He answered, that he knew not their names. He said there was forty on Long Island; and that Juanemo and three Nayantaquit sachims had Pequts, and that he himself had but twenty. Thomas Stanton told him and the magistrates, that he dealt very falsely; and it was affirmed by others, that he fetched thirty or forty from Long Island at one time. Then he acknowledged, that he had thirty, but the names he could not give. It pleased the magistrates to request me to send to Nayantaquit, that the names of their Pequts might be sent to Qunticut; as also to give Okace ten days to bring in the number and names of his Pequts and their runaways, Mr. Haynes threatening also (in case of failing) to fetch them.

Sir, at Plymouth, it pleased the Lord to force the prisoners to confess, that they all complotted and intended murder; and they were, three of them, (the fourth having escaped, by a pinnace, from Aquedenick,) executed in the presence of the natives who went with me.[1] Our friends confessed, that they received much quickening from your own hand. O that they might also in a case more weighty, wherein they need much, viz. the standing to the present government and liberties, to which I find them weakly resolved.

[1] The trial of the Englishmen was held on September 4, and they were executed on the same day. Bradford, *History of Plymouth*, II. 268.

They have requested me to inquire out a murder five years since committed upon a Plymouth man (as they now hear) by two Narriganset Indians, between Plymouth and Sowwams. I hope (if true) the Lord will discover it.

Sir, I understand there hath been some Englishman of late come over, who hath told much to Cutshamoquene's Indians (I think Auhaudin) of a great sachim in England (using the king's name) to whom all the sachims in this land are and shall be nothing, and where his ships ere long shall land; and this is much news at present amongst natives. I hope to inquire out the man.

Mr. Vane hath also written to Mr. Coddington and others on the island of late, to remove from Boston as speedily as they might, because some evil was ripening, etc. The most holy and mighty One blast all mischievous buds and blossoms, and prepare us for tears in the valley of tears, help you and us to trample on the dunghill of this present world, and to set affections and cast anchor above these heavens and earth, which are reserved for burning.

Sir, I hear, that two malicious persons, (one I was bold to trouble your worship with not long since,) Joshua Verin, and another yet with us, William Arnold, have most falsely and slanderously (as I hope it shall appear) complotted together (even as Gardiner did against yourselves) many odious accusations in writing.[1] It may be, they may some way come to your loving hand. I presume the end is, to render me odious both to the king's majesty, as also to yourselves. I shall request humbly your wonted love and gentleness (if it come to your worship's hand) to help me with the sight of it, and I am confident yourself shall be the judge of the notorious wickedness and malicious falsehoods therein, and that there hath not past aught from me, either concerning the maintaining of our liberties in this land, or any difference with yourselves, which shall not manifest loyalty's reverence, modesty and tender affection.

The Lord Jesus, the Son of righteousness,[2] shine brightly and eternally on you and yours, and all that seek him that was crucified. In him I desire ever to be Your worship's most unfeigned

ROGER WILLIAMS

[*Ca.* September 10–21, 1638]

All respective salutations to kind Mrs. Winthrop, Mr. Deputy, Mr. Bellingham, and theirs.

---

[1] Cf. *Journal*, 1. 286–287.

[2] In the Society's earlier printed version of this letter the word was given as "righteously."

RECEIPTS OF JOHN OLIVER AND OTHERS[1]

Received of William Wilks by the hands of mr. Lamberte for the vse } 18*li*
of mr. Tho: Flint eighteen pounds.[2]

JOHN OLIVER

vijth 17: 1638

viij 2: 1638. Received of mr. Lamberte by the hands of mr. Winthrop
for the vse of William Wilks and by his order thirty foure pounds.[2]

By me

JOHN HARDEY

Received of mr. Wilkes by the hands of mr. Lamberte for the debte of my
brother Sandforde the some of three pounds which was apointed to me to
be paide

per me

EDWARD HUTCHINSON

[*Endorsed by Governor Winthrop:*] Rec. for Mr. Lamberte.

HUGH PETER TO JOHN WINTHROP[3]

HONORED SIR, My sudden and humble request vnto you is that you would
bee pleased to accompany the deputy in putting your hand and seale to the
Testimony will bee presented vnto you for Mr. Humfrey, now bound for
England with his sonne only with him, and a very quiet contented mynd,
purposing to returne in the Spring, hauing left his family and estate in Godly
mens hands. I pray, Sir, fayle not herin. I meane the Country's Seale to it.
At next meeting I shall giue you better satisfaction about himselfe and his
departure. Thus with my humble respects and hartyest loue I leaue you
thus hastily saluted and am Yours in all duty

HUGH PETER

Salem vlt: Sept: [1638]

Your rundlet comes by the next.

[1] W. I. 123.
[2] The body of the document is in the handwriting of Governor Winthrop.
[3] Essex Institute; 4 *Collections*, VI. 102.

HUGH PETER TO JOHN WINTHROP, JR.[1]

GOOD SON, My truest loue vnto you and all yours in Jesus Christ our deerest lord. These may certifye you that I doe long for your company as much as the teeming earth for the rising sun. Let not your wife bee ouer deiected, for my part I am as deepe in my obstructions as at Rotterdam. I pray speake to your wife that Mat: Lake[2] and my mayd hope may bee with her and then I beleeue shee shall haue two tolerable seruants. my head is not well, nor any part at present for I cannot get sleepe: I would you should send mee word what you will doe therin but rather come ouer. Oh how my hart is with you. You doe not know how much I need frends and helpe.

tell my deere frend your sister Symonds that I am as low as euer, and wish I knew how to see her. Thus in much hast and perplexity I take leaue and am Yours euer

HU: PETER

SALEM vlt. Sept: [1638]

LUCY DOWNING TO MARGARET WINTHROP[3]

To her most honerd sister mrs. margret winthrop

DEAR SISTER, my cosen peters tells me mrs. cleare hath left you. I cannot much lament your lose, but if you be not prouided of one in her stead, I desier you if you pleas, to make vse of my mayde ellzabeth till you can be better fited and send susan downing to me, when my goods come   I pray present my seruis to my brother and all my cosens and command Your sister

L. D.

[*Ca.* October, 1638]

wee wear surprised on satterday night with your great lady.

---

[1] W. 2. 52; 4 *Collections*, VI. 97.

[2] Probably Margaret Lake, widow of John Lake and sister-in-law of John Winthrop, Jr.

[3] W. 4. 7; 5 *Collections*, I. 23. Lucy Downing was the wife of Emmanuel Downing and a sister of Governor Winthrop.

LUCY DOWNING TO MARGARET WINTHROP[1]

To her truly noble sister mrs. Margret winthrop this humbly giue

MOST WORTHY SISTER, I am so much obliged to you and so vnable to deseru your noble fauors that I blush to mention them. if god shall make me able to doe aney seruis for you I shall moste wellcomely imbrace it:

I hope you will honer poor salem and vs with your presence when our howes is but habitable, for handsom it will not be this year   I hear margret gostlin and my nan is a cominge and not my youngest whoe I expected would be a mayds work, and now I shall be ouer mayded: I hear you want one: if you doe I should be glad she might seru you till either some of our children or seruants wear disposed of: she doth all the worst work in her mothers howes and is very seruisable: but except you have nead of her I doe not wish it, for she is fit for any seruis. Your sister and seruant humble

L. DOWNINGE

[*Ca.* October, 1638]

RICHARD SALTONSTALL, JR., TO JOHN WINTHROP[2]

To the worthyly honoured John Winthrop Esq. Gouernour deliver

HON[OU]R[E]D SIR, Among some letters, and loving remembrances from our good freinds at Greenford wee received a letter to your selfe from my father Gurdon; and somthing bound up with it which my mother sends to Mrs. Winthrop: I hope they will bee carefully delivered by my brother Harry.

Mr. Bradstreet and George Carr being partners with my selfe in a vessell wherof Elias Parkman was master (who dwells at Conectecott; but is now in the bay, belonging to a vessell that came from thence; and is almost ready to returne againe:) wee are forced to crave your warrant for the stay of Parkman that hee may answer vs at the Quarter Court in an action of debt, as alsoe for the breach of his charter partie. Hee was lately at Ipswich and accompted with vs for 5 or 6 voyages betweene the Bay and Conectecote. I might soone tell you whatt our receipts have beene, though the providence of the lord hath beene good to vs; (if hee had beene as carefull as hee ought). He is in our debt 18*li* 10*s* by his owne accompt; the most part of this mony hath been long in his hand; and yet wee cannot receive a penny of him nor

---

[1] W. 4. 8; 5 *Collections*, I. 24.
[2] Essex Institute; 4 *Collections*, VII. 255–256.

a note of his hand that it is due to vs vppon demaund; vnlesse wee bee contented to take it at Conectecott when hee hath sould his house etc. or take it heare as himselfe appoynts. It is not the vse of the mony for my owne advantange; but the wrong I may doe where I owe it, that constrains mee to bee soe earnest for præsent payment (as I tould him often) otherwise I should not have beene soe troblesome to yourselfe and the Court as I am like to bee.

I shall not now add (what I have soe much cause) of my love and dutie to your [*torn*]. I know my engagments hervnto are great and my vnworthynesse alsoe, (though you are pleased soe vndeservedly) to accept mee herin. Yours vnfaynedly as I am ever bound in dutie

RICHARD SALTONSTALL

[*Ca.* October, 1638]

The whole summ that Elias Parkman owes mee is 5*li* vppon the last reconing, and 45*s* vppon a former; If hee bee willing to pay it (as I doubt not but hee can having fraight to receive) I shall make bould to entreat Mr. Stephen or Mr. Addam to receive it for mee; and to give him a receipt, and to send it by some that come this w[ay.] I am contented to adventur it with whome hee thinks me[et]. My Partners expect satisfaction speedily, or his appearan[ce] at the court.

ROGER WILLIAMS TO JOHN WINTHROP[1]

MUCH HONOURED SIR, Some while since I wrote to you a short narration of the Issue of my Voyage to Qunnihticut and Plymmouth etc. I desire only to know whether it came to hand. I haue bene carefully searching into that Rumour of the Plymmouth man slaine 4 yeares since. The persons to whome I was directed by our Plymouth friends for Informacion are yet absent on hunting: and Miantunnomu is but new returned from Qunticut, yet with what Instruction I haue already gotten I am this morning taking a Journey to the Sachims about it.

I heare of 3 Cowweset men in hold about Mr. Hathornes Cow. The Sachims affirme they can not discover the Partie   these 3 were 3 of six then there hunting, yet they say 2 things: 1st that many Northerne and Saugust Indians hunt there allso and 2ndly it may be that some adverse Person might out of subtle Envy shoot the Beast to render them odious to the English and to cause their deserting of the place which they would haue done, but that

[1] W. 2. 111; 4 *Collections*, VI. 252–253; *N.C.*, VI. 125–127.

the English were very desirous (especially Mr. Endicot) that they should kill and sell Venison etc.

For my selfe I shall faythfully enquire and disclose: although divers vnderstanding Persons of Salem haue affirmed, that the Cow dying about 3 monthes after, when so many head of Cattell dyed, it is very questionable whether the Arrow occasioned the Death etc.

Sir this is the occasion of this enclosed: I vnderstand that a Servant of yours Joshua —— is some trouble to your selfe, as allso to others and consequently can not (if he desire to feare the Lord) but himselfe be troubled and grieved in his Condicion, though otherwise I know not where vnder Heauen he could be better.

If it may seem good in your Eyes (wanting a Servant) I shall desire him (not simply from you) but for your Peace and his   I shall desire your best and full Satisfaction in payment, and what Summe you pitch on, to accept it either from this Bill, or if you better like from that debt of Mr. Ludlow for which he promised your Wo[rshi]p to pay me 800 waight of Tobacco but did not and I presume your Wo[rshi]p may with Ease procure it but I subscribe *Ex animo* to your choice and with respectiue Salutacions and continued Sighes to Heaven for you and yours rest desirous to [be] Your Wo[rshi]ps vnfained though vnworthy

ROGER WILLIAMS

[*Ca.* October, 1638]

Sir I am loath, but I presume once more to trouble you with that deceitfull man James Hawkings, crauing that you would please to lend an hand that by your selfe or the Court at Boston I may find mercy against such Iniustice.

Sir my wife (togeather with her best respects) to Mrs. Wintrop requests her acceptance of an handfull of Chesnuts: intending her (if Mrs. Wintrop loue them) a bigger basket of them at the returne of Gigles.

ROGER WILLIAMS TO JOHN WINTHROP[1]

For the right Wo[rshi]pfull and his much honoured friend Mr. Gouernour of the Massachusetts these

SIR, Vpon the receipt of your last (answering my Quæries) I haue acquainted the Sachims with the Busines: I am not yet furnished with Answere

[1] W. 2. 111; 4 *Collections*, VI. 254–256; *N.C.*, VI. 129–131.

sufficient: what I haue at present, I shall humbly and faythfully submit to Consideracion: 1 from them, 2 from my selfe.

From them: vpon sollemne Consultation with them about the 100*li* de-maunded of *themselues*: they say

First that they remember not that either in the first Agreement and League (in the beginning of the Pequt Warrs) or since, in any Expression, that euer they vndertooke to answer in their owne persons or purses what their Sub-iects should faile in.

2. Nor doe they belieue that the English Magistrates doe so practice, and therefore they hope that what is Righteous amongst ourselues we will accept of from them.

3. Therefore they professe that what Euill soeuer shall appeare to be done by any (subiect to them) against the Bodies or goods of the English, Satis-faction shall readily be made out of the Bodies or goods of the Delinquents.

For the 100*li* demaunded they say concerning the Salem Cow, they haue to this day enquired, and can discouer no guilt either in the persons ym-prisoned or the rest but doe belieue that it was falsly laid vpon them by such northern natiues whose traps they were, who themselues were guiltie.

For the horses, they haue sent for Wuttattauquegin who hath not bene with them these 3 yeares, but keepes at Massachusett they intend allso to call a generall meeting of the Countrey at his Comming, within few dayes, when I shall haue further answere from them.

Sir a word more from my selfe: I haue long since beleeued that as it is with the most High (Prov. 21. 3) so with your selues, To doe Judgment and Justice is more acceptable then Sacrifice. And therefore that it shall not be vngrate-full in your eyes that I humbly request leaue to say that I see the Busines is ravelld and needes a patient and gentle hand to rectifie Misvnderstanding of each other and Misprisions. The Sachims to prevent the feares of their Men in hunting or travelling etc. earnestly desired me to satisfie the English that if the Bearers of a writing from me should offend any wayes, that they the Sachims would, upon Informacion from my selfe, cause the Delinquents to make Satisfaction out of their goods or bodies: to the End that the English might not ymprison or transport away their persons, (which the Natiues suspect) 2 of their men hauing bene not long since caried away in an English ship from the Bay and 2 of their women the last Summer from Qunnunagut in this Bay.

In 2 particulars (as I conceaue) neither the Natiues nor my selfe were rightly vnderstood: First in the Scope of the writing which was not to aske leaue to hunt as before. 2ndly in the promise which was not to pay of themselues (I mean the Sachims) but to cause their men to deale iustly and to giue Satisfaction for offences committed out of their goods or bodies.

I hope it will please the Lord to perswade your Hearts to belieue what I affirme, and againe to review the writing: Howeuer, rather then any Labour or paines of mine (well meant to preserue peace) shall cause or occasion dissention, I resolue to be yet poorer, and out of my pouertie to endeauour and further Satisfaction. (The Earth is the Lords and the Fullnes of it.) To the Euerlasting Armes of his mercy I dayly recommend you and yours and rest Your Wo[rshi]ps most vnworthy

ROGER WILLIAMS

My respectiue Salutes to Mr. Deputie Mr. Belingham etc.

Sir I haue heretofore bene bold to request your helpe in recouering an old debt from Mr. George Ludlow: and you were pleased after dealing with him, to signifie that he had promised to deliuer ashoare for me 800*li* waight of Tobacco: I shall now humbly request that if Mr. Stratton desire it, or if he be againe bound for Virginia, that you would please to testifie so much as you remember in a line or 2 which may be of great vse for my recouering of the debt, and I shall desire to be thanckfull.

PROVIDENCE [*ca.* October, 1638]

JOHN WINTHROP, JR., TO MARGARET WINTHROP[1]

To my much honored mother mrs. Margaret Winthrop deliver In Boston

DEARE MOTHER, The occation of my writing at present is in the behalfe of this mayd Sarah Wing whom in respect of hir great desire to serve you, and my owne apprehensions of hir fitnesse for your attendance, in mary Cleers place, I make bould to commend to you, desiring you to make tryall of hir at least for a season. this I dare promise you in hir behalfe, that you will find hir as absolutely, and humbly at your command as any that ever you could have. I spake to my father of it when he was Heere, who was willing to it. I pray be pleased to receive her into your service, upon my word for her fidelity and trustinesse, hir tyme of 5 yeares service having given vp good experience therof. My wife had vpon her thoughts of her marriage hired another which now is disapointed. for wages she will referre

[1] W. Au. 74.

to your selfe or me what shalbe thought fitt. so with my humble duty to my father and to your selfe with my love to my brothers I commend you to the lord your obedient Sonne

JOHN WINTHROP

[*Ca*. October, 1638]

my wife remembers her duty also.

ABRAHAM SHURT TO JOHN WINTHROP[1]

To the Wor[shipfu]ll John Winthrop Gouernor of the baye of Messathusett deliver

ALDWORTH-TOWNE[2] the 8th of 8ber 1638

WOR[SHIPFU]LL, My dutie remembred ettc. Sir occasion presentinge to me for a parcell of Dutch tradinge cloth and wantinge there for the payment of it, shall desire you to paye vnto Mr. Tho: Milward the Thirtye pounds accorded vpon for the charge of the protest. I am informed by an easterne native that the Kerkes have taken two plantations in Canada   not presentinge else worthye your notice, I take leaue and ever rest Your Wor[shi]ps to be comanded

ABRAHAM SHURT

[*Memorandum by Governor Winthrop:*] mr. Keayne you may deliuer Tho: Wheeler his work.

JO: WINTHROP *Go[verno]r*

9: 26. 1638

STEPHEN BACHILER TO JOHN WINTHROP, JR.[3]

To my worshipfull frend John Winthrop Esqr. at his house in Ipswitch thes

WORTHY SIR, I commend me to you and yours in the Lord. So it is, that we are resolued (God so consenting) the second working day of the next weeke to set forward towards our plantation,[4] preparing therto the day

---

[1] W. 2. 183; 4 *Collections*, VI. 571–572.
[2] Pemaquid, Maine.
[3] W. 3. 26; 4 *Collections*, VII. 98–99. For Bachiler, see 4 *Collections*, VII. 88*n*.
[4] Bachiler and others had been authorized by the Massachusetts General Court on September 6, 1638, to begin a plantation at Winnacunnet (Hampton, N. H.). *Records of Massachusetts*, I. 236.

before. We intend to go by a shallop, so that, as our hope and desire is to haue your helpe and our Christian frends Mr. Brodstreet,[1] so we pray you both to be with vs (if possibly you can) the first working day, so to be ready to accompany vs the day following. We were there and vewed it cursoryly: and we found a reasonable meet place, which we shall shew you: but we concluded nothing. This day had not an hindrance falne out I had brought your father in lawes two stales of Bees to you, for that one of them hath robbed and spoy[l]ed a stall of mine (as the manner of Bees is) and I cannot tell how to proceed against the offenders to haue lawe and justice against them but by remoueing the theveishe stall, and keeping in the innocent till they be remoued. I pray you acquaint Mr. Bradstreet with our desire and purpose, that we may lay some foundacion, and the better by your helpe and assistance. The Lords good eye be ever vpon you and yours. And so I rest in him that is alsufficient. Yours in all christian office and service, his most vnworthy

STEPHEN BACHILER

This 9 of this 8th month 1638

RECEIPT OF JOHN SMITH[2]

Received of mr. Paylfre by the hands of the Governour 36s

By me

Jo: SMITH

8ber 14. 1638

EMMANUEL DOWNING TO JOHN WINTHROP[3]

To his Ho[nora]ble brother John Winthrop esqr. Governour at Boston

SIR, I thanke you for my bro[ther] Kerbyes letter, but before yt cam I had assigned him more monie, to serve his torne. the 50*li* I would exchange is of other monie, not of any I expect to be in his hands. I am not willing to send James of purpose about yt if I could other wise doe yt, before the shipp goes hence.

[1] Simon Bradstreet, Edward Rawson, and the younger Winthrop had been designated by the General Court to supervise the laying out of the new town. *Records of Massachusetts.* I. 236.
[2] W. I. 124. The body of the document is in the handwriting of Governor Winthrop.
[3] W. 2. 25; 4 *Collections*, VI. 49.

I thanke you hartilye for your kynde Invitation, but I hope there wilbe noe necessitye of my being there this winter. there is more cause of your coming hither, where I shall God willing acquaynt you with the secrets of the decoye.[1] I pray resolve to come ere winter. I doe rest vpon you for wheat and Rye, about 30 bushells of Rye and 10 bushells of wheate. I pray let my Cosen Stephen dispatch the perfecting of the accounts, and the remayne I purpose to dischardge with ready monie. Soe desiring the Good lord to preserve you to length of dayes and eternall Joy with my service to my sister and your selfe I rest your verie louing brother

Em: Downinge

Salem 22 October 1638

HUGH PETER TO JOHN WINTHROP[2]

To our noble Gouernour these present in Boston

Hon. Sir, I vnderstand by Mr. Pierse that Mr. Bellingham is very very greedy for more mony who hath already taken more then hee can answer: wherefore my humble request is that you would bee pleased to suffer none at all to touch it, synce the mony is properly myne and at the Court wee hope to bee all there; Mr. Pierse hath also promised to vndertake for all the Owners there, and I for those here, being iust halfe in eyther place and so to issue all.

I am bold besides to intreat you to let your seruant by your order to take all Mr. Lapthornes goods into your hands, that were at the ordinary, his trunke and other things are at your house already, and to pay 3*li* to the M[aste]r for passage, and what the ordinary demaunds, and to keepe all his goods safe because hee wholy belonged to mee, and my brother who sent the

---

[1] "Whereas Emmanuell Downing, Esqr., hath brought over, at his great charges, all things fitting for takeing wild foule by way of duck coy, this Court, being desiros to encourage them, and others, in such designs as tend to publike good, do give him full liberty to place the same duck coy in some convenient place within the bounds of Salem, as the towne and hee can agree, and that it shall not bee lawfull for any person to shoote in any gun within halfe a mile of the pond where such duck coy shalbee placed, nor shall vse any other meanes for disturbance of the foule there; and if any man shall offend against this order, hee shalbee fined, or otherwise punished by the discretion of such court as shall have the hearing of the cause; and if any person shall bee taken shooting, or going aboute to shoote, within the said limits, and beeing not knowne to the said Emanuell Downing, or his servants, which shall attend the said duck coy, it shalbe lawfull for them to make seizure of his peece, and detaine the same till the cause be h[e]ard and determined." *Records of Massachusetts*, I. 236.

[2] W. 2. 52; 4 *Collections*, VI. 97–98.

man ouer to mee vpon my letter will expect my faithfulnes. Thus making euer bold with you I rest Yours in all due respects and vtmost seruice

HU: PETER

SALEM 25. 8, [1638]

I pray salute your animæ dimidium and my noble Aunt. I pray intreat her or some body to buy mee 5 o[r] 6 doz: of Candles vpon any termes.

JOHN ENDECOTT TO JOHN WINTHROP[1]

To the right Wor[shipfu]ll our truely Honored Gouernour John Winthrop Esqr. deliver

DEAREST SIR, I humblie thanck you for your last Loving Lettre. I will not at present reply any thinge. It is well that your selfe and others of Gods Children with you are satisfyed in that dismission. I confesse I yet ame not, but more heereafter of this particular. At present I ame bould to entreate your fauour in a case of Mr. Bishopps the bearer heereof. It is a case of conscience. I haue laboured to giue him the best satisfaccion I can but it seemes hee is not satisfyed. I hope that hee is one truely fearing God and therefore I desire much (if God see it good) hee may be satisfyed in his scruples and feares: It concerne chieflie the Magestracie, concerninge their power in matters of Gods Worsh[i]pp. I leaue him to state the question, That you may the better satisfie him and the better understand him. As also if you please to take in the helpe of Mr. Cotton whom hee doeth much deseruedly reverence, as also your good Pastor That at least hee may be convinced of his error. Kindnes doeth much prevail with him. This Journey now into the bay is of purpose to seeke light as hee saith. The lord giue him light, if it be his will: Hee is come of from his former Judgment, That sanctification is not an euidence of our good estate: It may be hee may be brought of of this also: This being all at present but my true seruice to your selfe and dearest yoakefellow, I Commend you to the blessed protection of the Almighty and rest Yours euer

JO: ENDECOTT

29th of the 8th moneth 1638

[1] W. 2. 71; 4 *Collections*, VI. 134–135.

JOHN WINTHROP TO MARGARET WINTHROP[1]

To my Deare Wife, Mrs. Winthrop at Boston

MY DEARE, I prayse God we came safe to Salem, though we had very stormy windes. We found all well. I doubt I shall not returne before the 2d daye next weeke and then my broth[er] P[eter] will come with me. The Lo[rd] blesse thee and all our family, and send vs a happy meetinge. I kisse thee and rest thy faithfull husband

                                                         J: W:

Salem: 9ber 8, 1638

LUCY DOWNING TO MARGARET WINTHROP[2]

To her moste worthy sister mrs. margret winthrop this humbly present

MOSTE HONORED SISTER, it is the least part of duty to return you humble thanks for spareinge vs my brothers companye. wee reade your sweet affections to vs in it, and the nobleness of your spirit and it hath aded much to our former deep ingagements, and had it pleasd god to haue giuen vs your presence allso, our Joyes had bine compleet.

I am much obliged to you for your great care of my boye   I wish him or my self able to deserue it, but I desire if there be the least feare of ill, that he maye come right home.

I pray present my humble thanks to my brother. I was euer born to after witt, ells I should not haue parted with my brother without some refreshment for his Journie. I hope I shall haue more wit next time for it hath troubled me more then a little that I neclected it: but indeed I was confident of a day or 2 more. Your sister to seru you humble

                                                  L. DOWNINGE

[*Ca.* November 15, 1638]

---

[1] W. I. 125; *L. and L.*, II. 231; Twichell, 187.
[2] W. 4. 7; 5 *Collections*, I. 23–24.

WILLIAM SPENCER TO JOHN WINTHROP[1]

To his much Honored The Wor[shi]p[fu]l John Winthorpe Esqr. Governour off the Massachusts at his house in Boston deliver

WOR[SHI]P[FUL] SIR, After my humble seruice remembred vnto you with manny thanks for all your loue I make bould to troble you with theise few lynes. You may please to remember that not longe before I tooke my leaue off you you wear pleassed to advise me to doe what I could that their might bee a Vnion beetween you and the plantacions heer, and your resons wear verry waity with me and such as doe mutch stike by mee. now in rememberance of the same I tooke ocation vppon some Oppertunity to knowe the reson why it was not concluded when their men wear with you, vseinge some of those Arguments which your selfe vssed vnto mee but vppon debate I found A preieduse in the spirrits of some men concering your state as though you did not really intend such a thinge but onely pretended it which I laboured to beat offe as much as might bee ingadgeing my selfe that for your state in generall they did and doe as really intend their good as anny of ther neighbour plantacions wher vpon they propounded some resons to the Contrary that you only pretended and not intended such a thing. one was this that not withstanding you had said that god by his prouidents had soe disposed of it that you and the plantations vppon this river could not bee one body: yet when it came vnto the Isue you would haue Aggawame joynd vnto you or elce you would not conclud of the vnion, and to that purpose they say you haue written to dismise the same from them, this with some other which I forbeare to name vntell I speake with you because I presume they are but reports and soe may be false: but heering the other I could not tell what to say: only I their left it and spake no moore aboute it. now the truth is Sir, although for my owne part I do earnestly desier what euer may promote your good, and soe I hope shall doe yet I must confes I doe not yet see what benifit it canbee vnto you to haue a plantacion soe fare remote dependent vpon you which cann in noe kinde be seruiceable, and in the mean tyme may bee very preiedusall vnto the plantacion heer, For they cannot posible bringe aboute some of ther ocations as it wear meet they should if they bee severd from them   nay further I doe conceaue it may bee an ocation off some differts beetwixt you and them, but Ile say noe moore about it for present but leaue it vnto your wise Consideracion and when I know moore

---

[1] W. 4. 93; 5 *Collections,* I. 265–266. For Spencer, see 5 *Collections,* I. 265n.

I shall make bould to informe you. And what your wor[shi]p shall comand mee further I shalbe reddy to doe you what seruice I can.

Now further I make bould to troble you with another bussines. Their was due vnto mee from the Country for dyett for the Magestrats and Deputies in May was Twelve month[1] about 28*li*　now I haue often desiered it off the Tresurer but yet can gett but 17*li* 13*s* and that I had but at my comeing away. now ther is yet due vnto mee about 10*li*　now I gott very litle by it and have staied long for it　now I requested him to pay it for mee, and I vnderstand that he answrs: he cannot pay it vntell another Rate bee made now I doe humbly pray yow: that you wilbe pleassed to speake with him that it may bee paid, and I shall rest thankfull vnto you. soe fearing I have byne over tedious I comend you and all your wayty proseedings to the good blessing of god, and doe nowe and euer rest Yours in all bownden service

WILLIAM SPENCER

HARTFORD the 29th November 1638

I pray be pleassed to cause this leter to be sent.

[*Endorsed by Governor Winthrop:*] Wm. Spencer from Conectecott 10: 1638, about their Jelousyes.

THOMAS HOOKER TO JOHN WINTHROP[2]

RIGHT WORSHIP[FULL] WORTHY SIR, Though my experience be but little, and my observance small, yet it cannot but second that which you say in the entrance of your letter: Satan is not yet weary of compassing the earth to and fro: And he that is made vp of malice and hatred, cannot but show him self an enemy to the God of love, and the work of brotherly love, wherein lyes the life of all dutyes to God and man, and hence it is he turnes himself unto all shapes, to do mischeif this way, some time he vseth the lyons paw, somtyme he putts on the foxes skynn as the proverb is, somtyme he vseth violent opposition somtymes running circumvention, that he might ether openly or secretly blemish the vnity of the spirit, and eat asunder the syn-

---

[1] I.e., in May, 1637, during the session of the Massachusetts General Court at Cambridge, where Spencer at that time resided.

[2] Massachusetts Archives, Colonial, II. 196–203; *Collections of the Connecticut Historical Society*, I. 3–15. For Hooker, see *D.A.B.* This letter is an answer to the one abstracted by Winthrop under date August 28, 1638, and printed in this volume (pages 53–54, above). For Winthrop's rejoinder, see pages 99–100, below.

newes of society the bond of peace. I confesse my head growes gray and my eyes dymme and yet I am somtyme in the watchtower: And if the quære be Watchman what in the night as the prophet speaks, I shall tell you what I have observed, and shall be bould to leave my complaynts in your bossome, of what is beyond quæstion, and then I hope I shall give you a satisfactory returne of what you quæstion in your letter.

Before I expresse my observations, I must professe, by way of preface, 1. that what I shall write, are not forged imaginations and suppositions coyned out of mens conceits, but that which is reported, cryed openly, and caryed by sea and land: 2ly: my ayme is not at any person, nor intendment to charge any particular with you: because it is the common trade that is driven amongest multitudes with you, and with which the heads and hearts of pas- sengers come loaded hither and that with greif and wonderment: And the conclusion which is aymed at from these reproaches and practises is this, that we are a forlorne people not worthy to be succored with company, and so neyther with support.

I will particularize: If inquiry be, what be the people at Conitticut: The reply is Alas poore rash headed creatures, they rushed them selves into a warr with the heathen, and had not we reskued them at so many hundred charges; they had been vtterly vndone. In all which you know ther is not a true sen- tence: for we did not rush into the warr: and the Lord him self did reskew before friends.

If after much search made for the setling of people and nothing sutable found to ther desires, but towards Conitticut, If yet then they will needs goe from the Bay: goe any whither, be any where, choose any place any pattent, Naraganset Plymmouth, only goe not to Conitticut: we heare and beare.

Immediatly after the wynter, because ther was likelyhood multitudes would come over, and least any should desire to come hither: then ther is a lamentable cry raysed, that all ther cowes at Conitticut are dead, and that I had lost myne, and only one left, and that was not likely to live (when I never had but eight, and they never did better then the last wynter) we hear still and bear.

And least happily some men should be encoraged to come, because of my subsistence or continuance here, then the rumor is noysed, that I am weary of my station, or if I did know whither to goe, or my people what way to take, we would never abyde: whereas such impudent forgery is scant found in hell: for I professe I know not a member in my congregation, but sitts downe well apayd with his portion, and for my self I have sayd what now I write, if I was to choose I would be where I am.

But notwithstanding all this, the matter is not sure, and ther is some feare that some men will come towards Conitticut when shipps come over, ether some have related the nature of the place, or some freinds invited them, and therfore care must be taken and is by this generation, assoone as any shipp arrives: that persons hast presently to board them, and when no occasion is offered, or quæstion propounded for Conitticut, Then ther pity to ther countrymen is such, that they cannot but speak the truth: Alas do you think to goe to Conitticut, why do you long to be undone. if you do not, blesse yourself from thence: ther vpland will bear no corne, ther meddowes nothing but weeds, and the people are almost all starved: Still we heare and beare.

But may be these suddayne expressions will be taken as words of course and therfore vanish away when once spoken: Let it therfore be provided that the Innkeepers intertayne ther guests with invectives agaynst Conitticut, and those are set on with the salt, and goe of with the voyder: If any heare, and stay: then they be welcomed, but if these reports cannot stopp a mans proceeding, from making triall, they look at him as a Turk, or as a man scant worthy to live. Still we heare and beare.

I suppose you are not a stranger only in Israell, nor yet wholly ignorant of these things, being they are not done in a corner, but in the open streets, and not by some frantick forlorne creatures, or madd men, who know not, nor care what they say, but before the shipps can come to anchor wholl boats are presently posted out to salute persons ordinarily with such relations: The dayly expressions of Passengers report these with much greif of spirit, and wonder such wretched falshoods should be suffered amongest Christians.

Thus in N: E: but send over a watch a little into ould England, and goe we there to the Exchange, the very like trade is driven by persons which come from you, as though there was a resolved correspondence held in this particular: As the master and merchant who came this last year to Sea-brook fort related even to my amazement, ther is a toung battell fought vpon the exchange, by all the plotts that can be forged to keepe passengers from coming, or to hynder any from sending a vessell to Conitticut, as proclaymed an vtter impossibility.

Sir He wants a nostrell that feells not and sents not a sesmaticall spirit in such a frame of falsifying relations to gratifye some persons and satisfye ther owne ends.

Do these things argue Brotherly love? do these issue from spirits, that ether pity the necessityes of ther brethren, or would that the work of God should prosper in ther hands? or rather argue the quite contrary: If these be the wayes of God, or that the blessing of God do follow them, I never preached Gods wayes nor knew what belonged to them.

I suppose these premises will easily let any reasonable man see what the conclusion must be, that men would have to follow. The misery of the men of Conitticut would be marvellous acceptable to such, and therfore ther is little expectation they do desire ther good, and would procure it, who are not willing any good should come to them, if all the inventions of falshood can prevayle: Worthy Sir: these are not iealousyes which we needlessly rayse, they are realityes which passengers dayly relate, and we heare and beare: and I leave them in your bosome only I confesse I count it my duty, and I do privately and publikely pray against such wickednesse, and the Lord had wont to heare the prayer of the despised.

I shall now addresse my self to endeavour your satisfaction in the particulars propounded in your letter: you warne of the enemyes subtilty, that he pretends our honor with the heathen, and that equall to, if not beyond the greatest, but indeed intends the ruyne of all: I know the enemy wisheth vs no weale, yet I would do the divell himself no wrong, though he never did good. For I had hitherto thought in my most serious observation, that he pretended and intended the quite contrary: We have constantly and commonly heard his Indian Emissaryes vent such reproaches as these: That we were water caryers, tankard bearers, runnagates whipped out of the Bay: but of such Honor and that equall to the greatest: we know no such thing: we owne none, we desire none, we heare none such given and therfore if I may iudge the divells pretences by his practises, I cannot but conceave he pretended and intended the contrary.

The things of greatest consequence are three:

1. That you vnderstand from Mr. Williams, that our Magistrates denyed to the Naraganset that they were tyed to the agreement you made with them.[1] I suppose our Magistrates told Mr. Williams so much   And to evidence the reason of ther proceeding, you may be pleased to take notice of these 3 things:

1. That the copy of those articles came so late after the warr begunn by you (for to my best remembrance they came in the wynter by an Indian) that we had little liberty to consult, nor safety nor certaynty to send an answer, nor did we see any such necessity lead us thervnto being in the preface we were left vnto our choice, to take or refuse as we liked.

2ly: vpon the first occasion that our Magistrates had, when they mett Mr.

---

[1] Cf. Roger Williams to John Winthrop, August 14, 1638 (pages 52–53, above).

Stoughton commaunder of your forces at Pequoyt, they playnly and punc-
tually denyed to be tyed to that agreement in some things, according as they
had liberty and allowance from your selves: And this I suppose he ether did
or should have certifyed.

3 That they then gave reasons to him, why they could not so yeild because
they saw them apparantly preiudiciall to ther proceeding, and conceaved
they were so to him then: And therfore beleive it, for you will fynd this to be
true, that they pleaded ther owne priviledge because they were not tyed, and
conceaved him disadvantaged because he was tyed to the Art[icles] but left
him to his owne apprehensions: For when they observed Myantonymo to
withdraw him self and Indians, they wished Mr. Stoughton to presse him
with his agreement, he tould Mr. Stoughton expressely.

These passages being rightly considered, a ready answer may be applyed
to all your enquiryes.

"If ther was no article ther that could be preiudiciall: No present occasion
of performance, why should they disclayme? Why was not this signifyed
when the copy came to hand? Nay did it not imply a full consent when our
Magistrates obiected to the Naraganset his former breach of agreement, and
therfor our now denyall must be to advance our owne reputation and weaken
yours."

The answer will be in so many sentences, we could not at present signifye
our deniall because safe and certayne conveyance was stopped, but did it
with the first opportunity: we did then and do now conceave it preiudiciall
to be tyed to them all, we had present occasion to expresse the reason of our
non-performance of them at this tyme, to cleare our proceeding with them
according to our former expressions and therefore it was not to advance our
reputation and weaken yours, but to give a right apprehension of both, and
did by our Magistrates acquaynt Mr. Stoughton with our purpose, and give
reasons of our proceeding before we gave a deniall: The obiecting of the
breach of covenant to the Narag[ansetts] was not in respect of them selves
but that he kept not touch with you.

In the 2cond thing you propound in your letter ther be severall things, the
compasse wherof I do not so readily conceave and shall therfore take leave
to set them downe, and expresse my present thoughts, because I would not
mistake: Your words are

"A (2) is that having agreed to Articl[es] of confederacy with you, the
mayne end whereof was, that a certayne way might be established for the
ending of all differences by a peaceable meanes: Now because ther was some
small preheminence conferred vpon the Macheshusets, these articl[es] were

throwen aside, a new frame sent vs, wherin the sayd mayne end was vtterly neglected: the summe of all which amounts to thus much:

"1. Articles of Confederacy were agreed vpon:

"2. A certayne way propounded to end differences peaceablely

"3. These articl[es] were throwen aside, and a new frame sent

"4. And that because a small preheminence was given to the Macheshusetts:

"5. The mayne end wholly neglected:"

A free explication will give a right construction of all these according to the naked truth:

1. When then you say the art[icles] were agreed vpon: you cannot meane that they were concluded and established, for that was beyond the place and power of any that were at that consultation, but being by your self propounded, heard and attended by vs, it was agreed by consent on all hands, that they should be tendered to the consideration of the state with you, and of the magistrates and people with vs, and a return should agayne be made for a finall conclusion in that behalf, according to the ould rule quod ad omnes spectat, ab omnibus debet approbari: It being left to each partyes liberty to explayne or except.

Answerable to this determination the people here according to ther meannesse, were studious to take them into serious consideration and returned a comly account vnto you by ther Commisshoners.

In which account, all the explications they gave of the five first Articl[es] for the clearing of each others apprehension, found easy approbation, being no more but the meaning of the Art[icles] cleared.

The sixt Art[icle] wherin all the difficulty lay, vpon debate, in the issue appeared, by the ioynt iudgment of your court and our commissioners to exceed much the lymitts of that equity which is to be looked at in all combinations of free states: And were it not but that I do suppose the reasons then propounded, gave in vndeniable evidence that way: In my poore thoughts I have imagined, that it would not be difficult to demonstrate, that the meanes therin propounded to end differences, and to make and mayntayne peace would marvellously misse the end, in both: But it being, by the ioynt iudgment of all concluded, that it answered not a rule of equity, Another way that was subiect to lesse exception, and so in likelyhood to breed or occasion lesse heart burning, was attended and mutually assented to on all sydes:

This being the naked cariage of the cause: How a serious consideration of articles propounded in a way of love, and a rationall account given of ther conceavings, and that such wherin nothing was faulted, can be iudged a throwing away of articles, and sending a new forme: I confesse I see not.

How those meanes which by the ioynt approbation of all exceeds the bounds of equity and answers not the end of vnion, and treaty of combinations, should be an easy and peaceable meanes to end differences: I must confesse in the dymnes of myne owne apprehensions I am yet to seek: How in rationall charity I should conclude that the small preheminence of the Macheshusets should occasion men to alter ther apprehensions of any articles propounded, when the playnnesse and evidence of argument appeares to alter the cause even to the conceavings of such who have most interest in it: is yet beyond the retch of my reason, if I attend any rule I know.

From this seeming miscariage in these particulars you lead vs to looke vnto the fountayne from whence these and many other inconveniencyes will easily follow: Namely "to referr the dicision of a civill quæstion or controversy to wholl churches cannot be safe, nor warranted by any rule as you conceave." I confesse you are now lanched into a depth, and I have little to draw withal: And as far as I can ether see or observe, ther be few disputes that ever came to my view, that fynd any bottome here   An answer I suppose must issue from the right iudgment of the principles of state and church, as they are combined one with another or severed each from other, somthing I have some tymes thought of the poynt, but the full debate of it would be too large for an ordinary letter.

I shall attend only those things, which you seasonablely and pregnantly expresse in the cause: And here I fully assent to those staple principles which you sett downe: to witt: That the people should choose some from amongest them: that they should referr matter of counsell to ther counsellours, matter of Judicature to ther iudges: Only the quæstion here growes: what rule the Judge must have to iudge by: 2ly who those counsellors must be.

That in the matter which is referred to the iudge the sentence should lye in his breast, or be left to his discretion according to which he should goe: I am afrayd it is a course which wants both safety and warrant: I must confesse I ever looked at it as a way which leads directly to tyranny, and so to confusion, and must playnly professe: If it was in my liberty, I should choose nether to live nor leave my posterity vnder such a government: Sit liber judex as the Lawyers speake: 17 Deut. 10. 11: Thou shalt observe to do according to all that they informe according to the sentence of the Law Thou shalt seek the law at his mouth: not ask what his discretion allowes, but what the law requires: And therfore the Apost[les] when the rulers and high preist passed sentence agaynst ther preaching as preiudiciall to the state, The Apost[le] Peter made it not daynty to professe and practise contrary to ther charge, because ther sentence was contrary to law, though they might have pretended discretion and depth of wisdome and policy in ther charge.

And we know in other Countryes, had not the law overruled the lusts of men, and the crooked ends of iudges many tymes, both places and people had beene in reason past all releif in many cases of difficulty: you well knowe what the Heathen man sayd by the candell light of common sense: The law is not subiect to passion, nor to be taken aside with self seeking ends, and therfore ought to have cheif rule over rulers them selves.

Its also a truth that counsell should be sought from counsellors: but the quæstion yet is, who those should be: Reserving smaller matters, which fall in occasionally in common course to a lower counsell: In matters of greater consequence, which concern the common good, a generall counsell chosen by all to transact businesses which concerne all, I conceave vnder favour most sutable to rule and most safe for releif of the wholl   This was the practise of the Jewish church directed by God Deutr. 17: 10: 11; 2 Cron: 19 and the approved experience of the best ordered states give in evidence this way: Salomons one wise man, and the one wise woman in Abell that delivered the city showes the excellency of wisdome and of counsell where it is, but doth not conclude that one or few should be counsellors, since in the multitude of counsellors ther is safety.

The third thing touching the businesse of Agaam, comes last into consideration, in which I shall crave leave to open my self freely and fully, that the rule of righteous proceeding may appeare in vndeniable playnnesse, where it is: The summe of that cause is to be attended in two things: partly in that Jurisdiction we have exercised: partly in the iurisdiction which at this tyme you so suddaynly so vnexpectedly take to your selves:

The greivance in the former: Is expressed by you in these words:

"That notwithstanding your desire to our Magistrates to forbeare vntil the matter was tryed, and the consent of our commissioners to the contrary: yet they go on with more earnestnes, which seems to cary an appearance of some violence of affection, and setled purpose of opposition."

For a fayre and a full answer you may be pleased to vnderstand: 1: That I have advised with the Commissioners, and ther expressions to me were these, that they were so far from consenting, that you should take away the iurisdiction in Agaam from them to your selves, that to ther best remembrance ther was no such thing mentioned, nor were ther one sillable sounding that way in all the agitation of the businesse: when the Commissioners of other townes and amongest them one from Agaam, came to establish the iurisdiction which they now exercised, in reason it could not be ther commission, nor the intention of the townes to destroy ther owne iurisdiction, for that was to crosse the scope of the treaty, and overthrowe the combination for the establishment wherof they were now sent:

What ever limits should by mutuall allowance be agreed vpon, It was ever taken for graunted, and the nature of the treaty doth of necessity presuppose it, that the combination of the townes should be established not disannulled therby: And therfore vpon what ground you should conceave their consent in that behalf I cannot yet fynd out: For that speech of our brother Steele in private to Mr. Hauthorne affords no foothold at all to inferr such a conclusion: ne quid gravius dicam.

The act of Jurisdiction which hath beene exercised since your letter it was this: Ther was an inhabitant in Agaam apprehended in some misdemeanour, the towne sent the delinquent to the court to desire iustice, which they answerablely did and why they might not do it nay how they could avoyd it according to rule, It is beyond all my skill to conceave: For at the tyme of our election, the committees from the towne of Agaam came in with other townes, and chose ther magistrates, installed them into ther Goverment, tooke oath of them for the execution of iustice according to God, and engaged them selves to submitt to ther goverment and the execution of iustice by ther meanes, and dispensed by the authority which they putt vpon them by choice: Now when these men shall demaund iustice from magistrates so chosen and engaged, how in faythfulnes and according to ther oath they could deny it without synne: the covenant continuing firme on both parts, and renounced at this tyme by nether: It is beyond my compasse to comprehend, and vnder favor I do think beyond the skill of any man by sound reason to evynce: The magistrates who are lawfully caled, and stand bound by oath to execute iustice vnto a people, to deny the execution of iustice when it is demaunded by such is a greivous synne. But the magistrates were thus caled, thus by oath bound, and iustice was in this manner demaunded: Therfore had they then refused it, they had greivously synned: Yea taking it for graunted, that it is in each inhabitants liberty in Agaam to chose his iurisdiction (which is to me beyond quæstion): If I was ther an inhabitant, I should iudge my self bound in conscience to submitt to the iurisdiction of the river, and do beleive I should make a breach vpon the 8th commaund if I should do otherwise, because in so doing I should steale from myne estate, in that I should rush my self into needlesse and endlesse inconveniencyes: Namely to cast my self into that condition, that for a matter of five shillings (as the case may fall out) I should putt my self to vnreasonable charges and troble to seek for iustice a hundred myles of, in the wilderness: If Mr. Pynchon can devise wayes to make his oath bynd him when he will, and loosen him when he list: If he can tell how in faythfulnes to engage him self in a civill covenant and combination (for that he did by his committees in ther act) and yet can cast it away at his pleasure, before he give in sufficient warrant more then his owne word and will, he must fynd a law in Agaam for it, for it is writt in no law nor gospell that ever I read: The want of his help trobles not me, nor any man else I can heare of, I do assure you, we know him from the bottome to the brim, and follow him in all his proceedings, and trace him in his privy footstepps, only, we would have him, and all the world to understand, he doth not walk in the dark to vs: By this it is evident what the iurisdiction was which was exercised since your letter. [*The remainder of the letter is missing.*]

[THO: HOOKER]

[*Ca.* December, 1638]

[*Endorsed by Governor Winthrop:*] Received this from mr. Shepherd xth about the 1 weeke.

HUGH PETER TO PATRICK COPELAND[1]

To my Worthy and reuerend brother Mr. Copeland preacher of the Gospell In Bermuda

GOOD BROTHER, By these you may vnderstand that, wee doe not a little reioyce at any intercourse betwixt your selfe and vs. these bearers I pray bid welcome to you as any of yours should bee to vs. The M[aste]r[2] is an honest godly man of our church, and such as you will haue much ioy in, wee hope: and I pray helpe vs by prayers what you can. These can informe you of the state of things with vs, and how it is in England and Scotland even sad enough. wee haue a printery here and thinke to goe to worke with some speciall things, and if you haue any thing you may send it safely by these. our churches flourish, and the more by some late familisticall errors intruded by Satan: and truly troubles wee must look for on all hands, but wee know whom wee haue trusted. The God of all peace bee with you and all your worke for him.

[1] W. 2. 53; 4 *Collections*, vi. 98–99.
[2] William Goose of Salem, master of the *Sparrow* of Boston, who, with Stephen Winthrop, was at this time about to sail for Bermuda on a trading venture. *Notebook Kept by Thomas Lechford, Esq.* (Cambridge, 1885), 46–47.

our plantations doe reach a great way South and East, and I am perswaded will looke into the Indyes of which I would haue your opinion. Good Sir, bee earnest with the lord for vs, that wee may bee to his praise in Jesus Christ amen. Yours euer

HUGH PETER

SALEM 10 1ober 1638

JOHN WINTHROP TO THOMAS PRENCE[1]

To his verye worthye and lovinge freinde Mr. Prence Gou[ernou]r of Plimmouth deliver

SIR, This Lettre inclosed beinge deliuered to me by a mistake, was by the like mistake opened by me, but havinge read 3 or 4 lines I reveiwed the super-scription and founde my error, wherevpon I layd it by: and (consideringe how I would have another in like case to have dealt with me) I read no further of it, so as you may rest assured that neither my selfe nor any other since it came to my hands is privye to the contents of any more then the first 4 or 5 lines. So with my lovinge salutations to your selfe and all our worthye and reverend frends with you, mr. Bradford mr. Winslow etc: I commend you to the Lord and rest Your verye lovinge freind

JO: WINTHOP

BOSTON this 10th of the xth mo: 1638

This other Lettre to mr. Winslow came with it.

THOMAS DUDLEY TO JOHN WINTHROP[2]

SIR, Since my coming home I haue read over Mr. Lechfords booke,[3] and find the scope thereof to be erroneous and dangerous, if not hereticall, ac-cording to my concepcion. His tenet being that the office of Apostleship doth still continew and ought soe to doe till Crists coming, and that a Church hath now power to make Apostles as our Saviour Crist had when hee was heere. other things there are, but I pray you consider of this and the inseparable consequences of it: I heare that Mr. Cotton and Mr. Rogers know something of the matter, or man, with whom you may if you please conferre: I heare

---

[1] Winslow MSS., M.H.S.; *L. and L.*, II. 419.
[2] Belknap Papers, M.H.S.; 1 *Proceedings*, III. 311–312. For Dudley, see *D.A.B.*
[3] For Lechford's "Book of Prophesie," see *Lechford's Notebook*, xv–xx.

also that hee favoureth Mr. Lentall[1] and hath so exprest himselfe since Mr. Lentall was questyoned by the ministers: It is easyer stopping a breach when it begins, then afterwards. wee sawe our error in suffering Mrs. Huchinson too long: I haue sent you the booke herewith that instead of putting it to the presse as hee desireth it may rather be putt into the fire as I desire: But I pray you lett him know that I haue sent the booke to you, that after you haue read it (which I thinck you said you had not yet done) it may be restored to him: I received yesterday a lettre from my lovinge freind Mr. Burdett to excuse himself of the sclannder laid vpon him for baptiseing any, with some high straynes of other matter, which I haue answeared. This is all I haue at present, with due respect therefore I take leave resting Yours

THO: DUDLEY

ROCKSBURY dec. 11, 1638

I suppose the booke to be rather coppyed out then contryved by Mr. Lechford hee being, I thinck, not soe good a grecyan and hebritian as the Author vndertakes to be.

There was one heere to day of waymouth to buy treacle (as I heare) whoe reported that there are 60 persones sicke there of the spotted feaver except 3 of them of the small pox: If this be true the plague is begun in the Campe for the sinne of Peor.

THOMAS DUDLEY TO JOHN WINTHROP[2]

To the R[igh]t Wor[shipfu]ll John Winthrop esqr. Gov[ernou]r at Boston

SIR, I thancke you for your gammon of bacon, the outsides whereof I was forct to cutt of, it smelt soe restyly of the old Saxon reesing. I meant in my censure of your last booke noe resurreccion of unreasonable individualls, but a contynuance of those or some of them which should be aliue at the consummacion which I thinck is the same with your Species. The breaking open of your lettres was presumptuous if not hostile. For Mr. Gibbins I thinck I shall satisfy you at my next coming to Boston. For Mr. Lechford and his booke you say nothing, and I haue since heard that the worst opynion in his book, (which I thinck I shall proove to be heresy) is taken vpp by others: Nowe seeing that this is the way Sathan invades vs by (viz. new opynions

---

[1] For the episode involving the Reverend Robert Lenthall, see *Journal*, 1. 292–293.
[2] W. 3. 28; 4 *Collections*, VII. 111–112.

and heresyes) it behooves vs to be the more vigilant and to stirr vpp our zeale and stopp breaches at the beginning, least forbearance hurt vs as it did before. I desire to see the lettre Capt. Vnderhill wrote to Mr. Cotton. I take leave resting ready to doe you service

THO: DUDLEY

Dec. 24: 1638

EMMANUEL DOWNING TO JOHN WINTHROP[1]

To his much honored brother John Winthrop Governour deliver Boston

SIR, I blesse God for his tender Care of vs in preserving yours and myne in health and peace in these Infectious and stormie seasons. My Cosen Peter told me, this afternoone that there was not one sick in Salem. the Good lord graunt vs thankfull hearts, as for this, soe for all other his favours to vs; Mr. Ballard of Sagus lyeth verie sick of the pox; I found my sawes in a long Chest among the other things, the bundle of Sawes you sent me, are not myne, I wishe the owner had them.

For mr. Cooke, I, having noe other buisines to the Court, am loath to make a Jorney of purpose, therefore my hope is my Cosen St[ephen] Winthrop having a letter of Attornie will prosecute yt for me; If he goes for Bermodas, I must fynde out some other freind that will doe yt for me;

I haue soe manie things to retorne thanks for as I know not where to begyn, they deserve more then words. my hart is more willing to requitall then opportunity or abilitye can afoard. as an Indian said, Comaund me great things to the height of my strength, etc. I pray rem[em]ber my service with manie thanks to my sister, and soe with my love to all yours and mr. Harrison, with my dayly prayers for your prosperous condition in soule, body and all your affaires I rest Your assured loving brother whilest I am

EM: DOWNINGE

25. 10. 1638

---

[1] W. 2. 26; 4 *Collections*, VI. 49–50.

ROGER WILLIAMS TO JOHN WINTHROP[1]

For his much honoured and beloved Mr. John Wintrop at his howse at Boston

PROVIDENCE 10th 30, [1638]

SIR, Hoping of your Health this dead Season with respective Salutacions: I am bold to request a little helpe and I hope the last concerning mine old and bad Debtour about whome I haue formerly troubled your Wo[rshi]p, Mr. George Ludlow.

I heare of a pinnace to put in to Newport bound for Virginia, and I vnderstand that if you please to testifie what you remember in the case I may haue some hope at last to get something.

You were pleased after dealing with him at Boston to certifie me that he had promised to discharge vnto me 800 li. of Tobacco, which you afterwards thought to haue bene discharged: But he fayling, although my due came to much more, I request if you can remember in a line or 2 to testifie: and I shall desire to blesse the Lord for you and to beg of him a mercifull Requitall into your Bozome euen from his holy Left and Right hand especially: my writings are (from hand to hand about the busines) lost: so that all my Euidence will be from your hand, of his Acknowledgment and promise: Sir I rest vncessantly mourning that I am no more Your Wo[rshi]ps vnfaigned

ROGER WILLIAMS

Sir I may not omit my thanckfull acknowledgment of that Councell of Peace you were pleased to giue to a young Man who (when I was at Block Iland) repaired to your Wo[rshi]p for Advice in some Jar betweene him and his neighbours: Your Councell was prosperous and I desire you may haue the Joy of it, for so sayth the Lord To the Councellours of peace is Joy.

Sir I purpose within 20 dayes (if God will) to travell vp to Monhiggin: at my returne I shall trouble you with a line from Onkas, if I can speake with him about your Pequts.

Sir I pray let your Servant direct the natiue with this letter to Mr. David Yale Mrs. Eatons Sonn.

[1] W. 2. 112; 4 *Collections*, VI. 256–257; *N.C.*, VI. 127–128.

MARY CUTTING TO JOHN WINTHROP[1]

To the right wor[ship]full John Winthrop Esqr. at his house in Boston these deliuer

RIGHT WOR[SHIP]FULL, My seruice tendred unto you. I haue made bold to desire you to establish your promise in helping mee in an unexpected case, which is this. When I liued in Eng. my husband bound to us by Indenture a man, to bee our servant for eight yeeres. This servant hee brought ouer this yeere and thought fitt to leaue him heere, to accompany my other seamen. While my husband was in the Bay there came in a ship from Virginia: the Capt. of it was Capt. Thorneback, my servants neere kinsman. Hee spake with my husband that hee would free the man, that hee might bee with him: my husband answered that if hee would giue him content for the residue of his time, hee would willingly part with him. This second day hee is gon in my shallop to the Bay, and hath tooke his goods with him, contrary to my knowledge and will, with an intent to goe with his kinsman Capt. Thorneback, or else (as I since understand) to goe in some other ship to Eng. to a brother of his that is a captayne. I therefore desire you that you would bee pleased either to cause Capt. Thorneback to satisfye mee for my mans time in money, sc. for 3 yeeres and an halfe, or else to take some course that my man may bee returned againe. I think 20*li* is little enough for his time, but I leaue that to your wor[shi]ps disposing. I desire you to do the best you can for mee in the case. I rest Your wor[shi]ps seruant

MARY CUTTING

[*Ca.* 1639]

I haue made bold to acquaint the right wor[ship]full the Deputy Gouernour with this thing, more at large.

THOMAS JAMES TO JOHN WINTHROP[2]

To the right Worshipf[u]ll and much honord in christ Mr. Wintropp
Gouernour of Massacussett Bay deliver

SIR, May it please you. it is said of our maister Christ he will not breake the bruised reede, nor calcabit linum fumigans. Such as are in place and

---

[1] W. 4. 34; 5 *Collections*, I. 88–89. Mary Cutting was the wife of John Cutting of Watertown, a shipmaster.

[2] W. 4. 113; 5 *Collections*, I. 321–322. For James, see Morison, *Founding of Harvard College*, 384;

aucthority, haue a character of the almighty stamped on them especially they that hold it forth, where paternum regimen of the great God and gracious is expressed to such as vnder Gouerment. this makes me bold though meane and despised to discharg some part of my duty and affection which I beare and haue borne toward you in theise paper expressions and poore courtesies, vnbeseming your fatherhood if I were not perswaded of that sweete temper and disposition seated in an heart of bounty and goodnes, which is the Impresse of a gouernour mavult amari quam metui, for indeede (Sir) what greater argument of obedience, what cords, what bonds did euer long containe people in duty But where moderation and loue haue twisted both ends together.

Rehoboam delt ill for him selfe and posterity to lay the foundation of his Gouerment in austerity and harsh proceding. The Lord be blessed for all that good effected vnder your shadow, my harts desire and prayer is still for Gods blessing on your head and heart and family for the discharg of that trust which is the greatest, that I know hath bene committed to any mortall man on earth. I meane so many churches of Christ gathered in such an holy order vnder the Gouerment of the Lord Jesus. Concerning my selfe I humbly begg at your feete two things. first if a place called Seaconke be in your patent (which I can not say) but only heare by report I may haue liberty (if god geue me a calling) to haue your fauourable allowance and sitt vnder your gracious protection. the other is this that I may obtaine so much as common æquity and naturall Justice requireth which Job that president and patterne of æquity 29 Job 15 et 12 et 31 Job 13 granted to his bond slaues, that I neuer be punished in any kind causa inaudita before I am conuicted or haue liberty to speake for my selfe in a Judiciall way. I hope Sir, one day it will be no greife to you 1 Sam. 25. 31 etc. The lord Jesus preserue you blameles to that day amen.

So prayeth your Humble Seruant in all duty in Christ

THOMAS JAMES

I make bold to send mis. Wintrop a tame creature which she may dispose of as she please.

From PROVIDENCE [*ca.* 1639]

Matthews, *Calamy Revised*, 295. Neither of these writers mentions James's sojourn in Providence, whither he went after leaving the ministry of the church in Charlestown. Having been granted land in New Haven on November 3, 1639, he sold his "lands, rights, and privileges" in Providence on March 20, 1639/40. On June 11, 1640, he became a freeman of the New Haven Colony. Hoadly,

CERTIFICATE FOR JOHN OTIS[1]

Thes are to sertyfie your worships that the bearrer her of John Oates is trobld with an infermyty wherby he is desabled to serue in Armes   his infermyty is that vpon any small labbor ore toile he dos make reed water to his payne for which he desire to be excused   for the truth heare of we have heare vnto set our hands

JOSEPH ANDROWES
RICHARD BETSCOMB
DAVID PHIPPEN

[*Ca.* 1639]

[*Endorsed:*] Information.

JOHN SPENSER, ROBERT CRANE, AND OTHERS TO THE GOVERNOR AND ASSISTANTS OF MASSACHUSETTS BAY[2]

Copia Literæ

WORSHIPFULL SIRS, THE GOVERNOUR AND ASSISTANCE OF THE PLANTACION OF NEW ENGLAND IN MATATHUCHETS BAYE, You may bee pleased to remember that at a generall Court, houlden for the new England Company on Munday the last of November 1629 there was an agreement made by severall vndertakers as by their names herevnder written may appeare That they would vndertake to manage the whole stock, and doe and performe all those things which are there fully agreed vpon as by the order may further appeare. Now may it please you; wee whose names are vnder written did according to the desire of the Court lend to the Companie Mr. Cradock being then governor each of vs 25*li* as per the seale of the Company may further appeare;[3] to bee

Records of the Colony and Plantation of New Haven, 24, 35; *The Documentary History of Rhode Island*, Howard M. Chapin, Editor, 1 (Providence, 1916), 109.

[1] W. 10. 140. The signers of this document were all among the early settlers of Hingham.

[2] W. 4. 165; 5 *Collections*, 1. 484–485. For Crane and Spenser, investors in the Massachusetts Bay Company, see Frances Rose-Troup, *The Massachusetts Bay Company and Its Predecessors* (New York, 1930), 140, 154. The letter is placed conjecturally in 1639 because of the fact that Spenser, who came over to Massachusetts in 1634, remained here until sometime in 1638; and this letter was obviously written in England. Matthew Cradock, in his letter of March 15, 1636/37 (*Winthrop Papers*, III. 377–380), also refers to the issue which is the subject matter of this document, and it may therefore be that this document was written at about the same time and that it passed through Spenser's hands here before it reached Winthrop. Mrs. Rose-Troup discusses this document in *The Massachusetts Bay Company and Its Predecessors*, 107.

[3] See *Records of Massachusetts*, 1. 63–66.

repayd at 6 monthes now wee haue demanded our monie of the vndertakers here whoe by that order did vndertake the whole stock of the Company and promised to pay all those debts the Company was ingaged for, and they did act in paying some men their debts. Now wee haue demanded our monie but they answere they haue payd as farre as they received And put vs over to Mr. John Wentrop who was chosen presently after to bee governour whoe oweth 100*li* to the Companie out of which they say, our mony must be payd: Therefore wee pray you that considering wee did freely lend our mony for the good of the Company wee may not bee forced to doe any act for the recovery of our said monies, which may redownd to the dishonour of the Plantation for wee desire the prosperity of it as your selues but that you would (those of you to whom it belongs) take some order for the discharge of our mony and debt and that wee may by the Returne of the next shiping haue an Answeare of your Resolutions which way wee shalbee payd our mony or else wee shall commence a suite for an account of the Estate according to the order, or some other way for the recovery of our debtes Soe wishing, etc. etc. wee rest. [*No signatures*]

[*Ca.* 1639]

Wee forbeare to speake of that agreement which was made when it was ordered by the Court, and condiscended vnto by the vndertakers that the Joynt Stock being brought into a 3d parte of what was put in, Should bee Imployed for Seaven yeares and the produce devided, I say or that if any would take out his ⅓d parte of his stocke, hee might haue it but wee can get neither the one nor the other.

[*Endorsed by Governor Winthrop:*] Copy of Mr. Spenser Crane etc. lettre.

BILL OF JOHN TINKER[1]

Dr. My M[aste]r Jo. Winthrop Esqr.

	li	s	d
For Linen cloth twine and other comodities bought and other monies lide out and expences in his busines	11	18	6
for 2 firkins of suet	2	16	0
for 2 boxes of Candles waying 7 duz. 10 li. at 5*s* 8*d* per duzn	5	1	1

[1] W. I. 127; 2 *Proceedings*, XIII. 61–62. For Tinker, see 4 *Collections*, VII. 218*n*.

for 2 boxes	0	3	8
for a porter to cary them	0	0	10
for the fraite of the pack	0	10	0
	20	10	1
a parcell of shews sent	05	08	0
Received mony for 32 li. of beauer at 9s per li.	14	8	0
mony on mr. Rainsfords bill	9	5	0

1639[1]

	li	s
post 1 mr. Lokier minester		
For mony borowed of him Aprill	150	0
post 1 mr. Merideth hosier		
For a parcell of ware bought of him	11	12
post 1 mr. Hutchinson Linendraper		
For a parcell of linen ware bought of him Mar. 30th	53	5
mr. Andros Haberdasher		
[For a] parcell of ware bought [torn]		

[*Endorsed by Governor Winthrop:*] Jo: Tinker Bill 1639.

STEPHEN WINTHROP TO MARGARET WINTHROP[2]

DEARE MOTHER, My duty remembred to you etc. ha   inge this oppertunity to write I thought it my Duty to Acquaint you with what hath befell
us hitherto: it hath pleased god to give vs a very speedy and safe passage to
Quinipiack: we were but thre daye goeing thither   the lord was pleased to
watch ouer vs also when others slept in the night when we were runinge
rigt into great (though vnknowen) danger. the lord in mercy make vs truely
thankfull to him, that so he may be pleased to continue his Faviour to vs. I
have resceved much kindness from Mrs. Eaton and Mrs. Davenport. I know
not what else to write to you, but disiringe you would be mindfull of me in
your prayers, which is the greatist good you can doe for me I rest   I pray
present servis to Mr. Harrison and Mrs. Fitch my love to my brothers. Your
Dutyfull Sonne

STEPHEN WINTHROP

QUINIPIACK, Jany. 7, [1638/39]

⁂

[1] The following items, which appear on page 2 of these accounts, have been canceled.
[2] W. Au. 65.

SAMUEL WHITING AND THOMAS COBBETT
TO JOHN WINTHROP AND THOMAS DUDLEY[1]

To the right worshipfull our honoured Gouvenour and Deputy mr. John Winthrop and mr. Tho: Dudley at theyr houses in the Baye, Present these

RIGHT WORTHY AND MUCH HONOURED IN THE LORD, we the elders and brethren of the church of christ at Lyn haueing of late seriously weighed our greate need of a Faithful wise and wachfull magistrate to be among vs and of vs for our better furtherance in matters that concerne our owne and others good haue ioyntly pitched our thoughts vppon mr. Bradstreete for the man: and accordingly haue made the motion to him who as we perceiue principally sticketh vppon some Ingagements to others: though not clear therein whether ingaged to them at Ipswich (from whome he sayth his thoughts were that he had beene more fair than some would indeauour to perswade that he is) or whether Ingaged to others in the business of Mirimeck: for that he seemeth to question whether he be free from one of the two soe as to satisfy our desires of him; only he is resolued to take it into his serious thoughts and to aduise about it. wherefore we are bold to Intreate your worships for your further aduise and Incouragement herein not doubting but you will be pleased to take our present condition to hart and helpe what you may in a case soe nearly concerning vs and we conceiue also the common good: supposing it will be more for publique good that god hauinge lately lessened your number partly by death and partly by other prouidences that such an one as we Judge mr. Bradstreete to be should rather be nearer than soe far off. As for Accommodations some way suitable to such a worthy man we are freely willinge to come off that way to our vtmost ability and we hope to his content and soe perswadinge our selues that you will freely and fully aduise and further vs herein we humbly take our leaues and rest, your worships in all seruice according to God

SA: WHITING
THO: COBBETT
in the name of the church

If either of your worships please to Inquire of this our messinger concerning any particulars that you would be further informed in he will fully satisfye

---

[1] W. 1. 123. For Whiting, pastor of the church at Lynn, see Morison, *Founding of Harvard College*, 406–407; for Cobbett, see *ibid.*, 372.

you or if your worships please to Informe him in any particular that we haue omitted which might further vs we humbly desire you would be free that way and we shall desire speedily to set about the same.

LYNNE this 8th of the 11th m. [1638/39]

LETTERS OF ADMINISTRATION TO EDMUND AUDLEY[1]

Whereas it appears vnto me by diverse Listenings that Francis Dente late of Salem deceased did declare his minde and will to be that if he dyed without other disposition of his estate, the same should goe to Edmunde Adlye, I doe therefore hereby grant to the said Edmunde power to administer the goods and estate of the said Francis,[2] so as he cause a true Inventorye to be made thereof, to be deliuered in vpon Oathe, and to be accountable etc. when he shalbe required: This is allso to require all such as have any of the estate of the said Francis to deliuer in the same to the said Edm[un]de for which this shalbe sufficient warrant.

JO: WINTHROP Gou[vernou]r

xth 11th 1638[/39]

He is to bringe in an Inventorye and make further proofe etc: at the next Court of Assistants.

[*Memorandum by John Winthrop, Jr.:*] Memorandum mr. Hugh Peeters and mr. John Humfrie were Attornies for Edm[un]d Adly and gathered in some of his debts for the said Edmund Adly and paid the same to the said Edmund Adly being the summe of fourty pounds and if there were any more to be had of Francis Dents Estate he left it to the said mr. Humphries and mr. Peters to dispose of to any vse they should thinke good.

---

[1] W. 1. 125. This document was issued in accordance with an order of the Court of Assistants on January 5, 1638/39. *Records of the Court of Assistants of the Colony of Massachusetts Bay, 1630–1692,* II (Boston, 1904), 82.

[2] The original manuscript reads "Edmunde."

RICHARD GIBSON TO JOHN WINTHROP[1]

RICHMOND ILAND: 14° January, 1638[/39]

RIGHT WO[RSHI]P[FU]LL AND MY HONOURED FREIND, your health wished to Gods glory and the good of his people. Sir I am enforced at this time to crave your audience and judgement in a cause which nearely concernes mee, and wherein I haue no where to fly for right but to your selfe. And truly considering the many and weighty affaires which possesse you, I should be much discouraged to trouble you herein, were it not that your singular favour and clemency, the loue you beare vnto the truth, and the nature of the cause, being such as it is, haue emboldened mee out of measure. The case is this: By the prouidence of God and the Counsell of freinds, I haue lately marryed Mary daughter of Mr. Tho: Lewis of Saco, which marriage was thought a fitt meanes for the closing of differences and setling an order both for religion and goverment in these Plantations: Howbeit, so it is for the present, that some troublous spirits, out of missaffection, others, as is supposed, for hire, haue cast an aspersion vpon her, and generally avouch, that shee so behaved her selfe in the shipp which brought her from England hither some 2 yeares agoe, that the block was reaved at the mayne yard to have duckt her, and that shee was kept close in the ships Cabin 48 houres for shelter and rescue, which tends to her vtter infamy, the greif of her freinds and my great infamy and hinderance: which matter was once a particular iniury, and is now like to proue a generall quarrell:

My humble suite vnto your Wo[rshi]pp is: that (for the truthes sake vnto which wee are all bound to minister, for the publique peace, and the rescue of the Innocent, who is els like to suffer perpetually:) that you would please to call before you George Burdett[2] of Boston shoemaker, Anne his wife, and others whom they can name which came over in the ship with her, and examine them of these things whereof shee is accused, and I humbly entreat that you would giue a Testimoniall of these exacions: I married the mayd upon long demurres by advize of freinds, and if these imputations be iustly charged upon her, I shall reverence gods afflicting hand, and possesse my selfe in patience vnder Gods chastiseing. If false, both shee and many shall haue cause to blesse god for you, and for that goverment which shineth from you to us, and in that great day, there shall be many beare witnesse to the uprightnes, care, and godly zeale in which you spend your selfe amongst gods people.

[1] W. 4. 94; 5 *Collections*, I. 267–268. For Gibson, see 5 *Collections*, I. 267n.
[2] I.e., George Burden.

I had not stayed here so long, but that I was sent hither by a singular providence, upon engagement of time not yett expired, and for that it reigneth
in my hart, that god hath here some worke for mee yett to doe. Well, I pray
pardon my to much boldnes with you, And God almighty blesse you and
guide you with his eye, that you may long and long go in and out as a burning and shineing light amongst your people. Your Wo[rshi]pps ready to be
commaunded

RICHARD GIBSONN
Min[iste]r of the Gospell att Richmond Iland and Saco

EDWARD RAWSON TO JOHN WINTHROP[1]

To the Right Wor[shi]ppff[u]ll his much honored Lovinge Freind John Winthrop
Esqr. Governor of Mathatusetts present

RIGHT WOR[SHI]PPFF[U]LL SIR, Whereas there is one Walter Allen brother
in law to mr. Cutting Come ouer From berrye in old England hether this
yeere being lisenced by your Wor[shi]pp to live in this Jurisdiccon; and hath
bought a lott of one in our towne; the men deputed by our freemen to order
theire affaires hearing of some scandalous reports of him and that he had no
lisence to recyde heere wee sent for him to know, whether those reports were
true or no viz. whether within Five yeeres past he had two bastards the one
by a mayd the other by another woman acording to the report of his brother
in lawe Goodman Warde of Layford and who affirmed to a brother of our
Church that so he had and that he Came ouer hether becawse he Could no
longer abide in berrye: he Confessed that he had one bastard but denyed the
other afirming that he hoped he had made his peace with god therefore and
doughted not but he Could give sufficient of testimony of his Conversacon
since that time answerable to such profession of Repentance by mr. Ayres of
Watertowne; the towne therefore remembring the law made in may 1637:
and Considering the godly intents thereof which was as well to keepe out
such whose Lives were publickely prophane and scandalous as those whose
iudgements were Corrupt Least by the one the Comfortable societye of godes
people might be disturbed and by the other the iudgements of god procured
for the preventing of which it pleased the Lord to moove your hartes to enact
this Lawe, the towne therefore Considering the premises desired me to signifye vnto your wor[shi]pp what they knew in this particuler thereby mani-

---

[1] W. 1. 126. For Rawson, see Savage, *Genealogical Dictionary*, III. 510–511.

festing their faithfullnes in discouering of any thing which as they Conceave might tend to the nullifying of such a wholesome Lawe as also to desire your wor[shi]pp by a word or two at your Leisure and pleasure, that they may vnderstand thereby what satisfaccion your Wor[shi]pp hath or may receave herein of mr. Ayres For encouragement to receave him or elce For our orderly reieccon of him. Thus with the remembrance of myne and my wifes humble services remembred vnto your wor[shi]pp as also vnto your wife with our many humble thankes For all the manifestacons of your Love vnto vs desiring the Lord of heaven to encrease in yow such abillityes as whereby yow may be enabled to dischardge the place whereto he hath Called yow, to the Comforting of yourselfe and the people ouer whom the Lord hath sett yow Committ[ing] yow to his holy proteccon and remaine Your Wor[shi]pps Lovinge freind to thvtmost of his poore power to be Commanded

EDWARD RAWSON

From NEWBERY 7th Feb. 1638[/39]

AGREEMENT OF THE INHABITANTS OF SPRINGFIELD APPOINTING WILLIAM PYNCHON A MAGISTRATE[1]

February 14th 1638[/39]

Wee the Inhabitants of Aggaam vpon Quinetticott taking into concideration the manifold inconveniences that may fall vpon vs for want of some fitt magistracy amongst vs: Beinge now by Gods providence fallen into the line of the Massachusets Jurisdiction, and it beinge farr off to repayre thither in such cases of Justice as may often fall out amonge vs: doe therfore thinke it meet by a generall consent and vote to ordayne (till wee receave farther directions from the Generall Court in Massachusets Bay) Mr. William Pynchon to execute the office of a Magistrate in this our Plantation of Aggaam viz: To give oathes to Constables or millitary officers to direct warrants both process executions and attachments, to heare and examine misdemeanors, to depose witnesses, and vppon profe of misdemenors to inflict corporall punishment, as whippinge, stockinge, binding to the peace or good behaviour, and in some cases to require suirtyes, and if the offence require to committ to prison to committ dilinquents to the charge of some fitt person or persons till Justice be satisfyed. Alsoe in tryall of actions for debte or trespass to give oathes, direct Juryes, depose witnesses, take verdicts, and keepe records

---

[1] W. 4. 166; 5 *Collections*, I. 487–488. For Pynchon, see *Proceedings*, LXIV. 67–107; *D.A.B.* This document is in the handwriting of Henry Smith, Pynchon's son-in-law.

of verdicts, Judgements, executions: and what ever else may tend to the kings peace, and the manifestation of our fidelity to the Bay Jurisdiction; and the restrayning of any that shall violate Gods lawes: or lastly what soe ever else may fall within the power of an assistant in the Massachusett.

It is alsoe agreed vpon by a mutuall consent that in case any action of debte, or trespass be to be tryed, seinge a Jury of 12 persons fitt cannot be had at present amonge vs, that 6 persons shall be esteemed and held a sufficient Jury to try any action vnder the some of ten Pownds, till we shall see cause to the contrary, and by common consent shall alter this nomber of Jurers or shall be other wise directed from the Generall Court in the Massachusetts.

JOHN WINTHROP TO THOMAS HOOKER[1]

I received your large and lovinge Lettre.[2] I am sorry to have putt you to so much trouble considering your imployments, and little leysure to attend such extravagants as my selfe. I observe what you write in 2 parts. The 1 makes me a little merrye, the other calls me to more searious Consideration. in the 1 you compl[ain] of the slanderous and reproachfull speeches of some of ours. they report that your Cattle doe not thrive, that your ground is barrin etc: these are more like the speech of a prophet I will leave in her a poore and afflicted people etc. I know you trouble not your thoughts with these things, except it be for recreation. it is well they have no worse matter to laye to your Charge   if they had added that you had kept poluted night assemblys, and worshiped the head of an asse etc: then they had sett on with the weight of the old [illegible].

Yet if you could shewe vs the men that reproached you, we should teache them better manners, then to speake evill of this good land God hath brought vs to, and to discourage the hearts of their brethren: only you may beare a litle with the more moderate of them, in regard that one of yours Jo: Pratt[3] opened the doore to all that have followed and for that they may conceive it as lawfull for them to discourage some with vs from forsakinge vs to goe to you, and for yours to plott by incouragments etc: to drawe Mr. Shepherd and his wholl Church from vs. Sic fama est. For mine owne parte I knowe you have a most fatt and pleasant Country which you will finde, when ex-

---

[1] Essex Institute; *L. and L.*, II. 421–422. The letter is Winthrop's rough draft written on the blank inside pages of Emmanuel Downing's letter to him of March 2, 1638/39.

[2] See Thomas Hooker to John Winthrop, *ca.* December, 1638 (pages 75–84, above).

[3] For John Pratt, see *Winthrop Papers*, III. 240, *n.* 3.

perience (which vsually costs deare) teache you to improve it in the right kinde, for (as I sayd to some of yours longe since) you must turne your Cowes into flaxe and hempe, by which Course you may soone outstrippe vs, for that is a merchantable Comodity, and one acre with you will yield more then 4 with vs. (Provided allways that you secure Say brook.)

For the other parte of your lettre which concernes the differences between vs, I confesse I have sadd thoughts about it, which come to this issue, that seing we are brethren, one in consotiation, in the same work of God, in the same Community of perill, vnder the same envious observation, in the same relation for mutuall succour and incouragement in our waye, they must be composed, and if our feares prove true (for as yet we have not one shipp, no not for the fishinge) ere the 3 months be gone it wilbe no hard taske to reconcile vs, the fight will then be which shall have the comfort of yieldinge most but howsoever it fall out, yet we must live in peace and love, and blessed be God that hath fixt us in one minde in the trueth, which will make the matter the more easy. We all professe Christianity, we are now putt vpon some tryall for the practice of it. You know we have rules to walk by: one is that we should let the Cloke goe after the Coat; but (I suppose) you will not tye vs to that neither will we require it of you. we have another rule from the example of Ab[raham] who in the division gave Lott the choyse (yet men think it had better become Lott to have yeilded that to his elder) If this will not serve our turn, then we have a 3 Rule Thou shalt bringe it to the Judges, if there be none competent, then thou shalt set vp Judges etc. I should be very lothe it should come to this as being too public and too violent a remedye in our Case. I have thought of a 4th (which I conceive lawfull thoughe I finde it not prescribed) viz: that you should yield in some things and we in the rest, but it is like you may prescribe some other, therefore I [illegible] of nothinge. truly Sir, you have my naked thought of this matter, so farr as the Lord letts me see mine own heart, which I find very deceitfull when it is at best.

I would not meddle with the partic[ulars] for I had rather they were buried then aggravated, but if matters must come to be scanned, I doubt not there will app[ea]r some reason on our part, and that the occasion of your greatest greif arose wholly from your own Comission without any thought of ours tending that [torn] decline it never so confidently.

[JOHN WINTHROP]

[Ca. March, 1638/39]

JOHN WINTHROP TO [JOHN WHEELWRIGHT?][1]

SIR, Your lettere about W[innacunnet] I imparted to our General Court, who taking the same into Consideration have vpon mature deliberation ordered this answer to be returned to you.

1: It is verye strange to vs, that our lands which we have granted vs by his ma[jes]ties Patent, and which we have divers years since taken possession off, and declared them both by publ[ic] order of Court which some of your Company being then members of our Colony might or ought to have taken notice of: and others who are strangers might have doone the like by our erecting a house vpon the place, should now be Challenged by a new found title taken from the Indians: which Course how it will stand with Religion, good neighbourhood, or common honesty we leave to your selues and others to Judge, being not forward to express the Iniury which we iustly conceive hath been offered us herin.

2: Though we are not bound to plead our title of what we possesst before our neighbours who were after vs, yet to manifest our desire (as far as in vs lyes) to live peaceably with all men we are content to declare what right we have. 1: we challenge it by vertue of our P[aten]t as lying within 3 miles of the most n: parte of the river of merrimack, which though we have not yet surveyed, yet by relation of all who have travayled vp that River (and partic[ularly] mr. Wm. Hilton and mr. Joselin and Mr. Edw. Johnson) the place in question is within these bounds and more to spare then we intended to make vse off.

2: we challenge it by our possession, which we took peaceably, built a house vpon it, and so it hath continued in our peaceable possession ever since without any interruption or Claim of any Indian or other, which being thus taken and possessd as vacuum domicilium gives vs a sufficient title against all men.

3: For your title from the Indians, we deny it to be of any validity.

1: You cannot derive a good title to those Indians from whom you claym but men shalbe able to prove as good an Interest in some other Indians.

2: we deny that the Indians heere can have any title to more lands then they can improve, which we have stood vpon from the first, though to take away occasion of offence in some who are not so well satisfied herin, and for

---

[1] W. 1. 126. For the dispute between the town of Exeter, New Hampshire (of which John Wheelwright was chief settler), and the Massachusetts Bay Colony regarding the title to the land at Hampton, New Hampshire, where a settlement had been begun in the fall of 1638, see *Journal*, I. 293–294, 306.

other Considerations we have been content to give them some consideration in that kind. For clearing of this we conceive that man hath an interest to land 2 wayes: by a naturall right when God gave the earth to the sonnes of men, all men by this have a like right, by vertue whereof any man may make vse of any part of the earth, which another hath not possessed before him and [*illegible*] with it as our fishermans stages and his possession determineth his interest   The other is a Civill right, when men growing into Civill societies and by attainment of Artes and trades have therby means to improve more lands, and to [*illegible*] mens Interests to posteryty etc. if you ob[ject] that they have Commen[ced] etc. any there which are Civill Actions we Answear 1. that one or even some morall Actions make not a Civill bodye and ergo no Civill relation, no more than memory labour obedience to Commands, etc. doe declare a horse to be a reasonable Creature. These natives have no other but a naturall right, and that is only to so much land as they have means to subdue and improve.

1. A Civill relation cannot appertain to an incivill subiect: if it be obiected that a fool or rude man may have a civill right etc. it is granted, but that is by vertue of his [*illegible*] in some Civill body otherwise he cannot   therefore it is that the bodye is [*illegible*] to supply his defecte by appointing him a gardian, not only himself[1] but improvement of his estate: if you ob[ject] again

2. God gave the earth etc. to be subdued, ergo a man can have no right to more than he can subdue: if it be again ob[jected] that then it were lawfull in England etc: to take from any man such lands as he cannot vse. It is denyed vpon the former ground, for though the partic[ular] person cannot yet the Civill bodye can, and will, withhold not any our Indians for their whole bodye have no artes Cattle or other menes to subdue and improve any more of those lands then they plant with Corne.

[*Ca.* March, 1638/39]

EMMANUEL DOWNING TO JOHN WINTHROP[2]

To his much honored brother John Winthrop Gouernour

Sir, I thanke you for your kynde letteres, which I received yeasterday. I feare not the coming of shipps vnto vs, because I know, yt will not be in the

---

[1] The words "not only himself" have been substituted in the original manuscript for "to the end that the body may not be damnified for want of due."

[2] Essex Institute; 4 *Collections*, VI. 50–51.

power of any mortall man, (though as malitious as the Divill himselfe against vs) to hinder them. I am much more troubled that you write, how you are yet sometymes feverishe. I pray be more watchfull for your health, that you oppresse not your bodye nor spirits with the publique affaires, but rather spare yourselfe a while, that you may be the better enabled for tyme to come. cold and wett espetially of your feet are two great traytors to your health, and must be watched verie narrowly verie narrowly; The Good lord preserve you to vs, and I shall never feare foreigne malice, soe long as the trew worship of God is by authority upheld amongst vs, for he is faythfull and wilbe a sure rock of defence to his beloved. Mr. Rogers hath an overture of plantation[1] betwene Newberry and Ipswich, which I feare wilbe streightned, betwene Ipswich and N[ewbury] as Cambridge is, by hir Neighbour townes. now at Salem wee haue manie farmes to be sould, enough for all his Companie, and the Towne desires much his Joyning with our pastor. he may also haue with vs a plantation by himselfe, soe that I hope wee shall keepe him here or at Newberry. I pray present my service to my sister soe with harty prayers for your health desiring much to heare of your perfect recouerie I rest with manie thanks to your selfe and my sister, which I owe for more then my paper can hold. Yours assured whilest I am

EM. DOWNINGE

2 Martij 1638[/39]

PETITION OF THE INHABITANTS AND FREEMEN OF LYNN[2]

To our much Honoured Gouernour Deputie Gouernour, Assistants and generall Court now assembled

THE PETITION OF THE INHABITANTS AND FREEMEN OF THE TOWNE OF LYNNE

It is not vnknowen to a great part of the Countrey what hinderances, hazards and inconveniences do dayly accrew vnto such as passe ouer our Riuer by reason of the Flatts and rottennesse of the Marsh which are very hard to be prevented without much charge: and if they were amended would be yet still subject to dammage and decay. We thought meete therefore to suggest thus much vnto this Honoured Court that if they shalbe pleased to lend some competent allowance vnto so good a worke, as the erecting of a

[1] Rowley.
[2] W. 4. 167; 5 *Collections*, I. 488–489.

Bridge, Wee shalbe very willing to exceed our proportion in furthering the same: and had not the worke beene very weighty and our strength small we should not haue desired assistance in the same. But our confidence of your readinesse to further a publique good hath persuaded vs to present you these our desires, which we humbly leaue to your wise consideracion;[1] and rest Yours and the Common Wealths to be commanded

> THO: WILLES
> EDWARD HOLYOKE
> RICHARD SADLER
> EDWARD HOWELL
> EDWARD TOMLINS
> THOMAS TALMADGE
> *In the name of the towne*

The 11th of the first moneth 1638[/39]

ACKNOWLEDGMENT OF MASCONOMET[2]

This doth testify that I Maskonomett did give to Mr. John Winthrop all that ground that is betweene the Creeke commonly called Labour in Vane Creeke, and the Creeke called Chybecko Creeke, for which I doe acknowledge to have received full satisfaction in wampam peage, and other things: and I doe heereby also for the summe of twenty pounds to be paid vnto me by the said John Winthrop, I doe fully resigne vp all my right of the whole towne of Ipswich as farre as the bounds therof shall goe all the woods, meadowes, pastures and broken vp grounds vnto the said John Winthrop in the

---

[1] The General Court, on June 6, 1639, ordered "that those of Linn should have 50*li* from the country toward the building of a cart bridg over the ryver there, when the bridg is finished to bee allowed them." *Records of Massachusetts*, 1. 261.

[2] Essex Institute. The body of this document is in the handwriting of John Winthrop, Jr. For the Indian deed of Ipswich, June 28, 1638, for which this document is an acknowledgment, see page 42, above.

name of the rest of the English there planted, and I doe bind my selfe to make it cleere from the Claimes of any other Indians whatsoever.

MASKANOMETT X his marke

[*Ca.* March 13, 1638/39][1]

witnesses to this
GYLES FYRMIN
ADAM WINTHROP
HUGH X HILLIARD
     his marke
DEANE WINTHROP

[*Endorsed by John Winthrop, Jr.:*] Maskanometts Sale of Ipswich.

DOROTHY CRANE TO RICHARD CRANE[2]

To hir very loveinge husband Richard Crane seruant to Mr. Edward Rawsone at his house at Newbery be this deliuered New England

LOUEING HUSBAND, My love remembered vnto you withe Marey your daughter and all the rest of our Children remembrethe ther dewteyes vnto you, all of vs hoping of your healthe as we ware at the writing heare of   Thease ar to let you to vnderstand thatt I haue sent your clothes a pair of Breeches and a jurken and a Wascott and 2 new Shirtes and 2 paire of Shewes   But as for my cominge to New England, I cannot and the reason is Because I want meanes or Abiletey Besides that I am not as yet minded to com thither And further moore as for your coming houm I defare that to your owne mind for you know our Estatt how it is withe vs heare and likewise you know how it is thear with youe   thearfore vse your owne mind for that Mater. But as for that you sent to know how longe you sware to serue for your 35*li* your master knew at the first your Agreement that it was for 3 yeares seruices at our first knowledge. And afterword your master and you bothe told vs that you ware to serue hime for 5 yeares. And thenne your condition was that the 5*li* which was aboue 30*li* was to goe or be in part of the 2 last yeares wages which is 20*li* the which he promised that it should be left heare for the Benefett of your wife and children Excepteing that in parte of the 5*li* which wase

---

[1] Cf. *Records of Massachusetts*, I. 252.

[2] W. 4. 33; 5 *Collections*, I. 87–88. Richard Crane apparently later forwarded this letter to Governor Winthrop. See Richard Crane to John Winthrop, May 9, 1640 (pages 238–239, below).

to be Alowed you which was from the Annunciation of the vergen Marey
vntill the daye of your Ariueinge in New England which was at 4s a weeke
which we doe conceiue to be about 2li 10s   Soe we doe conceiue that at the
end of your 3 yeares thear will be 17li and ode mony due vnto you for your
last 2 yeares seruice   And furthrmoar we doe desiere to know whear your
master doe not pay you your 4li a year yearly during the said terme or not.
And so we leaue you to the protection of the Almightey   hoping that your
master and mistris ar in good healthe, I rest Your loveing wife

                                                           DOROTHY CRANE

STEASTON the 15th of Marche 1638[/39]

I haue sent your Clothes withe Walter Haimes Goodes.

DANIEL DENNISON TO JOHN WINTHROP[1]

*To the Wor[shi]pfull John Winthrop Esq. Govr. of the Massahusets these present
Boston*

SIR, Our Company wantinge some officers, haue accordinge to their
liberty, made choice of some, whom, they desired me to propound to the
Court or Counsell. They were willinge to expresse their loue and likinge to
Sargeant French and Sargeant Howlett proposinge the former for Leiuetenant, the other for Ensigne, yet esteeminge the Counsell better able to
judge, they agreed Likewise to propound 2 Gentlemen against their 2 Sargeants viz. Mr. Whittingham for Leiuetenant and Mr. John Hubbard for
Ensigne, willingly referringe it to the wisdome of the Counsell to appoint
2 of the 4, yet they were desirous that the Counsell might vnderstand that
the major part of them did rather desire the 2 Sargeants tho they did willingly refer themselfes to the Counsell   The Sargeants did modestly refuse
professinge themselfes ready to doe their best services in the places they now
hold, wherein I confess they are more vsefull, then I Suppose they would be
in other. The Gentlemen are not freemen yet of good report and esteeme.
your wisdomes will easily determine the matter. Consideringe Carpenters
worke not for respect I desire you would be pleased to intreate Mr. Salton-

---

[1] W. 1. 126. Daniel Dennison was one of the earliest inhabitants of Cambridge. He subsequently moved to Ipswich. He was for eleven years deputy from that town to the General Court,
and for the last twenty-nine years of his life he was an Assistant. For eleven years (including the
period of King Philip's War) he was Major General of the colony's forces. Lucius R. Paige, *History
of Cambridge* (Boston, 1877), 534.

stall or my Brother Bradstreete to install them in their places if you shall judge any of them meete. I will not further trouble you but present my service and remayne Your Worships to be Commanded

                                                          DANIELL DENISON

Ips. March 25: 1639

JOHN HAYNES TO JOHN WINTHROP[1]

To the Right Worshipfull his much honoured Freind John Winthropp, Esqr. Governour of the Mattachosett, these bee delivered

WORTHY SIR, In my jorney towards Quilipiacke, I mett with this Panaquanike Indian, who being bownde for the Baye, repayringe to your selfe, requested mee to signify to you what hee is and his erraund. The party is knowne to vs, and his busynesse in particular to trucke for certeine squaes that were taken when wee invaded ther coasts. I leave him and what hee hath to saye to your wisdom to consider of. Wee have lately hadd a great floode, that came vpp to some of our howses, and carryed away a good parte of our fences in our lowe grounds, otherwise, wee blesse the Lord, wee are generally in good health. I should gladly crave a word from you, if any newes by the fishinge shipps from England. In much hast, my service presented to your selfe, Mr. Dudley, with the rest of our good frinds, I take leave. Your assured Frind

                                                              JO: HAYNES

WETHERSFEILD, the 27th of the 1st month, 1639

JOHN WINTHROP, JR., TO JOHN WINTHROP[2]

SIR, These calling in this night intending to goe towards Boston tomorrow I am bold to present my humble duty and my wives to your selfe and my mother desiring to lett you vnderstand that we are in good health (blessed be god) with the rest of our freinds heere, and at my vncle Downings. heer is noe news to write you of. Joseph Grafton was on friday sevennight at Pascataway, having made his voyage hence thither and back againe in 3 daies, but there was noe ships come then to the Isle of Sholes. Just now one came to me that came from Quinipiack certifying that Mr. Goose was arrived

---

[1] Original not located; 4 *Collections*, VI. 355. For Haynes, see *D.A.B.*
[2] Essex Institute; 5 *Collections*, VIII. 34; *L. and L.*, II. 264–265.

there.[1] before he came thence he saw my brother Steven there well. the merchants there were about to hire Mr. Goose his Ship for England, but this party comming out of the bay I suppose it is not news to you; last weeke one having laded his canoe with wood coming where the sea was a little ruffe, she filled presently with water; but not sinking right downe he was succoured by an other boate, and so saved.

Goodman Giles of this towne came to me this day and told me he had order from Sergeant Watson by your order to pay me 10 bushells of corne, but having no notice therof from you, I doubted it might be some mistake. thus craving your praiers and blessing I commend you to the Almighty and rest Your obedient son

JOHN WINTHROP

[*Ca.* April, 1639]

Myselfe and wife salute our brothers and freinds with you.

JOHN WINTHROP, JR., TO ELIZABETH WINTHROP[2]

To my deare wife mrs. Eliz: Winthrop at Boston

MY DEARE WIFE, When my brother Steven went hence I was not vp nor well, so that I could not wright to the. I thanke god I am now much better then I was when he left me   though I much desire to enioy thy company yet I would not have the crosse thy intentions in staying till that tyme be past. I hoped to fetch the home my selfe, but am yet prevented. I can get noe garden inclosed, nor digged but I heare that in new ground it is best to begin when the weeds are sprung vp for then they will all be killed and grow no more that yeare. put my brother Steven in mind to send me my carbine, as he promised me. So with my best affections and love to the I commend the to the Lord and rest thyne in my best affections

J: WINTHROP

FROM THE SALTHOUSE[3] monday morning [*ca.* April, 1639]

my duty to my mother my love to my brothers and all freinds forgett not. my blessing to Betty and Fitz.
my brother Steven hath promised to bring the home when thou comest.

---

[1] Presumably on his return from his voyage to Bermuda. See above, page 84, *n.* 2.
[2] W. 7A. 61; Savage (1853), I. 473.
[3] See Calvin P. Pierce, *Ryal Side from Early Days of Salem Colony* (Cambridge, 1931), 36–42.

HUGH PETER TO JOHN WINTHROP[1]

To our noble Gouernour in Boston

SIR, According as I writ, yesterday in the afternoone Mrs. Ames[2] Mr. Phillips[3] and 2 more of the church our elder being one met here to deale with mee about Mrs. Ruth:[4] where Mr. Phillips with much violence and sharpnes charged mee home with this, that of all offences, such as were agaynst the widow and fatherles were greatest, aggravated it how he could, rememberd that which I never dreamt of that I should hynder the mayd of a match at London, which was not so, could not thinke of any kindnes I euer did her, though shee haue had aboue 300*li* through my fingers,[5] so as if God vphold mee not after an especiall manner, it will sinke mee surely. I told him, if hee had taken halfe that paynes with mee before, hee had done neighborly, and brotherly. hee told mee he would not stop my intended marriage but assured mee it would not be good: much wonder here is in the towne about it, though the elder thought my answear sufficient. Mr. Endecot haue likewise been dealt withall for the same thing, all which makes mee reflect vpon my rash proceedings with Mrs. Sh[effield].[6] Now (good Sir) let mee know what is best to doe, who am Your troubled and troublesome

H: PETER

SALEM 5 2d [1639]

JOHN ENDECOTT TO JOHN WINTHROP[7]

To the right Wor[shipfu]ll John Winthrop Esqr. Gouvernour deliver

DEAREST SIR, Your kinde lines I receaued by Mascanomet and your lovinge token formerly of trees, for both which I humblie thanck you as also for your kinde intertaynement of my wiefe. The Lord requite you for all. I cannot but acquaint you with my thoughts concerning Mr. Peter, since hee receaued a letter from Mrs. Sheffield which was yesterday in the eueninge

---

[1] W. 3. 53; 4 *Collections*, VII. 199–200.

[2] Joan Fletcher Ames, widow of the Reverend William Ames, the noted theologian.

[3] The Reverend John Phillips of Dedham, brother-in-law of the Reverend William Ames.

[4] Ruth Ames, daughter of the Reverend William Ames and Joan Fletcher Ames.

[5] After Ames's death, Hugh Peter had been active in taking steps to relieve the straitened circumstances of the Ames family. *Publications of the Colonial Society of Massachusetts*, XXV. 72.

[6] Mrs. Deliverance Sheffield, who subsequently became Hugh Peter's second wife.

[7] W. Au. 94; 4 *Collections*, VII. 157–158.

after the fast.[1] Shee seeming in her letter to abate of her affeccions towards him, and dislikinge to come to Salem vppon such termes as hee had written. I finde that hee begins now to play her parte, and if I mistake not, you will see him as greatly in loue with her (if shee will but hold of a little,) as euer shee was with him, but hee conceales it what hee can as yett. The begininge of the next weeke you will heare further from him.

I ame sorry to heare of Mrs. Winthrops sicknes, and Mrs. Downings feare of sicknes. The Lord doe good to them both and raise vp the one and keepe vp the other, if it be his will. We had yesterday blessed be our God a comfortable day of it. Mr. Humfryes voluntarily did acknowledge with many teares his cariadges of rashnes and hastines etc. in such a manner as hee drew teares from diuers. the Lord in mercy cary him further on in euery way of his to Gods glorie and his owne peace: I shall not further trouble you at present but committ you to him who is able to doe for vs all aboue what we can ask or thinck. With him I leaue you and your deare yoakefellow and all yours beseeching him neuer to leaue you till hee hath brought you home to himselfe in Glory. In whom I ame Yours euer whilest I ame

Jo: Endecott

[*Ca.* April 5, 1639]

My wief remembers her seruice to you and Mrs. Winthrop and Mrs. Downing. All heere are well blessed be God.

[*Memorandum by Governor Winthrop:*] Keepe this to your selfe.

HUGH PETER TO JOHN WINTHROP[2]

To the Noble Gouernor in Boston

Hon: Sir, I much thanke you for yours, and together am sorry for the sicknes of our frends. I am still troublesome to you. I haue sent Mrs. D[eliverance] Sh[effield's] letter which puts mee to new troubles for though shee takes liberty vpon my Cossen Downings speeches, yet (Good Sir) let mee not bee a foole in Israel. I had many good answers to yesterday's worke[3] and amongst the rest her letter; which (if her owne) doth argue more wisedome,

---

[1] The Fast Day was April 4, 1639. *Records of Massachusetts*, I. 253.
[2] W. 2. 54; 4 *Collections*, VI. 100–101.
[3] I.e., the Fast Day, April 4, 1639.

then I thought shee had. You haue often sayd I could not leaue her; what to doe is very considerable. Could I with comfort and credit desist this seemes best, could I goe on, and content my selfe, that were good: my request is that this bearer my harts-halfe may well obserue what is best. For though I now seeme free agayne, yet the depth I know not. had shee come ouer with mee I thinke I had bin quieter. This shee may know that I haue sought God earnestly, that the next weeke, I shall bee riper:

I doubt shee gaynes most by such writings: and shee deserues most when shee is further of. My very hart is with you and I am Yours euer

H: PETER

[*Ca.* April 5, 1639]

if you shall amongst you aduise mee to write to hir, I shall forthwith. our towne lookes vpon me contracted and so I haue sayd my selfe. what wonder the change would make I know not.

EMMANUEL DOWNING TO JOHN WINTHROP[1]

To his much honored brother John Winthrop Governour

SIR, I retorne you manie thanks for your kynde letter with a sorifull heart for my sisters sicknes   The Good lord blesse and sanctifie yt vnto hir. though I should be verie glad of my wives retorne, yet I dare not now call for yt. I haue nought to write but of planting sowing posting rayling etc.

My Cosen P[eter] is constant to his dayly charge, soe that all his freinds are resolved to leave him to his owne way, yet blessed be God his preaching is verie profitable and comfortable to all. I feare I shalbe disapoynted of 30 bushells of Indian Corne which I relyed on here. I pray let me be soe bold with you as to know if I may be supplyed thence   soe with my service to your selfe and my sister with harty prayers for hir health I rest Your assured loving brother

EM: DOWNINGE

SALEM 8 2di [1639]

[1] W. 2. 27; 4 *Collections*, VI. 51–52.

DANIEL PATRICK TO JOHN WINTHROP[1]

To the Honnored and Right Worthye Mr. Winthrope Gouernour deliver in Bostone thes

HONNOURED SIR, I confes I knowe nothinge in my selfe that shoulde in the least incouradge and imboulden mee to write vnto you for as publikelye soe priuatelye I am the same in acknowledginge my rougged vnequall and foolish carriedg toward your selfe, onelye now, as alwayes, beinge confident of your Clemencye and loue to reasone in or from anny, I humblye craue leaue to offer a propositione concerninge our towne boundes to your Con-sidderatione   In Deddam plott of there Neck, 2 lines is drawne, the last as Mr. Olliuer tels mee hauinge your Aprobatione, which allsoe is far better then the former. I haue presented a 3d to your farther vewe, which alsoe giueth the same quantety, and it may be as good in qualletye. Now good Sir I beseech you considder, Watertowne expeckts somethinge before Dedum as moore benificiall through Antiquetye; nether are they far behinde anny in improuinge theyre halfe soe much in quantety as they haue. agayne I knowe and fulley beleeue tis the great Joy of all godly rulers to see peace florish in the midst of Justice, therfore if in a just waye this 3000 Akers may be added vniustlye not preiudicinge Deddum whoes portione will still be the same and our to impatient spirrits therby quieted I thinke a farr better Consequence will followe then at the present in respeckt of troublinge you I may well express.[2] I feare I haue presuemd to far   therefore crauinge pardone if I haue bine needdless, and remayninge the same I was though fruetles, I leaue both the Case and your self with god to guide, and rest your Worships to commaunde

DANIELL PATTRICKE

WATERTOWNE this 9th of Aprill 1639

HUGH PETER TO JOHN WINTHROP[3]

To our noble Gouernour, Boston

SIR, Still pardon my offensive boldnes: I know not well whither Mrs. Sh[effield] haue set mee at liberty or not: my conclusion is, that if you find

---

[1] W. 3. 89; 4 *Collections*, VII. 325–326. For Patrick, see 4 *Collections*, VII. 321*n*.

[2] For the action of the General Court regarding the Watertown-Dedham boundary, see *Records of Massachusetts*, I. 257.

[3] W. 3. 53; 4 *Collections*, VII. 200–201.

I cannot make an honorable retreat then I shall desire to advance σύν θεώ.

Of you I now expect your last aduise, viz: whither I must goe on or of, salvo evangelij honore: if shee bee in good earnest to leaue all agitations this way, then I stand still and wayt Gods mynd concerning mee; if you find that cannot bee, then let our shee-frends come home, and I shall take what present speedy course I can to come ouer and labor to make vp all breaches. If I had much mony I would part with it to bee free till wee heare what England doth supposing I may bee called to some imployment that will not suite a marryed estate: for indeed (Sir) some must looke out, and I haue very strong thoughts to speake with the Duitch Governor and lay some way there for supplye etc. I heare all men complayning, few doing; if I goe to the Duitch, I pray let my Cossen Stephen goe along, if you thinke it not tanti disswade; why should wee not make some league with them? who are very probable to bee more then ordinary good or bad neighbours: once agayne I say wee must looke out, wee want necessary linnen cum multis alijs, and a voyage to the West Indyes would find vs wintere worke in Cottone etc. fishing will not yet or to purpose, manu-factures cannot sine manibus: I am sick to heare the complaynts   graunt ships doe come, eyther wee are too many to bee serued by so few ships; or theire supply will not bee quadrate, or we shall want mony to take them of: these things I say not out of want of faith for my selfe, but loue to the country. I resolue to quiet myne owne conscience about the state with what speed I can who haue made it my wife my life; the issue of our faste[1] should set vs vpon some singular things. I hardly haue seene more of Gods presence here, then on that day. The Lord hold our harts to the worke.

Once more for Mrs. Sh[effield]   I had from Mr. Hibbins and others her fellow-passengers sad discouragements where they saw her in her trim. I would not come of with dishonor nor come on with griefe or ominous hesitations.

Glad I am our sister is better. the Lord continue her to your bosome a blessed helper.

My sighes and harty desires are for you as for Your unworthy

H. P.

[*Ca.* April 10, 1639]

---

[1] I.e., the fast of April 4, 1639.

FRANCIS KIRBY TO JOHN WINTHROP[1]

*To the right wor[shipfu]ll John Winthrop esquire governour of the Massachusets bay
in New England*

LONDON this 11th of Aprill 1639

WORTHY SIR, I shall only in this paper salute you refferringe you to this
bearer Joseph Carter my loue deseruinge son and faithfull seruant, who so
soone as he was freed from my seruice had an earnest desire to come to N:
England. he can better or at least with more safty relate to you our Condicion
heer then I can write it. I knowe his desire is not to be chargeable to any of
his frends, neither doth his present Condicion require it, but what Courtesy
you please to do him, I shall take it as done to my selfe and be redy to
requite it in any seruice that I can do for you heer. Thus with my harty
prayers to the almighty for his blessinges vpon you and yours I rest Your
lo[ving] frend

FRANC: KIRBY

[*Endorsed by Governor Winthrop:*] Mr. Kerby. Received per Mr. Carter.

THOMAS COBBETT TO JOHN WINTHROP[2]

*To his much honourd Freind mr. Winthrop at his howse in Boston present theise
I pray you*

WORTHY SIR, I am bold to mooue you concerning that heifer calfe which
I mentioned formerly to you, that if it please your selfe to consider of the
vallewe of it as it was then or might haue beene since and that you please to
appointe it to be payd for my vse in corne either wheate or rye (if all you
can spare bee not otherwise disposed of) and send me word of what you shall
order herein I shall accordingly take order for your receiuinge of it by my
Brother Hill in whose debt I am and for the payment of which debt I am
put vppon it (at present) to request this at your wor[shi]ps hands. if your
wor[shi]p please to consider of me herein you shall doe me a great pleasure
(as matters now stand) and I shall soe acknowledge it. and thus not hauinge
more at present I desire to tender my best respects to you and to mris.

---

[1] W. 3. 9; 4 *Collections*, VII. 20–21. For Kirby, see 4 *Collections*, VII. 13*n*.
[2] W. 4. 94; 5 *Collections*, I. 268–269.

Winthrop leauinge you and yours vnder the comfortable shaddow of the wings of the Almighty   Yours in all Christian service

THO: COBBETT

LYNNE this 13th of the 11th m. [1639]

EDWARD HOWES TO JOHN WINTHROP, JR.[1]

To his much esteemed frind Mr. John Winthrop Junr. at Boston in the Massachusetts Bay or elsewhere in New England these deliver

SIR, Yours I receiued with 2 relations of Monstrous births and a generall earthquake.[2] When I had read them; they seemed to me like Pharaohs dreames; but whoe can tell certainely wherefore God sent them; where is there such an other people then in N: E:? that labours might and maine to haue Christ formed in them, yet they would giue or appoynt him his shape, and cloath him too. it cannot be denyed but we haue conceiued many monstrous imaginations of Christ Jesus, the one imagination sayes loe here he is, the other sayes loe, there he is, multiplicitie of conceptions, but is there any one true shape of him; and if one of many produce a shape tis not the shape of the sonne of $\frac{God}{man}$, but an vglie horridd Metamorphosis, neither is it a liuinge shape, but a dead one, yet a Crow thinkes her owne bird the fairest, and most preferre theire owne wisedome before Gods, Antichrist before Christ; to you I write with whome I may be bold; and is't a wonder the Earth should quake at this.   O Earth, Earth, Earth, heare the voyce of the Lord, a still silent voyce, yet where it comes it maketh the mountaines to quake, and the hills to tremble.

The bookes you writt for, I haue not mett with them as yet, at the shopps where I haue bin; I could wish you some bookes, but one booke were enough, if you could come by it. its written within and without, its calld by many names, but it is not knowne by the names, but to those that have the nature thereof; to giue you the name and nature in a word, its *The booke of life* (et est elixir vitæ), where you may read all within you and all without you; and him that is all in all; to whose protection I leaue you and rest Your frind in the best I may

EDWARD HOWSE

CURSISTORS COURTE neere Lincolnes Inn the 14th of Aprill 1639

---

[1] W. 2. 169; 4 *Collections*, VI. 505–506.
[2] I.e., Mrs. Dyer's and Mrs. Hutchinson's monsters and the earthquake of June 1, 1638.

Pray present my Loue to your best beloued wife. My father and mother are in health and salute you so doth my wife vnknowne to you, but by my relation; we should be glad to see you at our habitacion, if your affaires drawe you to London. For newes, I referr you to the vulgar Athenians. Vale.

Shall I hide any thinge from my frind, read this to Mr. J: S. and doe with it as you please. if it may doe him, or any other, good: God speed it.

THOMAS WELLES TO JOHN WINTHROP[1]

To the Right Wor[shipfu]ll Mr. Wynthroppe Gouernour at the Bay present these

RIGHT WOR[SHIPFU]LL, I cannot but condemne my selfe of great ingratitude, in this my so long sylence, after the receipte of many free and vndesearued fauors from your Wor[shi]p, for all which I haue not yet any oportunity to expresse my thankefull acknowledgement thereof but by these fewe lynes, wherein I desire humbly to present my harty and vnfeigned thanks vnto you. As for all other manifestations of your loue, so for your great Care and troble in restoreing vnto me my searuaunt out of the pawes of those desperat deluded Cretures at the Iland, wherein he was fearefully intangled and insnared; a Deliuerance, for which both he, and all his frynds, are euer bound to giue thanks to Almighty god, who made your Wor[shi]p so happy a Instrument as to accomplishe the same. What chardges ether your selfe or any by Order from you haue disbursed I shall most gladly satisfie. My deare Fryend Mr. Bellingham sent me word that he paid for his passage by water, the which I shall thankefully repay at his comming to Conectecott, which he hath appoynted before his Returne to the Bay.

I am sory to heare you haue such Ill Neighbours at Pyscataque which I feare will proue the Reseptacle of such persons as stand disaffected to this State. I should gladly be Aduised by your Wor[shi]p and my worthy Fryend Mr. Dudley what I might doe for the preuention thereof; haueing the disposeing thereof committed to my Trust (from the Company) with Mr. Whiting, if he bring no other directions at his returne from old Ingland, if your Wor[shi]p aduise yt may rest as yt is so long. thus craueing pardon for my boldnes I humbly take my leaue and rest At your Wor[ship]s searuice to be commaunded

THO: WELLES

HARTFORD this 16th of Aprill 1639

[1] W. 2. 186; 4 *Collections*, VI. 583–584. For Welles, see 4 *Collections*, VI. 583n. Welles had at this

JOHN ENDECOTT TO JOHN WINTHROP[1]

DEAREST SIR, I ame at your disposing about Plimmoth busines both for tyme and place and shall attend vppon you for direction in that busines.[2] I question whither we shall be able to determyne any thinge this first meetinge, for it is to be doubted whither in a generall Court they haue giuen any such full commission to any as the Court hath giuen vs. If you please to write a wourd to that effect, and that we might see their Patent, (They shall see ours, I haue the reduplicate) I thinck it will not be amisse. I will leaue it with you whither you thinck it not better to be at Hingham then Scituate. There are 2 men not so peacefull as I could wish, and I rather incline to the first, Hingham and so doeth Mr. Peter who I thinck will goe alonge with mee.

Sir If you please that Dauies[3] his punishment be deferred till the next Court, it being desired of many vpon his humble cariadge since his first punishment, I shall consent. The Lord in mercy keepe you for euer in whom I ame Yours truely

JO: ENDECOTT

[*Ca.* May, 1639]

JOHN WINTHROP, JR., TO JOHN WINTHROP[4]

To the right wor[shipfu]ll my much honored father John Winthrop Esqr. Gov. deliver In Boston

SIR, My humble duty to your selfe, and my deare, and honored mother. I thanke you for your love and kindnesse to my wife and her little ones. I expected them heere by the last pinnace, but I find it, as she hath told me she knowes not how to leave you, nor how to part with my mother, when

---

time a good proportion of the patents for Dover, New Hampshire. Savage, *Genealogical Dictionary*, IV. 478.

[1] W. 3. 39; 4 *Collections*, VII. 158–161.

[2] John Endecott and Israel Stoughton were commissioned by the Massachusetts General Court on March 13, 1638/39, to negotiate an agreement with Plymouth Colony regarding the disputed boundary between Hingham and Scituate. *Records of Massachusetts*, I. 254. Their first meeting with the Plymouth commissioners was at Hingham on May 15, 1639. *Journal*, I. 305.

[3] John Davies, "for grosse offences in attempting lewdnes with divers weomen," was, on March 5, 1638/39, sentenced to be "severely whiped" both at Boston and at Ipswich and "to weare the letter V vpon his breast vpon his vppermost garment vntill the Court do discharge him." On September 3, 1639, he was "vpon his good carriage . . . discharged from wearing the V which was formerly enioyned him." *Records of Massachusetts*, I. 248, 269.

[4] W. 1. 127; 5 *Collections*, VIII. 33–34.

she is with you; I desire you would please to lett her returne now. I doubt there will not goe any pinnace from hence this weeke, therefore I pray be pleased to speake to John Gallop to bring them: Joseph Grafton came from Pascataquacke the last Saboth day. there was noe other ship come, but one expected by John Treworthy dayly. one is at Richmond Iland. mr. Marshall and his wife being in a canoe there and one other man with them, the canoe was overturned but the 2 men holding fast vpon the canoe were saved   his wife was drowned, he having hold of her let her goe to save him selfe: the last day of the weeke there was a man almost drowned heere in the narrow river in a canoe having laden his canoe so deepe with dung that she sunke vnder him, scarce any wave stirring. an house was burnt heere last weeke in towne. Craving your prayers and blessing I commend you to the Almighty and rest

[JOHN WINTHROP][1]

[*Ca.* May, 1639]

[*Endorsed by Governor Winthrop:*] My sonne John.

ROGER WILLIAMS TO JOHN WINTHROP[2]

For his much honoured and beloued Mr. Governour of the Massachusets, these

SIR, In my last I gaue intimacion of another answere, which from the Sachims is this.

First, that although they remember not any agreements that haue passed about the natiues yealding vp their hunting places, advantages, etc. with in præscribed limits etc., yet, because satisfactorie agreements may haue bene vnknowne to them, betweene yourselues and the natiues about you, they haue sent for this man, Wuttattaaguegin, (who keepes most at Massachuset with Cutshamoquene, and hath not bene this 3 yeares with them.)

This man Wuttattaaguegin hath promised to satisfie in wampam, beauer and venison what it comes to.

But he belieues not the dammage can be so great, for thus he relates: hauing laid his traps, intending dayly to tend them, Cutshamoquin sent for him to be a guide to him in a hunting match about the Bay, where other natiues were ignorant. He went, yet sent a youth to view his traps, who saith

---

[1] The signature has been clipped from the original manuscript.
[2] Original not located; 4 *Collections,* VI. 257–259; *N.C.,* VI. 131–133.

that he saw the English men loose 3 horses out of the traps, and rode away vpon 2 of them, the third only was lamed.

Vpon this he desired libertie to returne to the Bay, to enquire more perfectly the dammage: and being not come back as yet, they haue this present sent againe for him.

Yet because they see not that Wuttattaaguegin broke any knowne couenant in laying his traps in that place, nor willingly wrought evill against the English, they conceaue it would be very faire and honourable in all natiues eyes, that it would please the English to make knowne as well their moderation as their justice in the case.

And for themselues they resolue if this man should not be faythfull or able to satisfie your demaunds, they promise (vpon perswasions and some offers of mine to them) to contribute themselues out of their owne, and to draw in helpe, that may in wampam, beauer, and venison make vp the whole summe before the next hunting be ouer.

So crauing humbly your loving acceptation of my poore service herein, or whateuer els you shall please to vse me in, I rest Your Worships most vnworthy

ROGER WILLIAMS

PROVIDENCE 2d 3, [1639]

My due respect to my honoured friends Mr. Deputie and the rest of the Councell.

GEORGE DILL TO JOHN WINTHROP[1]

To the Right wors[hipfull] the Hon: Gou[e]rn[our] Mr. Jon: Winthrop Esqr. at Boston

RIGHT WORSH[IPFULL], Hauing found your goodnes unto me I am bound further to implour your healpe in pittie of my poore estate. I haue suffered long the want of this monnie which is due unto me from Mr. Shurt and haue taken seuerall Journies into the Bay, and trobled my sealfe to my greate loss, otherwise to desire and seake my owne in the fairest manner. Your worship seeth how I am put of and I know unles I am healped by you I shall still suffer, who haue wanted it so much that I haue binn and am inforsed still to borrow to supply my nessessitie. I Besech your Worship therefore to grant

---

[1] W. 4. 95; 5 *Collections*, I. 269–270. For Dill, see 5 *Collections*, I. 269n.

me your warrant that Mr. Shurt may Answer me the Next Court. Betwene this and that he may either shew heare or Answer that which he pretendes (But I know he Cannot Doe) for auoyding my Demandes the thing is nothing to him But Much to me. Thearfore I humbly intreate your worsh[ip] in your Pittie and Iustise to healpe me so shall I be bound to pray to God for your worsh[ip] as I haue cause alreddy as Your poore yet humbly thankfull seruant

GEORGE DILL

from SALEM this 5th of the third month [1639]

ROGER WILLIAMS TO JOHN WINTHROP[1]

[For] his much honoured and beloved Mr. John Wintrop Gov[ernou]r of the Massachusets these

SIR, I am requested by Caunounicus and Miantunnomu to present you with their loue and respect (which they allso desire may be remembred to all the English Sachims) as allso with this Expression of the Continuance of their loue vnto you viz. 30 fathom of Beades (10 from Caunounicus and 20 from Miantunnomu)[2] and the basket a present from Miantunnomues wife to your deare Companion Mrs. Wintrop.

3 things they request me to desire of you.

First the Continuance of your ancient and constant friendship toward them and good opinion of their sincere affection to the English.

I obiected against this that I lately heard that 2 boates of English were cut of by Pequts and that Miantunnomu knew of the Act etc.

To this they answered that they haue not so much as heard of any miscarriage of the English this way of late and that 2 dayes since a Nariganset man came from Long Iland and brought no such tidings.

That they haue alwayes (and shall still) succoured the English in any such distresses: and that if but a single English man woman or childe be found in the woods by any of theirs, they should punish severely that man that should not safely conduct them and succour them etc.

2ndly That you would please to ratifie that promise made to them after the warrs viz: the free vse of the Pequt Countrey for their hunting etc.

3rdly That since there are many Pequt Sachims and Captaines surviving,

---

[1] W. 2. 113; 4 *Collections*, VI. 259–261; *N.C.*, VI. 133–135.
[2] Cf. *Journal*, I. 299, under date May 2, 1639.

many of whome haue bene Actuall murtherers of the English and (3 of them) which haue slaine some of their Sachims.

And that since the Agreement the last yeare at Qunnihticut with Mr. Heynes and the Magistrates you haue not yet pleased to come to Action.

And that the Pequts being many hundreths of them, may with these their Sachim[s *torn*] doe more mischiefe to vs and them.

They therefore request that you would please to write by them at present to Mr. Heynes, that so vpon your ioynt Agreement, they may themselues freely pursue those Pequt Princes and Captaines whome Mr. Heynes (who had the list of them from me the last yeare) shall name vnto them.

I obiected the report of great numbers of Pequts among themselues etc.

They answere, as formerly, that to cleare themselues from that, and to make it appeare how both the Monahiggins and the Nayantaquit men haue receaved the Pequts and their Presents (when they refused them) and so haue made presents to the English with the Pequt beades which themselues neuer did nor could: they will now fall vpon this Service and if the Monahiggins and Nayantaquit men will not ioyne with them in it, they will themselues pursue the Persons that shall be named to them wheresoeuer they find them although at Monahiggannick or Nayantaquit, without touching a Monahigganie or Nayantick man further then you shall please to advize them.

More they say, but I should be tædious and therefore with all due respect to your lo[ving] selfe Mrs. Wintrop Mr. Deputie etc. I rest Your Wo[rshi]ps faythfull and vnfayned

ROGER WILLIAMS

Caunounicus begs of you a little Sugar.

PROVIDENCE this 9th of the 3rd [1639]

ACKNOWLEDGMENT OF SAMUEL WILBUR[1]

Whereas I joyned with others in presentinge to the corte a writing called a petition or remonstrance,[2] I confes it was far beyond my place and range to vse such unbeseming exspresyons to those whom the lord hath set ouer me,

---

[1] W. I. 127.

[2] I.e., that in behalf of John Wheelwright in March, 1636/37. Wilbur was one of the large group of those signing this Remonstrance who were disarmed by order of the General Court in November, 1637. In March, 1637/38, he was, together with William Coddington and others, given "license to depart" from Massachusetts, and he went to Rhode Island. For his later career, see Savage, *Genealogical Dictionary*, IV. 544–545.

thearfor intreat your worships to vnderstand that it is only the cause which mad me to doe it, and for my rashnes and ofence thearein I humbly craue your worships prayers to the lord for pardon and pardon from your selues: I haue bene noe enimy to this state nor through the Asistance of the lord I hope neuer shall.

SAMUELL WILBORE

[*Endorsed:*] Samll. Wilbore Acknowledgment [*and in another hand:*] Saml. wilbore (3) 16, 1639.

ABRAHAM KUFFLER TO JOHN WINTHROP, JR.[1]

KIND SIR, Your 2 letters since your departure I haue Reciued and had Answred them [long] since but for my longe Sicknes occatisioned by the [*torn*] of a wall which brocke both my legg and Arme. [Your] vnckle Wintrope whome I mett the last weeke to[ld] of your helth and well-fare which I much joye to hea[r]   hee tould me that hee would convay a letter to you an[d] hauing so fitt ane opertunitie I could not but pres[ent] my servis to you and giue you thanckes for your pay[nes] in writing. I know you are desirous to heare of [my] prosseeding in Alchimie   all my proceeding therin is lost by reason of my longe sicknes so that I am now beeginning agayne   as for my other inventi[on] seeing all Christendome in Armes and all kings an[d] princes tacken that waye I was forst to leaffe o[ff] all curious inventissions   I now onelly follow die[ing] of scarrlett in which I hauc so much to doe that I ca[n] follow nothing elles except a generall pesse[2] were made whereby princes might tacke delight in A[*torn*]   I should bee glade to heare of your proseedings till when and for ever I rest Your Servant

ABRAHAM KUFFLER

LONDON the 12th of June 1639

---

[1] W. 4. 95; 5 *Collections*, I. 270–271. Abraham Kuffler (Keffler) was born in Cologne on October 4, 1598, the son of Jakob Kuffler, a merchant, who was councillor of the Elector of Brandenburg and his resident in Cologne. After graduating from Padua and taking a doctor's degree, Kuffler established himself in London. There he married the daughter of Cornelis Drebbel, Dutch physicist, who was then living in London and with whom he worked on the invention of a submarine. After the death of Charles I, he removed to Holland where he established a scarlet-dyeing business and where he also tried to sell a torpedo invented by Drebbel. He died in London on December 8, 1657. *Niew Nederlandsch Biografisch Woordenboek*, II. 739.

[2] Marginal note in the handwriting of John Winthrop, Jr.: "peace nere made."

ABRAHAM SHURT TO ROBERT KNIGHT[1]

ALDWORTH-TOWNE the 17th of June 1639

MR. ROBT: KNIGHT, When it shall p[l]ease god to send you to the Baye demand of Mrs. Milward for Mr. Elbridge his letter and shew it with the Invoyce vnto Mr. Winthrop togeather with his letter, and Dills account and his letter, and take vpon my note from Mr. Winthrop touchinge Dill   comend me to Mr. Mavericke and if Mr. Ludlowe be there demand his Account of him and procure an ende vnto it: and for Mr. Hickford be earnest with him and alsoe for the bill of 10s dew to me and to any one else that are indebted vnto vs: ratifyinge and conferminge what you doe therin as if I were present and thus wishinge you a safe retourne I ever rest Your Lo[ving] freinde

ABRAHAM SHURT

Witnes herevnto
HENRY CHAMPNEY

MR. MILWARD, lett me intreat you by vertue of this order, to call Gorge Dill of Salem before the gouerner and end the account which stands in shut betweane vs by reason that I am now bound for Pemaquid and cannot continew any longer in these parts my occations being vrgent to goe   whom and what you shall doe therin we shall allowe as well dun   he hath put vs to a great deale of charg in coming soe far to end his account and I hoope that you will recouer som what for it   soe I rest Your lo[ving] Frind to command

ROBERT KNIGHT

in BOSTOWNE the 11th July 1639

[*Endorsed by Robert Knight:*] A Remembrance from Mr. Shurt.

JOHN WINTHROP TO JAMES LUXFORD[2]

JAMES, heere wants yet 2 heifers and 2 steeres besides the Cowe and Bull which are at Tenhils. let me know presently what is become of them, for mr. Fenwick demands now Accompt of them.[3]

[JOHN WINTHROP]

[*Ca.* July, 1639]

---

[1] W. 2. 184; 4 *Collections,* VI. 573.
[2] W. 1. 190. For Luxford, see 5 *Collections,* I. 127*n.*; 2 *Proceedings,* VII. 127–140.
[3] There follow several obliterated lines in James Luxford's handwriting.

mr. Nye had 6 heifers

One died the 1 yeare.

The next yeare they had 4 Calves   [of] those 2 died the next winter one
in the begin[nin]g and the other in the end of the 1 mo:

The 2 rem[aining] were one a heifer and the other a steere.

The next year 4: 2 heifers and 2 steers (one of the steers was lost in the
11th mo:) rem[aining] 2 heifers and one steere.

The next yeare 3: 2 steers and a heifer.

The last yeare 3: 2 steers and a heifer.

Sould

The first heifer to mr. B[*illegible*] for 14*li*.

The steere to Brooks of Concord for 12*li*.

2 steers new this yeare to wheeler of B: for 23*li*.

a heifer sould this yeare for 15*li* to Toppin of Nubery.

a heifer Calf sould this yeare to Audly of Boston 7*li* 10*s*.

a Cowe to mr. Peck of Hingham this summer for 21*li*.

a Cowe to Edmund Jacklin last yeare for 22*li* deb: [*illegible*]

a Cowe last yeare to mr. Samll. Shepherd for 25*li* 5*s* with Calfe.

a Cowe to Griffin of Concord this yeare for 22*li*.

[*Endorsed by Governor Winthrop*:] mr. Nye his Cattle.

JAMES LUXFORD TO JOHN WINTHROP[1]

RIGHT WOR[SHIPFUL], hauinge beene this present morninge with Mr.
Phenick[2] about his cattell; it seemeth that soombody informed him ther hath
beene a greeter increase of his cattell, then is wont to coome of cattell in
ould England or new; but this great increase doth arise I suppose but rather
to the increase of my trouble and affliction from those that think they
can neuer haue Inought: now I suppose that the wronge is partly to your
wor[ship] for sayd hee, they that spake it had it soe from your wor[ship's]
owne moouth, namely that the last summer was two yeare they weare increased 20, a thinge vnpossible thought they had had 2 calues apeece soe
many as calued. I would to god that men would better weight and consider

---

[1] W. 4. 50; 5 *Collections*, I. 129–130.

[2] George Fenwick, coming to America for the second time, arrived at New Haven in July, 1639.
Journal, I. 308.

of things, if they be members that thus speake to please there frends; truly this will not passe when it shall coome before the Judge of all the world   then the prisoner case will be in matter of truth considered but to him I leaue them; knowinge that it could not coome from your wor[ship] soe great and playne a mistake, and for my selfe I doe not soe perentory conclude but that there may bee soome mistake which if any man can better helpe mee in them I will gladly for if the lord had not beene gratious to mee, I should not haue beene able to speak at all; neither will I perentoryly conclude that there may not be soome small mistake. I will not willingly err hearin; wheras I sould 2 heyfers to tappin of newbery of that Coompany, as I haue mentioned them; I sould alsoe a heyfer to mr. holyoak. now it may be that that which mr. holyoke had, might be on of them then tappin had but on of them and mr. holyoke on, which I am not able to resolue accept I see them; now if there should bee such a mistake, it is noe difference on the matter; thought mine Enemyes, that are not yet satisfyed, neither I think will be till they see mee closed in the earth, will not thinke me closd Inought. those I say would make much of such a mistake, and it weare Inought for them to bringe to your wor[ship] or the deputy that soe they might augment my sorrow and add affliction to my bonds, but if these men wear perswaded, that hearby they did me good (as intruth they doe) I suppose who euer they bee, they would crave the Lord in mercy forgiue them, and open ther eyes that they may see it; by that time they haue felt gods hand brekinge out agaynst them as I haue doone, for that sinn, they will haue cause to looke about them and bemoone it.

If ther should be that mistake that is abooue mentioned, then would ther be 20s difference; therfore I will absolutely conclude but soome such difference ther may bee, but very small if it be, which receiuinge any light I should be glad to correct: morouer, there may be soome debts in the book that are not in the note; as it seemeth Mr. Palmer of Charlestowne: also James Hawkins, that I am suer is not in the note, because I could not gett him to a reconinge till within this little time, and he did desier he might sett it of at Mr. Hills; which I told him if he could I thought it would be well Inought.

I think it weare not amisse if your wor[ship] did learne how it should coome about that Mr. Phenick should coome to haue it that 5 heigfer [*torn*] haue 20 calues in 2 yeare.

[JAMES LUXFORD]

[*Ca.* July, 1639]

JAMES LUXFORD TO JOHN WINTHROP[1]

RIGHT WOR[SHIPFUL], I humbly thanke your wor[ship] for the meeke and gentle note I receiued from your wor[ship]; I am sory that your wor[ship] doth looke on all as spent, espetially if your wor[ship] meane wastfully:

and wheras your wor[ship] saith I had beene as good haue doone nothinge in matter of accompt, I must be content to doe nothinge, for neuer keepinge accompt of Expenses, I doe not [know] how to make such an accompt as may content them; soe that I shall euen referr my selfe to the Lord and be silent.

for the marshalls he is debtor in the book 9*li* 12*s* 6*d*, wherof I did assigne him to pay 4*li* 10*s* for alewiues and another small debt to goodman Gibson, soe that that beinge payd he will be debitor 5*li* 2*s*.

Concerninge the [*faded*] secrett about the farme that your wor[ship] desired to know the ground of; I did speake of the farme at Concord riuer, neither did I mention secresie for any other cause but for that I would not be knowen to meddle in the prayse or disprayse of it; thought as I sayd, it will neuer benefit your wor[ship] nor your next heyer, saue that the medow that was last giuen you;[2] but for the vpland it is such as will not be of vse for corne, it will be soe chargable clearing, otherwise I minded noe secret: for while your wor[ship] might for a woord spekinge haue that, which for time present and to coome might be of more vse, and without charge, in a manner in the Improuement; I thought it best to take it while it might be had. I doe desier to be thankfull to god, that year will not add to my affliction. I trust god will giue me cause to be thankfull for soome abatement in his time as for mine affliction, whether the Lord haue sanctifyed it or noe: it must needs remayne doubtfull to your wor[ship] for I my owne self am doubtfull. the Lord helpe mee my fears weare neuer greter, lest my repentance should be ahabs, or Pharaohs, that would doe any thinge for the remoouall of a temporall Judgment, which beinge gone, forget ther promises and vowes made to god in ther Extremyty: and albeit I haue found by good experience that god hath bowed his Eare and heard mee in many things yet hear I find him a stranger in that I haue not founde soe humblinge my hart, as that I might for euer inioy his presence. he hath made a gratious promise that he will dwell in an humble hart. the humble soule shall alway haue his company, which my soule longeth for but I cannot inioy it: I earnestly desier that god will soe sanctifie his afflictinge hand, as that I may truly say it is

---

[1] W. 4. 51; 5 *Collections*, I. 132–133.

[2] The General Court had granted to Governor Winthrop on June 6, 1639, "a parcell of meadow . . . lying within a mile or two of his farme, beneath Concord. . . ." *Records of Massachusetts*, I. 261.

good for mee that I was afflicted. Wheras your wor[ship] doth giue me a caueat not to be ouer confident of my looue to your wor[ship] The Lord knoweth that I cannot bee ouer confident therof, thought in the efforts I fayld: this note I had layd by to send the last time but that I forgott to putt it in the other but heare I haue inclosed it.

[JAMES LUXFORD]

[*Ca.* July, 1639]

[*Endorsed by Governor Winthrop:*] James Luxford.

DEPOSITIONS OF RICHARD ALLEN AND OTHERS[1]

Rich: Allen Surgeon of the Globe sworn etc. Sayth

That Math: Cole who dyed in the Shippe sayd to this dep[one]nt about 2 dayes before he dyed that what he had in the Shippe he had disposed on allready, and for the rest he had made his will in England which he would not alter but Charles Turner told this dep[one]nt that he had given them to him, which he doth veryly think he did because he was very helpfull to him in his sicknesse.

Tho: Buxton sworn etc. Sayth

That the said Cole 3 dayes before he dyed told this dep[one]nt that he had given all he had in his Shippe to Charles Turner, and that he should satisfie this dep[one]nt for his paynes about him and he gave the said Surgeon four shillings.

Hugh Rowe sworn etc. Sayth

That 3 dayes before the said Cole dyed and again a little before he dyed, he told this dep[one]nt that the said Charles should have all he had in the Shippe save one 12*d* which he would send to his wife and that he should satisfie those that had taken paynes about him: and he sayth that the said Charles did tend him night and daye, and the said Tho: Buxton did take paynes about him allso. He said allso that he would have the said Surgeon to have 10*s*.

[*Endorsed by Governor Winthrop:*] Depositions taken (5) 2: 1639.

[1] W. 1. 128.

JOHN WINTHROP'S MEMORANDA ON COURT CASES[1]

(5)   7 3*s* Rich: Hamon

      3*s* Edward Simonds   taken loytering and sleeping abrod in tyme of

      3*s* Wm. Firnwell   exercise vpon the Lords daye   this last bought
out his tyme of mr. Ball of Newbury I Committed him for not
[*illegible*].

16 Jo: Jones and Eliz: Furness of Concord for fornication 2 years since
she was returned and inioyned to appeare at next Court.
qu: she confessed it not of Conscience   he was Committed until next
5 daye.

23 Neipnosset sach: of Agawam brought me 6 fath[om] wa[mpum].

25 N: Davison for swearing submitted to a fine of 20*s* before me and the
deputy.

26 Wm. Quick and Robt. Gillham [*illegible*] vndertook in 10*li* a peece
for Edward Eldon that he should appear at the next Court of Assistants to abide etc. the next in the meane tyme he should satisfie such
as he hath stolen goods from and depart with his frends out of this
Jurisdiction.

29 Francis Doughty of Dorch: and Hen: Webb: de Boston 500*li* [*illegible*]
Condition for Fr: Doughty his appearance at the next Court of Assistants to answer Wm. Cole and Eliz: his wife in an action of the
case etc.

(6)   1 Mr. Wm. Hibbins vndertook to answere at next Court to the Action
of Jo: Knight against Jo: Morecroft.

(6)   1 Jo: Baker 40*li*   for Jo: Baker his appearance at next

      Capt. Edw: Gibbins 30*li* Court.

5 Peter Pickford

   Rich: Redman   5*li* [*illegible*] to appear at next Court except called

   Tho: Warner   in the mean tyme.

8 Wm. Cockram had Jo: Neal his servant delivered to him and he
vndertook in 5*li* to bring him in at next Court. Tahans sent me by
squ[*illegible*] 7 fath[om] wampom.

---

[1] W. 1. 192. Cf. *Records of Massachusetts*, 1. 268–270, and *Records of the Court of Assistants*, 11.
85–88, under date September 3, 1639, where there are references to four of the cases mentioned in
these memoranda by the Governor.

(6) 23 Rich: Willson inioyned [*illegible*] to appear next Court for stealing from mr. Wade of Linne his master.

[*Memorandum by Governor Winthrop:*]

Remb:

Commissioners at gen[eral] Court for Plimouth to meet at Scituate.
Mr. Chancy his business at Cambridge.
Recorders affairs.
Armes sent home by Jo: Sanford.

RICHARD ANDREWS TO JOHN WINTHROP[1]

To the Right Wor[shipfull] and his much respected good frind
mr. Winthrop Esquire theas deliver

LONDON this 8th of July 1639

RIGHT WOR[SHIPFULL], Sir my service remembred and your health and prosperitie in the Lord desired. although vnknowen I did by my letter of the 10th of Aprill laste per your servant John Tynker make bould to intreat your Wor[ship]s Favor in receavinge of some parte of satisfaction from mr. William Bradford of Plymoth Gouernour and mr. Edward Winslowe with some others for 5 or 6 Hundred pounds principall money, besides Forberance therof and as much more allsoe for many yeares due to me as I then writt,[2] and thearwith to provide heyfores about 2 or 3 yeares ould or yonger, and them to deliver forth one a peece soe farre as they would reach vnto godly poore men whoe have none of theire owne, and cannot procure such a kinde-nesse from frinds, that they might keepe them for me for halfe the increase for 4 5 or 6 yeares as might bee conceaved moste meett, and at the tyme aforesaid to receive backe the stocke with halfe the increase, and to dispose of the said stocke againe with all the increase of the yonge Heyfores which maye falle to me at the devition vnto other the like godly poore in the severall Townes and villadges theare. and for the steares and steare calves which maye falle to me at the said tyme I doe freely give the one halfe of them vnto such poore mynnesters theare as have moste need, and the other halfe of the steares for such publike good vse and disposal as shalbe con-

---

[1] W. 4. 96; 5 *Collections*, I. 271–274. For Andrews, one of the adventurers for New Plymouth, see 5 *Collections*, I. 271*n*.
[2] Cf. *Journal*, II. 70; Bradford, *History of Plymouth*, II. 288–293.

ceaved moste needfull and fitt, and if your Wor[ship] please to excuse my
said former bouldnes thearin, I maye hope of the like favore the second tyme.
soe presuminge of your Wor[shi]ps readines to further a small kindenesse
to the poore, I have lately sould some comoditie vnto mr. John Beachamp[1]
of London which amounteth vnto the some of 384*li* 06*s* 00*d* one Condition
to take satisfaction in New England either for the whoale or ellse for so much
thearof as mr. William Bradford mr. Edward Winslowe or some other or
others of them shall either paie or secure to paie vnto your Wor[ship] to content, at or before the 20th daye of June next which shalbe in the yeare of
our Lord 1640 in parte of moneys they owe and are indebted vnto mr. Jo:
Bechamp one account between him and them, and vnto me in parte or in
full of the said some of 384 06 00 which mr. Jo: Beachamp oweth me for the
foresaid comoditie sould him. And so much of the said some of 384*li* 06 00
as they shall not have paied or secured to paie vnto me theare for him before
or vppon the 20th daye of June nexte, mr. Jo: Bechamp hath covenanted to
paie me heare vppon the 24th day of June nexte in full of the said some of
384*li* 06 00. And if your Wor[ship] or asseignes doe receive the said some of
384*li* 6 0, or what parte therof shalbe received to content, either in heyfores
worth the Rates, or in any good comoditie worth the price to sell, or wher-
with Heyfores may bee had in exchange at indifferent rates as they are sould,
or so much as good men of Plymoth doe secure soe to satisfie vnto your
Wor[ship] for me to content, and for so much thearof as shall at any tyme
bee received in comoditie, I desire that yonge Heyfores about 2 or 3 yeares
ould or vnder may bee thearwith bought, and that all of them may bee
disposed of and distributed to and amonge the godly poore in the severall
townes and villadges in America: one a peece vnto svch as have not any
before and have moste need, to bee kept for mee for halfe the increase, for
4 5 or 6 yeares as shalbe conceaved moste meett, and after, in all things to
bee disposed of with theire increase at the tyme of devition accordinge to
thoase before mentioned which are to bee provided with what may bee received of mr. Bradford mr. Winslowe and the reste vppon my owne account
and in parte of the said Fyve or Sixe Hundred pounds principall money
they doe owe me besides Forberance, boath which said somes the former and
the latter are due to me from them as somuch redy money lent for theire
Trade and suply, although the latter bee now for comoditie sould mr. Bechamp, and thearfore they have good reason to give verry good content in
the satisfactions they deliver for boath the one as well as the other. I ame

[1] Beauchamp, like Andrews, was one of the adventurers for New Plymouth.

ashamed to bee soe troublesome vnto your Wor[ship] as I feare this bussines
is like to bee, yeat seinge I intend more the good of the poore herin then any
to my particuler, I hope your Wor[ship] will excuse my bouldnesse herin,
but if our frinds at Plymoth cannot satisfie the whoale in one yeare lett them
doe it in 2 yeares, and if they cannot doe it in 2 years lett them doe it in 3
years yearly, soe that they would perfect accounts with vs, either as parte-
ners, or allowinge our principall disbursements for them with so much Forberance for the same as shall indifferently bee thought meett, that I might
knowe how much to expect from them, and soe humbly takinge leave doe
eand and reste Yours in humble servis to bee comaunded

RICHARD ANDREWES

DEPOSITION OF WILLIAM KNAPP AND HUGH TILLEY[1]

Wm. Knopp and Hugh Tilley testifie vpon Oath That on the 5th daye of
the last week, one Robert Wright servant to Mrs. Glover of Cambridge did
overtake them beyond Charlston neck, and brake out into filthy and rayling
speeches without any provocation, howling etc. and bidding 2 of the neighbors there kiss his ars, and calling this deponent Knopp bast theavish knave
saying that all his Children were so, and calling him dogges-pricke slave,
and other reviling speeches, and raylinge allso vpon this other deponent
calling him rogue and raskall and iostling him divers tymes, so as they conceiued he was in drink for he was often ready to fall, and smelt of drink etc.

Taken vpon Oath before me

JO: WINTHROP Gov[ernou]r

(5) 8: 1639

Jo: Hall affirmed the substance of this.

SAMUEL WINDES TO JOHN TINKER[2]

To my Very louinge Freind Mr. John Tinker in New England this deliver

MR. TINKER, my loue remembred to you with hope of your safe arrivall
in New England allsoe my loue to all the freinds of myne in the shipp where

---

[1] W. 1. 128. There were at this time in Watertown two William Knapps, father and son, the
elder of whom was a carpenter. Savage, *Genealogical Dictionary*, III. 34. Hugh Tilley, formerly of Salem,
had been a servant of Sir Richard Saltonstall. *Ibid.*, IV. 302.
[2] W. 1. 127.

you went   I haue sent the shooes by the g[*blank*] shipp with Mr. Tinge beinge vndertaker thereof   Mr. Harbert your Freind is in the same shipp a passenger therefore I pray you to harken after the receipt of them for my discharge that I bee not questiond about them no moor   so with my loue to you and prayers for you in hest I sease Your truly Louinge Freind

SAMUELL WINDES

LONDON this 10th of July 1639

THOMAS HAWKINS TO JOHN WINTHROP[1]

WOR[THY] SIR, After my humble servis presented, these are to acquant your Worship that the bearer hereof John Warner hath bin this day with me and giuen me[2] satisfaction conserning a small debt he was indebted to me, vppon which I haue dellivered him his bill I had vnder his hand for payment (this att his request) and I rest yours in all Bounden dutie

THOMAS HAWKINS

DAURTCHESTER the 12th of the 5th month 1639

ISRAEL STOUGHTON TO JOHN WINTHROP[3]

To The Right Wor[shipfu]ll our Honored Gouernour John Winthrop Esq: These present

RIGHT WOR[SHIPFU]LL, Hauing beene at Waymoth in person with Brother Millet to demand 100*li* of Tho: Richards vpon a Bond committed to my Trust and by Letter of Autorny assignd to me to receiue and dispose to Mr. Cornish his vse: by which bond he is bound in 200*li* for payment of the 100*li* vpon demand as hath beene performed, So it is that he hath refused payment vpon this grownd, he saith he gaue Mr. Cornish 2 bonds, one to remayne heere, and the other to carry with him, and because he hath not sent him that bond he will not pay the mony vpon this: But will first be advised, and will come to your Wor[shi]pp for advice.

Now my occasions detayning me I make bold to informe you what concernes my part, and so you hearing both may advise as God shall guide you.

---

[1] W. 14. 22. For Hawkins, noted shipwright in the early days of the colony, see Oliver A. Roberts, *History of the Military Company of the Massachusetts Now Called the Ancient and Honorable Artillery Company of Massachusetts*, 1 (Boston, 1895), 63–64.

[2] The word in the original manuscript is "be."

[3] W. 4. 96; 5 *Collections*, 1. 274–277. For Stoughton, see 5 *Collections*, 1. 274*n*.

The bond in my hands he cannot deny to be his act and deed. vpon this I require performans seing the mony allso is truly and really due and legally assignd to me by Mr. Cornish his Letter of Attorney vnder a publique notarys hand: where by allso I haue full power to giue all manner of Release etc: and if he haue giuen an other bond for the same thing it might be his weakenes, and yet it may allso so far as I know be some custome among sea men etc: Now Mr. Cornish acknowledgeth that bond and writes to me that vpon notis of the performence here, he will cancell it, or do with it as I shall direct, and I offered Mr. Richards both to giue him Release from this and that in Mr. Cornishes name, absolute, and to be bound in all that ever I am worth that that bond shall never be required, this being performed: Here he knowes it cannot, and in England the bond it self runns in that forme that it will be nothing worth but lyable to diuers manyfest exceptions. The Condition of the bond being this that the mony be paid here or in Old England vpon demand the 30th of July 1639 Such and such articles [and] conditions being kept, which afford evasions too many there, tho the mony should not be paid here at all. But much more if release therefrom be produced.

Besides he is not going to England, nor is there person or place mentioned where to demand it in England The simple intent was this (and exprest) that if shipping came not hither this yeare so as Mr. Cornish could take a course to demand it here, then Mr. Richards was oblidgd to take a course to pay it him there, as the wittnes testifyeth.

Now that makes him the more presume is because he perseiveth the mony is like to abide here and he hopeth to haue the vse there of a longer season: allso they presume forfeitures will not be taken in N: E: and so make a nothing of refusing payment: and makeing a mock of me and my words and paynes etc. For Brother Millet gaue him notis expresely I had not the bond in England. this was on wensday last, and on thursday I spake with him at boston, and he bore me in hand I should haue the mony, yea before your wor[shi]pp that day For I told him I would come downe my self: yea being there the Evning before to conferr and see if all were cleare that I might receive it on the day, I told him and we disputed the case of the other bond: and after this parted with this same promise from him, only that he would attach the mony in my hands to answer a plea about Land: but we should haue the mony. It was ready in gold the most, we should only stay the telling of it. In these very termes he spake as we 2 cann depose: yet on the morrow he denyed it, as he or shee saith vpon better consideration:

Now may it please you, I did obserue great Carefullnes and faithfullnes in Cornish for Sallanova (whose mony this is realy tho it be turnd into

Cornish his name, by Richards his meanes, and so lyable to Mr. Quoitmore ells I suppose it were not) and because I was by Sallanova from the beginning by letter joyned Assistant with Cornish that he might haue right etc. I take my self bond in faythfullnes to see the vttmost least I fall short of others in so good a vertue as faythfullnes   And were the mony free I could send it home by as good a hand instantly as I could desire, Mr. Woolcot by name that goeth into those parts.

But if it will not be freed, seing providence hath cast it so, I recon it my duty and right to do what an autony should and may for the speedy takeing it into my owne hands for suppose it miscarry and I omit my trust how can I answer it   therefore resolue if he do not forthwith pay it, I will by the Lords leaue sue this bond the next court,[1] and tho I expect not forfeiture, yet I doubt not the principall and sufficient Charges, for default: For if it ly here it shall not ly vnimprooved to his Benefit that owes it, for the power I haue I will improove (takeing care for my owne safety) with what faithfullnes I cann attayne.

Thus much I thought meet to informe, and leaue your worship to aduise as God shall direct: So with my due respect and service Remembered I leaue you to the Lord   Yours for ever oblidgd

ISRAEL STOUGHTON

DOR[CHESTE]R July the 31th 1639

NATHANIEL SPARHAWK'S ACCOUNTS, 1638–1639[2]

	li	s	d
Reckind the 5 daye of the eight moneth 1638 and ther was dew			
vnto me fower skore poundes sixteen shillinges seaven pence	80	16	7
Item the 10th of December,			
30 yds. of brodcloth the one half at 11s the yard and the other half at 11s 6d yd.	16	17	6
2 tillets about the clothes 3s 6d a pece of cloth to pack yt in 18d	0	5	0
4 li. of candle at 7d per li.	0	2	4
To William Coles 4s 8d 4 li. candle 2s 4d	0	7	0

[1] Richards discharged his obligation to Cornish on September 3, 1639. *Lechford's Notebook*, 159–161. Since there is no mention of the case in the court records, he presumably paid just in time to avoid being sued at the Court of Assistants which met on that day.
[2] W. I. 124.

Item by your order to goodman Bullocke	3	0	0
Item to mr. Wintroppes man black thrid	0	0	7
Item To Thomas Kinge by your order in goods the 12th of February	3	16	3
more to Thomas Kinge in goods	1	12	5
Item 4 hogsheds 10s 2 li. of candell 14d a skine of silke 1d	0	11	3
2 koops 2d nayles 2s 4d 3 li. candell 21d	0	6	1
6 thousand of nayles 14s 2d 3 li. candell 21d	0	15	11
Tobaco 18d an axe 2s 8d 2 li. candell 14d	0	5	9
2 thousand of nayles at 21d per hundred	1	15	0
	110	11	3

Item 1 payer of hose 3s 6d	0	3	6
by your order to John Champney in wars	0	5	7
Item a doeskine 3s 5d 3 yds. $\frac{1}{4}$ of lase 6d ob. claspes ob.	0	4	0
2 li. candell 14d	0	1	2
Item To mr. Padue the 15 of the second moneth as by a nott in goods	4	3	0
Item To your man 18 C 4 skore and 10 of ten peny nayles at 11d per Co.	0	17	0
Item 3 li. candell 21d 1 peyer hose 3s 2d 1 li. candell 7d	0	5	6
1 li. of glue 10d 3 li. of hoops 3s 6d 6 li. candell 3s 6d	0	7	10
1 yd. bindinge 1d 3 li. candell 21d	0	1	10
Item To Thomas Kinge the 17 of the 4th moneth by your order	1	8	0
1 li. candell 7d 1 gallon of vinnger 22d	0	2	5
$\frac{1}{2}$ li. shott 1$\frac{1}{4}$d 3 quire of paper 18d	0	1	7$\frac{1}{4}$
Item the 26 of the 5 moneth to Thomas Waytes in cheese and other thinges	0	15	0
Item To your Lad 11 pyntes of vineger 2s 4d 1 yd. locrum 16d	0	03	8
1 payer of shoes 4s	0	4	0
The charge yt cost the protestinge the bills	0	10	0
The 3 bills that fayled one of mr. Collets of 30li and 2 of mr. Ingall of 20li a pece	70	00	0
	190	05	4$\frac{1}{4}$

	li	s	d
Reseived by goodman Rice	67	10	0
Res. by Elder Chempney	6	14	0
Recs by mr. Sheperd	42	00	0
Recs by Elder Champeys brother	36	00	0
Recs by that the Govo[rno]r for the Bullockes by			
my brother Stone	40	00	0
	192	4	0

This is a true accompt:

per mee JAMES LUXFORD

[*Ca.* August, 1639]

[*Endorsed by Governor Winthrop:*] mr. Sparhawks Account.

ROGER WILLIAMS TO JOHN WINTHROP[1]

MUCH HONOURED SIR, You were pleased some while since to refer me to Mr. Heynes for a Lyst of such Pequt as were Authors and chiefe Actors in the late Murthers vpon the English.

Accordingly I haue sent vp once and againe to Mr. Heynes and we are come to a period: The Child is come to the Birth: a little strength from your loving hand (the Lord so pleasing and blessing) will bring it forth.

This Lyst here inclosed (which I request may be returned) was drawne by my best Enquirie and Tho: Stantons in the presence of the Magistrates at Qunnihticut the last yeare.

This List he was pleased to send me with the Addition of 7 more vnder his owne hand.

Some Quæries I made vpon some of the 7: as allso [*torn*] Sasacous his brother Puppompogs (now vpon Long Iland) whome Mr. Heynes desired might be spared and I applauded the Desire in many Respects only I desire for many other respects that he might be sent to some other part of the world.

Allso, since that the Nayantaquit Sachims who harbour many of these and Okace, Caunounicus and Miantunnomu requested that a pinnace might lye some few dayes at Pequt to promote and countenance the worck while Miantunnomu pursued them.

Vnto all which Mr. Heynes in this last is pleased to answer, so that we are come to a period.

[1] W. 2. 113; 4 *Collections*, VI. 261–262; *N.C.*, VI. 135–137.

This weeke I went vp to the Nanhiggonsick about other busines; there I found a Barr which I thought good to request your Wo[rshi]p to remooue by a word or 2.

Your Captiue (which was Maumanadtucks wife) now at Pequt, presuming vpon your experimented Kindnes toward her, informes all Pequts and Nayantaquits that Mr. Governours mind is, that no Pequt man should die, that her 2 Sons shall ere long be Sachims there etc. Your wisedome (now by a fresh line or 2) declaring that none but these (who by the best of Intelligence appeare to be deeply guiltie) shall die may facilitate the Execution to the Honour of your Mercy and Justice and the clearing of the Land from Bloud, either that of our Countrimen allready spilt or that may be hazarded by these wretches: I might but will not trouble your Wo[rshi]p with some presumptions that way: the Lord be pleased to further and blesse: and helpe your precious Soule and mine to remember that Vengeance and to long and expect for it vpon the Enemies of Jesus, when Blood shall flow out of the Wine-press to the horsebridles by the space of 1600 furlongs. Your Wo[rshi]ps vnfayned hietherto

ROGER WILLIAMS

[August, 1639]

Mine humble and true respects to Mrs. Wintrop, Mr. Dudley Mr. Belingham etc.

The messenger is ignorant of the matter and is satisfied.

[*Endorsed by Governor Winthrop:*] Mr. Williams about the Pequods to be killed (6) 1639.

AFFIDAVIT OF SARAH HOBART[1]

Sarah Hubbard wife of Edmund Hubbard of Hingham in New England Planter aged about fifty three yeares sometimes the wife of John Lyford Clerke deceased and mother of Obadiah Lyford Clerke deceased and of Mordecai Lyford sworne saith upon her oath that the said Mordecai who hath this day chosen the said Edmund Hubbard to be his guardian is brother and next heire of the said Obadiah. Jur. 1 (6[i]) 1639 Coram

JO: WINTHROP *Gou[vernou]r*

---

[1] W. 1. 127. The handwriting of the body of the document has not been identified.

JOHN HARRISON, JR., TO JOHN WINTHROP[1]

*To the honourable my truely noble freind John Winthrop esqr. Governour of
Masecusets bay and Agawom humbly present these Boston*

THRISE HONOURED SIR, had an oportunity sooner presented it selfe, sooner
I should have tendered my humble servise to yow beside which I am sorry,
that I haue nothing else to offer in thankefullnesse for so many noble favours
wherewith it hath pleased yow perpetually to ingage mee to your goode-
nesse. having met with shipps that are come out of England later then any
(I suppose) which come to yow, I am bould to informe yow of the newse
which they bring. the 2 armys lying some while one against the other in
Scotland, the King beeing 50000 strong, and the Scotch 18, they skirmisht
3 times but to litle purpose, som men beeing hurt on either side and neither
much prevailing, the K[ing] hath recovered his Scotch crowne and septer.
the people have greate hopes of peace both parts inclin[in]g that way, especially because the K[ing] of Danemarke and his sonne are both dead,
and that Kingdome doth descend to our K[ing] in right of his mother, to
which purpose there are greate preparations. Sir John Penington hath
made a greate fight with the French whom hee hath beaten, taken 7 of their
shipps and sunke two, all bound for Scotland laden with powder and shot
and other provision. Sir Davy Kirke hath sent 3 shipps to the French that
fish towards the Southermost parts of the land, and one pinnace, for his
impost beeing the 10th fish, but they beeing 14 saile were to strong for him
and empty made them fly home againe. hee exersiseth great tyranny especially amongst the planters so as hee is seldome spoken of without a curse.
I beseech yow Sir even for gods sake, if ever yow bore any love to mee remember mee now in your prayers, my condition is in the world bad but
spiritually worse, through your prayers, and the rest of my freinds, gods
faithfull servants with yow, I hope to find comfort. forget mee not Sir I beseech yow in this request. if I may bee to yow serviseable in England pray
make vse of mee, for I am confident that there lives not a man more zealous
to do your commands then your humble and affectionate servant

JO: HARRISON

FERMOUS this 11th of the 6t 1639

[*Endorsed by Governor Winthrop:*] J. Harryson, Junr.

---

[1] W. 4. 47; 5 *Collections*, I. 119–120. For Harrison, see *Winthrop Papers*, III. 517, *n.* 1.

EZEKIEL ROGERS TO JOHN WINTHROP, JR.[1]

HONOURED SIR, I was at Ipswich this weeke to haue attended on you, but you were gone to the Court before I came.[2] I humbly thanke you for your kinde purpose to haue seene our poore Towne. In regard of your many buisinesses, much company, and short time, I could not exspect such a fauour at this time. But God may afford some opportunity, when you may haue more freedome. The season yesterday, and this day, hath hindred my fixed resolutions of wayting on you, my body being not strong; especially since my sicknesse. Therfore I beseech you to excuse me and so with my seruice to your selfe, and the rest of our hon[oure]d Magistrates, I committ you to God, and rest at Your Commande

EZ. ROGERS

This present [*ca.* September, 1639]

HUGH PETER TO JOHN WINTHROP[3]

To our Noble Gouernour these present Boston

HON[O]R[E]D SIR, Synce my last I haue nothing to certifye you but what fell out the last day of the last weeke in our congregation at a church-meeting where Mr. Holgraue denying some thing that was cleere to the Congregation (hee being then dealt with) was suddenly struck by Gods hand with the losse of his memory, and such fumbling in his speech that wee were forced to send him forth, and at his house hee talked very idly slept, and is still weake but recouering: it did sadly affect vs all: The lord helpe vs to make vse of it to his praise.

I pray salute all our deerly beloued with you and bee pleased to tell this story to honest Mr. Wilson whom I salute in the lord.

My wife desires my daughter to send to Hanna that was her mayd, now at Charltowne to know if shee would dwell with vs, for truly wee are so destitute (hauing none but an Indian) that wee know not what to doe. Thus with my deerest respects I am Yours as you know in all duty

HU: PETER

SALEM 4° Sept. [1639]

¹ W. Au. 93; 4 *Collections*, VII. 205. For Rogers, first minister of Rowley, see 4 *Collections*, VII. 205*n.*

² Probably the Court of Assistants which met in Boston on September 3, 1639, and the General Court which convened the following day.

³ W. 2. 54; 4 *Collections*, VI. 101.

HUGH PETER TO JOHN WINTHROP[1]

To our noble Gouernour these present at Boston

RIGHT DEERE AND HON[ORAB]LE, I haue receiued yours, and this bearer Mr. Knolls[2] coming to mee from Pascataway, and wholy depending vpon your selfe and mee for some directions in his matters, I would in his behalfe desire your wonted lawfull tendernes to which wee are inuited by all the 3 parables in Luke 15, and heathens teach some thing when they say Cæsar dando, sublevando, ignoscendo, etc.

I shall bee ready to attend your mynd for my coming over about it at any tyme, and I suppose it were not amisse I should bee there when hee speakes with the ministers vnles hee be referd to vs this way which I should thinke farre better for the man. But the busines will bee to satisfye the State, which how it will bee before a Generall Court I cannot tell. I think dispatch will bee comfortable for him. Captayn Vnderhill intends likewise to come.

I need not cast my drop into your ocean, who knowe how to deale in these matters, only I tender the man etc.

I still beare my share with you, though truly I am burdend in my spirit with your acknowledgments of I know not what to call it.

We are iust now about meeting Mr. Hubbard and 3 more of Ipswich to sell your sons Castle hill to them, but you would wonder to see their dodging. If they haue it they must pay for it in some measure else it were more hon[ora]bl[e] for him to giue it.

Good sir bee cheerfull in the Lord, the whole world shall change, but our God neuer, in whom I am Yours or no

HU: PETER

SALEM 6o Sept. [1639]

I pray exceedingly salute our worthy sister etc.

GEORGE FENWICK TO JOHN WINTHROP, JR.[3]

For his very loueing freind Mr. John Winthrope att Salem thes

SIR, I thanke yow for your kind letter and am as glad to heare of your welfaire as yow of my safe arriuall in thes partes, as I should also be to se

[1] Essex Institute; 4 *Collections*, VI. 103-104.
[2] The Reverend Hanserd Knollys of Dover, New Hampshire. Cf. *Journal*, I. 295-296.
[3] Yale University; 4 *Collections*, VI. 365. For Fenwick, see *D.A.B.*

yow and other good freinds there with yow; I thanke god I find noe want heare but company which I hope the lord in his owne tyme will supplie. imployment I haue enough, if not too much, for my weake number, which takes vp both my tyme and thoughts. I hope heare after I shall find a vacation to visit my freinds. I am glad to heare yow are about your salt workes and wishe yow hartilie all good successe of which I shalbe exceeding glad to heare   If there be any thing wherein I can pleasure yow I shalbe glad to doe it. In the mean tyme recomending my loue and respect to your selfe and bedfellow with Mr. Peters and Mr. Endicott, I rest Your loueing and assured freind

GEO. FENWICK

CONECTICUTT Sept. 13th 1639

My wife remembers her respect to yourself and wife.

GEORGE FENWICK TO JOHN WINTHROP[1]

SIR, I thank yow for your continued offices of loue in your counsaile to my servant while the lord granted him health, and your kindnes and respect to him in his sicknes. as the lord shall offer me opportunitie you shall euer find me reddy to performe the lik or any other fruit of reall affection for yow or yours. The change that his death hath mad in my occasions putts me vpon much new labour that I thought I had done with, and therfor I must be very breife att present. I shall desire that those catle that are in your hands or any others may be continued as they were till next springe, when I shall if the lord grant life take order for them. I wrott to you concerning powder that was left in the bay. the store we had heare grows short, but I hope we shall haue noe nead till next springe, vntill when I leaue it also, only I directed my man that if he saw it were decaying, haueing bene longe keept (though that we haue heare holds yet well) he should sell 8 or 10 Barrells of it. Concerning the last part of your letter I can yett say litle, only thus much that what soeuer tends to mutuall defence and shall conduce to the setling and mentaineing vnfained loue, yow may expect from me and all those who are intrested in this place. for other matters, as they are of greate consequence, and neare concernement to others as well as my self, I can att present say thus much only, that if ther be any thing betwixt yow and the townes aboue,

[1] Miscellaneous MSS., Bound, M.H.S.; *Hutchinson Papers* (1769), 107–108; (1865), I. 120–121.

about bounds, what soeuer is concluded without us heare I shall account invalid, and must protest against it. I speak not this out of any feare either of wrong or neglect from yow or them, but to tell yow in short (haueing many other busness) what I hold my self bound to doe in that particular, and when ther shalbe a fitt tyme for any thing betwixt vs yow shall find vs in all things to submitt to right and good conscience. I am lastly to thank yow kindly on my wifes behalf for your great dainties. we both desire and delight much in that premitiue imployment of dressing a garden, and the tast of soe good fruits in thes partes giues vs good incourag[emen]t we both tender our loues and respects to your self and bedfellow. if there be any thing wherein yow can vse me I am Yours in any real office of loue

GEO. FENWICKE

7 October 1639

This young man came by a providence in the bark that brought me newes of Richards death, and haueing bene versed in bussines while he was an aprentice I hope will ease me of some occasions that I send him ouer to dispatch.

JOHN ENDECOTT TO JOHN WINTHROP[1]

DEAREST SIR, Vnderstanding by diuers heere That Mr. Eaton[2] hath ingaged himselfe to diuers within this Jurisdiccion in great sommes of money as also abused others by his base cariadges and now escaped the hands of such officers as were sent after him; I thought it my dutie to write vnto you onely to demaund whither it be not needfull to send after him where hee is gon: For I ame certainly informed that hee is gon in Neles barke to Virginea. Now If you and the deputie thinck meete to send to the Gouernour and state there to send him back together with one Samuell Eale a man of Mr. Natha: Rogers which Nele hath caryed with him: (though hee was informed whose seruant hee was, as Mr. Nathaniell Rogers tells mee). Mr. Younge his shippe is like to stay theise 2 or 3 dayes yet, who is bound for Virginea. I pray you if you thinck it meete and fitt that you will be pleased to send with what speede you can: I thinck if there be no other effect of it, yet it will satisfie many men of the care this State hath of the welfare of there members. But

---

[1] W. 2. 72; 4 Collections, VI. 135–136.

[2] Nathaniel Eaton, first head of Harvard College. For Winthrop's account of Eaton's disastrous career in that position, see Journal, I. 310–315.

it may doe the partie good to bring him vnder Gods ordinances, and it may be a meanes of procuring parte at least of their estates who haue trusted him. As also prevent him from wronging others where hee may come. But I leaue all to your wise and Christian consideracion: And rest thanckfull vnto yow for your louing tokens. I shall neuer come out of your debt. I must leaue another to repay all into your bosom, our good God, To whose blessed protection I leaue yow, euer remayning Your Wor[shi]pps truely while I ame

Jo: ENDECOTT

10 of 8ber 1639

JOHN UNDERHILL TO JOHN WINTHROP AND THOMAS DUDLEY[1]

To the Right Wor[shipfu]ll John Wenthropp and Tho: Dodli Gofornor and Depoti of the Macetusets these in Boston

HONNORED IN THE LORD, Youer Silenc onc more admirse me. I youse chrischan Playnnes. I know you loue it. Silenc can not reduce the hart of youer bore brother: I would the rightchous would smite me espeschali youer slfe and the honnored Depoti to whom I also dereckt this letter together with youer honnored slfe. Jasos Christ did wayt and god his father did dig and telfe bout the barren figtre before he would cast it of: I would to god you would tender my soule so as to youse Playnnes to me. I wrot to you both but now answer: and I here I am dayli abused by malischous tongse: John Baker I here hath rot to the honnored depoti, how as I was dronck and like to be cild, and both falc. vpon okachon I delt with Wannerton for intrushon and findding them resolutli bent to rout out all gud among vs, and advanc there superstischous waye, and by boystrous words indeferd to fritten men to acomplish his end, and he abusing me to my face, dru vpon him with intent to corb his insolent and dasterdli sperriti, but now danger of my life, alth[ough] it might hafe bin just with god to hafe giffen me in the hanse of youer enimise and mine for thay hat the wayse of the lord and them that profes them, and therfore laye trapes to cechte the pore in to their debayst corses, as Isterdaye on Pickren there Chorch warden caim vp to vs with intent to make som of ourse dronc as is sospeckted, but the lord soferd him so to misdemen him slfe as he is likli to li by the hielse this too month. I

---

[1] W. 3. 44; 4 *Collections*, VII. 178–179. For the proposal to bring Dover, New Hampshire, under the Massachusetts jurisdiction, a move to which this letter relates, see *Journal*, I. 320–321.

latli was with Mr. Williamse[1] which here we would goyne with youer state: but serious protestachons ar made to pregise vs in case we gife you intrest in this Riffer: my hombel request is that you will be charitabel of me when the work of the Lord is don you shall I trost hafe all these clammors to sese with satisfacchon to gods pepel: let Justies and merci be goynd. bannisment is past vpon me, and by the apoyntment of the lord. I freli confes my contumeli to the Cort, but more here after of this. by this barer I am requested to hafe a full answer from vnder youer hanse, that cuch percons as we shall send to tret with youer state maye hafe free egres and regres with out mollestachon: youer letter sent to Mr. Knolse we hafe sene, and both of vs labrod to advanc the work which we hope will redound to the glori of god and the sopresing the wicked among vs, but we are prifat in oure prosedingse tel a conkluchon: and so desier you: for we ar threttend. You maye plese to soggest youer will to this barer, you will find him tracktabel. We shall not rest vntel this work be finnist and youer slfes pouer here. in hast I rest youers to comand

JO: VNDERHILL

DOVER 12 of 8 mont 1639

STEPHEN BACHILER TO MARGARET WINTHROP[2]

To my very loueing and worthy Christian frende Mrs. Alice[3] Winthrop wife of our Worshifull and Reverend Governour these

Grace, mercy, and peace in our Lord Jes. Christ.

AUNCIENT AND CHRISTIAN FRENDE, I present my great respect, and thankfullnes vnto you, in a little token. And though it be little in it selfe, yet doth it conteine greater waight of true worth, then can easyly be comprehended, but of the spirituall man. As god gives you leasure to reade any thinge that may further your piety, and hope of a better lyfe then this, if you shall please to vouchsafe a little part of that tyme to reade this by degrees, I shall judge it more then a sufficient satisfaction to my loue and desire of furthering you in the waye of grace. And as I do both dayly and dulye pray the God of heaven (and that by speciall [*torn*] and remembring of our worthy Governour, your selfe, and blessed fruites of your Loue) and I blesse the Lorde without

---

[1] For Francis Williams, Governor of the Mason and Gorges plantation on the Piscataqua, see 5 *Collections*, I. 325n.
[2] W. 3. 26; 4 *Collections*, VII. 99–100. For Bachiler, see 4 *Collections*, VII. 88n.
[3] I.e., Margaret.

many (if any) fayleing—so shall I ad this to my prayers, that my token may
in some thing helpe you forward (as a sweet gale of winde in your backe) in
the way of God. Looking among some speciall reserued bookes, and lighting
on this little treatice of one of myne owne poore children, I conceaued nothing
might sute more to my loue, nor your acceptance. I desire my seruice in
Christ may be remembered to Mr. Governour, with blessing on you and all
yours and so I cease, and rest Yours euer in the Lorde Jesus his vnworthy
servant

STEPHEN BACHILER

This 17 or 18th of this 8th month 1639

HUGH PETER TO JOHN WINTHROP[1]

To our noble Gouernour these deliver at Boston

DEEREST SIR, I humbly thanke you that you would please to mynd mee
for my sheepe.

For this bearer Walter Baker hee hath demeaned himselfe very fayrly
with vs, and our Elder who was to hyre him finds not the least fault with
him, but that hee was to imploy him vpon the water in a Canow, which hee
likes not of. I like the man very well, and you shall meet with many that
will bee farre worse. I can safely commend him, so farre as I can heare or
discerne.

I shall bee bold to communicate diuers things to you about the Court,
before the Court (God willing)   For present I cease to bee further bold and
with my truest affection and due respect to yourselfe and all yours I rest
Yours in all duty

HU. PETER

SALEM 25 of 8, [1639]

I craue this bearers helpe about the shipping my ram. Your son and little
are well gone yesterday to Ips:

Mr. Cotton etc. wee see not.

[1] W. 2. 53; 4 *Collections*, VI. 99–100.

WILL OF JOHN WINTHROP[1]

I John Winthrop of Boston in New England being (through the blessing of the Lord) in good health, yet considering my change approaching and the vncertainty thereof, and desiringe (according to the good pleasure of the Lord) so to settle the affaires of my famyly, as when the Lord shall call me to himselfe, I may neither be troubled with the Care of these outward thinges, nor for want thereof may leave any occasion of strife or evill reporte behinde me, doe in the name and feare of the Lord ordaine this my last will and Testament, though I cannot make it so full and exacte as I would in many particulars, in regarde of those engagements which now lye upon me, and the incertainty of my estate in England, yet my intent is that this shall stande for the present to be some direction to my executors etc. till God may please to give opportunity of altering the same in a more cleare way.

First my Care is that all my debts and duties be payd, and for that ende, I give power to my executors to sell the house I dwell in at Boston and the lande beyond powderhorn hill, and any of my stock and moveables, Corne on the grounde, my part of the windmill, and interest in the weere at mistick. And for my deare wife, who hath been a faithfull helpe to me, though I lefte an estate for her in England, yet being doubtfull what may become of that, and havinge had 400*li* of it allready my will is she should be maintayned in a comfortable and honorable Condition, according to her place, and as my estate will beare therefore I give vnto her halfe my farme Tenhills during her life, with the vse of such stock as shall be left vpon it (my debts etc. payd).

And for my good sonne John, who hath alwayes been most loving and dutyful to me, and to my wife as if she had been his naturall mother, and hath cheerfully departed with all his interest both in his mothers inheritance and mine to a great value, and that without any recompense, I doe commende him to the Lord in all that the blessinge of a father may obtaine for an abundant recompense upon him and his. And I do give unto him the other moitye of my farme Tenhills with the stock thervpon, and after the decease of my wife the whole, to remaine to him and his heires forever.

I give to my sonne Adam my Iland called the Gouernours Garden, to haue to him and his heires forever: not doubting but he will be dutyfull and loving to his mother and kind to his brethren in letting them partake in such fruits as grow there. I give him allso my Indians there and my boate and such household as is there.

---

[1] W. 7A. 63; Savage (1853), II. 439–441; *L. and L.*, II. 250–252.

I give to my sonne Stephen my moiety of the Ile Prudence in Naragansett Bay, which with his parte of the reversion of his mothers estate in England wilbe a good portion: for it wilbe fitt she should dispose some parte of it to her other sonnes, according to our first intention, and I hope they will all rest satisfied at their mothers disposall therof.

I give to my sonne Deane and his heirs my lande at Pullen point with the 40 acres of marsh on the other side the hill there, and I must leave him to his mothers care to furnish him with some stock, and if my lande beyond Powder-horne hill shall not be solde etc. then I give it to him and his heirs.

I give to my sonne Sam[ue]ll my lot at Concorde which I intende to build upon if God give life and meanes, and the half of my farme of 1200 acres vpon concord River, and my 3 oxen in Eph: Childs keeping.

All the rest of my lande vndisposed of (there being aboue 2000 acres still due to me from the Country) I give to my sonne John and his heirs, whom togither with my wife I make executor of this my last will and Testament, and my will is that all my plate and other household and bookes shall be equally devided between them: and my wife to dispose of her parte (besides her own Jewels and other peculiar things fitt for her owne vse) as herself shall think fitt.

I will that Jo: Gager shall have a Cowe one of the best I shall have, in recompence of a heifer his father bought of me: and an 2 ewe goats and 10 bushels of Indian Corne.

(8) 29, 1639

My estate becoming since much decayed through the vnfaithfullnesse of my servant Luxford, so as I have been forced to sell some of my lands allready, and must sell more for satisfaction of 2600*li* debts whereof I did not knowe of more than 300*li* when I intended this for my Testament, I am now forced to revoke it, and must leave all to the most wise and gratious providence of the Lorde, who hath promised not to faile nor forsake me but wilbe an hus-band to my wife and a father to our Children, as he hath hitherto been in all our struggles. Blessed be his holy name.

Jo: WINTHOP

(4) 25, 1641

[*Endorsed by Governor Winthrop:*] my will [*and further, at the top:*] this is since Revoked.

EDWARD TYNG TO JAMES LUXFORD[1]

To Mr. James Luxford deliver this with speade at Medford

Mr. Luxford and loueing freind, I am Fre for the disposing of my Cattell   therefore yf you please to aquant your m[aste]r and to Com to me that we may treate further Concerning them I shall for reson forbare my mony whate time you thinck fit. so it is with the partey that was to haue them just as you sayd his m[aste]r was willing but not his m[ist]r[es]s. I haue but a short time to stay   therefore pray let me heere from you this day without fayle. Your Loueing freind

Edw. Tynge

[*Ca.* November, 1639]

[*In another hand:*] kind and Louing frend this is to let you understa [*unfinished*].

JAMES LUXFORD TO JOHN WINTHROP[2]

Right Wor[shipful], The letter in question I cannot find which for the thinge suspected would haue much cleared it, and since I haue labored otherwise ther is on Hawkins an ould man that came from those parts, which in the time of my prosperyty did frequent the towne, who I did thinke could haue cleared it, but I haue beene with him and he cannot, but he hath promised to enquier out on that came this last year from thence, with whome he had lately talked, and sayd that he will send him to mee or let me know wher; my selfe did send letters to the same towne to soome of the best which weare my frends there, and for safe cariage did get Goodman Linte the Barber to inclose them in a letter of his to one Richard Kinge of Bostone who euer goeth thither; butt I neuer had answer of them; but he had answer of his wherin they weare inclosed throught a letter to the sayd Richard Kinge, wherin I made mention of my purpose of marriage;[3] and such is the trouble and greefe that I am in partly in regard of your wor[ship] partly my wife in this present condition, that I am in a strayt, neither as yet can I find any man that knoweth mee, that can accuse or excuse mee in this thinge. and thought ther may be peace within, yet as Vriah sayd in another case, soe

<hr>

[1] W. 1. 115. For Tyng, a Boston merchant, see Savage, *Genealogical Dictionary*, iv. 356–357.

[2] W. 4. 50; 5 *Collections*, i. 130–132.

[3] On December 3, 1639, Luxford was haled before the Court of Assistants on a charge of having two wives. For the disposition of his case, see *Records of the Court of Assistants*, i. 89.

how cann I be at rest while ther may the lest suspision of jelosie remayne to
your wor[ship]   wherfore if I had it as the Lord knoweth I haue not, I would
beare the charge of any faithfull messenger that might be sent vnto the place
for a certificate, but as I ever tould your wor[ship] I would not soe the Lord
knoweth, that I haue not reserued on peny for that purpose or any other;
but could such a thinge be I would be a faithfull seruant and prisoner, till
his returne; in the mean time I hope that I shall find soome other I hope
soombody that can speak more then yet I can find any; and I hope yet the
letter will coome to my hand; But I must not wholy neglect your wor[ship].
mr. Tinge beinge put to a sudden pinch, would sell me for your wor[ship] a
bargen that is worth between 2 Brothers 30 if not 40*li* the byinge and doth
offer it mee on your wor[ship's] woord, at 9 months day of pay; it is eleuen
heighfers at 16*li* 10*s* a peece. goodman write had bought them for himselfe,
but not at the same prises nor rates, as now they are, and he promised mr.
wilsons security and mrs. wilson will not let him. mr. meyhew and my selfe
did prise the heighfers at a redy mony prise beinge chosen by Goodman
write, it is lawful for your wor[ship], ther as good as I haue seen; and in the
springe or before your wor[ship] may sell as many cowes as will pay for
them   I haue sent mr. Tings letter, which he now sent to me.[1] I desier that
ther be noe speech of the former businesse till my corse be layd. If possible I
can I will be with your wor[ship] in the morninge.

[JAMES LUXFORD]

[*Ca.* November, 1639]

[*Endorsed by Governor Winthrop:*] James Luxford.

EZEKIEL ROGERS TO JOHN WINTHROP[2]

[*To*] *the worsh[ipfu]ll, our much [honoured] Gouernour, John Winthorpe, Esqr.,*
these present

WORTHY SIR, It was no small trouble to me, at my last being in the Bay,
that your buisinesses were so many that I coulde not haue conuenient time to
speake with you. The loue which you haue shewed to me, by so many expressions and so constantly, euer since my coming hither, as it was a greate motiue
to me, to stay in these parts, so I holde my selfe bounde in all obseruance, and

---

[1] This letter is printed above (page 148).
[2] W. 3. 55; 4 *Collections*, VII. 206–209.

vpon all occasions to acknowledge the same. I may well say, I thinke of you often, when I see you not, making often mention of you in my poore prayers; which indeede your place requireth though I had no other ingagements. This place is a place (as of mercyes, so) of tryalls; The devill is very buisy; and I suppose and hope thatt you haue angred him, as much as another, and therfore may neede prayer against him.

I doe hartily reioice for all that good, of which God hath made you an instrument to this Colony; and which also he hath done to your owne soule; which (I hope) prospereth dayly; and the Lorde cause it to thriue and prosper still, that you may bring forth more fruites, euen in your age, and hauing serued your generation and God in it, may obtaine a more then ordinary measure of glory. For let not (I beseech you) glory alone content you, since you haue so faire an aduantage for measure and degree; and the Lorde shall assuredly giue it you, if you be not wanting to your selfe. And since I haue thus begun, giue leaue to him whose poore labours you haue accepted in publique, and from his soule wisheth well to yours, to speake a fewe words from God vnto you. Let it not seeme a small thing in your eyes, that the Lord hath giuen you a principall place in these Churches of Christ; and this place (though poore and despicable in the eyes of some haughty ones, yet) honoured of God aboue most, if not any in the worlde. Certainly your account wilbe greate: though if good, the greater the better. To which ende, I beseech you in Gods feare, be much and strict in the obseruing and examining your estate, hart and wayes. Your estate, that finding still more clearly Gods loue in pardoning and accepting you through Christ, you may be constrained to loue him, and wholly taken vp with the zeale of his glory. Your hart, that no euill may insensibly creepe in, to the defilement of it, and your estrangement from God, or greeuing his spirit. Your wayes also, to the euidence of your faith, and comfort of the Churches.

There is a peece of Godlinesse, called the Dayly Direction, which your vncle Egerton so much commended that I hope you are well acquainted with; and indeede without it, a Christian shalbe maimed at the best. Concerning your Ciuill actions, this may be one Rule among many, to iudge of the lawfullnes of them, when we dare aduisedly commende them to God in prayer, and on the contrary.

Sir, your godly hart will pardon my boldnes: somwhat I woulde haue sayde to the expressing of the truth of my hart; though I finde my selfe at this time lesse fitt, being weary this night after some Sabbath labour. Let them that loue you not be afradde to speake to you; I am not, and I am persuaded you doe willingly accept me. I might also tell you, that the exspectation of the Country is generally raised touching this Court. Especially touching oppression, and what wilbe done against it. For my part, I beleeue that if there were a Law to hang vp some before the Lord, they deserue it, and it would to him be a sacrifice most acceptable. Shall the already perse-cuted and impouerished pretious members of Christ be made a pray to Cor-morants? Vnderstanding persons doe thinke that one of them woulde will-ingly pay a fine of 100*li* per annum if he might be suffred to goe on as he hath done. I am sure God is displeased, and woe to them by whom it is. The Lord keep your good hart from pertaking at all in other mens sinnes (espe-cially of such a nature) by the least indulgence. A body of Lawes is now of all much desired; and all maturenes of proceeding therin wished. Your forward-nes to communicate to the Elders such things as they may be capable of, doth as much indeare you to them (who must be a greate meanes of your strength) as honour you. One thing I should be bolde to intreate, that wheras some that came newely ouer haue bene bold to vent Arminian and the like fowle errors, and then goe their way vnquestioned, leauing an infectious sauour behinde them (as Mr. Hewett[1] for one) some order may be taken, if not to sett a brande on such as haue so offended already, yet to preuent the like, by calling to account any that shall dare so to offende. Sir, Mr. Lamberton[2] did vs much wrong; I exspected his comming to the Bay; but it seemes he sitts downe at Quillip[iack] yet he hath a house in Boston: I woulde humbly craue your aduise to Mr. Will. Bellingham about it, whither we might not enter an action against him, and (vpon proofe) gett helpe by that house: For Bartlet, I referre him to your wisdome, but we smart deeply by him, hauing no place to meete in. Concerning the name of our Towne, to keepe our poore Name. I am loth to trouble you with our troubles further from some Newbery men: But I beseech you knowe, that our charge valued first by our incouraging freinds, to be about 500*li*, is at least 900*li*.[3] It was some greife to me, that any thing was payde by any of our company toward the last Rate, considering our weake estates.[4]

None doe know (or fewe) what we are impouerished by this purchase, and Quillipiake, and the fayling of some exspected freinds. I only commende it to your louing thoughts: If we be disabled at our first sitting downe very

---

[1] The Reverend Ephraim Hewitt, who had come to Boston this year and had then gone on to Windsor, Connecticut, where he became a colleague of the Reverend John Warham.

[2] George Lamberton, a merchant of New Haven.

[3] For Winthrop's account of the difficulties attending the settlement of Rowley, Massachusetts, see *Journal*, I. 297–298.

[4] The following year the General Court granted Rowley "immunity from publike charge in regard of their great loss, and charge by purchasing of land, and hinderance of planting the last year." *Records of Massachusetts*, I. 289.

farre, I see it will not be easy to rise after in this Country: but the Lord who knoweth our vprightnes, will take care for vs. Thus my distance from you, and now inforced absence, makes me too tedious and bolde with you. Pardon it I beseech you. My seruice to yourselfe, and your worthy companion remembred, I committ you to God, and rest Yours euer in Christ to be comm[an]d[e]d

Ez. Rogers

Rowley, Nou: 3: 1639

I purposed to haue written to the Deputy, but am not able. Some (it is thought) are backwarde to appeare against one of the Delinquents, because of the relation to himselfe, not knowing his worth, and opinion of the party, as I doe.

Sir I humbly thanke you and Mris. Winthorpe for this pretious token, your dainty fruite; and doe beseech the Lord [*torn*] hande. I haue [*torn*].

JOHN TINKER TO JOHN WINTHROP[1]

To the Right Wor[shi]ppffull and his much honerd Mr: Jno. Winthropp: Esqr: Go[vernou]r deliver

RIGHT WOR[SHI]PPFFULL, After my humble duty and servis to your sellfe and my m[ist]r[es]s presented, I think it a part of my ingagement to your wor[shi]pp to aquainte you with the dispensation of the lord, and his good providence in our voyage, and our safe ariuall: we hadd for the most part blessed be God faire and comfortable winds and wether, only aboute some 400 leagues from the lands end of N. Engl: we had such a strong NW winde we could not beare saille for 4 or 5 dayes together, and when we came to the Lands end of England the Lord did in mercy very remarkably deliver vs from shipp rack, which we hould euer worthy our Remembrance, and doe accknowledg our sellfes with all his people bound to blesse his name for the same, which happened thus; after we sounded, and had found such depth and ground wherby our m[aste]r and all his company did conclud they weare the soundings of Vshan on the French side, the next day came vpp with vs a shipp of Dartmoth, from Rochell bound home, whoe joyntly concluded the same, and soposed we weare some 30 leages of from Dartmoth to the WSW. he being soe neere his owne coast, we concluded to follow his light; soposseing by morning to make the Start, which is a poynt of land

---

[1] W. 3. 58; 4 *Collections*, VII. 218–220.

twixt Plimoth and Dartmoth. the wind being faire and fresh at SSW and our corsse N *b* E: aboute midnight we heard the other Sipp make a great shoute, which some few of our company heard, and sudenly looking aboute, espyed closse vnder our lee bowe the breach of a greate rock, which they sopossed to haue beene the edy stone which lyeth 2 or 3 leauges of from the harbers mouth of Plimoth, which afterward appeered to be a great rock called the Woolfe or Gulfe betweene Silly and the Lands end, some 3 or 4 leauges south, and had it not beene that per the speciall prouidence of God he, then, at the helme hadd made a great yawe toward the wether at vnawares, we hadd vn-avoydably beene cast away but the Lord whoe neuer slumbreth did gra-cyously watch ouer and deliver vs. Oh that we might therfore praise him for his goodnesse and walke answerable to his mercys soe largely extended toward vs: 2 days after the wind scanting vppon vs we put into Plimoth being saterdy the 9th of nouember 5 weekes and a day from our waying Anchor att Nan-tasket: the cheefe news we heare is of the peace made with Scotland and a great ouerthrow the Hollander hath giuen to a fleete of the Spainyerds of 70 great shipps waiteing vppon the coast of England, to aide the plate Fleete the sircomstance of which I supose your wor[shi]pp wilbe better informed of per some opertun[it]y, per which I hope to send this my leter viz: per a shipp of Bastable. I shall not truble your wor[shi]pp farther but humbly craueing your Fauour leaue you to the euerlasting protecion of the Allmighty and euer rest Your Wor[shi]pps humble servant to my poore power

JOHN TINKER

PLIMOTH 12th 9th m. [1639]

I humbly intreat your wor[shi]pps Fauour thesse inclosseds may be con-vayed per the next opertunyty.

NEHEMIAH BOURNE AND THOMAS HAWKINS
TO JOHN WINTHROP[1]

To the Wor[shipfu]ll and his muche honored Freind Mr. John Winthrop Esqr.
Gouernour of the Mattachusetts Baye att his house in Boston deliver

EXON. 14th 9br 1639

RIGHT WOR[SHI]PP[FU]LL, After our due Respects remembred, and our best desires for your good health and happines, These may serue to intimate

---

[1] W. 3. 79; 4 *Collections*, VII. 297–299. For Bourne, see 4 *Collections*, VII. 297*n*.; for Hawkins, see *ibid*.; page 132, *n*. 1, above.

to your wor[shi]pp our safe arriual att Plymouth through gods riche mercy
and good prouidence being all in health on the 10th day of this Instant
month: Being so deeply ingaged by so many bonds we could not pass by
this opertunity to acquaint yow with suche newes as is brought to our hands:
hauing suche short time to express our desires we humb[l]y craue your
wor[shi]pps kind acceptance here of: So it is that vppon our arriual we heare
that the 6th month last past there arriued 70 sayle of the king of Spains
Armado all great shipps in the Channell. as they came along about the Ile
of Wight there mett with them about 35 sayle of Flemings and interchanged
many blowes but they left and went vp into the Downes, and the Flemings
followed them and they both anchored there: only there being then Sir John
Pennington Viceadmiral of the narrow seas with 4 shipps and they came and
rode between them and suffred them not to fight: the General of the Spaniards sent vp with speed to the king for protection, and for Conuoy by his
Ma[jes]tis shipps, pretending they were bound to Dunkerk with 20000 men
and some Treasure for the Emperors forces (but what there intentions were
god knowes, but its not without suspition that there ends were worse they
hearing how things stood between the 2 kingdoms) but the king and state denyed them any Convoy, only gaue them leaue to take supply of prouision and
munition they wanted and gaue them leaue to stay there vnder his protection
suche a certaine sett time and then he would leaue them; but great hast
there was made to expedite many shipps of the kings and marchants into the
Downes, to keep the narrow seas: and al the Coast in that quarter was raisd
vp in arms not knowing there intentions: there time being expired that the
king had limited, the king sent downe to Sir John Pennington to take no
further protection of them and so he waghed Anchor and the hollenders lett
slipp and also the Spaniards and imediatly fell to it.

Now before this time the states of Hollond had dispatcht away so many
shipps to the other that they were 120 shipps. they hauing putt themselus
into such an order appointing euery ship to there quarter: 6 of them presently
boarded the Admiral of the Spainards and left hir not till they sunke hir
downe right. 8 or 9 more they burnt and sunk: 8 or 10 they putt ashore
some on our coast, some on the Cost of France: 18 more they tooke and
caryed away to Flushing: al the rest escaped to Dunkerk, al but one that
now is [at] Plymouth that we were aboard on and spake with the Capt[ain]
being attended by diuers of the states shipps that narrowly watch hir in so
muche that she cannot escape them.

As touching the Scotch buisnes: it is as we heard the warr is seased and
forces withdrawne: but what the Issue wilbe we know not but its muche

feared, it wil breake out afresh againe: as we heare they do demand allowance from the state towards the great Charge they haue bin necessitated vnto for their defense: thus in muche rudenes and brookenes we haue made bold to acquaint your wor[shi]p with such news as we haue intreating your accept-ance and your remembrance to god for vs. with our seruice to your wife to Mr. John Winthrop to Mr. Cotton and Mr. Wilson wee comend you to god and rest Att your Wor[shi]pps seruice to our power

NEHEMIAH BOURNE
THOMAS HAWKINS

Your otter you were pleased to comend to me to present to the Kinge after we had kept her very carefully in the ships hold 3 weekes, one day while we were att dutie she gott vp betwene decks and run out in to the sea through a little scuttle hole in the ships counter that I conceaued she could nott haue gotten out of and was drowned   itt mutch trobled me for the present but it cold nott be helped.

[*Endorsed by Governor Winthrop:*] Mr. Bourne from England.

JOHN WINTHROP, JR., TO JACOBUS GOLIUS[1]

Clarissimo Doctissimoque vire Domino Doctori Golio professori Mathematicæ Lin-guæque Arabicæ in celiberrima Academia Lugduni Batavorum amico suo observando

SALEMI IN NOVA-ANGLIA Novemb: 20, 1639

CLARISSIME DOMINE DOCTOR GOLIE, Decimus iam annus est a quo, post iter nostrum a Constantinopoli in nave, quam dicunt London, tecum Venetijs fui, primo quidem in valetudinario (Lazaretto vocant Itali) circa mensem, post autem in vrbe ipsa: omnium mihi dulcis recensque memoria est pro suavissima quam tecum habui consuetudine. Ipse quidem mense Aprili anno 1629 illinc in Angliam navigans, tibi Venetijs commoranti et oportunitatem

---

[1] W. I. 129. Jacobus Golius (1596–1667) was an eminent orientalist and traveler. After grad-uating from the University of Leyden he taught Greek at La Rochelle, and in 1622 accompanied an embassy of the United Provinces to the Sultan of Morocco, where he remained two years and ac-quired important manuscripts. He succeeded Erpenius as Professor of Arabic at Leyden in 1625 and the next year departed on a voyage to the East in order to procure Arabic manuscripts for the uni-versity. He spent considerable time at Constantinople and evidently on his return voyage in 1629 fell in with Winthrop. He was an indefatigable scholar, interpreter of oriental languages for the Netherland government, author of an Arabic-Latin lexicon and a Persian dictionary, and editor of many Arabic texts. J. C. F. Hoefer, *Nouvelle Biographie Général*, XXI. 120–123.

commodi per Germaniam itineris expectanti animo quidem tristi valedixi: non autem sine certa spe me brevi tempore te in Hollandia visurum; quod quamvis maxime in votis fuit (et semper et adhuc est) hunc tamen mihi gratiam negavit, qui sapienti suo concilio, et voluntate nos, nostraque regit, dirigetque Deus. Postquam enim in Angliam reversus sum, non diu ibi manere, nec in Europa licuit, brevi enim singulari numinis ductu, ad hanc coloniam translocatus sum, vbi adhuc etiam hæreo. Hocque est quod te sæpius scivisse cupiebam, nec defuit industria, et te per epistolas compellandi, et de tua valetudine inquirendi sed frustra, nisi quod intra paucos dies, per quendam D[omin]um Matrell (nescio an nomen recte teneo medicum se profitetur et gradum ibi cepisse dixit) a Lugduno huc nuper adventum, de tua salute maximo profusus gaudio intellexi: Jam autem non dubitans quin ad manus tuas hæ litteræ nostræ perveni[r]ent, et te salutatum per eas vellem, nostrique in te amoris testimonium præbere, et vt intelligas me adhuc dei gratia in vivis esse, atque in hac Americæ parte Nova-Anglia colonia Anglorum celeberrima (cuius nec te possit latere fama) manere: multa de rebus nostris hoc in orbe tibi scripsissem, sed, vt plenius omnia acciperes, hunc Juvenem Franciscum Higenson qui hic a pueritia per decennium vixit tibi commendatum habere mallem, ingenuus est, et (pro discendi ratione hoc in deserto) mediocriter literatus optimè novit omnia, et de colonia nostra, et de regione ipsa, et de barbaris incolis, vt ab illo quicquid in hisce cognitu dignum sit verè intelligere possis: obsecro te, vt illum amanter accipies [sic], et, si qua possis, in studiorum cursu promoveas, discendi enim studio hinc peregrinatur:

Quæ de me scire cupis ab illo etiam multa, intelliges [six words deleted] scias autem preter medicinam Opticen aliasque mathematicas disciplinas Hermeticæ philosophiæ (qua de superiorum et inferiorum Harmonia docemur, vt optime nosti) me maximè studiosum esse: sed ad varias etiam vertor inventiones, pro vt coloniæ conditio exigit, Jam compendium in salinis quæro, ad salem ex aqua marina faciendum [several lines illegible] sed de his forsan satis. hoc verum [five words erased] a te peto, vt me de valetudine tua, prima occatione [sic] certiorem facias, nihil enim mihi gratius si vel lineam a te acciperem. Deus te incolumem servet vale. Tui Studiossissimus

JOHANNES WINTHROP

PATRICK COPELAND TO JOHN WINTHROP[1]

*To the worthy and wor[shipfu]ll Mr. John Winthop Gouernour of Boston
in new England deliver this*

Grace and peace from the rich fountaine of both.

WORTHY AND WOR[SHIPFU]LL SIR, I perceive by yours your remembrance of vs in sending 12 New-England Indians to vs, which were left at Providence; if they had safely arrived here, I wold haue had a care of them to haue disposed them to such honest men as should have trained them vp in the principles of Religion; and so when they had been fit for your Plantation, haue returned them againe to haue done God some service in being Instruments to doe some good vpon their Country men: The Dutch in Amboino in the East-Indies haue gayned many to God and his Truth after this manner. Their Preacher Danker and Scholemaisters (when I was in those parts in the East India Companies service) learned first the Molaya tongue (the current language of India, as the Latine tongue is of Europe) and their Preacher bestowed halfe of his labors vpon the Indians (who were conquered by the Dutch) and the other halfe vpon the Dutch: Their scholemaisters likewise taught the Indians the Dutch tongue; and they taught the Dutch children (whereof there were then, and still are yeerely sent from the Low-Countries some hundreds) the Molaya tongue, both Dutch and Indians being brought vp in the same schole together: and having thus taught them to read and vnderstand the Dutch character, their Preachers penned the grounds of Christianity in the Molaya tongue and dutch letter which they sent to Holland to be imprinted there, and transported to the Molacca Islands; so that by these meanes many thousands of them are converted to the Christian faith: This practise the Dutch learned of the Jesuits whose practise it was to get the children of great personages to tutor them, and teaching them the Latin Roman letter they penned the grounds of Popery in the Goyriah, Molaya, Japan and other languages, but in the Roman letter, and having their printers in Goa, Nangesack and other Cities vpon the Continent of Asia, and the Isles of Java and Japan they caused those Catechismes of Popery to be imprinted there, wherewith they poysoned thousands, and so in a manner became Maisters of the sweetest places of the Continent of Asia, and Japan, as I observed by my travels in those places: so that being my selfe in Nangasack, a famous City of Japan, I saw with my owne eyes the monu-

[1] W. 4. 97; 5 *Collections*, I. 277–280. For Copeland, see *Publications of the Colonial Society of Massachusetts*, XIII. 16, *et passim*.

ments of many faire Churches and an vniversity which sometimes they had there, but by their pragmaticall intermedling with state-matters were banished from Japan by Augusheshama the then Emperour, being informed by our Countryman Capt. Adams (who made Shipwrack on Japan, and there lived many yeers at the Emperours Court) of their treacherous practises in Christendome: so that their Churches and vniversity which they had in Nangesack were ruined at the Emperours Command, but that whole City to this day speaketh the Spanish and Portugal tongues, and are all seasoned with Popery: there I had of Capt. Cox, our Cape-merchant a Popish Catechisme imprinted in Nangesack in the Italian letter, and Japan tongue, which Catechisme I have now in my study. With the practise of the Jesuits in perverting, and of the Dutch in converting Indians I acquainted the Earle of Southampton Governour of the Virginia Company, Sir Edwin Sandys and the Council of Virginia, who liked well of it, and gave order to Sir Francis Wyat their then Governour in Virginia to follow this practise, but in a better manner. Thus briefely I thought good to acquaint you with this practise of the Jesuits and Dutch in the eastern parts of the world, which if it be followed by your Preachers and Scholemaisters, through Gods blessing vpon their labours I doubt not many of your heathens may be gayned to the Christian faith. I would to God that his worke did thrive so well with vs as you write it doth with you: wee haue within these two yeeres many that seeke to vndermine vs, and to ruine the good that wee have endeavoured to doe here, as Mr. Cotton will acquaint you, to whome I have written somewhat more at large of this matter.

I have sent you a small Poesie[1] of one of our Preachers, whom the Lord hath taken to himselfe: hee hath left behinde him a hopefull sonne of his owne name who is reasonable well entred in the Latine tongue. if there be any good Schole and Scholemaister with you, I could wish with all my heart that hee might have his education rather with you, then in old England,[2] where our Company there have by their letters this yeere to our Governour Capt. Thomas Chaddock (who desires the continuance of your love) promised after a yeere or two to take charge of his education with them: hee is a fatherlesse childe and of good expectation, if God sanctifie his spirit.

---

[1] George Stirk, *Musæ Somerenses* (London, 1635), *Publications of the Colonial Society of Massachusetts*, XIII. 56.

[2] George Stirk (or Starkey), son of the Reverend George Stirk of Bermuda, came to Harvard College and graduated in the Class of 1646. For his later career, see John L. Sibley, *Biographical Sketches of Graduates of Harvard University*, 1 (Cambridge, 1873), 131–137, and the references to him in two articles by George L. Kittredge: "George Stirk, Minister," *Publications of the Colonial Society of Massachusetts*, XIII. 16–59; "Dr. Robert Child the Remonstrant," *ibid.*, XXI. 1–146.

If you send vs any more of your Captive Indians, I will see them disposed of here to honest men; or if you send mee a couple a boy and a girle for my selfe, I will pay for their passage, so they be hopefull.

Thus in some haste, our London ship being neere ready to set sayle, and I having many of my friends to visite by letters, I commit you to the blessing of the Almighty, and blesse God for raysing you from the gates of Death to doe him some further service. Yours in the Lord

PAT. COPELAND

PAGETS-TRIBE this 4th of Decemb. 1639

[*Endorsed by Governor Winthrop:*] Mr. Copeland. Received per Mr. Babb (5) 7 40. Resp. per Allegiance.

EZEKIEL ROGERS TO JOHN WINTHROP[1]

To the right worsh[ipfu]ll our honoured Gouernor John Winthorpe Esqr.

RIGHT WORTHY SIR, AND MUCH HONOURED IN CHRIST JESUS, I humbly thanke you for your acceptance of my poore hasty and indigested lines, wherin you coulde finde nothing, but my faithfull desire of all increase of true worth and honour to you. You haue by your long labours, trauailes, and aduentures, deserued much of this Lande; and my prayers haue bene of late more then ordinary, and my spirit raised, to begge that the Lorde woulde cause all of vs to be conuinced by the powring out of his graces on you, that you are euen that man, whose person and posterity he meanes to make an example to after ages for worth and Blessings.

Certainly this worke of the Lorde in bringing so many pretious ones to this place is not for nothing: But I am assured, that a blessing it shalbe to none but downright godly ones; for in that notion we gaue vp our inherit-ances to the Lorde. But truly Sir we are not yet (the body of the land, I mcane) as we must be. And if magistracy and ministry preuaile not to clense our mixtures and filth, a sore scourge we shall most certainly haue. My Spirit is oft troubled about this. And hauing not many dayes (as I haue cause to thinke) here to passe, I earnestly labour, that I may dy with this testimony that I haue indeauoured to the vttmost to discharge my duty in this Lande, which (I doubt not) is your better aime. I shall desire (if God permitt) to see you as soone as the season permitts. We reioice and haue blessed God for the Labours of the Court, which I publiquely gaue thankes for. We haue cer-

---

[1] W. 3. 56; 4 *Collections*, VII. 209–211.

tainly many Anabaptisticall Spiritts among vs and other base persons, who woulde diligently and yet secretly be searched out. I tooke occasion at the ordination[1] to speake somwhat earnestly about Catechizing, which (if God meane vs good) must be a maine helpe. The backwardnes of many therin, is to me a sad signe.

I humbly thanke you for your louing letter, which doth much stirre me vp to pray for you; for (as you say) I am sure your place doth neede it, and we all owe it. Touching the two things you propounde in the ende of your letter; though you best vnderstande both the difficulty and cure, yet if (vpon thoughts at leisure) any thing occurre, I wilbe bolde to write.

Since I am putt vpon this Lords day at night to write this for a messenger in the morning, I cannot omitt to tell you my Text this day, and doctrine which out of 1 Pet. [1], 15, was this, that The Saints patterne for holines is no lesse then the holy God himselfe. The very naming wherof is an astonish-ment to my soule; who knowe that I come so farre short of many men. Yet the gospell requires nothing but what it affords. O what persons then might we be, if the Promises were improoued! But you will better inlarge this. It is late and I am weary. My seruice and faithfull well wishes to yourselfe and your worthy yokefellowe; so I rest Yours in Chr[ist] to command

Ez. Rogers

Rowly, Dec. 8. 1639

We had a little snowe this weeke, but it is all melted. I suppose you heare of a new sad Crosse from Quillip[iack] in Jo. Hardyes Pinnace, wherin may be much of my estate, for ought I knowe; but the Lords will be done, who will not faile me.

WILLIAM CODDINGTON TO JOHN WINTHROP[2]

To the Right Wor[shipfull] and his much estemed John Winthrupe Esqr.
Governour of the Massachusets deliver in Boston

Right Wor[shipfu]ll, haueing so opertune a measseinger as your owne Indean, being by my pinnice returned from Blocke Iland and doth now hast to returne vnto yow I doe make bould to salute yow, haueing littell else to informe your wor[ship] of. Mr. James being returned lately from Quinepage,

---

[1] For Rogers's ordination, see *Journal*, I. 325.
[2] W. 3. 74; 4 *Collections*, VII. 278–279.

doth informe that the Inhabitants did giue their power to the Church and the Church hath chosen Mr. Theophilus Eaton their Magistrate, for so they cale him, Mr. Newman, Mr. Fugall, Mr. Gilbard Captin Turnor, assistants.[1] he did lickewise informe that they haue taken one of the Pequit Murderes Nepawbuck by name, and haue putt him to death. I haue the names of 12 of the Pequits Morders that are yet aliue. Your Indean knowes some of them his Brother more and wher they liue. our Indeanes here are peaceable, though we trust them not. Could be glad to here from your worshipe, If any thinge be attempted aginest them about two Maires and Cowe we heare they haue killed, that we might stand vpon our gard. I am remoued 12 myles further vp in to the Iland ther they haue gathered a Church and doe intend to chuse officers shortely, and do desire better healpes in that kind when the lord is pleassed to send them and would gladly vse what meanes doth lye in vs to obtayne them. things are in fare better passe conserning our ciuill governmentt then they haue bene diuers Famelyes being come in that had revolted from ther owne acte and haue giuen satisefaction. Mr. Gorton and Mrs. Huchson doth oppose it. it wos hached when I wos last in the baye, and the Lord I hope will shortely putt an esew to it. being in great hast with my loue to yourselfe, Mrs. Winthrupe and all that doe remember me, I take leaue and rest, yours to be commaunded wher in I maye

WILLIAM CODDINGTON

ACQUEDNECKE Decmr. 9, 1639

Mr. John Cogshall Mr. William Brenton, and Sergant Balstone doe desire to haue their service presented to your wor[ship].

DEED OF JOHN WINTHROP TO JOHN NEWGATE[2]

Knowe All men by these presents that I John Winthrop Esqr. Governour of the Jurisdiction of the Mattachusetts Bay in New England for fower score pounds of lawfull money of England to me in hand payd by John Newgate of Boston in New England Feltmaker Doe hereby graunt bargain and sell unto the said John Newgate All that my Lott of upland lying neare Rumney marsh in New England conteyning One hundred and Fifty acres be it more

---

[1] Cf. *Records of the Colony and Plantation of New Haven, 1638–1649*, Charles J. Hoadly, Editor (Hartford, 1857), 11–21.

[2] Original not located; facsimile in Winthrop Deeds, 30; 2 *Proceedings*, VII. 139. For Thomas Lechford's record of this transaction, see *Lechford's Notebook*, 232.

or lesse,[1] abutting upon the highway there leading to Divers mens lotts on the East, and upon the lands perteyning to Charlestowne towards the west, and the Lands now of Nicholas Parker sometimes Mr. Vanes towards the south, and partly upon the lands of James Pen and partly upon the lands of the said John Newgate on the north parte, with the appurtenances. To have and to hold the said Lott with all the appurtenances unto the said John Newgate his heires and Assignes for ever. In witnesse whereof I have hereunto sett my hand and seale the Eightteenth Day of the tenth moneth in the yeare of our Lord One thousand six hundred thirty and nyne and in the Fifteenth yeare of the Raigne of our Soveraigne Lord Charles now King of England etca.

JO: WINTHOP

Signed sealed and Delivered
in the presence of:
STEPHEN WINTHROP
et mei THO: LECHFORD scriptoris hujus

NATHANIEL WARD TO JOHN WINTHROP[2]

To our much honored Gouernor att Boston

SIR, I thanke you very much for your loue and liberality by Mr. Rawson you sent me more then I desired   I haue 2 more earnest requests to yow, 1 That yow would please to advise throughly with the counsell whether it will not be of ill consequence to send the Court busines to the common consideration of the freemen.[3] I feare it will too much exauctorate the power of that Court to prostrate matters in that manner. I suspect both Commonwealth and Churches haue disended to lowe already. I see the spirits of people runne high and what they gett they hould: they may not be denyed their proper and lawfull liberties, but I question whether it be of God to interest the inferiour sort in that which should be reserued inter optimates penes quos est sancire leges. Yf Mr. Lachford haue writt them out I would be glad to peruse one of his copies if I may receiue them.[4]

The other is that yow would not passe your promise nor giue any incour-

---

[1] Cf. *Report of the Record Commissioners of the City of Boston*, II (Boston, 1881), 27.

[2] W. Au. 93; 4 *Collections*, VII. 26–27. For Ward, see 4 *Collections*, VII. 23*n*.; Samuel E. Morison, "Nathaniel Ward, Lawmaker and Wit," *Builders of the Bay Colony* (Boston, 1930), 217–243.

[3] Ward's reference is to the Body of Liberties adopted in November, 1641, which was now in draft form and had been ordered by the General Court to be sent around to the several towns for the criticism of the elders and other freemen. *Records of Massachusetts*, I. 279.

[4] Cf. 3 *Collections*, III. 88.

agment concerning any plantation att Quichichacke or penticatt,[1] till my self and some others either speake or write to yow about it which shalbe done so soone as our counsilles and contrivalls are ripened: In too much hast I comitt yow and your affaires to the guidance of God, in whome I rest Your Wor[shi]ps in all Christian service

NATH. WARDE

M[s] 10[i] 22[o] [1639]

There is a necessity that the Couenant if it be agreed vpon should be considered and celebrated by the seuerall Congregacions and Townes and happily the [*illegible*] but I dare not determyne concerning the latter. I meane of putting it to the Suffrage of the people.

ACKNOWLEDGMENT OF RICHARD BELLINGHAM[2]

23. 10. 1639

There is due to mr. Wm. Tinge ten poundes which he payd to}
mr. Day for the Country to be putt on mr. Winthrope G. account.} 10 0 0

I am to repay it the latter end of the next moneth

R: BELLINGHAM *Tr[easurer]*

[*Endorsed by Bellingham*:] this bill paid and received in againe by me R. B.

GILES FIRMIN TO JOHN WINTHROP[3]

MUCH HONOURED AND DEARE SIR, But that I thinke it needlesse (God hauinge more then ordinarye fitted you for such trialls) my letter might tell you with what greife of spirit I receiued the news of that sad affliction which is lately happened to your wor[shi]p, by means of that vnfaithfull wretch;[4] I hope God will finde a shoulder to helpe you beare so great a burthen. But the little time there is allotted mee to write, I must spend in requestinge your

---

[1] Andover and Haverhill.

[2] W. 1. 130. For Bellingham, see *D.A.B.*

[3] Miscellaneous MSS., Bound, M.H.S.; *Hutchinson Papers* (1769), 108; (1865), II. 122–123. For Firmin, see 4 *Collections*, VII. 273*n.*

[4] James Luxford, whose defalcations while in Winthrop's employ were now threatening to bring financial ruin upon the Governor.

wor[ship]s Counsell and fauour. my father law Ward since his sonne[1] came
ouer, is very desirous that wee might sett downe together, and so that he
might leaue vs together if God should remoue him from hence. because that
it cannot bee accomplished in this Towne, is very desirous to gett mee to
remoue with him to a new Plantation. after much perswasion vsed considering
my want of accommodation heere (the ground the Towne hauing giuen mee
lyinge 5 miles from mee or more) and that the gaines of Physick will not
finde mee with bread; hee besides apprehendinge that it might bee a way
to free him from some temptations, and macke him more cheerefull and
seruiceable to the Country or church haue yeelded to him heerein as I
desire your Counsell, so I humbly request your fauour, that you would bee
pleased to giue vs the libertye of choosinge a plantation; wee thinke it will
bee either Pentuckett, or Quichichchek, by Shawshin: so soone as the season
will giue vs leaue to goe, wee shall informe your wor[shi]p which we desire:
and if that by the Court of Election we cannot gather a company to begine
it, wee will let it fall. Wee desire your wor[shi]p would not graunt any of
them to any before wee haue seene them. if your wor[shi]p haue heard any
relation of the Places, wee should remaine thankfull to you, if you would
bee pleased to counsell vs to any of them. Further I would entreate your
aduise in this: the Towne gaue mee the ground (100 acres) vpon this Condition that I should stay in Towne 3 yeers, or else I could not sell it: now my
father supposes, it being my first heritage, (my Father hauinge none in the
Land) that it is more then they cann doe to binde mee so when as others haue
not beene so, but range from place to place on purpose to liue vpon the
Country. I would entreate your Counsell whither or noe I cann sell it. Further:
I am strongely sett vpon to studye Diuintie. my studyes else must bee lost:
for Physick is but a meane helpe. In these Cases I humbly referr to your
wor[shi]p, as my Father, for your Counsell. and so in much hast, with my
best seruice presented to your wor[shi]p, wishinge you a strong support in
your affliction and a good and comfortable issue I rest Your wor[shi]ps in
what hee cann to his power

                                                    GYLES FYRMIN

IPSWICH: 26 10th 1639

    wee humbly entreate your secrecye in our desires.

---

[1] The Reverend John Ward, son of the Reverend Nathaniel Ward of Ipswich.

HUGH PETER TO JOHN WINTHROP[1]

To our noble Gouernour, Boston

Honred Sir, You must giue mee leaue to inquire of your welfare agayne and to intreat you still to looke at him that is gone before vs in greatest sorrowe. I did reioyce when I obserud that same Compositum ius fasque animi, sanctosque Recessus Mentis. The lord bee with you still. James Luxford was at Sagust when I came by I haue layd out for him. Mrs. Lake will come speedily and truly (Sir) you haue many frends Thomas Reade would haue hartily come and done your busines, and if there bee cause stands ready.

Wee are all here well, and are yours. let not Mrs. Strattons busines trouble you. I hope you will find wee loued you, and still shall, but alas wee fayle basely when wee come to proofe. Salute our deere sister, and let her not now bee despondent, least the deuill bee gratifyed. My wife is very thankfull for her apples, and desires much the new fashiond shooes.

Good Sir, if there bee any thing wherin I may bee more yours quid mi impera: bee you euer saluted in the Lord by Your

Hu: Peter

Salem 26. 10. 39

EXAMINATION OF WILLIAM BROWNE AND OTHERS[2]

Wm: Browne, Tho: Warner and Peter Pickford did affirme that to morrow 14night about one of the clocke, they were called vp by Seaburne about a great noyse on the water, and comming out they heard a party cry he hath allmost killed a man, and another answered through the Rogue over board, and presently the boat was sculled on shore by the party and they asked him what was the matter, and boye tould them that the 2 men had been fighting and had lost an oare (and one of the men lay along in the boate, and the other sate by but neither of them spake, for they seemed to be drunken) so

---

[1] W. 3. 54; 4 *Collections*, VII. 202–203.
[2] W. 1. 191.

they stayed there till neer Daye and then the boy sculled the boat to Mr. Luxons shipp to which they said they did belong.

[*Ca.* 1640]

[*Endorsed by Governor Winthrop:*] Examination.

JOHN HUMFREY TO JOHN WINTHROP[1]

MUCH HONOURED, I was both yesterday morning and night to have attended you but at both times too late. This morning I doubted I should have beene as much too earlie for you, as I was by some unexpected detention too late for my owne occasions. You being further necessitated to stay at Charlestowne, I thought good to satisfie my selfe rather then you in revolving the cause of that diminution of your wonted respect which upon unapprehended premisses I could not divine. So that now contrarie to my former apprehensions, I rather wonder you were not more alienated from mee, conceaving mee to be under that guilt (which I blesse god I am not) then that you were so much. However I know your greater latitude both of parts and pietie steares your practice beyond my reach; yet why (so conceaving of mee) should you not with compassion or feare (pulling out of the fire) explicate and set in ioint a forlorne and sin deceaved wretch. Your tendernes in other kindes hath sometimes manifested it selfe; for which I have blesde god and you in my feeble expressions. The proportions of the bowels of Christ mee thinkes should have much more expresd themselves herein. And yet I must acknowledge your Joseph like tendernes in this with all due thankefulnes, both in regard of my owne particular, and my relations to our common engagements. Wherein the lord shall be pleased to enable and enlarge mee to further expressions of thankefulnes to him and your selfe, I trust I shall studiously and sincerely endeavour to husband his grace. Onely I beeseech you in the name, and for the honour of our common saviour not to suffer mee to goe blindfolded with the deceipts of anie sinne, where eyther your clearer light or godly iealousies may have occasion to expresse themselves. For though I know no sinne my soule desires approvingly to make anie league withall; yet I experimentallie know my heart is desperatly deceitful, and god the searcher of harts can discover more of mee to others, then hee may be pleased to doe unto my selfe, at least for a time. If anie such case and time fall out

[1] W. 2. 6; 4 *Collections,* VI. 17–18. For Humfrey, see *Winthrop Papers,* II. 153, *n.* 4.

by the permission of god in the revolution of anie of my fibrous corruptions, though you should not (which yet I ever hope you shall) have thankes from mee, yet you shall not (you know) goe without a full reward from him who covers a multitude of sinnes in them who seeke to reduce and save anie sin-sicke soule. My paper and time (though your patience should not) confine mee. I am, Though your weake and gods wicked, yet I hope (at least out of gusts of temptations) the sincere servant of both.

Jo: HUMFREY

[*Ca.* 1640]

My busines yesterday morning was to tender the paiment of that debt of love to you which you have wished to mee, viz: to supply you (if your occasions requirde) with such monies as I had to spare from my pressing necessities: your least word or intimation shall commaund what is left.

SAMUEL MAVERICK TO JOHN WINTHROP[1]

WOR[SHIPFU]LL SIR, My Service beinge remembered, you may be pleased to vnderstand that there is a difference betwene one Ralfe Greene and Jno. Peirse each challinginge a promise of mariage from a maide servant left with me by Mr. Babb beinge daughter vnto a freind of his. either of them desired my consent within a weeke one of the other, but hearinge of the difference I gaue consent to neither of them, desiringe there might be an agreement first amongst themselues, or by order from your wor[shi]p: the maide hath long tyme denied any promise made to Greene, neither can I learne that there was euer any contract made betwene them, yett I once herd her say shee would haue the said Greene and desired my Consent therevnto, but it rather seemes shee first promised Peirse and still resolues to haue him for her husband. for the better clearinge of it, I haue sent all such of my peopell as can say any thinge to the premises, and leave it to your wise determination, conceivinge they all deserue a checke for theire manner of proceedinge. I take leave and rest Your Wor[shi]ps Servant at Commaund

SAMUEL MAVERICKE

[*Ca.* 1640]

[*Endorsed by Governor Winthrop:*] Mr. Mavericke about his servants marriage.

---

[1] W. 3. 82; 4 *Collections*, VII. 307–308. For Maverick, see 4 *Collections*, VII. 307*n.*

CERTIFICATE OF EDWARD NORRIS[1]

These are to Certifie that William Whyte and Marye Ware, (both lately aryved in this land), have with the consent of parents on both sydes, agreed togyther, to enter into the state of mariage, as soone, as the wor[shipfu]ll Governor here should be pleased to give admittance which they rather chose then any other waye else had it bene done before theyr setting forth which vpon request, I am bold to testifye on theyr behalfes

EDW: NORICE

[*Ca.* 1640]

DANIEL PATRICK TO JOHN WINTHROP[2]

RIGHT WORSHIP[FU]LL AND MUCH HONNORED SIR, Least through greeff I shoulde trouble your Attentione with abrupt languadge I humblye craue leaue to vnfoulde my reall thoughts in a few lines breffly vnto you. I am still in doubte of your continued displeasure towards mee. if my Groundes will nott afforde such a constructione, I shall at once be both glad and sorrye for my mistake; Worthye Sir is my faulte soe great that I cannot be reconcilde; I doe confess I am a man of manny faylinges, and certaynelye I am not ignorante of that vnbesseeminge Cariadge once, nay twise towards your selfe, but as time ripneth frute soe haue I through gods goodnes since that throughlye considderd the folly of such rash and proudlike Actions. Therfore I beseech you pass by whats past for I am vnfaynedlye sorry for myne offence, and I hoope and resolue in time to come to be moor carefull if the Lord inable mee. I am loath to vtter anny thinge in myne owne behalfe, nether can dutye extennuate my faulte, yet cann I bouldlie pleade Innocencye in anny other thinge to my Knowledge. Accept what you haue hearde your selfe from mee. If I haue priuily Instegated, or by Aspertions sought to wrong you, lett your harte be hardned, for ther should be cause. Nay if I haue secretlye giuen waye to anny disloyall thoughts, justlye lett mee reape stuble in stead of a frutefull haruest from this my Acknowledgment. I knowe the diuell is readye to imploye bad mindes by whisperings to preiudicate your Thoughts agaynst mee; perticculars I knowe none, butt if there ether hath or shoulde, I humblye beseech you lett Christiane Charretye from the groundworke of thees

[1] W. 1. 140. For Norris, fourth minister of the Salem church, see 5 *Collections*, 1. 306n.
[2] W. 3. 89; 4 *Collections*, VII. 326–328.

vnfayned expressions, confounde ther motions as but false, or (at best) suppositions. Nether doe I by this make waye for my followinge propositione, for it is butt commone; onely a dutye is heerby intended in the first place, and next my owne peace, which I ame to seeke with all men: Your sunn Dudlee when in the baye last, verry kindly desirde mee to come and liue at ther plantione.[1] A good lott he promisde to procur mee. Now Honnoured Sir my full resollutione is nott to remoue to anny plantatione in the Pattent if you are not willinge. What Nueberrye once offerd me was ther owne volluntarye ackt, and noe wayes sought by mee; a little lande will serue my Turne, peaceable Competency I onelye seeke of god. If I may haue your good will therein, with Cheerfullnes, I shall proceed, and how soe euer rest your Worships in all hartye Affectione and Christiane seruice to commaunde

DANI. PATTRICKE

[*Ca.* 1640]

[*Endorsed by Governor Winthrop:*] Capt. Patrick for reconciliation.

JOHN WINTHROP TO HENRY PAYNTER[2]

REV[EREN]D SIR AND MY GOOD BROTHER, My selfe and wife doe most heartyly salute you and our deare sister and all our Cosins. Sir I received your lovinge Letter dat[ed] 9ber 15, 39 this present daye in a shippe which now arr[ive]d from the Ile of Maye: I am very gladd to heare from you, and of your healthe and wellfare; and your good inclination towards N: E: which gives vs hope, we shall one daye see you h[ere] [*torn*] may be assured of most kinde wellcome, which (I hope) you doubt not off. and thoughe I will not vse any Arguments to perswade you (for I have been allways slowe in that exercise) I would gladly remove one block, which seemes to lye in your waye, and that is about our Church Covenant: Your Letter comes so late to my hande as I shall not have opportunytye to have answar from mr. Hooker (being 100 miles from vs) tyme enoughe to certifie you of it this yeare: but I will tender you mine owne thoughts about it: and I suppose I may saye to you as experience hathe proved in many other bothe learned and godly tu si hic esses aliter sentires: It cant be that the Covenant (if it be rightly knowne) should give offence, if it did not seeme to strike at the foundation of the Churches in Engld. which (as wee heere conceive) is but in semblance

[1] Salisbury.
[2] W. I. 111; *L. and L.*, II. 416–418. For Paynter, see *Winthrop Papers*, II. 196, *n.* 2.

only, for we acknowledge many true Churches in Engld. which are ioyned only by an implicite Covenant, but let the Covenant be examined which is this: I doe renounce all former corruptions and polutions   I doe promise to walke togither with this Church in all the ordinances of Religion according to the rule of the Gospell, and with all the members heerof in brotherly loue. this is the substance of the Covenant   now if a father should require this of his child or a master of every servant he receives into his house or a Company of Christian neighbors in Engld. of such as they receive into their private communion, what offence were here? seeing heere is nothing required of the partye but what he is bound vnto by the worde of God. besides it is of the nature and essence of every society to be knitt togither by some Covenant, either expressed or implyed: now to leave it vncertaine, where men have opportunytye to expresse and cleare it, were a faylinge (at least).

But it is ob[jected] that there is neither precept nor patterne of any suche Covenant in scripture; Answ: Admitt there were none, yet there is warrant sufficient for gatheringe of Churches, and therefore all things necessaryly incident therto are warr[a]ntably implied. What other warrant had Neh: 5: 12: to binde the people by an oathe to release their vsurious gaine? or the people at his appointment to binde themselves by an Oathe and a Curse to walk in the Lawe of God? which example may be warrant sufficient for Ch[ristia]ns when they enter into Church fellowshippe to binde themselves by promise to walke accordinge to the rule of the Gospell, and what evill can be in it, if the Churche require suche a promise of them? Let that place in Neh: 10: 1: 29: etc. be well considered. I suppose it may satisfie any that is not vnder temptation, of the warrantablenesse of such a Churche Covenant as ours is.

Again leave out the Covenant and let vs see what manner of Churches you will constitute: suppose 10 or 20 Christ[ian]s were desirous to constitute a Churche, these being mett togither, every of them makes confession of his faith, will this make them a Churche? I conceive it will [pass the skill of]¹ a good logitian, to make these a Churche, without some contract or agreement such as will amount to a Covenant.

Againe if a man enters no covenant, then is he not tyed to one Churche more then to another, and then may he depart without leave or offence, nor can he be reputed to be of that Churche any longer then while he is in the Assembly, and so consequently, vpon the dissolvinge of the assembly, the Church hath no beinge till they assemble again.

Now whereas I expresse my feare of temptation in suche as scruple our

¹ The words in brackets are crossed out in the original, and the single word which Winthrop interlined as a substitute is illegible.

covenant, so far as for that verye Cause to shune Communion with vs, I doe it not without good grounde, for when I see them leape ouer greater matters, as communicatinge with all parochiall members, whereof many are no Saints neither by callinge nor profession: submitting themselves to Canonicall obedience, whereby they evidently betraye the libertye of the Gospell, and enervate the power of Ch[ris]t his holy ordinances, of ordination, Admonition, excom[munication] etc. putt the case allso (as it often falles out) that a godly patron when he bestowes a benefice vpon a min[iste]r, takes a soleme promise of him to be resident vpon it, to teache dilligently etc: who is there amonge you that will scruple to accept a livinge vpon suche a Covenant as this, which hathe neither precept nor patterne in Scripture? So when the Clerck comes to the B[isho]pp for Admission, if he requires a promise (nay an Oathe) of him to doe that which the dutye of his place requires, none of you would sticke at suche a Covenant as this.

Besides There is a great mistake in the order of our Covenant, for it passeth for granted everywhere that none can be admitted heere before they enter into this Covenant, whereas in very truth they are tryed and admitted by the vote of the wholl Churche before any Covenant be tendered or mentioned to them. Lastly it is sometymes tendered to them as a declaration of their purpose and intention only and not in the words of a Covenant or promise, so willinge are our Churches to please our brethren in all things to our mutuall accord and edification.

[JOHN WINTHROP]

[*Ca.* 1640]

[*Endorsed by Governor Winthrop:*] Lettre to Bro. Painter.

LUCY DOWNING TO JOHN WINTHROP[1]

To her most honerd brother the gouerner this present Boston

SIR, I am most sadly affected with james luxfords perfidious dealeing with you: I must confes I should not haue bin apt to expect better in such a way of dealeing, yet I did hope god had blest your selfe with the phenix of the age. but I see god will not haue vs expect miracles whear meanes may be had: yet your call from your ocasions hath bin of that nesessitye and wayt for the honer of god, and the good of this collony, as far as I am able to iugd, that I

---

[1] W. 4. 8; 5 *Collections,* I. 24–25.

think you haue many promises in bank for support. I think god hath gifted you with much self denyall for his name, and that cannot fayle of reward from him that hath so firmly promised it: but howeuer god is only good: only wise, only able to deliuer and prosper: and he vseth not to fayle whear he giues a wayting spirit: standing still is somtimes the way to reach saulluation from god: he hath allso blest you with many experiences of former mercy, and experience may well breed hope: Ohe hapy pitch, could wee indeed say with Job, though he kill vs yet to trust him, and to take the stem of bitter as willinglie as the stem of prosperity becaus from god   I think this wee ought to indeuor but for my part the scripture it selfe hath not conuinct me of a president of such a temper att all times, and he that best knowes our frame knowes wee can return but what he is pleasd to furnish vs with: yet good sir remember the perill and disaduantage of deiection of spirit. many by strenght of resolution and composednes of spirit, without anny better principles haue waded in depths, and clymed heights: how much easyer may it be to those that are compast with cloudes of witneses, and promises as that author sayth cast of all that preseth downe, and annimat vs to aspire his steps that contemned all sublinarie changes: but what doe I troubleing you with thees wheerin you are so much better furnisht then I can supply: I much bewayell my insufficiencie to be assistant in anny kynd to you. I owe you much but must submit to prouidence: Yours to commaund

L. Downinge

[*Ca.* January, 1639/40]

LUCY DOWNING TO JOHN WINTHROP[1]

To her much honnerd brother the gouerner this present Boston

Sir, meer indulgence to an akeing head hath caused my long silence whear I moste desire conuers. I thank you for your good aduise. the former are safe I am confident, thoughe not so facill when most nessesary, the later wich is the infusion I haue prepared but not yet experimented but I think to try it very shortly: thes frequent strong distempers and the hazard of my condition otherwise doe now call for preparation for a greater change, whearin I craue your most effectuall help, that wee may one day meet in that eternall bless, wich neither siknes, depts, or deaths can dismall or deuide: I should be very glad to hear of a good Ishue of your troublesome ocasions. I cannot but be

[1] W. 4. 12; 5 *Collections*, I. 33.

saded att my owne vnhelpfullnes to you theerin: but what I haue I wish at your seruis and as opertunity will permit, I shall be glad to make a readyer tender theerof. I haue seen the time I have bin a mrs. of some mettall. nowe wee trade all in land wich is not so currant: but god knowes what is best for vs. it is very bad that is not better then I deceru or can vse well.

I should be glad to hear of my neeses safe deliuery.[1] I pray present my humblest seruis to my good sister, wishing her fullnes of action may be a means to fre her of all mellancholly ease: wee haue expected my nephew this 3 or 4 dayes, but I presume he stayes for good newes. I am in some hope of the hapynes to see you hear att ower ordination.[2] I should be most glad theerof: in the interim I pray pray for and commaund Your great sister

L. D.

[*Ca.* January, 1639/40]

I pray commend my harty affections to all yours and all our Boston frinds.

EMMANUEL DOWNING TO JOHN WINTHROP[3]

Sir, I haue deferred writing vnto you, in hope to haue ben at Boston 'ere this;

I remember when this plantation began, Mr. Isake Johnson said, more then once, that he was resolued to spend and be spent in this buisines; what he then said you haue effected. Now if the Country should fayle I am confident the Lord will in his good tyme give meanes of freedome out of all your Cares and feares; I haue a Cow Calfe at Mistick, I pray accept of yt, and were I in monie as I haue ben, I should doe that, would become a loving brother; Job was raised to a full estate in this way by his freinds, soe I conceiue tis a dutye and debt the Countrye stands in to free you, and being a way of God you may with Comfort accept yt; however the Country may deale with you, I pray doe not you nor my sister oppresse your spiritts herewith, but wayte with cheerfull patience on the lord, who alone can and ordinarily doth bring good out of evill, and confident I am, he will in his owne way and tyme performe yt to you.

I know not how the buisines stands for mr. Eatons debts, whither I must

---

[1] Lucy, daughter of John Winthrop, Jr., and Elizabeth Winthrop, was born January 28, 1639/40.

[2] The Reverend Edward Norris was ordained at Salem on March 18, 1639/40. Frederick L. Weis, *The Colonial Clergy and the Colonial Churches of New England* (Lancaster, 1936), 152.

[3] W. 2. 27; 4 *Collections*, VI. 52–53.

loose that 10*li* or noe. I am not willing to trouble you therein. I pray speake to my Cosen Stephen to looke after yt for me; soe craving pardon for this boldnes with my love and service to your selfe and my sister I rest Your assured loving brother whilest I am

EM. DOWNINGE

SALEM 9. 11. 39[/40]

GEORGE PHILLIPS TO JOHN WINTHROP[1]

To the r. w. our worthy gouernor Mr. Winthrope at Boston these

RIGHT WOR[SHIPFULL], I receiued a note from you the last sixt day wherin you moued mee to send you the notes which you heard I had gathered concerning the body of Lawes intended   I confesse I had done a little as good as nothing against the last generall court in September and brought them downe with mee to a meeting of the Elders at Mr. Cottons thinking others had done the like but none were produced but mine which with much importunity (in regard of my backwardnes) they gatt out of my handes and there I left them   And not thinking them worthy the looking after (beeing soe suddayne and vnpolished a transcript) I neuer enquired after them, nor know where they are   Had I iudged them worth any thing I shold haue made more enquiry or If I had conceiued they wold haue beene lookt after I shold haue more minded them and taken a course in this interim to haue given myselfe a little better satisfaction in attending to what I cold haue attayned. I pray you to accept of this my Apology and iust excuse   And soe praying the Lord to blesse you and all yours I humbly take my leaue, Resting Yours in all obseruance and vnfaynd loue

GEORG: PHILIPS

WATERT: 13º vndeci: 1639

JAMES LUXFORD TO JOHN WINTHROP[2]

RIGHT WOR[SHIPFUL], The Lord blesse you, and yours. And soe helpe mee to beare this and all other tryalls, as I haue intended good to your wor[ship] and been faithfull to you in respect any wilfull preiudicinge your Estate; I

---

[1] W. 4. 48; 5 *Collections*, I. 124–125. For Phillips, see 5 *Collections*, I. 123*n.*; Henry W. Foote, "George Phillips, First Minister of Watertown," *Proceedings*, LXIII. 193–227.
[2] W. 4. 52; 5 *Collections*, I. 139–140.

receiued a note the last night by mr. Dauis wherby I did vnderstand that your wor[ship] did propose to speak with me at the farme, but the wise god hath disposed otherwise, who is good and all his doings are good, hath brought me neare to you thoughe he hath stopped my passage to you   I will quietly beare, and abide the wrath of the Lord for I haue sinned: I am afrayd of the poore wooman in your house, but your wor[ship] may perswade hir that the cage doth soome burds good, beinge therin better to haue, and by restraynt of liberty are brought and taught a better note. the good Lord I am perswaded will helpe me at last to make a right vse and for your wor[ship] my loue is noe lesse to you, but I am still perswaded, that thought you should follow me to the death I should looue you. I doe desier to know whether bayle may not giue me liberty till the daye of my apearinge, it hath doone it for theeues and murderers. it is not my mind to escape as god shall helpe me   I thank your wor[ship] for the liberty I had that I am not in the common house   it is a mercy the Lord blesse you for it. I pray let me vnderstand that and what bayle will be asked or what your wor[ship] thinke best, and soe the Lord Jes. euer bee with you. A poore prisoner

James Luxford

[January 14, 1639/40]

[*Endorsed by Governor Winthrop:*] Jas. Luxford Letter at the prison. (11) 14. 39[/40].

JAMES LUXFORD TO JOHN WINTHROP[1]

Right Wor[shipful], now hauinge vntyed the last knott, If your wor[ship] can now forgiue it will take away soom part of my greefe and calamyty which is in soom measure vnsupportable: to speake with your wor[ship] I thinke it in vayne to desier supposinge that your wor[ship] will not vouchsafe soe to doe: for bayle I see it is but in vayne for me to seeke, for great ons I think will not and meaner dare not because euery on that doth shew me any kindnesse is suspected, soe that I thinke it my best way to betake mee to misery at first. that little mony that I had, I haue putt into goodman Brackets[2] hands. as the widow sayd, when I haue eat that I am redy to dy. 22s part wherof your wor[ship] gaue me 10s ould bullock mooud with pitty gaue me and as I euer sayd, If a peny more that I cann remember be found with me in ould England or new, hange me for that: 3s 6d more I thinke I haue: more then that

---

[1] W. 4. 51; 5 *Collections*, I. 134–135.
[2] Richard Brackett, keeper of the Boston jail.

22s. my cloths doe ly at rice morris all I haue. I[f] god take me hence, I wish they may be caled for theare Be mercyfull as your heuenly father is mercyfull and soe indeed you are; I beseech you forgiue as god for Christ sake forgaue you: if it be possible to hide it from hir lett not that poore wooman know that I am hear, lest to all other sorrow this be added that I murther the mother and child: the burden is alredy beyond my strenght, if an almighty power helpe me not as blessed be god he doth in soome measure for I beare about mee the sadnesse of you and yours, the lamentable condition of my wife and children, beside the Burden of mine owne sinn, the cause of all [*torn*] the feare alsoe of corporall punishment. suffer me therfore I pray you wor[ship] to make as the treasurer yesterday aduisd mee a breef narration of my charges at the farm, and be not offended if hearin I do make it apeare that I haue not falsly taken any thinge from your wor[ship] which if I haue I ever desier more then man is able to inflict. When I haue doone I shall shew your wor[ship] before any other, for beinge doone I must leaue it to the true censur and tryall of mankind.

[JAMES LUXFORD]

[*Ca.* January 17, 1639/40]

[*Endorsed by Governor Winthrop:*] James Luxford about his account.

HANSERD KNOLLYS TO JOHN WINTHROP[1]

To the Right Wor[shi]p[fu]ll and his honoured friend John Winthrop Esq.
Gouernour of the N. England bee these deliver

HONOURED SIR, Duty bindes mee to returne humble thankes to your wor[ship] for your vndeserued love manifested to mee in your letter I lately received; wherein also you againe certify mee, that for your owne parte you are fully satisfyed in my repentance and acknowledgment. I would the Lord (in mercy to my poore afflicted soule) were pleased, to give mee soe much fauour in the eyes of all, who are offended by that my letter, that my eares might heare, or mine eyes may see from them, as I doe from your Wor[shi]p, to witt, That they were fully satisfyed: Till then I am not, (nay I cannot be) satisfyed. By these delayes, I thinke god would haue mee more humbled for my sinne. the Lord of his rich mercy give mee what he requires of mee, and what I see not teach mee, that wherein I haue done Iniquity, I may doe noe

---

[1] W. 4. 97; 5 *Collections*, 1. 280–283. For Knollys, see 5 *Collections*, 1. 280 on.; *D.A.B.* For Winthrop's account of the episode which gave rise to this letter, see *Journal*, 1. 295–296, 309, 328.

more; And as a meanes needfull to be vsed, to lett mee see, that which (it may bee) I yet perceiue not, as also to help on my further humiliation and godly sorrow. I once more yea againe and againe humbly beseech you for the Lord Jesus Christ his sake help me to a Coppy of that my letter; Oh deare Sir, the Consideration that I was called out of my Natiue Country etc: and led into the wildernesse to be tempted is not my sorrow, but that I haue sinned in the wildernes, and tempted my god in the desart is the greife of my heart; my sorrow and my shame it is, that I who professe loue to Christ and to the brethren, should pearce him, and his members by that my sinne, The roote of which sinne was the Relicts of that Curssed Emnity in my heart against the Lo[rd] Christ and his people, for certainly had not the Devill (that old accuser of the brethren) fyered his temptation vpon the tinder of that Corruption, he could not (I thinke) haue caused my wretched heart to conceaue nurrish and bring forth such a monstrous Imp soe like himselfe (to witt) an Accusation of the Brethren; this woefull experience of the vanity of myne owne heart, I haue gained at a deare rate. the good Lord sanctifye it to mee, and cause mee more narrowly to examine the sines of my Nature and Practice, and to looke diligently least any Roote of bitternesse spring vp, That I may gett the blood of Christ applyed therevnto for the mortification thereof.

Loving Sir since I writt to you It pleased our Gouernour[1] to send the Marshall for mee at the generall Court being sett the first day of this 11th moneth, And I appearing was questioned about that my letter, etc. I answerred that I had not a Coppy of it, but what I had received from your Wor[shi]p wherevpon I voluntarily shewed the Court your letter, wherein you related sundry passages of that my letter, which being read publiquely amongst them, after some Considerations the Court pleased to enioyne mee, to answere the said Matter, when I shall be therevnto called by the Court. I told them, I had written diuers letters to your wors[hi]p about that matter, and by my last letter to your wor[shi]p had desired a conduct from the Honoured State, to the end I might come and manifest my vnfained Repentance with my presence as I had done in writing; The Court replyed, that in as much as the Matter did not depend in your Court, they might without any wrong to your State or to my selfe cause mee to answere it here. I answered that I doubted it would not giue them soe good satisfaction (as I thought I stood bound in Conscience to doe,) because they were none of them here present; The Court replyed againe that they would write forth-

---

[1] I.e., John Underhill, at this time Governor of Dover, New Hampshire.

with to your Honoured State, that they had taken notice of such a thing and had questioned mee for itt, and the Cause should depend in their Court, And if soe bee, they had not received satisfaction about it, They might (if they pleased) send their deputies hither and here receaue such satisfaction from mee as the word of god required according to their best light in the hearing of such a Cause. And withall our Gouernour charged mee (in the presence of the Court) not to goe into the Bay, nor write any more about this Cause, without the Consent of our Court or at least of our Gouernour and assistants, because now it depended in this Court. I humbly beseeched them for leaue to speake, which given, I told them sadly It was much trouble to my Conscience, that I should be hindred from seeking Reconciliation (by any lawfull meanes I might) with those whome I had iustly offended, and to be deferred or delayed therein was a sore trouble to mee, Telling them, that it lay heauy vpon my soule euery tyme I came into the presence of god either in publique or private, When I remembred that my brethren had such a thing against mee, and I was not reconciled to them, wherewith some of the Court then present was touched with bowels of brotherly Compassion toward mee And vpon my humble request, the Court promissed mee to write forthwith to your State, but engaged mee as before not to goe nor write without their Consents; Wherevpon I forbore to write (though with much trouble) till now that I received your letter, wherevpon I went to the Gouernour and assistants and desired leaue to write, and haue read vnto them this my letter before I sent it to you according to myne engagement; Wherefore I doe humbly beseech your Wors[hi]p to compassionate and commiserate my afflicted Condition (not that I would make hast out of affliction for I beleeue god hath and will doe mee good thereby) but that I would not lye vnder sinne. Wherefore when you receiue the letter which our Gouernour sends concerning mee I earnestly entreat you to vse all lawfull meanes your wor[shi]p shall think meet to putt an end to my expectation of Reconciliation with you all whome I haue offended, and so forced in strates of tyme to breake of abruptly, humbly desiring your prayers for mee and a speedy answere to our Gouernour and myselfe concerning mee, with a Conduct which I much desire,[1] I take leaue, praying for your wor[shi]ps increase of honour and happines I rest on gods mercy. Your poore afflicted and vnworthy friend in the Lo[rd]

HNSRD KNOLLYS

DOVER 11 m. 21, 39[/40]

[1] Knollys was granted "letters of Public Assurance" on January 29, 1639/40. *Suffolk Deeds*, 1 (Boston, 1880), 3.

JOHN UNDERHILL TO JOHN WINTHROP[1]

To the Right Wor[shipfu]ll John Wenthrop Esquire Gofornor of the Macetusetes
at boston these I praye

RIGHT WOR[SHIPFU]LL AND MUCH HONNORED IN THE LORD JESOUS CHRIST OUR LORD, Vnderstanding by Mr. Elms, Mr. Calkard and Ed: Starbock that Mr. Knolse had from hear wrot a letter for Ingland[2] wherein it Justli aperse that God is dishonnored youer commonwele and cherches cast vnder reproch, we cald him to acount as in equiti we were bound to answer this offencif paschegs of his. he not fulli abel to answer the pertickelers I am apoynted by the cort hombli to crafe the coppi of his letter of you, that we maye the more thorrily dele with him whom we find injenious to confes his falt and gif du satisfacechon not onli to vs, from whencs he wrot it but to youer whole state which we shall dilligenli furder him in, and shall be willing to my pouer to dow the like to the glori of God and my farther humelyachon: not that we intend to weken youer pouer by bringing it dependant in oure Cort but this we were forst too in regard it was rot and ackted vnder this Jurisdicchon: so as the Chorch and combenachon might be thorroli informd of his ofenc so that by his repentanc the word of god might hafe free pascheges without pregedice. thous much I am bound to signifi to youer honnored s[e]lfe and take lefe comending you to the infinite merci of God in Christ Youers to comand

JO: VNDERHILL, *Gouer:*

DOUER, 22 the 11 mon. 1639[/40]

JAMES LUXFORD TO JOHN WINTHROP[3]

RIGHT WOR[SHIPFUL], I beeseech you in the executiotion of Justice that yet you will remember mercye: and remember the promise which your wor[ship] solemly made that thought your wor[ship] will not forgiue the wronge, as soomtime you promised to doe, yet that I might coom forth to receiue such punishment as the country and your wor[ship] please to inflict. I am constrayned to trouble your wor[ship] agen, hearinge by diuers that I am not like to be caled for this Court.[4] If your wor[ship] will not be per-

---

[1] W. Au. 95; 4 *Collections*, VII. 179–180.
[2] See the references in *n.* 1, page 176, above.
[3] W. 4. 52; 5 *Collections*, I. 135–139.
[4] There was a meeting of the Court of Assistants on January 30, 1639/40.

swaded, but that I and my poore innocent babes must suffer: the Lord I
trust will yet looke on my misery, for your wor[ship] I neuer intended your
wor[ship] harme   I leaue the lord to perswade your wor[ship] of the truth
of that which you are yet hard to beleeue, but god that searcheth the hart
and tryeth the reynes, before whome cursed Doeggs and flateringe Zibaes,
without tru and sound repentance, shall not be able to stand vp right,
knoweth that I haue not taken from your wor[ship] any thinge more or
lesse   I haue not with soome growe great with my m[aste]rs decay, but in
my ould age my self wife and children if god doe not mightyly helpe, beyond
mans expectation, may coome soone to perish for extreeme want; I am very
sensible of your wor[ship's] condition more euery day and that God hath
made mee an Instrument hearof, it is soe breakinge of my hart, and I doe
vnfeynedly professe, that soe farr as I know my hart if the losse of my life
might reedeeme it I could willingly giue it vp which since it cannot doe, if I
myght but suffer with your wor[ship] in the manyfestation of my vnmoouable
affection to your wor[ship] in soome improouement of my trauells in any
way that might be aduantagious for you or yours yet I would be gladde;
thought I haue beene chased out as a dogge not worthy to coome neare the
house wher your wor[ship's] seruants dwelt; those who did it manyfestinge
great willingenesse, as expression did manyfest, of the ruinge and destruction
both of soule and body, soomwhat contrary in my apprehention; I pray God
forgiue it, at which time, on my returne, the tender compassionate caryage
of your wor[ship] cannot be forgotten of mee nor I hope shall not while I
liue; and truly as soomtime I sayd to soome, when I little thought of these
things that are now falen out, that if the state should euer requier it I would
spend my trauells in your wor[ship's] affayers, for bread and water rather
then any other for 100*li* per Annum: my hart is still the same and though
soome of the wisest and holyest haue concluded that ther cannot be ann
Expectation of any blessinge to goe with my labors; it is soomwhat rashly
concluded, allbeit I doe highly reuerence him and his Judg[ment] yet if it
had beene in the case of another, I could of sayd truly that Israell on the
same ground might haue beene perswaded to haue reiected Dauid and that
it could not be that euer the kingdoome could prosper while he did gouerne.
A greeuous sinn committed a heuie Judgment inflicted, and sadd things
dayly ensued, Butt God that pardoned his sinn, wrought saluation for him,
and for all Israell by him. The like might haue beene sayd of Joabb. It might
haue beene obiected that he had beene the instrument vsed by god to bringe
that heuie calamety on kinge and people, in Absoloomes Rebellyon, nay if
they might of gone on probabilityes as now is vsuall without ground, but

brayne sick fansies, ther might haue beene much to mooue the scruple; for if Joabb had not beene, Absolom might haue then farr inought from hauinge such power to put his father to flyth. Joabs subtillty was the cause of his cominge to the Court; he might haue beene not only thought by this to be a mann not fitt, with any hope of successe, to haue the whole guidance and orderinge of the battell agaynst him; but rather haue beene suspect of treason, for that he had beene soe intimate with him: but neither Dauid nor the people stopte him. But Dauid doth continue his comission: and he goeth forth and with successe returneth   the obiectyons heare made, are not hard to Answer, wher charety is but wher that is wantinge, the strongest Arguments are of little or noe force; Truly I could yet desier, from that vnfeyned looue that I haue borne to your wor[ship] and haue doone since I saw your face, and doe at this present day; that I might be permitted to enter on soome improoue-ment, with small charge, where there could be noe great danger of losse and see whether or noe the lord haue cursed my labor. If I should say that my labors formerly had beene cursed, or should soe now conclude; I should much dishonor god, but god that saw and knew, that the way was not right according to him, the snarre that I had brought my selfe into, did blast it. I hope in mercy to my soule, thought it haue falen out much to your wor[ship's] trouble, disquiett and damage; and which is noe small greef to mee, I feare to the detractinge of soome honor and esteeme, which other-wayes might haue continued longer matter to mee of deep humyliation and farther ingagement; to indeuor if possible I may be yet an instrument of soome good to your wor[ship] before I leaue this troublesoome world; consider that my last labors that yet doe remayne, doth not seeme to be cursed. I found the lord both in the house and field; I found as little cause of just complaynt as any ouersear in the land, either of stubbornnesse or idlenesse of those that weare vnder my charge. If I had walked closly with god, and had not beene vnmindfull of his woord and wayes, I might haue had that coomfort that now I want. But I trust god will yett restore your wor[ship] double and that these eyes of mine may see it, by what way or meanes seemeth best to him.

I could hartely still wish that your wor[ship] had your farme wher it hath beene spoken of: you may, if not you, yet yours find the benefitt, but your selfe I doubt not: for the wronge that I haue doone to your wor[ship] which is great many wayes, I doe refer thee mentioninge of it to a time and place, where god may haue more glory and it may tend more to your wor[ship's] honor and satisfaction when euer I shall be caled, which that I may not be sparinge in, the Lord whome I seeke I trust will helpe mee, and that with an vpright hart as in the presence of god I may doe it I desier the helpe of your prayers: I am sorry that my poore babes with ther mother are now as I heare redy to be turned forth of doors, miserable wretch I, that am like to bringe sorrow and misery to soe many, but my trust is in the lord, who is redy to heare the prayers and pardon the iniquityes of his seruants   poore lambes what haue they doone; ther is a great brute that I should haue 2 wiues in ould England, which is a crime deseruinge noe lesse then death. goodwif Bullock did report that my mrs. should tell hir soe, who because I know hir to be a notoryous lyer I the rather mention it beinge confident that therin as in many other things shee hath belyed both your wor[ship] and my mrs. as shee is a wooman makinge as little conscience therof as any in new england. I would your wor[ship] would aduise mee, euen as you would aduise on whom you looue, what I might doe in this. It is as certenly false as that ther is a god in heauen; as will be prooued, and thought the lord sent such things for the chastisement of them that he looues, yet without repentance the can looke for noe better reward then Cayne or Judas. I beseech you yet for the Lord sake be mindfull of my bonds, and be soome meanes for my deliuerance, if they haue hopes or feares, to haue farther matter agenst me, lett them apoynt me my limitts which if I passe let me dy: but I will trouble your wor[ship] noe farther entreatinge the lord to open your wor[ship's] hart to shew mercy.

Your wor[ship's] in All humble and hartey seruice, thought in any other kind yet held vnwoorthy

JAMES LUXFORD

[*Ca.* January 25, 1639/40]

THOMAS SHEPARD TO JOHN WINTHROP[1]

To the M[uc]h Honoured Mr. Winthrop at Boston be these delivered

SIR, I doubt not but that yow will haue the harts and prayers of many in the compiling of the History tho yow be left alone in it. As for those objections; 1 That some mens virtues cannot be commended with modesty because they are now liuing; I suppose the Historian may without any just offence giue them there due, especially in those cases where there vertues are exemplary to others, and the expressions modestly setting them out without swelling of the socket where such lights are set vp.

2 That some persons errours cannot be mentioned without prejudice to

---

[1] W. Au. 95; 4 *Collections*, VII. 269–270. For Shepard, see *D.A.B.*

there places; I confesse tis some what, yet let the History make its progresse till it comes to such persons times and practises; and then vpon serious thoughts spent how to carry on that busines, I doubt not but god will manifest himselfe on way or another by that time, that there will not be much cause of sticking here what to doe;

3: That some things may prejudice vs in regard of the state of England if divulged; I know not what they be which can do so, more then what is known to all the woorld already; if there be any secret hid things which may be prouoking; it may be left to the judgement of others how far it will be fit to divulge them when the coppy is priuately examind;

surely Sir the woorke is of god and many eyes and harts will be now expecting it with prayers; the good Lord guide and encourage yow in your way and recompence it abundantly to yow.

When I came to write this letter I perceiued that he that tooke a coppy of what yow sent, had sent it away by Edw. Mitchelson to you, which was without the least notice I had of it; and sory I am it was returned so rudely; if I had known yow desired any answer to it I should haue before this time haue sent; but I looked on it as a Law made by the Court and therefore I knew not how acceptable or safe it would be to reply; and if I know myself I know I desire peace with all but especially with such whose wisdom I prefer aboue mine own folly who can see little: 1: This only I meruayle at that that should be condemnd as a sin simply in itselfe, and yet by order of court liberty giuen to men for some few dayes to commit that sin; as in case freends come fresh out of England, they may then drinke to them without being liable to punishment:[1] 2: This also I doe humbly intreat that there may be no sin made of *drinking in any case one to another*; for I am confident he that stands here will fall and be beat from his ground by his own arguments; as also that the consequences will be very sad and the thing prouoking to God and man to make more sins then (as yet is seene) God himselfe hath made: if more be desired of me then this I should not be vnwilling to write but I desire yow would consider I am alone, and that I am desirous of as much ease and peace I can: I am in extreame hast. The Lord guide and direct and blesse yow in all your thought [al]wayes for his prayse. Yours

T. SHEPARD

CAMB: Jan: 27: [1639/40]

[*Endorsed:*] Mr. Shepard about the History and health drinking etc.

---

[1] Shepard, in this portion of his letter, is referring to the order of the Massachusetts General Court against drinking healths which was passed on September 9, 1639 (*Records of Massachusetts*, I.

WILLIAM HOOKE TO JOHN WINTHROP[1]

To the Wor[shi]p[fu]ll John Winthrop gouer: be delivered in Bostone

Wor[shi]p[fu]ll Sir, Vnderstan[d]i[n]g that mr. Winselowe and some other gent: haeth power from your Worshipp to grant out lottes at merimake to newe commers, Sir if you shall thinke it fitt to lett me haue a portion of land in that plantation I will remoue and about June next to bild there   I haue written vnto mr. Winselowe allredy about it expecting an answer euery daye that I maye order my bisnesse accordenly for my remoueall   I desier noe great quanitie of land but that I maye haue that which is sufficient for the manigine of that estate which I haue. I haue fead my selfe a longe time with v[a]ine hopes   there is noe posibelity here with vs for the geathering of a Church except god in mercy open there eyes and lett them see there supersticious waye which they desier to goe. Sir desireing your worshipp to helpe this poore man the berer here of which haeth bine much damnified by the master of Gallopes pinnas Sir I leaue the matter vnto the party to relate vnto your worshipp   to my knowled[ge] haeth Caried himselfe here amoungst vs verie shamefully the master and gallope Sonne twoe, Inuited some of our naybours aborde his pinnas and made them dronke and dronke themselues twoe   he heath not it answered for it but some stands bound for them   I rest leaueing your worshipp to the lords protecktion Yours to command

WILLI. HOOKE

ACCOMENTICUS the 28 January 1639[/40]

Sir If I might not be to troublesome vnto your worshipp desiring an answer by the first.

271–272). The provision in that order to which Shepard takes particular exception is the one stating that the ban on health drinking was not to apply to those arriving in the colony after the publication of the order until they should have had "one weekes residence heare." For Winthrop's discussion of this order, see *Journal*, I. 325.

[1] W. Au. 96; 4 *Collections*, VII. 196–197. For Hooke, see 4 *Collections*, VII. 195n.

EDWARD STARBUCK TO JOHN WINTHROP[1]

To the Right worsh[i]p[ful] mr. Winthrop
the Gouerner of the massatewsetes giue this I pra

WORTHEY SIR, My humbel Seruis presented to your worship Returning
many thankes for all your louing respectes shewed mee and my felowes with
mee. You may iustly chaling mee for ingratitude becaues I seeme to haue
neglected to write to your worship but now hauing an oppertunity I thinke
it my deuty to writ and there with allso to manefest the Caues of this delay.
Retourning home in saftey from your Courte[2] wee did acquint our gouerner
and neighboueres with the pleasur of your honred Court and after som
agitationes wee with diueres otheres of our naighboueres to the number of
29 consented vnto your Articeles and determined to send forth with for mr.
Broadstreet and a mesenger was nominated and apointed to that end to ac-
companey mr. knowles[3] to ipsich according to your order to haue conferred
with the elderes of the Church and otheres, who weare prepared accordingly
to set forwardes on the second day following but that which leted was A
scruple springing vp in the Consience of our gouernor which as hee saied much
troubled him soe that hee had no Rest in his spiret where upon th[e pe]opel
at his Commaund was willed to meet againe the 5 day folowing and mr.
knowles and the mesenger stayed from their apointed Journey and A strict
Charge was giuen by the gouerner him self that noe man within our Juris-
dicktion should write into the bay thereby to giue intelegence of the buesnes
in Agetation and mr. helmes stricktly questined by him vpon suspition that
hee had writen somthinge into the bay which strict Charge was the Caues
that I did not write to you before now, wherefoure I prayou do [n]ot take it
ill from mee neither impute it to me as neglect   If I had had liberty as I haue
had oportunetey you should haue Read my lynes eare now   may it pleas
your wor[shi]p therfore to vnderstand that the 5 day aforesaide the peopel
meeting according as the weare comanded held a court purpouesly about the

---

[1] W. i. 187. For Starbuck, see Savage, *Genealogical Dictionary*, IV. 171–172; Alexander Starbuck,
The History of Nantucket (Boston, 1924), 656–658. This letter from Starbuck putting on Underhill,
then Governor of Dover, the blame for the failure at this time of the attempt to bring that town
under Massachusetts jurisdiction brought forth in reply a letter from Governor Winthrop which,
according to Winthrop, was the most important evidence used against Underhill in deposing him
from his office early in 1640. *Journal*, I. 330.

[2] For Winthrop's account of the negotiations in September, 1639, between Massachusetts and
the settlement at Dover, see *Journal*, I. 320–321.

[3] See Hanserd Knollys to John Winthrop, January 21, 1639/40 (pages 176–178, above).

saide buesnes which being set our gouerner makeing a speech to the peopel
conserning the saide Artickeles which wee brought from youre Generall Couert
and presed them with thees Artickeles folowing 1 how it could stand with
their Alegence to their kinge to giue them selues and theires to the State of
the masatewsetes for euer to becom one bodey polytick withe them. Their answer was that the state of the masatusetes being the kinges loyall subiectes and
for ought the knew the best that hee had the thought it noe breach of theire
Alegence to subiect them selues and thereres to be laufully gouerned by them
vnder his magestey 2 qu. in as much as it was expected that pouer from the
king by Comision might ere longe com to establish gouerment in the Riuer
and for ought the know this yeare, how could the answer this their Act of dis-
pouesing of them selues and thereres vnder a[n]other Jureyesdicktion without his Consent And not breake theier Alegence which at the first somwhat
feared the peopel. But answer was made that such A pouer had beene long
expected from his magestey by som, but in as much as his magestey did not
Answer their expectationes but Rather seemed to neglect them the might
therefouer the thought lawfully take the best Cource to liue vnder such A gouerment as was authoriesed by his magestey without feare of being called to
acounte by him for breach of their Alegence.

But if pouer did com indeed from his magestey to settel gouerment heare
in this Riuer and by vertew there of the peopel shall be comanded to be subiect to that Authoretey then how will the keepe theier Alegence with his magestey and there league with the masatewsetes their answer was that if the could
not haue leaue to com of from theier voluntuarey Subiecktion to the masatewsetes to liue vnder the poure and Athoratey that his magestey shall be pleased
to sett vp in the Riuer according to god which the hoped would not be denied,
then the could sell their estates and houses heare and Remooue to the masatewsetes without breach of theire Alegence soe long as the obayed in doing or
sufering and not breakeing Couenant or league made with the state of the
masatewsetes. And here vpon it was Replyed that if his magestey doe indeed
send and establish gouerment in thees northerne pertes or but in this whole
Riuer, Comaunding all his faithfull and loyall se[rvan]tes to be subiect to that
his authoratey soe estableshed then in Case the State of the masetewsetes will
not as here is no Claues binding them in thes there Articeles so to doe, giue
the peopel leaue to fall of from theier gouerment and to be subiect to the
kinges Authoratey then heare established, the must eaither breake theier Alegence with the king or theier league with the masatewsetes or at least sell
theier houses and soe tourne theier backes of the king and his Authoratey.
This the peopel could not for the present tell how to deney but desired som

further Consederation before the gaue a full answere, whearevpon at last it was conclewded that the buesnes should be demured and time was giuen by an unanemoues Consent of all the peopel to demur deliberate and consider there of vntill our next generall Couerte which was the 1 day of the 11 month And it was then allso agreed and ordered that the gouerner should forth with write to mr. Broadestreet to acquinte youer state or Couensell with this demur about your first Articell which leter was sente to exeter to be sente to goe by the firest opertewnitey. this leter being sent our gouerner being vpon som occasion at Agamenticus mr. hooke toulde him that his father[1] certefyed in a leter out of ingland that there was Comision granted and gone out from his magestey for the gouerment of thees northerne partes. Allso mr. wanerton had Receued as the said leteres from a ship and with them A box with a comission in it as was suposed directed to mr. Vines wherevpon our gouerner haueing some Conferance there, was advised to perswade the peopel to confirme there owne Combination least those to whome the king had granted his Comision finding them vnsetled should setel such A gouerment among vs or Joyne vs to such a gouerment wee should not like of And the gouerner to efect this caled a couert to that end which being asembled and he haueing propounded the same thinges to the peopel and the being suddenley afected with it yellded presently to his proposition and propounded 6 of the freemen to be chosen assistentes to our Gouerner whereof 2 Refused and 4 weare elected magestrates with him After which election the gouerner and asistante as I heard haue writen to your honored Councel of the state a full and finall answer to the Artickeles you sent but what is therein contained I am alltogether ignorant of it being sent before the Court held the 1 of the 11 month was the Reason. I thinke y[our] Aticele weare not mentioned at all then as was before intended Reuerend Sir this is the som of all paseues so neare as I can Relate them I am sorey that youre artickeles weare not Receued of our peopel yet I hope still that the lord will one waye or another bring it to pas and I doe think[2] that It might yet be efected if one thinge would be granted which is libertey of Consience in one pointe which is the sp[torn] the first euedence not that I am an enemy to the graces of god or to those that euedence there estates that way. Right worshipfull I would I might beg 2 or 3 lines from youre worship I should thinke my self muchonored by you I haue a grea[t] desire that this Riuer might be youeres and could be glad if the lord would be pleased to use mee as an unworthey instrewment of doing anithing that

[1] Humphrey Hooke, alderman of Bristol, England.
[2] The spelling in the original manuscript is "thing."

way　t[h]erfore Sir make vse of mee and by godes help you shall finde mee faithfull. soe with my prayeres to god for you and youers I take leaue beging pardon for my Rewdnes　I am no Scoler. Youer worshipes seruant in the lord

EDWARD STARBUCK

[*Ca.* February, 1639/40]

JOHN ENDECOTT TO JOHN WINTHROP[1]

To the right Wor[shipfu]ll and my truelie honored Friend Jo: Winthrop Esqr.
Governour deliver

DEAREST SIR, What construction you may put vpon my silence I dare not conclude, but I hope the best. The wise man saith that a Friend loueth at all tymes, and a Brother is borne for aduersitie. And heere is my griefe, That I cannot shew my selfe either, as I desire or as my dutie binds me. I cannot excuse my not writinge (though not out of neglect). But the present want of a more reall comfort and effectuall expression of my loue and seruice hath hither vnto hindred mee. If I should say I doe not truelie and heartilie reverence and loue you and yours, I should speake against my conscience. Yet I cannot satisfie my selfe with sole verball expressions But I desire to waite vppon God who will in his tyme bring all our matters to passe, and work all our works for vs. I haue had many sad thoughts about your affliccion yet I neuer doubted to this howre of your comfortable deliuerauce. I ame thinking sometimes that the Lord is trying of the whole Countrie, not but that hee knowes their hearts etc. well enough, but hee will haue you to see their loues and affeccions towards you also. Sometimes I ame thincking hee is vppon the tryall of your selfe in the exercise of your faith and patience and other graces: That as you haue bene beneficiall and helpfull all your tyme since you came over, in the course hee had sett you, now hee will make you beneficiall another way to vs all in an exemplarie cheerefull vndergoinge of Gods afflicting hand in wisdom and patience. Sir let mee say thus much to you. That your last Sicknes did you not good alone, but many others also obseruinge the lords guidinge of your spiritt vnder it: I blesse the Lord I can truely say I gayned by it, and I know some others that exprest the same. This I ame confident in The Lord is now louinge of you deerely. And his corrections are the corrections of a louing Father. If hee will haue you to be

[1] W. 2. 73; 4 *Collections,* VI. 116–138.

poore for a little while It is to make you richer hereafter, not onelie heere as hee did Job, but for euer heereafter to all eternitie. I ame glad to heere you are chierfull. Yet I know (in respect of others) your cares cannot be a few and I feare griefs also. The lord our good God in mercie cary you through them to his praise and your true comfort. I should haue bene with you at Court, but I ame aduised by all my friends to stay at home this tyme. And I was the more easilie drawen vnto it, because I finde my selfe worse and worse within this senight then I haue bene this moneth: my cold which I haue had this moneth or 5 weekes increasing vpon mee and head out of order vpon euery little wett in my feete. I therefore shall desire you good Sir to excuse mee to the Deputie and the rest of the Court, beseeching the lord in mercie to sitt amongest you and to guide you all in his feare to doe his will. To whose blessed protection I committ you, And rest Your Wor[shi]pps truelie and vnfeagned whiles I ame

Jo: ENDECOTT

SALEM the 2d of the 12 moneth 1639[/40]

Myne and my wiefs service remembred to Mrs. Wintrop your deare yoake-fellow and to Mr. Jo: Wintrop and his wiefe and our true loues to all yours with you. Your sisters Sonne[1] is named after your name, John.

PETER DE SALLENOVA TO JOHN WINTHROP[2]

To the Worshipfull Mr. John Wintropp Gouernor in new England att Bostone deliver

WORSHIPFULL, Aftar my harty Comemdations to you and yours nott for-getting Mr: Pettors, my Earnist requeist to you, is when I was last in new England I left a kindsman of my wifes with one Mr: Steauens of Maruill head a shipp Carpintar for hee was bound to me to teach him his trad   I undar-stand he haue neclected him, and nott taught him his trad according as he

---

[1] John, son of Emmanuel and Lucy Downing, who was baptized at Salem, March 1, 1639/40.

[2] W. 1. 130. Captain Peter de Sallenova of Dorchester, England, where the records refer to him variously as captain, chirurgeon, and apothecary, was in the colony in 1635, at which time he was consulted by the General Court in connection with the proposed expedition against the French at Penobscot. *Records of Massachusetts*, I. 160. The following year he was reported to be in the West Indies (*Winthrop Papers*, III. 275), and he subsequently returned to England. Charles H. Mayo, *Municipal Records of the Borough of Dorchester, Dorset* (Exeter, 1908), 516–517, 544–545; *Minute Books of the Dorset Standing Committee* (Exeter, 1902), *passim*. There is a reference as late as 1642 to his owning land in Weymouth, Massachusetts, where he may earlier have been employed in building the mill or dam owned by Henry Waltham and Thomas Richards. *Lechford's Notebook*, 2, 2n.

was bound to me for hee haue sett hime to keepe Cabarretoes[1] and nott to bee a Carpintar. I haue Intreated Mr: Angill Hallott to call him before you to gett a warrant to bring him before your Worsh[i]p Ether to release ore to teach him his trad. and all soe I haue a 100*li* in Mr. Izerill Stotons hand   he receud it for the sellinge of my Land att Wayemouth. he haue neauer re-turned it to me, and if you know any bodye that will tacke the mony there, and send a bill to be payd heare by a sure Freind, and if I had my mony I should be with you this yeare therfor the next yeare I will be with you Leav-inge you to the proticktion of the Allmighty I rest Your uerey Loueing Freind

P. SALLENOVA

DOCHESTAR the 5 Febr: 1639[/40]

HENRY WALTON TO JOHN WINTHROP[2]

To our honnoured Gouernour the right wor[shi]p[fu]ll Jno. Winthrop Present in Boston

MOST RESPECTIUE SIR, I pray be pleased to pay to the bearer hereof, Mr. How, the somme of thirty one pownd tenne shillings in full, if it may be with your wor[shi]ps Conueniency. if not, as much as you canne, my occasions beinge Somewhat vrgent, and soe with the presentment of my humble serui-ice to your wor[shi]p I humbly take my leaue and rest Your humble Seruant to Command Till Death

HENR WALTON

LYNNE this 11th of the 12th Moneth 1639[/40]

[*Endorsed:*] Receud of this 30*s* in mony and thirty pounds by Jo: Gallop per me[3]

DANIELL HOW

---

[1] Probably "cabaret," in the obsolete sense of "a drinking house." Cf. *N.E.D.*

[2] W. 1. 130. Henry Walton and Daniel Howe were members of the Lynn group who, in 1640, founded the town of Southampton, Long Island. Walton, by the time of this letter, had returned to Lynn, but subsequently, as appears from his letter of June 4, 1644 (pages 460–461, below), he lived in Flatlands, Long Island. Howe also left Southampton, becoming one of the founders of East Hampton. James Truslow Adams, *History of the Town of Southampton* (Bridgehampton, L. I., 1918), 46, 47.

[3] This endorsement, with the exception of the signature, is in the Governor's handwriting.

GILES FIRMIN TO JOHN WINTHROP[1]

To the Right Wor[shi]p[fu]ll and our honoured Gouernour John Winthrop Esq.
att his house in Boston deliver

MUCH HONOURED AND DEAREST SIR, I cann hardlye thinke of you, much
lesse write to your wor[shi]p, without some greife of Spirit; I am glad yet
to heare, and cannot but looke vpon it as a great power of a God to carry
his Creature thorough such a triall, without discontent, or frettinge against
his Prouidence. I haue heard a Conclusion gathered against these Plantations, because the Lord hath so sadlye afflicted the founders of them in their
estates; that therefore it was not a way of God, to forsake our Countrye, and
expose ourselus to such temptations, as wee haue done, so long as wee might
haue enioyed God in any comfortable measure in the place whence wee
came, alledginge that it is scarcely knowne that any church in a way of
Separation as wee are did euer yet thriue in grace. at first hearinge the
thinge, I was a little affected, onely when I came to consider, that those who
haue thus suffered in their estates, haue beene no seekers of themselus, but
the commonnesse of their spiritts or vnfaithfullness of seruantes, as a means,
haue beene the onely cause I haue againe gathered my thoughtes to rest,
hopinge still that God will finde out a way to make your burden lighter. for
the letter which your wor[shi]p sent mee, and for your vndeserued loue
therein manifested, I humbly thanke you. your Counsell carriinge reason
and your owne experience in it I cannot sett light by, hauinge beene a means
to calme my disquiett thoughtes, and to stopp them in their hurrye: my
Father law still holdes his owne, and would yet haue mee rise from hence.
my brother Ward wauers much, but rather declines it from your arguments,
and some others which wee finde out together: howsoeuer if time will giue
vs leaue (the Lord willinge) some of vs will veiw Pentuckett in the Springe,
because euery one that hath seene it giue it such large commendations for a
small Towne, the way also thither beeing passable for a great pinnace: onely
my feare is that Passaconnaway liuinge there sometimes hee will hardly bee
bought out with a little. my brother Ward hath beene offered the place at
Marblehead, when the minister goeth away to Jefferies Creeke who is there.
the message was first done to my Father Ward, who should haue enformed
my brother of it, but hee kept it in his owne breast, and did not reueale it,
till long after by accident hee heard of it: so that now hee fears the opportunitie is slipt: diuers enticements hee hath to returne to England, but his

[1] Essex Institute; 4 *Collections*, VII. 273–274.

wife is vtterlye against it; and hee is willinge, if hee might but haue any employment to stay still. if your wor[shi]p did but put in a word for him, if you thinke the place conuenient for him, your word would doe much: hee did helpe at Rowlye, but because hee was not in Couenant some tooke offence, and hee layed it downe at my vnckles desire and his church who else would gladly enioyed his helpe. this letter I would desire your wor[shi]p might bee safely deliuered to your Sonne, containinge in it some money which I ought him. thus still crauinge pardon for my boldnesse, with due thankes for your loue and care of mee; my due seruice being presented to you, desiringe the Lord to support your Spirit vnder your affliction, and to giue a fauourable issue out of it I rest Your wor[shi]ps in any seruice

GILES FIRMIN

IPSWICH: 12th of the 12th 1639[/40]

EDWARD WINSLOW TO JOHN WINTHROP[1]

WORTHY SIR, Had not the Almighty (who is righteous in the middest of mans unrighteousnes) stirred up certaine malicious and slanderous persons to defame me with impudent false and shameles reports to my no smale griefe and trowble I had been with you before this day, knowing right well how comfortable the face of a friend is in such sad conditions as yours at present. How I haue been and am affected with those losses and crosses are befallen you by your unfaithfull servant he that made the heart best knoweth; But when I consider how unhappy a man may be in the fullest and most plentifull enjoyment of worldly treasures then I judge you neerer happines in the losse of them; not dowbting but our gracious God will sanctefie his hand unto you, assuring my selfe it will be good for you in the end. How prone would Gods people be to haue their hearts ensnared and taken up with the world and the riches and honors thereof if he should not sometimes shew us their vanity. He that brought Job so low (after he was humbled before him) blessed his latter daies more then his former. We haue to doe with the same God: He can doe what he will, and let this be our comfort he will doe what is best for us: therefore let us shew foorth his praise by patient submitting to his hand, joyning therewith a diligent enquiry after the cawse twixt him and our selues. I haue too often used a foolish proverb, I had rather be envyed than pittyed: but I finde by lamentable experience Gods word

---

[1] Miscellaneous MSS., Bound, M.H.S.; *L. and L.,* II. 256–257; *Hutchinson Papers* (1769), 110; (1865), II. 123–125. For Winslow, see *D.A.B.*

true, That none can stand before envy, and therefore prefer your condicion far before mine owne, whom I conceiue to be compassed about with Friends. But alas however a Friend loues at all times, now is the time of tryall; and heerein (as many other waies) I dowbt not but you will gaine by your present condicion, which the Lord in mercy grant. What you wrote to our Governour he imparted to me. Few or none of note haue commen from your parts this way of late by reason of the season. So that we heare not what order you haue taken in your busines. If my presence may any way stand you in steed you may command it and my best service therewith. I pray you Sir take it not ill that I am thus plaine. If I faile tis occasioned by my loue knowing right well how such an unexpected streight may pinch a good estate which I should be very sorry to heare. Be you and yours saluted in the Lord, to whom my prayers are that his comforts may exceed your crosses: And so desiring your prayers take leaue remayning your assured Friend simpathizing with you

EDW. WINSLOW

CARESWELL[1] this 17th mo. ult. 1639[/40]

JOHN HARRISON, JR., TO JOHN WINTHROP[2]

HON[ORA]BLE SIR, I have received your letter, with much thankfulnesse, accounting myselfe not a litle ingaged to you aboute my former bonds, that at so greate a distance I am so neere your thoughts. your good counsell was very seasonable and helpe much to stay my not altogether quieted consciense which for the spase of above 3 months laboured of much paine contracted by the remembrance of my evill life (blessed bee god for his goodnesse to mee in revealing my selfe to my selfe)   that love which yow expressed to mee the evening before my voyage so much wrought with mee as that the seas and discommoditys of a suddenly-vndertaken voyage were not comparatively so trobblesome to mee as my owne thoughts, which yet I could well beare till my second ship was ready for England which had not beene 2 dayes at sea before a storme broke out and it scarsely ended till wee had beene of home which presenting mee the possibility of death, and the horrours to come after as it denyed mee stomacke, sleepe, and any other rest so did not it leave mee but added to my other greifes a feaver, in which agonys the L[ord] helped mee very much, for though the ship had neither surgeon, nor fresh

---

[1] The name Winslow gave to his farm in Marshfield.
[2] W. 1. 131.

meate or any confection to alay the fury of my desease, before my arrivall, my health returned, and by the meanes of a gent[leman] of Wales, a minester who this summer intends to bee with yow, my inward man received much rest, and sense that heere in London by the constant helpe of a faithfull preacher, both in publique and private much more, which that it may continue I humbly begge your prayers: and having discovered to yow my spirituall estate, I will bee bold to disclose my temporall. Vpon my first coming to London my father was so much displeased with mee that I almost altogether dispaired of any Looane from him, but the L[ord] was not absent at so greate neede, and moved his heart to continue 50*li* a yeere to mee, which without increase lasted till now, and as I am informed the next quarter it shall bee doubled. but as yet I have not obteined leave to visit my father. I am bold to become an humble sutor to yow, that if yet yow have them, it may please yow to send mee those letters which yow received from my father while I was with yow.

by a ship that went to your parts from Barnestaple I presented yow a letter and in it signified the peace, and such other newse as I could gett. at my coming to London the downes were stuffed with a greate Armado of Spannish shipps full of souldiers some suppose, their intent was when his M[ajes]ty should be busy in the Northerne parts, to have landed in the Southerne. the Hollander met him at sea and for safeguard forsed him in to the K[ing's] chamber where by the regall command they were suplyed with what they would. amongst the rest they had much powlder and shott, not with standing which helpe a tenth part of them scarse returned home, for the flemings sett vpon them againe as soone as they had weighed anchor even in sight of the K[ing's] shipps, and forst 25 of them a shoare which never came of, 15 they burnt, and tooke 7. The generall of Naples was slaine   Trampe him selfe the flemmish Ad[miral] was hardly beset, but hee came of bravely. it is suspected that wee shall have warrs with france, for some iniurys donne to the P[rince] Palatine whom with his 2 bretheren they deteine prisoners. Normandy is lately in Rebellion expecting English aides, but that fier is now quenched and garrisons put into most of their townes, at the cuntrys charge. the Prince of Oringe hath some noble designe [in] hand, for hee hath commanded all the English Captaines, vpon forfeeture of their places to returne, by the first of Aprill the 11th daye of which month our Parliament is to beginne for which the writs are already drawne with blankes. The L[ord] Deputy of Ireland that is now L[ord] Leutenant, and hath powre to asigne a deputy; hee is also created Earle of Strafford. Sir Hen: Vane is tresurer of the houshold, and Sir Thomas Germaine Controller, both of them are to bee made Barons

against the next year. my L[ord] Coventree is dead and in his place my Sir
Lo[rd] Finch that was cheife iustice of the common pleas, in whose rombe
there, Sir Edward Litleton that was Solicitor is put   My L[ord] Keeper
that was, left 12000*li* a yeere in lands, beside 8000*li* a yeere which hee had
got with mariages for his sonnes. and in ready mony there was found 40000*li*
the L[ords] amongst them have lent the K[ing] 300000*li* my L[ord] of Northumberland, 20000*li* my L[ord] of Pembrook 20000*li* Cant. 3000*li* and my
L[ord] Keeper but 6000*li* at which offer the K[ing] gave him some unkind
words the greefe whereof as tis reported kild him. my L[ord] of Dorset lends
10000*li* and very carefully payeth his debts. my Lady Dutchesse of Ritch-
mond is dead, and the Dutchesse of Lenox the Dukes mother. The B[ishop]
of Lincolne should have had an other sensure this last terme but vpon his
humble petition to the K[ing] it is deferred till the next. and as tis thought,
hee shall bee no more trobled, hee is still a L[ord] B[ishop] but sine officio
and beneficio. for his maintainance hee hath out of his lands (which are extended at halfe the value to pay his fine of 11000*li*) 800*li* per annum and hee
either hath or faines an humility next basenesse, which maketh him now the
subiect of each mans pitty. Prage is taken. there are six armys on foote in
Germany lying in severall places. there were the begining of the last month
200 soldeers prest, to augment the garrisons in the castles of Garnsy, Jersy
and Silly where the 3 prisoners yet continue. Dr. Mickletwaite is dead, at
his new living of 300*li* per annum and in his rombe wee have a man, nulli
impietate secundus.[1] but our hopes are that hee will shortly bee a B.B.
and then tis possible that honesty may creepe in to the Temple church. The
greatest grand in Spaine is dayly expected heere an Ambassador, there are
greate preparations of rich clothes bespoken by his agents, for forte boyes,
pages, and gentlemen. my L[ord] of Arundel was this last winter goeing to
Matagascar, with his wife and yonger childeren, there hee would have
found[ed] a common-wealth of which him selfe was to bee Prince, but at last
his Lordship was content to send and stay at home. my L[ord] of Marle-
borough hath letters of Mart and is gone to the West India. other newse
then this I call not now to mind. yow writ for a booke of Mr. Dudleys which
I left in my chamber with Mr. George Downings Plutarch, and a booke of
Mr. Maverickes. if it may bee my good happ to do yow servise or any of gods
people with yow, assure your selfe I shall bee more ioyfull of such imploiment
then I can expresse. my creditors there I shall with what speede I can satisfy,
(god knowes my heart)   there is nothing at this time more trobles mee than

---

[1] John Littleton.

these ingagements   I have received no letter from Mr. Peter which maketh mee much marvell considering that I left with him some bills for my creditors p[aya]ble some 2 yeeres after the date. some of them had bills before but I was then vnder age and therefore the bills void, which delivering the new Mr. Peter should have taken vp the old and sent to mee   I humbly beseeche yow Sir to mind him of this, and to remember mee in your prayers for which for ever command Your true freind and servant

[JOHN HARRISON]

INNER TEMPLE LONDON Feb: 18º 1639[/40]

pray present my best servise to good Mrs. Winthrop and all yours.

[*Endorsed by Governor Winthrop:*] Mr. Harison.

GEORGE JENNEY TO JOHN WINTHROP[1]

To my much honored and worshipfull Brother in Law Jhon Winthrop Esqr. at Boston in new England giue this

RIGHT WORSHIPFULL AND WORTHY BROTHER WINTROOP, salutation in the lord giuing thanks vnto our blessed god from the best sinseritie of my harte for the prosperitie and blessed suckses of you and your worthy assosiates in the christian plantation in Newe Enggland wher I vnderstand the word of god grace and the gospel of his deer sonn in the puritie and power of it doe prosperusly flurrish which maketh me much to reiose and draweth from me much thankfullnes vnto god, and am very glad that I put in my poor mite of 25*li* for furtheranc of that blessed worke. You know that I am a freeman in that plantation and haue as due vnto me a hundered acres of ground to be assighned vnto me[2] which in regard of my age I neuer looke to Inioy which I hope my children and posterity hearafter may Inioy if they will. In the meantym I desier your happy further suces in this blessed worke and that you would ryde on with the spirit of meeknes and power in the vse of the sword of the spirit which is the word of god that the arke of gods truth may

---

[1] W. Au. 72. George Jenney of London married Mary Clopton, sister of Thomasine Clopton, Governor Winthrop's second wife.

[2] The records of the Massachusetts Bay Company make no mention of Jenney's investment in the Company's stock, nor do they refer to him in any other connection. His name, furthermore, does not appear in Samuel F. Haven's list of adventurers in the Company (*Transactions of the American Antiquarian Society*, III. cxxxiv–cxxxviii) nor in the list compiled by Frances Rose-Troup (*The Massachusetts Bay Company and Its Predecessors*, 130–162).

flourishe amongst you and the dagones of heathenes Idolaters and false wor-
shiper and all aduerse powers may be suppresed to the glory of god and your
endles saluation: in the meantyme I would intreate a curtesie of you for a
spetiall frind of myn who is a tenant vnto me and in his house I doe lye
when I am at London   his nam is mr. Robert Downes a good able christian
both in knowledge and practis and hath at his own charg breed vp a young
man his brother in skooles in the country and at the Vniversity and ther
hath taken his degrees and is now a worthy preacher in London   now such
as he is being so worthy a member in the church in doing of good it is pitie
to hinder   now ther is one Robt. Howet[1] who cam from Sudbery in Suff[olk]
and as I vnderstand liues neer vnto you in the same towne who oweth my
frind mr. Downes x*li* by bond and did very dishonistly depart away without
giuing him Satisfacon. now I would Intreat you to doe your best Indeuours
to helpe him to his money and I will take it as thankfully as if it were don
for my self. and so I abrubtly Conclud commending myself and loue vnto you
and to my good Sister your wyf, my Cosen John Wintrop your elder sonne
with all the rest of your Children and I pray salut from me reuerent mr.
Peeteres, and mr. Phillepes late precher of boxted and mr. Phillepes late
preacher of Wrentum and so comending you all to the blessing of our great
god in Christ Jesus our blessed sauiour and redemer   I had almost forgot
your good brother and Sister mr. Downing and his wyf vnto whom I pray
Commend my tru loue Your tru louing brother not only Law but also in
Jesus Christ

GEORGE JENNEY

from the trinity minores in LONDON without algate to which place If you
direct any Leter to me to the house of mr. Robt. Downes he will send it
vnto me the 18th of February Anno 1639[/40]

[*Endorsed by Governor Winthrop:*] brother Jenneye respecting mr. R: Howin
he saythe the debt was 34*li* and he hathe paid him all the rest and leave
goods in Sudbury with his wife to satisfie him, and will paye so soone as he
is able   he sent by J. Tinker etc.

---

[1] The correct name is "Howen," or, as Winthrop states in his endorsement, "Howin."

SAMUEL FONES TO JOHN WINTHROP[1]

To the Wor[shipfu]ll his much respected Vnckle John Winthroppe Esqr.
these in Boston New England

WORTHY SIR, I receiued your louinge, and kinde letter, then which I doe
assure you I know not any thinge that could haue bin welcomer, except
your personall presence. I doe blesse god for you, in as much as hee hath
stirred up your heart, too seeke, and wish my good, soe that hee hath not
left mee freindeles, although hee hath taken away my parents, and remooued
my neerest freindes farthest from me: I doe earnestly desire of him, that my
heart may bee affected with his goodnes toward mee: and I beseech you Sir
to continue your earnest supplications to the throne of grace for mee, that
the lord would bee pleased to direct mee in the good way, that I may in my
life and conversation, walke answerable (in some measure) to his goodnes,
and mercy soe abundantly manifested vnto mee. I am as yet in a doubt
what profession to betake my selfe vnto, I am at a stand betweene Divinity,
and Physicke. I haue aduised with my father-in-law what course I were best
to take. hee did consider of it, and aduised with some godly ministers of his
aquaintance about it, but hath not yet determined what will bee my best
course. hee hath therefore perswaded mee to study the groundes of boath,
a little while, till I can be resolued; Sir I would gladly haue your iudgment
likewise; a mans callinge is a thinge of great importance, and not rashly to
bee determined of, and beinge entred upon, not with out good groundes to
bee altered. You wrote vnto me in your letter, that once heeretofore you
sent vnto mee, but receiued noe answer. I thinke I did receiue the letter,
but was then destitute of meanes of conveighance of an answer: since that
time liuinge in Oxford, I became acquainted with mr. Francis Kerby of
London, by reason of his sonnes beinge of the same house with mee, soe that
by his meanes, I haue opportunityes of sendinge more frequently then heeretofore. If you please to direct your letters to him (in London, at the signe of
the three pidgeons in Bishops-gate-street) I shall be sure to receiue them:
and if you please by some trusty messenger, to send my fathers ringe to him
for mee, I shall bee very thankefull to you for it. I haue much desired it for
my fathers sake, and it will be dearer to me now, then if I had first had it, in

---

[1] W. Au. 73. Samuel Fones was the son of Thomas Fones and Anne Winthrop, sister of the
Governor. He took his B.A. degree at Oxford (New Inn Hall) in 1638 and his M.A. in 1641. He
married Mary, daughter of Eleazer Dunkon, a draper of Harleston, Norfolk, and became curate of
Woodbury, Devon, from which post he was ejected in 1660. He died in 1693. Arnold G. Matthews,
Calamy Revised (Oxford, 1934), 204–205.

regard of your enioyinge it, and my receiuinge it from you, to weare it in memory of you boath. I cannot determine of my cominge to N:E: I doe confesse I earnestly desire to see you, and the rest of my neare, and deare freindes, (whom it hath pleased god in his good prouidence to place there with you:) but there are soe many hindrances to withstand my resolution, that I feare I shall not breake through them all. howeuer, I am dayly with you in desire, and make dayly mention of you in my prayers, desiringe the lord to blesse and prosper you, in your vndertakinges. I am for the most part resident at Oxford, but am at this present with my father, and mother[1] at Exeter whither your letter was sent mee. I was this last summer in Suffolke, where to my great comfort I found my Aunt Gostlin, to whom I was truely welcome: it was a great comfort to mee, to see some of my Freindes: and yet I greiued as much, when I considered what an alteration there was since my last beinge there: the house that I had soe often made my home, looked sadly as if it had mourned for the absence of its master. my father and mother kindely salute you. I thanke god for them, I haue truely found a father, and a mother in theire loue to me, and care for me; I beseech the lord to recompense them in a plentifull maner. I pray remember my duty to my Aunt, my hearty loue to my brother, and to all my cousens: and in your prayers at the throne of grace forget not Your poore nephew vnfaynedly honouringe and reueringe you

SAMUELL FONES

After my letter was written before I could send it I came to Oxford where I now am. if you send to mr. Kerbyes I shall not fayle of your letters.

OXON: Feb: this 21, 1639[/40]

GEORGE ROSE TO JOHN WINTHROP[2]

To the worshipfull and his honorable worthey Freinde a Publicke Freinde
the Church and Cuntreyes Freinde,
Mr. Winthope, Gouerner of Matetuset Beay at Boston I wish theise

My humble Dutie and Seruis with beste affection. May it please your worshipe to conceaiue that I haue Cause to simpothise with you in your extraordinarie damage as allsoe your worships soe longe Forebearance not

---

[1] The Reverend Henry Paynter and his wife, Priscilla, who was Samuel Fones's stepmother.
[2] W. 4. 99; 5 *Collections*, I. 283–284. For Rose, see 5 *Collections*, I. 283n.

in callinge to acount your vniuste stewarde beffore such extreame out Runinge   this giues mee to vnderstand you did conceaiue the man to bee honeste
allthough I knewe to the Contrarie in some parte, and that from the Comon
out Crie of the Cuntrie as thus hee and they that make noe acount what
wages the giue to mean and insoficient parties are not to Bee trusted. but
hee gaue 20s wages for Driueinge beasts from Duxburie to your Farme:
ergoe, not to be trusted   I bewaiele frome my verrie hart the passages of my
knowledge in some perteculers, but I steay heare: and take it for truth
through the good hand of our god: your worship is now soe provided as
you maie Reste well Satisfied: as brother Wright giueth mee to vnderstand.
yet I besseech you trie beffore you truste and I hope you will   for my owne
part vnworthey I ame to make cleane your shooes and soe Reste intreatinge
the lord to vphold your worship vnder soe greate and vnacusstomed triall
for whome manie doe implore the Throne of grace: and I vnworthey wretch
amongst manie fare the better for your worshipe euerrie daie I doe arise in
that our god hath giuen you a hart and a hand: a Sworde to mayntaine the
ordinances of the lord in puritie peace with power. manie maie your daies
bee with much inlargment, to be more refined with partinge with drosse
and in Conclusion to be a greate gainer by soe bad a bargain and soe all
shall worcke together for the beste to them that loue and longe for the
apeareinge of our lord Jesus Christe to yours and our Imortalitie. euen soe
be your part from the Bottom of my poore hart. Amen. yours to command:
hart purss and hand

GEORGE ROSE

MOUNT WOLLISTON this 21th of this last month 1639[/40]

Reuerend Ser yf teares would haue sealed wax mighte haue ben spared:
yours and you be blessed together and a part   manie are they that wish soe
in hart.

FRANCIS KIRBY TO JOHN WINTHROP[1]

*To the right Wor[shipfu]ll John Winthrop esquire Gouernour of the Massacusets bay
this present at Boston in New England*

LONDON this 22th of Feb: 1639[/40]

KIND SIR, Yours of the 12th of the 6 month I receiud with the inclosed to
Mr. Tindall which I sent accordingly, also I receiud yours of a later date

1 W. 3. 9; 4 *Collections*, VII. 21-22.

with a packet to Jo: Tinker which I likewise deliuerd to him, who is now
an vndertaker in a ship bound to Conecticot but will touch at the bay first
and land there some parte of her ladeinge (Deo assistante [*sic*]). this bearer
Mr. Cuttinge I suppose is freighted wholy (or for the most parte) by Mr.
Foxcrofte, the next will be Mr. Bab who will be redy about a month hence
per whom I shall write to you againe and that I thinke wilbe at least a
month before Jo: Tinker. we haue now greate hope of a parlament and we
hartily desire your praiers vnto God to direct the heart of his maiesty and
the house of parlament with one vnanimous consent to aime at Glory of
God and saftie of this kingdome. the difference between his maiesty and the
scots is not yet appeased I pray God put such an end to it as may be most
for his Glory and the Good of both kingdomes. your frends at Groton are
well as I vnderstand per Ben: Gostlin who was there lately. Thus haueinge
not else to you at this time I commit you and all yours to the protection of
the almighty and shall euer rest Your lo[ving] frend

Franc: Kirby

[*Endorsed by Governor Winthrop:*] Mr. Kirby per the Desire.

RECEIPT OF EDWARD CARLTON[1]

Received of mr. Winthrop in parte of a greater Summe twentye powndes.

Edward Carlton

(12) 24, 39[/40]

EMMANUEL DOWNING TO JOHN WINTHROP[2]

To his ever Honored brother John Winthrop Governour

Sir, I doe retorne you manie thanks for your kynde letter of the 13th of
this Instant, and doe blesse God for the continewance of health to you and
yours, and doe much reioyce in this, that the lord hath enabled you with
patience and chearfulnes to beare your burthen he knowes well what service
you haue done for his people and Churches here. he hath promised requitall
for a Cup of cold water given to any of his. I need not tell you of his riches,
ability and faythfulnes in the performance of his word and promises to the

---

[1] W. 1. 128. For Carlton, see 5 *Collections*, 1. 303*n*. This document, with the exception of the
signature, is in the handwriting of Governor Winthrop.

[2] W. 2. 28; 4 *Collections*, VI. 53.

meanest of his servants, nor of his trew and tender love vnto you, soe that I am assured he will repaire and fully repay all your losse, Costs and charges spent in his service. I pray be confident hereof and doe him that right, in being as chearfull and contented now, as when you had the world most at comand; and soe with pardon for my boldnes and faythfull service to my good sister and your selfe I rest Your assured loving brother whilest I am

EM: DOWNINGE

24. 12. 39[/40]

EDMOND FREEMAN TO JOHN WINTHROP[1]

*To the Worshipfull my very good frend Mr. John Winthrope at Boston
in the Bay deliver these*

SIR, these may pleas your worship to vnderstand that I have appointed my Son William Paddy to receue of you for the Corne which I was to haue of the last yeere. I desire you would satisfy to him for so much as I paid for yt long sins which is I think 11*li* 13*s* 4*d*. Ther was A Cow appointed by Mr. Andrewes for Mr. Williames of Providens.[2] I desire you would be pleased to send me word wheather you haue any or noe. Or mony to buy for him. I haue directiones from him to that effect that Mr. Williames may haue a Cow to keepe her for haulfe the Calfe. I the rather make bold to intreat your answer because Mr. Williames hath sentt to me often tymes abought yt. With my salutacions to you in the lord and to all thos that feere the Lord with you I take my Leaue. Your Worshipes to vse

EDMOND FREEMAN

Last moneth 25th day [1639/40]

EDWARD HOWES TO JOHN WINTHROP, JR.[3]

*To my verie louinge frind Mr. Jo: Winthrop at his house in Salem or elsewhere
in New England these deliver*

SIR, To tell you quid scribitur, quid agitur de terra ista Adamica fere incognita what I heare, what I see, what I knowe; would be as tedious for

---

[1] W. 1. 140. Edmond Freeman, who came to Massachusetts in the *Abigail* in 1635, settled first in Lynn and two years later became a freeman of New Plymouth, for which colony his brother-in-law, John Beauchamp, was an adventurer. He was one of the founders, in 1639, of the town of Sandwich. Bradford, *History of Plymouth*, II. 336.

[2] Cf. Richard Andrews to John Winthrop, July 8, 1639 (pages 129–131, above).

[3] W. 2. 170; 4 *Collections*, VI. 507–508.

you to read, as for me to write; but to tell you where I am? and what I doe; and when you shall see me, is a shorter worke. my bodie is at London, my soule in my bodie, and my mind in my soule, etc. and if you will, in mind I am and canbe euery where, while I am writing this lettre, I am with you; and what doe I? Outwardly, I am writing, inwardly I am meditatinge; and still with you and doe you aske when you shall see me, if you know not I will tell you. When you can see your selfe, or you and I all one; longe since you termed me Alter idem, and will there neuer be an vnion thinke you. because I account few words best, I haue sent you a little booke or two more by Mr. Kirbies sonne [*seven lines mutilated*] more then one, there is all goods to be found in vnitie, and all evill in duallitie and multiplicitie. Phoenix illa admiranda sola semper existit. therefore while a man and she is two, he shall neuer see her   the Arabian Philos[opher] I writt to you of, he was styled among vs Dr. Lyon, the best of all the Rosicrucians[1] that euer I mett with all, farre beyond Dr. Euer; they that are of his straine are knowing men; they pretend to liue in free light, they honor God and doe good to the people among whome they liue, and I conceiue you are in the right that they had theire Learninge from Arabia. But they come much shorte of the people that haue theire learninge from heauen, from God, from the Sonn of his Loue, such as I meane as are liuinge men, whose life and Conversation caracter-izeth them, and not theire knowledge, for 'tis written (and we beleiue) knowl-edge puffeth vp, and Loue buyldeth vp. they haue knowledge as much as any, but it is not theire essence, theire life: theire All ☉. But more of this hereafter, and for other newes I referre you to your sister Fekes [*seven lines mutilated*] What can I say more ☉ Remember my humble service to your father and mother and my louinge salutations to all your brothers and sisters, and to Signior Humfries, Mr. Rich: Saltonstall, etc. Haue with this as much loue as a man can yeild to his frind, and the Lord giue you a right vnderstanding in all things; this is and shalbe the harty prayer of Your euer louinge frind

EDWARD HOWSE

25⁰ Febr: 1639[/40]

Direct your lettres to me neere Lincolns Inn.

Coats lyned with fur [*torn*] among gent[lemen], I pray helpe me to some Otter or [*torn*] winter, as may lyne me a Coate, and I will retorne money or Bookes. Vale in Christo.

---

[1] This word is represented in the original manuscript by symbols.

EDWARD PAYNE TO JOHN WINTHROP[1]

To the Right Wor[ship]full John Winthrope Esquir deliver in Boston
New England per Mr. John Cutting whom god preserue

from LONDON this 26th of feberuary 1639[/40]

RIGHT WOR[SHIPFULL] AND MY MOST LOV[ING] FRIND MR. WINTHROP, my
Love And Best Respects remembred vnto you Sir And Allso vnto mistres
Winthrope with all the rest of your family wishing and praying for your
healthes And weallfar ass for my owne. Sir I give you much thankes for your
love and for your leater, Butt for the Otter which you seant she was lost in
coming hom for the which I ame very sory yett Sir your Love I do seatt much
by and Desir to serue you in whatt I can to my power. Sir I haue seant you
by Mr. Cutten A small token of my Love, 6 Gares of zant oyle. Sir my Request vnto you is that you wold be pleased to healp me in that busnes betwen
Mr. Eatton and me for the bill which I had of him for three hundreth pownds
vnto Mr. Adames and Mr. Gough is protested and theay will not pay Itt
And I vnderstand that Mr. Eatton is flead, so that I fear I shall loos my
monie which I haue ben long geeting with much Labor and paynes   I did
part with my monie for the good of the Cuntry and my frinds therin which
ar many. I shall not ned to inlarg much   your wor[ship] knowes what I
said   Sir Mr. valentin hill hath all my bills att boston. I shall not see you
this yeer. I do determyn to build A new ship against the next yeer And so
god willing to see you which I long to doe   I wold fayn se what this parlament will efect   Sir I haue treated with your brother About some land of
yours   he is in very good health I mean your brother Mr. Dean Tindall   he
hath paid me the 50 pownds and desires to be hartily Remembred vnto your
wor[ship] and vnto his sister   I ame to goe to se the land, etc. Sir If wee doe
Agree I shall pay part her and part in new England which by my owne ship
your wor[ship] shall farther vnderstand   in the mean tyme not to inlarg
any farther desiring your wor[ship] to be A meanes for me otherwiss I know
I shall go ner to loos that monie: Sir I wold your wor[ship] had bought all
the indigo that came vpon condicion I had ben your wor[ship's] halfe. if any
more should come if your wor[ship] pleas or any other comodities for to
deall and seand them I shall tak so much paynes ass to send you the returnes

---

[1] W. 4. 98; 5 *Collections*, I. 285–286. Captain Edward Payne was a shipmaster engaged in the
transportation of passengers to New England.

and shall desir to go halfe   thus comiting you and all yours to the good
guidanc of the lord I rest Yours to command

EDWARD PAYNE

I Desir Sir to be remembred vnto all my loving frinds in Boston and ealc
wher.

[*Endorsed by Governor Winthrop:*] Mr. Edw: Payne received per the Desire
(4) 12. 40.

JOHN TINKER TO JOHN WINTHROP[1]

To the Right Wor[shi]ppfull and his much honered Mr. Jno. Winthropp Esqr.
Go[vernou]r of the Matachuses thesse deliver in Boston N: Engl:

LOND: Febr: 26th 1639[/40]

RIGHT WOR[SHI]PPFULL, Haueing an oportunyty wherein to aquainte you
with the Lords goodnesse in our wellfare, I thought it not good to neglect
it though I haue nothing to present to your wor[shi]pp for present, but thesse
few lines, haueing effected nothing as yett eyther for the Receiueing of monys
or paying Mr. Rowe or buying of any comodytes, it beeing a very dead and
hard time for monyes generally, and like to bee a yeare in which (so farr as I
can see for the preasent) there are like to come but a small quantyty of Passengers ouer, in comparison of what hath beene formerly, and the reasone I
conceiue to be the hopes of some reformation in England by the intended parlament, the which cann hardly bee expected per judicious and wise men (by
reason of that great stroak the Prealacy haue in poynting out the Countrys
choyce of Parlament men:) but rather see trublesome times aproaching both
within and without the Kingdome. The lord teach vs to make a saintyfyed
vse of his vissitacions, and to learne righteoussnesse by all his Judgments
abroad in the World. There ware Comissioners sent from the Scotts which
after some long continuance the King vouchsafed them Audience this last
fryday being the 21th of febr: and after some discontented speeches at last
obteined Fauour to kisse the Kings hand, which was a hopefull signe of
Reconsillment but they resolue they will neuer haue more Bishopps, but I
shall not truble your wor[shi]pp farther with any discourse of news there
being so litle certeinty in any thing we heare. I haue carefully delivered all

---

[1] W. 3. 59; 4 *Collections*, VII. 220–222.

your wor[shi]pps letters: I was at Mr. Tindalls about the 11th and 12th of Jenuary at Maplested and they ware all very well blessed be God, and doe desire to be remembred to your wor[shi]pp and to my mistris with thankes for the Indian baskett she sent to Mr. Tindall. hee hath not as yet sould your wor[shi]pps Land, but doth indeauour to put it to sale, which if it be sould I doe intend according to your Wor[shi]pps apoyntment to request 100*li* or 2 to convert to your vse. I haue bene diuers times with Mr. White the Layer and he doth not as yett giue me an Answer concerning the letter your wor[shi]pp sent to him. The Otter you sent per Mr. Cutting was lost ouerbord, which Mr. Paine doth much bewaile haueing intended it a present to the King. if your wor[shi]pp could by any meanes purchasse the like againe in the Cuntry, it would be worth the adventureing once more, if possible it might be preserved to that purpusse. Mr. Harrisson doth remember his servis to your wor[shi]pp   he hath so farr obteined fauour at his Fathers hand as to haue his vsuall pention of 50*li* a yeare and his Chamber in the Temple: I heare Goodman Luxford hath charged bills of exchange vppon men in London for some hundred Pounds, of which some is for the vse of Mr. Vallentine Hill, for so much received of him there and was to be paid to Mr. Huchinson Linen draper in Cheapeside. now the partyes seeing so litle reason why he should charge any thing one them haue protested his bills, and doe think it to be litle better then a cheate. his brother allso by vertue of a letter from him did desire to take vpp some mony for him to pay in N. Engl: against which I advised some partyes he spake to, soposeing if it hadd bin your wor[shi]pps minde you would at the lest haue giuen your hand testymoniall to a matter of so great consiquence but I shall craue your wor[shi]pps pardone if I haue [done] amisse in it. I shall by Gods leaue come to the Bay a part vndertaker with Mr. Paine in the Susan and ellin. we shall intreate the Churches prayers for our safe and speedy conduct, and so with my humble servis to your wor[shi]pp and to my mistris I mekely leaue you to the Allmightys protecion and rest: your faithfull seruant to my poor abillity

JOHN TINKER

I would intreate your wor[shi]pps fauour that this leter to my mother may be conveyed by the first opertunyty for it is mater of consequence and I shall rest bound to your wor[shi]pp.

We intend to set out aboute the 20th of Aprill.

[*Endorsed by Governor Winthrop:*] Jo: Tinker Recd. per Mr. Goose (4) 6. 40.

MATTHEW CRADOCK TO JOHN WINTHROP[1]

To the Right Wor[shi]p[fu]ll Jno. Winthrop Esqr. Gouernour of Londons plantacion
in the Mattachusetts bay in New England in America deliver per the Desire of N. Engl.
Mr. Jno. Cutting whome god preserue

RIGHT WOR[SHI]P[FU]LL, My Loue and seruice presented to you   yours
of the 8 8th I haue Receiued by my Cussen Cooke by which and other
relacions I fynd my selfe still grow deep Indebted vnto you, which I wish it
lay in my power to requite. I was lateley caled vppon by mr. Mutyes Clarke
of the Counsell for answere to the Letter sent you, but I Replyed I had received none[2] and sence heard noe more thereof from him. The Writts for a
parlaiment are nowe abroad   I heare there hath beene great adoe at Westminster theise 2 dayes about there burgesses and not yeet agreed on. One
tuesday next the burgesses of London are to bee chosen beeing the 4 March.
god in mercy dyrect them and the whole kingdome in their Choise that this
parlament may produce good to the Realme, approching Euills being much
to bee Feared great preparacions are in hand against the skotts as Is doubted.
god in mercy graunt all may bee Concluded in pease. some 3 dayes past this
Inclosed was and still Contynues to bee openley sould and are exceedingley
bowght vp. In pervsing of it you will be able to Judge more   yf you shall
thinke of owght fitt to be mooued in parlament Consider seriousley of it with
the Court there to whome I pray you tender my best seruice with all dewe
Respects and vppon nottice of your desires I doubt not but to fynd meanes
to furder the same, wherein my best Indeuours shall at leastwise not bee
wanting. I ame behoulding to the Court and I harteley thanke them for
Easing me in the Cuntrey rates this last yeere.[3] Truley as I once delyuered at
a full boord at Counsell tabell, so I haue great Cause to accknowledge gods
goodness and mercy to me in Inabling me to vndergoe what I haue and doe
suffer by N. E. and as I spake then openley so I profess sincereley yf my heart
deceyue me not, I Joye more in the exspectacion of that good shall Come to
others there when I shalbee dead and gone then I greyue for my owne
Losses thowgh they haue beene verry heauey and greate seeing God hath
Inabled me to beare them; I vnderstand there Is voluntary contribucions
towrds a Colledge in Cambridge which I must Confess Is a worthey worke.
I pray your wor[shi]p bee pleased to mooue the Court to Cleere that debtt

---

[1] W. 2. 67; 4 *Collections*, VI. 128–130. For Cradock, see *D.N.B.*
[2] Cf. *Journal*, I. 300–301.
[3] Cf. *Records of Massachusetts*, I. 257.

dewe to me by the Cuntry, out of which money I ame Content and doe Freeley geeue Fyftey pounds to the sayd Colledge and for the aduansment thereof; I shall not troble you further at present but wish some serious course might be thought of howe Returnes may bee prouided whereby trade may bee Incoraged   I speake not for aney partyculer end of my owne but for the publique good and ame of opynion to cherish a Magazine for Fish to bee the oneley way by Gods assistance   The well ordering of it Is all and noe better meanes I thinke then that some beginning bee made without exspectacion of present proffitt oneley that the Fishermen may be assured the Fish shalbee taken of there hands as Fast as they take it. this by degrees will drawe Fishermen to plant themselues there and some must bee dealt withall to begin to plant and to haue incoragment herein but I submit to grauer Judgments of your selfe and those there who are better able to Judge what may bee done next heerevnto pipestaues if the tymber be fytt when well sesened would be thought vppon. I Craue Leaue and with tender of my seruice and best Respects shall euer Rest Your wor[shi]ps to be Comaunded

Mathew Cradock

London 27 Febr. 1639[/40]

Remember my loue I hartely pray you to mr. Downing   I doubt I shall not haue leisure to write him herewith   my selfe wiffe and mother desire to be Remembred to your selfe and mrs. Winthrop.

[*Endorsed by Governor Winthrop:*] Mr. Cradocke Recd. per the Desire   Resp. per the Desire.

JOHN WINTHROP TO EZEKIEL ROGERS[1]

Rev[eren]d and Deare Sir, I received your lovinge Lettre, for which and all other fruits of your Love I kindly thanke you, especially for your prayers, which (I hope) shall not be lost vpon me. mr. Nelson and mr. Carlton have been with me, and I have given them what satisfaction I can for the present: I prayse God, it dothe not greive me to departe with any thinge, to pay my debts. yet there is somethinge troubles me a little, that some of my Christian frends should take advantage of my servants vnfaithfullnesse, to gett suche bargaines, as some of them have (vpon better con-

[1] W. 1. 146; *L. and L.*, ii. 419–420.

sideration) been sorrye for, and have released them, and withall holpen to ease my burden, by lendinge me freely: but others call strictly and hastyly for the like, which thoughe I looke at it as an Iniury yet I have not complained of it to any, nor doe I intende to doe, being perswaded that they are suche as doe abhorre all oppressinge practizes, (thoughe a good man may steppe aside that waye vnawares especially in N: E:) and knowinge your wisdome and integritye, I will make you Iudge in the case: it may be you will not meet with the like (all circumstances weyed) and thus it stands: some of them let my servant have monye, without my desire or privitye, till they come to me for their security and they acquaint me with it in suche manner, as I could apprehende no other, but that they lent it freely to doe me a Courtesye; (havinge then no present occasion to make vse of it themselves) so now they have engaged me to requite this kindnesse some other waye, but withall, they privately contracte with my servant, for large interest, and take a bill of him for deliuery of so muche Corne at an vnder rate, but no mention for what Consideration: nor was I ever like to have knowne it either from them or from my servant, had not a stranger (greivinge (as he sayd) to see how my estate went awaye) given me notice thereof, lately, wherevpon I examined my servant, who then confessed it to me: otherwise I had payd interest for mony, and yet been engaged to them for that, which it seemes now they lent for their owne advantage: for why would they not els have acquainted me with the Interest as well as the principall? except they held it either not to be so lawfull, or not of so good reporte to take interest, as to lende monye. thus my Corne that I had provided for the food of my famyly is sould awaye without my privitye (thoughe I was neere enoughe to have been spoken with) some at 2s the bushell vnder the market, some 12d some more some lesse, whereas if they had tould me when they tooke securitye for their mony, that I must have payd suche rates for it, I could have served my occasions otherwise, and could as well have made vse of my frends or other means then for 2 or 300li as I am forced now to doe to paye their principall and vse withall: Now thoughe my purpose be (God inablinge me) to satisfie all so fast as I can raise mony and provide Corne, yet I thinke it but reasonable that suche as have bargained for Corne at such vnder rates, should staye till others (whose bargains are more equall) be first satisfied, so I leaue this matter to yourselfe to iudge off. For your owne debt, I suppose you intended me a Courtesye in offeringe to accept a heifer for your 2 Calves and 4li and accordingly I desired mr. Carlton to choose one for you: and I thinke if you value your Calves viz: a Bull and Cowe Calfe of a weeke old at 5 or 6li (which is the most they can be worth) and my heifer (as I sould her fellowes before winter) at 13*li* you will finde yourselfe mistaken, but that is a small matter between yourselfe and me.

[JOHN WINTHROP]

[*Ca.* March, 1639/40]

[*Endorsed by Governor Winthrop:*] To mr. Ez: Rogers not sent.

EMMANUEL DOWNING TO JOHN WINTHROP[1]

SIR, I thanke you for your loving letter and doe blesse God for peace and health to you and yours: I am confident you having spent your selfe and estate in this ho[noura]ble service; that yt will redounde to your greater creditt and honour with God and man, then if you had gayned riches as other Governours doe both in Virginea and elswhere, and yt will rise vp in Judgement against extorting Governours that shalbe sett over the people in succeeding generations, when your selfe shalbe at rest reaping the fruits of your present labours;

The noate that Edr. Dillingham gave you, I never saw yt. I pray therefore take his affid[avit]. yt had ben done here if wee could haue mett with mr. Endicott, who is much trobled with a Cough and Cold and cannot be at this Court. He rem[em]bereth his trew love and service to your selfe and my sister.

I cannot leave my wife now to attend Dillinghams buisines and I feare if I should haue ben there, the tryall would be putt of with one devise or other because I did not serve mr. Saltonstall and his partner to the Court. If he can he will keepe Dillingham from you. I pray keepe the affidavit or send yt me for I can depose he would haue sworne to yt if wee could haue founde mr. Endicott. Yeasterday my wife was in a feavor, this day shee is pretyly well; so with my service to your selfe my sister and all yours I rest Your verie loving bro[ther]

EM: DOWNINGE

2. 1. 39[/40]

[1] W. 2. 28; 4 *Collections*, VI. 53–54.

THOMAS GOSTLIN TO JOHN WINTHROP[1]

To the right worshipfull his very Loving and much respected Brother
John Winthrop Esqr. at his house in Boston this present in niw England

MOST LOVING BROTHER, I receyved yours bearing date the 1 octo: wheareby I perceiue that myne had much distasted you (which much greeved me) to thinke that you should so misconstuer my meaning and to conceyve the worst of me in all things for for my owne parte I never questioned your loue or conceyved ill of you but allways accounted you my Cheifest freind and still doe howsoever you conceyve of me   neyther can I tell why you should conceyve me to be resolued never to see N: E: I am suer it haue allwayes beene and still is my desyer and should think my selfe happy to inioye both yours and others sweete sosietie whom I truly and dearely loue   neyther to my knowledg did I ever Charge you with vnkindenesse or offended with you for not taking off sum of my Children but only thought that God had not apoynted my cominge thether because I Could never finde an opertunitie to send any of my Childrin (hauing many) beforehand, having much de-syered it. I must confess your last but one did much trouble me. whearfor neglecting, once writing to you, you censored me to be alltogether regardles of you and one that was alltogether taken up with the world and therfor would (as I conceyved) leve me to the world which did much greeue me neyther did we ever doubt of our owne or our Childrins wellcom to you for yf ever we could haue found an opertunite fitting we had exercised your loue therin   neyther have we so set vp our rest in ould En: but yf it would please God to make a waye for vs we should be as glad to intertayne such an oper-tunitie as ever we weare of any   and yet to deale playnely ther is something that hath and still doeth much discoureg me and that is in keepeing diuers from being of your congrigation and such as be of good iudgment and con-versation (as we have relation) and not admitting ther yong Children the sacrement of habtisme seing Christ would not haue such forbidden to be brought to him. and grant that the Father and mother be not beleevers (and yet desyer to haue ther Children babtized) happely it may be that the Grand-father or Grandmother or ther predecessors maye have beene beleevers. then are not such the seede vnto whome the Couenant apperteine or belonge? I desyer herein to be satisfied. for I will assuer you rather would I liue with breade and water wheare I am (inioying that meanes I yet doe) then to liue elsewheare delissiousely not being admitted in to the Congregation and com-

---

[1] W. 1. 134. Thomas Gostlin, a Suffolk clothier, married Jane Winthrop, the Governor's sister.

munion of saynts. I thanke our good lord I yet liue vnder a faythfull minister
one that faythfully labours and earnestly desyers to enlarge his masters kingdome   the Lord giue vs grace to bring forth frute in some measuer answar-
able to that cost he hath bestowed vpon vs that when our change shall be
we maye be counted worthy through Christ Jesus to reigne with God for
ever more for the attayning wheareof we humbly and earnestly intreate you
to solicite the Lord for vs That he would lead and gide vs by his counsell
untill he bringe vs to glory. And now my deare and loving Brother I hartely
thanke you for all your loue shewed to me and mine, and am hartely sory
you should conceiue or once think that we should slight your good will which
I allwayes highly prised and doe earnestly still desyer to haue it and that at
any time you shall heare any ill of vs spare not to admonish vs or to quicken
vs vp in the waies of holynes (for I confesse we are too remisse therin the Lord
forgiue vs) for I acknowledge the reproofe of a freind is better then the kisse
of an enemie and hope we shall be willing to lissin to good counsayle at all
times   and seeing you would not haue vs scrupulous in frequenting your
loue or acquainting you with what you might doe vs good you shall vnderstand that we have a greate desyer to send you your godson our Sonn John
to be imployed by you and indeed we had sent him now but for want of
meanes (for we weare never worse for monyes then now for I know not well
what shift to make.   formerly I had Freinds heere as your selfe and brother
Downing who haue lent me 50*li* at a time but now haue none so to pleasuer
me   I thanke God for it I haue good store of good Corne but monyes being
scarse and Corne plentifull it will now yeald me noe mony to speake of   I
haue oft wished J. and our selues with you but wishes and teares haue both
one propertie they shew ther loue but want the remedye)   and to deale
truly with you it is that that have beene the only cause of our staying   I
have wished a hundred times that I had gone with my Sister Winthrop for
I see the longer the worser but formerly my wife was very backward when
we might better have gone and now having less means and more Charge
she is very desierous of goeing   I praye God direct vs and giue vs grace to
submit to his blessed will in all things   heer have bin and still are troubell-
some times the Lord helpe vs   heere is now in all likelyhood to be a parle-
ment   I praye God prosper it and cause some good efect by it otherwise I
see nothing but all wilbe nought but the Lord can doe what it pleaseth him
the Lord giue vs fayth to rely wholy vpon him and allwayes to stand vpon
our watch that come lyfe come death Christ maye be to vs advantage   I
praie remember our best respects to our good Sister your wife and to my
Cozen John and his wife and I praye excuse me for not writing to him and

tell him yf I could as easely wright to him as he can to me he should have twoe for one but never was Beare draune to stake with more vnwillingness than I to wrighting of letters whear it not so I would wery you with letters and never vndergoe any more such censures for that Commend me allso to my Cosen Pheakes and tell her she haue still an Ante in ould E: though I think she haue quite forgotten her for she promised that she would wright and we should haue all the nuse from her but I am suer it is longe when it come I hope it wilbe large for as yet we never had one word from her remember our loue to my Cosen Dudly and his wife and I praye tell her as much also Commend vs allso to Stephen Addam Deane Samuell and all the rest of our Cosens and freinds and thus with our kinde salutations to your selfe we leve you to the good blissing of God and ever remayne your assured loving brother

THO: GOSTLIN

GROTON martch 2, 1639[/40]

The wid[ow] Grigly remembers her sarvis to you and desyers to heare how her children doe I pray when you write let vs heare of them.

[*Endorsed by Governor Winthrop:*] Bro: Gostlin (4) 6, 40.

NEHEMIAH BOURNE TO JOHN WINTHROP[1]

To the Right Worthie Mr. John Winthropp Gouernour of the Mattachusetts Baye these present in Boston

RIGHT WOR[SHI]PP[FU]LL AND MY VERY MUCH HONOURED FREIND, After my due respects presented to your selfe, and vertuous wife: hauing so fitt an opertunity, and being ingaged by so many obligations therunto I cannot omitt, but do make bold to present these few rude lines vnto yow: wishing all increase of grace and peace with all the fruites of righteousnes which are by Jesus Christ to the praise and glory of god, and humbly intreating the lord to double his Spiritt vpon yow, according to the greate importance of your imployments and affaires; with muche prosperity, and long dayes; to his glory, and the Comfort and rejoicing of that greate people you are intrusted with: I am att present in health and so haue bin since my departure, through the riche mercy of our god; but haue looked many times toward that good

---

[1] W. 3. 79; 4 *Collections*, VII. 300–301.

land, and not altogether without some breathings and longings, after those pretious liberties once injoyed (though uery vnproffitably)   truly sir my thoughts are sadned to recount them, and what little improuement I made: but I hope this long abstinence will make me sett a higher price vpon New England then euer   Its deploreable to se what we are forced to behold: Concerning Newes: att present there is little but what you haue heard (I suppose) ere now: as touching the Spanish Armado, of which I made bold to aduise yow formerly from Dartmouth: Concerning the Scotts: here is great preparation for warr, and is out of doubt against them notwithstanding the parlament which is like to proceed the 13th of the next Month, which makes many wise men stand not knowing what to iudge of things: and att present I think mens hearts are shaken more then euer notwithstanding the parlament. many that haue kept themselues fast in their ingagements waiting and hooping for a good issue of this great desighne that would now willingly disingage themselues, but cannot: the times that are approaching threaten heauy and sad things: the good lord be intreated to thinke vpon his poor people that yett apprehend it not: If god giue an opertunity I shal speake more att large: in the mean time I thinke it behooues al the lords people to double their duty and improue all the interest they haue in heauen for this poore land. I haue made bold to appoint my wife to wait vpon your wor[shi]pp about Eatons buisnes if she need: Thus not to be ouer bold and tedious: with my desire to present my seruice to Mr. John Winthropp and Mr. Stephen, To Mr. Cotton and Mr. Wilson humbly intreating your prayers and the continuance of your remembrances att the Throan of grace for vs as we haue greate need; in regard of that we meet withal within, and from without: with harty thanks for all your former loue and Respects I comend you to god who is the great Councellor and to our lord Jesus who is the great Sheepheard of his Flocke, and humb[l]y take my leaue and rest Your Wor[shi]pps most Obliged in all Duty

NEHEMIAH BOURNE

LONDON 4th 1st Mo. 1639[/40]

[*Endorsed by Governor Winthrop:*] Mr. Bourne per Mr. Goose.[1]

---

[1] The following paragraph, in a different hand, is written on the verso of Bourne's letter and seems to have no connection with it: "That which I can testifie is that ther was a plaine bargan for ought I could see for Mr. Bridges bid him to fetch the money and one to cary it away; the Reason as I conceive that hee sold it to Mrs. Hudsons was because Mr. Canes man brought not the money beefore Mr. Bridges had presant ocation to goe out of the towne and told him soe."

EZEKIEL ROGERS TO JOHN WINTHROP[1]

To our honoured Gouernour John Winthorpe Esqr. at Boston, these present

R[IGHT] WORTHY SIR, I humbly thanke you, as for your care to answere the necessityes of my neighbours, so for your plaine dealings with my selfe, in expressing how you conceiue concerning my due from you; which is both gentlemanlike and christian; and therby I knowe how to satisfy you.

Now therfore for my bargaine about the Cowes, it was as reall as I coulde make it; and all the mony paide by Mr. Nelson or myselfe, a good time before I was to haue the cowes deliuered. They were to be very good ones and two calues that were to come in Jan. or Febr. My neighbours that then had calues, will not now take 10*li* a peece for them, and therfore my right and due was to haue as good, and not to be disaduantaged by my long stay and suspense. Neither therfore did I mistake my selfe in the moderate demande of a heifer; and addition of the 4*li*. I also thinke it requisite that in a worde, I doe lett you knowe that the young Cowes I had were not such as your man intended me; and I persuade myselfe he was then reall, therfore I pardon and pitty him. Besides the goates were bad (diuers of them) in comparison of what we bargained for. And one of the oxen I bought, had some blowe or hurt aboue the vpper iawe, which since groweth in a great wenne, and it is feared, it may kill him, swelling now vp to the ey. These things I was loth to trouble you with before; but now thinke it fitt you should knowe, that I am a looser by him. Yet I am very well satisfyed with the young heifer, and doe most earnestly and dayly begge of God, that you may haue cause to say, It was good for me that I was afflicted.

Sir, there is one thing that is a newe trouble to vs; though the Court doe giue vs but three miles of the eight, that we go into the Country, yet we heare that some woulde take somwhat of from that. It seemeth they thinke vs very vnworthy neighbours. But I made knowne my minde to your selfe; of whose worth I doubt not. And for any other, they shall knowe that in a iust cause, I will not be afraide to pleade the right of my suffering neighbours, God assisting vs. To whom (with my seruice to yourselfe and worthy companion) I committ you and your affaires, and rest Yours in Chr[ist] to be commanded

EZ. ROGERS

ROWLEY, this 4th of the 1, 1639[/40]

---

[1] W. 3. 56; 4 *Collections*, VII. 211–212.

Sir, The mony that Mr. Nelson paide for me to your man, was that I lent him, when he coulde gett none of your man for this vse.

I craue pardon, if you thinke me earnest, in the matter of those that would depriue vs of our measure of lande; because I thinke such doe very little compassionate our many losses and tryalls.

BENJAMIN GOSTLIN TO JOHN WINTHROP[1]

To the wor[shi]p[fu]ll his Lovinge Vncle mr. Jno. Winthropp
giue this in Newe England

from LONDON this 6th March 1639[/40]

MOST LOVING VNCLE, I Reced your loving letter for the which I thanke you and likewise for your good Counsell which I desire of God grace to followe   I am hartely gladd to heare of your well being and your hopefull procedings and earnestly desire of god to goe alonge with you and direct you in all your enterprises that you may doe nothing but what may tend to gods glory and the good of the plantation which per gods appoyntement you haue bin Called vnto that when ther shall be a period putt to your dayes you may inioy the happines which is laide vp for gods servants. Remember my kinde love to my Ante Winthrop and to all my Cosens in generall   I shold be verry gladd of some good Occation to come to Newe England that I might inioy your sweete sosiety which once I did but then was not Capable of but as yett I am in soe good imployment and in so hopefull a waye that I shold be much blameable if I shold thrust my selfe oute of it   I shold be verry glad to Rece[ive] a letter from you if you wold doe so much as wright to me and send it per mr. Midleton for I Know he will Conveye it to me onely Direct it to Ben: Gostlin Aborde the shipp Henry Bonadv[entu]r[e] at Leghorne or elce where   I haue a Jarr or 2 of good Oyle which I doe intende to send per James Brocke which is all that I haue for you at presant yett I wold intreate you to accept as my love   I am now bownde for Rushia and from thence to Leghorne   I haue bin at home these six months for trading haue bin verry dead and is still   I thinke that ther will be but fewe passengers Come ouer this yeare being in hope of soome good vent of this parliament which is now towards which I desire god may not be frustrated but if this shold not take effect to my Knowledg ther will come Abondance the next Spring. Ald

[1] W. I. 132. Benjamin Gostlin, a sea captain, was the son of Thomas Gostlin and Jane Winthrop, sister of Governor Winthrop. See Joseph J. Muskett, *Evidences of the Winthrops of Groton* (1894–1896), 92–94.

Some and mr. Craddocke[1] are Chosen Burgesses for the City   I know not as yett whoe is Chosen for Suffolke but I thinke Sir Nathaniell Bampston[2] will be one   I haue nothing elce worth trobling you with all   I bles god we are all in good helth and thus in hast I Comitt you to the protection of the Almighty desiring you to Remember me in your Prayers your trewe Loving Nephewe

BEN: GOSTLIN

[*Endorsed by Governor Winthrop:*] Cosin B: Gostlin to be answ: by mr. middleton.

STATEMENT OF ROBERT PENOYER[3]

(1) 12. 39[/40]. Inter mr. Cradock and wm. Bartlett

Robert Penoyre sayd that Wm. Bartlett was lame and not able to doe any thinge for about 6 weeks, but after that he did goe forth and helpe to work but could not doe as formerly: and further he sayth that his brother did helpe him with some diet, as a cheese of about 20 li. and some Biskett, because he might not eate of the full diett of the famylye.

SIR NATHANIEL BARNARDISTON TO JOHN WINTHROP[4]

To my Honored and assured loving freind John Winthrop esqr. gouernor
in New England present these

DEARE BROTHER AND INTIRELY BELOUED, I receaued two letters from you the last returne: at that tyme it pleased the Lord to visit me with a great and long sicknes, to the great hasard of my life, but it pleased the Father of Mercies and God of all Consolations to heare prayres, and to rayse me from the gates of the graue, and to lend me (most vnworthy) sume longer tyme the better to fitt my selfe for Hym, and to try how farr that correction would worke my vnruly and poluted hart to better obedience, and frame it to improue the remaining talant of my tyme in the glorifiing of Hys name, and advan[c]ement of His Honor, for which I euer desyre I may acknowledg

[1] Thomas Soame and Matthew Cradock.
[2] Nathaniel Barnardiston. See his letter to Winthrop, March 15, 1639/40 (pages 217–218, below).
[3] W. I. 128. This document is in the handwriting of Governor Winthrop. For Penoyer, see Savage, *Genealogical Dictionary*, III. 390–391.
[4] Original not located; 4 *Collections*, VI. 547–548. For Barnardiston, see *D.N.B.*

with all thankfullnes, and bless and prayse His abundant free grace and goodnes to me, and provocke all that know and affect me to ioyne in assisting and helping me in the same, which I humbly craue of you with confidence and assurance. And now the Lord hath put me vpon a tryall, by caling of me, with Sir Phillip Parker, (alltogether vnsought for) to serue for my countrey in the Parlament which is to begin the 13th of Aprill next. I haue nothing to supporte me in this great busines, being contious to my self of my most vnfitnes euery way, but the allsuffitience of Hym that caled me cann inable me, who deliteth to manifest His powre by contemtable and weake meanes. His couenant and cale is the only supporter of my fayth hear in. Help, I beseech you, Sir, with all the might and force you can make, this great work; which if it suckseed not well, is like to proue exeding perrelous and dangerous to this church and kingdome. Now we see and feele how much we are weakned by the loss of those that are gonn from vs, who should haue stood in the gapp, and haue wrought and wrasled mightely in this great busines. My neighbor Mr. Pepis desyreth me to present his loue to you. We both thanke you for your loue to his sonnes. I know not yet how the Lord will dispose of me. This parlament will beget a resolution in vs, but I fear; I could wish sume of you wear hear before it endeth. Mr. Waldegraue soiorneth with me. I forget not you in your apoynted tyme. I doubt not but you doe the like for vs. The Lord hath made me a grandfather by my daughter. My son is yet a single man. I often consceaue in my sleep that I am with you. My self and wife salute you and Mrs. Wintrope with our best affectiones, beseeching the Lord to prosper you all in all your vndertakinges to His glorey. Salut in the Lord all our dear frindes with you, as if I named them in perticular. So resteth Your most assured loving frend and brother

NATH. BARNARDISTON

KETTON, March 15th 1639[/40]

[*Endorsed by Governor Winthrop:*] Sir Nath: Barnardiston. Resp. per the Sparrow, J. Bradshawe etc.

SIR FERDINANDO GORGES TO JOHN WINTHROP[1]

To the Wo[rshipfu]ll and my much respected frend John Wintrupp Esqr. at Boston
in the Bay these present

WORTHY SIR, The soddain approach of our longe wished for Parlament inuites me to attend the happy issue therof, that otherwise had a Resolution to haue visited you this Springe, but I haue sent a neer kinsman[2] of mine own name with other necessary Seruants for the better orderinge of my affaires, and makinge of my prouision agaynst the time it shall please God I come my selfe. In the mean while I am bould to intreat of you to second this my Cosen Gorges in any Just and reasonable occasion he shall haue cause to vse your fauour in, I hauinge giuen him Command to be carefull to doe his best that all fayr Corrospondency be maintayned between those two seuerall Plantations, as a speciall means by Gods fauour to giue furtherance to the happiness therof, and when God shall be pleased that I may arriue I doubt not but you shall perceaue my greatest Ambition shall tend (next to the seruice of God) by what wayes or means an vnion or Conformity of all parties may be established, or at the least a patient or charitable bearinge with each others Errors or selfe Affexions, that soe our Soverainge L[or]d the Kinge may be ashewred of our subiections, the publique be not disturbed the common course of Justice made free, and the countries defenses prouided for, which worke beinge finished I shall willingly commend my selfe ready to giue an account of all my Actions to him that is only able to forgiue all our offenses and giues vs ashewrances of his mercies through the sufferances of his blessed son our only sauiour Jesus Christ to whose sacred and gracious assistance I commend you and all your Endeuours, and to whom I wish as becommeth Your very louinge frend

FERDE. GORGES

ASHTON March 26, 1640

[*Endorsed:*] Sir Ferdinand Gorges Resp. per the Desire.

---

[1] W. Au. 103; 4 *Collections*, VII. 331–332. For Gorges, see *D.N.B.*; 4 *Collections*, VII. 329*n.*

[2] Thomas Gorges, who arrived in Boston in the summer of 1640 with a commission for the government of the province of New Somersetshire. *Journal*, II. 8.

LAWRENCE WRIGHT TO JOHN WINTHROP[1]

To my verie loueing Cosen Mr. Jo: Winthrop the Elder in New England
These deliver

26 March 1640

SIR, I thanke you for your kind entercourse of lettres; I pray continue it: I haue placed the lame man you recommended in Bartholmeus hospitall, wher he remayned vntill now, with some aduantage in his strenght, able to stand not to goe. I haue now recommended him to an Hospitall at the bath, wher he hath hope of farther cure. Wee are now neere our parliament. For the most part good men are chosen in euery place for that imployment. Our King vppon his own charge prouides for warr thirty Thowsand foote and 7 or 8 thowsand horse We say against the Scotts; but we know not: a few monthes will discouer: the Scottish Comissioners or petioners are yet heare; some say Episcopacie is the great controuersie others say more then that otherwise ther would be no warr and some thinke all will end for the good of both countries; but we pray to god almighty who only knowes: to whose prouidenc I recommend you and yours as your loueing Kinsman

L. WRIGHT

My wife remembreth hir loue etc.

I prayse God my selfe and child liue and are in health and do hope he may liue to see better tymes in this Kingdome. I pray remember vs in your prayers. according to my weake measure I do you and yours.

[*Endorsed by Governor Winthrop:*] Dr. Wright Resp. per the S[p]arrow.

JOHN VENN TO JOHN WINTHROP[2]

To the Wor[shi]p[full] his much respected friend Mr. Jo: Wynthrop Gouernour of new
England present these att Boston

WOR[SHI]P[FU]LL AND WELBELOUED IN THE LORD JESUS CHRIST, havinge this oportunitie I could not omitt (by my Christian neighbour) to be preasent with you in a few lynes, acknowledginge with thankfullnes yours, now longe

---

[1] W. 3. 107; 4 *Collections*, VII. 390–391. For Wright, see *D.N.B.* Wright's relationship to Governor Winthrop came through his marriage to Mary Duke, second cousin of the Governor. Muskett, *Evidences of the Winthrops of Groton*, 82.

[2] W. 4. 100; 5 *Collections*, I. 288–289. For Venn, see *D.N.B.*

since receaued, wherin you expresse the affections of the whole plantion vnto our present Condition, and we are fullie perswaded of your Loue and the Contynuance theireof, for we know what is true is lastinge, and we stand in need of your stronge Cryes vnto the Lord both in regard of Church and Comonwealth   I shall not need to incist on particulers, those whom god now sends to you, are able at large to relate our Condition. the Lord fitt vs for euill dayes, and our last Change. its true we are not yett come to open and common sufferings, but yet our burdens within and without are manie, the Lord help vs to beare them, or in his tyme deliuer vs out of them. I pray that as we desire to pray and especiallie to prayse god for you, so you would be intreated to remember vs in a speciall manner to god againe: God hath caled a parlamente appointed to beginne the 13th of this Instant, how longe it will contynew we are not worthy to know, nor what it will bringe forth; we are full of feares, and haue little ground of Comfort or hope of Good, saue onlie in the Lord, that is the fowntayne of all happines and giuer of euerie good, yea he can bringe good out of euill. greate preparations we haue for warr voted to be against the Scotts, but lookinge on the manner of its goeinge on with other things that doe adhere, makes vs all stand amazed. here are 4 Comiss[ione]rs from Scotland that wayte his Ma[jes]ties pleasure, but after often hearings are not dispatched. here is on greate Don come from Spayne: annother greater is landed at Plimouth   Some proiect is in agitation which tyme must discouer   good from them we cannot exspect: I must now conclude   I desire with all hartie affections to be remembred to your wor-[shi]p and to all our brethren with you, and doe remayne Your Wor[shi]ps to comand

JOHN VENN

[April, 1640]

[*Endorsed by Governor Winthrop:*] Capt. Venne Resp. per the Sparrow.

NATHANIEL WARD TO JOHN WINTHROP[1]

To the Wor[shipfu]ll our Gouernour att Boston

SIR, We are bold to continue our suite concerning the plantation I lately mencioned to yow. our company increases apace from diuers townes, of very desirable men wherof we desire to be very choise. this next weke if God

---

[1] W. 3. 11; 4 *Collections*, VII. 28.

hinder vs not we purpose to view the places and forthwith to resort to yow[1]
and in the meane tyme we craue your secrecy and rest Your Worships

NA: WARDE

[*Ca.* April, 1640]

We haue already more then 20 families of very good Christians purposed
to goe with vs if God will and we heare of more.

Our neighbour Townes are much greiued to see the lauish liberality of
the Court in giving away the Countrye. some honest men of our towne
affirme that in their knowledge there are 68 townes in England within as
litle compasse as the bounds of Ipswich: I knowe neere 40 where I dwelt:
Rowly is larger then Ipswich 9 or 10 miles longe and will haue other plantations within it tributaries to it and intend as we heare to stretch their wings
much further yet and will spoile Qutcthicqute vtterly if not Pentucket. We
earnestly pray yow to prevent it. We should incourage many to come ouer
if many plantations were not spoiled by the extreame largnes of those that
are already giuen   our purpose is to haue no great bands.

NATHANIEL LUFKIN TO JOHN WINTHROP[2]

To the Right Wor[shi]pp[full] and Worthy Mr. John Winthrop the Elder now or late
Governour in new England giue theise with hast at his house at Boston
in Mathechuset Bay

WORTHY SIR, My best observance and respect premised. Though I am
vnknowne to you, yet I am bold to wright a few lines vnto you in the behalfe
of a poore kinsewoman of mine whoe cometh with the Bearer herof to new
England a servant vnto him by couenaunt for some yeares. Soe It is, that
there is one Thomas Blower who now liveth (as I heare) at Boston in new
England where your Wor[shi]pp dwell: This Thomas Blower oweth mee
twenty fower pounds of currant English mony. I hope the man hath soe much
honesty in him that hee will not denye it. Suer I am that hee often protested
while hee was in England that hee was more ashamed of my debt then of any
els: but if hee should soe farr forgett himselfe as to denye it (which I am far
enough from iudgeing of him) there is one Edmund Rice and Henry Bruning

---

[1] Giles Firmin, in his letter to Governor Winthrop, February 12, 1639/40, says that "some of
vs will veiw Pentuckett [Haverhill] in the Springe." The petition for the grant of land for the new
settlement came up before the General Court in May, 1640. *Records of Massachusetts*, I. 290.

[2] W. 4. 100; 5 *Collections*, I. 286–287.

whom this Bearer knowes well whoe can tell of this debt as well as my selfe, and will, (I am confident) bee ready to testifie their knowledg herein, If cause shall require: Now my humble desire vnto your worship is that you would stand my kinsewomans friend in this matter. I doe intend to make her M[aste]r a Letter of Attorny to receiue the debt for her vse: to whome I doe freely giue it. I hope if your Worshipp doe but speake with the sayd Thomas Blower hee will pay the mony without farther troble: if not my humble desire is that the Bearer hereof may haue the benifitt of a faier way in lawe according to the orders of new England for the recouery of the same. I am bold with your Wor[shi]pp being a stranger peradventure more then I should, but knoweing your pious disposition and that you are a true friend to Justice and equity and a hater of the contrary I haue presumed this farr what favour you shall shew vnto my kinswoman herein whose name is Mary Tompson my Sisters daughter I am confident though shee bee never able to requite yet shee will remember it with thankefulnes even vnto the ende, and I for my part shall euer bee bound vnto you in any service that lyes in mee for the same. Thus being heartily gladd with a very great number here in England to heare of your Worshipps prosperity and of the prosperity of the church and commonwealth in new England I humbly take my leaue, comending your worshipp and all yours to the gratious protection of our good God alwayes ours in Christ Jesus, And rest At your Worshipps service

NATHANIELL LUFFKIN

from my house at HITCHAM in Suffolke, this 1 of Aprill 1640

JOHN TINKER TO JOHN WINTHROP[1]

To the Right Wor[shi]ppffull and his much honnered Mr: Jno: Winthropp Esqr: Go[vernou]r of the Matachuses, these deliver At Boston in N: Engl:

LOND: Aprell 13th 1640

RIGHT WOR[SHI]PPFFULL, Though my occations are not many to wright vnto you, I thinke it my bounden duty to neglect no opertunyty to present my servis. I did thinke I should haue presented my persone beffore thesse lines before your wor[shi]pp, but such sadd and dangerous times as nowe are in England, will occation our demourage beyound our time Appoynted: I writ your wor[shi]pp word per Mr. Goosse that I had joyned with Mr.

[1] W. 3. 59; 4 *Collections*, VII. 223–225.

Paine a part vndertaker in the susan and ellin, and our intentions ware to haue set forth the 25th of Aprell, but I feare it wilbe mid may beffore wee shall gett of: passengers and frait coming in very slowly, partly staying to see what the ishue of the Parlament wilbe, and partly becaues of the dead marketts men haue for the puting of of theire estates: all which expence of time and monyes I feare wilbe to me a great losse rather then a gaine, yett I desire to submit my selfe to the good prouidence of the Lord to deale with me as it pleaseth him, and to rest satisfyed if hee shall only carray mee through all thesse cares and paines and set me downe in the place and con-dicion whence he tooke me vpp: presumeing if I should faile of prosperity in this pressent way for my advansment I shall finde exeptance with your wor-[shi]pp as formerly: I haue effected nothing as yet for you, eyther for the paying of Mr. Rowe or the buying of comodytys according to your appoint-ment, there is soe litle mony stiring to be exc[h]anged for the Plantacion and soe many hands to catch for it, that there is noe hopes of obteineing any in that way, nor of Mr. White the Layer in whitefryers it being dispossed of some other way: only I heare that Mr. Tindall is vppon salle of your wor-[shi]pps land, by whome my last hoppes is to be fur[n]ished with what is requisite. I doe heare a dayly complainte of Goodman Luxford vppon the Exchange for charging bills vppon men for the payment of great somes of mony heare for soe much taken vpp there of some new comers ouer for your wor[shi]pps vsse, which doth apere to men of vnderstanding to haue an ill face of deceipt, the men to [w]home he sends being such as he neuer had deallings with for a peny, nor doe se any reason why he should charge any such bills vppon them eyther in your wor[shi]pps or his owne name. I speak not any thing out of preiudice to the man but to informe your wor[shi]pp of what is related to me being tender of your detryment per any such vnfaith-fullnesse of which you may be ignorant: and that it may appeere it is noe groundlesse asspercion I shall indeauour eyther in this leter or at my coming, to shew your wor[shi]p the coppys of his bills vnder their hands to whome they ware sent, but I only whisper this to your wor[shi]pp intreating (if he proue himselfe an onest man) it may not come to his heareing as from me least he be insenced against me, if otherwise it is a timely warning to your wor[shi]pps preuenting what euells may ensue: I omit to wright of any nuse soposseing your wor[shi]pp will haue it plentyfully by word of mouth: Mr. Kerby haueing a sonn in this shipp the William and George with Mr. Babb: only this, this preasant day the 13th of Aprell is the first day of the Parlament and I heare the first request the King doth make in his speech to shew the ocation of meeting, is to require ayde against the Scotch faction, pretending to make it apeer they intend rebellyon against the King, the which with many other passeges, both seene and heard of, doth make vs feare sadd times. the lord fitt vs to suffer and stirr vpp the harts of you in generall and particuler to importune him at the throwne of his grace for a preuencion from, or deliuerance out of those iud[g]ments we dayly expect: and soe for the p[resen]tts I leaue your wor[shi]pp to the lord and the power of his grace who is able to saue our soules to the day of his coming, and with my humble seruis to you and to my m[ist]ris desire euer to rest Your Wor[shi]pps Faithfull servant to my poore power

JOHN TINKER

EMMANUEL DOWNING TO JOHN WINTHROP[1]

To his Hon[oura]ble brother John Winthrop Governour

SIR, I praise God my wife had a good day to retorne home, but yeasterday shee was as ill. last night shee slept prety well, and is chearly this morning. The Good lord open our eares to heare his rod speaking vnto vs;

I thanke you hartily for the spade; Daniell playd the foole to aske yt, having enough to serve our tornes, yt was putt a shore, but in theire hast coming home, I suppose tis lost, for I cannot heare of yt.

I haue not yet had tyme to speake with my wife scarce about my seuerall occassions in the Bay as flax seed hemp Corne etc. which I must referr to the next the boate being vnder Saile   soe with harty thanks for your great and vndeserved love vpon euerie torne manefesting yt selfe with my service to your selfe my sister etc. I rest Yours assured whilest I am

EM: DOWNINGE

15. 2, [1640]

GILES FIRMIN TO JOHN WINTHROP[2]

To the right Wor[shi]p[fu]l and our honoured Gouernour John Winthrop Esq.
at his house in Boston

RIGHT WOR[SHI]P[FU]L HONOURED AND DEARE SIR, I receiued your louing letter with many and heartye thankes for your remembrance of mee; it is

[1] W. 2. 29; 4 *Collections*, VI. 56.
[2] W. Au. 101; 4 *Collections*, VII. 275–276.

no small comfort to mee that I haue a roome in your thoughtes, and that my welfare should bee so much desired and regarded by you, as your letter intimates. for the Corne which your wor[shi]p haue procured mee, I am sorry I should put you to trouble, but humbly thankefull that you will doe it, and that you haue answered my bold request: what price it carry, your wor[shi]p mention not, yet I suppose it will bee as cheape as any. I thanke the Lord I haue louinge freinds who doe supply my necessitie, and doe send in beyond my thoughtes. for your counsell about my remouinge into the Bay, I doe not sett light by it, consideringe from whom it come, hauinge a deeper reach then my selfe: onely for matter of imployment, I haue as much heere as I desire, and loue my plantinge more then it, onely the highest ambition of my thoughtes and desires are to bee vsefull and seruiceable heere in a common way. Freinds I haue verie louinge ones and mr. Rogers ministry very searchinge: yet if your wor[shi]p shall please to lend mee your thoughtes, I shall receiue them thankefully, and veiw them well: Wee haue diuers very ill: and Fluxes and Feuers, I obserue are very dangerous. My hast is much onely I shall waite for your arguments, and in the mean time with my best seruice and due respects presented to your selfe and second selfe desiringe the Lord to answere all your loue I rest: your wor[shi]ps vnworthy kinsman

GYLES FIRMIN

IPSWICH: 15: 2 mo: [1640]

JOHN HARRISON, JR., TO JOHN WINTHROP[1]

To my truely honoured freind John Winthrop esqr. these at his howse in Boston

SIR, in the Desire I was bold to present yow with my humble servise, and to aquaint yow with such newse as I then knew, the greate good also that god hath donne both for my inward and outward man in those lines I also notifyed to yow, and as then so now I most heartyly and humbly begge your prayers to the almighty for his assistance against the strength of temptation, in all sorts.

on Monday last beeing the 13th of Apr. our Parliament began. the K[ing] with the P[arliament] and such of his nobility as the vast land-floods would suffer to come to London rid from Whitehall in greate magnificence to Westminster. his M[ajes]ty made a longe speech, and drew forth out of his pocket a letter sent by the Scotch L[ords] to the French K[ing] for aide to invade

---

[1] W. 4. 47; 5 *Collections*, I. 121–122.

Engla. tendering their best servises to that effect. this the K[ing] intercepted, and thervpon imprisoned the Commitioners of Scotland in the Towre whose handes were to the letter, amongst which the L[ord] Lowden was one, reputed a man of extraordinary partes, all which as tis thought will scarsely save his head. they presse soldiers in all partes of England, some say 30000 foote and 7000 horse, others adde to this number few or none substract, the preparations are greate of all sorts of amunition. the E[arl] of Northumberland is cheife generall, and my L[ord] Conoway commands the horse, there are in the army very able soldiers from France Spaine and the Netherlands, especially of the Irish who in their last Parliament held some 5 weekes sinse have freely given the K[ing] 4 Subsidys, with promise of a farther suply if hee shall have ocation. 8000 foote are levyed there and 2000 horse. in Germany the 2 greate armys are parted without fighting almost, and on both sides forage what they can. the turke makes greate preparations but against whom none knowes. there arived heere lately a Spannish Ambasador in greate state and magnificence with such gorgeous Aparrel as from Spaine would scarsely bee expected. what his businesse is I know not, but it is generally voted that hee comes to intreate the Lady Mary for his M[ajesty]s eldest sonne and to offer the Emperors daughter for the Prince. this Spanniard return'd in bills of exchange (as tis sayd) 4000*li* for gold lase which his foote men wore. The P[rince] Palatine some reporte is at liberty the certeinty of that newse I know not. sure I am that hee is not in England. in France there is very greate provision against Spaine, and so e contra. their exactions are so greate as the Normans are scarsely yet in quiet   both there and in Ireland and heere too so much raine is fallen as a greate dearth is generally feared. this is all the newse I have at this time   I shall heere therefore end in all humblenesse begging your prayers for mee, and resting Your servant to the vtmost of my strength

Jo: Harrison

Inn: Temple: Lon: Apr. 15, 1640

[*Endorsed by Governor Winthrop:*] Mr. Harryson [*and in another place:*] Mr. Harrison at the Catheryne Wheele in Gratious street 8o*li*.

FRANCIS BACON TO JOHN WINTHROP[1]

To my very worthye and much esteemed friend John Winthrop Esq. at Boston in New Englande

SIR, Mr. Tyndall offering a Farme to sell that it seemes was purchased with your money, although it was much worse then when it was bought by him by reason of the woode and Tymber cut of which did discourage me; yet because it did lye in the towne where I dwell I haue bought it the rather alsoe because I wold further the occasions of you my old friende and Acquayntance, accordeinge as Mr. Tyndall hath ordered the payments. I know you vnderstande by many the state of things heere And I must confess when I considder it I condemne my selfe for purchaseing for if a goode change come not by the parliament I shall wish my money in my purse agayne And both it and my selfe with you. Because the Farme it seemes was a trust for Mrs. Winthrop I therefore sende a relese for her and you to seale. My mother and my selfe present our true loues and best wishes to your selfe and Mrs. Winthrop And prayeing god for a blessinge vpon you and yours I shall euer remayne Your assured freinde

FR: BACON

From SHRUBLAND Aprill 16th 1640 the 2d day of our parliament

[*Endorsed by Governor Winthrop:*] Mr. Fr. Bacon Resp: per the Sparrow.

EDMUND BROWNE TO JOHN WINTHROP[2]

To the right Worship[fu]ll Gouernour and my much honoured friend John Winthrope Esqr. deliuer this in Boston

RIGHT WORSHIPFULL, my humanity commands mee to apologize in the entrance of my letter. Your promptitude to assist mee with your letters in my honest attempt obligeth mee to all gratefull displayes, as in all deserued christian seruices, soe especially in this to present you with a relation of my proceeding in the suit[3] I motioned your testimoniall for; but because time hath yet not matured any thing worth the informing, and my occasions verge

---

[1] W. 4. 102; 5 *Collections*, I. 289. For Bacon, see 5 *Collections*, I. 289*n*.
[2] W. I. 194. For Browne, see Morison, *Founding of Harvard College*, 368–369.
[3] For a lawsuit upon which Browne was embarking in the summer of 1639, see *Lechford's Notebook*, 130–133.

homeward I humbly craue your pretervition of my silence, and want of attendance, assuring your worship that I shall be ready to tender my seruice
in that or any other action vnto you whom I finde soe reall. thus with my
humble respects vnto your worthy selfe, and indeered friend Mrs. Winthrop,
with my thankes vnto you and prayers for you I rest Your obliged in all
Christian seruice

EDMUND BROWNE

the 18th of the 2d month [1640?]

JOHN UNDERHILL TO JOHN WINTHROP[1]

*To the Right Wor[shipfu]ll John Wenthrop Esquier, gofornor of the Macetuchets baye
these present I praye*

RIGHT WOR[SHIPFU]LL AND MUCH HONNORD IN THE LORD, among the rest
of my aflickchons jusli imposed by my sinnfull lif and backsliding prodigalliti
in my whole corce this is on that doth and will agrefate my grefe that I am
deprife of that chrischan liberti I once had; boght by the preschous blud of
the Lord Jusous. but I hafe made the blod and deth of Christ of non efeckt
therfore I am justli depriued of liberti to visset you, nor dare I aproch youer
presenc tel the lord mofe you there vnto: to here the rumers and fliing reportes gon out agaynst me ar not so much admirabel to me becase it is
Sathans time now or nefer to wage ware agaynst my soule, and prefent my
reconsilement with his pepel by his falce alarmse: which sound ale the con-
tri ofer: sir be plesd to here mee in the matters of excetor and douer and
let not mallics and fare words take place in the bosem of the wise. I know it
doth not yet with youer slfe. I am trobeld that chuch hard reportes should
gooe out agaynst me and my slfe not thorroli vnderstand mense displesure
tel this morning: I came simpli to satisfi the Chorch, not thincking to haf
herd cuch hard reportes agaynst me, thogh som smale Ingling I had before:
and therfore was aduised to bring with me that which will both satisfi youer
slfe and the Chorch in those late rumers: I expeckt the mind of God at youer
lesure in this matter I request of you and rest Youers to comand

JOHN VNDERHILL

From Capt: Gibons house BOSTON: 20 of 2 mo. 1640

[1] W. 3. 45; 4 *Collections*, VII. 180–181. For the circumstances of this letter, see *Journal*, I. 328–330.

SIR JOHN CLOTWORTHY TO JOHN WINTHROP, JR.[1]

For mr. John Winthrop the yonger, my very worthy freind this deliver

WORTHY SIR, Yours off 25 7bris last I lately received by this bearer, cannot but much wonder, what should becom off the letters I haue long synce, and att seuerall times retourned, all importing the receipt off your both letters, and thinges sent; I account myselfe more then satisfied in doing you any seruice, and iff your dysbursements bee not equntized in the mony lent and horse, iff hee were sound, then am I your deptor, and shall most gladly know your minde [torn]   but for Sir Rich: Saltonstall, hee neuer opned his mouthe in the matter; and I must confess, I neuer moued itt to him; I am sory for the loss off the ships sent by them, [mutilated]   however the Lo[rd] rules, and thats strong consolation; I [torn] humble seruice to all knowne freinds worthy Mr. H[torn] Bellingam; And iff any off my interposition heer [be] the least vse vnto you freely command mee as Your most affecti[onate]

                                                          JO: CLOTWORTHY
DUB: 21 Ap: 1640

WILLIAM PAINE TO JOHN WINTHROP[2]

To the Right Worshipful and much onred Loving freind the Governer

RIGHT WORSHIPFULL AND MUCH ONERED IN THE LORD, Thes are to giue your Woorship to vnderstand that wher as Goodman Medcalfe mad som spech of your not hauing 40 bushil of Corne he should not a neded for althow Coleg ded not deliuer his that I might a had of him when I was there it how som ever I would fal short of this 40 soe it wil be deliuered acording to your derecion   Sir ther is an other bisnes which I here your worship is to haue the hering of which is betwixt on Smith and my brother Hammond dauter which when I was in the bay he mad a gret stir about it and much desired that we could goe to Mr. Philipes or Mr. How to haue them to here the bisnes that was betwixt him and the mayd: resolving if he might not safely leaue her when he hard Mr. Philipes he would then be ruled by his iugment: and soe he teld his tale   Mr. Philipes his Answer was that he could not leue her exsept she ware wiling or eles that he could proue somthing that would mak an nulity: and then he resolued at that time to goe on and prosed: but

---

[1] W. 12. 9. For Clotworthy, see 5 *Collections*, I. 203n.
[2] Essex Institute; 4 *Collections*, VII. 401–402. For Paine, see 4 *Collections*, VII. 401n.

more I might say but I shall not at this time: this I am sure he had don the mayd a gret dele of rong and for my part I think had thay bine wis as thay should she may mak as good a mans wife as his: but I could desire that it might be mad an end of that the Cort might not be trobled with it: but if it should com to the Cort then I should desire that I might haue word: but thus leving and commending you and al your afayeres to the Lords good Gidance: thus Remaning youers to command to his power with my Servis to your worship

WILLIAM PAINE

From IPSWICHE the 21 of the 2 month 1640

GEORGE PHILLIPS TO JOHN WINTHROP[1]

RIGHT WOR[SHI]P[FU]LL SIR, Neighbour Hammond comming vnto mee with a note you were pleased to send to him about a case of difference between him and Mr. Smith wherin you intimated that it was needfull that I shold write something in the case of my knowledge: and being desired by him I was willing soe much the rather to yeeld to him because I perceiue you iudge it meete. Mr. Smith acknowledged that himselfe and the yong mayd did mutually consent and gaue their promise one to another and further confessed that he really did take her to be his wife and this by his owne act or allowance was publikely sett vpon our meeting house where other things rendered to publike notice are vsually affixed myself viewed it and generally was taken notice of But after this he tooke some distast and wold breake of againe and pleaded two thinges as making in his apprehension a nullity. The first was that the promise was conditionall if the parents and he cold agree but her mother affirmed that her daughter denied that there was any condition The publishing of it seems to eneruate that exception The second thing was that he had heard of some misdemeanor of the yong mayd I turned him Deuter: 22. 13, 20, and wisht him well to consider what he did alleadge and he vndertooke to proue it entreating mee to giue the hearing of the witnesses. I was not very willing to meddle in it but vpon entreaty of her vnckle Payne I yeelded to assist him to cleare the case as farre as I shold be able: he went away resolued to performe it but I neuer heard of him till this time and father Hammond sayth that he came to them and desired that there might bee a mutuall passing by of things as finding it

---

[1] W. 4. 49; 5 *Collections*, I. 125–126.

difficult to make proof of the reports and hereuppon further proceeded as they say   more I know not vpon present remembrance   One Mr. Deacon who I thinke is with him was present at all this discourse betwixt him and mee soe was alsoe Mr. Payne who if he were heere might mind mee of some-things I suppose which wold aduantage mee to a clearer expression   This I perceaue he hath much entangled the yong mayd put her parents to a great deale of trouble and griefe brought an euill fame vpon the mayd and giuen offence to many in dallying with matters of soe great wayght   I leaue all to your wise and Christian considerations and with my prayers to God to guide and blesse you in this and all other your affayres that they may all issue to peace and righteousnes I humbly take my leaue and rest Your worships in all Christian obseruance

GEO. PHILIPS

WATERTOWNE this 24: 2: 1640

[*Memorandum by Governor Winthrop:*] Mr. Smith confessed before me and the Treasurer that her father and he did agree vpon portion.

MEMORANDUM ON THE CASE OF WELTHIAN RICHARDS'S MAID[1]

(2) 24. 40

Mrs. Richards brought her mayde Edye white to me for her misdemeanor. her man Jo: Gill about 21 years of Age affirmed that she being sett to keepe the 7 Cowes of her masters she left them in the woods and went awaye to the house of one Carpenter in Weymouth, and there lodged, and he wished her to goe home, and brought her neere home, but she went awaye againe, and wanderd in the woods till the 7th daye at night, and then she went to one Dyers house, but they would not entertain her but sent her home, but she came not home till the Lords Daye in the afternoone. This she confessed, and said she was afrayd to goe home, yet she sayth her master and Mrs. never beat her since they were before me etc. but onely hir Mrs. gave hir a blow or 2 on the eare.

her Mrs. charged her further with discovering the secretts of the famyly. one thing she confessed about a mayd that drank to much there.

Jo: Gill charged her also with ordinary lying and lazynesse.

[1] W. 1. 132. This document is in the handwriting of Governor Winthrop.

She sayth the reson why she lost the Cowes was that she sate downe and slumbered, and the while they went awaye.

NICHOLAS JOHNSON TO JOHN WINTHROP[1]

To his very deare and much respected good freind Mr. John Winthrop an esquire at his house in Boston in new england theise deliuer with care I pray

Most louinge and kind and deare and much respectted good freind, my best seruis and affecttions in the lord remembred vnto your worshippe with greate hope of your continuall healthe and wellfare and still wishinge that you may thriue and increase in all thinges both spirrituall and temperall and that you all soe increase which truly feare the lord then the Lord fill all of our hearts that doe feare him with prayses and thanksgiuinge that shall as hyther to hath wrought exceedeingely for his peoples good. and wheareas it hath pleased god to sett vs far remote one from another heere in this world yett I still desire that we may be in presence together to sitt and singe hallaluiiahs and prayses to the god that liueth euer more and louinge freind thought we are far remote heere yet lett vs be remembred of you to god in your prayers as you are of vs and I wish that the lord would in mercy looke vpon all the Israell that are of you and vs that the lord would in much mercy looke vpon vs and perfect our hearts that all of our liues might be very much to Gods glory that we might walke in the feare of his Ma[jes]tye that we may growe in grace and perfect holines in his feare. the lord make vs all wise to saluation and direct vs by his spirritt to order our liues aright that in all thinges god may haue glory and the end may be to our eternall peace and louinge freind wheareas I have receaued many and great kindnesses from your worship I would not haue your worship thinke that because they are past and longe since reseaued and therefore forgotten by me noe I would not haue your worship thinke but that I haue many thoughts of your loue and kindnesses to me which I doe exceedingly thanke your worship for desireinge the lord fully to recompence you for them. and I doe exceedeingely thanke your worshipe that I am not yett forgotten by you that you doe somtymes remember me by a letter which I receaue as a token of great loue and with much reioyceinge still craueinge the same curtysy at your worships hand for I much reioyce to heere of your prosperyty and these are further to intreate a kindnes at your worshipes handes that wheareas the bearer heereof

[1] W. 4. 101; 5 *Collections*, I. 290–291.

is a younge man and hath beene once before in your Plantation and did returne with hopes to haue inioyed his fathers and mothers company there
and occations be soe that they could not prouide to put of thinges to come
and they beinge my very deare and good Christion freinds therefore if your
worship would some wayes direct him in the best I should take it as done to
my selfe and euer rest as I haue iust occation to doe behouldinge to your
worshipe   and soe in great hast I leaue you to god and to his holy protecttion
who is able to keepe our soules safe vnto the cominge of his Ma[jes]ty in
whome I rest Your louinge freind

NICHOLAS JOHNSONNE

From BIDDENDEN this last of Aprill 1640

LUCY DOWNING TO MARGARET WINTHROP[1]

To her most honerd sister mrs. margret winthrop hum[bly] tender this Boston

MY MOSTE HONERD SISTER, I maye well blush att my longe silence beinge
your deptor for so many noble fauors both when I was with you and since.

it is truth I sometimes forbear you trouble by writinge, because I see it
pleaseth you better to pleasure your frinds in acsions then in words. I could
wish my selfe mrs. of that faculltye allso, but barrennes in both is a bleamish
intollerable. I hope I shall studiouslie desire to doe you better seruis: my
frequent and exquisit messeryes I presume you haue often heard of. they
keept me in a habit of complayninge, but I bles god I haue had much re-
mission for 4 dayes past, and should be moste glad if it would pleas the lord
to giue me strenght to wayt apon you, but rather that I maye euer submit to
his will that makes all conditions blesings, to whom I pray commend your
vnworthy sister and seruant

L. D.

[*Ca.* May, 1640]

your lemmons wear allmost as rare as drops of life. I am the more sensible
of your depriuement of them.

---

[1] W. 4. 9; 5 *Collections*, I. 26.

MARY COLE TO JOHN WINTHROP[1]

To my verye louing and mutch respected good frend mr. John Winthrop
gouernour of new england giue this

WORTHYE SIR, I receiued your louing letter which was most wellcom to me, and doe blese god that you and mrs. winthrope are yet aliue, and in health and prosperitye: Jacob was not more Joyfull of Josephe I thinke: I wish it might haue beeine my portion: that you might see my eyes closed as he did his fathers: but the lord hath apoynted me other worke: by reason of my sonnes condition that he is in: I pray God sanctifie it vnto me, and not only helpe me well through that but fit me for greater tryalls: I know not what I may liue to see, the dayes are dangerous and we haue not yet resisted to bloud: I humbly thanke you and mrs. winthrope for all your abundant loue to me and mine euer since I knew you: and especiallye now in sutch a time of abundance of businesse you would be pleased to take the paynes to wright to me: that is vnworthye of so great loue from you, that you shoulde so louingly condole with me, euer in myne afflictions: and haue sutch a sim-pathy and fellow felling of the distressed condition of one so vnworthye and now so far from you: The lord reward your loue into your bosome seuenfolde and giue me a thankfull hart for his great mercies and loue in christ jesus which is the ground of all comfort: I neuer had more need of good counsell and incouragement then now: for I am often in a conflicting condition: I cannot yet attayne to full asurance of my salluation, but still am doubting: I still find sutch a corupt hart, and strong inclinations to sinne, and weak-nesse to resist temptation that vpon euery new asault I haue new fears: I cannot yet atayne to selfe denyall, nor get an hart trulye humbled for these things in these sad times which make me feare I shall not hould out, because I feele my fayth so weake. yet I haue had abundant experience of gods mercyes to me, in all my necessties, which makes me abhore my selfe for my vnthankfullnes and deadnesse of hart and vnbelefe: for in my greatest tryalls he hath sent some moderation and mixed some comfort to allaye the bitter-nesse of it   we ought to prise small fauors   they come from the same loue of god that great ons doe   if I weare not blind I might see his great good-nesse to me: therefore I besech you helpe me by your prayers that my hart might be like a spirituall echoe answering the lord agayne with cherfullnesse in thanksgiuing and holy obedince for the lord loue no blind sacrifice   I be-

---

[1] W. 4. 34; 5 *Collections*, I. 89–91. Mary Cole was the wife of Joseph Cole and had been a neigh-bor of the Winthrops in Groton. For various references to the Coles, see *Winthrop Papers*, I, II.

sech you plead hard with the lord for me and mine and for our church for wee neuer had more need   wee want our moses in our towne to helpe our aron our whole countrey want phyneas. the lord turne all our harts vnto him by true and v[n]feined repentance and thus with my dutifull and best respect remembred to your selfe and good mrs. winthrop I commit you and all yours to the protection of allmightie god and euer rest your louing frend to my power

MARYE COLE

GROTON this 2 of maye 1640

I pray remember my best respect to mr. downing and mrs. downing and all your sonne and daughters.

[*Endorsed by Governor Winthrop:*] Wid. Cole. Recd. per the Sparrow.

DOROTHY FLUTE TO JOHN WINTHROP[1]

WOR[SHI]P[FU]LL MR. WINTROPP, I am sorry being but a strainger that I am forced to make soe bould as to bee troublesome to you by writing, yet my occasion being Considered I hope my boldness shalbe pardoned. that good report that I haue alwaise heard of your redines to doe Justice is my present incouragement. My occasion is this   about 5 years past I had a sonn went to sea with my brother Hurlestone who left my Child with one Mr. John Humphries who then liued att Saugust in new England who hath euer since deteyned my Childe to his great hindrance there being some meanes here due to him which cannot bee receaued withowt his beeing here and by reason of his longe absence is like to bee lost   I cannot mencon how many letters I haue sent to Mr. Humphries for the space of theis 3 or 4 yeares for my Childs coming home but I cannot inioy[n] him soe that I haue noe other refuge but this of flying to your wor[shi]pe for your ayde in graunting my Child leaue to come home, that soe that little estate which was left him by his late father may not bee alltogeather imbeazealed away from him. It is my great greif also that Mr. Humphryes should promise my brother soe faithfully to bringe my Child vpp att schoole and hee euer since imployed to keepe hoggs and goates,[2] and by this meanes hee is like not only to bee

---

[1] W. 1. 133.

[2] In the case of Edmund Thompson *vs.* John Humfrey heard before the Essex County Court on December 31, 1639, John Flute testified that "he drove out eight Marblehead cows and eight

depriued of his meanes but also of educacon or any Calling by which hee may hereafter subsist; I know a word is enough to the wise   I am Confident I shall not need to inlarge, therefore resting vppon wor[shi]ps redines to helpe the fatherless and of your willingnes to graunt my Child liberty to come home by the first, desiring your wor[shi]pe to send for Mr. Humphryes and inioyne him to the like for which fauor I and my poore Child shalbe bound to pray for your wor[shi]pe: If my Child haue a desire to bee there lett him but come ouer and settle his estate here and if hee will hee shall retorne thither againe thus I rest Your freind though vnknowne

DOROTHY FLUTE alias MILWARD

May 5th 1640

My sonns name is John Flute.

BENJAMIN GOSTLIN TO JOHN WINTHROP[1]

*To the wor[shi]p[fu]ll his very Loving Vncle Jno. Winthropp
in Newe England*

LONDON May 8th 1640

SIRR, since my last letter per mr. Goose I doe vnderstand that you are in good helth and all yours for the which I bless god and desire god to continew it if it be his blessed will but I am verry sorry to heare that your man hath delt so ill with you as I vnderstand per mr. Kerbys letter and Tho: Tinker   I haue sent you a small Rondlett of Rise which I wold intreate you part be-tweene your selfe my Ant Downing and my Cosen Jno. Winthrop and accept of it as a small token From a loving Kinsman   I haue also sent 2 Jarrs of oyle which if you doe love oyle I wold intreate you to take [*torn*] if not lett my Ante Downing take as her dew f[or] to my Knowledg it is good oyle for I putt it vp my selfe onely for Freinds and this is all at present that I haue to present to you   I had other things which I had intended for you but my Long liing at home and my Freinds heere haue deseved me of them and now I praise god I am bownd out speedyly I hope within ten dayes the sooner the Better for the Lord be m[e]rcyfull vnto vs and turne the Kings hart or else to this Land in my foolish Iudgment is nothing to be expected but confushion

---

calves from Mr. Thompson's." *Records and Files of the Quarterly Courts of Essex County, Massachusetts,*
1 (Salem, 1911), 14.
    [1] W. 1. 133.

and as for the Roote of all this and the prodigious Frute that from it spring will be nedles for me to relate for I Know you Know it all redy in part and the rest will suddenly be related   therefore I will be silent onely I speake trewly it greue my hart to thinke of the misery that is approching if god be not the more favorable for he alone must doe it the other mayne hope being now frustrate   therfore I beseech you to pray for vs for if euer mother had neede of Dawghters helpe now it hath and I prey god the Dawghter be not burdened by her and thus for present I committ you to the protection of the almighty desiring to be remembred to my Ante Winthrop and to my cosen Jno. and Steven and Adam and Deane and An: and the rest if ther be any and Samm: and my Cosen Elizabeth Fones and all the rest in ienerall all which I shall be gladd to here from: but much more to see   I prey excuse the bowldnes of your Affectionate Nephew

BEN: GOSTLIN

all our Freinds here are well and I shold be gladd to here per mr. Midleton at our meeting in the straights of your welfares.

[*Endorsed by Governor Winthrop:*] Neph: Ben: Gostlin Received per mr. middleton   Reply per mr. middleton.

RICHARD CRANE TO JOHN WINTHROP[1]

To the right wor[shi]pp[full] Mr. Winthrop at Boston Governour of this Patten

MR. GOVERNOUR, my service attend you   I desyre your Wor[shi]p would bee pleased to pardon my boldnes herin. these are to lett your wor[shi]p vnderstand that I have truly served my m[aste]r mr. Rawson according to covenant. my time will bee forth on fortnight before midsomer next, therfore I desire your wor[shi]p to stand my frend (beeing destitute of any other in this land) that I may part from my m[aste]r without any trouble, because I have a wife and five poore Children in England which will not come to mee, and I desyre to goe to them   now because I feare my m[aste]r will oppose mee in this my purpose, I have thought good to appeal to your Wor[shi]p whom the lord hath sett in place to iudge the cause of the poore and the rather because I am a poore man and not able to spend mony in sute. I desyre your wor[shi]p to give mee leave to have access vnto you, if my

[1] W. 4. 103; 5 *Collections*, I. 291–292.

m[aste]r shall oppose mee which I much feare. I have sent my lettre[1] which you have read, which doth express 5 yeares but I am sure I aggreed for noe more then three, nether can I serue any longer by reson of a fall one the yce, and age alsoe, beeing 54 yeare old. my m[aste]r intended to imploy mee to make powder. I am sorry I could not have materials wherby to improve my skill for the good of the land. thus desyring to pardon my boldnes and to stand my freind, I rest Your poore

RICHARD CRANE

May 9, 1640

ISAAC LOVELL TO JOHN WINTHROP[2]

To the right Wor[shi]p[fu]ll Mr. Wintrup Gouerner of New Ingland
I pray deliuer this

SIR, not knowing whether in these trublesum times it will please God I shall longe inioye life or liberty to wright vnto you againe I am glad of this my ocasion to truble your Wor[shi]p with a few lines althoug I hope you will counte it no truble my busines is this my wiues Vnckel Goodman Fuller of Ony[3] in Buckingham sheare desired me to wright vnto you concerning a sonne of his John Fuller for whome he hath purchased land in Saugust[4] and hath furnished him with cattel and other prouisions out of Ingland to his great cost which hee intendeth hee shall inioye liuing in that obeadience vnto his father which God commandeth and hee hath promised the which obeadience hee hath not obserued in these too thinges first in his intended marradge for whareas hee beinge scarse twenty years of adge will marry a stranger when his father alreddy hath made a worthy choyse for him heare in Ingland secondly in his remouing frome Saugust or Bostone to goe with Mr. Woster[5] if hee liketh better to bee at Bostone his father will thare purchase for him if hee will follow his owne will rather then obeadience to his fathers lawfull commandes hee doeth profes hee will take all from him which was intended both of land and cattel etc: and disinherrit him in ould Ingland his fathers intent and mine both is for new Ingland before long if

---

[1] See Dorothy Crane to Richard Crane, March 15, 1638/39 (pages 105–106, above).
[2] W. 4. 103; 5 *Collections*, I. 292–293. All that is known of Lovell is certain biographical information given in his letter to Governor Winthrop, May 2, 1637 (*Winthrop Papers*, III. 408–409).
[3] Olney, Buckinghamshire.
[4] See *Lechford's Notebook*, 152–153.
[5] The Reverend William Worcester, formerly a fellow townsman of the Fullers at Olney, came to Massachusetts in 1639 and became the first minister at Salisbury.

God giue life and liberty   the party who gaue his father noties of this his name
is Henry Person sonne in law to goodman Cooper dwelling at Sawgust   it is
his fathers desire and mine (who haue beene alreddy to bould with your
Wor[shi]p) that you will be pleased to doe God this good seruis in your place
as to exammine the say[d] John Fuller concerning these thing and to admonish him vnto submition. thus commiting you and your to the protection
of our mercifull God with the remembrance of my humble loue I take my
leaue Your Worships in the union of the Lord Jeasus

ISAACK LOUELL

From FINSBERRY hard by More fildes neare London May the 11th 1640

[*Endorsed by Governor Winthrop:*] Mr. Isack Lovell, Resps. per the Sparrow.

THOMAS MAYHEW TO JOHN WINTHROP[1]

To the Right Worshipfull John Wynthropp governour this deliver

RIGHT WOR[SHIPFU]LL, I am to pay my owne Rate and some 5*li* for other
men that I owe it vnto and allthough that I haue had bills due from the
Countrey one yeare and 7 monethes synce for 70 and od pownds I must now
haue my goods solld except I pay out this money: which seeing I haue mony
to rec[eive] from the countrey methinkes it is verry hard measure. I cannott
see equitie in it. I may safely say that If I had had my money as was then
fully intended being then 100*li* it had donne me more good in name and state
then now wilbe made whole with double the money but yf there be noe
remedy but my goods must be strayned and solld, I desire your worshipps
aduice per this bearer which is the Constable what course is to be taken in
putting it of. I thinke he comes vnto yow for counsell in that behallfe: thus
with my due respecte in some hast I rest Your wor[shi]pps to command

THO: MAYHEW

11th of the 3d 1640

Mony is verry hard to gett vppon any termes. I know not the man that
can Furnish me with it. I coulld not gett the 100*li* of Mr. Gibbins. I gott 30*li*
sett of inconueniently: and when I was syck and in necessitie I coulld not
gett any of the tresurer. I delight not to compleyne.

[1] W. 3. 13; 4 *Collections*, VII. 32–33. For Mayhew, see 4 *Collections*, VII. 30*n*.

EDWARD HOWES TO JOHN WINTHROP, JR.[1]

LONDON May 12, 1640

DEARE SIR, Yours of the 16th of March last, this day I received per Mr. Kirbie, and am sorrie to vnderstand by you and him, that the vnfaithfull steward hath mett with you or your fathers estate; I could wish my selfe with you (till the storme here be ouer) but I doubt I should be in the stewards case, though not vnfaithfull yet vnprofitable, for I cannot digg and to begg I shalbe ashamed, nor howe to ymproue that little God hath lent me, if I were with you for Lawyers and Phisitians haue noe gaine with you, and I thinke Clergie men as little, vnlesse they be such as shall speake and doe to please men, hauinge an excellent forme of Godlikenes, but denye the power thereof. But my good frind; the word saith; Godlienes is greate gaine, if a man be content with that which he hath; tis to you I write this, as to a frind whome I entirely Loue. As for the Magneticall instrument you writt of; it is alsoe sympatheticall and therefore magneticall; we vse to say good witts iumpe, though heads touch not; many can say soe, some find it soe, but fewe enquire into the true reason whie it is soe. I haue sent you a booke by Jo: Tinker that will sett your witts on wollgatheringe, or rather to shew you howe some mens witts runne a wollgatheringe, vntill like the Astronomer gazing vpwards doe fall into the pitt of Death. I know the gent[leman] one Mr. Wilkins of Maudlin Hall in Oxon made the Booke;[2] and he pretends to haue the perpetuall motion, and the magneticall Alphabet, sed cui commodum in tempore confusionis. I allwayes forbeare to contradict the wilfull, tis to reproue the scornefull, and to cast pearles to swyne. But to our sympatheticall busines whereby we may communicate our minds one to an other, though the Diameter of the Earth interpose. Diana non est Centrum omnium. I would haue you soe good a Geometritian as to knowe your owne Center. Did you euer yet measure your euerlasting selfe; the length of your life; the breadth of your Loue; the depth of your wisdome; and the hight of your light; Let Truth be your Center and you may doe it otherwayes not. I could wish you would nowe begin to leaue off being altogether an outward man; that is but Casa Regentis; the Ruler can drawe you straight lynes from your Center to the confines of an infinite Circumference, by which you may passe from any parte of the Circumference to an other, without obstacle of Earth

---

[1] W. 2. 170; 4 *Collections*, VI. 509–511.

[2] The book referred to was probably the third edition of John Wilkins's *Discovery of a World in the Moone; or, A Discourse Tending to Prove That 'Tis Probable There May Be Another Habitable World in That Planet* (London, 1640).

or secation of lynes if you obserue and keepe but one and the true and only Center, to passe by it, from it, and to it. me thinkes I nowe see you intus et extra, and talke to you, but you mind me not, because you are from home, you are not within, you looke as if you were carelesse of your selfe, your hand and your voyce differ, tis my frinds hand, I knowe it well: but the voyce is your enemies; O my frind, if you loue me, gett you home, gett you in: you haue a frind at home, as well as an enemie; know them by theire voyces, the one is still driuing or enticing you out, the other would haue you stay within. Be within, and keepe within, and all that are within, and keepe within shall you see, knowe, and communicate with, to the full, and shall not neede to straine your outward sences to see and heare that which is like themselues vncertaine, and too too often, false, but abidinge for euer within, in the Center of Truth, from thence you may behold conceiue and understand the inumerable diuerse emanation within the Circumference; and still within; for without are falcities, lyes, vntruths, doggs, etc.

I sent you lettres and 2 bookes by Mr. Kirbies sonne   I hope ere this they are come to your hands. I pray present my vnfeigned Loue and humble seruice to your honored father and mother alsoe to Mr. Dow[ning] and your good aunt; and tell her I hope we shall doe some good for her this terme in Cheneys Busines. I desire to knowe what became of my lettres to Jo: Sand[ford] and to the rest, what you knowe thereof send me word, for I would not haue the persons of men perish, for theire sinnes sake, if possiblie I could preuent the same. My wife and I haue noe Child yet, my father and mother are both liuinge and hartie, I thanke God; and as longe as they liue looke not for me, the word is gonne out of my mouth and I cannot recall it; yet assure your selfe I am present with you in prayer, hartie good wishes, and other thoughts for your reall welfare and safety. my loue is soe to you I am loath to parte; yet being alsoe loath to be troublesome and frinds must sometymes parte, that they may againe renew theire frindshipp. Salute your wife for me, and wish well to Tuissimum

ED. HOWSE

I pray rem[ember] to send me some furrs to lyne a Close Coate withall in the winter; and the price of them I shall pay to whom you will, or send it in bookes.

Remember my Loue to Mr. Humfries and Mr. Fowles, and Mr. Rich: Saltonstall, when you see them.

BRAMPTON GURDON TO JOHN WINTHROP[1]

To my worthy good frend Mr. Winthrop the Gouernor in neu England be thes

GUNFORD this 13 of May 1640

MY WORTHY GOOD FREND, Your letters writ in the begeneng of marc[h] wear verry welcoum to me, but I asseuer you I was muche taken with sorrow for your great losse thearin expressed, but that is not enoff, except we doo extend boueles of compacyon to a destressed frend for which I am verry redy to joyen with any in so christyan a deuty. Sir Nathaniele Barnston and I haue had often speche about it. we are bothe willing ayther to geu or to lend a greatter soum, only we would be glad to haue soum frend hear to vndertacke for the repayment at a year or 2 year if yow so desyer it. I haue had speche about this with your scearuant Tinker   he put vs in hope that your brother Tindall will doo it for you, the which if he will I shall wellingly lend 100*li*. now Sir Natha[niel] would willingly vnderstand which wear the best for yow, to lend or to geue. we cannot thinck to hear from yow so sone, as your necessyte m[a]y requyer soum more spedy cors, thearfore, I resolue thus   I will now deliuer to your scearuant 10*li* for him to employ to your ewes till I hear further whot is your desyer   if you desyer by way of geft rather then to lend I shall be welling to returne you 10*li* more bothe of geft or to lend yow a 100*li* hauing sceceuryte to repay it at a year or for longer tyem. We are hear in verry hard condicyon in regard our parlament is desolued, but let me tele you it comforteth the hartes of the honest men of bothe housen that thay yelded not to geue a pene to help the K[ing] in his intended ware agenst the Skottes, nor the cortyers of the hous durst not moue to conscyder whether to haue ware or peas, but the K[ing] fyending the hous was bent for peas as not sceing any caus of war, he desolued the hous. The K[ing] scent erly in the morning to speacke with the speker. when he was coum to him he tocke him into his barg and carryed him in to the vpper hous to macke sceuer he should not goo into the nether hous to preuent the howes from protestyeng aganst the ware, ship mony, and conduct mony, which greu burdensoum all the kingdoum ouer. on teuesday the 5 of this the parlament was dissolued. the next morning on of the Scecretaris cam to the L[ord] Brockes hous thear by the Lord Say and scearched bothe thear stodyes and lickewis others went and scearched Mr. Jhon Hamden Mr. Pem and Sir Walter Earles closet   Sir Water was abrod when thay cam. thay tocke away a trunc from

---

[1] W. 2. 181; 4 *Collections*, VI. 565–566. For Gurdon, see 4 *Collections*, VI. 559n.

Mr. Pim, thinkeng thear had ben that thay sent for but it proved aparrele.

I doo not hear thay haue gayned thear payens. on weddensday in the eueninng a messenger cam with a Scecrataris leter to Miles Corbetes chambur warneng him with sped to repayer to him and to bring all papurs that he had resayued. Miles was called to the chayer, for matter conserning religyon, and thear cam many biles agenst B[ishop] Wren. he apered, and cam well off. yow shall hear of wors doinges, and so I pray God to kep vs in pes. Good Sir pray for vs hear in ould england. I pray commend me to your selff and wiff. I rest your louing frend

                                                                B. GURDON

[*Endorsed by Governor Winthrop:*] Mr. Br: Gurdon. Resp. per the Sparrow.

EDWARD COOKE TO JOHN WINTHROP[1]

To the right wor[shipfu]ll my most Honoured friend, Mr. John Winthrop Esqr.
Governour in New England present these

WORTHIE SIR, Yow were pleased to give mee soe good encouragment by your letter of my sonns deportment in New England and the hopes of his well doeinge in that Cuntrey, being stockt with thinges fitting his Callinge, as I have now sent him back againe, fully accomplished with all provisions for his profession, and otherwise, giving yow thankes for your kindeness shewed to him, not doubting but that hee willbee a very vsefull mann amongest yow, and to your selfe and yours serviceable vppon all occations, as indeede hee stands most oblieged for your favours. his purpose is to sitt downe in Charles Towne. I entreate your good favour to him with your good advise in som perticulers as his howse, or what els may concerne his good, and I willbee ready vppon all occations to express my thankfullness. Let mee entreate your acceptance of a poore token of my love, which my sonn will deliver vnto yow and soe for this present, presenting my Service to your selfe, I commend yow and all yours to the divine protection, and rest now and ever Your wor[shi]pps assured friend to serve yow

                                                                EDWARD COOKE

LONDON, May 15° 1640

[*Endorsed by Governor Winthrop:*] Mr. Cooke. Resp. per the Sparrow.

    [1] W. 3. 104; 4 *Collections*, VII. 383.

WILLIAM CODDINGTON TO JOHN WINTHROP[1]

To the Wor[shipfu]ll and his much respected frind John Winthrape Esqr. at his howse in Boston deliver

WORTHY AND BELOUED, I haue recaiued your letter sent by my Cozen Burt in Ans[wer] wher vnto I would not haue yow troubled how to write vnto me, seeing at this distance we knowe not how other wayes to confer to geather. Many loueing letters haue passed betweene vs at a fare greater distance of place then nowe we bee at. possibely yow may conceiue of things deeper or other wayes then ther is cause for. I doe intend to answer for my selfe (by neighbours) I doe not knowe howe yow doe meane, vnlesse it be the brethren that did remoue with me. It may be they are better able to answer for themselues then I am. I was sick when the measinger[2] yow mention came to the Iland, who said they had onely one Question to put to me, which wos whither I did hould my selfe to stand a member of the Church of Boston or not. I answered to my best rememberance to this effecte that the Quest[ion] wos very considerable, and needed my best health to answer to it, but for these grounds I did scruple it, viz: after serous debate at 2 solomon meeting in which very few of the members wos wanting (to my best rememberance, and so others afferme allso) which meeting wos first accationed by the motion of one of the members nowe resident with yow, and as I toucke it in the name of others, my selfe and Mr. John Coggshall being to geather at my howse, with some other brethren, that wee two, and some others he mentioned, would remoue, for their peace and settelement, etc. I did Inquire how that might be without offence. he said he would procuer vs a Church meeting, in which it should be transacted. At the Later our teacher being out of the towne when the former wos, it wos with the generall advice and consent of all (as I take it) we were commended to the grace of God in christ Jesus in our remouall, and it wos the substance of mr. Cottons sermone the next Lords Day, wher ther wos not Churches to commend their brethren two, ther they might commend them two the grace of god in Christ Jesus, which I have related to some Elders and brethren of other

[1] W. Au. 97; 4 *Collections*, VI. 312–316.

[2] William Hibbins, Edward Gibbons, and John Oliver were delegated by the Boston Church, February 16, 1639/40, "to goe to the Iseland of Aquethnicke to inquyre of the state of matters amongst our Brethren there, and to require some satisfactory Aunswer about such things as wee heare to be Offensive amongst them." MS. records of the First Church of Boston, copy in the Society's library. Winthrop's account of this embassy is given in his Journal (I. 330–331). An abstract of the report which the messengers gave upon their return to Boston can be found in Robert Keayne's MS. volume of notes on sermons preached by John Cotton which is in the Society's library.

Churchs amongest your selus, as else wher, some by word, others by writing, and though they differ as I haue to show, "1 Elder sayth it wos a dumbe dismishon. 2 Elder sayth it wos because most of them wos departed in their spirits then from the sents here. the 3d Elder sayeth directly that it wos a dismishon,[1] and that your church had not further to doe" etc. And trewely I would seriously moue this Question, that if the Church Covenant did reche me being remoued vpon what grounds they did first advise and motion my departuer, which must of nessetye cutt of that relation.

for that place aleged by yow Mathew 18, it doth remayne yet to be proued by scriptuer that any Church did ever clame power over their brethren, remoued by their consent, more then over those that wos never in fellowshipe with them. It wos tendered by Mr. Hibings and accepted by me, that some thing should be donn in this kind, but I haue hard no thing of it as yet. I could therfore wish my brethren knewe it, and that I wos not thus charged.

2ly I may to your selfe answer my dismishon out of the Commonwealth, and when I wos departed the feare that the Cuntrie expressed, which stands vpon recourde in your Court booke, that my selfe and others of vs wos gone out of the way (when wee went to seeke out a place for our abod, and though I haue it to shew vnder your selfe and the Go[vernor]s hand that nowe is, that I had a yeares libertye for my remoueall) to escape onely the Censer of the Courte for the present, and therfore it wos inacted that vnlesse we were departed by such a tyme we were to appeare at the Courte.[2] for my owne part, I wos not willing to liue in the fyer of contention with your selfe (and others whome I honered in the Lord), haueing liued 7 yeares in place of Goverment with yow. But chose rayther to liue in exsile, and to put my selfe vpon a sudayne remouall, vpon 14 dayes tyme, to a place with out howseing, chuseing rather to fall in to the hand of god, which what my selfe and wife and famelye did induer in that remoueall, I wish nether yow nor yours may ever bee put vnto. if after all this vnder taken of my part for peace, we must Clash, and make it appeare in the Christan world, we that are as a Citty set of hill: (the will of our god be donn) I could wish for the good of both plantations that it wos other wayes, and muteall Loue and helpefullnes continued.

For the letters you mention, they haueing said before that they had onely one thing to propound to me, and not profering me any leters, I might not possibely attend being sicke to what passed aboute them; as indeed I do not remember now, would they that wos aboute me haue bene willing, if

---

[1] In the margin: "and all 3 agree its a dismishon."
[2] Cf. *Records of Massachusetts*, I. 223.

they had profered me them, that I should then haue read them, feareing it would doe me hurte, sence my recovery I haue desired a copy of them, and haue bene promised one. The other thing yow mention conserning our vn-curteous entertayment of your Churchs measingers I haue enquired into it and cannot vnderstand but that they were recaiued with respect and cur-teousely entertayned at both plantations.

For the Indeans I could wish all lenety towards them, which vnderstand not possibely the natuer of a promise. they saye it was that if any iniueryed the English they would not protecte them but deliuer them vp to make satise-faction ether in their persons or estates. Ther is a lude Felowe, one Tho. Saverye, whom I heare is now in durance with yow, who haueing stolne a paire of showes from my howse of the lords day, and heareing it wos dis-covered fled from the Iland to the 7 myles riuer, and ther being afflicted in consence (as he pretended) for what he had donn, came to acknowledge the evill of it, and giue satesefaction. I susspected though he seemed to Crye, he did but dissemble therfore searched him and found of him a silver s[*torn*] marked 1639 which he said he had had 6 yeare which wos [a]boue 4 yeare before it wos mayd allso a bugle purce and a gould ringe (which he said he found as theefes use to fynd their goods) but wanting a prison he mayd an escape from vs before punishmentt, aboute 5 weekes sence; Lately I wos in-formed, that at a place caled Puncataset vpon the Mayne Land wher he keept the last sumer and wos much freequent in folowing etc. he hath had a child by an Indean womon, which is a boy and is not black-haired lick the Indean children, but yelow haired as the English, and the womon being laitely deliuered doth say English man got it, and some of them name him, and when he ranne away from vs, he would at Titecute haue lyne with knowe Gods mother, which doth speake of it in detestation and that those that pro-fesse them selus to be Christians, should be more barberous and wyld then Indeans, to the proproch of our nation, and the dishoner of god   seing God hath deliuered him into your hands I thought meet to informe yow, that yow might se Justice donn of him.[1] thus with my due respect to thc Go[verno]r, your selfe, the Debty Go[verno]r, Mr. Endecote, Mr. Humfreyes, Mr. Nowell, and Mr. Bradstreete etc. I sease from writeing but not from remayne-ing Your loueing frind till death

WM. CODDINGTON

NEWPORT this 22th of May 1640

---

[1] At a Court of Assistants on June 2, 1640, Thomas Savory, "for breaking a house in the time of exercise, was censured to bee severely whiped, and for his theft to bee sould for a slave vntil hee have made double restitution." *Records of Massachusetts*, I. 297.

Ther is a lude person one Hugh Durdall that Mr. Pamer brought in to the Cuntrie being bound over to answer some misdemenour at the next Courte hath mayd escape awaye about 2 dayes sence, and is feared will git passage in the West Indean shipe. he is much indebted here also. Vale in Dom. Jesu.

[*Endorsed:*] Mr. Coddington Resp. (4) 11. 40.

EDWARD PAYNE TO JOHN WINTHROP[1]

To the Right Wor[shipfull] John Winthrop Esquir Governer Boston in New England

RIGHT WOR[SHIPFULL] AND MY MUCH RESPECTED FREND MR. JOHN WIN-THROPE, My Love Remem[bere]d vnto you Sir allso vnto Mistres Winthrop with all your children wishing your wellfar ass myn owne. Sir these few Lines I haue mad bold to writ vnto you too sertifie you of some pasages her the tymes ar very troublesome and the parlament is Broken vp and some of the aldermean wear imprisoned and towe of the birges of the Lower hows butt shortly deleverid her hath ben great stir the prentises did Rise and wold have puled downe the bishop of Canterburis hows and did begin and allso pulled down one or two prisones and leat the Prisoners all loss, and forced one alderman to Depart the prison or eallc they swore they wold pluke downe that prison allso: so the alderman cam forth to quiet them and re-turned to Prison again and the next day he was relesed Itt wass alderman Atkines Burges for norwich the Lower hows of parlament stod very strongly for the Priviledg of the Subect and for Reaestablishing of Religon the King is much displeased noe monie will be granted the wares for Scotland goes one butt with a very ill will from the subect what will insue I know not the lord in mercy Look downe vpon vss and Sir if ever ther wear ned of prayers and teares for a poor Kingdome, now is the tyme and therfor Sir remember our poor nation I know Sir you ar not wanting in that Behalfe who knowes but the lord may turn in mercy vnto vss again the papists increas in abun-dance, and ther is great fear in the citty and a strong watch keept every wher and great search mad: Sir I hop to se your wor[ship] next yeer. I stay this yeer att home to order my buisnes, for I fear I must come away att last Sir I haue vndertaken for the transporting of the pasengers and goods in our ship only John Tinker hath a sixtht part now Sir when wee came to grauesend

[1] W. 4. 104; 5 *Collections*, I. 294–295.

the pasengers puting me of to pay ther fraight ther att the very pinch they had no monie so that I could haue noe monie and being loth to turne them ashore, seing theay wear poor people allthoughe I am sur theay gaue me iust Caus soe to doe, wass forced hauing noe other remidy to tak severall bills for my monie the which I ame out of to pay me ther for the which theay haue ingaged ther goods. Sir I wold desire your Wor[ships] Assitanc allso for mr. Eattones Bill   Itt is vnpaid and I haue seant the protest over with the Bill   I hope Sir your Wor[ship] will see that I may haue a proportion acording to my dept for I wass loth to cary the monie out of the Cuntry and therfor wass willing to leaue itt but I had litle thought that mr. Eatton had ben such a man. Sir allso her is a frind of myn the Bearer herof one of our owners sonnes mr. Tho. Dutchfeld his father is one of the Captaynes of the Cyti of London he cam out of the Est indies having ben out 7 yeeres and desiring to trauell again I covnseled him to come too new England and he hath some 1000 pownds worth of goods with him, and Desired me to adviz him what to doe when he cam ther. I haue advized him to be att mr. Leverits hows But when god sends him Sir I desir your wor[ship] to adviz him for the beast   his father will be very thankfull vnto you: for he is a very honest godly man and desires the wellfar of him   Sir I pray excus my boldness   I ame much ingaged vnto you for all your Kindness, desiring to requit you if it Lyes in me. Sir I have ordered my man to stay ther to look vnto my buisnes   I desir your wor[ships] love in advizing him in douptfull things when he shall adres himselfe vnto you. I haue given him a leatter of Atturney to recover my Depts in and to order my buisenes: I hop next yeer Sir to see you; your frinds her ar all in health, ass far as I can her. Sir I commit you with all your family vnto the good guidanc of the lord and rest yours to command to my power

EDWARD PAYNE

from THE DOWNES this 28th of May 1640

JOHN TINKER TO JOHN WINTHROP[1]

To the Right Wor[shi]ppffull and his much honnered Mr. Jno. Winthropp Esqr.
Go[vernou]r of the Matachuses thesse deliver At Bostone in New England

RIGHT WOR[SHI]PPFFULL, To whome I must euer acknowledg my selfe deeply ingaged for your greate kindnesse and respect vouchsaffed me, and for [w]home I shall reioyce to doe any servis acording to my poore power

[1] W. 3. 60; 4 *Collections*, VII. 225-228.

and it is my greife I canot doe that servis which suts my desires and your wor[shi]pps occations. I am very sory to heare of that great vnfaithfullnesse of Goodman Luxford, whome I doe confesse I did feare for a great while agoe, though I did not declare my thoughtes or was I inquisatiue to finde the truth least I should be iudged an intruder into other mens ocasions: but the lord knows my hart had I forsene the extent of such a disaster beffalling your wor[shi]pp I should neuer haue departed from you: neither doe I yett thinke any strenth or abillity the lord hath afforded mee to much to doe your worshipp servis: I haue received your letters with your orders for the payment of 800*li* to seuerall men, which I was to take vpp of Mr. Tindall if the Land weare sould: or if not to borowe of such gentlemen as ware your Frends, as Mr. Gurdon Dockter Wright etc: I was with Mr. Tindall, and the land is sould: yett he standing ingaged as a Fefee in trust for the stateing of my mistress and the chilldren in the meanes at the time appoynted, will not disburce any more then may stand with his security vntil he haue a releace from my m[ist]ris and the chilldren: Mr. Stephen being at age he hath sent a release for him to signe to: and vppon the retur[n]ing of it will part with more. he hath now paide Mr. Cradock and Mr. Jno. Dodd 50*li* per peece and will pay to Mr. Cradock 80*li* more and to Mr. Meclethweit per my strong perswation 50*li* more: for I doe perceiue it should haue beene paide in aboute michaltide last and the forbearance of it is a great rong to him: I haue allso spake often with Mr. Gurden and Docter Wright about the borowing of monyes and because your wor[shi]pp did not request them to it possatiuely: they doe require some securyty and are willing to lend 100*li* apece as allsoe Sir Nathaniell Bramstone which is 300*li*. I writ to Mr. Tindall to know his minde aboute it, and he was vnwilling to doe thatt of all other things. Dockter Wright allsoe propounded to me this that I should goe to those gentlemen seuerally to [w]home these somes of monys are to be paid, and bring them to some Composition: but I finde the debts are not directly from yourselfe to them: soe they seeke not imediatly to you but to those whoe are indebted to them and therfore it is not proper to propound it to them: and since this time I haue not binn with them: only Mr. Gurden hath sent your wor[shi]pp 10*li* for a token the which I receiued as allsoe 50*li* of Mr. Tindall for your vse and for want of time to disburce it for your proper vse, I would intreat your wor[shi]pp to take what goods of mine you please to that quantyty of 60*li* and pay only what consideracion vppon them you please, for the Fraite Customs and all other charges vppon them: It hath pleased God to disap[oin]t me in the throw effecting of my businesse so that I could not come with Mr. Clay in the Susan and Hellin of which I haue a

part in vndertakeing for the setting of her forth: yett I haue sent in her
diuers servants and goods to the value of 560*li*. I would intreat your wor-
[shi]pp to doe me all the Fauour you cann in the assisting of my servants
and Frends in the manageing of my affayres by your Councell and advice:
my businesse I haue declared at large and directed to your wor[shi]pp in a
booke to the end you might see what it is: howsoeuer it should please God to
deale with mee befor I come to you or thay whome I betrust in the manageing of my businesse should cary themselues, it being a matter of great
Consequence my credit being great and my estate but smalle: I would intreat your wor[shi]pp soe sone as my servants and other Passengers that I
am allied vnto are landed to lett one of your servands prouide some lodging
for them at some of the Neighbours houses and I shall giue good satisfaccion:
vntill such time as they shalbe dispossed of according to my direccion in my
boke. If any of my Agents in my busines should stand in neede of any mony
for a small quantyty just at theire ariuall as I sopose they will: I would intreat
your wor[shi]pp to lend them some, to the vallue of 5 or 6*li*, and they shall
pay it againe: I am very sory I haue Failed of sending such tokens as I had
prepared for your wor[shi]pp and my m[ist]ris and some other, but I hope
the Lord will bring me safe to the place of my desires againe: I haue sent all
my leters by a yong marchant whose Father viz: Mr. Duchfeild is parte honer
of the Susan and hellin: I would intreat your wor[shi]pp to shew him respect
partly in regard of his Father and partly in Respect of his courtyous cariage
toward me: I shall not faile Good willing to doe what I can in your wor[shi]pps
busines to know fully what wilbe done in it before I come: It is a very greate
greiuanc and generall Complainte among all the Merchants and dealers to
New England that they can haue noe Returnes, and theire bills are very
naught insomuch that if there be not some Course taken for beter payments
of our Creditors our tradeing will vtterly cease: thesse bills from James Luxford and Mr. Nathaniell Eaton, charged falcely one men heare, haue done
a great deale of hurt and ocationed a great deale of slacknesse of men about
London for sending of goods this yeare: I pray God saintyfy his dealing
toward vs and fitt vs for any Condicion. I haue soe intangled my selfe in
businesse depending vppon some whoe disapoynted me, that I canot come
away till the next shipps, but the times are desperatly dangerous in all respects: I shall but truble your wor[shi]pp to relate any news   I rather reffer
you to discorce with Mr. Duchfeild whoe I supose wilbe a good Intelligencer
and therfor I craue your wor[shi]pps pardon for my bouldnesse and with
my humble servis to you and to my m[ist]r[i]s I leaue you to the lord and
to the power of his grace for a returne of all your kindnesse in your bossome

many fould and rest: Your wor[shi]pps euer obleiged in any servis to my poore power

JOHN TINKER

From THE DOWNES the 28th of May 1640

JAMES LUXFORD TO JOHN WINTHROP[1]

RIGHT WOR[SHIPFUL], I did vnderstand by goodman Brackett, after I came to my lodginge, that your wor[ship] had sent to speake with mee but it was then to late to trouble your wor[ship] this morninge I came downe and perceiuinge your wor[ship] to be busie with soombody in the hall and soe durst not attempt to coome in, but if your wor[ship]s will be to speake with mee I shall attend your wor[ship] in the eueninge, or at your best leasure. otherwise if my coominge be offensiue to any if your wor[ship] please to write a woord or two of your mind I shall accordinge therto so doe as god shall helpe mee whether to answer any obiection: or if it be to hasten my departure. I am determyned suddenly to depart by gods helpe; thought yet I know not which way to turne my foote, I doe resolue god willing not to offend that way. I was not well and thoroughly whole which was the reason I went noe sooner,[2] and soe the Lord your god foreuer be with you and yours, and send you such as may be accordinge to his hart and yours to follow all your occasions, who alsoe in his time, I am confident, will shew not only your wor[ship] but other of his servants, that I am cleare in the thinge wherof I am accused to wronge your wor[ship] if not it is my coomfort that the Lord knoweth it and this I leaue as the last woord for ought I know, that euer I shall speake or write to your wor[ship] (it is in gods brest what shall bee) that besied my owne conscyence god which is much greter, bearinge mee witnesse, that my father was neuer more deare to mee then your wor[ship] That I haue beene as faithfull to your wor[ship] in all my Improouements, as euer seruant was to his m[aste]r thought I erred in the way, yett this is a truth whether you will beleeue mee or not, that neither my selfe nor any for mee to my knowledge hath perloyned any thinge from you and as I goe with an emty purse soe I thanke my god on my knees day and night that in that

---

[1] W. 4. 53; 5 *Collections,* I. 140–141.

[2] At the General Court on May 13, 1639, "James Luxford, for his forgery, lying, and other foule offences, was censured to bee bound to the whiping poast till the lecture from the first bell, and after the lecture to have his eares cut of; and so hee had liberty to depart out of our iurisdiction." *Records of Massachusetts,* I. 295.

my conscience is cleare and my poore compannyon that was I know hath
that to coomfort hir, whose labors together with mine, which soe much looue
and faithfullnesse imployed, will speak when wee sleepe in the dust. Now
agayne the God of all consolation and coomfort be with you and yours, and
thought I might not labor with my hands for your wor[ship] yet with my
whole hart shall I labor with god in prayer for your wor[ship] till I dy:
Soomtime your wor[ship's] belooued seruant but till death yours vnfeynedly
louinge, poore desolate disconsolate

JAMES LUXFORD

[*Ca.* June, 1640]

THEOPHILUS EATON TO JOHN WINTHROP[1]

*To the Right Wor[shipfu]ll John Wynthrop Esq: Governour of the plantations
in the Massachusetts Bay deliver*

SIR, I can neither write nor indeede thinke of my brothers[2] miscariages
without much greife and shame. He who searcheth the heart knew what
sapp ranne within when the fairest leaves appeared outwardly, but his late
and I feare present fruite hath bin exceeding bitter and his state the more
dangerous because I feare he is but a litle sensible of it, besides much dishonour to the great name of God. I heare he hath bin very injurious to sundrie men, the particulers I fully vnderstand not, nor as yett how farr my
self am interressed in his sinfull projects. Some moneys he received for me,
some goods he had of mine, some goods by my order he sent me, and some
without order. how these reconings stand he never sent me any account
though I wrote to him for it into the Bay and since to Virginea. other moneys
I payd him upon his [*torn*] such security as gave me present satisfaction
supposing him faithfull partly by a bond partly by a deede of Bargaine and
Sale, which I suppose to be good, though the witnesses heard them not read,
when they saw him seale and deliver them as his deeds. I am not privie to
any the least indirect ayme on my part in that cariage nor did I foresee that
inconvenience which hath since followed. I formerly wrote to Mr. Bellingham
desiring a share in the estate he hath left, according to my interest, and I
desire from your self all lawfull furtherance herein. beyond Justice I know
you cannot grant nor doe I desire. he hath also received Fowerscore pownds
for Mr. Foxcroft by Mr. Lings order from goodman Lyne as I take it of

---

[1] W. Au. 98; 4 *Collections*, VI. 344–345.
[2] Nathaniel Eaton.

Charlestowne, and severall sommes of Mrs. Woolcott for Mr. White. I assure
my self they also (with others) shall have satisfaction so farr as the estate will
goe. I pray you excuse this boldnes. might I doe you any service in these
parts I should gladly imbrace the opportunity. with my due respect to your
self Mrs. Wynthropp and other freinds I rest Yours in all service of love

THEOPH: EATON

I have intreated my Cozen Malbons help in my buisnes   what he doth
in it I shall allow.

QUINYPIOCK this first June 1640

GEORGE MOXON TO JOHN WINTHROP[1]

To the wor[shipfu]ll his much respected frinde mr. Winthroppe at his house
in Boston be these delivered

WORTHY SIR, Salutations in Christ Jesus. Sir I make bold to trouble you
with these few lynes, in them intreatinge your helpe to clearre this poynt
whether we of Agawam were dismissed out of the Bay with this proviso to
continue of the Bayes iurisdiction. if there be any order of Court touchinge
that matter it may giue light. the grounde of my request is thus much. I
haue heard that some of our neighbours in the River are doubtfull whether
we lye not in Sin, (not in fallinge from theyre government but) in fallinge
disorderly from them without first orderly debaytinge the matter and our
greiuances if we had any: I would therefore gladly haue such groundes as
may be convincinge to any that shall desire a reason of vs if any shall hereafter speake of it to any of vs. I conceiue some obiection may be grounded
on this, that they were possest of vs at that tyme. Through gods mercy we
all well in our plantation only mr. Pynchon lately lost a boy, who tendinge
Cowes neare our river too venterously went into a birchen Canowe which
ouerturned, and he was drowned. remember myne and my wifes truest loue
to your selfe and Mrs. Winthrop. The lord sanctifye the passages of his providence to you, and beare vp your spirits in close walkeinge with him. soe
prayes Your lovinge freinde to vse in the service of the Gospell

G: MOXON

SPRINGEFELD mens. 4ti die 2do 1640

[1] W. 4. 105; 5 *Collections*, 1. 296. For Moxon, see Morison, *Founding of Harvard College*, 390.

BOND OF MATTHEW ALLYN[1]

Noverint vniversi per præsentes me Mathew Alline de Branton in Comit: Devon: gen: teneri et firmiter obligari Johanni Hill de Pilton in Comit: prædict: gen: in octoginta libris bonæ et legalis monet: Angliæ Solvendis eidem Johanni Hill aut suo certo Atturnato Executoribus Administratoribus vel assignatis suis. ad quam quidem Solutionem bene et fideliter faciendam obligo me hæredes executores et administratores meos firmiter per præsentes Sigillo meo Sigillat: dat: die nono Junij Anno Regni domini nostri Charoli, dei gratiæ Angliæ, Scotiæ, Franciæ et Hiberniæ regis fidei defensor: etc: decimo Sexto, Annoque domini 1640.

The Condition of this present obligation is such, that If the aboue bounden Mathewe Alline his heires executors, administrators, or assignes, or any of them, shall trulye paye or cause to be payde vnto the aboue saide John Hill his executors administrators or assignes, the full and whole Summe of fortye pounds Lawefull monye of England, within the space of on month after the arrivall of the saide John Hill into the place or countrye commonly called Newe England beioynde the Seas that then this present obligation is to be voide and of none effect otherwise the same is to stand in its full force power effect and virtue.

MATHEW ALLYN [Seal]

Sealed and delivered In presents of
   THOM: AYSHEFORDE
   TRISTRAM POLLARD

I arrived at Charelston in Newe England on mondaye beinge the 17th of August 1640, and the next daye Sevennight followinge, beinge Tusedaye, and the 25th daye of the Saide Moonth of August, I received five pounds of Mr. Mathewe Allyne, as part of payement of 40*li*, which remainder of fourtye pounds, beinge 35 pounds I am to receive of the Saide Mathewe Allyne, on the 14th daye of September next followinge beinge then the full moonth after my arrivall into this land of Newe England, accordinge to the obligation within written.

[JOHN HILL][2]

---

[1] W. 1. 134. The body of this document is in the handwriting of John Hill. For Allyn, see *Winthrop Papers*, III. 249, *n.* 1.

[2] Hill very likely wrote this paragraph on the second leaf of the folio sheet on which Allyn's

THOMAS DUDLEY TO JOHN WINTHROP[1]

To my honoured brother John Winthrop esqr. at his howse at Boston

SIR, I haue received the 20*li* you sent now by your man for which I thanck you. The truth is, I owe the whole 50*li* to be paid the end of this moneth and haue noe other money to pay it: The money is not yet gathered vpp here for you, and how much will be in money I yet know not: For the other things you wryte of I likewise retourne thancks, and purpose to conferre thereof with you at my cominge to Boston, and in the meanetyme and ever shall rest Yours very assured

THO: DUDLEY

ROCKSBURY, 4 mo: 15 day 1640

RICHARD VINES TO JOHN WINTHROP[2]

To the Wor[shi]p[fu]ll John Winthrop Esquire at Boston these present in
Massachusetts bay

SACO the 25th of June 1640

WORTHY SIR, You may please to vnderstand that whereas Captaine Vnderhill hath bin with me and the rest of the Counsellors for this Province desireinge here to inhabitt and enioy the priuiledges of the same, we heareinge of some engagements of his to the Massachusetts bay haue thought good to acquaint you therewith, desireing to heare from you how farre those his engagments doe extend, that soe we may know how to proceede with him therein according to law and equitie, for we desire in this and the like cases to doe as we would be done vnto, which if you wilbe pleased to send vs your answeare herein, we shall then vpon further consideracion proceede accordingly. thus with my due respects remembred I committ you to the protection of the Allmighty resting Yours to my power

RICHARD VINES

bond was written. Subsequently it was cut out and pasted on the verso of the bond. For another document relating to Allyn's bond, see John Hill to John Winthrop, October 13, 1640 (page 293, below).

[1] W. Au. 100; 4 *Collections*, VII. 112.

[2] W. 3. 92; 4 *Collections*, VII. 337–338. For Vines, see 4 *Collections*, VII. 337*n*.

EDWARD WINSLOW TO JOHN WINTHROP[1]

To the W[orshi]pp[fu]ll his much honored Friend Joh. Winthrop Esq. at his howse
at Boston these be delivered

SIR, Yours of the 18th of this pr[ese]nt I lately rec[eived] being perswaded as you write that if it were your owne case you would not stand with me but in a case between a stranger and you wherin you are betrusted and for the publick etc. I hope you conceiue of me as of one that would not desire any thing that should appear to be unjust: but for the Cattle to be valued by two publick persons of your owne might haue satisfied the publick; And for Mr. Andrews[2] tis true he desired cattle of such an age and price; but the price at that time was under their worth by a yeares growth: for yearlings and the advantage were ordinarily sold for 15*li*. Againe Mr. Andrews is well acquainted with payments in Engl. and how easie a thing it is to turne any valuable commodity into money but it is otherwise heer, and especially at this the most hard and dead time of all other these many yeares: I speak as it is with us: but if you conceiue the Gent[lemen] valued them too high I am contented to let them goe as I offered to your selfe at 18*li* per head the fiue. If you say it is too high, truly I marvell at it, being this weeke Mr. Hatherly made payment to Mr. Freeman and Mr. Atwood in Cows (and in a busines Mr. Andrews, if I be not much mistaken, is interested) at 18*li* 15*s* per head. Nay since these valued some passed in account between Mr. Paddy and some of your parts at 20*li* per head; and therefore I pray you take it into further consideracion, and remember you may fall into an extreame. Truly Sir it is my desire to discharge it that makes me importune you neither doe I conceiue how you can justly suffer in it: and to avoide suffering I see is not possible: for I finde innocency (by lamentable experience) will little helpe amongst men. Yea wherein I haue been most carefull therein most abused and therefore in discharging a good conscience we must leaue all events to God. If I had any hopes of a chapman I would make money of them but haue none, however I thanke you that haue been so kinde to giue me time: but I feare that time will rather hurt then helpe me, and therefore beseech you againe either to accept them or acquaint Mr. Stoughton with it that he may write to Mr. Endecot about it: for they may doe it as well by letter as presence, onely I pray you conceale what I offer if they must value them: and if you please I will send them upon the first notice.

---

[1] W. 2. 90; 4 *Collections*, VI. 165–168.
[2] Cf. Richard Andrews to John Winthrop, July 8, 1639 (pages 129–131, above).

I thanke you for your loving manifestacion about mine owne busines. There hath nothing been done in it since the Gent[lemen] (to whom I am much bownden) were heer. As there shall be any thing done I take it my duty to acquaint them who have taken so much paines therein. Onely my purpose is to study waies to satisfie for words so far as a good cause will permit. The Lord in mercy direct me who haue need of more then humane patience to beare these things from this people: For ten times more from others were not a tenth part so much, nor can any beleeue that seeth not, that I should suffer as I doe from them; The Lord lay it not to their charge and giue me wisdom and patience to beare it. Be you saluted and yours together with those Gent[lemen] (espec[ially] my respects to your Govr.) Good Sir let me haue your pra[yer]s who remaine yours till death

EDW: WINSLOW

(4) 27. 40

I thanke you for your Engl[ish] news. I rec[eived] a letter from Mr. Sherley this yeare. he writes that in steed of a letter he had thought to haue seen me, but is glad I came not, for if I or any partner had commen Mr. Beauchamp had trowbled him and had for that end entertayned a Soliciter etc. He writes me of the lord keepers death and that Secretarie Cooke hath letters of ease which is to me very sad: for new England in those two is stripped at once of our best friends at the Board: so that now we must live by Faith without any dependance on meanes at all. Mr. Downing to whom I desire to be remembred with all thankefulnes, can better informe you about it then my selfe.

I would haue written to the Gent[lemen] about our busines, but knew not how you would take it, but what you shall write in it I will stand to, and therefore I pray you let it be dispatched and let me haue word that I may send them.

WILLIAM BRADFORD TO JOHN WINTHROP[1]

To his worthy and much Honoured freind Mr. John Winthrop Esquire these be delivered

SIR, not knowing of this conueiance till they were ready to goe, I thought good to scrible a word or tow by candle light, rather then not to aduertice you of so serious a mater; I am Informed by good Intelligence, that the Narhiggansetts haue made a great colection amongest ther people; and sent a great presente, both of white and black beads to the Mowhakes, to entreate

---

[1] American Antiquarian Society; 4 *Collections*, VI. 158–159.

their help against you, and your freinds, if they see cause. And they Mowhaks haue receiued their presente, and promised them aide, biding them begine when they will, and they will be ready for them, and doe encourage them, with hope of succese. The thing is true but I may not reueile the auther. It would cost the liues of some if it shoud be known, neither would I haue it voulgarly knowne that it came from hence least it should be susspected; their owne commone people doe not know it. I fear they are too well furnished with peeces by too much remisnes. Thus in hast I take leaue, with my harty saluts to you and yours, and many thanks for my kind entertainmente when I was last with you Your euer louing freind

WILLIAM BRADFORD

PLIM: 29 of 4 month 1640

I pray you remember my loue to the Gou[ernou]r and aquainte him hear-with. And if you haue any spetiall news from England I would be glad to know it.

[*Endorsed by Governor Winthrop:*] Mr. Bradford about the Indians (5) 40.

WILLIAM HUTCHINSON AND OTHERS TO JOHN WINTHROP[1]

To the Right wor[shipfu]ll John Winthruppe Esq. at Boston deliver this

RIGHT WOR[SHIPFU]LL, We haue laitly received a letter from Barborah Davice, the wife of James Davice, now resident in Boston with yow, wherin we vnderstand that he hath made complaint of her, if not falce accusations laid against her,[2] theirfor we thought good to testefy, being desired theirvnto, what he confessed vpon exammination, before vs whose names are heare vn-derwritten; The ground of his exammination was from some falce reports he had raised vp against his wife, we call them falce because they prooved so to be when they weare inquired into, but not to troble yow with those: A word or tow of what he did confesse; when the question was deman[d]ed of him, did your wife deny vnto yow due benevolence, according to the rule of

---

[1] W. 1. 135. William Hutchinson, the husband of Anne Hutchinson, and the other signers of this letter were among those who left Massachusetts for Rhode Island as a result of the Antinomian controversy in 1637.

[2] At the meeting of the Court of Assistants on June 2, 1640, James Davies, "for his unquietnes with his wife," had been "enioyned to appear at the next Court of Assistants." *Records of Massachusetts*, 1. 296.

god or no, his answer was she did not, but she did and had given her body to him. this he confessed, and did cleare her of that which now he condemmes her for, and this may evince it and proove it to be so, for he did heare likewise reporte his wife was with childe, which we vnderstand he doth also deny vnto your wor[shi]pps   And that will also proove him to speake falcely if he shall say his wife did deny him mariage fellowship vntill he did come vnder your gouerment; 3dly this we must witnesse, That his wife was not the ground of his being sett in the stockes; but for his disturbance of the peace of the place at vnseasonable howers whenas people weare in bedd, and withall for his curssinge and swearing and the like; Againe a word or tow concerning his life when he was with vs. It was scandolus and offencive to men sinfull before god; and towards his wife, In stead of putting honour vpon her as the weaker vessell, he wanted the natural affection of a reasonable creature. We also found him Idle and indeed a very Drone sucking vp the hony of his wifes labour, he taking no paines to provide for her, but spending one month after an other without any labour at all. it may be sometimes one day in a month he did somthing being put vpon it, being threatned by the govourment heare; and Indeed had he not bene releived by his wife and her freindes wheare shee did keepe, he might haue starved, besids he is given very much to lying, drinking strong waters; and towards his wife shewing nether pitty nor humanetie, for Indeed he could not keepe from boyes and servantes, secrete passages betwixt him and his wife about the maryage bedd. And of these things theire is more wittnesses then vs. And concerning her; she lived with vs about 3 quarters of a yeare, whose life was vnblamable befor men for anything we know, being not abel to chardg her in her life and conversation, but besids her masters testemony who best knowes her is this, that she was a fathfull, carfull, and panfull both servant and wife to his best observation, during her tyme with him. Those things we being requested vnto, we present vnto your wise considderations hoping that by the mouth of 2 or 3 wittnesses, the innocent wilbe accquitted, and the guilty rewarded according to his works; thus ceasing further to troble yow we take our leaues and rest Your wor[shi]pps Lo[ving] Freinde

WILLM. HUTCHINSON
WILLIAM BAULSTON
WILLIAM ASPINWALL
JOHN SANFORD

PORTSMOUTH the 29th of 4th mo. 1640

[*Endorsed by Governor Winthrop:*] From Portsmouth about Davis and his wife.

GEORGE FENWICK TO JOHN WINTHROP[1]

For his honored freind John Winthrop esqr. att his house in Boston, thes

SIR, When I was with yow I did not know, how Mr. Whitefeild and I should devid.[2] I thought it most equall that he should haue had part stock and part of your debt, but he being vtterly destitute of Catle and relyeing vpon those he expected vpon his bargaine with my wife, I haue condiscended to lett him haue all the 5 Cowes that remained of my wifes whole stock, and haue taken your debt wholly vpon my selfe beinge confident that as your occasions will inable yow, yow wilbe mindfull of it. I speak not this to straiten yow, for the Lord knowes that from that respect I beare yow for your publique mindednes and personall worth I could be very reddi to doe a greater Courtesie for yow if it were in my power yet my occasions are such, and my disappointments haue bene soe great that I haue bene and am lik to be more straitned for moneyes this yeare then in that litle tyme I haue liued I haue ever bene, for of 1000*li* and aboue I ordered to be returned into the Bay I haue receaued but 326*li* and it is very doubtfull what is become of the rest; as also after the death of my servant, I sent another for Engl. to bring me some returnes, who was forced to goe about by Spaine, and I heare noething of him, though I haue a letter from John Wood, who mentions provisions he hath to bring for me from some freinds but mentions not my man; which makes me the rather feare because the letters I wrott by him were left behind and sent by another Conueyance and by them such freinds as I wrot to may provid for me. The Lordes wilbe done in all. If he se not meet my occasion should proceed according to my owne order and provision, I hope he will giue me a hart with all humblenes to be contented to haue them stayed or caried on after his good will and pleasure. I haue receaued the Cow that was with you (by my servants) and shall not trouble yow now further, but presentinge my true respects to your selfe and bedfellow I rest Your lo[ving] freind

GEO: FENWICK

SEABROOK 6° July 1640

My wife remembers her loue to yow both.

[1] W. 2. 145; 4 *Collections*, VI. 365–366.
[2] The Reverend Henry Whitfield, founder of Guilford, Connecticut, and a close friend of Fenwick. In 1639 Fenwick, planning his return from England to Saybrook, had arranged with Whitfield and the latter's company for "their joint immigration to Connecticut in the same ship, and made joint stock of their cattle and other effects necessary for the supply of their plantations."

CERTIFICATE OF JOHN MAYO[1]

DORCHESTER the 6° of the 5 moneth 1640

These are to Certefie those whom it may any wayes concerne that the purposse of marriage betwixte Mr. Tylly of Barnestable and mrs. Blower of Boston hath been three seuerall times published In the meeting at Barnestable

JOHN MAYO

[*Endorsed by Governor Winthrop:*] Certif. for mr. Tilly and mrs. Blower.

EDWARD WINSLOW TO JOHN WINTHROP[2]

To the W[orshi]pp[fu]ll his much respected Friend Joh. Winthrop Esqr.
at his howse at Boston these be delivered

WORTHY SIR, Your last letter I received and giue you thanks for your continued loue in imparting unto us such news as you heare from Engl. What will be the issue of these sore beginnings the Lord onely knoweth, but it concerneth us deeply to be affected with them as a people that must share with them in weale and woe. The Lord in mercy so order and dispose as what is amis may be reformed, and his name may be glorified.

Concerning your acceptance of the Fiue Cows I am willing to send them and becawse the wether is so hott, the flie so busie and the woods so thick I haue agreed with Robert Waterman to bring them by water. I pray you send me a receipt under your hand for them upon the back of the note or bill I left with you. Thus with my kinde saluts to your selfe and all yours whose wellfare I desire as mine owne, with all due respects to you and them take leaue remayning Yours assured

EDW: WINSLOW

PLYM (5) 7. 40

Bernard C. Steiner, *A History of the Plantation of Menunkatuck and of the Original Town of Guilford, Connecticut* (Baltimore, 1897), 22.

[1] W. 1. 135. For Mayo, see Morison, *Founding of Harvard College*, 390; *N. E. Historical and Genealogical Register*, XCV. 39–49, 100–108.

[2] W. Au. 101; 4 *Collections*, VI. 168.

EDWARD NORRIS TO JOHN WINTHROP[1]

*To the R[ight] Wor[shipfu]ll John Winthrope Esq. at his house these be deliuered
in Boston*

WOR[SHIPFU]LL AND R[IGHT] WORTHY SIR, I have receaved letters from
some speciall frendes in Bristol with this request: that whereas one Mr. Long
an Alderman of that Citie, of great estate, and very good esteeme there, hath
sent over his eldest sonne (one addicted (as it seemes) to traveyl) to recyde
for a time in these partes, and hath desyred above all, that he might (yf
possible) be entertained by yourselfe vppon what termes yow shall sett downe:
and that I should doe my best to further the same: these are with intreatie
to tender the sayed motion vnto yow by waye of letter being not well able
to traveyle my selfe (which else I would, and should have done) that yf great
inconveniences stand not in the waye, yow would be pleased to fullfill the
request of such as are well able and (I believe) as willing to make satisfaction,
with respectfull thankes, and love vnto yow. the yong man I knowe not, being
in foraigne partes at my being in Bristoll but is there readye to present himselfe vnto yow, as I have given direction, and the m[aste]r of the ship with
whom he came. Thus, craveing leave for this boldnes with yow vpon such
an occasion, I commend yow, with good Mris. Winthrop, to the grace of God
in Jesus Christ, resting Your Wor[shi]ps in all due respect and observance

EDW: NORICE

SALEM, 9no 5^{ti} M[ensi]s [1640]

LORD SAY AND SELE TO JOHN WINTHROP[2]

WORTHY SIR, I received a letter from you dated the 20th of March[3]
whearin vppon hearsay you fall into a reproffe of me backed with intimations
that I may expect and fear Judgements as the 10 princes of [I]srael founde,
for bringinge vp an ill report vppon your lande, and diverting mens intentions from comminge to you as they did discorage the Israelites from goinge
into the lande of Canaan. and as befell Moyses and Aron for [*torn*] gods

---

[1] W. 4. 106; 5 *Collections,* 1. 306.

[2] W. Au. 99; 5 *Collections,* 1. 297–303; *L. and L.,* 11. 422–427. For William Fiennes, First Viscount
Say and Sele, see *D.N.B.*

[3] For Winthrop's account of his controversy with Lord Say and Sele over the latter's attempt
to persuade New Englanders to move to his settlement at Old Providence in the Caribbean, see
Journal, 1. 334–335.

people to have ielovs thoughtes of his goodnes to them, thorough theyr owne
unbeleefe: and that you may fix it deaper you desire me to consyder the 4
of Nehemiah 1. 2. 3. 4. 5. whearin the example of Sanballat and Tobiah are
sett before me to fright me. and indeade good cause had I to be frighted,
and much humbled if any of these wear iustly applyed to me, or theyr actions
and myne in this particular of like nature and consequence, and soe rightly
paralelled. But wheras you speake in your letter of taking the name of god
in vayne, I pray consyder seriously, and lett our frendes thear be Judges
betwene vs, wheather this be not a taking of godes name in vayne to misaply
scriptures in this manner (a thinge that when I have heard of it elswhear in
speaches and letters hath greaved me) by assuminge (for that must be granted
you) that thear is the like cal from god for your goinge to that part of America
and fixinge thear, that thear was for the Israelites goinge to the land of
promise and fixinge thear: the like grownde for your staying in that place
and others comminge theather to you, that thear was for Nehemiahs buildinge the walls of Jerusalem: and for you to plant thear, and noe whear else
is as much a worke of God as his building Jerusalem in that place and now
whear else, although the meanes and probabylities in humane reason for
your owne good, and inablinge to doe much more good for the advancement
of the gospell wear surpassinge what is thear neaver soe much. is this to be
offered vnto men of Judgement? Whoe knoweth not that in the one case
fayth only was to be used, and reason layd asyde; but in this of yours it will
on the other syd, be a want of fayth and tempting of god not to exercise
reason in the consyderation of possibylyties, yea, and probabylyties. Thus
much to your instances out of scripture which give me leave to intreat you
to vse with more care. for the matter it selfe the substance of what you charge
me with is, that my authorytye (which you advance as very effectual) hath
diverted many from coming to you and cast theyr affections another way:
this you say you envy not, but wish they may speed well in a better choyse;
and yet presently add that this hath caused many a hart to be trobled and
greaved. and also this causeth you to lay this charge vppon me; why should
you or any other man be greaved that men followe theyr Judgements in
transplantinge themselves when it is free for them soe to doe: and when
they think another place more commodious then that for them thearfore
pitch vppon it rather. and if I think soe too why am I soe sharply dealt
withall only for speakinge that which is a truth in my Judgement to any that
shall advice with me. But you will say I disparrage that plantation to advance
another: it is meet for him that will Judge to hear both sydes fyrst and to be
sure of his groundes: if you knewe how basely and falsely that other plan-

tation of Provydence hath bin disparraged by those affected to yours for the
ende for which you suspect I had don the like to you, then you would better
knowe whear to place and apply your reproffes. For my part my prayers and
[*torn*] have bin and shall be for the good and advancement of those faythefull
people, and pure churches that I know to be thear; and to that very ende
have I accordinge to my Judgement persuayded men to thinke of a more
southerly part of that Continent whear they might fitt a commodious place
for such a body as they already are, and are likely to growe vnto quickly by
accession of those whoe would thear come vnto them, or they would be able
to bringe vnto them if poore, by the abylytie that such places would afford
them: whearas nowe they are soe placed that rich men growe pore and poore
men if they come over are a burthen, the rich only mayntayninge the market
for a time vntill that be spent which they bring out of Englande, which land
floude will have an ende, and then wantinge a springe, and havinge a con-
tinual wast the water will all run out of the poole; in a place whear staple
commodyties already are, and the soyle and clymate knowen to be fitt to
produce the richest, and thearby to carry on soe great a worke as the fram-
inge of a commonwealth and the setlinge thearof for posterytie, thear will
be noe place for this [*torn*]; and by this I hope alsoe I shall not be thought
to have a little Iland and the advancement thearof only in my contemplations
in all this proposition   What may iustly be vrged agaynst me by the arguments you have vsed and pressed which doth not as much concerne them
whoe dayly leave you att the Bay and goe many miles southward for better
accommodations only may you not aske them wheather they dowbt the
worke be of God? wheather his gracious presence be not amongest you etc.?
these arguments conclude not at all a condemnation of what they have don:
or what I desyre might be don by you all when it shall be soe prepared that
you may see it feaceable and profitable, not for outward thinges alone (though
that will be founde necessary as I veryly thinke) but most of all for the advancement of the gospell and puttinge downe the great adversary thearof
that man of sinn, whearvnto as you are now you neather are able nor are
likely to be to putt your handes to the least wheele that is to be turned about
in that worke otherwayse then by well wishinge thearvnto: All the rest of
your proffes to prove it a worke of God are meerely besydes this question,
and nothing to the pourpose: it is good in argumentation, especially when
you will presse Judgements vppon any, to examine fyrst wheather your
reasons conclude the poynt in question, or are soe far besydes the matter as
that they may all be granted and yet the case remayne the same it was: I will
grant that God is with you, that you are glorious churches, that he sent you

theather in handfulls vntill you might grow vnto a body fitt to doe him service; that he hath blessed you thear with some testimonyes of his favour vntill you wear soe augmented: will it att all be concluded from thence that you are bounde to stay thear, or that that is the place which he hath designed out for you: and whosoever discorageth others from cominge to you fighteth agaynst God? noe such thinge, I will more probably argue the cleane contrary! god hath carryed you theather in parts, one company after another, whear you might be gathered togeather in safty, vntill you wear growen vnto such a bodye as wear able to doe him service, and sitt downe in safty in such places as may be most fitt for the worke he hath in hande, and for your owne comfortable subsistinge: this you could not have don by handfulls as you went out, thearfore att the fyrst you wear cast vppon this place: and caryed out into this wildernes to be increased and fitted for the worke intended for you: now you are thear you fynde it but a wildernes (which causeth many of you to straggle), that soe when an opportunity is offered vnto you you might not neglect it, but see your selves called to it, as you have bin hear sheltred by a gracious provydence vntill you wear growen fitt and able to vndertake it, which opportunity if you neglect by pretend[ing] [*torn*] while you neglect to serve provydence, which offereth you meanes another way, and discovereth to you the want of meanes wheare you are: you will doe noe other then cast your selfes downe from the pynacle and refuse the stayres which are before you: for it is as likely that you have in provydence bin cast vppon that place to remove from thence vppon due occasion, as to stay thear, and much more likely when in some other you may doe more service, and receave more meanes by much of comfortable subsistence. hear you see which way all your arguments may be turned with as much convincinge evydence, as to conclude that you bringe them for. for the barrenes of the lande and the coldnes of the ayre in the winter it will be testyfyed from those whoe have had experience of it, your owne losses may be sufficient witnes of it, but I pray tell me, be it as it is, is thear any impiety in me to move men to live in a warmer clymate and in a more frutefull soyle when it is fre for them to make theyr choyse, why are you angry with me for this? for your goverment it is a very plausible way to win vppon the [*torn*] that affecteth popularyty, to persuayd them that other men goe about to enthral them, and theyr posterytie, but he standeth for theyr libertye; when it may be neather he nor they rightly vnderstande what true goverment is and desyrable liberty, such as wise men would wish to inioy, and live vnder: I wonder you should conceave any man would desyre to advance his owne posterytie by enthraling other mens whoe have moved any alteration of goverment with you: and theyr posterytie with you, or like to be with you, or to be advanced by beinge thear? hath any gon about to inslave you? You say your forme of goverment you hear is much blamed but whearin you expresse not, only you ende with this that you woulde not be enthraled to advance other mens posterytie: and I say agayne noe wise man shoud be soe folish as to live whear every man is a master, and masters must not correct theyr servants; where wise men propounde and fooles determine as it was sayde of the Citties of Greece. for my part if you ayme att me I doe Judge and thinke I can mayntayne by good reason that to be the best forme of goverment which hath in it the good of all three, so fittly limitinge each other, and thearby preventinge the evills of eather, that beinge equally poysed one by the other, they shall all yealde forth what is good in eather for the settlinge and preservinge of common right and liberty to all and every particular. it may be you ayme att this that some ranckes shoulde be hereditary and that you think woulde enthrale others: not att all when it should be in theyr giftes vppon meritt and well deservinge of the common wealth, and in theyr power to resume vppon demerritt; that thear is power in a state to reward virtue hereditaryly and for disservice to lay a punishment that shall extende to posterytie, this constitution doth not abridg power in those that give it, though they injoy it not themselves, but advanceth theyr liberty to theyr owne good. Thear is noe danger in such different degrees (which will be founde necessary) so longe as they are allwayes accomptable to parliamentes consisting of all estates vnited yearly and havinge in that vnion supremam potestatem: For what you say of the Church not compatible with another frame of goverment, I pray putt away that error; these govermentes must be, as in theyr owne nature they are, keapt and exercised soe distinct, as that movinge within theyr owne sphæres, the church goverment beinge wholly spirrittual, can consist with any forme of outward goverment good or bad soe did they in the time of the Heathen Tyrants. I have trobled you with a tedious and scribled letter, you must excuse me I cannot for the hast of the bearer whoe stayeth for it while I write it transcribe it   my hast also may cause me to give you lesse satisfaction then oth[erwise I] might. You may please to make the best interpretation of all, and to accompt of me as one that wisheth all happynes to your plantation and to your selfe shall remayne Your very lovinge frende

W: SAY AND SEALE

July 9, 1640

[*Memorandum by Governor Winthrop:*] To my Lo[rd] Brooke that their estates were gone allready. Aske mr. Gurdon mr. Darlye etc. what is become of their adventures. What content those have who be there. What Conveniences they return with   what staple Comodyties for livlyhood. What is become of their 120000*li*.

CERTIFICATE OF WILLIAM TOMPSON[1]

5.14.1640

These are to certefie that a purpose of Marriage betweene Joel Jenkins and Sarah Gilbert both of Brantree hath beene published aboue the Space of a fortnight. ita testor

WILLM. TOMPSON

[*Endorsed by Governor Winthrop:*] Certificate Jenkins marr[iage].

EDWARD COOKE TO JOHN WINTHROP[2]

To the right wor[shipfu]ll my most Honoured friend, John Wintropp, Governour in New England, present these

WORTHIE SIR, I hope my sonne Robert Cooke is safely retorned into New England longe before this letter commes to your hands, and that his deportment shall bee such, as will purchase your good favour, etc. the occation of this letter, is in the behalfe of a learned Gentleman of my acquaintance Mr. Bird, who I vnderstand hath written to your selfe to bee entertayned of the people in your parts as a phisitian, and well knowinge his sufficiencies in the practize of phisick, my request to yow is, that yow would bee pleased to further him in his desires, which if yow shall please to doe, I am assured yow will not repent therof, and I shall take this your kindenesse as an espetiall favour to my selfe. I commend all to your wise consideration, and commend yow and all yours to the divine providence, and rest Your Wor[ship's] ever ready to serve yow

EDWARD COOKE

LONDON the 20 Julij, 1640

[1] W. 1. 135.
[2] W. 3. 104; 4 *Collections*, VII. 384.

ROGER WILLIAMS TO JOHN WINTHROP[1]

PROUIDENCE, 21. 5, [1640]

MUCH HONOURED SIR, Your Runnawayes (as I before surmised) are at Monhiggin and the Squa Sachims daughter is married to the Sachim Onkas. I know the match hath bene long desired (although the Sachim hath 5 or 6 wiues allready) which makes me feare that all Indian meanes will not reach your iust desires: May you please to rest a litle for Miantunnomu (as he pretends out of loue and respect to your Person) is very diligent about a peaceable returne of them that he may bring them with him and as many more of the Runnawayes as he can gett. Onkas was gone to Qunnihticut so that a litle patience is requisite.

Sir This you may please to signifie to your much honoured brother Mr. Gouernour[2] that this busines only hinders Miantunnomues Comming. He is (not satisfied but) perswaded to trust to Interpreters whom he feares to trust, and to come without my selfe.

As allso may you please to vnderstand that the Nayantaquit Sachims still refusing to yeald vp any of those Pequts to death to whome they had promised Life: Our Friends of Qunticut (as I haue heard by 2 letters from Tho: Stanton) intend present Revenge vpon them: Caunounicus and Miantunnomu still perswade (to mine owne knowledge) the Sachims at last to be wise and yeald vp their Pequts, but in vaine For the Nayantaquit Sachims resolue that for so many liues as are taken away by the English or the Monhiggins and Pequts with them they will take revenge vpon Mr. Throckmorton at Prudence, or Mr. Coddington etc. or Prouidence or elsewhere.

I haue dealt with Caunounicus and Miantunnomu to desert the Nayantaquits in this busines. They answer they would if they had shedd the bloud of the English, but as they are their Brethren so they neuer hurt the English, but ioyned with them against the Pequts etc. Only they haue bene greedie vpon the Prey against the English mind: and lastly they say the English Partialitie to all the Pequts at Monhiggin is so great and the Consequences so grieuous vpon the Abuse of the English Loue, that all their Arguments returne back (which they vse to the Nayantaquit Sachims) as Arrowes from a stone wall.

Tho: Stanton informes me of another cause of Warr vpon the Nayantaquits

---

[1] W. 2. 114; 4 *Collections*, vi. 263–264; *N.C.*, vi. 137–139.

[2] This reference to Thomas Dudley fixes the date of this letter as 1640, in which year Dudley was Governor. By the time he again held that office (1645), Miantunnomoh, who figures prominently in this letter, was dead.

viz: Wequash affirmes that one of the petie Sachims of Nayantaquit was aboord Mr. Oldams pinnace, and that some goods and gold are at Nayantaquit. Gold I neuer heard of but the Pinnace Skiff and other Luggage and small particulars I had word of at first which were (by reason of distance) let alone: and in case that any one of the Sachims or more knew of Mr. Oldams death and that due Evidence be found, I yet doubt (now since the Comming of the Lord Jesus and the Period of the Nationall Church) whether any other vse of Warr and Arms be lawfull to the professours of the Lord Jesus but in Execution of Justice vpon malefactors at home: or preseruing of life and liues in defenciue warr as was vpon the Pequts etc. Isay, 2. Mic. 4.

If the sword rage in Old or New E: I know who giues out the Commission, and can arme Frogs, Flies, Lice etc. He be pleased to giue vs Peace which Earth neither giues nor takes. In him I euer desire to be more vnfaigned and faythfull Your Wo[rshi]ps

ROGER WILLIAMS

JOHN ENDECOTT TO JOHN WINTHROP[1]

DEAREST SIR, Hearing of the remarkeable stroake of Gods hand vppon the shippe and shipps companie of Bristoll,[2] as also of some Atheisticall passages and hellish profanations of the Sabbaths and deridings of the people and wayes of God, I thought good to desire a word or two of you of the trueth of what you haue heard: Such an extraordinary Iudgment would be searched into what Gods meaninge is in it, both in respect of those whom it concernes more espetiallie in England, as also in regard of ourselues: God will be honred in all dealings. We haue heard of seuerall vngodlie carriadges in that ship as, First in thee way overbound they would constantlie Jeere at the holie brethren of New England, and some of the Marriners would in a scoffe ask when they should come to the holie Land? [2.] After they lay in the harbor Mr. Norrice sent to the shippe one of our brethren vppon busines and hee heard them say, This is one of the holie brethren mockinglie and disdainefullie. 3. That when some haue bene with them aboard to buy necessaries, The shippe men would vsuallie say to some of them that they could not want any thinge, They were full of the Spiritt. 4. That the last Lords Day, or the Lords Day

---

[1] W. Au. 94; 4 *Collections*, VI. 141–142.
[2] The *Mary Rose* of Bristol blew up in Charlestown harbor on July 27, 1640. For Winthrop's account, see *Journal*, II. 9–10.

before there were many drinkinge aboard with singinge and musick in tymes
of publique exercise. 5. That the last Fast the Maister or captaine of the
shippe with most of the companie would not goe to the meetinge, but read
the booke of common prayer so often over that some of the company said hee
had worne that threedbare with many such passages. Now if theise or the
like be true, as I ame persuaded some of them are, I think the trueth heereof
would be made knowen by some faithfull hand in Bristoll and else where.
For it is a very remarkable and vnusuall stroake. Pardon I pray you my
boldnes heerein. You shall command mee in any seruice I can doe. I write
the rather because I haue some relation that way and shall therefore be glad
to be throughlie informed of theise things. This bein all at present I leaue
you with the Lord desiring myne and my wiefs heartie loue and seruice to be
remembred to your selfe and your dearest yoakefellow, and rest, Yours euer
assured

Jo: Endecott

Salem the 28th of the 5th moneth 1640

BILL OF WILLIAM HUDSON, SR.[1]

Bought of Wm. Hudson viz.

	li	s	d
Impr[imis] 3 C of lardg 6d nayls at 8d per C	00	02	00
Item 42 li. of smirna raysons at 30s per C	00	11	03
Item 5 payer of hooks and hinges qt 11 li. ¾ at 5d per li.	00	04	10
Item 6 squar staples	00	01	06
Item 6 hasps and 12 stapls	00	02	00
Item 3 C of hob nayls	00	00	09
Item 2 C of repair nayls	00	00	06
Item ½ C of 2s 6d nayls	00	01	05
Item 8 li. of pruns at 3d ½ per li.	00	02	04
Item ½ C of 10d nayls	00	00	5½
Item ½ C of 20d nayls	00	00	11
Item ½ C of 2s nayls	00	01	2
Item ½ C of 2s 6d nayls	00	01	04
Item ½ C of 3s 4d nayls	00	01	10
Item 1 C of 20d nayls	00	01	10

[1] W. 1. 136.

	li	s	d
Item 1 C of 2s nayls	00	02	04
Item 1 C of 10 nayls	00	00	11
Item 1 C of 6d nayls	00	00	07
Item 1 C of 2s nayls	00	02	04
Item 1 C of 2s nayls	00	02	04
Item 1 C of 2s nayls	00	02	04
Item 1 C of 20d nayls	00	01	10
Item ¼ li. of nuttmegs	00	02	00
Item 1 li. of Curants	00	00	08
Item 1 C of pruns at	01	05	00
Item 3 C of bisketts 24s per C	03	12	00
Item 12 yrds ½ of kersey at 3s 8d per yrd	02	05	10
Item For bread meale and flower	23	14	02
Item mor for bread	01	16	00
Item For iron ware delivered to Thomas Painter of Hingam	00	09	00
The whole somme is	35	11	06

Wherof I haue receaued   20li

[*Endorsed by Governor Winthrop:*] Wm. Hudsons Bill delivered to me (5) 28. 40.

LUCY DOWNING TO MARGARET WINTHROP[1]

To her much honerd sister mrs. margret winthrop this present Boston

MY MOST DEAR AND HONERD SISTER, I did intend to haue bin with you last
week, to gayne the best aduise I can for my head, but being preuented by the
hast of some others, and much busines of hay and harvest, and some mitti-
gation of payne for present, I am willinge to seru the times as far as god shall
pleas to inable. I know your self are now in the height of busines allso: I
thank you I receiued your great dayntyes of roswater and aples. I am much
obliged to you for them I wish I could as well deseru them. I pray excuse all
my bouldness with you:

I sent a box last week to your howse wich I desire may be set safe for me.
I allso sent my nephew winthrops cote and sadle theerwith   I hope he hath

¹ W. 4. 10; 5 *Collections*, I. 27–28.

it ere this. I pray present my seruis to my brother and all my nephews and euer command Your sister and seruant

L. D.

[*Ca.* August, 1640]

I haue a letter in my box for my brother from docter Wright.[1]

I would intreat you if you can hear of a good mayd seruant for all work: that is dayry and kitchin to stay one for me or send her to me.

ROGER WILLIAMS TO JOHN WINTHROP[2]

PROUIDENCE 7. 6. (so called) 40

SIR, About (from Portsmouth) I receaued yours. As I lately advertizd to Mr. Gouernour, the hurries of the natiues thoughts and consultations so continue, about the 3 Nayantaquits, prisoners with our friends at Qunniticut; that your runnawayes are longer secure in their escape then otherwise they should be.

The Monhiggin Sachem, Onkas, refuseth to part with his prey: And whereas Miantunnomu was going vp to Monhiggin himselfe with a sufficient company for the runnawayes, Onkas sent word that it was your worships plot to bring him into the snare at Monhiggin, that there the Qunnihticut English might fall vpon him.

Miantunnomu still promiseth me to come ouer to you, and his purpose (to his vtmost) to bring them with him. My occasions lead me within these 4 or 5 dayes to Qunnipiug, when (the Lord so permitting) I purpose to goe vp to Monhiggin and try the vtmost my selfe. The yssue of all is in that Euerlasting Hand, in which is our breath and our wayes, in whome I desire to b[e] still Your Worships [vn]faigned

ROGER WILLIAMS

I thanck your worship for the Scotch intelligence: The issue (I feare) will be generall and grieuous persecution of all Saincts.

Mine and my poore wiues best salutes to Mrs. Winthorp and all yours.

[*Endorsed by Governor Winthrop:*] Mr. Williams, (6) 10. 40.

---

[1] Cf. Lawrence Wright to John Winthrop, March 26, 1640 (page 220, above).
[2] Original not located; 4 *Collections*, VI. 265.

WILLIAM HOOKE TO JOHN WINTHROP[1]

To the Wor[shi]p[fu]ll John Winthrop Es: in Bostone

Wor[shi]p[fu]ll Sir, Mr. Dexter haeth bine at me for a longer tim for the payment of the 436*li* which is dewe vnto my father from him   I am willing to doe him all the good I canne in the thing to writ vnto my father to forbare him some serten time longer   I cannot conseue howe he canne paye it moneys being soe scearse in the Countrey without time   it make me the redier to helpe him finding him soe willing in doeing what he canne to make payment makeing noe question but my father will harken vnto what I shall desier him in the forbarance of this mony   Sir if I maye craue soe much at your hands by letter to giue my father notise of the scarcitie of monyes in the Countrey it will be a greate meanes to preuayle with him the more to harken vnto my letter and likewise that I haue done my Indeuer for the getting in of his moneys ore else my father maye thinke I might haue done more then I haue done.[2]

Worthy Sir one Courtise more I would desier your worshipp to doe for me if you thinke it conuenient   Mr. Godfree haeth informd my father of many false thinges by letter against me in my remoueing from Accomenticus   nowe ser you knowe vppon what grounds my remoueing was and what ends I propounded vnto my selfe in regeard of the vnsettellnesse of the Church and state   praye Sir satisfie him in your wisdome what you thinke meat   good Sir if you shall thinke it fitt send a letter by Mr. Dexter that I may send it to my father with my letters.

I found by my fathers letters which I receued this sommer my father was informed by some that pretended a greadell of loue vnto me that the Church Couenant did deney boeth king and prince and likewise bindeth a man from remoueing vppon any ocation to ould england   these are the thinges that makes my father soe vnwilling to my remoueing   And soe rest in hast leaueing your worshipp vnto the Allmity Lords protecktion Your seruant euer to command

WILLI. HOOKE

Dated In Lin 15 daye [August?] 1640

---

[1] W. 3. 52; 4 *Collections*, VII. 197–198.

[2] On August 20, 1640, Thomas Dexter mortgaged to Humphrey Hooke, alderman of Bristol, and others, as security for payment of £500, his eight-hundred-acre farm in Lynn with all the appurtenances, together with twenty head of cattle and his crops. *Suffolk Deeds*, I. 15.

WILLIAM BRADFORD TO JOHN WINTHROP[1]

To his worthy and beloued freind mr. John Winthrop Esquier these be delivered

WORTHY SIR, I most kindly thanke you for your loue and paines, in aquainting me with the newes from our owne Countrie   the Lord be mercifull to them, and vs, and teach vs to make that vse thereof that is befitting so sade a condition. I had sundrie courrantoes came to my hands out of holand: In one wherof (bearing date in Nouember last) ther is mention made of an Inquision, and search made through all Englande of all the papists in the land, and the number giuen to the king weer aboue tow hundred thowsand families; and of them were found to be 16000 of the spiritualitie (as they call them)   what may be the reason of this search is not expressed, but is not hard to be conjectured. We hear a rumorie that our freinds of Coonightecute Intend to begine a warr with the Narrigansets speedilie; If you know any Certaintie therof, I desire you would be pleased to aquaint vs with it, that we may the better looke to our owne defence. I wish they may goe vpon good grounds least they bring euill vpon them selues, and their Nighbours. but If Justice, or necessitie compell them; they shall not (in my judgmente) doe well to linger so longe as to giue them time to geather in their corne. But the Lord direct them to doe, and you to counssell them as may be for the best in so waighty a case. Thus with my humble thankfullnes vnto you for your loue, which I esteeme precious, I rest Your vnworthy freind

WILLIAM BRADFORD

PLIM: 16 6 month 1640

RICHARD VINES TO JOHN WINTHROP[2]

To the right wo[rshipfu]ll his honored Freind John Wentrop Esqr. thse Boston

RIGHT WO[RSHIPFU]LL, Your letter concerning Capt. Vnderhill received and another since about the attatching of Mr. Purches his estate, wherin you desire to be certified the truth by mee. that and much more you may command of me. Mr. Purches engaged himselfe to come to Saco at his retourn from the bay to answeare to such Complaints as was against him or else to giue Security to appeare at our next court. Mr. Greenesmith was by when

¹ W. Au. 100; 4 *Collections*, VI. 159–160.
² W. 3. 92; 4 *Collections*, VII. 338–340.

this promise was made: at that present tyme I received a letter with a greate Complaint from Capt: Thomas Young, how that Mr. Purches had endeavored to hinder his discoveries by many [*torn*] Suggestions and he feared to the overthrow of his designes promising to produce many witnesses to proue it, and desired iustice from our Court for that the wrong was offred within our Province. Ther ar likewise some accions of debt against him, and an accion of the Case to the value of 20*li* at the least, and one other matter of great moment I haue against him, which I forbeare to prosecute or mencion till I speake with your selfe, which shalbe with the first Conveniency. Now when we heard that Mr. Purches had carried away his Cattell and other goodes for the Massachusetts, and was intended to fetch away the rest with all Speed, we sent vp our marshall to his house to require Security for his appearance at our next court (for the Causes aboue specified) if in case no Security would be given then to attach and sease vpon soe much goodes as might secure his appearance. the goodes left were attached, whervpon Mr. Jordan a minister (that kept the house in Mr. Purches his absence) went with the marshall to gett some of the neighbours to be bound for the appearance, but none would. he carried one hundred twenty od yeards of Indians beades with him to be a pledge if in case his frend fayled. no Security being had the officer seased vpon the beades and brought them away. Since which tyme I sent to Mr. Purches who came and gaue security for his appearance. I offered him his beades, he would not receiue them but answeared me he would come by them by law: and this is the truth of the matter. I vnderstand by your letter that he hath put himselfe vnder your goverment, notwithstanding I conceiue that soe long as he hath goodes, Chattells house Land and servants within our Province, he is like wise within our goverment, and lyable to it. I desire your answeare and opinion herin, for that I shalbe very vnwilling to entrench vpon your Priveleges in the least measure, having found your selfe far dissonant from the like vnneighbourly acts. Thus ceasing farder to trouble you; with my respectiue service to your selfe I rest Your assured freind and servant

RICH: VINES

ACCOMINTICUS 21th Aug: 1640

EZEKIEL ROGERS TO JOHN WINTHROP[1]

To the worsh[ipfu]ll his much honoured freinde John Winthorpe Esqr. these

WORTHY SIR, Hauing no opportunity last weeke to speake much with you; and hauing founde both acceptance and courtesy from you; and being in this holy and neere bond of communion in the Churches with you, I thinke my selfe bound in all Christian duty, to acquaint you with two things, which I shall commende to your wisdome and thoughts, especially hauing a messenger that I dare trust.

First, that many of Gods people did thinke that some of the Court were very sharpe in dealing with Mr. Hawthorne, and aboue that he deserued, if matters be well scanned.

Secondly, some haue also reported, that Mr. Hawthorne alledging that he tooke aduise concerning some buisinesse with the Elders, yourselfe shoulde reply to this effect, That his so aduising with the Elders woulde be to the ouerthrowe of you all.[2] Because I am assured that you suffer in the minds of many for this, I durst not but lett you vnderstand thus much, that you make vse of it, as shall seeme good to you; and as I doe desire you will be pleased, to acquaint me with any thing that may, in the like or any other kinde concerne me.

Sir, my God is wittnesse (which is a greate expression, and to be vttered aduisedly) that I doe vnfeinedly wish your welfare and prosperity both spirituall and temporall, and that this my aduertisement proceedes from no other grounde. And if you knewe how many my businesses are and exercise about my owne hart, you woulde beleeue that I needed not make my selfe any newe worke, which I did not thinke God doth putt on me. But I will not now be further troublesome to you. My seruice and loue to your selfe and worthy yokefellowe, so I committ you to God Yours in Him to command

Ez. ROGERS

ROWLEY, 23 of the 6, 1640

[*Memorandum by Governor Winthrop:*] My answer in the other side.

I thanked him for his faithfullnesse. That I remembred not Mr. Hawth: matter, that I was sure I vsed no suche expression, it being against my Iudgment and practice. I confessed that for a man to oppose the Iudgment

---

[1] W. 3. 57; 4 *Collections*, VII. 213–214.

[2] Cf. Winthrop's statements about the part played by the elders in the election of a governor in May, 1640. *Journal*, II. 3.

of some Elders to the Iudgement of the Court openly in Civill matter (which might be the Case) was worthy reproofe, and I think likely I might saye something to that purpose. I desire him to produce my accusers that I might be cleared or iustly condemned. That if I heard not from him I would cleere myselfe publickly.

WILLIAM CODDINGTON TO JOHN WINTHROP[1]

To the Wor[shipfu]ll and his much respected Frind John Winthrope Esqr. at his howse in Boston deliver Per Mr. Jer. Gould

NEWPORT Aug. 25, 1640

WOR[SHIPFU]LL AND BELOUED, Your leter of the 11th of the 4 mo. I recaiued the substance of your whole leter to me falles into these 2 heads.

First will conserne your Church Covenant. this I aleged in my former leter as that which wos the princepale force with me, which you did not answer vnto, viz. That it doth remayne to be proved by the rules of the gosple, that any Church ever clamed power over their brethren remoued, more then over those that wos never in fellowshipe with them. Mr. Hibings promised, and I accepted, That your church Covenant should be sent, with grounds to prove this poynte. the other that yow answer tow, of the advice I had taken with Elders and brethren in the poynt, and of the consent of the maior part of the Church wos but subordenate to this.

2 head of your leter doth trench vpon the passages concerning Mr. Weelewrights Banishment. what I did therin wos in discharge of my conscence in my place. and trewley Sir to my deserneing whither yow did well or I, depends of the trewth of the cause, the way of souluation and Evidenceing therof, which Mr. Cotton and he affermed, and the rest of the Elders opposed, which remaynes yet controvered for ought I knowe. I well approue of a speech of one of note amongest yow, that we were in a heate, and Chafed, and were all of vs to blame. in our strife, we had forgoten wee were brethren not further at this present.

I wos advised by leter first out of the Baye that the governor, and the deputy, and other of the magistrates had adviced and incouraged the towne of Brantree to commence a sute aginest me after I recaiued a note from the Governor that it wos for a promise. I knowe no thing of it, in regard wherof I desire that the Plantiues may put in their Complant in answer and that I

---

[1] W. 2. 129; 4 *Collections*, VI. 316–318.

may haue tyme giuen to put in my defence, seing, for these Reasons I haue
aleged to the Governor, and others, I cannot be free to come and plead my
cause and seing it is according to what is practized in our Natiue Land, and
the Courts of Justice ther established. I could wish that we, that haue liued
7 yeares in place of magistracey to geather might not multeplye greveances
one aganest an other, but I shall not ade further therin I haue sent over
the Berer Mr. Jer. Gould, who is desirous to confere with your wor[shi]p
about it. the Naragansets and Nantequits keepe constant wach sence Conect-
ecute men touck 3 Nantequits. ther be 12 notorious murder[er]s yet liueing
4 at Nantequite and 8 of them at Mohegen according to my best intelegence,
whose names I haue   the Nanteqets would deliuer vp their 4 but they would
haue Ocas first deliuer vp his 8, that they may see its Justice the English
seekes. With my loue and my wifes presented to your selfe and yours I rest
yours

Wm. Coddington

[*Endorsed by Governor Winthrop:*] Mr. Coddington about the Church etc.
(6) 25. 40.

EDWARD CARLTON TO JOHN WINTHROP[1]

To the Right wor[shi]p[fu]ll Mr. John Winthrope esqr. att Boston giue this
in hast I pray you

RIGHT WOR[SHI]P[FU]LL, my purpose is by reason of some speciall prouidence for to goe into england by the Sparrow (if the lord will) the time
that I haue to prepare my selfe for that longe and tedious iorney, is not lik
to be aboue 7 dayes, otherways I thought for to haue come my selfe for to
haue reckoned with you: but haueinge soe much to doe at home that I could
not possibly come, therfore I doe much intreat you as my case requires for
to send me by this bearer the remander of what is betwixt vs: first you know
that there was betwixt vs in money 79 pounds: but after there was 5 pounds
to be taken of: soe the sume was 73 pounds: of which I haue had 28 pounds
in money: one heifer which at this day will not giue 14 pounds: I thinke if
any would buy hir shee may be sold for 20 markes: as for the Cow and Calfe
which you sent me: I gott one to look vpon hir that day shee came too me:
and thei did thinke that if hir age and pouertye with the price that Cattell
then did beare she and hir Calf would not giue much aboue 20 pounds: I

---

[1] W. 4. 106; 5 *Collections*, 1. 303–305.

am willing to sell them now for 22 pounds: soe that if you doe account the Cow and Calfe to 20 pounds and the heifer too 14 pounds: the money which I haue receiued beinge 28 pounds: amountinge in all to 62*li*: then there remaines in that 11 pounds: the quantitye of Corne that was due too me was 150 bushells: of which I haue receiued 70 bushells: soe there remaines 80 bushells of which I am willinge accordinge to your desire for to take after 4 shillings a bushell for 60 bushells, tho I payed too pownd 6 shillings a bushell; and for the other 20 bushells I shall giue order to some for to receiue of you for the vse of my familye: soe that in all there is 23 pounds due vnto me: there was a steare calfe which I was to haue had of Luxford with the cowe that I bought of him: which yit I neuer had: tho I might of had of him a heifer calfe if that I durst haue taken it but I would not for that he told me it was his wiues: but if you be pleased I shalbe willinge to cast it in with your cow price att 20 pounds: yett as I sayd you shall haue her for 22 pounds: and I am confident that she is better like than shee was when she came be 40 shillings: good Sir I beseech you for to lett me know in what I am or haue beene [*illegible*] in. I shall endeuor for to giue you full satisfaction in it: for truly I haue counted it no small mercye that prouidence did soe order it that I fell into the hands of such an one as I did: but sorry I am for what you haue and doe suffer still in regard of that cross prouidence towards you: now my comfortable goeinge for my outward man consists in your sendinge me the moneys that is due too me: which is 23 pounds for I haue not any to help me forward in that iorney: I did not think for to haue troubled you about it this long time: but now the lord is pleased to try me sadly by some vnexspected newes: therfore I beseech you that you would help me: truly I was neuer putt into such a straite in all my dayes: that I know of. I hope for to see you before I goe: somwhat I haue at home to discharge and alsoe to buy before I goe   thus with my truest seruice to my selfe I rest Yours to vse in what he may

ED: CARLTON

I purpose for holland if that you will be pleased to comand of me any seruice.

Sir I doe humbly intreate you for a beagle that will hunt the wouls well: ether that you lend me one: or that you will giue me one. I desire that you can doe soe that he might come by this bearer.

From ROWLEY the 7 day of the last weeke [*ca.* August 29, 1640][1]

[1] This date is based on Carlton's statement at the beginning of his letter that he hoped to go

Received with mr. Carlton and made over for all debts and things between him and James Luxford, and made over for all save 80 bushels of
Indian corne at 4*s* the bushel which is to be delivered him at the water side
in the Massachusetts at the rate of the markett.

EDWARD CARLTON[1]

8. 10. 1640

[*Endorsed by Governor Winthrop:*] Mr. Carltons Account for all matters.

FRANCIS DOUGHTY TO JOHN WINTHROP[2]

To the much honoured Magistrat Mr. John Winthrop these deliver in Boston

SIR, my service remembered to your Worship, may it please you hearinge
my sister Cole hathe petitioned against me,[3] I make bold to intreat you doe
me the fauor to let me vnderstand theffect of her proceeding and whether I
shall need to attend the next Court and what you guesse she will doe then
and when the Court is. I pray God increase your honour and perpetuate
your happinesse resting, till you Command

FR: DOUGHTY

Towards the end of August 1640 from TAUNTON

EZEKIEL ROGERS TO JOHN WINTHROP[4]

To the Worsh[ipfu]ll his worthy freinde John Winthorpe Esqr. at Boston these present

WORTHY SIR, I blesse God for your Christian acceptance of my simple
expression: He haue all the glory therof, and ourselues incouragement to
deale vprightly in any the like cases, yea in all. Your iudgment concerning
consultation with the Elders in waighty cases, is sounde and according to
the worde; and though you shoulde gett little else but prayer, it woulde be

to England "by the Sparrow" (William Goose, master) and on the evidence (*Lechford's Notebook*,
304) that Goose, on the first of September, was making arrangements for his departure.

[1] All but the signature of this receipt is in Governor Winthrop's handwriting. The handwriting of Carlton's signature here differs from that of the signature to his letter.

[2] W. 4. 107; 5 *Collections*, I. 308. For Doughty, see 5 *Collections*, I. 308n.

[3] For documents in the case of William and Elizabeth Cole *vs.* Francis Doughty, see *Lechford's
Notebook*, 137, 171–174, 256.

[4] W. 3. 57; 4 *Collections*, VII. 214–215.

no losse. Godly wisdome shoulde teach vs, both not to intermeddle where we haue no call, and to knowe what respect belongs to Christian Magistrates. If they and we shalbe taught of God to ioine together in all things with loue and consent, it wilbe no small pledge of Gods being among vs; I tremble to adde the contrary; quod Deus noster auertat. Touching the buisinesse of the Bounds, which we haue now in agitation; I haue thought, that a good fence helpeth to keepe peace betweene neighbours; but let vs take heede that we make not a high stone wall, to keepe vs from meeting.

Wheras you speake of clearing your selfe in publique, I shoulde desire (if you please) to speake with you first: which I hope to doe before the Generall Court. So with my respects and loue, I committ you to God, and shalbe glad if in any thing you will vse or commande Your poore freinde

Ez. Rogers

Rowly last of 6, 1640

EDWARD CARLTON TO JOHN WINTHROP[1]

To the right Wor[shi]p[fu]ll Mr. John Winthrop Esq. att Boston giue this

Right Wor[shi]pp[fu]l, I am willinge still that the Cow may be looked vpon and prised as shee might be worth at the time shee came too me   as for bullocke of Salem I know not: but this I know that there is diverse euen for your mris. sake is apt to bid more and alsoe to giue more for a commodytye than it is worth: for my selfe[2] I haue not as yit found hir to equallise much lesse to exceed any Cow that I haue: which Cowes I prised at 20 pounde a yeere before the time that your Cow came to me: yit I say I am willing that any should prise hir as she was worth when shee came too me: and wher as you writ of your takeing offence and the Cause which you say was my takeinge interest for my money: first I say that which your man borrowed of me in your name was most of my estate: out of which I had a familye to meanteine, that I am to take care for in a way of the lord: againe when I told you that he did owe me money; I did not tell you of the interest that I was to haue for it   my reason was that I did thinke that you were priuye to all his doeinges: and as for the quantitye of money that I was to haue for the interest of a sume of a 170 pounds od money, was but 24 pounds accordingto as Corne ruled about the time that he had the money of me: the time that he had the money of me was nye a yeare and a halfe: soe that I know no grounde that

---

[1] W. 4. 108; 5 *Collections*, 1. 308–309.
[2] This is a doubtful reading.

you should take offence att: and besides I suppose that you are not ignorant what rate the country hath alwayes giuen for the interest of a 100 pound for a yeare: which is now 20 pound a yeare; it was sore against my mind that he had my money soe long as he had.

I doe belieue that if any one had gained no more by him then my selfe I thinke your estate would not haue beene impayred by him: soe that I hope there is noe just cause why you should be offended: my necessitye of my money putts me on exceedingly for to writ vnto you for it   the want of it in regard of my present necessitye is no small trouble too me: in that it came not by goodman Swane was one meanes that did stay me for goinge with Mr. Goose: I am loth to vrge you: but this I must say that my want was neuer soe much as now, considering what a matter lyes vpon the haueing of it: Sir I am but a stranger in the land; and therfor cannot doe as others may: soe that my hope for the present for the accomplishment of this bussiness comfortably relyes upon you   therfor my desire is that you would send it by this bearer: thus in [*illegible*] haist I rest Yours to vse in what hee may

ED: CARLTON

[*Ca.* September, 1640]

EDWARD CARLTON TO JOHN WINTHROP[1]

To the right Wor[shi]p[fu]l Mr. John Winthop esqr. att Boston giue these

RIGHT WOR[SHI]P[FU]LL, It is no litle trouble to me that my necessitye is such in regard of my iorney that I cannot be silent for the want of my money: I profess vnto you in the simplicitye of my hart if that I could haue procured moneyes any otherwayes, I would neuer haue beene soe vrgent with you as I haue beene: I doe bleiue if that you were but fully possossed with my condition and alsoe with the occasion that moues me to goe into England: you would very much commiserate my case: few intimate freinds I haue in this land: as for kindered none: a stranger I was to those of our owne plan-tation soe that my desire is that you would help me, and alsoe that you would not be offended with what I haue or doe write now vnto you: for as I haue sayd, soe I say still that if I had any other way to procure it: I should will-ingly haue lett it remaine in your hands till that you sent it me without any demaunding of it: and as I did formerly write vnto you, that the want of the moneyes was one prouidence that did hinder me for goeing in the Sparrow:

---

1 W. 4. 107; 5 *Collections*, I. 307.

but I am to goe (god willinge) with the next ship that goes for england which wilbee the next weeke: soe that I sent this bearer a purpose to you   thus good Sir I pray you consider of my necessitye: and passe by any weaknesses, which my necessitye and straite may moue me to fall into   Soe with an Expectation of what I haue and doe now writ for I rest Yours to vse and command in any thing that he can

ED: CARLTON

[*Ca.* September, 1640]

HENRY WALTON TO JOHN WINTHROP[1]

To the right Wor[shi]p[fu]ll John Winthrop Seneor in Boston these present

MOST RESPECTIUE SIR, My humble Seruice presented. Sir the occasion of these few lynes is humbly to entreate your wor[shi]p in the behalfe of our Company[2] to peruse these inclosed Lynes, and to be pleased In two or three words to Informe the bearer hereof whether it be needfull for vs to require any more of Mr. Forrett,[3] than to Subscreibe to this Inclosed writeinge, For Mr. Forrett beinge in some Straites desired vs to vndertake the payment of thirty pownds for him which wee haue donne In Case that your Wor[shi]p doe Conceaue that Mr. Forrett hath done that which is meete on his part, which writeinge is an agreement betweene him and vs, Concerneinge the bownds of our Towne.[4] Thus humbly Craueinge pardon for our often Troubleinge your wor[shi]p in this buisnes I humbly rest Yours to Command till Death

HENR WALTON

LYNNE 3th 7ber 1640

[*Memorandum by Governor Winthrop:*] my advice was to paye the 30*li* and to take a receipt as payd vpon the purchase because it was a valuable consideration which would strengthen their title against all men.

[*Endorsed by Governor Winthrop:*] about the 30*li* to mr. Forrett Long Iland.

---

[1] W. 1. 136.
[2] I.e., the founders of Southampton, Long Island. For Winthrop's account of the settling of that town, see *Journal*, II. 4–5
[3] James Farrett, agent for the Earl of Stirling, the grantee of Long Island.
[4] Adams, *History of Southampton*, 263–265 (Appendix IV).

HUGH PETER TO JOHN WINTHROP[1]

SALEM 6° Septi: [1640]

HONORED AND DEEREST IN THE LORD, Wee receiued your basket of bounty and loue to those who must dye in your debt, but leaue requitall of all to him who must discharge our greatest skores. I had both written, and seen you before now but that deepe melancholy is getting fast vpon mee agayne, and tethers mee at home, and much occasioned by my brethren ingaged before this time to come in with the discharge of your matters, but they try my patience in waiting. I hope not to bee long from you, and the rather to aduise for Mr. John Winthrops going with Mr. Bois to which I wholy inclyne: it will bee vsefull and exemplary. One mayne occasion of my writing at this tyme is in behalfe of Mr. Paddy this bearer, who earnestly desires some course may bee taken for what is due from the Country to his father Freeman for his Armes they had in the Pekot seruice for which hee might haue had 40*li*, and now desires but 15*li* of the Country to bee payd as they please for species. Good Sir, let him haue reliefe by what meanes you can, synce you know the Case and this present Gouernour doth not.

I thinke I shall neuer leaue to bee troublesome vnto you, pitty and pardon, and salute your deerest with all yours. Our strong and mighty Helper the God of Israel keepe vp your hart, and spirit, sweeten all your sowres, euen all your pathes and carry you through all difficultyes through Jesus Christ. In whom I am Yours fidelissime

H. PETER

I take it Captayn Gibbons can tell best of these arms.

INQUEST ON THE BODY OF WILLIAM RICHARDS[2]

An Inquisition taken at Boston the 15th daye of the 7th mo: 1640 vpon the veiw of the bodye of Willm. Richards lyinge dead vpon the Oathes of 12 freemen herevnder named, before John Winthrop one of the magistrats of this Jurisdiction as followethe

The Jury doe present that the said Wm. Richards, not havinge God before his eyes, but beinge seduced by the malice and instigation of the devill in and vpon the 14 daye of this 7th monthe in the after noone did enter into an

---

[1] W. 2. 56; 4 *Collections*, VI. 104–105.

[2] W. 4. 167; 5 *Collections*, I. 489–490. The body of the document is in the handwriting of Governor Winthrop.

outhouse of one Tho: Buttolfe his master and there with a rope which he fastned to one of the rafters or purleynes of the said house, and tyinge the other ende thereof about his neck he hanged and strangled himself and so the Jury doe find that he murdered himself and was guilty of his owne deathe.

JO: WINTHOP

EDWARD HUTCHINSON	JAMES EUERILL
ROBERT SCOTT	RICHARD COOKE
SAMUELL SHARMAN	HUGHE GUNISON
EDWARD BELCHER	GEORGE BURDON
RYCHARD HOGGE	NATHANIEL HEATON
THOMAS SCOTTO	ARTHR PERY

THOMAS MAYHEW TO JOHN WINTHROP[1]

To the wo[rshi]p[fu]ll Jno: Wynthropp senior Esquire

SIR: It hath beene three times published at Water towne meetinge howse that this Bearer Richard Gale and Mary Castle intended to enter into a Couenaunt of marriadge   not haueing els I Rest Your wor[shi]pps to Command

THOMAS MAYHEW

WATER TOWNE the 16th of the 7th 1640

PROPOSITIONS CONCERNING EVIDENCE OF GOD'S LOVE[2]

1: A Ch[ristia]n may have (vpon the manifestation of Gods free grace in the offer of the Gospell) some Comfort and staye of heart, by restinge vpon it: alltho he hath as yet no grace in himself.

2: A man can h[ave] no Evid[ence] or Ass[urance] of Gods special loue to his soule bef[ore] he doe beleeve in Christ.

3: After a man dothe beleeve there is a testimony of Gods sp[iri]t touching a mans good estate.

4: This testimony of the spirit is given only to beleevers, and suche as are adopted by Faith.

[1] W. 1. 136.
[2] W. 4. 168; 5 *Collections*, 1. 490–491. This document, including the signatures, is a copy in the handwriting of Governor Winthrop.

5: The most vsuall Testimony of the Sp[iri]t is togither with our Sp[iri]ts, or by the sight of Graces.

6: A Ch[ristia]n not doubting but supposing and takinge it for granted that he hath Grace in himself, may have Testimony of Gods love by the Sp[iri]t, without present actuall reasoninge or mindinge of his Graces.

7: To a Ch[ristia]n doubtinge of his Grace or not knowinge it, there is no Testimony of Gods loue by the Spirit, without cleeringe vp in some measure of the truth of his Graces allso, either precedent or concommitant togither with the wittnesse of Gods love.

8: A Ch[ristia]n (by neare and immediate revelation of Gods love to him) dothe not thereby see his faith and sanctification, without experience by the helpe of the Word and Sp[iri]t of the truethe of their worke in his soule.

9: That the Test[imony] of Gods love which is not conf[erred] by foll[owin]g Grace is not the witt[ness] of Gods Sp[iri]t but a delusion.

10: There is no test[imony] of the Sp[iri]t in [*illegible*] that is without the word, either in the lettre or sence thereof.

11: When the Sp[iri]t witt[nesse]s Gods loue by the word in the sence of it, yet this test[imony] is to be tryed by the written word: that so it may be discerned to be indeed a test[imony] of the Sp[iri]t, and not a delusion. We conceive that these are agreeable to the truthe.

Jo: Philipps	Rich. Mather
Tho: Weld	Jo: Burre
Jo: Allen	Jo: Willson
Tho: Sheppard	Jo: Eliot

Roxbury (7) 23. 40

[*Endorsed by Governor Winthrop:*] About Evidence etc.

EDWARD HOPKINS TO JOHN WINTHROP[1]

*To the Wor[shipfu]ll his much Respected freind Jno. Winthroppe Esqr.
att his house in Boston deliver*

HARTFORD the 25° of 7[i] 1640

SIR, There was about 9 weeks since a suspitious fellow came into these parts, whom wee then examined and tooke order for his forthcomming when we should heare further concerning him. Since which wee haue vnderstood

---

[1] W. 2. 133; 4 *Collections*, VI. 333–334. For Hopkins, see *D.A.B.*

from Mr. Hatherley that he is a servant of his and ran away from him   he desires he might be sent backe and directed to your selfe which accordingly I haue now done. the mony which he hath earned since his coming into these parts hath beene for the most part layd out by him in apparrell which he hath with him   the rest I conceaue will scarcely suffice to pay for his passage.

I haue by the same pinnace also sent a small bundle of apparell and a white hatt which belongs to two Boyes of Mr. Thomas, who were returned backe to him. I pray you be pleased either to giue him some notice of it that he may send for it or to cause it to be sent to Mr. Bradford att Plymouth.

I shall not trouble you further att present but with remembrance of my best respects to your selfe and our other freinds there, doe take my leaue Resting Yours in what I may

EDWA. HOPKINS

JOHN TAYLOR TO JOHN WINTHROP[1]

To the Righte Worshipfull Mr. John Wintrope these be delivred I praye att his house in Boston

RIGHTE WORSHIPFULL, my servise remembred Vnto your selfe and Mrs. Wintrope, with many kind thankes for your last loue shewed to me att Boston att you house.

These are to intreate you to send vp those goods I left with you, by Goodman Grafton, or Goodman Codmore this returne I praye. if anye of the Caskes bee not hedded I praye lett me intreate soe much that you would bee pleased to lett some of your men to see them mended and putt into the pinnes.

soe at this time I leave you with my servise remembrd to your Worshipe and rest you[r]s to Comande in anye servise that I maye to my power

JOHN TAYLOR

From CONNECTICUTT this 28th of september 1640

[*Endorsed by Governor Winthrop:*] Jo: Taylor for Jo: Tinkers goods.

---

[1] W. 1. 136. The following memorandum by Governor Winthrop, written on the verso of this letter, appears to have no connection with it: "1000 acres vpon Shawshin river with 100 acres of meadow and the rest of such lands as the next Courte will to the house there, with liberty of fishing in a great pond lying about a mile and a half to the west of the said River; and that I may haue leaue to take the rest in some other place where it may be found."

HUGH PETER TO JOHN WINTHROP[1]

To the right wor[shipfu]ll John Winthrop Esqr. this present Boston

DEEREST SIR, I should not haue needed your last as a spurre to mee to write, had not my thoughts about yourselfe bin so succesles that I lost all courage that way, and am also at present fallen into a sore fit of my old hypocondriacal melancholy, through cold and care. My hartyest desires are for you and yours, and I could wish I knew what to doe to compas my purposes.

What my aduenture was at Pascataway I suppose Mr. Larkham[2] hath told you, and if death preuent not, I shall my selfe shortly. In the meane tyme remember mee where you may doe mee the most good, and I shall striue to retaliate.

The last newes sayes the Convocation[3] made 17 new Canons, wherof one is that all ministers shall preach 2ce per annum for conformity, and 4 tymes for the Kings prerogative: what past betwixt Mr. Williams at Pasc[ataway] and my selfe I shall tell you. The Lord bee with your spirits. Yours euer and euer

HU: PETER

SALEM vlt. Sept. [1640]

De nuptiis, nihil habeo præter ætatem quod displicet, videntur satis optandæ.

Salute the good gentlewom[an] and all with you.

EZEKIEL ROGERS TO JOHN WINTHROP[4]

[To] his much [honoured] freinde John [Winthrop] Esqr. these present

WOR[SHIPFU]LL AND WORTHY SIR, vpon my motion at the last Generall Court for an Exposition of our Grant (occasioned by the questioning of some) Mr. Broadstreete desiring some of the land granted to vs on the one side, and

---

[1] W. 2. 57; 4 *Collections,* VI. 107–108.
[2] The Reverend Thomas Larkham, leader of the church faction in Dover, New Hampshire, which was opposed to the Reverend Hanserd Knollys.
[3] The Convocation of the Province of Canterbury, which met in April and May, 1640. Samuel R. Gardiner, *History of England from the Accession of James I to the Outbreak of the Civil War* (London and New York, 1904), IX. 108, 142–148.
[4] W. 3. 58; 4 *Collections,* VII. 215–217.

Mr. Woodbridge on the other, opposition was made contrary to my exspectation, and noise raised to my greife; though the lesse because we were but the occasion, and others the cause. Yet to preuent euen that also, if it be possible, I am bolde to make this addresse to yourselfe; rather then to come personally to the Court, except I shall heare it to be necessary.

You best knowe how oft we expressed ourselues, and how plainly, concerning our desired bounds, as Ipsw[ich] Riuer and Merimack; without which we woulde vpon no termes accept of a Plantation here. Ipswich men desiring our neighbourhood, coulde shewe vs little desireable here (except we purchased it at a deare rate) but the Name of Merimack and some considerable places there, as a Neck of land, and the like. This first to your selfe, and after to others being expressed, you were all forwarde to testify your loues (as before, so) therupon, and we left the procuring of the Grant to yourselfe, who doubted not, but more, rather then lesse, (if it were desired) woulde be yeelded to. Wherupon I wrote many letters to my freinds in England, wherin I tolde them precisely of our bounds; and the sound of Merimack we made not a little vse of. Herupon we proceeded simply to our worke, and made a too-costly purchase: digested (though hardly) our too much straitning towards Ipswich etc. Now therfore to heare that questioned, which was especially looked at in our Grant, I say after all these our costly proceedings, your wisdome will thinke how welcome it is to vs: Besides my owne credite, which hitherto God in mercy hath maintained, must be now of no value among my freinds. Two things especially seeme to be objected to vs. First the largenes of our Plantation, if we haue our desire. To this I say, First, suppose it so, yet no lesse was accepted of vs. Secondly, I say, so farre as I can discouer, no plantation hath had lesse granted of the Court, though we haue our desire. For our largenes comes from our owne purses, or the gift of those that desired our neighbourhood, and would incourage vs in the purchase. Neither doe we purpose to keepe this lande vnimployed so long by halfe, as others haue done, if God prosper vs.

We are loth to say all we might, except we be vrged. The second thing objected is, the words of the Grant, as it is recorded, that mention (they say) only eight miles euery waye. I answere that I suppose that might (if it be so) arise from hence, that many in the Court did not doubt, but that eight miles did afford vs our desired bounds: but this we say, that if we could not haue them vnder eighteene miles, we were to haue so much as did reach them. And it seemes the Register only looked at the Text not comment. And it wilbe prooued by good wittnesse, if neede be; That Newbery men desiring two miles more by Merimack, your selfe instantly replyed (which I heard hisce auribus) that that could not be, because it was granted already to vs. So that the notion of eight miles was not the main matter, but Merimacke.

Sir, I am hartely sory thus farre to trouble you: but your wisdome will see a necessity, and therfore pardon. I humbly beseech you to acquaint our worthy Gouernour herwith, and so many of the Court, as you see fitt, or the whole.[1] I am sory also to thinke how harsh such things are like to be in England and Quillipiake, as they are like to be carryed thither quickly, if they be noised in open Court, so that it were well if that were preuented. It hath bene a trouble of late to my poore neighbours (though a quiet people) to heare of this, after their purchase and building, and returne from Quillip-yake. Especially, since they heard that Mr. Broadstreete plainly in open Court saide he exspected land there, and therupon opposed vs; as I haue signifyed to himselfe, and doe thus write, because he still saide he intended to doe so. Though happily, if your selfe doe satisfy him, he will forbeare. But I forgett your trouble, therfore againe crauing pardon, with my seruice I rest Yours to commande

Ez: Rogers

ROWLEY, 5 of 8, 1640

EDWARD WINSLOW TO JOHN WINTHROP[2]

To the w[orshi]pp[fu]ll his much honored Friend Joh. Winthrop Esqr.
at his howse at Boston these be delivered

Sir, By the enclosed you may perceiue the ernest request of your unfaith-full servant Luxford who hath no lesse but much more importuned me since I rec[eived] his lines using Pauls plea for Onesimus etc. but you know the man and his manner of importunity, pleading his paines and care so many yeares, and however his faylings were great yet I perceiue he thinks his paines to be greater and that in his extreame necessity you should take compassion on him, but I refer him to your mercy and yet would haue you consider well what you doe. The truth is I thinke he is very pore: for he worketh not, yet offered me his labor this harvest for his dyet which for some reasons I durst not accept but pitty the man. He hath taken a Farme of Mr. Hanbury which was Mr. Browns at 40*li* per annum, but how he will pay it or raise it I know not, especially when he hath neither stock security foode nor credit. He saith

---

[1] The General Court took action on October 7, 1640, to satisfy Rowley's grievances regarding the boundaries of the town. *Records of Massachusetts*, I. 305; *Journal*, II. 15–16.

[2] W. 2. 91; 4 *Collections*, VI. 169–170.

there are some in the bay that will affourd him some help but who they are or what it is I know not.

I suppose you haue heard what was the issue of the day of humiliacion concerning the eleccion of Mr. Chancey;[1] But things are like still to goe ill for on the 2d day of this weeke a mocion was made by Mr. Paddy and some that inordinately cleaue to him for his setling at Jones river some three miles from Plim[outh] who purposeth there to lay the foundacion of an Academy, and reade the Arts to some that are fitt for that purpose that so they may also haue use of his gifts. I manifested my dislike to the Gov[ernour] who still pressed his gifts, but I told him they must still retaine his errors etc.[2] with his gifts which were like to weaken if not destroy both the Congregacions of Plym[outh] and Duxburrow being seated in the midst equally between both having already manifested his judgement to be more rigid then any Separatists I ever read or knew; holding it lawfull (nay a duty for ought I heare) to censure any that shall oppose the major part of the Church whether it be in eleccion of officers or receiving in or casting out of members if they will not be convicted and yield by which meanes 10 or more may be cast out to receiue in one. But what will be the issue of these things the Lord onely knoweth; I feare the Lord hath a quarrell with us, and the rather becawse Mr. Bradford and Mr. Reyner are both drawn to yield to the mocion which is so contrary in my apprehension to the peace of the Churches, especially when I consider the confidence or rather selfewillednes of the man. Truly Sir I conceiue if you conceale how you come by your informacion, and giue your christian advice to Mr. Bradford spedily about it you may be the instrument of much good. For my selfe however I am ready to demand a dismission from them, yet I simpathise with them and desire their welfare as much as ever, and for me to oppose he hath such a party as I might rather expect dismission with a Censure then otherwise: But entreating you to conceale your author, and commending you and it with all yours to the blessing of the blessed God with many thanks for your last loue take leaue remayning Yours till death

                                                          EDW: WINSLOW

CARESWELL this 10th of 8th 1640

Mr. Blindman salutes you.

[1] The Reverend Charles Chauncy, at this time assistant to the Reverend John Rayner in the Plymouth church and later (1641–1654) minister of Scituate and (1654–1672) President of Harvard College.

[2] For Chauncy's "errors" on the subject of baptism, see *Journal*, II. 321–322; Bradford, *History of Plymouth*, II. 300–307.

JOHN HILL TO JOHN WINTHROP[1]

October 13, 1640

On the 16 of August last, I arrived at Newe England.

On the 25 of August last, I received 5*li* of Mr. Mathewe Allyne, as part of of 40*li*, due from him to me, on the 13 daye of September then next followe-inge, vpon the Forfaiture of a Bond of 80*li*. But my principall mony was not answeared, till the 10th daye of this present month of October, beinge a full month after the time of due payement.

And the Forfaiture of my Bond, or my losses or dammages arisinge ther-vpon, ar not answeared to this daye nor will they be ever answeared, vnless some frind doe helpe me. And my dammage is as followeth.

On the 24th of September last, beinge Thursedaye I had passed for Bris-towe in mr. Willkinge his Shipe, but wanting my mony, I have stayed here, till this daye, which will be 3 weekes next Thursedaye and I shall be very like to staye here 3 weekes or a month longer to my owne cost and charge; which is much to my small stocke of 30*li*, all my temporall State, to sustaine me.

But Mr. Allynes answeare, and all his answeare, is this because he payed me 5*li* of my 40*li* 20 dayes before my 40*li* was due.

Therfor he thinkes it Lawefull for him to keepe the other 35*li* of my 40*li* from me, 28 dayes after it was due; not regardinge herein, either the forfai-ture of his Bond of fourscore pounds or my losse and dammage of 6, 7, or 8 weekes charges for want of my mony or that he hath had my mony this halfe yeare gratis, payeinge noe vse for it   Your humble Servant

JOHN HILL

[*Endorsed by Governor Winthrop:*] Mr. Jo: Hill and Mr. Allyn.

JOHN PHILLIPS TO JOHN WINTHROP[2]

To the right w[orshi]pful Mr Winthrop

SIR, these 2 persons Thomas Paine of Salem and Rebecca Ware my servant, were contracted at Dedham above a moneth since, and their contract pub-

---

[1] W. 1. 138. The writer of this letter was doubtless the John Hill to whom Samuel Haskell, a silk throwster of London, gave a bond on October 26, 1640, to pay Hill £7 "upon the Arrivall of the ship the green Lyon in England aboard the said ship." *Lechford's Notebook*, 327.

[2] W. 1. 137.

lished thrice in the several townes; may it please yow to accomplish their marriage. so I remaine yours in Chr[ist]ian Service

Jo: Philip

Roxbury 8ber 17, 1640

ARBITRATION
BETWEEN MR. NORTON AND RICHARD ARRESBY[1]

(8) 20. 40: Inter Norton Defendant and Richard Arresby

Mr. Norton

That he offered Ar[resby] 20 nobles per annum and he seemed well pleased.

that his passage was not granted to his knowledge.

that his tyme was to begin when he came to vndertake the businesse which he thinks was Augt. 10.

That he married since, and his wife hath been a charge and no benefit, haveinge nothing to doe but milk Cowes. He charges hir not with any vn-faithfullnesse, and the Cattle have thriven well. He was contented his wife should be there and have her diett.

For the 8*li* Arresby disbursed 12 months since he had his owne and his boyes passage allowed which should have been payd in England and he had sope etc. 2*li*.

For the boyes Clothes which dyed he did not meddle with them, but if he knowes where they are he may have them.

Arresby

That his tyme was to begin when he landed.

That he landed at Dorchester June 23 in the John 1639.

That he went to Conectecutt with mr. Nortons leave and was here again 3 weeks after, and went presently to Pascat[aqua].

That his wife was entertained by mr. Nortons consent, she provided diet for 5, 6, 7, 8 workmen in hay tyme. She made butter and cheese and some sent to Mrs. Norton. she holpe tende the Cattle while the boye was offe in the baye. They are agreed from the 7th of this monthe to the 25 of the 1 monthe for 20*s* the monthe and a bushel of Corne.

---

[1] W. 1. 137. The body of the document is in the handwriting of Governor Winthrop.

Arbitrated

That his tyme shalbe accounted to begin July 1 his tyme at Conecticutt restored.

That his wages for him selfe and wife for that yeare shalbe 20*li*.

That he shalbe allowed 20*s* above the boyes passage which dyed.

That his mony for his owne and his boyes passage (which is vsually payd before hand) shalbe sett against the mony he disbursed for his wife.

That he shalbe allowed 20 nobles for him selfe and wife for the tyme since his year ended to the 7th of this month.

Jo: Winthrop
Wm: Tynge

INVENTORY OF JOHN WINTHROP'S GOATS[1]

Ocktober 28, 1640

Sir ther be of yor old [*illegible*] of gotes:	6
of your [*illegible*] of gotes	6
of yeline kids	6
of wehther kids	2

by me Jo: Porter

[*Endorsed by Governor Winthrop:*] Goates (8) 31, 40.

JAMES COLE TO JOHN WINTHROP[2]

To the right worshipfull mr. John winthurpe in bostowne this be delivered at his house

Right worshipfull, I haue receaued a leter from you by mr. browne, conseringe a deet due vnto you of 62 pound: mr padey haue apounted me to pay vnto Daniell Coall of plemoueth 30 pound: before your leter came, and I haue payed him on thurd of it and the rest with as much speed as I can: and for the other 32 pound I desier you to forbear me in regard that mony is so carse, and the wine which I had of goodman luxford I had a hard bargaine of it   I lost thre hoegsets of it by the resonn of rotinge Caske that it

[1] W. 1. 139.
[2] W. 1. 138. For Cole, see Savage, *Genealogical Dictionary*, 1. 427.

was in, therfore I desier you forbeare me   I will god willinge macke you satisfaxtion in Corn or other commodytis by the springe or a litell after so in hast I rest

JAMES COALL

From PLEMOUETH nouember second day of the moneth 1640

I talked with mr. browne about it and he tould me that he would writ vnto you about it for in trueth I haue it not at present to pay.

HENRY SMITH TO JOHN WINTHROP[1]

To the Right Wor[shipfu]ll John Winthrop these be delivered at his howse in Boston

RIGHT WOR[SHIPFU]LL AND DULY RESPECTED, yow lately wrote a letter to my Father[2] wherein yow intimate that yow have seene a sufficient letter of Atturny from the 2 sisters of John Alline to John Porter of Hingham to receive theyr brothers estate and to give a discharge. Now I was made Executor by his will in my Fathers absence, and the most of his estate lay in goods and land as the Inventory will declare, soe that I putting off the most of his goods, have received verry little mony, and soe bin forced to take it in worke or such like payment, and some depts are yet due, and those have nothing to pay but corne: there is only seaven pownds which my Father will take order to be forthwith payde in to yow, and for the remaynder I shall either send corne to be delivered at Boston at the price the market affords at springe, or else pay in any other goods I have as it shall be judged worth by indifrent men, For mony is not to be gotten with vs for any goods we have. I shall desire to heare from yow how the Atturny accepts of this course of payment, and accordingly I shall address my selfe for performance, and with all deliver vp the accounte, dependinge on what yow wright for my discharge. thus forbearinge to be further troublsome at present I rest Your worships in all due respectiveness

HENRY SMITH

SPRINGFEILD this 2th November 1640

	li	s	d
The totall some of the Inventory is	38	13	03
His Depts Are	05	03	08
Soe ther resteth due	32	09	07

---

[1] W. 4. 109; 5 *Collections*, I. 310.
[2] I.e., his father-in-law, William Pynchon.

JOHN BROWNE TO JOHN WINTHROP[1]

COHANNETT the 3th of November 1640

WORTHY SIR, your letter to James Cole I haue deliuered but haue noe hope of getting Any money of him: he saith he did Owe you 62*li* but three munthes since Wm. Paddy gaue him Order to pay 30*li* of it to Daniell Cole of Duxbery, part wherof he hath Alredy payed. for the 32*li* he saith he hath hope to get you to spare him yet A yeare longer   he saith he hath payd for goods had of Luxford by Mr. Paddyes Appoyntment neare 100*li* soe that if Mr. Paddy should seeme to you that hee would giue mee satisfaxtion hee is worthy blame, for he never spake word to mee tending to such an End worth receuing An Answer from mee: I thought fit to certefy you herof having soe fit An Oportunity as this bearor by whome I desyre to heare from you if your Occasions will permit Soe resting your loving Frend

JOHN BROWNE

EVIDENCE AGAINST HENRY WALTHAM[2]

As conserning the old mr. Waltham there are 5 women of hingham that if they be called out they can speake of his lacivious cariage. the 1 is the wife of Andrew Lane, who when she was a mayd she wanting a payre of shooes she heard that mr. Waltham had a payre and she coming to the house he was with out the dore and she asked him if he had any shooes, he sayd he had and so he went in and she went in after him   now the house was remote from other houses and it had 2 romes in it and he went into the roome wher his bed was and would have her to com in but she was loath but he told her that else she could not see the shooes and so with much adoe she went in and when she came in he showed her a payre of mans shoes. then she told him those would not serve her and so turned about to go from him out of the roome but he caught hold of her and told her that he would kisse her and he held her close to him with his left hand and kissed her and when he had so done he did grope her all about her body with his other hand and she being much affrayd did not know what to doe beleving that he would offer her abuse: and she could not call to any   then by the providence of god ther did a man come in while he was so doing to her and then he let her goe.

---

[1] W. 4. 109; 5 *Collections*, I. 311. For Browne, see 5 *Collections*, I. 311n.
[2] W. 1. 139. For Waltham, see 5 *Collections*, I. 311n.

the 2 next are the wifes the one of Thomas Lincolne the goate keeper, the
other of Goodman farrow: which were at his house together to buy biskett
and some other things now he was so audacious that he sett hands in both
of them and did grope ther bodyes likwise in a very lacivious manner and
would not give them the things that they came for but would have them to
lye ther all night, and would have had goodman Lincolne his wife to have
promised him when she would come to him agayne. the other was the wife
of William Buclan she was sent by her husband to buy tobacco of him, and
when she came he likwise sett hands in her but whatt his words were to
him [*sic*] she will not tell but if she be called on her oath I doubt not but she
will tell, but she being wroth with him flung from him the last is the wif
of George Lane she likwise being sent by her husband for tobacco she came
first to the mill and asked the milleard if ther were any milk to mr. waltham
his house for she was very dry and he told her noe, but when she came to
his house he would faine have her to come in to the inner roome and ther
she should have some milke and watter to drinke and with that she suspected
him and would not go in because the milleard told her they had no milke
and she would not go in but stood at the doore then he came to her and
went to plucke abroad her bossome and she was much afrayd of him and
did labour to come nearer to the dore but he kept fidling about her bossome
and asked whither she was with child or no and moreover loked in her face
and asked her wher she did pray or no then at length when she saw her
opertunity she ran from him being much afrayd and therfor I would pray
you to consider of it whither he be fitt for honest company or else should
be confined and I would intreat your advise whether you can grant warrants
for these women this court or els that he should be presented for it.

[November 14, 1640]

[*Memorandum by Governor Winthrop:*] For these wittnesses, it were needfull they
should be examined.

[*Endorsed by Governor Winthrop:*] against mr. Walton of Weymouth Mrs. R:[1]
(IX) 14. 40.

---

[1] Probably Welthian, the wife of Thomas Richards of Weymouth, partner of Waltham in the
mill there. On other occasions she referred unflatteringly to Waltham as "a cozener and a cheater"
and as one that "never feared God nor never will." *Lechford's Notebook*, 321, 373.

ARBITRATION AGREEMENT[1]

We Hendry Neale, Hendry Hobson and Willm. Penn do bind our selues in twenty pound apese to stand to the arbitterment of Alexander Winchester James Penyman Steven Kinsle Gregory Baxter Samvell Bass Thom. Matson and Willm. Chesebrough all oth[e]r covenants betwene vs the said Hendry Neale and Hendry Hobsonn to be of none effect witnes our hands this 25th of the 9th 1640.

Wittnes   Hendry Neale X his mark
  Willm. Chesebrough   Willm. Pen X his mark
  Matthew Barnes   Hendry Hobson X his mark

It is ordered by vs hose names are vnderwriten that Hendry Hobson shall be released From Hendry Neale soone as we can provide him of a Fitt m[aster] with home the said Hendry shall serve out his hole tyme[2] that he was to serue the said Hendry Neale the said Hendry Neale haveing six pownd alowed him For the said Hendry Hobsons servis in witnes wherof we haue set to our hands this 26th of the 9th 1640.

Willm. Chesebrough
Gregory Baxter
Alexr. Winchester
Jams Peniman
Sammuell Bas
Thomas Matson
Steuen Kinsley

[*Endorsed by Governor Winthrop:*] Hen: Neale and his Apprentice.

NATHANIEL WARD TO JOHN WINTHROP[3]

Sir, I thanke you much for your letter and loue and those of the plantation for their good esteeme of mee, which I trust I shall not be backward to requite to my poore power: when I came out of the bay matters were left thus be-

---

[1] W. I. 139.

[2] Hobson was not finally released from his service to Neal until April 27, 1642, at which time he was put out to Thomas Meakins for the remainder of his time. *Records of the Court of Assistants,* II. 122.

[3] W. 3. 12; 4 *Collections,* VII. 29.

tweene Mr. Shepheard and mee, that if there might be any subsistence there[1] this winter, I should heare from him: speaking both with him and some of the plantation I discerned that they thought it too difficult to adventure thither till the extremity of the winter were abated. I acknowledge I am tender and more vnfitt for solitarines and hardshipp then some others especially att this tyme through many colds and seeds of the bay sicknesses I brought from thence yet if God and counsell cast me vpon any worke or condition I should labour not to wayue his good prouidence. I heare there is no priuate roome there, litle prouision and not a woman to dresse meate or wash linnen, and the cheif of the men are like to be absent for the most parte att their owne homes. I am much troubled what to doe, but vpon Mr. Shepheards letters I shall take aduise and doe what God shall direct and inable me vnto. In the meanetyme iterating my thankfull respect to your selfe and them craving your prayers I rest Your wor[shi]ps in all Christian service

NATHL. WARDE

IPSWICH 9is: 26, [1640]

TESTIMONY OF ELIZABETH STURGIS[2]

First I Elizebeth Sturges do Afirm that when I lived with my master Cumines I was sent to Cap: patricks to help his wiffe and having busines in the seler he cam down presenlie After mee and tooke mee about the midel and wold kisse mee and put his hand into my boosome at which I was much amazed at his Carage to mee beeing but young yet striving with him he let me go   then presentlie After I went home to my masters and being trobeled at it when we wer in bed I aquanted my dames sister with his Carage to me Afterwards my dame sending mee thether againe I refused to go   my dame desyerous to know the reason hir sister standing by told hir, and shee made hir husban aqunted with his Carag to me and hir husban told a neybor of it and that man told master Carter and Mr. Carter deals with him about it wher vpon he comes to my master and cals him to speak with him   then my master cals mee out and sayed to me I wonder you shold deale so with me, and I replied to him and sayd you cannot be Ignorant of these thinges and After many pasages he sayd if these thing be trew I was in a great temtation and then he sayd to me he cold troble me but he wold not and so left.

2lie some tym After I living at home with my father I went into the lot to

---

[1] Probably the new settlement at Haverhill.
[2] W. 1. 144.

gather sucking stalks and he cam sudenlie vpon me and asked me whether I
spake those things that I had spake for anie hurt to him or not   I sayd no I
amed not to hurt him nor anie other and the things being past I intended to
speak no more of them   then he ofered to kisse mee   I refusing he sayed vnles
I wold kisse him he wold not beleeve but that I wold speak of it againe.

3lie som tyme After I being maryed vpon some occation coming into the
bay to my fathers I going to watertown to the lecter he overtooke mee on the
way and spake to mee to call in as I went backe to see his wiffe which I did
and sudenlie he cum in and desyered mee to go into the next room to speake
with me about our plantation and when I was there hee cume to kisse me   I
desyered him to forbeare and told him such things wer not fit but he wold
and did and wold have had mee to set in his lap but I did not   then he replied to me that it was lawfull so to do to expresse love on to another   then
I rose vp to go away but he sayd I shold tarry for hee had sent for sacke and I
shold drinke with him   I told him I must be gon   he told me if he had tyme
and oportunitie he wold make it apeere to mee the lawfulnes of it   I still
desyering to be gon hee wisht me not to be offended for if I did love him but
as well as he did love mee I wold not take it so ill but wold rather pittie him
then be offended. then hee was at me to meet him in the Evening in the way
and he wold further labor to convince me of his love to me but with much
adoe I got away and presenlie made my father and all the house aquanted
with it and durst not go out into the way that night for feare.

[*Ca.* 1641]

[*Endorsed by Governor Winthrop:*] Sturgis wife against Capt. Patrick.

DANIEL PATRICK TO JOHN WINTHROP[1]

RIGHT WORSHIPFULL AND MUCH HONN[OUR]ED SIR, hauinge considdered the
messenger that brought your louinge summons I thought good to avoyde
superfluous wordes, by expressinge my minde vnto your Wors[hi]p in a fewe
lines as followeth. I hearde onely by one partye of some Aspertions cast on
mee by this woemane. hauing noe other proofe I coulde make noe slaunder
of it, yet dide I write a letter to her husbande that if such thinges wear spoken,
soe far as I could obtayne I should expeckt Sattisfactione. In the meane time,

[1] W. I. 147.

this Reporte came to one of our towne, betwixt whome and I, Difference had bine to longe and to greate, whoe amongst many other Bitter words, proffest hee woulde worke my Disgrace, as far as it laye in his powr, and forth with this woemane was sent for, with a messadge of Incouradgment, that shee shoulde not feare but stande firmlye to the matter, though in the manner shee did Accknowledg her faulte. shee beinge come Resorted to that parte, but of her Comming or beinge in the Baye I knew not of till Accedentallye I sawe her, yea and then shee indeauorde to conceale her selfe as much as shee coulde, till after Inquirye beinge informde shee was att her Fathers Howse, I went thether and offerd to goe with her, and her Father, to the Elders, or before whome shee pleasd if shee had ought to obieckt agaynst mee. But deserninge noe willingenes then in her to goe before witnes, I thought it noe wisdome to force my owne Name vppon the stadge seeinge by testimonny god gaue mee noe callinge thervnto, neither haue I hearde anny thinge moore of it this date that coulde be a wittnes, saue that one man, whoe is nowe in Plimmouth pattent; which Partye towlde mee, shee had sayd, and vnsayde, the words, and that hee coulde proue shee had serued others in the same Nature in there towne. Butt indeed if my owne testymonny woulde serue, I am certayne I coulde sattisfie your worship fully of the Abuse of this woemans Chardge. Howe soe euer Right honnord Sir As a Father to this Common wealth I thinke my selfe Happy that I maye open my greeuance vnto you, knowinge that in Respeckt of your selfe, I shall not be vnderstoode to desire the least fauour in anny sinfull practise proued. sir the Casse is thus, I finde as a practise to common (to moore deservinge then my selfe) Those whoe prossecute moore Bitterlye agaynst mee, then to my Knowledg I haue deserued at there handes, yet knowinge nothinge nothinge cann be but through gods leaue. I desire and through his mercye have fownde some benefite from the same; I haue sufferred much allreadye, that little means which by suruayinge I was growne into is stopt; Boasts are made to this purpose, I haue vncaptaynde him, and vnhorst him, hee is out of the Gouernors Fauour, hee is nowe pretty lowe, and indeed they saye true, for if god Rayse not vp some frinds I see noe end of ther farther pressinge mee lower still. Therfore doe I beseech you sir soe far as Justise will permitt lett mee begg what I noe wayes haue deserued, eauen as much Fauour as your Christiane Charrety cann Afforde in such a Casse. But not to be Tedious vnto your Wor[shi]p, As I knowe by this woemane I am wrondged, soe doe I knowe you are nott Ignorante, howe fare such Reports woulde creep in eauen amongst Maiesty and Minnistrye, if Godlye wisdome should not chill them in the hatchinge; and as I see ther wisdomes, whoe att anny time haue had to doe in that kinde, nottwithstandinge noe proff coulde be brought, Rather chuse to pass by much then publikely opose a slaunderous tounge, which neuer soe vniustlye cast out, yett neuer fayles to leaue some spots in the Aprehentions of some behinde. I therfore beseech your worship to considder that poynt in anny thinge that concernes mee vnfaynedlye desiringe noe other Judg then your selfe vnto whose Voyce I shall Attende, and willingly submit if I knowe myne owen harte as Readylye as to the Courte, if you finde anny defeckt in mee. This I made boulde to offer to your Christiane Considderratione, not Questioninge but god will Dereckt you in all his wayes. I rest your worsh[i]ps Readely to my powr to Commaunde

DANI. PATTRICKE

[*Ca.* 1641]

[*Endorsed by Governor Winthrop:*] Capt. Patrick about Sturgis his wife.

LUCY DOWNING TO JOHN WINTHROP[1]

To her most honerd brother Jhon Winthrop esq. this humble Boston

SIR, I am very glad to hear the constant good newes of your health my good sisters and all your familye, the lord long continue it: for my selfe constant paynes thoughe not so sharp as some former fits yet doe much weaken; and smaller changes doe the more affect. the Lord only brings good out of euill, and strenght out of weaknes, and then I shall yet reioyce in him. Sir James Downing is desierous to marie with rebecca coper[2] whoe liues with Msr. Endicot. Nowe wheather Msr. Endicot be trusted in her estate or no I am ignorant, but I haue heard he is not, only Msr. hauthorn and some others but questionles Msr. Endicot will expect to be sought to in the thinge, and his countenance theerin will be of moment. theerfore my husband would humble desire your selfe if you haue noe exception against it, that you would be pleasd to doe him the fauor to writ to Msr. Endicot to desire his furtherance theerin. The dispotition of the mayde and her education with Mrs. Endicot are hopefull, her person tollerable, and the estate very conuenient, and that is the state of the busines: allso James is incouraged by the mayds frinds to prosecute the sute, but I think he hath not yet spoken to the mayd as I hear.

---

[1] W. 4. 10; 5 *Collections*, I. 28–30.
[2] For an earlier letter relating to Rebecca Cooper, see John Endecott to John Winthrop, August 15, 1637 (*Winthrop Papers*, III. 483–484). See also Mayo, *John Endecott*, 108–109.

allso I fear wee must intreat you to work with my cosen peters for his consent and the churches, wich is indeed all in him that wee maye haue some meanes att our farms for the education of our familyes. nowe to put such a charge apon only familye as that is profferd to our perticuler is as much as nothinge because it is beyound our grasp. but a few familyes joyninge through gods blesing so setled apon theer busines might be better able to support the charge and with more comfort by much then in this remotnes wee are in when I dare saye wee haue not 3 days in the week fre from either wholle distraction or much discomposure theerby both in temperall and allso spirit-uall ocasions, whearin I spare respect of your owne experience and only desier you to inlighten his iugdment in the thinge. I question not your owne, ells I should be more perticuler. allso sir Jo. Downing is very eager for sea Imployment. my cosen Peters wisht me to put him to msr. allerton for a whille, so I moued it to Msr. Allerton, and he doth earnestly aduise I should rather haue him taught first to writ and acoumpt well, and such like, that so he might allso be fit for merchandize. nowe what I humble request of your selfe is that you will pleas to aduise with Msr. pierce in the thinge: and Msr. pierce they saye is the moste able to teach him in this country. nowe if it be for a childs beinge, I shall be as ready to bestow a cowe or 2 apon him that waye as another, and if he hath it in an art I hope it maye be less casuall and I shall take it for a very kind respect in Msr. Pirce if he pleas to help hearin.

Sir I am very frequent in troubleing you butt I pray excuse me, and I shall euer desire to be your more seruisable sister

L. D.

[*Ca.* January, 1640/41]

I pray my euer humble seruis and thanks to my sister and all my nephews and neec. it is very late ells I would write to my nephew Stephen. I thank both him and your self for his good newes.

HUGH PETER AND EMMANUEL DOWNING TO JOHN WINTHROP[1]

To our honored brother John Winthrop sen: esqr: these present in Boston

DEERE SIR, Wee are bold to intreat your furtherance in counsell and other helpe for the suppressing pipe staffs riuers and clabords in our towne; because

---

[1] W. 2. 48; 4 *Collections*, VI. 90.

wee haue 2 or 3 ships building. wee desire that within 2 or 3 miles neere any riuer they may not fell great tymber fit for shipping, for they may as well cut it further of it being so portable, and ship-timber being so heauy. your letter to Mr. Endecot by this bearer will helpe vs very much.[1] This bearer will giue you more reasons then wee can, to whom wee intreat you would bee pleased to listen.

These men cut downe but halfe of the tree for their vse, and the rest lyes rotting and spoyles our Comons, with many more inconveniencyes then wee name. Thus crauing your wonted and lawfull favor herein, with our due salutations doe rest Yours in all duty

HU: PETER
EM: DOWNINGE

SALEM 13. 11. 40[/41]

EMMANUEL DOWNING TO JOHN WINTHROP[2]

SIR, I haue here in Salem a desire to Match my sonne James to a Maide[3] that lives in mr. Endicotts howse. hir sister[4] is maryed here who sayes the mayd was left to hir dispose by hir parents, but they dying intestate, the administration and tuition of the maide was by the Court comitted to mr. Hathorne, mr. Batter and Goodm[an] Scrugs, and to helpe mr. Endicott with some present monie, you wrote to mr. Hathorne to putt hir to Mr. Endicott to board, who therevpon receved 40*li* aforehand for 2 yeares. I haue moved mr. Hathorne, and mr. Batter for my sonne, who are well pleased therewith   I purposed to haue acquaynted mr. Endicott therewith, but that a freind in great secrecye told me, that mr. Batter had in my sonnes behalfe told yt to mr. Endicott, and as mr. Endicott said to my good freind mr. Hathorne that he had the wholl dispose of the maid and would provide a better match for hir, mr. Hathorne answeared him that they the Feoffees were trusted with the person and the estate vntill the maid should be of yeares to dispose of hir selfe, which said he, that shee now was of full yeares to dispose of hir selfe, being past 16, for shee is about 17 yeares of age; then mr. Endicott replyed that he would write to the Gouernour and your selfe about yt. mr. Hathorne desires not to be knowne of this councell revealed to me etc. I should first haue advised with mr. Endicott in this, but hir freinds

---

[1] Cf. John Endecott to John Winthrop, January 28, 1640/41 (pages 311–312, below).
[2] W. 2. 30; 4 *Collections*, VI. 56–58.   [3] Rebecca Cooper.
[4] Mercy Cooper Felmingham.

desired he should not yet be acquaynted therewith, nor now vntill I heare an answeare from yourselfe, and the Governour that the Maide be left to hir owne dispose of the Feoffees to whom before hir full age shee did apperteyne. I pray let me be beholding to you to acquaynt the Governour herewith, with my humble dutye to him, that he may doe me right and answ[er] mr. Endicott without offence that the mayde is of full age, but I leaue the matter and manner myselfe and all to your better Judgement, submitting wholly to the will of God herein; I desire much to see the yssue hereof and to match some of my elder Children because some thinke me to blame that none of them are disposed of. I have provided a verie good Match for my neice Nab. Goade. he is old Moulton his only sonne, a member of our Church, of 4 or 500*li* estate. if my sonns buisines proceede I may about a moneth hence, haue both cowples maried on a day.

I feared the losse of your accounts which my wife now hath found being in hir custodye. I purpose now according to promise send in my next the abstract thereof, that you may understand how yt is betwene vs. I pray let my Cosen Stephen take a receipt of mr. Treasurour vpon deliuerie of the 40 bushells of Corne for vij*li* in parte of the rate of Salem, for myne owne parte thereof comes to but 4*li* 10*s*. Soe with my humble service to yourselfe and my good sister I rest Your assured loving brother

EM: DOWNINGE

20. 11. 40[/41]

LUCY DOWNING TO MARGARET WINTHROP[1]

To her most honerd sister mrs. margret winthrop this present Boston

WORTHYLIE HONERD, I humble thank you for all your fauors whearin both I and myne are sempiternally ingaged allso I humble thank you for the mayde   I haue good hopes of her. My cosen nab and she wear fellow trauillers in the ship from eng: nab. giues her the report of a very good carigd theer: allso my brother got[2] and his wife wear near neighbours to hir frinds in eng. and they repute them to be people of a very godly conuersation, and many times hereditary blesings are perpetuated and vertue followes them: my mayd abygall is suddaynlie to be maryed to robert Moulton of this towne: and I hope it maye proue a blessinge of comfort to her for the parents and

---

[1] W. 4. 11; 5 *Collections*, I. 31–32.
[2] John Goad, who married Abigail, sister of Emmanuel Downing.

sonne are people of a religious peacable life, and prouident in theeir estates:
I haue felt more generall weaknes within this fortnight then euer formerly
without violent distemper. but I suppose age and constant infermitye can
produce noe less. the Lord giue me to liue only by fayth in him, and that will
preuent the king of terors force. when our life is hid with him that liues foreuer, why should wee fear a happye appearance. but my death maye produce
the more trouble to so dear and noble a frind as your self with myne: but excuse all my bouldnes I pray, and blame me not for makeing the best choyce
I can for them, and he that commaunds charitye and promiseth requitall to
cups of water, I hope will be your full reward. theer lyes my refuge ells durst
I not presume so far apon your patience.

I pray present my seruis and thanks to my dear brother and nephewes whom
I should be glad to see: and my seruis to my neec and hapye wishes to her
and hers. I rest yours in all seruis obliged

L. D.

[*Ca.* January 20, 1640/41]

I desire 2 red caps that are in the trunk, wich I pray to be sent me, allso by
Msr. Pester I beged garlick and sage and to borrow a gander. I haue 3 gooses
and not a husban for them, wich lost me at least 40 egs last year and very
generall is the loss.

I am very glad to see your pattern of vertue and exquisitnes. It is worthy
all prayses and Immitation. I am purchasing of toolles wich I could not till
very latly hear of, and then I could wish strenght to wayt apon you for instructions, but I fear Luce is not dilligent wich I should take both very ill
from her and for a presage of the like. slothe is a loathsome disease in young
people both in the eyes of god and man.

RICHARD VINES TO JOHN WINTHROP[1]

To the right Wo[rshipfu]ll his honored Freind John Wenthrop Esqr.
at Boston thes in Massachusetts

RIGHT WO[RSHIPFU]LL, I received your letter concerning Mr. Jenner,[2] acknowledging your former Courtesies to my selfe, and for your furtherance of

---

[1] W. 3. 93; 4 *Collections*, VII. 340–342.

[2] For Thomas Jenner's account of the beginning of his ministry at Saco, see his letters to Governor Winthrop, February 4, 1640/41 (pages 319–320, below), and April 26, 1641 (pages 331–332,
below).

a minister for vs our whole Plantacion ar greatly behoulding vnto you. We haue ioyned both sides of our river together for his mayntenance, and haue willingly contributed for his Stipend 47*li* per annum hoping the lord will blesse and sanctifie his word vnto vs, that we may be both hearers and doers of the word and will of god. I like Mr. Jenner his life and conversacion, and alsoe his preaching, if he would lett the Church of England alone. that doth much trouble me, to heare our mother Church questioned for her impurity vpon every occasion, as if men (ministers I meane) had no other marke to ayme at, but the Paps that gaue them suck, and from whence they first received the bread of life. I wish they would follow the Counsell you giue me in your letter, (To improue that which is profitable to them, and cover the rest with loue,) for why should a Son betray his mothers weaknes. Noah his Son lyes still vnder a curse for discovering his fathers shame his brothers eternall blessings for the Contrary. good sir pardon mee, I hope pardonable; I haue pleaded for our mother, which I beseech the almighty god to purge from her errors.

We haue not pressed Mr. Jenner to any manner of Church discipline but to preach and teach as seemeth good to himselfe. The Sacraments we desire to haue administred amongst vs, as beleiving Christians, although great Sinners. at present we doe not moue him to it, but for my parte I profes my selfe to be an opposite to Church Covenant, and Seperacion, holding it sufficient that I am allready a member of the Church of England, and so consequently of the Church of Christ, and soe capeable of the benefitts of his Sacraments. This is my opinion, till I shalbe therof convinced. I will both loue honour, and cherrish Mr. Jenner in his Calling, both for his Function and worth sake, and allsoe to gratifie your selfe, and the rest of my worthy freinds that by gods providence comended him hether. I must confes that I knew nothing of his comming t[i]ll I saw him, and doe beleiue I should haue refused him whome now I embrace with intire affecion, had not your selfe and Mr. Humfrey encouraged me thervnto by your letters.

It seemes the governour makes a question that Sir Ferdinando Gorges was not in the French wars in his tyme. Capt. Bonython intreates me to write a word or two therof. I beleiue it was before Mr. Dudley his tyme, Sir Ferd: being now nere 80 yeares ould, and he went to those warres very young, and ther he received his honour; I haue often heard him discourse of those warlike accions, and that the King of France himselfe fetched him of from a breach being wounded, either at the seige of Amiens, or before Paris I know not whether.

Thus ceasing farder to trouble you, with my respectiue to your selfe, I rest, your assured freind and servant

RICH: VINES

SACO 25th of January 1640[/41]

RICHARD VINES TO JOHN WINTHROP[1]

For Mr. Wentrope

SIR, Three or[2] 4 yeares since Mr. Cleiues being in England procured a writ out of the Starr chamber office, to command Mr. Edward Godfrey, Mr. John Winter, Mr. Purches, and my selfe, to apeare at the Counsell tabel, to answear some supposed wrongs   Mr. Godfrey went over to answeare for himselfe Mr. Winter and my selfe, and out of the same Court brings a writt to command Cleiues to pay vnto him 20*li* for his Charges, which he refuses to doe. now Sir Ferdinando Gorges gaue me order to see Mr. Godfrey haue Right in this case. Cleiues sayes we haue nothing to doe, neither haue wee any power to levy money here vpon any writts that come out of England, for he will answeare it from whence it came. I shall humbly intreate your advise herein, what Course is to be taken that I may free my selfe from blame and the malice of Cleiues, who is a Fire brand of dissention and hath sett the whole Province together by the yeares. I make bould to trouble herin, as a case of greate difficultie, desireing your answeare by the first Convenience.

I vnderstood by Mr. Shurt that you desired some gray Pease for seed. out of my smale store I haue sent you a bushell, desiring your acceptance therof, From Your Freind and servant

RICH: VINES

SACO 25th Janu: 1640[/41]

HENRY WALTHAM TO JOHN WINTHROP[3]

To the Woo[rshi]p[fu]ll John Winthrp Esq. Assistant of Newe England deliver in Boston

WOO[RSHI]P[FU]LL, Maye it please you, I Receaued yours sente mee by M[is]tris Richards. perseaing of some mise Information of my vnwillingnes

---

[1] W. 3. 93; 4 *Collections*, VII. 342–343; *G.S.*, II. 231–232.
[2] The word in the original manuscript is "of."
[3] W. 4. 110; 5 *Collections*, I. 311–313.

to pease, I should bee sorrie to profes vnto yow desire of pease, yf it wheare not sinceare, Althoughe my aydge and condition did not calle for it. I haue euer bine vnwilling to bee contentious, much les to nurrishe it. I doubte not but what yow shall here From An Envious persone, shalbe more then this loue, which out of your Innate goodnes maye bee Abused by A longe tonge, ore pen, vntle yow heare both. I doe truly profes vnto yow, I haue Indeauored all I cane for pease; my sealfe and my sonne hauing soffered much with patiance, which ill natures, for private ends (Joyned with pride and Malles) the more Insulte, Roling downe ther power one the deiected, presuming (As it semes) one ther wealth, and I conseaue not without Abusing, in sayeing shee had power giuen her to detayne the Tolle Corne since my sonne deceased, and would not lett vs haue halfe a busall of Corne to make vs Breade, but constrayned to borrowe it. I haue bine soe fare from Reviling her, that I often goe from her, and giue her noe Answare, althoughe shee continewes Ralling, which wilbe to troblesome to Relate att presante. Wheras I am charged to Incoureadge our servants, ore suffer them to carrie them sealfes scournefull to wards her I neuer did, Althoughe shee hath often Abused them, not with ill termes only, but in striking, and distorbing them in ther bussines, vnbeseming a moddeste woamanes carreadge, I should humblie beseace yow to here the differance betwixt vs, and then yow will soune Judge whoe ys in Faulte. I was laste weake with her aboute the deviding the howse, which shee Refuseth to doe, and since I receaued yours haue written her, yf shee please to permit Mr. Neweman, Mr. Parker and Goodman Batts to devide it, maye saue her Jurnie, and refer all other things to the Maiestrates.[1] ther are some that would Rente, and some that would buye the Mill, but none will Joine with her, and shee will doe nothing but what shee please her sealfe, wherfore I shall desire some ouer Ruling power maye order it, not doubtting As yow will not see her wronged, soe yow will see shee maye not doe wrong Especially to one in soe dessolate Condition, wherof I am Confidente, doe hartely praye the allmightie to continewe your long lyfe to his Glorie the Contries good and your owne Eternall Hapines, vnto whose protection I leaue yow, and euer reste Your poore freind in all obseruance

HENRY WALTHAM

WAYMOUTH, the 25th of the 11 month 1640[/41]

---

[1] For the action of the Court of Assistants in the disputes between Henry Waltham and Welthian, wife of Thomas Richards, see *Records of Massachusetts*, I. 313.

LUCY DOWNING TO JOHN WINTHROP, JR.[1]

To her most honerd nephew Jhon Winthrop esq. this present Boston

SIR, wee now expect you stay for 6 boyes; you are gone so longe. Indeed wee want your company very sensible: my lady Susan I hear is now deliverd,[2] theerfore in poynt of good manners your wife may now presume to be eased of her load allso. If ocasion be for your longer stay I pray sir let georg know I expect him with this bearer Msr. Ruke: or the next conueniencie: allso my husband desiers to know if you will part with some hay that you haue   wee are in much want ells. I pray your spediest answeer. I haue experimented the crocus this 2 nights and found much though not a totall fredom of payne theerby. I pray let me know if I may safly aply it to the mould of my head. I thank you much for your aduise, and I pray to my brother allso giue my many thanks and to all my seruis and best wishes is Yours

L. D.

Jan. 28 or tuesday [1640/41]

all our newes is out of eng: I hope you haue it before vs: wee haue put his grace of canterbury fast in the tower[3] and if our St. Peter keeps the keyes his grace is like to coolle his shins ere he gets in this could weather; for we speak only of his confusion and vnpardonable sins.

JOHN ENDECOTT TO JOHN WINTHROP[4]

To the right Wor[shipfu]ll and my worthie and much honoured Friend,
John Winthrop Esqr. at Boston deliver

DEARE SIR, I called our towne together before your Lettre came seeing the spoile of timber which might serue for many good vses. And the towne agreed not to cutt any great tymber which is fitt for shipping planckes or knees etc. nor any for clapboard within twoe miles of the towne eury way, nor to fell any other timber but for their owne priuate vse.[5] I think it were well if the

---

[1] W. 4. 11; 5 *Collections*, I. 30–31.

[2] Lydia, daughter of John Humfrey and Susan Clinton (daughter of the Earl of Lincoln), was baptized April 25, 1641. *Vital Records of Salem, Massachusetts*, I (Salem, 1916), 456.

[3] Laud was impeached of high treason on December 18, 1640, and was at once sequestered from Parliament by the House of Lords and committed to custody. He was not actually committed to the Tower until March 1, 1640/41. Gardiner, *History of England*, IX. 249, 297.

[4] Original not located; 4 *Collections*, VI. 143.

[5] Cf. Hugh Peter and Emmanuel Downing to John Winthrop, January 13, 1640/41 (pages 304–

Generall Court would make provision heerein. I pray you Sir if you heare any certaine newes by any Lettres concerninge the taking of Newcastle and Durham, and the winter parliament or any other newes out of England, that you will be pleased to let mee vnderstand of it. All the newes comes to your partes first.

I am told that you are sollicited in a busines concerninge the girle[1] which was put to my keepinge and trust, whose estate was also committed to the trust of Mr. Hathorne [and] Mr. Batter. I have not bene made acquainted with it by you know whome, which if there had bene any such intendment I think it had bene but reason. But to let that passe, I pray you aduize not to stirre in it, for it will not be effected for reasons I shall shew you afterwards. The Lord in mercie keepe you and yours, to whose blessed guidance I committ you and rest. Yours truelie and heartily euer to commaund

JO: ENDECOTT

28 11 mo. 1640[/41]

EDWARD WINSLOW TO JOHN WINTHROP[2]

*To his much honored Friend Joh: Winthrop Esqr. at his howse at Boston
these be delivered*

WORTHY SIR, When I remember your constant and long continued loue I cannot but blame my selfe that having no speciall busines into your parts this winter season and thereby debarred sight haue not so much as written these two moneths unto you. This later I must needs confesse is inexcusable, but for the former however it is busines enough for me to see the face of your selfe and yours together with the many godly and pretious friends and br[ethre]n I haue both in Boston and elsewhere amongst you, yet the many businesses I haue had (and the more in regard of mr. Blinmans friends that are come to liue with us and the streightnes of place to receiue them) and our preparacons to enter into Cov[enan]t together with many afflicions in my Family God being pleased still to exercise me under his hand by taking away one of my children by death and some others in my Family exercised with sicknes, together with some other outward losses in my cattle, may rather cawse me to stay at home and consider, then to be exercised abroad. But God willing I

305, above). For earlier timber regulations adopted by Salem, see *Essex Institute Historical Collections, Second Series, I, Part I* ("Town Records of Salem"), 107–108.
    [1] Rebecca Cooper.
    [2] W. 2. 92; 4 *Collections*, VI. 171–172.

shall take a due season to see you and them. In the meane time let these my lines witnes my continued loue to you and them, whose welfare if my heart deceiue me not I desire as mine owne.

I received letters lately from mr. Endecot and your brother Peters, and make bold to trowble you with conveyance of my answers to them together with many smale pamphlets bownd up together which we printed in the netherlands occasioned by one of them called the peoples plea for the exercise of Prophesie, which he much desired me to procure and send him, and which I entreat you to convay by the first opportunity, for it was long before I could call to minde where I had lent it, and could not procure another in all Plimoth.

There is a Friend of mine that desired me to crave your advice in two particulars: the one in case he hath sold a parcell of goods of some value to one upon day and hath but a bare bill for his security and the person['s] sufficiency suspected, whether your court allow not an arrest for better security? or if he cannot be that way relieved, then by what other? The 2d is of greater consequence, vizt. having an estate of lands still in wales, tho as formally made over to another as advice of law could passe it, and acknowledged before a m[aste]r of the Chancery; yet since his comming away is credibly informed that he was called in Court of Star-chamber and fined 200*li* for not appearance, but was never served with any precep[t] nor heard of it till within these 14 daies nor can conceiue any thing saue malice should be alledged against him now what course you will advise him to take in it. I pray you Sir pardon my boldnes with you, and let me receiue a word or to from you as your occasions will permit. Be you kindely saluted also mr. Cotten, mr. Wilson, your sons mr. Joh. mr. Steph. and mr. Adam with all other my beloved Friends with you, whose pr[ayer]s I desire, especially in that great and weighty worke which doth so much concerne the glory of G[od] in raysing up his church amongst us. And the Father of mercies and God of comfort raise and keepe up your spirit aboue all the crosses of this life, and fill you with his comforts in C[hrist] Jesus. Amen. Yours in many bonds

EDW: WINSLOW

CARESWELL 11. 28. 1640[/41]

[*Endorsed by Governor Winthrop:*] Mr. Winslow Rec. 12. 13. 40.

JOHN ENDECOTT TO JOHN WINTHROP[1]

To the right Wor[shipfu]ll and my much hon[ou]red Friend John Winthrop Esqr.
deliuer theise at Boston

DEAREST SIR, I haue according to your desire aduised with Mr. Downinge and Mr. Hawthorne concerninge Mr. Peter his Voyage for England.[2] And we haue imparted our thoughts each to other about it: And we haue (according to the tyme) considered First of the proiect it selfe and 2dlie of the persons to be imployed about it. For the proiect (if we mistake it not) viz. For an agent or agents to be imployed by the Country or Counsell to procure men or money or both for vs from England, wee (submittinge to better Judgments) thinck it may proue more hurtfull then helpefull vnto vs diuers wayes. For First it will confirme my Lord Say and others of his Judgment, that new England can no longer subsist without the helpe of old England; espetiallie they beinge already informed of the forwardnes of diuers amongest vs to remoue to the West Indies bec[ause] they cannot heere maintayne their families: 2dlie. It is likelie to tend to the dishonour of God, when Ill affected persons shall vnderstand that our necessities are such as we are forced to seeke for Reliefe as before. 3dlie. It may be a meanes (instead of sending over more persons and money vnto vs) of discouraginge and diuerting both from vs; The report of our pouertie having bene alreadie a manifest cause of debarringe most from vs. 4thlie. It is to be feared that vnlesse the money we expect [they] would sollicit for, be freelie giuen vs, It will rather impouerish vs and so bringe dishonour to God by such ingagements not duely satisfyed Then doe vs good though it should come vppon easie termes. Plimmoth plantacion may giue vs some light heerein. But to looke amongest our selues if there were noe other ground but this, the due consideration how vnprofitablie the monies we haue had haue bene layd out, as namelie in wines and liquours, and English prouisions of dyett and vnnecessarie brauerie in apparell: all which tends to the scandal of religion and pouertie: much more might be said.

Yet thus farre we thinck Gods prouidence might be serued, that if priuately some Godlie wise men in seuerall townes were spoken to (who are well knowen in England, and haue bene men of eminency and esteeme ammongest them, As Mr. Cotton, Mr. Esek: Rogers, Mr. Norrice, and many others such) to

---

[1] W. 2. 74; 4 *Collections*, vi. 138–141.
[2] For the proposal, early in 1641, to send agents to England in behalf of the colony, see *Journal*, ii. 24–26.

write to their acquaintances who are likelie to doe vs good, by way of Counsell to aduize them, that it might be pleasing to God to further the worke of
the Lord heere by their purses and persons etc. This we thinck wilbe more
effectuall then the other:

Touching the persons some of them who are thought to be most fitt
to be imployed in this dissigne we thinck (with submission) most vnfitt,
which we are assured you will also be of our myndes when we shall
speake together, but I forbeare to write for letters may miscarry. Onely
in generall to take notice That they are men well-affected to the West
Indies. other thinges hereafter. Theise few quæres I propose to your best
thoughts.

1 Quære. Whither prayinge and waytinge (as the case stands) were not
more agreeable to our state and condition then to runne vnder so many
dangers to relieue our selues. The Lord hauing hitherto bene verie good vnto
vs beyond expectation.

2 Quære. Seeing it is likelie that the Merchants in England and others are
lookinge this way alreadie: whither it be not a forestallinge of the prouidence
of God to run before it, and to hasten the worke our selues, [which] the lord
would better effect in his tyme that his hand might be seene in it.

3 Quære. Whither it be not somewhat preposterous to goe from a place of
safetie prouided of God, to a place of danger vnder the hand of God to seeke
reliefe for vs.

4 Quære. Whither it be proper for [*torn*] minister to leaue his worke and to
attend to secular businesses which may be done by others. Whither it be not
something Jesuiticall.

5 Quære. Whether the noice of procuring money out of England will not
procure with it much envy from that State and stirre vp against vs and the
godlie there the chiefest amongest them, moneyes being denyed them by such
men in case of such danger and waighty affaires in hand there.

6 Quære. Whither our scarcitie of money leads vs not rather to some more
frugall course heere at home and to the strict reformation of the mispending
of money then to seeke abroad for more to maintaine vs in our disorders which
I feare will hardlie be avoyded.

7 Quære. Whither there will not be more peace vnto vs and blessing vppon
vs in a patient waiting vpon God, then in a (seeming at least) distrust of his
prouidence.

Theise thinges I leaue to your more serious considerations, the Lord in
mercie direct you in all to whose blessed guidance and preseruation I leaue
you with my due and best respects and seruice to your selfe and deare yoake-

fellow and rest Your wor[shi]pps truelie and heartily euer to be commaunded

JO: ENDECOTT

[*Ca.* February, 1640/41]

Mr. Steephens man Anchor I haue called before mee a moneth since and I haue examined him, and threatned to haue him to Court, fearing hee should not speake the whole trueth but conceale something. Hee cannot witnes of any miscariadge towards Bennetts wiefe [*torn*]: But I gaue him not an oath bec[ause] hee professed hee could not witnes any such thinge in the least measure, yet if this will not satisffie vppon your intimation I will giue him an oath.

HUGH PETER TO JOHN WINTHROP[1]

To my honord brother John Winthrop se: Esqr. these present in Boston

HON[O]R[E]D SIR, These are to accompany Mr. Knollis. What aduise I gaue at my being there[2] Mr. Wilson can informe you, whose letter I would desire you to reade, I being to giue an account to them that sent mee. Now my earnest request is that this bearer and 3 or 4 more of his frends may haue the liberty of sitting downe in our Jurisdiction. hee may [be] vsefull without doubt, hee is well gifted   you may doe well to heare him at Boston.

They there are ripe for our Gouernment as will appeare by the note I haue sent you. they grone for Gouernment and Gospell all ouer that side on the Country. I conceiue that 2 or 3 fit men sent ouer may doe much good at this confluxe of things. These will relate how all stands in these parts. alas poore bleeding soules!

I haue desired Mr. Endecot to write to your gouernour. I thinke this worke falls naturally vnder the Care of the Counsell. If Mr. Larkam say and hold hee hath promised mee to close with vs, but Malè audio. What are men?

I haue a neere Cossen with him a Justice of Peaces daughter with him very hopefull, and as handsome as any in the Country, 200*li* for present and hopes to haue 100*li* more   I wish your sons any would take her, and it   I am now seeking out a husband for her But wish yours farre better euery way. shee is lately by her frends my kindred commended to my care; I am somtymes thinking of Thom: Reade though I haue my feares. if you please you may

---

[1] W. 2. 57; 4 *Collections*, VI. 106–107.

[2] I.e., at Dover, New Hampshire. For an account of the disturbances created in that town by the hostility between the Knollys and the Larkham factions, see *Journal*, II. 27–28; Jeremy Belknap, *The History of New Hampshire*, I (Boston, 1792), 46–54.

write me a word. Thus with my hartyest and humble salutes I rest yours as your loue hath made me

H: Peter

[*Ca.* February, 1640/41]

THOMAS LARKHAM TO JOHN WINTHROP[1]

To My Ever Honoured the Worr[shipfu]ll John Wintroppe Esqr.
present these in Boston

Grace and peace in Christ Jesus

Honoured and Gracious Sir, I am bold uppon both what I have seene in you and heard of you, to desire you to heare and declare my just defence of mine innocency, in and concerninge some unhappy differences lately risen in this our poore dissevered and therefore distracted plantation betweene my brother Knollis and my selfe. Lest I should be guilty of my owne wrongs by not timely apologizinge, yet I will write as in the presence of the Lord. Beinge by Gods providence brought hither I found a people in a Church-way and a Pastor and so joyned to them to partake of and submitt unto the ordinances of our Lord and Kinge amonge them according to his will to be administred, and (lest I be tedious) some time after received a call to office viz. to be teacher to the Church, and (though not suddainly) yet at lengh yeilded to become so as was desired, withall desiringe that mine ordination might be deferred untill I might both be better satisfied in some things about it not to me so cleare as to other my Reverend brethren, and also might have it solemnely done (if done at all) in presence of some other Elders which I intended to advize with and invite hither in time convenient, conceivinge that without offence I might prophesie and dispence by the key of Charitie, though not by a key ministeriall as I perceive most thinke I cannott by virtue of mine former dedication to God by the layinge on of the hands of the presbetery in England, leavinge all ministeriall administration (for feare of offence) to my Brother, ordained by one of them pastor of the said church. So we went one together lovingly A While, untill My poore brother began to ball about that prime evidence etc. and under the name of Legalists to fire the comfort and shake the faith of such poore weake ones, as yet might be possessed of the faith of Christ, though not of that reflect act, etc., the controversie is not new,

---

[1] W. 4. 110; 5 *Collections*, 1. 313–317. For Larkham, see *D.N.B.*; Morison, *Founding of Harvard College*, 387.

you know. Well, as if he had studied nothinge else or thought nought else needfull to be discoursed of in publique he setts to it with might and maine, to the offence of not only my selfe but all most every member of our church, callinge mourninge and prayinge etc. an Idole in one Sermon and in another interpretinge Jer. 12. 2 to be meante of beinge rooted and bringinge foorth fruits in the church, which plainly is meante of outward prosperitie as to me seemeth. (But lest I cloy you) I after exercise on the Sabboth, beinge the 3d of the 11 moneth, tooke occasion to lay before the church the errour at least danger as I said of his discourse, havinge before privately often reasoned with him about the point. A short answere he gave and it was accepted in that part of it in which he offered to submitt to other Churches, and so we went one in the afternoone as before quietly. But his spiritt beinge impatient of conceited disgrace, breakes out in private incredibly to one John Baker not unknowne to you to this purpose that his Doctrine was of Christ and would stand when mine would fall to the ground that he would preach it and preach it againe that he would no more come to humour me in my pride that I might depart when I would for soe I did differ in 22 things which he had to shew etc. After proceedinge there was a church meetinge; I craved Satisfaction, he insteede thereof sitts downe and begins a complaint, consistinge of many branches, which he read out of a Paper and so goes to a table and craves mine Answere and said he would write it. I som whatt amazed to see such wild doings, spake what the church disliked nott and so we spent one whole day which was the fifth day of the weeke puttinge of what was further to be done unto the Sabboth, intendinge after the eveninge exercise but He gave foorth Words that he would deale with one of our Magistrates and mee first of all before any exercise should goe one and indeede was ready in the meetinge house so to doe in a marvelous stiffe way had not the Magistrates interposed wherevppon, protestinge against the Church he went out and some 2 or 3 more the rest stayinge. We went on with Gods Worshipp as God enabled, apointinge the next whole day for a meetinge mixt of the church and also of the Magistrates as magistrates which day beinge spent untill eveninge our Magistrates were pleased to enjoine him silence untill some course were taken to appease these hurliburlyes. But so farre was his spiritt from stoopinge as that foort with he departs to goe to the bay sayinge that he would goe to all the Mag[istrates] and elders, to spreade abroade my opinions which, as they are not to the businesse in hand so neither can his weake head I doubt me easily understand them. What the Opinions be that he hath by this time blazed I hold I doe not certainly know, but I heare of some few scattered in the way towards the Bay, viz. that Christ is not the Head of the visible Church, That the church of

Rome is a true church, That Ordination must be performed by Elders, That there is not an Absolute necessitie of sett private meetings, that the Church cannot excommunicate kings, that kings and Princes and also Magistrates, are Gods Ministers in church affaires, That they haue power to call Counsells and appoint Church meetings and to sitt not only as members but Magistrates, That they may silence suppresse and Banish Ministers in some Cases, That It is not a Barr to hinder Church fellowshipp to be vnregenerated allwaies, That the Callinge of Ministers in England is not Antichristian and the like. As he divulgeth them, I cannot tell what to say for some things I have said like unto all this, But desire first to set[tle] plainly what he layeth to my charge in these or a[ny] other suggestions and then I shall I hope give satisfaction to all Gods people one way or other. Errare possum hæreticus esse nolo, God beinge my helper, to whom I can appeale with a good conscience in my proceedings professing that his wild and weake and pope-like carriage in this Church, and Odde Phrases in Sermons, unwarrantable and unpatternd expositions of Scripture, and other Absurd yet impudent practizes have putt me in private reasoninge upon the heate of oppositions, wherein if I have in that heate spoken things unsound (which yet I am not conscious of) when light shall be sett up I hope the spiritt of trueth will guide me to walke accordinge to it. In the meane time as you can I shall desire you to prevent my hanginge, untill I have answered for my selfe which I the rather hope you will doe because you know what in his passion he wrote of the Bay into England etc. Verbum sapienti sat. The Lord Jesus blesse you truly noble Sir and all yours and continue you still a Worthy Champion and father in his Israell. Yours to be disposed of in the Lord

THOM. LARKHAM

[*Ca.* February, 1640/41]

THOMAS JENNER TO JOHN WINTHROP[1]

To the Right Worsh[i]p[ful] his very loueing and kind friend Mr. Wintrop at his howse in Boston in N. E. giue theise I pray

WORTHY SIR, my due respect being remembred to you: I heartily salute you in the Lord, giueing you humble thanks for your favourable aspect which

---

[1] W. 3. 97; 4 *Collections*, VII. 355–356. For Jenner, see Morison, *Founding of Harvard College*, 384–385. A catalogue of Jenner's library, which was bought in 1651, after Jenner's return to England, by the Corporation for the Propagation of the Gospel in New England for the use of John Eliot, is printed in *Publications of the Colonial Society of Massachusetts*, XXVIII. 113–136.

hath alwaies bin towards me, (tho: of me most undeserued,) and especially
for your late kind letter on my behalfe; for which sake, I was kindly imbraced,
aboue the expectation of my selfe, and others, and am still (I thank God)
loueingly respected amongst them: but not with out some hot discourses,
(especially about the Ceremonies,) yet they all haue ended (through mercy)
in peace: and for aught I can perceiue, doe prize the word, and relish it,
dayly better then other, and some promise faire, euen in Mr. Vines his
family. But generally they were very ignorant, superstitious, and vitious, and
scarse any religious. Fre leaue they giue me to doe whatsoeuer I please: im-
poseing nothing on me either publikly or privately which my selfe dislike
onely this, Mr. Vines and the Captaine¹ both, haue timely expressed themselues to be utterly against Church-way; saying, their Patent doth prohibit
the same: yet I for my part neuer once touched upon it, except when they
themselues haue in private discourse put me upon it by Questions of their
owne, For I count it no season as yet to go build, before God send vs materials
to build with all. Thus being in some hast, I end, humbly craueing your
prayers: and so committing your selfe and all yours to him, who hath promised to Guide vs by his Counsell here, and afterward to receiue vs vnto glory,
in whome I rest your worsh[ips] to command

THO: JENNER

Remember my loueing respect (I pray) to Mrs. Wintrop, also to Mr.
Wintrop your eldest sonne, to Mr. Cotton and Mr. Wilson.

SACO, 4th of the last 1640[/41]

JOHN ENDECOTT TO JOHN WINTHROP²

To the Wor[shipfu]ll my truelie honoured Friend John Winthrop senior esqr. deliver

DEAREST SIR, Both your Letters I receaued, for which I humblie thanck
you. And in answere to them both thus. I shall (according to your desire in
the one) call the old planters together assoone as convenientlie I can. And we
will recollect what the Lord shalbe pleased to bring to our memories. And
with what speede I can I shall send it you. I feare it will not suddainelie be
done because they liue at their farmes, but I will hasten it what I can.

---

¹ Richard Bonython.
² W. 2. 76; 4 *Collections*, VI. 144–145.

Touching that in the other about Rebecca Cooper, the Lord knowes I haue alwaies resolued (and so hath my wiefe euer since the girle came to vs) to yelde her vp to be disposed by yourselfe to any of yours, if euer the Lord should make her fitt and worthie, and you accept of, which also I know Mr. Peters can and will fully satisfie you in from both our expressions from tyme to tyme. And that is our purposes and resolutions still if God hinder not. Now for the other for whom you writt.[1] I confesse I cannot freelie yeald therevnto for present, for theise grounds. First the girle desires not to marry as yet. 2dly shee confesseth (which is the trueth) herselfe to be altogether yet vnfitt for such a condition, shee being a verie gerle and but 15 yeares of age. 3dly when the man was moued to her, shee said shee could not like him. 4thly You know it would be of ill report that a girle because shee hath some estate, should be disposed of so young espetiallie not hauing any parents to choose for her. Fourthlie I haue some good hopes of the childes comminge one to the best things; and on the other side, I feare, I will say no more: Other things I shall tell you when we meete. If this will not satisfie some let the Court take her of from mee and place her with any other to dispose of her, I shall be content, which I heare was plotted to accomplish this end, but I will further enquier about it, and you shall know of it if it be true. For I know there are many passages about this busines which when you come to heare of you will not like. But I leaue heere. The Lord our good God keepe and preserue you and yours blamelesse to the comminge and appearing of his sonne: And giue vs all faith hopefullie to waite vppon him who will doe for vs aboue what we can aske or think. In whom I ame Yours in true and heartie loue and affeccion while I liue

Jo: ENDECOTT

Salem 5. 12. 40[/41]

My wiefe desires to haue her seruice remembered to you and Mrs. Winthrop.

---

[1] Cf. Hugh Peter's reference to his "neere Cossen" in his letter to Governor Winthrop, *ca*. February, 1640/41 (pages 316–317, above).

THOMAS GORGES TO JOHN WINTHROP[1]

To the Right Wor[shipfu]ll and my much honoured frend John Winthropp
these present in Boston

AGGAMENTICUS 23 12 m. 1640[/41]

MOST HONOURED SIR, Your loue to me, and the respects I owe you haue commanded me not to omitt the first opportunity. I haue talked with my neighbour Dixy[2] concerning that which you desired me and he tells me thus, for his passage you payd 4*li*, and he brought you one Mr. Jams to repay you for his freedome, and to place him with one Mrs. Higgison, but you replied that you would keep him for yourselfe, and giue him as much wages as any other man would. now he sayth that he might haue had 13*li* per annum of one Mr. Wright, after his years seruice you freed him, and let him haue some tools which [he] beleeus came to some 40*s*, likewise a suit of cloth and some other thinges, all which with the 4*li* he beleeus did not amount to aboue 13*li*, as he might haue had of Mr. Wright, but he sayth if ther be any thing due to you from him he will not fayl to giue you satisfaction to the vttermost of his power, for he acknowledgeth your loue towards him and the fauours you did him. I hear that Mr. Winter the disturber of our little common wealth, is now bound for Boston, he is either gone already or he goes with Mr. Campion. now I would desier you, if you thinke fitt to send him by Campion to be deliuered to me or to our Constable at Pascattaway, or to send him by my neighbour Mr. Page or by some other conueyance, and in it you will doe me and the whole prouince a great fauour, and I shall be ready to the vttermost of my power to obey you in the like request. I cannot send vnto you at this present news at large from Ingland, because the contrariety of the winde hath hindered it from comming from the Iles of Shoals only this I beleeue you hear that the Parlaiment is like to proceed. And a letter came to one of our Riuer, that the Lord Deputy of Ireland hath 3 bills preferred against him, and tis thought will hardly come of: Mr. Burton Mr. Prin and Mr. Bastwicke are called to the Parlaiment to relate theyr causes ther, and great hope ther is that Religion will be more countenanced then it hath binn. as I receaue more I will not fayl to certify you.

Mr. Jenner I hear is like to remain at Sacoe   it is an argument I hope that God intends good vnto these parts. we haue sent younge Mr. Ward of Newbury a call. I hope the Lord will be assistinge to vs in it. Mr. Burdith is at

[1] W. 3. 91; 4 *Collections*, VII. 333–334. For Gorges, see 4 *Collections*, VII. 333*n*.
[2] William Dixon. See Charles E. Banks, *History of York, Maine* (Boston, 1931), I. 108.

Pemiquid which lyes on the borders of this prouince. he is grown to that
height of sinn that it is to [be] feared he is giuen ouer. his time he spends in
drinking, dauncing, singing scurrulous songes, and for his companions he
selects the wretchedest people of the country. at the Springe I hear he is for
Ingland. I haue sent you some of that stuff which with vs supplies the want
of hempe. our Indians make theyr snow shoes, nets and bags of it, alsoe of a
bigger stalke called silke Grass which makes very fine hempe. The former is
as plenty with vs as ferne, the later grows not very plenty, espeacially about vs,
but ther is very much of it in the country. I hear both sorts are plentifull with
you. Thus with my humble seruice tendred to your selfe and to Mrs. Winthropp with many thankes for your loue to me, desiringe the Lord to reward
you, and to take you in to his sacred protection, I rest Yours in all due
respects

THO: GORGES

THOMAS GORGES AND EDWARD GODFREY TO
JOHN WINTHROP[1]

To the Right Wor[shipfu]ll John Winthrope Esqr. these present speed in Boston

AGGAMENTICUS 1 March 1640[/41]

MOST HONOURED SIR, one Reuben Guppy of late comminge into our plantation and pretendinge much Religeon and a great zeal for the Ordinances
of God was entertained by a planter, but since ther haue come diuers reports
vnto vs of his misdeameanors with you, and that fear of punishment droue
him away, and likewise this day I haue receaued a letter from Captain Vnderhill which expresseth the desier of Mr. Endicott to haue him returned
which letter I haue sent you heerinclosd. the desier we haue to satisfy his
request, and to ridd such fellows out of our Prouince, which haue brought
such a scandall on it haue caused vs to omitt noe opportunity of sendinge him,
therfore by Sampson Salter, M[aste]r of the Makeshift you shall receaue
him. resolued we are that this Prouince shall be noe refuge for Runn-
aways, for none comminge from another Plantation shall be entertained
heer without a Certificate of his good demeanour, or vppon the knowledge
of some of the Inhabitants. thus with our seruices tendered to you: com-

---

[1] W. Au. 102; 4 *Collections*, VII. 335–336. For Godfrey, founder of York, Maine, see 4 *Collections*,
VII. 377n.; Banks, *History of York, Maine*, 41–52 *et passim*.

mendinge you to the protection of the Almighty we Rest Yours in all due respects

THO: GORGES
EDW: GODFREY

SAMUEL MAVERICK TO JOHN WINTHROP[1]

To the wor[shipfu]ll Jno. Winthorp Esqr: these present, Boston

SIR, I vnderstand there is a report abroad that I should be privey to the flight of one Bell who was bound to appeare this court[2] he and one Morecroft I found at my howse one day last weeke who acquainted me with the buisines they are bound over for, craved my advise. my answar was, Inocencey was a bulworke, wished them if cleare of the fact, to stay, if guiltey left it to theire owne discretion. they professed innocencey and as I vnderstoode resolved to stay, as morecroft can testifie. be pleased to certifie so much if occasion be. I assure yow it is truth. I know there want not those which hunt after any thinge which may redound to my discreditt. your selfe euer honored Sir and honest Capt. Gibones are the only men which ever dealt plainely with me by way of reproofe and admonition, when you have heard of any thinge in which I have beene faultie which I hope hath not beene water spilt vpon a stone, and by it yow have much oblidged me. There are those which take an inquisition like course, by indeavoring to gaither what they can from malcontented servants or the like, which course I conceive is not warrantable. the former course is more commendable and will worke better effects   I hope God will enabel me in some measure to walke inoffencively, but findinge by 10 yeares experience that I am eie sore to diverse heare I have seriously resolved to remoue hence assone as I have dispatched away Mr. Allies ship with fish which ship is daily expected. al other hinderances are already remoued. My well wishes shall euer attend the Plantation, and your selfe and yours in particular, howeuer. be pleased to passe by my to longe neglect of visitinge yow, havinge not beene in Boston these fower monethes. as there is no one more engaged to yow, so there is none which more honores you then Your worshipes reall freinde and servant

SAMUEL MAVERICKE

March 1th 1640[/41]

[1] W. Au. 102; 4 *Collections*, VII. 308–309.
[2] Cf. *Records of the Court of Assistants*, I. 103.

EMMANUEL DOWNING TO JOHN WINTHROP[1]

To his much honored brother John Winthrop Governour Boston

SIR, this day I had a meeting with mr. Saltonstall about Dillinghams buisines, and chardging him with your noate sent me into England   he said there was deliuered James Luxford 20 Cowes, whereas your noate doth mention but 15, soe it was conceived that Dillingham or Luxford should deceive me of 5 Cowes, but after they were gone I founde Luxfords noate of my Catle he deliuered me which doth mention 19, soe there is but one wanting, which, (if he did not deliver James Luxford,) mr. Saltonstall must pay me for; I haue sent my man of purpose with these notes which I pray retorne by him againe. Dillingham wilbe with you to morow of purpose to cleare himselfe of these 5 Cowes, if yt shall apeare that Luxford hath cosened you and me of that one Cowe which is yet wanting, let yt never trouble you. that you may vnderstand how 20 Cowes should be deliuered to Luxford; the account is thus viz: In May 1633 there were deliuered to Dillingham

$$\left.\begin{array}{l} \text{9 Milch cowes} \\ \text{2 heifers} \\ \text{7 Cow calves} \end{array}\right\} 18$$

Of these 18 there dyed 2, soe there remayned 16   of these there was the first yeare with Dillingham 9 Calves, 5 Cow calves, and 4 bull calves.

In June 1636 Dillingham deliuered as he saith 4 of the said 5 Cow calves with the former 16 being then growne to be Cowes, in all 20 Cowes to James Luxford, who accounted to me as per his noate apeareth for 19, soe there wants but one, of this reckoning, but manie more are wanting to me of Dillinghams account which he said did dye and were killed by woolves etc. I doubt I must come to a Jury at Boston with mr. Saltonstall at last. he confesseth he hath 100*li* left of Dillinghams in his hands to satisfie me if neede be, and that there is almost as much more leyable to my satisfaction, elswhere. wee parted verie good freinds after all our debate of the buisines, soe for this tyme being over troublesome with my service to your selfe and my good sister I rest Your verie loving brother

EM: DOWNINGE

10. 1. 1640[/41]

[1] W. 2. 29; 4 *Collections*, VI. 54–55.

My wife and sonne John present their service we being all in health, blessed be God.

JOHN TINKER TO JOHN WINTHROP[1]

To the Right Wor[shi]ppffull and his much honnored Mr. Jno. Winthropp Esqr. thesse present in Boston

RIGHT WOR[SHI]PPFFULL, I am deeply ingaged for your great kindnesse the lord only can reward it and I only return thankes: I was sory I tooke not my leaue of your wor[shi]pp at my coming away haueing thoughts since you might possibly haue hadd some more servis to haue comanded me but I intreat your wor[shi]pps pardon: we are through vnseasonable wether per Gods prouidence put into Sallem there waiting a fitt Season which we hope will fale this night we humbly intreat your wor[shi]pps prayers for our saffe Conduct. we canott but take notis of the lords preuenting our being at Sea this last extremity of wether: we are affraid Mr. Lambertons Jurny by land will proue Ill: all our Frends at Sallem thanks be to the lord are well and desire to be rem[embered] to your wor[shi]pp and thus with my humble servis to you and to my m[ist]ris presented I shall euer rest Your Wor[shi]pp obleidged to Comand in any Servis to my poore power

JOHN TINKER

SALLEM: 10th Mar: 1640[/41]

[*Endorsed by Governor Winthrop:*] Jo: Tinker at his departure to Conetecutt.

JOHN ENDECOTT TO JOHN WINTHROP[2]

To the Wor[shipfu]ll John Winthrop senior Esqr. deliver at Boston

DEARE SIR, I hope I shall euer honour and loue you for your great care over mee and your wholsome counsell giuen to mee, which I haue through the mercie of God followed, so farre forth as I could vppon my best search chardge my selfe of the least appearance of giuing offence, either to the honoured maiestrates or ministers that subscribed the letter. I think the Church and all that heard mee will cleare mee of the things layd to my chardge. And I blesse God so hath my honoured brother Mr. Humfries already done and

---

[1] W. 3. 60; 4 *Collections*, VII. 229.
[2] W. 2. 77; 4 *Collections*, VI. 145–146.

hath giuen me full satisfaccion in his free acknowledgement of his failing heere, as also of his vniust chardges layd vpon mee there: which we were all glad to heare, and do praise the name of God for him, And my heart is neerer knit to him than euer.[1]

Yet Deare Sir let mee in loue tell you that you seeme in your Letter to tak all for granted that was related vnto you, which is not your wonted custome to doe: And that did at the first not a little greiue mee: Salomons rule would haue bene obserued. Proverb 18. 17. If you had in the least measure suspended etc. till I had written, It would haue sauored more of Justice. But I cannot but think you in wisdome did it to put mee to a deep search whereby the more to humble mee which I confesse I haue need to be: The Lord in mercie make mee thankfull for all good helpes for my soul, and requite into your bosome all your labour of loue shewed to mee in this or in any of your former kindnesses. With him I will leaue you and in him rest Yours most obliged

Jo: ENDECOTT

SALEM the 15th of the 1 moneth 1640[/41]

JOHN WOODBRIDGE TO JOHN WINTHROP[2]

To the right wo[rshipfu]ll John Winthrop sen. Esqr.,
at his house in Boston, these present

RIGHT WORTHY SIR, After my service præmised, etc. I am bold to write a few lines to you, with desire that you would advise vs the best you cann, and as speedily as your occasions will permitt. Some of vs haue desired to plant at Quichichuick,[3] and accordingly notwithstanding all the oppositions and discouragements that wee haue had hauing viewed the place since the court were intended this spring to haue built there: but there are two things that yett stand in the way to hinder vs; the proceeding of either of which may be so great an anoyance that will quite cutt off any hopes of being to a plantation there. The first is the intended takeing of a farme by Rowley men (which the court allowed them to doe in lieu of a farme which Mr. Vaine had within their bounds) adioyninge to their bounds, which though it be not plainely expressed yett wee are credibly informed they intend to take neere Quichi-

---

[1] For Winthrop's account of the quarrel between Endecott and Humfrey arising out of Endecott's opposition to Peter's being sent to England as an agent for the colony, see *Journal*, II. 26.

[2] W. 4. 111; 5 *Collections*, I. 317–319. For Woodbridge, see Morison, *Founding of Harvard College*, 409–410.

[3] Andover.

chuick, and so to take away 100 acres of meadow from that place which at best will entertaine but a small company by reason of the little quantity of meadow. The second is that notwithstanding all the agitations of the last Court, Mr. Rogers being demanded whither he yett expected any more answers that the contention the last court was onely about the neck and whereas he afterward expressed to the court that his first grant was 8 miles into the country (he sayes) no body speaking against it he tooke it for granted that he should haue 8 entire miles into the country besides what was giuen, and they purchased from Ipswich and Newbery. These onely are the impediments and reason of our not proceeding. Now that which wee would desire of your wo[rshi]p by way of advice is an answer to these 3 Questions. 1. Whither you apprehend that the Court will allow of their so taking the farme afforesayd in such a place as will be so much præiudiciall to a plantation. 2. Whither the Court will make good the grant of 8 miles intire to them, or compell them to stand to those bounds onely which were specifyed the last Court. 3. Whither you would advise vs neuerthelesse to proceed and trust to the Court more, or to desist and leaue it either alltogether or till things are cleered by the Court. I haue desired to propose these things first to yourselfe rather then the Gouernour because I know that he hath allwayes heeretofore bin opposite to my going thither. And the reason why I desire your speedy advice is because some of our company haue sold themselves out of house and home, and so desire to bee setled as soone as may be. Diuers others would gladly know what to trust to, and seeme with some resolution to affect Long Iland intending speedily to be gone thither if they settle not heere: and for my owne part I haue strong solicitations thither and by some not of the meaner sort: and (being resolved that I cannot comfortably carry things along as I am) though not there yett elsewhere I thinke I must resolve to labour to better my selfe. Thus leauing to your serious consideracion what I haue written desiring your speedy advice I humbly take my leaue and rest, Your wo[rshi]ps to command

JO: WOODBRIDGE

NEWBERY this 22th of 1 mo. 1640[/41]

DEANE TYNDAL TO JOHN WINTHROP[1]

To my assured louing Brother Mr. John Winthrop att Boston present this

LOUING AND GOOD BROTHER, I hope you vnderstand by my letter and by Mr. Tinker what mony I haue disburst since the sayle of your land. I haue payd since I receiued your last letter xx*li* to Mr. Kerby, and a 100*li* to Captaine Raynsborow, and I was with Mr. Harris att the Signe of Kathern wheale in gratious streete to haue payd him a 100*li* according to your direction, but he heard nothing of it, nor had no authoritie to receiue it, soe I keepe it in my handes, and since that time I haue binn sent to by one Mr. Cortman for a 120*li* but haueing no directions from you to pay it him, I did denie him, but I tould him that there was a 100*li* in my handes, which I would keepe till I heard whether you would haue me pay it him or Mr. Harris. I haue set doune this 100*li* in my account to you as if I had payd it to Mr. Harris, but I doe acknowledg I haue it in my handes and will neither pay it to Harris, nor Cortman till I heare from you which of them you would haue, to haue it. My Cosin Deane Winthrop not lyking a tedious sea voyage was set a shore att Maligo and is com safe to me in to England   I know not whether he can prouide to com in this ship but he sayth he will make speede to you. I will send you a boy or two when he coms if I can get them but I know not what wages you use to giue there, nor how long you would haue me indent with them to serue you. I will doe my best, and if I faile in anie thing you must pardon my ignorance. I send you my accounts by which you may see what is layd out of the 1300*li* and what is remayning. The mony that is remayning in my handes I desier to keep for my sister, and the yonger Childrens portions if you please but not soe strictly but that if you haue occasion to vse 30*li* or 40*li* you may haue it with all my hart for I protest brother I loue you from my hart and tender your reputation as my owne. I thank God my selfe and all my familie are in good health. my wife desiers your prosperitie and remembers her faithfull louc to you. The Parlament is yet siting and there is an act past for to haue a parlament every third yeare. 4 subsidies are granted and the Leiutenant of Ierland is now vppon his tryall, but nothing yet concluded on. It is reported that the Bishops shall haue no more voices in parlament. The Scots are still at New Castle. what I heare more you shall know by my Cosin Deane. and now desiering the almightie

---

[1] W. 1. 144. For Tyndal, brother of Margaret Winthrop, see *Winthrop Papers*, II. 300n.

to power his blessings plentifully vppon you I rest Your assured louing brother

DEANE TYNDALE

From MAPLESTED this 7 of Aprill 1641

[*Endorsed by Governor Winthrop:*] Br. Tindal Received (6) 10. 41.

DEANE TYNDAL TO MARGARET WINTHROP[1]

To my deare and louing sister Mris. Margaret Winthrop att Boston in new England present this

LOUING SISTER, Thoughe I writ latly to you yet I can not let this messenger passe without bringing my respects and loue to the. I would willingly haue had my Cosin[2] haue stayd here, but I perceiue his affection to Father and Mother will not let him stay from them. I haue furnisht him with such mony as he requiers to carrie him ouer. he is much grone and verie ciuill. I hope you will haue a great deale of comfort of him. it would be well for him if my brother would bread him vp in som calling and then with Gods blessinge howsoeuer the world went, he might make a shift to liue. my wife remembers her tru loue to you, and hath sent such things as you writ for, and she says if she knows your wants you shall haue what she can help you to. and now de-siering the almightie to blesse you and yours I leaue you to his protection and rest Your assured louing brother

DEANE TYNDALE

From MAPLESTED this 13 of Aprill 1641

HENRY SMITH TO JOHN WINTHROP[3]

To the Right wor[shipfu]ll and duly respected John Winthrop Esqr. these be delivered in Boston

RIGHT WOR[SHIPFU]LL, After my due respect remembred, I have by my Father bin made acquainted with what, in your letter to him, yow write about John Porters busyness. In answer wherto this I returne as formerly: I shall

---

[1] W. 4. 44; 5 *Collections*, I. 113.
[2] Deane Winthrop.
[3] W. 18. 76.

endevor to satisfy the debt in the best maner I can, though it was a busyness put vppon me contrary to my desire, and I can truly say I have not received 30s in mony for all his goods and yet I have payd 7li in mony by Goodman Johnson and some depts are yet vnpayed, and the partys for the present vnable to satisfy it, one especially who owes a good summe, had lately his howse and goods burnt. mony we have none with vs, nor means to procure any. The best means I can at present thinke on is corne: which if John Porter will appoynt any Pynace that comes into the river to call for it, I will deliver heere as much corne as the dept comes to at 3s per bushell which is the setled price amonge vs. the cariadge of it downe from vs to Hartford doth vsually cost 6d per bushel, and I alsoe will take order with some of our towne to carry it downe to the Pynace as I shall have direction from him: for I thinke it is as much as in equity can be required of mee to make payment in the place where I received it, and not be put to any further charge or trouble. for a coppy of the will[1] I cannot at the present send it because of the messengers hast. Mr. Moxon only tooke some noates from his mouth which he hath, and at his cominge into the Bay in June shall be brought with a coppy of the Inventory. thus forbearinge to be further troublsome at present I rest Yours in all offices of due respect

HENRY SMITH

SPRINGFEILD this 25th Aprill 1641

My Father desyrd to remember his due respect to yow who hath received your letter and kindly thanks yow for your care in that busyness.

THOMAS JENNER TO JOHN WINTHROP[2]

WORTHY SIR, Your pious and good letter I received for which I humbly thanke you. Your judicious counsel therin I loueingly imbrace, as concurring fully with mine owne Judgment: hence have I not troubled the people at all with Church discipline, or constitutions of Churches, etc. but haue bent my whole studdies to shew them their miserable and lost estate with out Christ, etc. Nor haue I enveyed, in the least measure against the Church of E[ngland] (to my remembrance) but haue ben (and still am) very fearefull to giue one word of distast about those things; but altogether do seek to gaine them

---

[1] I.e., that of John Allen. See Henry Smith to John Winthrop, November 2, 1640 (page 296, above).

[2] Miscellaneous MSS., Bound, M.H.S.; *Hutchinson Papers* (1769), 111–112; (1865), I. 125–126.

to Christ. True I do acknowledge that after I had ben here for the space of a month or 6 weeks, and perceiuing them very superstitious: (performing mans invention rather then the instituted worship of God:) now that I might gaine their good esteme of Gods pure ordinances and make them see the evill and folly of their superstition and willworship, I made choise of Ps. 19 and 7 to handle it at large. And in one of the uses of reprofe, I bent myselfe as strongly as I could against the religion of the papists, and condemned those practices which I saw the people here were superstitiously addicted to, in that use against the papists whose religion I shewed at large, consisted either of a new invented worship not mentioned in the law of God, or of Gods instituted worship miserably abused either by their additions or diminutions; and shewed the perticulars wherin. Now (I heartily thank God for it) it tooke a generall good impression: excepting Mr. Vines and one more: who told me that I struck at the ch[urch] of Engld., though I mentioned her not. wherupon he pressed me to dispute with him about one part of Baptizing infants with God-fath[ers] and Godmoth[ers] the which I was very loth to discourse about: yet I saw that either I must, or else sit downe with shame, for he had caled to gether his whole family to heare it. now it pleased God so to strengthen me (through the riches of his mercy) that he was utterly silent: and since that time hath manifested more respect and loue to me and my master then formerly, and doth take notes of the sermons dayly, and repeate them in his family very orderly, as I am informed.

Thus sweet sir I make very bold to enforme your worsh[ip] with the truth of things, though not worth the writing. I haue ben solicited both from the inhabitance of Stratens Plantation, and from those of Caskoe to be a meanes to helpe each of them to a godly minister, wherfore I do make bold to intreat your worship to do your endevour to furnish them both.

Thus hopeing err long to se your face, I leaue you in the arms of our blessed Saviour, in whome also I rest Your worsh[ip's] to com[man]d till death

Th. Jenner

Saco, 26 of the 2d 1641

ROBERT CHILD TO JOHN WINTHROP, JR.[1]

To his honoured and much respected freind Mr. John Winthrop
at his fathers house in Boston deliver this New England

WORTHY SIR, I received by Mr. Euans letters from you, and am glad to heare of your good health, and shall most willingly doe you any service here that lyes in my power. in the letters I received a note inclosed, of those bookes you desire I should procure for you. I haue inquired at most of the book-binders shops in London, but scarce find one of them. I found two peeces of Faber, viz. Alchymista Christianus et Hercules Chymicus, but because you haue not seene them, and according to my iudgment they are bookes of noe great value, I bought them not, but will send you them with his Abrege des secrets to pervse from myne owne library. I found likewise Franciscus Georgius de Harmonia mundi   I know not whither you haue seene him. the title promiseth much, but (me thinkes) the matter contained in it is not much worth, its in Fol. of 20s price. Della Brosse at this time is not in my hands. I count it an excellent booke, and haue sent to Fraunce for it, and Burgravius workes, which you mentioned, and the rest of the bookes, which I have not: From myne owne library I likewise send you to pervse till I come to new England, Dr. Dauisons workes, the French Jesuits voyages in Canada in 3 volumes, that you may see how they proceede in the conversion of those Heathen and how little the Lord hath blessed them in there proceeding; Gassarells Secrets inoyies des Persans: Rochas des eaus minerals, excellent bookes both in French: likewise Arca aperta in High Dutch, which I desire you to keepe tanquam Sybillæ folia, item a little book of vrines. Mathesius, Solea, and the rest I neither inioy nor as yet can find, but I shall doe my best indeauours to procure them for you: These bookes you shall receive by Mr. Evans shippe, which (god blessing them) will arrive at the port so soone as this: I haue sent you likewise a Catalogue of my Chymicall bookes.[2] if you like them, they are at your service   I should take it for a great fauour, if you would send me a Catalogue of yours, that I might know what excellent bookes are in your hands. I Intend if I haue leysure to goe to Burdeau, from thence to Tholouse to salute Faber, to procure vines and a vigneron, who can like-wise manage silkewormes, if it be possible. if I can doe you any pleasure there, pray let me heare from you speedily. I intend when I returne to you (god

---

[1] W. 4. 54; 5 *Collections*, I. 148–151. For Child, see 5 *Collections*, I. 148n.; George L. Kittredge, "Dr. Robert Child, the Remonstrant," *Publications of the Colonial Society of Massachusetts*, XXI. 1–146.
[2] See pages 334–338, below.

willing) to prosecute the planting of vines throwly, to try somewhat concerning silkewormes, and would to my power helpe forward the digging of some good mine, if you haue found any in the country. Wee haue here very much good newes (the Lord be praised). Euery 3 yeares wee shall haue a parliament. the deputy is condemned by both houses, the Archbishop is in the Tower, and will certainly be punished severely, the statute against papists is to be executed many of them therefore, and for some treacherous busines are fled the kingdome: Mr. Prin, Bastwick are at liberty and haue 5000*li* apeece for satisfaction.

The prince of Orange son hath maried our kings eldest daughter.[1] The convocation house, which presumed to set after the Parliament house was broken vp and made new Canons are fined 150 thousand pounds and vpward to helpe toward the payment of the scots 300000*li* graunted by the parliament. Lord prelates, deanes, prebends are fallen, and whither bishops shall follow, sub iudice lis Ẽ. the sweedes in Germany haue suffered a defeat by the Emperour but haue well repaired there forces againe.

Portugall is totally revolted from the Spaniards, and haue taken two great Citys from him. Catalonia likewise is ioyned with them, so that at this time the proud Spaniard is desperate, and hath given Flaunders to the Emperour. wee haue some suspition of the French because of there very great forces in Normandy therefore 25 ships are preparing: more particulars new you shall heare by the shippe. Remember my service to your father Mr. Dudley Mr. Bellingham, Mr. Humphreys, Mr. Cotton, Mr. Wilson, Mr. Peters, vnto whome I am much beholden. yours

ROBERT CHILD

[*Ca.* May, 1641]

ROBERT CHILD'S CHEMICAL BOOK LIST[2]

Libri Chymici, quos possideo sunt

Germanici

1 Aureum vellus. 4°
2 Rosarium nouum. 4°
3 Triumphwagen ☿ⁱ. 8°

---

[1] William, Prince of Orange, married Mary, eldest daughter of Charles I, May 2, 1641.
[2] W. 5. 177. See William J. Wilson, "Robert Child's Chemical Book List of 1641" (with an Introduction by Charles A. Browne), *Journal of Chemical Education*, xx (March, 1943), 123–129, where full titles, in so far as identification has been possible, are given.

4 Turba ph[ilosoph]or[um]. 8°
5 Gab gotts. 8°
6 Opuscula Chymica. 8°
7 Promptuarium [Al]chy[miae]. 8°
8 Ph[ilosoph]ia Chymica. 8°
9 Cabala Concordantia Chy[m]ica. 8°
8 Promptuar[ium] pars alt[era]. 8°
9 Suchtenii de ☿°
12 Arca aperta Jesuer Mehung. 16
13 Pract[ica] ☉ˢ R[oger]i Baconis. 8°
14 Richard[i] Anglici Lulli. 8°
15 Secreta ph[ilosoph]icali[a]. 8°

Italici

M: S: II. 4°
il mondo magico. 4°
Inganni d'Alchymisti. 4°
Nazari de transmut[atione]. 4°
Thornei de sublimat[ione]. 4°
[Oliverus de] Oliver[iis] de ☉ pot[abili]
    [De]lap[ide] ph[ilosoph]orum
Braceschi Exposit[ione] Geber

Gallici

Flamell, Alph[abet] d[e] Chym[ie]. 4°
Cham. Plan. eschole transm[u]t[atoire]
Bo[u]quet Chymique
Quercetan[us] preparat[ion] Chymique
Toyson d'Or
Nuisement tratte du sel
Fabri abregè
Tratte des experiences
Prototype chymique
Cosmopolite
Sommaire della med[icine] chymique
des eaux minerales Rochas

Anglici

Ripley 12 gates MS.
♂all Cup. Primrose
Revelation secret spirit
Plats hiden treasure
of Bathes
Cotta Cont[ra] Antony

Latini

Agricola de Re metall[ica]. Fol. i
de ortu subterraneorum uocum. Fol. i
Mylij Basilica. 4°
  Medica
  Ph[ilosoph]ica. 4°
  Chymica
  Ph[ilosoph]ia reformata
  Anatomia ⊙ˢ
Libavij Alchymia docimasima. 4°
Ep[isto]l[a]e vol. 2°. 8°
Not[a]e in Raym[undum]. 4°
Galen[us] Temp. 4°
Panacea Antigra[mania]. 8°
Not[a]e libavian[a]e. 8°
Liba[vius] singularia. 8°
Fabri Myrothecium, Curat[iones]. 8°
  Palladium
  Abrege des secrets
Hercules Chymicus
Alchymista Christianus
Hartman[n] in Croll[ium]
Hartman[n] praxis
Disputat[iones] eiusdem
Davis[s]on Chymia[tricus]
Severini Idea
Mayeri Hyero[gly]phy[ca]
Septimana ph[ilosoph]ica
  De physico circulo quadrato
  Examen pseudochymicorum

Rubei de distillat[ione]
Caranta de ☉s
Carerii disput[atio]
Panthei alchymia[m]
Abraham de ☉s
Lacinii collectanea
Margarita pretiosa
Rulandi disputat[iones]
promachomachia Bruschi
Theat[rum] Chymicum 5 vols.
Fallop. de aq. miner.
Guntheri paradoxa
Phaedronis Chymica
volum[ina] 2º Alchymi[ae]. 8º Basel
Cesalpinus de metallicis
potier apologia
veredarius
Furichii Carmina
nihil, aliq[ui]d, om[n]e
Tetras Chymiat[rica] Kerneri
Wittestein de 5 ess[entia]
Evonymus
Augurelli Carmina
Geber vol. 2º. Rom[a] Argent[orati]
Beguini Tyrocinium
Antonii Apologia
Gro[ss]schedelij Proteus Chym[icus]
Dornei Congeries Paracels[icae]
Dela Brosse
Chrisypi
Animadv[ersiones] de alchym[ia]
Horn de ☉s
demonst[ratio] Chy[mico] in Riolan
Nolli Systema Hermet[icae]
Iatrochy[mia] luis venere
Drebbel de Elem[en]tis
Harmonia Chymica
Spagyrica Pharm[acopoea] Potyeri

Zuingeri Exam[en] Chymicorum
Rog[er] Bacon Chymica
Mouffet, Chymica
Zynesii et Democriti, Chymia
Bornelli Chymia. 4°
Zenerti opera omnia partim Chymica
Rhena. 4°

[*Ca.* May, 1641]

GEORGE FENWICK TO JOHN WINTHROP[1]

For his much respected freind John Winthrop esqr. att Boston thes

Sir, Robert Saltonstall hath bene [*torn*] that land he hath disposed w[*torn*] the Countrie gaue to his father [*torn*] bought of Capt. Pattrick the c[*torn*] my letter to yow was, to manifest [*torn*] and his sone which his letter de[*torn*] all to prejudice either I wrott [*torn*] wherby he desires me to take care [*torn*] which I wonder he should doe w[*torn*] of all to his sonne by the letter [*torn*] The truth of the bussines vpon the [*torn*] and discourse with Rob. I [*torn*] did really giue him such pow[*torn*] verball reseruation to him-self [*torn*] not to answere his promises to h[*torn*] and good behauiour for the tyme to com[*torn*] of him. he is att present very se[*torn*] passages and I would gladly hope) d[*torn*] promise reformation, and to doe noe [*torn*] advice of freinds, his present strait [*torn*] discharge his present ingagments he [*torn*] with me to helpe him out of them, and although [*torn*] neuer to haue had any dealings with him [*torn*] some experience of his setlednes yet vpon [*torn*] promises of future care in his occasio[*torn*] more to performe them I haue consent [*torn*] what I can, therfor sir If it stand any [*torn*] conveniency to cutt of what he owes you [*torn*] wayes with any other to further him I shall allow [*torn*] account. I haue also consented to lett him haue some other moneyes that are oweinge to me, if he can make vse of them. He also intreats me to be sutour to yow on his behalfe, to further him to such moneys as may be dew to him from the cuntrie, for his purpose is to dispatch as sone as he can, that he may returne and attend the aggrement with Stiles which Mr. Haynes and others aboue conceaue wilbe for his advantage. I nead not say any more to yow whom he hath euer found soe much his freind. I haue receaued the trees yow sent me for which I hartily thanke yow. If I had any thing heare that could pleasure yow, yow

---

[1] W. 2. 146; 4 *Collections*, vi. 367–368.

should frely comand it. I am prettie well storred with chirrie and peach trees
and did hope I had had a good nurserie of Aples of the Aples yow sent me
last yeare but the wormes haue in a maner distroyed them all as they came
vp   I pray informe me if yow know any way to preuent the like mischeife
for the future. Your sonne was with me befor your letter, and acquainted me
with your owne and his desire. I did but express my hart when I told him I
should be glad any way to pleasure either of yow, and soe farre as it did concerne me gaue my consent (with this reseruation which I know in his own
disposition he would be reddie enough to yeald to) that if there were any
fishing neare it (which soe farr as I se we must all suddenly seek after) you
might [grant] me a liberty to make vse of part of it for that imployment but
whither euer there will be any such occasion or noe I know not: soe with
tender of my owne and wifes loueing respects to your selfe and bedfellow I
rest your assured frend

GEO. FENWICK

May 6th 1641

your bill I left with Mr. Bellingham.

[*Endorsed by Governor Winthrop:*] mr. Fenwick for mony [*illegible*] payd to
mr. R. Saltonstall.

[*Endorsed by John Winthrop, Jr.:*] mr. Fenwicks Consent for Fisher's Iland.

WILLEM KIEFT TO JOHN WINTHROP[1]

Al Molto Mag: Sig:, il Sig: Gio: Wintrop Bostoni

SIGNORE, Ho hauuto molto cara la lettera di Vostra Signoria di 10 di
maggio per la qúal la mi da molti aúiso che mi ê statto gratissimo hauer
inteso, e peró la Ringratio Sommamente di questo suo gentil officio, qúella
sia certa che non mi potra far maggior piacere offerendomi alli súoi com-
mandi prontissimo; vn de Nostri Vesselli ê Venútto de gli indi occidentali,
Confirma la Reuolta de portugual, e che gli Signori portuguesi hanno man-
dato imbassadori in Hollande e Francia cossi ancora hanno fatto quello dela
Baya Todos los Santos in Pharnambúcco.

---

[1] W. 1. 145. For Kieft, Director General of New Netherland, see *D.A.B.*

Altro non occorro   a V. S. di continoúa mi Racommando, state Sano,
de Vostri Signore affettionato Ser:

GUILL: KIEFT

NOVA BELGIA alli 17 di Júny 1641

[*Endorsed by John Winthrop, Jr.:*] from the Governour of the Dutch plantation
vpon Hudsons river.

EMMANUEL DOWNING TO JOHN WINTHROP, JR.[1]

To his euer honored Cosen John Winthrop Esqr. [torn]

[*A few lines destroyed*] to be soe full to [*half a line defaced*] nothing further or
hinder your sale with them as the Case stands.

My sonne is not yet retorned from Ipswich whom I expect euerie howre
and soe haue done these 3 dayes; If you goe for England before yt be done,
yet I will if God permitt pursue yt to the vtmost, and send per the next shippe,
that you may receive your monie of his Father.

My deare and hartye beloved Cosen if I see you not before you goe, yet
know you carrye my hart and true affections with you, and shall count eurie
day, three, vntill you retorne againe. Reade and seall if you can my Cosen
Peters letter before you deliuer yt. Soe wishing you a prosperous Jorney and
safe retorne I rest your assured loving vncle

EM: DOWNINGE

SALEM 29 July 1641

EMMANUEL DOWNING TO HUGH PETER[2]

To his verie loving Cosen Mr. Peter at Boston deliver

MY GOOD COSEN, vnderstanding you were resolued to goe by water into
the Bay or at least to the shippe, I sent my wife yeasterday with my Cosens,
purposing my selfe to haue accompanied you by water to the shippe, but
though you haue altered your Course and prevented me and some others,

---

[1] W. 2. 31; 4 *Collections*, VI. 59.

[2] Massachusetts State Library; 4 *Collections*, VI. 58. The original manuscript of this letter was
given by Robert C. Winthrop, Sr., to Charles Deane, March 13, 1880. It was item No. 4065 in the
catalogue of Mr. Deane's library which was sold at auction in March, 1898, and was purchased by
Mr. Robert C. Winthrop, Jr., who presented it to the Massachusetts State Library.

yet shall my hart and prayers ever attend you, early and late at Sea and at land, in the Court and in the Countrie vntill you retorne againe vnto vs. remember my service to mr. Weld and mr. Hibbons, whom I had embraced on shipboard had you not thus stollen from vs.

The Bishop caused a *Quo Warranto* to be sued forth in the kings Bench against our Patentees, thinking to damme our patent, and putt a generall Governour ouer vs, but most of them that apered I did advise to disclayme, which they might safely doe, being not sworne Magistrats to governe according to the patent; and these Magistrats which doe governe among vs being the only partyes to the patent were never Summoned to aper. Therefore if there be a Judgement given against the patent, Its false and erroneous and ought to be reuersed, with a motion in the kings benche without any long suite by writt of Error may set right againe   farewell my deare Cosen, soe wishing you a prosperous Jorney and safe retorne I rest yours assured whilest I am

EM. DOWNINGE

SALEM 5th day morning [July 29, 1641]

THOMAS MAYHEW TO JOHN WINTHROP[1]

WOR[SHIPFU]LL SIR, I haue deliuered mr. Russell my accompt And doe hereby intreate yow to sattisfie him and this shalbe your Full dischardge   I suppose I Left a Coppy of the accompt with your wor[shi]pp. not haueing ells at present I Rest your wor[shi]pps to commaund

THOMAS MAYHEW

CHARLESTOWNE 23 of the 7th 1641

[*Endorsed by Governor Winthrop:*] Mr. Mayhews Assignment to mr. Russell of my debt for which he hath my Bill.

JOHN WINTHROP, JR., TO ELIZABETH WINTHROP[2]

[*To my*] *deare Wife Elizabeth Winthrop* [*at*] *Tenhills neare Charlstowne*

BRISTOL Octob: 8, 1641

MY DEARE WIFE, I wrote to the from Newfoundland concerning our arrivall there, but know not whether my letters that I sent by 2 severall boats,

---

[1] W. 15. 59.
[2] W. Au. 74; 5 *Collections*, VIII. 35–36.

to be conveied to a ship bound for new-england, were delivered. therfore
concerning our arrivall there I shall breifely mention it againe. we were 14
daies from New-england thither. we staied there thre weekes before we found
a ship ready to sett saile for England. from thence we were 20 daies before
we arrived in England, having very foule weather, continuall stormes betweene Newfoundland and England and our ship very small about 60 tunnes.
but it pleased God to deliver vs out of all those many dangers we were almost
every day in: so as we are now at Bristoll in safety (praised be his name) where
we arrived the 28 day of September, and meeting with mr. Boole, who is going
to Barstable, I leave this letter with him to be sent, if any fishing ships doe
goe to New-Engl: before winter that thou mightest vnderstand of my welfare
by the first. I shall write more largly to my father. remember me to all my
deare freinds brothers sisters cozens, and specially to thy deare selfe with my
blessing to my children. God keepe you all. Thy affectionate Husband

JOHN WINTHROP

heere is a ship to goe from Bristoll (as we are informed) about a month
hence by which God willing I shall write the more, being vncertaine of the
conveiance of this. be thankefull to God for vs, for [*torn*] he hath delivered
from great and often dangers.

Prythe forget not to send my particular salutations and love to my brother
and sister Symonds and all my cosens there, my vncle and aunt Dow[n]ing
and all there, mr. Humphries and all his, mr. Endicot and mrs. Endicot, my
sister Lake, and Martha. If you se my brother or sister Dudly or send to them
my cosen Cookes both and theirs, with mr. Dunstan and his wife mr. Sheap-
herd, mr. Lines mr. Allen and mr. Nowell and theires also Capt: Sedgwick,
mr. Coitmore mr. Norton my cosen Parker Capt. Keine mr. Coggin mr.
Tomson mr. Rainsborough mr. Haines cosen George Downing with all at
home with you cosen Hanna Lake and the rest. I cannot write to any of them
now. Farewell my deare wife it is midnight and time to sleepe. I pray be carefull of your Journies to Cambridge or else where, and remember what I desired you, to stay with the children one part of the day your selfe. Let betty
lerne to read by any meanes but keepe hir not too close to it.

LUCY DOWNING TO JOHN WINTHROP[1]

To her much honoured brother the governer this present in Boston

Sir, I receiued yours of the 15. I am sory to hear matters are so ill, but it is easier born att distance, then in near relation. I hope it will shortlye appeare more euidently whear the mallady lyes, an the discouerers to appear more inocent. The good lord assist his poor seruants in his owne worke, for the enemy is still vigilant to peruert and blemish by one means or other, what is of god.

Your good sister[2] is gone to visit the bay and it seems was more willinge boston should haue her brauery then poor salem, but was at present a little preuented, but I doupt not but hauinge possesion she maye and will in short time attayne her ends, and why she should be molested in it is much disputed and Mr. Peters much censured and condemned in crosinge his deed to her, but whilst men make our lawes they are fitest to jugd of them. but certaynly the woman is daungerously affected, and they that haue experience will finde noe less. I hear she hath an intent to present my sister with a gowne, and tould the party she heard her former present was acsepted, therefore if she could giue, she would try her power to sell. I hope some piggions are come to your hands and more had bin sent if I had had a larger thinge to put them in, but if you pleas to return the cage it shall be filld agayne. so with my best seruis to my good sister and cosens all, I rest yours to command

L. D.

[*Ca.* 1642]

an allmenick maker wear conuenient but it is 27 or 28.

NATHANIEL ROWE TO JOHN WINTHROP[3]

To the worshipfull, and much respected Freinde Mr. Winthrope Magistrate, liueing att Boston in New-Ing:

Most loueing and kinde Sir, my humblest seruice remembred to you: I now with much consideratione (and thinkinge of all thinges, and businesses) doe write to you. First of all; my father sent mee to this countrie verie hastelie, (and ouer-much inconsiderately) indeed it is a sore greife to mee, that I

[1] W. 4. 9; 5 *Collections*, I. 26–27.
[2] Mrs. Hugh Peter, whose husband Winthrop often called "Brother Peter."
[3] W. 4. 112; 5 *Collections*, I. 319–321.

should charge my prudent and most deare father with the euill of rash doeinge of thinges: but yet beinge compelled in this time of straighteness, I must say itt. My father sent with mee provitiones enough for to serue mee a yeare or towe; as Meale, Flower, Buttar, beefe. I haueinge lost my meale and flower was compelled to sell the rest of my provicion, and indeed being counselled soe to doe, I immediately did itt; Then Mr. Eaton, and Mr. Dauenport haueinge noe direct order what to doe; wished mee, and sent mee vnto Mr. Eaton the marchants brother to be instructed in the rudiments of the Lattine Tongue (in which, with practise, I shalbe prettie skilfull). I liued with him about a moneth, and uerily in that space he spake not one word to mee, scilicet, about my learninge, and after he went awaie, I liued an idle life, because I had noe instructour. After all this: I was sent (by Mr. Bellinghams order) vnto Mr. Willis of Linne, the Schoole-maister: and theire I liueing priuately gott the best part of my lattine-tongue, but yet not by his instructiones, butt indeed onelie by seeinge his manner of teachinge, and gatheringe thinges of my selfe, and alsoe by bribeinge (or giueing gifts to) his sonnes for patternes; of which Mr. Willis neuer knew, as yett: This last half yeare hath binne spent in receiueing instructiones frome Mr. Dunster, whoe (blessed be god for itt) hath binne a guide to leade mee onne in the waie of hummane litterature, and alsoe in diuine: Thus much for my cours in this lande: Seeing Sir you out of youre fountaine of wisdome, doe adiudge that it is my fathers will and pleasure that I should betake my selfe to one thinge, or other, whereby I mighte gett my liueinge (*O Tempora O Mores!*) why! for my part I shall be willinge to doe anie thinge for my father (God assistinge mee) att Quille-piacke, as to help to cleare grownde, or hough upp grounde, quia enim, qui humiliatur, is uero tempestiuô exaltabitur: But I pray you Sir to make the waie cleare for mee to goe to England, soe that I may speake more fullie to my father; and with my freinds, soe that and if my father hath caste his affectiones off frome Mee (which if I had but one serious thought that waie, it would be the distractinge of my spireite all the daies I haue to liue. the curse of the parent is the greatest heuiness and burden to soule of a childe that is, my father neuer made anie such thinge knowne to mee) that I might not loose those opportunities that are offered to me by one of my Vncles, whome I am certaine will doe mee anie good, and if that my father be offended with mee, then if I be att London I feare not but that my Vncle will pacifie my fathers wrathe. thus I end. your obseruant seruant

NATH. ROWE

[*Ca.* 1642]

THOMAS SHEPARD TO JOHN WINTHROP[1]

To our much honoured Gouernour Mr. Winthrop

R[IGHT] W[ORSHIPFU]LL AND MUCH HONOURED, I haue sent yow according to your desire the apprehensions of those at the riuer, together with mine own, about the questions now stirring:[2] what I haue writ I am not wedded to, but if better light appeare, I fall down to it; In discussing these questions, we generally walke in vntroden paths few Casuists speake ἀκριβῶς to them; the whole Christian woorld hath hitherto not attended to Moses Judicialls as there rule, and therefore haue bin wanting to cleare vp there proportions; I haue therefore spoken many things to see of what weight they might be in other mens ballances who are best able to judge: determining nothing without concurrance of thoughts and apprehensions of brethren for whom (and not for the court) I prepared them; I could not but satisfy your own desire, intreating yow to peruse them your selfe and to communicate them to none (at least for the present) vnles it be to the Deputy who I thinke desired to see them also:

Mr. Wilson also let me see a discourse writ with your hand concerning Fornication, Rape etc: at first I desired to see it only and consider; but perceiuing that invndation of abominable filthinesses breaking in vpon vs; my spirit was pressed to returne an answer to the question about single Fornication; and the punishment of it; letting passe other things which I haue no time to peruse; I haue therefore sent yow that answer I haue drawn vp which should haue come to yow long since but I haue bin hindred; but now I knew not how safe it was any longer to keepe it by me; he that hath transcribed it hath done me much wrong by blotting of it, and I have no leysure to write a better: I hope yow will accept of my good will: only do not mistake my ayme; my scope in this answer to the discourse is not to define any thing, but to enquire and to propound to your wisdom some things considerable, and to be considered of, at your leysure, that so if yow find them weake and inconsistent with truth yow may cast them by, without any offence to me; if any thing of weight be in them, yow may be pleased to consider of making some Law for the punishing of that sin which I feare else will soone poyson these societies; you may keepe this Answer by yow; but I pray send me the other two vnto me when yow haue done with them: the god of all wisdom and

---

[1] W. 3. 72; 4 *Collections*, VII. 270–272.
[2] Cf. Savage (1826), 45–47; Bradford, *History of Plymouth*, II. 310–314.

mercy counsell guide direct yow in your more weighty aff[a]yres: Yours euer

THO: SHEPARD

[*Ca.* 1642]

Your apprehensions agaynst reading and learning heathen authors, I perswade myselfe were suddenly suggested, and will easily be answered by B[rother] Dunstar, if yow should impart them to him:

JOHN WILSON TO JOHN WINTHROP[1]

To our honored Governor, [John Winthrop Esq.,][2] these deliver

HONORED SIR, I perceaue the reason why I receaued not answer hitherto from mr. Shepherd was, because he was desirous the answer might be if it were the will of god according to your desire. He delayd not to mooue her in the thinge, and seriouslie to Commend it to her serious thought, and perceauing her inclined aversely from marriage, or the motion therof, he desired she would not presently answer at all, much lesse resolue. But rather take time and Consider therof as a matter of Great moment, and of such Inducements waightie, which before her were præsented. neyther did she returne him Answer till this morning. Which was to this effect: that she did account her selfe greatly bounde to yourselfe who did expresse toward her so great loue, as to make her such an offer. and was very thankfull in that behalfe, but declareth a firme resolution for sundry reasons not to entertayne any thoughts of marriage, nor doth find any inclination to this or any motion, (though Sundry besides this she hath had) as not able to Bury her husband so soone as she Cals it. and she hath written letters to her father whom she expecteth now shortly at lest to heare from him, to whom she hath engaged her selfe by promise, to reserue herselfe wholy to his Counsell and direction in her affaires. And if she had not so written, yet would she thinke her selfe Bound neuer the lesse to walk by that Rule (ther being it seemeth extraordinary dearenes and Tendernes betweene them in him as a father et Contra.) And though It be not mentioned, yet I beleeue what I hinted to you before, that their is some speciall likelihood of Some body or other to Come with or from her father, whom he may Commend to her. So that I neyther see nor gather any probability of further Successe in this Ayme. Wherin I doubt not but you are and will be ready (as in all thinges) to resigne vp your desires to the

---

[1] W. 1. 141. For Wilson, see *D.A.B.*
[2] The words in brackets are canceled in the original manuscript.

Good pleasure of God, whom as you serue in a good conscience so neyther will he be wanting to you nor yours in any seasonable [*illegible*] Vnto whose sweet Grace, and rich reward recommending you, and your honorable yoke-fellowe, I do rest Vnfaynedly at your Service in Christ Jesus

JOHN WILSON

[*Ca.* 1642]

JOHN WINTHROP TO ——— ———[1]

REV[EREND] AND DEAR SIR, I heartyly thank you for your loving payns in resolving my obiections, which were, some of them I see, ouer curious and needless: I am clearly satisfied in that which was the main occasion of my trouble, and your laying open the grounds and reasons of the particular parts of your Answer makes it clear to me, that your intentions were sincere, without partiallity, and your main ayme, truth and peace for which I bless the Lorde, and crave pardon for my [*illegible*] iealousyes; and though I cannot concur with you in every thing yet being satisfied in the main, I can well be silent in the rest. the Lord will clear his own truth in his own tyme. For matter of Temptation, it may be as you suspect, but truly I cannot find wherein the strength of it should lye, for as for the gent[leman] hims[elf] he hath euer been, and still is deare to me, and many friendly affairs have passed between vs, both former and later and so we are like to continue (for aught I know.) For the Office of C[ouncillor] I am no more in love with the honor, or power of it, then with an olde friese Coat in a summers daye: therefore, when it was propounded to have the power taken away, I never opposed, but presently drew vp the order for it, and shalbe as ready to doe the like for the abrogation of it, if it be so dissolved. Neither will those speeches I vsed in the Court about the book or the author (if I might be iustly dealt with to be heard before I were censured) argue any indulgent affection in me towards the Office, or disaffection to the Author for I professed my concurrance with those that cleared him; only I differed in this that I would have had it doone in an orderly way. I would have had the book first read and the Court to have determined of the matter of it, before they had medled with the Author but finding the Court to be bent the contrary way I drew vp an order for his clearing as full and safe for him as himself could have drawn. As for any conspiracy against his life or etc. I never heard it (to my best remembrance) so much as propounded by any of the magistrates for that or any other Censure

---

[1] W. 1. 148; *L. and L.*, II. 274–276. For Richard Saltonstall's treatise on the Standing Council, the subject of this letter, see *Journal*, II. 59–60, 86–88; *Records of Massachusetts*, II. 5, 20, 21; *New England Quarterly*, IV (January, 1931), 68–71.

but only that he might be questioned for it. The Lord knowes, that that which I write is the truth, whatsoever you have heard to the Contrary: If you discern any Tempt[ation] to lye elswhere, I shall take it as one fruit of your love to discover it and help to heal me. So desiring still to enioy your faithfull Counsell and prayers, I heartyly salute you and rest

[JOHN WINTHROP]

[On the Verso]

1: I conceived that verum et sanum were not convertible.

2: That lawfull ordinary power could not be said to be transcendent, only in respect of the Officer to whom the dispensation of it is committed.

3: That though the matter of the scripture be always a Rule to vs, yet not the phrase, for I should not say, that a man who should sleep 40 ho[urs] did sleep 3 days and 3 nights; or that he who breakes on of the kings laws breakes all etc.

4: I supposed that an example or similitude if it agreed in the thing intended, was proper, though it agreed not in all parts.

5: That infirmity maintayned with obstinacy may prove wickedness, therefore principiis obstare might be according to prudence in such a Case.

6: That such a dispensation of power as in the Aduice is presented could not be adequate to all the ordinary occasions of the commonw[ealth].

7: I could finde nothing omitted that might save the authors reputation (being but one and the youngest in authority amongst us) and nothing inserted (more then one worde of ordinary complement) that might vindicate the Credit of that Stand[ing] Councell though they be 3 to one, and ancientest in p[rac]tice of government.

8: I did not conceive that liberty for Advice would have been taken so largely as to be a shelter to all that is in that book, so far as it is applied.

That whatsoever is transcendent is above all Rules, and so *[torn]* Transcendent power must be above all Laws and that [can be] no other but Tiranny.

That such an observation of all the Elders, in so solemn a way would make vs more obnoxious to the peoples Censure, then all that the book can fix upon vs.

That though the Answ[er] should prove so exact, as it might be written vpon (as now it is reformed) in nullo erratum, yet it might have been of vse to have added some such Apologie as might haue prevented the misapprehensions of weaker Judgments.

[*Ca.* May, 1642]

JOHN WINTHROP'S SUMMARY OF THE CASE BETWEEN RICHARD SHERMAN AND ROBERT KEAYNE[1]

Att the generall Courtt (3) 18—1642

A breaviate of the Case betwene Richard Sheareman pl[aintiff] by petition and Capt. Robert Keaine defen[dan]tt aboute the title to A straye Sowe supposed to be broughtt from Deare Iland about (9)ber 1636

The poynts in the Case agreed

1 The pl[aintif]f had a Sowe all white, Saue a black Spott vnder the eye of the biggnesse of a Shilling and a ragged Eare.

2 This Sowe was Carryed to deare Iland.

3 Noe profe thatt it was brought back. onelye probablie itt might be though neare 40 Swine miscaryed there thatt yeare.

4 The defendant had a straye Sowe soposed to be brought from Deare Iland that yeare.

5 This Sowe was Cryed divers tymes, and many came and sawe her, in the tyme the defendant keept her, which was betwene one and 3 yeares.

6 The defendant had before this tyme, a faire white Sowe of his owne which he keept in his yarde with the straye Sowe aboue a yeare.

7 The defendant killed one of these Sowes about (8ber) 1637.

8 The pl[ain]t[iff]s wife soone after, charged the defendant to haue killed her Sowe.

9 The defendant shewing the pl[ain]t[iff]s wife the Sowe which remained aliue she disclaimed itt.

10 Upon Complaint of the pl[ain]t[iff]s wife, the cause was brought to the Elders (as matter of offence) and vpon hearing all Allegations, and the most materiall wittnesses on booth parts, the defendant was Cleared.

11 The cause thus rested till (2)—1640 and then the pl[ain]t[iff]s wife brought itt to the Inferyer Courte att Boston where (vpon a full hearinge) the Jurye founde for the defendant and awarded him about 3*li* costs.

12 Now (about 2 yeares after) the pl[ain]t[iff] brings the cause (by petition) into the generall Courte declyning the Court of Assistants to which itt

---

[1] American Antiquarian Society; *L. and L.*, II. 284–287; *Proceedings of the American Antiquarian Society*, Second Series, XXX. 231–234. The entire document is a copy in an unidentified contemporary handwriting. For Winthrop's account of this celebrated litigation, see *Journal*, II. 64–66, 116–120. See also Arthur Prentice Rugg, "A Famous Colonial Litigation," *Proceedings of the American Antiquarian Society*, Second Series, XXX. 217–230.

properlye belonged, and declares againe for the Sowe which was killed (8ber—37.)

The Evidence

pro pl[ain]t[iff] Two or three wittnesses that the Sowe killed (8ber 37) had sume such black spott vnder the Eye and some cutts or ragges on the eare.

pro def[endan]t 1 This contradickted by more wittnesses (which yet may be reaconsiled by other wittnesses of thee pl[ain]t[iff]s (viz.) that the defen[dan]ts owne Sowe had sume such spott there aboute in the skinne butt not in the haire and soe might not be easy to discerne when the haire was thick, but apparent when the heire was off.

2 proued by 6 or 7 wittnesses whoe then lived in the defen[dan]ts famelye, but are all gone since (but one or two) that this Sowe was the defendants owne and bought of one Houghton.

For the other Sowe which was
aliue a year after

pro pl[ain]t[iff] diuers wittnesses that this Sowe had such markes as the pl[ain]t[iff]s.

pro def[endan]tt 11 more wittnesses (and of as good credytt) that this Sowe (which was the straye) had other markes and not such as the pl[ain]t[iff] Claimed itt by.

2 Itt was clearelye proued that this was the onelye straye Sowe the defendant had, that this was offered to be shewed to the pl[ain]t[iff]s wife before the first Sowe was killed though att another tyme denyed her, for some reasons then alledged by the defen[dan]tt and that she was shewed itt after, in thee defen[dan]ts yeard and confidently disclamed itt as none of hers. And now againe, vpon her Oath in the Courtt did claime A Sowe by other markes, and not such as this Sowe had.

For A 3 Sowe never spoaken off
before this Courte

pro pl[ain]t[iff] A wittnesse or 2 that they sawe a 3d Sowe in the defen[dan]ts yarde.

pro defe[ndan]t 1 This can be of noe waight against soe manye wittnesses to the contrarye.

2 This 3d Sowe is not proued to have such markes as the pl[ain]t[iff]s.

3 This might be one of the breede of the other sowes, or some Neigh[bo]rs swine taken in the defen[dan]tts garden and keept vp with his owne, till the owner fetched it awaye.

4 the pl[ain]t[iff]s claime and the scope of his Euidence being for the Sowe killed aboute (8)ber—37 if he faile of that, the Courte is not to seeke out a Sowe for him.

The whole Eauidence is thus Ballanced

pro pl[ain]t[iff] The testimony considered apart amount to a probable eauidence, that the defen[dan]tt had and converted to his owne vse the pl[ain]t[iff]s Sowe.

Ball[anc]e The testimonyes reaching noe further, maye albe true, and yett the defen[dan]tt not guiltye, nor anye of these Sowes the pl[ain]t[iff]s.

pro def[endan]tt The testimonyes (whither considered apartt or with the other) afforde Euidence of Certaintye, raised vpon certaine grownds, as occasion, oppertunitye, familiaritye, freaquencye, etc.

Ball[anc]e If this testimonye be true, Itt is not possible the defen[dan]tt should be guiltye or anye of these Sowes the pl[ain]t[iff]s.

For Instance

Joseph wanders alone in the wildernesse his Coate is founde torne and bloudie, he is never heard off for manye yeares: vpon this probable euidence, Jacob concludes that Joseph was deuowred of a wilde beast: But when evidence of certaintye comes out of Aegipt that he was ther aliue, and Lord of Egipt the former æuidence was invailed and the Spirit of Jacob reviued, and now he concludes he was liuing: though he knewe not how he should come thither, or how he should be soe aduansed there. Now lett anye impartiall hande hold the Scales while Religion and sounde reason give Judgment in the case.

Yett (if neede weare) this might be added, that whereas the pl[ain]t[iff]s wife was allowed to take her Oath for the markes of her Sowe, the defendant and his wife (being denyed the like libertye) came voluntarelye into the Court and solomelye in the preasence of god declared 1 that the Sowe which was first killed was there owne. 2. that the Sowe which remained and was shewed the pl[ain]t[iff]s wife and which she disclaimed was the Straye Sowe. 3. that they never had anye other straye Sowe.

This cause (after the best part of 7 dayes spent in Examination and agitation) is by the breakeing vp of the Courte dismissed, not by occasion of A negatiue voate in the Magistrats (as is misreported) but by A fundamentall and Just Lawe agreable to sounde reason as shall appeare (the Lord willinge) in due season: The Lawe was made vpon searious consideration and Aduise with all the Elders (1) 1635 to this effect.

Noe Law Sentence, etc. shall passe as an act of the Courte, without the consent of the greater part of the magistrates of the one parte and the greater number of the deaputies on the other parte.

There were present in the courte, when the voate was to be taken 9 Magistrates and 30 deaputies whoe had all heard the Cause examined and argued, soe as noe centance could be legally passed without Consent of 5 magistrates and 16 deaputies which neither pl[ain]t[iff] nor defen[dan]tt had, for there were but 2 magistrates and 15 deputies for the pl[ain]t[iff] and 7 magistrates and 8 deputies for the defendant the other 7 stood doubtfull. yett was there noe necessitye, that the cause might not haue bene brought to an issue, for eyther the Court might haue Argued the Case againe by which meanes some who were doubtfull might haue come to a reasolucion or others might haue changed there Judgments and soe haue proceeded to a new voate, or else Committyes might haue bene Chosen, to order the Cause according to Lawe.

That this is the true state of the Case for the substance of itt, as it hath bene considered and allowed, by other of my breethren and Assotiates booth Magistrats and deaputies with our proseedings therein and which we shall not be ashamed (by the Lords helpe) to avouch and maintaine, before all the world, I doe heare affirme vnder my hand: dated att Boston this 5 – 15 – 1642.

JOHN WINTHOP go[verno]r

JOHN HUMFREY TO JOHN WINTHROP, JR.[1]

To his worthy deare friend Jo: Winthrop Esqr. these in hast

DEAREST AND MOST DESIRED SIR, you are a thousand times wellcome home, and should be 1000000000000000 times to mee if you would goe along with mee. I beseech you if you see the wind chops about contrarie, and hold there, come downe, I will beare your charges of the Post, and you shall doe no worse (but as much better as you will and I can helpe it) then I. Indeede I thinke you should have beene with us before. I have laine wind bound here these 5 weekes yet not daring to budge an inch, expecting everie day our ships comming, which have laine in like case this fortnight at Cowes. But this morning the wind springs up faire, and I hope the ships will be suddenly in with us. Good deare loving Sagamore, let us have your companie if possible. If you can be helpefull anie way to my poore familie I know you neede not be intreated. I heare they want monie. I pray speake to my good freind mr.

[1] W. 2. 7; 4 *Collections*, VI. 18–19.

Waring (to whome with his my best respects with all thankes for all manner of kindnes)   I know hee will not see them in miserie that are cast upon them about six pounds a month I suppose will doe their turne sufficiently, the rest I would gladly should goe to the paying of debts except that which you shall neede thereof and by vertue hereof I inable you to take for your (if) emergent necessities. With my love and my love over and over and through and through I rest Your most affectionate foolish faithfull

Jo: Humfrey

Waymouth July 21, 42

JOHN WILSON TO THOMAS WELD AND JOHN ELIOT[1]

To my reuerend louing brethren mr. Tho: Weld and mr. Jo: Eliott
with the rest of the Elders at Roxbury

Brother Weld and Eliot, My loue in the lord.

Vpon G[oodman] Comptons[2] speach with your selues and the deputy Gouernor, I went to the Gouernor, to desire his fauour to that end that he might be licensed to come with his people into these parts, wherby he might himselfe be the more fully satisfied in case any scruple remayne in the matters betweene him and the Church, which doth make your selues vnsatisfied to- wardes him. Wherunto the Gouernor is very willinge (and thinkes it would be good for the man) only he conceaues it not fitt to receaue such a ones tes- timony (as touching your consent or encoragement herin) it being his owne Case, vnles he had brought hither the handes of the Elders (I meane your selues etc. of Roxbury) I as so wishinge and aduising. I tell him I doubt not but yf I had made mention therof it had bene done nor doubt I but that you will now do so much, that the Gouernor and the Deputie may be the more encoraged to make him the grant. your very louing brother

John Wilson

[*Ca.* September, 1642]

---

¹ W. Au. 104; 4 *Collections*, VII. 3–4.

² John Compton of Roxbury became a freeman of the colony on September 3, 1634. Because of his adherence to the Wheelwright faction he was included among those who on November 20, 1637, were ordered to be disarmed and later (March 12, 1637/38), together with Coddington and others, was "licenced to depart" from Massachusetts. *Records of Massachusetts*, I. 212, 223. On September 25, 1642, "vpon Lettres of Dismission from our Sister Church of Rocksberry and vpon his open declaring of his Condicion and profession of his Faith in the Publique Assembly," Compton was admitted to membership in the Boston church. Records of the First Church of Boston, copy in the Society's library.

[*On the verso, in the handwriting of Eliot:*] If in synceryty and vprightnesse he intendeth to listen to, and imbrace the truth of Jesus Christ, we think it will much tend to his comfort and ours to remove hither: But if he have a secret reservation in his breast to hould to mr. Wheelerights opinions more or lesse which we much feare we think otherwise of it:

> JOHN ELIOT
> THO: WELDE
> JOHN MILLER
> ISACK HEATH

RECEIPT OF THE DEACONS OF THE CHURCH IN BOSTON[1]

BOSTON in N: England (7) 20: 1642

This is to certifie, that we the Deacons of the Church there have received of mr. winthrop our Governor a twenty shillings piece in golde sent from mr. Sparrowe of Ipswich to Nath: Greygoose late a member of our Churche, now deceased, who in the tyme of his sickness was maintaynd at the Churches charge a longe season.

> WILL COLBRON
> VAL: HILL
> JACOB ELIOT

[*Endorsed by John Winthrop, Jr.:*] Deacons of Boston: receipt of 20s for N: Graygoose.

MARTHA SYMONDS TO JOHN WINTHROP, JR.[2]

To my loveing brother John Winthrope Essqr. in England or Elswhere deliver

September 27 1642

LOUING BROTHER, I could not but rit thes faue lines vnto you being verey desierus to heare from you it being so I cannot see you heare but I hop it will not be long but you will bee heare wee thinke the time verey long since you wint and wee know it cannot but be verey greues to my sistar to be so long

---

[1] W. I. 149. The body of the document is in the handwriting of Governor Winthrop.

[2] W. Au. 75; Waters, *Sketch of John Winthrop the Younger*, 68. Martha Reade Symonds, second wife of Samuel Symonds of Ipswich, was the daughter of Edmund Reade and Elizabeth (Cooke) Reade (who later became the first wife of Hugh Peter). Her first husband had been Daniel Epes. Elizabeth Reade Winthrop, the second wife of John Winthrop, Jr., was her sister.

absent from you thoth she bares it verey well before company   therfore I
pray hastin to vs and let not watestill wat any longer[1]   you know I soppose
your sones name is so   I must be brefe becas I am vnfit to rit much. I haue
laine in and have another lekill girll and haue kept my chambar this nine
wekes and haue had a sore brest but the lord hath bin verey good to mee.
my husban is well and is at the bay at the court aconsulting what to doe about
the Ingines   wee are in fare of thim   my sistar lake is heare and desiers to be
remembared to you   this with my loue to you remembard, I commet you
to the lord and rest your euer louing sistar

MARTHA SIMONS

THOMAS FOWLE TO JOHN WINTHROP, JR.[2]

To my worthy freind John Winthrope Esqr. these deliver

SIR, I vnderstand that you had neede look to your selfe. tis ill dealing with
Citizens. I hope your longe stay wilbe to the better successe. I wish you well
and a prosperouse sucesse in your Interprizes. I thank you for your letters
which I haue receiued   I haue 2 thinges for my selfe to recomende vnto you
first to be ameans to pro[cure] my 15*li* of mr. Peters to be payed to my brother
Potter or mr. John Book but I hope tis payed longe agoe so I vnderstand they
had it from the passengers as soone as they came ashore. it much concernes
me   2ly I expect a ship from my brother from london   therefor I pray helpe
him to as many passengers and Goods to fraight as you cane as I hope you
will doe wherin you shall Ingage me to doe you any service of loue and speak
to mr. reade and mr. Peters therefore and lett not absent freinds and former
discourse euer be forgotten. I say noe moor but shall rely vpon you for all
your assistance therin   soe not else but comending you to Gods protection
I rest your very loving freind

THO: FOWLE

1642 Sept. 30

For your black leade business I am ready to joyne with you th[er]in, and
I shall attend your further directions.

---

[1] Wait Still, son of John Winthrop, Jr., and Elizabeth Winthrop, was born February 27, 1641/42.
[2] W. 1. 149. For Fowle, a Boston merchant, see Savage, *Genealogical Dictionary*, II. 192–193.

DEPOSITION OF JOSEPH STEYNS[1]

Op huyden den Eersten October anno xvj twee en veertich, Compareerde voor my Joseph Steyns, Openbaer Notaris, by den Hove van Hollandt geadmitteert, t'Amsterdam residerende, in presentie vande onderges getuygen, Claes Claesz van geluckstadt out omtrent negentien Jaren, bootsgesel geweest opt schip genaemt sint Jan van Hamborch, daer Schipper op was Jan Alberts, Ende heeft ten versoeche van mr. Jan Winthrop Student, Engelsman, verclaert, getuycht, ende geattesteert hoe waer ende hem getuyge seer wel Kennelyck is, Dat den producent omtrent een maent geleden tot Hamborch voors Ingeladen heeft int voors schip seecker scheepskist met cleederen, boecken, ende andere dingen, om naer Amsterdam gevoert te worden, welcke kiste hy getuyge selffs tot Hamborch ontfangen ende Ingenomen heeft vanden producent, wetende oversulcx Dat de voors kiste met cleederen, boecken, ende anders hem producent toe comt. Verclaert noch Dattet voors Schip int herwers comen van seeckere duynkerckers (daer Capiteyn op was Cornelis Jansz) genomen, ende tot nieupoort opgebracht is, ende Dat de voors kiste in zee van de Duynkerckers geopent is geworden, daer hy getuyge bystont ende gesien heeft Datter cleederen ende boecken in waren ende meer andere dingen. Presenterende tgeene voors (ist noot) by eede te stercken, Gedaen t'Amsterdam ter presentie van Goris van Hoeck ende Jan Purdis getuygen hier toe versoocht—*Quod attestor rogatus*

STEYNS [illegible]
Anno 1642

[1] W. IB. I. Mr. Arthur L. Bigelow of Princeton University has kindly established the text of this document (the original Dutch of which contains elements of the coastal dialect between Amsterdam and Rotterdam, with Saxon vestiges) and has also supplied the following translation.

"Today, the first of October, Anno 1642, appeared before me, Joseph Steyns, Notary Public, attorney at the law court of Holland, living at Amsterdam, in the presence of the witnesses mentioned below, Claes Claessen from Glückstadt nineteen years since, seaman on the ship named *St. John* of Hamburg, whose skipper was Jan Alberts; and he has, at the request of Mynheer Jan Winthrop, student, Englishman, declared, witnessed and attested how truly and well known it is to him, the witness, that the plaintiff about a month ago at the aforementioned Hamburg had put on board the aforesaid ship a certain chest with clothes, books, and other things to be brought to Amsterdam, which chest of the plaintiff he himself, the witness, received at Hamburg and took in, knowing that the aforesaid chest with clothes, books, and so forth belongs to him, the plaintiff. He further declares that the aforesaid ship, on its hither voyage, was taken over by certain Dunkirkers (with Cornelis Janssen as Captain) and was brought to Nieuport, and that the aforesaid chest was opened at sea by the Dunkirkers, for he, the witness, stood by and saw that there were clothes and books and other things too therein. Presenting the aforesaid (if necessary) to be strengthened by oath, done at Amsterdam in the presence of Goris van Hoeck and Jan Purdis, witnesses requested to this end—*Quod attestor rogatus*

STEYN [illegible]
Anno 1642"

MARGARET WINTHROP TO JOHN WINTHROP, JR.[1]

To my good Sonne Mr. Jo: Winthrop Iunr. in London deliver

LOUINGE SONNE, Your longe abcenc giues me opertunytye of manyfestinge my loue to you which I have to much neglected by the former shippes, expectinge your desyred prescence longe before this tyme, but we must wayt still, till god see good to let vs enjoy you. I haue sent my sonne Stephen to despeach some bisinesse which he wil acquaint you with, and I hope we shall in gods tyme, see you both to our comfort. your wife thinkes longe for your cominge, yet it pleaseth god to help hir to beare it pretty cherfully hir little boye is so mery that it puteth many a sad thought from his mother. When I thinke of the trublesom times and manyfolde destractions that are in our natiue Contrye I thinke we doe not pryse our happynesse heare as we have case, that we should be in peace when so many troubles are in most places of the world. I wish we ware more sencible of the calamityes of others that we myte crye the more mytylye to god for them. I haue no ocasion of businese to troble you with. I receiued a box with some aparel, and i thanke you for your care. my brother rote me word he would paye for them I pray let Mr. Smith send hime his bill, if he haue not. and thus desyringe the lord to preserue you these perylous tymes, I commend my best affectons to you and rest Your loving mother

MAR: WINTHROP

BOSTON 8ber 10: 1642

ADAM WINTHROP TO JOHN WINTHROP, JR.[2]

To his much honoured Brother John Winthrop Esqr. giue this I pray

KIND BROTHER, I haue reseued toe letters from you this somer wherin I cannot but take notise of youer loue and mindfullness of me. it hath bene a great comfort to us heer, that in youer absence we haue heard sumtimes from you we did exp[e]ct to haue sene you heer this somer which was the caus that I and the rest of youer frends did neglegt sum oppertunities of wrighting but now wee are informed to ouer grefe that we must waight still. my sistir is very desiros to see you heer vpon any condition, and yet thankes be to god

---

[1] W. I. 150; *L. and L.*, II. 303–304.

[2] W. I. 150; 5 *Collections*, VIII. 221–222. Adam Winthrop was the second son of the Governor by his third wife, Margaret Tyndal.

she is pretly cherly in exp[e]cktation winter will pass away and the time will
aproch when shee may more sertainely exp[e]ct youer rettune. my brother
Steuen I thinke will be the bearer of these letters. I suppose by this time you
haue heard of my mariage with Mrs. Elizibeth Glouer. I haue sent a letter
of atturny to my vncle tindall mr. kirby and dockter wright to take up those
monies that wear lefte hir by hir fathres will and by sum other frendes. now
I haue giuen a letter of atturny to my vnkle douning and youer selfe and my
brother Steuen whear I haue giuen full power to take up the monyes to giue
releses and discharges   I haue giuen sum diricon to my brother Stuen for
the laing out of the monis who I think will be at most laisuer   of youer care
and helpfullness to him I doe not doute   thus with my many thankes for
youer many fauors, and praier for youer saftie in these trublesum tymes, I
rest youer louing brother

ADAM WINTHROP

BOSTON this 10 of October 1642

ELIZABETH WINTHROP TO JOHN WINTHROP, JR.[1]

To her much honored Brother John Winthrop Esq. these present

MY MOST DEARE BROTHER, Since it hath pleased the Good Lord (by whose
providence all things are ordred, for the best) to joine me in such a nere relation to your selfe, I make bold to trouble you with these few rude lines, by
them to signify my vnfeigned love and servise to you, and further to intreat
you would favorablely imbrace me as youre vnworthy sister. were my poore
abillyties answerable to my wishes you should find me not inferior to my
relation, but such happinesse is not to be expected, espetially consider[i]ng
your merits, the least of which deserves incomperable recompence   what
lyes in my poure I hope you shall in no wise find me wanting. only be pleased
to owne me as one that desire to shew her selfe worthy even to the very vtmost
of her poore indeavors, of so great honour as to be brought into so nere relation with your selfe. my hands are little able to helpe your selfe or youres, yet
what love and tendernesse I am able to showe to your children and deare
wife my most kind Sister and Cosens I shall count it my delight to manifest.
My poore prayers and harty petitions are yours, amongst which it is none of
the rarest, that that God who in safety caryed you forth, would in his mercy

[1] W. Au. 75; 5 *Collections*, I. 91–92. Elizabeth Winthrop, whose marriage to Adam Winthrop had
taken place in February, 1641/42, was the daughter of Jose and Elizabeth Glover. The latter, following her husband's death on the voyage from England, became the wife of Henry Dunster.

restore you againe to all your freinds and espetially to your truly loving Wife which with many prayers and teares wishes your returne, which tyme whenever it shall be the Infinite God temper with as much joy as we beare your absence with sadness. in the meane tyme I rest Your truly loving Sister

ELIIZABETH WINTHROP

Dated CAMBRNGE October 11: 1642

[*Endorsed by John Winthrop, Jr.:*] this was from my brother Adams his first wife mr. Glovers daughter.

JOHN WINTHROP TO THE ELDERS OF THE MASSACHUSETTS CHURCHES[1]

. . . generall Councell of the State onely: and therefore, in their first institution, they were appointed, as the representative bodye of the Freemen, and therefore, where the people cannot exercise Judicature in their owne persons, thoughe they have power to substitute others, there their deputyes are not Judges in waye of such an Ordinance and I feare least this hathe been a great Cause of Gods withholdinge so muche of his presence from vs, since that Court hathe dealt so frequently in judginge private Causes, to which they have no ordinary callinge, that I knowe: for our Saviour teaches vs, that everye man that shall exercise power of Judgment over others, must be able to prove his Callinge thereto. Not that I deny that Court all power of Judicature, (for the bodye of the freemen may exercise it, in some transcendent Cases, where other remedye fayles) but in small and ordinary Causes, which properly belonge to other inferiour courts, I see no Rule to warrant our practice (but of this onely obiter). Now you may iudge, how muche it concerned the honor of the Court that (when so much blame was layd vpon it throughe the wholl countrye) it might be knowne, how the opinion and advice of the magistrates, or the greater parte of them, stood in the Case.

One thinge more I shall make bould to Commende to your wise consideration, as a matter of great Concernment: I vnderstande, there is a purpose in some to possesse the people with this opinion, that it is the power of the Neg: vote in the magistrates, that hath occasioned all the late troubles, and therefore they should take it awaye, at the next Court of Elections, and be-

[1] Fragment in Harvard College Library; *L. and L.*, II. 277–279. For Winthrop's account of the meeting of the elders, convened at Ipswich on October 18, 1642, and of their deliberations on Richard Saltonstall's treatise against the Standing Council, see *Journal*, II. 86–88. See also Winthrop's earlier letter on the subject (pages 347–348, above).

cause it is knowne that diverse of the magistr[ate]s are not like to consent
to it, they must therefore be lefte oute (which wilbe very acceptable to some
of them) and others putt in their places, etc.

If it should so fall out, I may bouldly saye, I knowe not any thing could be
more dishonorable and dangerous to our State; dishonorable it would be,
to take the power from those whom the Countrye pickes out, as the most able
for publ[ic] service, and putt it into the hands of others, whom they passe by,
as the more weake: dangerous allso it wilbe, for it will raze the foundation of
our Goverment, so as, I can make it appeare, that whatsoeuer the deputyes
shall determine without the consent of the greater parte of the magistrates,
wilbe of no validitye: for if our power be derived from, or have any relation
to, our Patent, it is so fixed in the Governor and assistants, as (how many
soeuer shalbe ioyned to them, as coadiutors or Counsellors etc. yet) the maine
strengthe of Aut[horit]ye (in pointe of dispensation) will rest in them, and
can by no lawe be avoided, vnlesse we will erecte a new frame of Goverment
vpon a new foundation, which (I suppose) is far from our intentions. As for
the inconveniences, which are obiected, they are but vngrounded suppositions, as first This: what if the magistrates should growe Corrupt etc.? this is
no more to be feared, then of the deputies, and if of bothe, then of all the rest
of the people, and if so, then it is past remedye.

Againe, if the Court of Assistance doe injustice, or mistake in any cause,
what help is there, if the magistrates have a Neg: vote in the generall Court?
To this it may allso be Answer[ed] what remedye will there be, if the generall
Court should erre, or doe injustice? there must be a stoppe somewhere: yet
this Remedye there is, if the magistrates have erred it is not vnlike but they
will hearken to better advice in the generall Court; but if they will not, they
may be turned out and better putt in their places, and then they may be
called to Acco[unt] for any miscarriage.

The last thing that I will trouble your patience with at the present is about
a position maintained in the Countrye, (and those none of the worst) that it
should be dangerous for the Com[mon]w[ealth] to have the magistrates
vnited in Love and affection, therefore care to be had, that there be no kindred, affinity, or close amity betweene them: but that they should rather be
devided in factions etc.: If this past for good doctrine, then let vs no longer
professe the Gospell of Jesus Christ, but take vp the rules of Matchiavell, and
the Jesuits, for Christ saythe Love is the bond of perfection, and a kingdome
or house deuided cannot stand: but the others teache (or rather the Devill
teacheth them) deuide et impera etc. I need write no more of this: your owne
observation, of what advantage hath come to the countrye by the late di-

visions and oppositions amongst vs, will call vpon your Care and faithfullnesse, to putt your hande for tymely preventinge the like.

The ende of my writinge to you about these matters, is both to discover to
you the dangers I have discerned, and allso to crave your advice and helpe,
so far as the power and dutye of your place in the Churches, doth call for it
from you: If in any thinge I be mistaken, I shall thankfully accept your lovinge corrections, but for the sinceritye of my heart, and searious intentions,
for the publ[ic] good of all estates, my witnesse is heaven, to whose Judgment
I must stande: So earnestly cravinge the continuance of your prayers, with
a thankfull acknowledgment of the many testimonyes of your love towards
me, beseechinge the Lord in my dayly petitions, still to owne and blesse your
selues and your labours, for the further advancement of the kingdome of his
sonne in this parte of the world, I take leave and rest your brother and fellowe
helper in the Lords worke

JO: WINTHOP

BOSTON (8) 14—1642

JOHANNES TANCKMARUS TO JOHN WINTHROP, JR.[1]

Clarissimo Viro Domino Johanni Winstrop, Amico meo unicè dilecto

CLARISSIME SIMUL NEC NON CHARISSIME D[OMI]NE WINSTROPI, Ut priores
binæ tuæ: sic et posteriores per Dominum Dogget (et quidem pergratæ omnes)
recte ad has manus pervenêre. Utinam et mea, per Petrum Petersen, Amb-
stelodamensem tabellarium, ad Clarit[atem] Tuam missæ, redditæ sint tibi:
quibus condolentiam meam cordialem de (proh dolor!) perdita tua arca,
sum testatus. Precatus sum animitus et etiamnum precor, ut cum Deo re-

---

[1] W. 19. 47. Tanckmarus's letters to Winthrop furnish few biographical facts, and no formal
account of his life has been found. Dr. Harold S. Jantz of the Department of Modern Languages
and Literatures of Princeton University, from his extensive research in this period, has kindly supplied the following information. Tanckmarus was a Doctor of Medicine, but of what university is not
known. During the years 1632–1635 he is known to have been at Lübeck, where in official documents he is referred to as "Paedagogus" of Heinrich Ottendorff (friend of the poetess Anna Owena
Hoyers) and where, like Ottendorff, he was closely associated with a group of mystics and heretics
(including Joachim Morsius) who were followers of Jakob Böhme and Valentin Weigel. As a result
of these connections he was on more than one occasion in difficulties with the Lübeck authorities,
and there is record of his having twice made formal recantation of his errors. Kaspar Heinrich
Starck, *Lübeckischer Kirchen-Historie* (Hamburg, 1724), 796; Heinrich Schneider, *Joachim Morsius und
sein Kreis* (Lübeck, 1929), 48–57. In 1642 he is known to have been in Hamburg, where Winthrop
presumably met him upon going there to study (see Sir William Boswell to the Chevalier De Vic,
November 1, 1642, printed immediately following). In 1649 he was living in Lauenburg (John
Doggett to John Winthrop, Jr., September 25, 1649), and there is trace of him there as late as
1652 (John Doggett to John Winthrop, Jr., February 3, 1651/52).

cuperare eam queas. Dolendum est homines sic cum hominibus agere, sic homines ab hominibus spoliari. Deum immortalem quò impietatis â Diabolo seductis et tam horribiliter lapsis devenitur! Semper et ubique, Diabolum opera sua per suos peragere videmus. Beatus ille, qui filius existit lucis, et omnia temporalia caduca et fluxa, quatenus id fieri queat, flocci pendit. Faxit Deus inprimis, ut animo ditemur, filium ipsius Jesum reverâ possidentes. Ah crede mi amantissime Winstropi, quod de hoc tuo infortunio impensissimè doluerim et doleam. Utinam ego ê diverso re quapiam hoc recompensare queam: certè si voluntati facultas responderet, etiam in hoc, quantopere te amem, experireris. Intereà loci, qua ego non possum, ut Deus ter opt[imus] max[imus] ea præstet, rogo. Suavissimæ tuæ conversationis non possum oblivisci: utinam eâ, dum vivam, frui [possim] Quod polliceris, te operam esse daturum, an in Angliâ aliquid præstare possis, quo in præsens possim sublevari, ex eo (ut et omnibus reliquis) cognosco benevolum tuum in me animum quam gratissimo corde amplector, rogoque ut id agere perstes: Quod si, ut nullus ambigo, feceris, nullus et tu dubites, quin adhuc aliquid sim facturus, quod et gratissimum arridet Tibi. quo citiùs me sic juvare poteris, eò gratiùs arridet mihi. Quibus, optime mi Amice, vale, et quidem in Deo, (in quo millies millema prospera et secunda tibi ex animo precor) â me et uxore meâ amicissimè salutatus. Deus sit tecum, et Te in posterum pro paternâ ipsius affectione et voluntate, ab omni malo et infortunio custodiat, Amen. Tuissimus

JOH. TANCMARUS

HAMBURGI die 28 Octobr. Anno 1642

[*Endorsed:*] This Letter was Let fall in the durt per A woman that brought it.

SIR WILLIAM BOSWELL TO THE CHEVALIER DE VIC[1]

A Monsieur Le Chev. De Vic Resident pour S. M. De la Gr: Bret: etc. A Bruxells

SIR, There is one Mr. Jhon Wenthrop a Suff: gentleman and student in Physique, who coming lately from Hamburgh into these parts by land, embarqued vpon a shippe of that towne bownd for Amsterdam, a chest conteyning in It apparell, books, and other n[ecessa]ries appertaining soly to him, and his personall vse, no way contrebanded, which a ship of Dunikerk (or

---

[1] W. 1B. 2; 5 *Collections*, I. 323. For Boswell, see *D.N.B.*; for Sir Henry De Vic, see 5 *Collections*, I. 323*n*.

other place of Flandres) toke at sea, and haue brought into that or other port of Flandres.[1] Wherupon my earnest suit vnto you is, to lend Mr. Wenthrope your aduise, and assistance as shalbe requisit for the recouery of his said goods, for which himself (if possible) or frend, whom he employes for this end, will wayt vpon you. wherein you will not only doe a work worthy of your self, but particularly oblige him, and mee Your most aff[ectiona]t[e] frend and seruant

WILLM. BOSWELL

HAGHE 1 Nou. 1642 st. no.

[*Endorsed by John Winthrop, Jr.:*] Sir William Boswell, the Kings Agent at the Haghe his letter for me to the Kings Agent at Bruxells.

SIR CHARLES COOTE'S ACCOUNT OF HIS IRONWORKS[2]

There was in Ireland discovered these severall sorts of Ironston at Sir Charles Cootes workes.

First a rock mine which lay neere day in an ordinarye yellow mould which was plowed land; the bend laye thicke, and continued without any earth intermixed, and lay without any other rocke, of limeston, sparre, or slate, it was of a blew coulor very hard and ponderous, and beinge calcined would stick extreamly vnto your toung.

This Ironston was extreamly Rich, and yeilded great store of Iron and wrought very well and gently, in the furnasse, and would make both gray motly or white sowe Iron without any trouble or vndercharging the furnasse: yet when it came to the fineryes it was very dangerous Iron, for it was apt to runne cleere, and not to incorporate though you vsed Hammerslag (the scales of the hammer worke) therewith. When it came vnder the hammer it would flye extreamely, and hardly hold to make a bloome, and commonly was a rotten redshire, and a staring coulshire, both in one barre without any intermixture of tuffnesse at all, and truly was fitt for little vse; yet this mine mixed with white Ironston, bloomers sinders or bogge mine yelded extreamly well incorporated readily at the fineries, and made as good Iron as your sussex Iron in England provided there were not above one halfe of the Rock-mine vsed in the furnasse at a charge, and a good proportion of limeston or

---

[1] See note 1, page 356, above.

[2] W. 5. 198. This document is in the handwriting of John Winthrop, Jr. For Sir Charles Coote (d. 1642) and Sir Charles Coote, Earl of Mountrath (d. 1661), see *D.N.B.*

sparre, which was every where in that country, where these are wanting you must vse your furnasse sinder to qualifye the hardnesse of your rocke mine, which will produce a good greene running sinder at the furnasse which is the maine part of the worke.

Next we had two sortes of white mine the one was full of scales and that riseth in small pinnes about the bignesse of ones hand and vnder, and had a core in the middle blew, and being broken was like an hunnycombe this was our best mine wrought gently in the forge and furnasse made a good mixed coulshire and tuffe Iron somwhat better then vsually your sussex Iron, this Ironston lay in a blew slaty marle in a mountainous and wett countrye in vaines one vnder an other, some neere day, was easily raised, for the deepest lay not above 30 foote deepe.

The great white mine lay in the same kind of ground but in greater vaines and riseth in great stones, or pinnes of halfe an hundred waight, and had little or noe scales at all, this mine wrought by it selfe made a very couldshire Iron, and wrought so very hott in the furnasse that it burnt the twire stones in an instant, tympe and hearth, that many admirable founders, which we had out of severall partes of England were not able to make a blowing of above 10 or 12 weekes at a tyme yett we had good hearth stones, but this Ironston being mixed with the small Ironston above specified, and some limeston yeilded abundantly, wrought gently, att furnasse and forge, and made good Iron; and our blowing lasted 3 quarters of a yeare and cast 12 tunne of sow Iron a weeke one with an other.

We had a fourth kind of mine which was a bogge mine, which if wrought by it selfe at a furnasse would choke a furnasse, but mixed with other mines in a furnasse made as good Iron as Spanish Iron; this lay in our greatest bogges vpon the superficies of the earth like a scurfe on a scauld head, about 4 or 5 inches thicke, and being lett lye dissolved into a small sand of a black coulor.

The charge was this.

We paid the founder 5s a tunne for casting and 10li a yeare standing wages: the finery man 6s 8d per tunne for refining and 5li standing wages. the hammerman 6 per tunne and 20li per annum standing wages. The carpenter 25li a yeare standing wages for his repairing of things. The smith 25li per annum standing wages, for keeping things in repaire.

for cutting of wood we paid 9d a coard.

for making a load of coles 2s 3d 22 barrells at the fall.

Cheefely take care so to place your furnasse that there be noe water springs or dampes vnder hir for it will spoile all which if your ground will nott admitt, you must make a false bottom with severall pipes to carry away the dampes and water or springs.

[*Ca.* 1643]

[*Endorsed by John Winthrop, Jr.:*] Sir Charles Coote discourse about Ironston in Ireland.

ADAM OTTLEY TO JOHN WINTHROP[1]

To the Right Wo[rshipfu]ll his Much Honord Freind John Winthropp Esq.
Gou[ernou]r of the Matachuset Bay deliver

HONORD SIR, Beinge conscious of my owne indezert (that any thinge concerninge my occacions) though my weale or woe consist therein, (should borrowe soe much tyme from your weightier affaires to graunt a thought much lesse a tender consideracion of my more then youthfull (I might say grosse) folly) yet am I bold to present you these lines, beleeuinge that your candid disposicion loues open plaines. my hart therefore declares the some of what it thinks. sir, I haue knowene, (I would I could soe still) I haue moovd in these sphæres of your noble fauour, which had god beene pleas'd to haue vouchsafed mee accordinge to the integrity of my cause, I might haue still gloried in his grace therin, and retourned him the praise therof. But thus it is, adventuringe with my owne compasse beyonde the Card of judgment I am fallen into the twoe daungers Sylla and Carybdis (the losse of truly willinge and affectiond Frinds with hazard of my owne lyvely hoode.) If the cry of my involluntary offence bee not pardonable in your just brest, yet pitty may finde a harbour for one whose relacion streames from the vaines of him I knowe you loued well, and liues or dys in mee. I beseech you Sir giue eare with patience and let these fewe rude expressions begge soe much favour that I may, at your favorably appointed tyme haue accesse to your presence, and you shall much engage Your servant to loue and honour you

ADAM OTTLEY

[*Ca.* 1643]

[1] W. 4. 116; 5 *Collections*, I. 327–328. Ottley was the son-in-law of John Humfrey. Sidney Perley, *The History of Salem, Massachusetts*, II (Salem, 1926), 198.

JOHN WINTHROP TO JOHN WINTHROP, JR.[1]

You are the Chief of Two Families; I had by your Mother Three Sons and Three Daughters, and I had with her a Large Portion of outward Estate. These now are all gone; Mother gone; Brethren and Sisters gone; you only are left to see the Vanity of these Temporal things, and learn Wisdom thereby, which may be of more use to you, through the Lord's Blessing, than all that Inheritance which might have befallen you: And for which this may stay and quiet your Heart, That God is able to give you more than this; and that it being spent in the furtherance of his Work, which hath here prospered so well, through his Power hitherto, you and yours may certainly expect a liberal Portion in the Prosperity and Blessing thereof hereafter; and the rather, because it was not forced from you by a Father's Power, but freely resigned by your self, out of a Living and Filial Respect unto me, and your own readiness unto the Work it self. From whence as I do often take Occasion to Bless the Lord for you, so do I also Commend you and yours to his Fatherly Blessing, for a plentiful Reward to be rendred unto you. And doubt not, my Dear Son, but let your Faith be built upon his Promise and Faithfulness, that as he hath carried you hitherto through many Perils, and provided liberally for you, so he will do for the time to come, and will never fail you, nor forsake you.

My Son, the Lord knows how Dear thou art to me, and that my Care has been more for thee than for my self. But I know thy Prosperity depends not on my Care, nor on thine own, but upon the Blessing of our Heavenly Father; neither doth it on the things of this World, but on the Light of God's Countenance, through the Merit and Mediation of our Lord Jesus Christ. It is that only which can give us Peace of Conscience with Contentation; which can as well make our Lives Happy and Comfortable in a mean Estate, as in a great Abundance. But if you weigh things aright, and sum up all the Turnings of Divine Providence together, you shall find great Advantage.

The Lord hath brought us to a Good Land; a Land, where we enjoy outward Peace and Liberty, and above all, the Blessings of the Gospel, without the Burden of Impositions in Matters of Religion. Many Thousands there are who would give Great Estates to enjoy our Condition. Labour therefore, my good Son, to increase our Thankfulness to God for all his Mercies to thee, especially for that he hath revealed his Everlasting Good-will to thee in Jesus Christ, and joined thee to the visible Body of his Church, in the Fellow-

---

[1] Original not located; Cotton Mather, *Magnalia Christi Americana* (London, 1702), Book II, 32–33; *L. and L.*, II. 319–321. The italics of Mather's text have not been retained.

ship of his People, and hath saved thee in all thy Travails abroad, from being Infected with the Vices of these Countries where thou hast been, (a Mercy vouchsafed but unto few Young Gentlemen Travellers.) Let him have the Honour of it who kept thee. He it was who gave thee Favour in the Eyes of all with whom thou hadst to do, both by Sea and Land; He it was who saved thee in all Perils; and He it is who hath given thee a Gift in Understanding and Art; and he it is who hath provided thee a Blessing in Marriage, a Comfortable Help, and many Sweet Children; and hath hitherto provided liberally for you all: And therefore I would have you to Love him again, and Serve him, and Trust him for the time to come. Love and Prize that Word of Truth, which only makes known to you the Precious and Eternal Thoughts and Councils of the Light Inaccessible. Deny your own Wisdom, that you may find his; and esteem it the greatest Honour to lye under the Simplicity of the Gospel of Christ Crucified, without which you can never enter into the Secrets of his Tabernacle, nor enjoy those sweet things which Eye hath not seen, nor Ear heard, nor can the Heart of Man conceive; but God hath granted unto some few to know them even in this Life. Study well, my Son, the saying of the Apostle, Knowledge puffeth up. It is a good Gift of God, but when it lifts up the Mind above the Cross of Christ, it is the Pride of Life, and the High-way to Apostacy, wherein many Men of great Learning and Hopes have perished.

In all the Exercise of your Gifts, and Improvement of your Talents, have an Eye to your Master's End, more than your own; and to the Day of your Account, that you may then have your Quietus est, even, Well done, Good and Faithful Servant! But my last and chief Request to you, is, that you be careful to have your Children brought up in the Knowledge and Fear of God, and in the Faith of our Lord Jesus Christ. This will give you the best Comfort of them, and keep them sure from any Want or Miscarriage: And when you part from them, it will be no small joy to your Soul, that you shall meet them again in Heaven!

[JOHN WINTHROP]

[Ca. 1643]

AUGUSTINUS PETRAEUS TO JOHN WINTHROP, JR.[1]

To his much honoured and respected friend Mr. John Winthrop
at Mr. Joseph Carter his house at the 3 pigeons in bischopgate strete ouer against
the black bull London

HOCHGEERTESTER HERR Allerwertester, vertrawester und allerliebster freundt Mr: Wintrop, dem herren zu dienen, weis ehr mich zum aller hohesten verobligiret, sein liebestes schreiben, das erste datieret im Januario at Ipswich undt das andere im februario aus london seint mihr alle beide mit hohesten freuden vndt grossesten contentament eingehendiget worden ausserhalb dise 2 hab ich keines von dem herren weder aus Brabandt, flandern oder Engellandt bekommen. wir sint alzumahl wegen des herren sehr bekummert gewesen, weile wir kein schreiben haben bekommen undt haben gantz vermeinet das ihm etwa ein ungluck ware zu handen gekommen ich hette auch vorlengest an dem herren gescrieben, habe aber nicht gewust wa der herr anzutreffen ist. Es ist mihr sehr leidt seinenthalber das ehr so wenigh von seinem sachen itzundt in Engellandt hab ausgericht. Erfrewe mich aber zum hohesten seine gute gesundtheit undt gluckliches wolergehen, interim mus man von dem andern patientia haben, es kan geliebt es God, dermal eins widerumb zum friedlichen stande kommen, unsere sachen stehen noch zimlich woll. wir sint noch alle wol auff, Des herrn doctors iungeste kindt ist ungefehr 14 tage nach seiner wegreise gestorben. wir laboriren wenigh wegen der grossen discommoditet eines guten laboratorij. ich habe 2 diuerse mahlen schreiben, kurtz nach des herren wegreise bekommen aus Crabaten undt Dalmatien von dem grafen, warinne mihr mein begehren so als Luna fixa promittiret wurdt wan ich seluest will hinkommen, werde also diese woche dahin reisen, ich reise durch franckreich undt Italiam zu ihnen umb dasselbige zu erlangen ich wolte wunschen das ich darnach gelegenheit hette meinem allerliebesten freunde dieses auch zu communiciren, wolte wunschen das ich darnach bey euch in Americam were. die herren Kuffler haben mich gebetten dem herren freundtlich zu salutiren sie seint itzundt gantz resoluiret nach America zu reisen mehr als zuvor haben begehret das

---

[1] W. 1. 152. It has not been possible to find information about Petraeus beyond that kindly supplied by Dr. Harold S. Jantz of Princeton University. According to Dr. Jantz, Petraeus, one of Winthrop's closest scientific friends, belonged to the group of Dutch and German chemists who assembled in Amsterdam during the Thirty Years' War and formed a society which was one of the predecessors of the Royal Society. This society included Johann Morian, Johannes Sibert Kuffler, his brother Abraham Kuffler (see page 122, above), and, somewhat later, the well-known Johann Rudolf Glauber.

ich an dem herren schreiben solte das der herr die farkens vel hogges oder
porcos fein solte mesten lassen damitt sie wol fett waren wan sie alda solten
kommen. Der herr mus dem Gouverneur uber die hogges alias porcos com-
manderen das ehr sie wol zu essen gibt. des herren Jodoci von Rhee proces
lasse sich der herr zum hohesten befohlen sein dan ehr sich bey uns gar wol
lesset ansehen ich habe die beste hoffnungh da zue als ich zu ein proces
iemahls gehabt habe, der herr halte ihn zum hohesten secret. der herr
schreibe nichtes hinfuro an mihr das etwa secret ist without our clauis, dan
ich nun diese woche von hier auff Calis undt vollendt durch franckreich
reise, werde also keine briefe mehr von dem herren alhie bekommen, nicht
eher bekomme ich sie bis ich wider zu ruck komme, aus franckreich wil ich
dem herren auch noch screiben, der herr gedencke doch meiner wan ehr in
America ist, ich sol dem herren nimmermehr vergessen, undt wunsche alle-
zeit, das ich widerumb bey dem herren muchte kommen undt stetes in seiner
compagnie verbleiben. Es kommen alle tage einen grossen hauffen neue
Philosophos alhie aus Hoch teutshlandt, darunter viele sein die gar grosse
kunstler sein. ich hoffe ich soll auff meine reise guten succes haben. Es lassen
dem herren freundtlich salutiren. Domini Kuffleri cum uxoribus atque
familijs, Dns Haberfeld, Dns Saarburgh, Dns Caesar atque omnes boni amici
salutant te maxime. der tinctor van Amsterdam undt der ander van leiden
sind hier beide gewest haben nach dem herren gefraget, recommendiren dem
herren gar hoch undt glauben gentzlich, der herr habe ein particular tinctur,
der herr lasse nicht nach und schreibe mihr aus America ehr sende es nuhr
an die herren Kuffler so sal ichs wol bekommen, wa ihr etwes secretes darin
schreiben wollet das thut cum clave nostro nempe vitrum Veneticum.   salutiret doch freundtlich in Engellandt euren lieben bruder meinentwegen
undt meldet ihm meinen unbekanten doch willigen dienst an, alle meine
bekanten in Engellandt salutiret meo nomine, In America eure liebe haus-
fraw, vatter, mutter, bruder undt schwester undt alle eure gute freunde.
ich hoffe ich soll euch alda einmahl sehen   ich habe noch kein weib das
machet ich hab noch kein particular ruff dismal nicht mehr ohne ich befehle
euch gottliche protection and I remaine iour bounden seruant for euer weil
I liue

                                                          AUGUSTINUS PETRÆUS

HAGAE COMITIS den 1 martij A[nn]o 1643 [N.S.]
                    ———————
                        9 martij

   Remenber mi veri kindle to Mr. Joseph Charter and his lovingh wife and
daughter.

DEED OF JOHN WINTHROP, JR., TO EDWARD PARKS[1]

This Indenture made the One and Twentieth day of March 1642 In the Eighteenth yeare of the reigne of our Sovereigne Lord Charles by the Grace of God King of England Scotland France and Ireland defender of the faith etc. Betweene John Winthropp of New England in America in the parts beyond the Seas Gent[leman] (but now resident in the Citty of London) of the one part And Edward Parks Citizen and Merchanttaylor of London of the other part Witnesseth that the said John Winthropp for and in Consideracion of the summe of Two Hundred and Fifty Pounds of lawfull money of England to him before the ensealinge and delivery hereof well and truly satisfied and paid by the said Edward Parks Whereof and Wherewith the said John Winthropp acknowledgeth himselfe to bee fully satisfied and paid And thereof and of every part and parcell thereof Doth Heareby acquite and discharge the said Edward Parks his heires Executors and administrators and every of them by theis presents Hath graunted bargained and solde alyened enfeoffed and confirmed And by these presents Doth fully Heareby and absolutely graunte sell alyen enfeoff and confirme vnto the said Edward Parks his heires and assignes forever All those his Lands Meadowes Pastures Woods and Woodlands with their appurtenances lyinge and beinge in Toppesfeild within the parish and bounds of Ipswich in New England aforesaid in the parts beyond the Seas, Conteyninge by estimacion Three Hundred Acres bee they more or lesse And all the estate right title interest Revercion Revercions clayme and demaund whatsoever of the said John Winthropp of in and to the said Lands Meadowes Pastures Woods and Woodlands and of in and to every part and parcell thereof, To Have and to holde the said Lands Meadowes Pastures Woods and Woodlands with their and every of their appurtenances vnto the said Edward Parks his heires and assignes To the only vse and behoofe of the said Edward Parks his heires and assignes forever. And the said John Winthropp for himselfe his heires Executors and administrators and for every of them Doth Covenant promise and graunte to and with the said Edward Parks his heires and assignes by theis presents in forme followinge that is to say That hee the said John Winthropp now is and standeth lawfully rightfully and absolutely seised of and in Three Hundred Acres or above of Land Meadowe Pasture Wood and Woodland lyinge and beinge in the Hamlet Village or Place called Toppesfeild in the Parish of Ipswich in New England aforesaid, of a good sure absolute and indefeazable estate in the

[1] Topsfield Historical Society. For Parks, see 4 *Collections*, VII. 385n.

Lawe in fee simple To the only vse and behoofe of himselfe his heires and assignes for ever And that the said Edward Parks his heires and assignes shall or may to his and their owne proper vse and behoofe peaceablie and quietly enter into have holde occupye possesse and enioye all the said Lands Meadowes Pastures Woods and Woodlands and every part and parcell thereof without any lett trouble expulcion evicion or interrupcion of or by any other person or persons whatsoever And free cleare and clearely acquitted and discharged of and from all former and other guifts graunts bargaines sales leases estates Charge and encumbrances whatsoever And that hee the said John Winthropp and his heires and Elizabeth his wife and all other persons any thinge havinge or lawfully clayminge of in to or out of the said bargained premisses shall and will at all times hereafter vpon reasonable [*torn*] make and doe all and every such further and other lawfull and reasonable act and acts thinge and things for the further and better assuringe and conveyinge of the said Lands Meadowes Pastures Woods and Woodlands with the appurtenances and every part and parcell thereof to the said Edward Parks his heires and assignes As by the said Edward Parks his heires or assignes or his or their learned Counsell in the Law shalbe reasonably devised or advised In Witnes whereof the said partys to theis presente Indentures have herevnto interchangeably sett their hands and seales Given the day and yeare first above written

JOHN WINTHROP

Signed sealed and delivered in the presence of us
    THO. SMITH Sen[ior]
    R. MOUNTGOMERY servant to Thos. Smith Sen[ior]
    BEN: SMITH [*illegible*]

AGREEMENT OF JOHN WINTHROP, JR., AND OTHERS WITH NICHOLAS BOND[1]

Know all men by these presents that whereas John Winthrop Junior of Boston in New England esqr. doth purpose at his retorne with all convenient speed to erect and build a worke for the making of Iron: and hath taken in divers Copartners for the advance and effecting thereof, whereas alsoe Nicholas Bond of the Citye of Westm[inster] in the Countye of Midd[lesex]

[1] W. 2. 171; 4 *Collections*, VI. 516. The handwriting of the body of the document has not been identified.

esqr. hath before the sealing hereof delivered and payed vnto the said John the some of one hundreth pounds of lawfull monie of England to be imployed in the said Iron worke for the best benefitt and advantage of the said Nicholas Bond his executours administratours and assignees, which said some of one hundreth pounds, and all the benefitt advantage and encrease, that shall from tyme to tyme and at all tymes hereafter arise and growe, Wee the said John Winthrop Emanuell Downinge and Hugh Peter doe hereby for our selves our seuerall and respective executours and administratours promise and agree to be accomptable vnto the said Nicholas Bond his executours administratours and assignees for the same, according to the trew entent and meaninge of these presents, without fraude, Covenn or Collusion; witnes our hands and seales this 23d day of March Anno D[omi]ni 1642.

JOHN WINTHROP
HUGH PETER
EM: DOWNINGE

Sealed and deliuered in the presence of vs:
   THO: WELDE

[*Endorsed:*] Mr. Wintrop Mr. Peters and Mr. Downing assignment of articles about the Iron woork in New England.

JOHANNES TANCKMARUS TO JOHN WINTHROP, JR.[1]

Clarissimo Viro, Domino Johanni Winstropio, Amico meo singulariter dilecto

CLARISSIME D[OMI]NE, AMICE SINGULARITER DILECTE, Unde tam diutinum silentium tuum? nam per tot menses nil quicquam literarum â Te vidi. Superstitem adhuc te esse spero; cur taceas haut scio. Rogo a[h] ut gratissimis tuis literis me quamprimum bees, condictique memineris. Doleo res Anglicanas ita turbatas; te verò in iis pace tamen et salute frui confido. Ego quidem adhuc cum meis valeo; sed nimis, scholastico nimirum munere, distractus: unde nimis me sublevatum velim. Vale dulcissime Amice et illico rescribe. Tuæ Claritat[i] amantissimus

JOH. TANCMARUS

HAMBURGI 27 Martii, vet. stili, Anno 1643

Uxor mea amicè mecum salutat. Spero priores meas epistolas Te accepisse.

[1] W. 19. 47.

JOHN HAYNES TO JOHN WINTHROP[1]

To the Right Wo[rshipfu]ll Jo: Winthropp Esq. Gov[ernou]r at the Mattatusetts Bay
these present

HONOURED SIR, Since your former I received lately by an Indian messendger your last, wherin yow mencion the Claime that is made to the Mattabeseicke Sachims[2] land, lately deceased, mediating that they might not be preiudiced in ther Rights. the truth is we are most vnwillinge to offer them the least Iniury in that kind. the case is really this, we have a pretty space since in the life time of that Sachim that is nowe departed, bought his land, and have it vnder his hand with witnes etc. and are at the time of his death to enter vppon the whole, and it being the most considerable place of the River for Plantation not yet planted, we can by noe meanes tollerate ther residence in that place I cannot advise as the Case stands for Miantonimo to send his sonne hither for ther will vndoubtedly be greater hasard of the safety of his person, then he is aware of. I shall acquaint yow with the reason of my thoughts when I see yow which I hope will be with the rest of the Company about the begin[nin]ge of the 3d month next. In the interim I Recommend yow to him that is able to keepe yow and Rest Yours affectionatly

JO: HAYNES

HARTF[OR]D the 29th of the 1st mo: 1643

[*Endorsed by Governor Winthrop:*] mr. Haynes Rec. (2) 7—43.

WILLIAM WALDERN TO JOHN WINTHROP[3]

To the Right Honoured Mr. John Winthrop Governour at Boston theise present

HONOURED SIR, Wee haueing examined some witnesses vpon a suspicion of a Murder according to your order I haue sent them desiring your advise what further should be done therin. for my owne parte I am perswaded that what some of the witnesses affirme the Circumstance of the matter was extracted from them privately, by some not favoring Mr. Larkham for the yong woman sithence haueing spoken with her I perswade my selfe what

---

[1] Chamberlain Collection, Boston Public Library; 4 *Collections*, VI. 355–356.
[2] Sowheag, sachem of the Indians living at what is now Middletown, Connecticut.
[3] W. I. 154. For Waldern, see Savage, *Genealogical Dictionary*, IV. 390–391; *Journal*, II. 288–289.

she spake was meaning her selfe being with Childe   I leaue it to your wisdome to consider of: but thus much I thought my selfe bound in Conscience
to write to you humbly craving your Counsell herein   thus with my service
to you remembred I humbly take leaue and rest Yours to Command

WILLIAM WALDERN

NORTHAM[1] 3º 2º Mo: (43)

[*Endorsed by Governor Winthrop:*] Mr. Walderne about the Examiners.

RICHARD STORER TO JOHN WINTHROP, JR.[2]

*To the right Worshipfull and his very Good Freinde Mr. John Wintropp,
lodging att one Mrs. Goffs in Filpott Lane in Fanchurch street
deliver these I pray London: post paid 4d*

MUCH HONOURED SIR, Haueinge Receiued your letter and heareinge that
you are not yet gone I make bould to wright these few lines vnto you wherin
my wife and I desire to present our Seruis to yow and all soe to be thankfull
for all those many vndeserued kindnesses we haue from time to time receiued
from yow. Loueing Sir these are to let yow vnderstand, that the Lords hand
hath laine very heauy vppon my wife euer since I came into England, but especially since I came from London that now she is in such a weake Condition
that I much Question whether she will liue tell this letter come to your hands.
She hath a stronge Consumtion with an extreme Cough of the Longes, and
a great feauer that she is worne away to nothinge but skinn and bonnes, that
if yow should now see hir yow would wonder   it is now att the righinge
hereof 12 or 13 nights since she tooke any rest. I knowe the Lord is able to
raise hir vpp againe, but in the Judgment of men there is but smale hopes
she hath beene vnder the doctors hands, and he hath giuen hir vp   what the
Lord will doe we know not as yet. the Lord helpe vs to submitt to his Chas-
tisinge hand with patience, yet I blesse[3] the Lord she wants nothinge, that
canne there be gott for hir Comfort. att first indeed when she tooke hir bed

---

[1] I.e., Dover, New Hampshire.

[2] W. 1. 155. The writer of this letter has not been positively identified. He may, however, be the
Richard Storer whose widowed mother married Robert Hull, father of John Hull. After having
served some years as an apprentice to a London goldsmith, Storer came to Massachusetts with his
mother and stepfather in 1635. The latest positive evidence of his being here is in November, 1639,
when the town of Boston granted him land in what is now Braintree. *Report of the Record Commissioners
of the City of Boston*, II. 43. At some subsequent time he returned to England. Hermann F. Clarke, *John
Hull, A Builder of the Bay Colony* (Portland, Maine, 1940), 30–31.

[3] The spelling in the original manuscript is "plesse."

it was somethinge hard with vs, that we was faint to sell our flocke bedd and other thinges to make mony to helpe vs, but then I entered in to Corronall Finnes Seruis, which is only a messengers place for the City, to runne of messeges for him and the Counsell of warr and that hath beene my subsistance and is at this present. all the helpe that I could heare of both by phisicke and other meanes I haue had for my wife but I cann see noe amendment at all. I intreat yow Sir to let my freinds vnderstand our poore destressed Condition, and intreat them, if they euer did intende to be helpfull to vs to shew it now in Contributing to our necessety, for it cannot be in a more seasonable time, and for our goeinge to New England this yeare it cannot possible be expected, though we desire to giue yow humble thankes for your Loue and kinde profers in that respect, and in the meane time we shall desire your prayrs to god for vs, desireinge the Lord to guide and prosper yow in all your vndertakinges and rest Your poore servant to command

RICHARD STORER

From BRISTOL: 29 of Aprill 1643

I pray yow let vs heare from yow once more before you goe: direct your letter to Mr. Abele Kelly:

RECEIPT OF NEHEMIAH BOURNE[1]

Received 5th May 1643 of Mr. Jno. Winthrop the some of Fifty pounds in part for passage of men and goods to New England

NEHEMIAH BOURNE

FRANCIS WILLIAMS TO JOHN WINTHROP[2]

For the Righte Worship[fu]ll Mr. John Winthrop Esquir Gouernour
of the Massachusetts present these

SIR, Though A stranger A long time to your person, I am no stranger in my thankefull harte (to the All glorious Maiesty of Heauen) for such as you: you whose knowne worth and inward candor, nor frownes, nor flatterie, could euer force from its trew goodnesse for the generall good. Monster Ingratitude cannot say I flatter   wittnes not only this colloneys approb[a]tion,

---

[1] W. 4. 115.

[2] W. 4. 115; 5 *Collections*, I. 325–327. For Williams, see Savage, *Genealogical Dictionary*, IV. 559–560.

but all forayners that hath dealte or conuerst here. your constant Zeale for the things of God and man, may trewly intitle you to be the Father, and first Founder of this flourishing coloney and will haue the happiness to leaue behind you a lasting memory, but such as Honour God he will Honour: 1 Sam. 2: 30: (Right worthy Sir) It hath not bine out of neglect in not addressing my selfe vnto you by letter, in Answer of yours, but feare of troubling your more weighty Affayres with my vnnessasarie Lines. I tacke my selfe to be obliged that you are pleased to giue me notice that I lye vnder Jelousies of some of my neibours, and that they suspect my Affection, and Integrity towards them: Two things A man ought to respect whiles he liues here: his Inward Integrity: and his outward righteousnesse his piety towards God and his Reputation towards men: To haue euery man speacke well of me is vnpossible: because howsoever I carry my selfe: some Cynick will barke at my course. who can scape the lash of censure: If I should camelion licke, change my selfe to euery object, I might well be censured for A timorist, yes surly: and that Justly. I would if I could please all, but I had rather please one good man then content A thousand bad ones: How is it possible I should be loued of some, since diuersityes breed nothing but disvnion: and sweete congrewity is the mother of Loue. I will neuer professe what I will not striue to practice: and will thinke it better to be but crocked Timber: then A strayte blocke, and after lye to stumble men, as my Accuser hath done, for A supposed honest man being found lewde: is hated as A growne monster, but he that keepeth his mouth, sayth the wise man keepeth his soule: Perhaps the reporters are honest, and then I feare I haue deserued it: If it be so, I will labour to shacke off that corruption: and be glad I haue so by your meanes discouered it, and indeauor to win them by humanity, and gentilnes: Our blessed Sauiour hath taught me to love my enimyes: and to ouercome euill with good, and by loue to serue one Another but wee all know nature to be so composed that wee see more of others then ower owne, but trewly (Sir) I am sensible of my owne vnsufficiency (for maney respects) to haue Any charge or trust in the managery of Any office in your colloney, and therfore, as before, so yett, they would be pleased to passe me by, and macke choyce of some fitter man to doe them seruice. you desyre to know wherin you might pleasure vs, and that you are carefull for the weale of Pascattaque, then thus, as when the Romans indennizond any nation they commonly Adrest themselues to some select senator for ther patron, (So Sir) we apply our selues to you and therfore I am once more A suter, that you would be pleased to give your Ayde and Assistance vnto Mr. Parker our Deputy in the confirmation of this necke of land intire, for A townshipe, and that it may not be curtayled on the syde, by the pattentees of the greate house, or mangled on the other, by them of Douer, therby vtterly to macke it vnfitte to mayntayne ether A ministery or the inhabitants now living, or to come on it. Douer men vppon A treaty frely yelded vp the necke, prouided they might inioy that marsh which they haue propiety in, and to hould the sayd marsh of this Township which wee condesended to, but here only wee differd, and that them and thers would neuer pay any Rates for the sayde marsh: Accept then (vertuous Sir) this my good will, tacke it from him, who (leauing you and yours, all your fayre Actions and occasions present to the all Pure God which neuer leaues his) Remaynes Euer Deuoted to your Worthey vertues

FRANCIS WILLIAMS

PASCATT. May 9: 1643

BILL OF THOMAS HILLER TO JOHN WINTHROP, JR.[1]

sould vnto Mr. John Wintrop By Thomas Hiller At the thre leges in the Poultrey the 10th of May 1643

	li	s	d
4 flockes Beds and boulsters large	04	02	0
2 lesser flock beds and boulsters	01	12	0
5 plaine Rougs	02	05	0
3 pare of fine midell blankets	01	07	0
1 border	00	09	0
3 plaine mats	00	01	6
paid the porters	00	00	8
	09	17	2

ARTICLES OF APPRENTICESHIP[2]

This Indenture witnesseth That Mary Gore daughter of Samuell Gore late Citizen and Grocer of London deceased hath putt herselfe Apprentice vnto John Winthrop Gentleman and Elizabeth his wife or their assignes to doe and performe All their affaires and businesses whatsoever And with them after the manner of an Apprentice to serve from the Feast day of the Nativity of St. John the Baptist next ensuing the date hereof For and during the terme and space of Nyne yeares from thence next following and fully to

[1] W. 1. 152.
[2] W. 1. 151.

be compleate and ended during which said terme the said Apprentice her said Maister and Mistresse faithfully shall serve, their secrets keepe, and their lawfull Comaunds gladly doe she shall doe noe dammage to her said M[aste]r and M[ist]r[es]s nor suffer to be done of others, butt to her power shall it lett, or forthwith give notice thereof to her said M[aste]r and M[ist]r[es]s Their goods she shall not waste, nor to any vnlawfully lend; She shall not committ Fornicacion, nor contract matrimony during the said terme. She shall not play att the Cards dice tables nor any other vnlawfull games. She shall not haunt Tavernes nor Alehouses, nor absent herselfe from her said service day or night vnlawfully, Butt in all things as a good and faithfull Apprentice towards her said M[aste]r and M[ist]r[es]s and all theirs shall meekely and mannerly behave herselfe during the said terme And the said Maister and Mistresse their said Apprentice in the true knowledge Feare and wayes of God and godlines shall carefully and conscionably teach and instruct, or cause to be taught and instructed Fyndeing to their said Apprentice meate drinke apparell lodgeing washing and all other necessaryes during the said terme And for the true performance of all the Covenants and articles abovesaid the said parties bynde them selves each to other by these presents In witnes whereof the said parties have to these present Indentures interchangeably sett their hands and seales Gyven the Nyneteenth day of May Anno Domini 1643 And in the nyneteenth yeare of the raigne of our Soveraigne Lord King Charles of England etc.

The X marke of
MARY GORE

Sealed and delivered in the presence of
    RICHARD HILL
    CONSTANCE HILL

AGREEMENT BETWEEN ELIZABETH GORE AND JOHN WINTHROP, JR.[1]

This witnesseth that itt is agreed betwixt John Wintrop and Elisabeth Goore that shee is willing to refer herselfe wholy to his disposing and prouiding of a place for her as hee in his Iudgment shall thinke good: and that shee doth wholly submitt herself to him as a freind to take care for her dis-

[1] W. 1. 151.

posing in witnes hereof shee hath hearevnto sett her hand this 20 day of may 1643.

ELIZABETH GOORE

[*Endorsed by John Winthrop, Jr.:*] Eliz. Gores note [*and, in another place:*] Servants indentures.

JOSHUA FOOTE TO JOHN WINTHROP, JR.[1]

LONDON this 20th of May 1643

MR. WINTHROPE, I comend me vnto you etc. herinclossed is my accounte of my disburstements and layings oute and besides my 100*li* as I haue your acquitance For and besides the 50*li* mr. Folly haue acquitance For it there Rest due to me From you that I ame to Racaiue of you in mony Just 9*li* which nine pounds I pray leaue out For me and besides if you will haue som stonnes bought leaue 5 or 6*li* mor to by and pay For and about Charges For stones land I pray 5*li* in mony with my man if I be not at home, and desier mr. docter child to leaue that 10*li* with me that he is to paye you For if you make accunte that I shall prouyd stones and do bisnes and send them after you you must leaue me mony to do it with all my paynes which I vallue at a grat Rate in Raspicte of such a multitud of bissnes of min owne as I haue vppon me, yet not whithstanding now I haue begon to set affoot into this bisnes it shall not perrish For want of what assistance that I can giue to it in Raspect of my time. now For these 3 workemen and the Founder sonn I haue Fitted theme with all there weckly alowance For there diate and logging and have payd them tell mundaye next so if thay be not taken in to the ship diate a tusdaye next then you must alowe them the 3 men 12*d* a peece a day and the boye 6*d* a daye tell thay be enttrtayned a ship bord, and with all the much grombell because that thay haue layne so longe here and haue lost ther laber and haue had but bare 12*d* a day for ther diote and loging which thay say thay haue spent all and more. so I tould them that I would writ to you to giue them som thing towards it which I pray do   I thinke about 10*s* a peece will plase them and 5 or 6*s* the boye and tell them when thay com in new England that when you se som good proced and proffit com in of the workes that you will further Raward them. all the other 3 men are Runawaye   I pray see that these 3 men and boye

---

[1] W. I. 154. For an earlier document in the *Winthrop Papers* relating to Joshua Foote, a London ironmonger, see *Winthrop Papers*, III. 208–209.

haue good bedes bought them and that thay [have] all acomendation in the ship that you can posibly aford them to kept them in health. I praye giue them good Raspict   so for present I rest yours to vse

JOSHUA FOOTE

now I laue these workemen to your musry   laue sombody to tend vppon them to acompany them to graues End to diricte them to and in the ship tell you are settled at sa with them   you ware best to gitt som new England man and giue him 5s to acompeny these men tell thay be settled aship bord.

JOHN WINTHROP'S DEFENSE OF THE NEGATIVE VOTE[1]

A Replye to the Answ: made to the Discourse about the Neg: vote

Vpon Consideration of the substance of the Answ: I finde that the maine difference will fall into these 4 questions

1: whither a Neg: vo[te] be reserved to the magistrates by the Lettres Patents.

2: whither it be a fundamentall part of our Goverment.

3: whither it be Lawfull and expedient for vs.

4: what is the proper place and power of the Dep[u]tyes.

Then I shall cleare some of the Answearers mistakes.

And in this Replye I shall still retaine the title of Magistrates, which the Answ: declines, and that professedly, which I knowe no reason off, seinge the Patent allowes it, and himselfe invests the Dep[u]tyes with it. (18)

The 1: Qu: wilbe best cleared by the Patent it selfe, wherein I will sett downe the verye words themselues (so far as concernes the state of the Question) and not leave out what may make against me, as the Answ: often doth.

The Patent runnes thus.

Any 7 or more persons of the Assistants, togither with the Governor or Dep[u]ty Gou[erno]r so assembled etc: shalbe a full and sufficient Court etc: And the said Gov[erno]r or Dep[u]ty and 7 or more Assist[ants] may hould 4 generall Courts etc: And the said Gov[erno]r or Dep[u]ty Assistants and freemen, or the greater number of them etc: wherof the Gov[erno]r or Dep[u]tye and 6 of the Assist[ant]s to be allways 7 may admitt freemen and make Lawes etc:

And it shall and may be lawfull to and for the Gov[erno]r and suche of

[1] Massachusetts Archives, CCXL; L. and L., II. 427–438. For Winthrop's account of the circumstances leading to the writing of this document, see Journal, II. 120–121.

the Assist[ant]s and freemen etc: as shalbe so Assembled etc: or the greater parte of them, whereof the Gover[no]r or Dep[u]tye Gov[erno]r and 6 of the Assist[ant]s to be allwayes 7 to make etc: all maner of whollsome Orders etc: not contrary to the Lawes of Engld: as well for setlinge the formes, and Ceremonies of Goverment and magistracie, fitt and necessary etc: willinge and commandinge etc: that all suche Orders Lawes etc: as shalbe so made by the Gov[erno]r or Dep[u]tye etc: and suche of the Assist[ant]s and freemen as aforsaid etc. shalbe observed etc:

From these seuerall branches of the Patent it appears, that the consent of such 7 magistr[ate]s is required to euery Lawe etc: and not their presence onely to make a Court, as the Answ: pretends: and that for these Reasons

1: Because in the 1 Branch 8 such magistr[ate]s are required to be present for the Being of a Court, and not 7:

2: Because in this and the other Branche, where it declarethe their Actinge power and not their capacitye, as in the 1 Branche, it requires the Consent of 7 onely.

3: This proviso beinge expressed in bothe those Branches, where all the Acting power is given to the Court it must needs be intended to be for some vse: but if it be not to give a Neg: vo: to those magistr[ate]s it is vaine and vselesse, nay contradictory to the former, which requires the presence of 8 suche magist[rate]s to make suche a Court.

4: It sayth that the Court being so Assembled, they etc: whereof the Gov-[erno]r or Dep[u]ty and 6 Assist[ant]s to be allwayes 7 may make Lawes etc: so that it dothe not speake heer of constitutinge a Court (for that is taken as in beinge now) but of what power they shall have in this Court.

5: The like proviso will admitt no other interpretation in any like Case: As if this Court should decree that the Gover[nor]s of the Colledge or the greater parte of them (whereof the President to be allwayes one) may make orders etc. heer the Presidents consent is required as well as his presence. So if an Order were, that the milit[ary] Companye etc. whereof the Captain or Leiutt[enant] and 2 other of the Officers to be allwayes 3, might receive in any to their Company, this gives those Officers a Neg: vo: without all Question.

6: This forme of proviso and no other is vsed in all Commissions or Patents where a Neg: vo: is granted, as in the Commissions of Oyer and Termi-ner, where though there be vsually aboue 20 ioyned with the Judges of Assise, (who are onely of the Quorum) yet they all can doe nothing in the Court without the Judges consent　So it is in many like Cases, if it were needfull to recite them: so it is in the Commis[sion]s of the Peace where vpon

20 yeares experience, I never knew any Cause Carried by vote against such
as were of the Quorum   if the Answ: hath knowne any I wish he would produce it. It is true, that the Judges in every Court are all of equall power by
the first Assignauimus in their Commission, yet where the Kinge or the Lawe
shall in some Cases enlarge the power of some, and restraine others, by the
same Commission, their power must be exercised accordingly. whence I
must Conclude, that either these words in our Patent doe give the magistrates a Neg: vo: or els there was never any Neg: vo: granted by any Patent
or Comission by any kinge of England since Edw: the 3ds tyme: let the Answ:
shewe some other forme of words vsed to that purpose, or he must yeild the
Cause.

As for that which he alledgeth out of the stat[ute] of 33 H: 8 it is nothinge
to the purpose: beinge made for Colledges Deaneryes etc: and extends onely
to such Affaires, wherein they Acte meerly as Corporations, as leasinge their
lands etc: but it extends not to the Acts of Courts in Corporations: for then
it had taken awaye the Neg: vo: from the Houses of Parl[ia]ment, for these
are allso a Corporation (as mr. Prine shewes in his late booke in defence of
the Parliament.) And besides, the Statutes of England doe not binde in any
other parts out of that kingdome, So as the Kings Lettres Patents are not
included in that Statute.

The 2 Question is, whither this forme of Gouerment be fundamentall in
our Com[mon] w[ealth].

That it is such thus I proue.

1: Such forme of Goverment as is rightly built vpon the first foundation,
is fundamentall. But this is so: therefore it is fundamentall.

The proposition is vndenyable.

The Assumption I proue by the words of the Patent and the Order of our
Court made An[n]o 1634.

2: That which makes a specificall difference betweene one forme of Goverment and another, is essentiall and fundamentall But the Neg: vo: in the
magist[rat]es doth so in our Goverment therefore it is essentiall and fundamentall.

The Assumption is proved by this, that if the Neg: vo: were taken away
our Government would be a meere Democratie, where as now it is mixt.
This I proue thus:

Where the Cheif Ordinary power and administration thereof is in the
people, there is a Democracie: This I prove thus, If it be in the Dep[u]tyes
it is in the people, but it wilbe in the Dep[u]tyes: ergo etc., for they are but
the representative body of the people, and the matter lyes not in the number

of people Assembled, but in their power: Againe the people are not bounde
to sende their Dep[u]tyes, but they may come themselves, if they will. And
thoughe the magistrates be ioyned with them in the Court, as they were in
Athens and other popular states in Greece etc: yet they serve but as Councellors, seinge they shall have but their single votes, as every one of the
people hath. Lastly the Answ: himselfe confesseth, that the Dep[u]tyes are
the Democraticall parte of our Gouerment. (19)

Now if we should change from a mixt Aristocratie to a meere Democratie:
first we should haue no warrant in scripture for it: there was no such Goverment in Israell.

2: we should heerby voluntaryly abase our selues, and deprive our selues
of that dignity, which the providence of God hath putt vpon vs: which is a
manifest breach of the 5th Com[mandmen]t for a Democratie is, among
most Civill nations, accounted the meanest and worst of all formes of Goverment: and therefore in writers, it is branded with Reproachfull Epithits
as Bellua mutorum capitum, a *Monster*, etc: and Historyes doe recorde, that
it hath been allwayes of least continuance and fullest of troubles.

And whereas the Answ[ere]r would helpe this, by investing the dep[u]tyes
with office and magistracye (18) I shall shewe his mistake heerin in itts
proper place, and with all how it would overthrow the power of the Dep[u]-
tyes, and so of the generall Court, if suche an opinion should be allowed.

To the 3 Qu: whither the Neg: vo: in the Magistr[ate]s be lawfull, and expedient for our State, I shall referre the reader to what is allreadye written
in the Discourse etc: for I conceive the Arguments there are not weakened,
by any thinge in the Answ: Seinge the maine strength of all that is obiected
depends vpon his misinterpretation of the Patent, and of the Order of 34
which (I hope) wilbe sufficiently cleared in this Replye: and for what may
need any further light, I shall afforde a word or 2 about it, in its proper place.

The 4th Qu: is about the proper place and power of the Dep[u]tyes.

For clearinge of this I shall need onely to explaine more fully, what I
wrote in the Discourse: least some others might fall into the same mistakes
which the Answ[ere]r hathe.

Thus therefore I lay it downe.

1: They have the same place and power which the Freemen assembled in
a Generall Court ought to have: according to the Order of 34:

2: These, ioyned with the magistrates in any generall Court have (together
with them) all the power legislative, and the cheife power Juditiall, of this
body Politick.

3: Neither the Magistr[ate]s alone, nor the Dep[u]tyes alone without the consent each of other, in any generall court, have any power at all.

4: The Dep[u]tyes are no magistr[ate]s nor (considered alone) have any iudiciary power. this Is proved,

1: By the Patent which gives the freemen (whom they represent) no such power, in any generall Court. It allso provides that every magistrate or officer of the Court, before he exercise his office, should take the Oath therevnto belonginge: but neither the Freemen in Engl[an]d, nor the Dep[u]tyes heer haue used to take any suche Oath, nor is there any Oathe appointed for them by Lawe: nor is there any power in this Goverment, to administer an Oath to them, in such maner as the Patent prescribes, for it must be administred to them, before they exercise any Aut[horit]y, and then there is not any Aut[horit]y sufficient to give it them: and let any indifferent man Judge whither the Patent (which looked at the wholl bodye of Freemen) did ever intende, that they should take an Oath as Officers in the Court: which if it had, it would sure have been putt in practice, in the first Courts in London, when they did all things by learned Counsell in Lawe, there would have been an Oath framed for them, as well as for the Gov[erno]r Dep[u]tye and Assist[ant]s, or there would have been some such Clause incerted to the Oath of freemen, so as it is plaine, that by the Patent, where was no such office, or Juditiary power given, or intended, to them, as the Answ: pretends, but onely that they should Acte as Freemen etc.

And if the Answ[ere]r had considered, what would necessarily followe vpon this newe office and magistracye, to which he would have the Dep[u]tyes to be sett aparte from the bodye of Freemen (as well as the magistr[ate]s) he would rather have lefte them still in their proper place: For whereas the Patent allowes none to be members of the generall Court, but the Gov[erno]r Dep[u]tye, Assist[ant]s and company of Freemen, if the Dep[u]tyes be invested with any other Office (as the Answ: would have them) they can be no members of that Court, nor have any vote there,

But leaving him to retracte this error, amonge many others (as I shall manifest heerafter) it is without controversy, that the Dep[u]tyes are the same company of freemen whom the Patent intends, and neither have, nor (I suppose) doe seeke any other office or power, then what belongs to the Fremen, bothe by the Patent, and by the orders of our Court.

This shall suffice in waye of Replye to the substance of the answears. I would haue stayd heer, but that I finde (amonge his many mistakes) some, which for want of clearinge, may perchance mislead the reader   for the readye findinge of them, I haue put to them such figures as I haue noted them by in the Answer:

(1) In the Discourse I bringe an Instance of the Elders Judgment in a like case, to this effecte, that the choosing of a man to the office of a Councellor dothe not make him a magist[rate] from whence he inferrs (not observing the similitude) that I make the Dep[u]tyes to be no more but Councellors.

(2) When I saye, that the foundation of the peoples power is their liberty, he inferres, that I denie them to have any power: whereas my meaninge appeares clearly to be onely this, that their freedome from any other power, makes them no otherwise subiecte, then accordinge to their will, and Covenant.

(4) He demands what will become of those Lawes, to which the maior parte of the Assist[ant]s have not agreed? I Answ: If they have not expressed their Consent to every Lawe, yet seeinge there is no Recorde of their dissent it is enoughe, and this q[ue]r[y] might have been spared.

(5) He reproues vs, that in our begininges we sware, such as we Admitted to freedome, to the Aut[horit]ye of the Gov[erno]r and other the magistr[a]tes etc., and not of the Gov[erno]r etc. and companye etc:

I answ: 1: we did not sweare them to the persons but to their Aut[horit]ye, which was no other (nor was any other challenged) then what was established by Patent, and every man that tooke the Oath, could vnderstand it no otherwise, though the express words of the Patent were not observed, nor could so properly be at our first comminge, when we had no freemen, besids the magistr[ate]s (that I remember) nor were there any Considerable company of them, for a good tyme after: 2: those who sawe the multitude of our other vrgent Affaires and difficultyes we encountered with, and the little Court businesse we had, would easyly allowe vs pardon of that, or greater errors (which are incident to all Plantations, in their beginninges) especially seeinge our Readinesse to reforme them, and to conforme to the right Rules of our Goverment.

(6) He denyethe that by the Order of 34 the power given by Patent to 7 mag[istra]tes is so altered, as that the maior parte should stand instead of the 7: Answ: It is true, it is not in the same words, but the same clearly in effecte: for the Patent saythe the 7 must be allwayes a parte of the maior parte etc: and the Order of 34 saythe that no Lawe etc: without consent of the maior parte. such contentions about words had been better forborne. he that will nodum in stirpes querere, may finde himself worke enough, but to little purpose.

(8) Heer is another obiection eiusdem farinæ with the former: about the words Neg: vo: not beinge expressed neither in the Patent nor in the Order of 34 which I shall speake more fully vnto heerafter.

And heer he thrusts in an Argument or 2 against the Order of 34 in respecte of the common construction that is made of it, for the Neg: vo:

1: That (if it be in that Order) it was so inuolued amongst other things, that the intent of it was not so distinctly discovered, nor so clearly established: For Answ: I will sett downe the words of the Order; No Lawe etc: shall passe, as an Acte of the Court, without the Consent of the greater parte of the magistr[ate]s of the one parte, and the greater number of the Dep[u]tyes on the other parte: now, (to cleare the Court of that ignorance, or vnwarinesse which the Answ[ere]r would cast vpon it) I wishe the reader to Judge, how the Neg: power of the magistr[ate]s could have been more distinctly sett downe, or more clearly established.

2: That by the Neg: vo: the entire vnion would be dissolued. Answ: 1: It will as well be dissolued by the Neg: power of the Dep[u]tyes (which cannot be taken from them) and then disparitye in any society or bodye will doe the like: which is a Tenet against all experience, and the very Course of Nature: for heerin would the Lord our God, have his excellent wisdome and power appeare, that he makes (not the disparitye onely but) even the contrarietye of partes, in many bodyes, to be the meanes of the vpholding and vsefullness thereof.

3: such a vnion as he aymes at, to consist of Individualls of the same kinde, is bothe against the Patent and the Order allso: for bothe doe expressly distinguish the generall Court into severall parts: as the words declare.

(9) He denyes the Neg: v: to be a fundamentall Lawe, by this Arg[u]ment that the Court in 34 wherein this Lawe was established restrained the 4 generall Courts to 2:   Ans: by the same Reason it would followe, that one Lawe in any Court beinge void, all the Acts of that Court should be voyd allso.

(10) He denyes the Judgment of the Elders about the changinge any forme of Goverment to be as I have reported it: for this I referre the Reader to their Answeare.

(11) (13) He saythe that we may not imitate the Parliament of Engld:

1: because of the disproportion betweene that Court and ours.

2: because our magistr[ate]s are not of the Nobility, as the vpper house there is. Answ: He will not denye, but we may and must imitate our Lord Jesus Christ, where there is a greater disproportion: And reason will teach vs to imitate those, in whom is founde the greatest measure of wisdome and vertue: and thoughe our Court holds no proportion with that, in degrees, yet it dothe in parts: and so a child may strive to imitate a man in speaking, walkinge, temperance etc: But the Answ[ere]r forgatt his owne Rule, when he holds forthe our Court in imitation to that in their Stile of High and Eminent: which is too far aboue our Capacity. And if he would yeild them a Neg: v: in respecte of their Nobilitye: the reason is stronger for our magistr[ate]s: for those Nobles represent onely their owne familyes, but our magistr[ate]s doe represent the Aut[horit]ye of all the people as well as the dep[u]tyes doe that power and Libertye which they have reserved to themselves.

(12) He would seeme heer to Affirme that the house of Commons in Engld. have Ordinary Juditiary power: and sure, he would have spoken it out, if he had knowne it had been so: but he would have vs shewe that ever they made any vniust Lawe, or putt any innocent person to death: Ans: when he shall shewe vs any Lawe made by them, (in ordinary course) or any person (innocent or nocent) adiudged to death by them, I will then satisfie his demande: In the meane tyme, I am readye to shewe him some vniust Lawes made, and some innocent persons put to death by their consent.

And whereas he doth taxe me with likeninge that High Court to a grand Jury because, when I speake of their impeaching any person, I explane it by the word indite, as more commonly knowne, and of the same signification. I leave this to equall iudgment.

Further it may be observed, that when he speakes of the safetye etc: in the Iudgment of the Dep[u]tyes, rather then in the magistr[ate]s, he reckons them 40 and these onely 4 or sometymes 5 whereas he knowes the magistrates are 10 or 11 and as they are not allways present, no more are the Dep[u]tyes. Besides, his Argument from the disproportion betweene 40 and 4 is a meere fallacye: for it was never knowne, that the magistr[ate]s have stood alone in any opinion, without a considerable parte of the most able Dep[u]tyes concurringe with them: Nor have the magistrates any such power, ouer the peoples lives and libertyes by their Neg: vo: as the Answ[ere]r pretends: but onely to preserve them, if by any occation they should be in danger: I cannot liken it better to any thinge then to the brake of a windmill: which hath no power, to move the runninge worke: but it is of speciall vse, to stoppe any violent motion which in some extraordinary tempest might otherwise endanger the wholl fabricke.

(13) Heer he chargethe me with Crossinge my selfe: because in one proposition I saye, that in the magistr[ate]s and Dep[u]tyes ioyned etc: is the wholl power iuditiary etc: and after I denye the people alone to have any Iuditiary power in the generall Court where this Crossinge lyes, I confesse, I cannot see.

(15) Whereas I saye we should incurre Scandall, by vndervaluing the gifts of God, as wisdome, learninge etc., and the Ordinance of magistracye, if the Iudgment and Aut[horit]ye of any one of the Com[mon] ranke of the people, should beare equall weight, with that of the wisest and cheifest magistrate: this he layethe to my charge, as a Scandall indeed: and heer and in (17) he makes a longe discourse, besides the scope of my Argument and intention: For I acknowledge (and have allways so doone) that there are of the Dep[u]-tyes men of wisdome and learninge sufficient, and it may be, not inferiour to some of the magistr[ate]s: but yet, if in Com[mon] repute (especially in forreine parts) the magistrates be looked at, as men precedinge in gifts and experience (for otherwise the people are misguided in their Choyce) then the Scandall will remaine not withstandinge. and besides I speake not posi-tively but hypothetically: so as if there be at any tyme one or more Dep[u]-tyes so weake, as will holde no proportion with the most able of the magis-trates, then my Argument will hould good, without any Scandall or offence given on my parte. And whereas I stile suche a Dep[u]tye of the Com[mon] ranke of Freemen: I hope it is no disparagement to any, to be counted in that Ranke, which is allowed equall power with the Governor and Assistants in our highest Court, althoughe a Dep[u]ty in Court be of more value then any one freeman, seinge he represents many: yet before and after the Court, he is but as another freeman, and so cannot be counted in the same ranke with the magistrates. And I should be willing to learne of the Answ[ere]r, or any other, how I might have spoken more modestly, in thus and suche like passages, and not have lost the force of my Argument: which (the Lord knowes) was the onely thinge I intended, and not to extoll the gifts etc: of the magistrates, nor to debase those of the Dep[u]tyes: for I acknowledge it my duty, to honor the gifts of God where euer I finde them, and I hope, my ordinary practice hath not been different.

(16) He mistakes Demurringe for Democratie, and yet the Sentence might have easyly guided him to the worde.

(17) He sayth, that the Order of 34 is obsolete, because it was never putt in practice. I suppose the vse of it beinge knowne (for it hathe been ofte spoken off in Court) hathe kept proceedings in that good Order, that there hath been small or no occation to make vse of it. But if this were a good Ar-gument, many of our Capitall lawes would soone be obsolete: and by the same reason, we should slight all fortifications, which had not been Assaulted in 10 or 20 yeares. and men should laye by their swords after they had worne them suche a tyme without any occation to make vse of them. and many suche absurde conclusions would followe vpon such premises. but to helpe

the feebleness of his Argument, he tells vs, the Neg: vo: was once called for, but denyed in Court: for which, seeinge he Cites not any Record or other proofe, It shall need no Answ: especially seing he tells vs not, what parte, or member of the Court denyed it.

(19) He denyethe the Neg: vo: to be any forme of Gov[ernmen]t because it is not (as he saythe) forma constitutiva Gubernandi, but vox constituta: that is: It is not such a forme as giues beinge to the Goverment but onely a vote constituted.

Answ: Heer againe I must give the Reader notice of a fallacie, in takinge advantage now of the stricte meaninge of those words, which in all the former dispute haue been taken accordinge to the Com[mon] acceptance. For howsoeuer we haue carried on our discourse in the Termes of a Neg: vote, (the Question beinge first started, and since debated, vnder that notion) yet it is an Affirmative vote, which is indeed controverted, and which is granted, bothe by the Patent, and by the order of 34: for bothe doe declare, that the Consent of so many magistr[ate]s shalbe necessarye to everye Lawe, order etc: Now if the Lawes etc: be essentiall to our Goverment, and these can haue no beinge, but as they are Affirmed, or assented to, by the magistr[ate]s, then is this Assent (concurrent with the rest) forma constitutiua, for thus composed, it dothe dare esse quod sunt. He is allso mistaken in denying, that vox constituta can be essentiall to a Goverment: for then he may as well denye that the freemens votes in Elections are essentiall: and suche a vox constituta is not a bare Negation, or posse impedire, quod non transit in Actum.

(15) For that probable instance I bringe out of Jer: 26: it will hould still, for aught is alledged against it: for though the Princes ioyned with Ahikam, yet he onely is named verse 24: (for it is like he was President) and their Neg: vo: (if not his alone) saved Jer: against the minde of the Preists: as for the people they onely gave their approbation to it: for it is without question, that the people had no Juditiall power nor vote in their Courts: for the Lord Commandinge them Deut: 16 to appoint them Judges in all their Tribes, and those should iudge them etc: he excludes them from all ordinary power of Judicature themselues.

Diverse other passages I omitt, as being of no weight in this controversye, and I leave them to the readers Judgment.

There are 2 or 3 Arguments more (which I haue mett with otherwhere) which may heer allso receiue Answeare.

1: Magdeburge changinge their Democratie into an Arist[ocracy] were soone after destroyed. Answ: 1: Their destruction did not arise out of their new Goverment, nor for it; but meerly from an externall cause: viz: the Emperors displeasure against them, for refusinge to choose his sonne their Administrater or Prince. 2: if this had befallen them for changing that forme of Goverment which the providence of God had setled them in; it is a good warninge to vs, to take heed how we attempt to change our owne.

2: The Judges in Engld. have no hand in makinge those Lawes, by which they are to Judge.

Answ: The Judges of the Kings Benche, Com[mon] pleas and Eschequer have not, and the reason is because they onely intende it, and are to attende the vpper house vpon all occations: but it is vndenyable, that aboue ⅔ of the members of both houses are Judges of the laws they make, in one Court or other.

3: The greatest power is in the people: therefore it should be in their Dep[u]tyes.

Answ: originally and vertually it is: but when they have chosen them Judges, etc: their Juditiary power is actually in those to whom they have committed it and those are their magistr[ate]s in such order as before is declared.

There Remaines one obiection, which for better satisfaction, I shall endeavour to give a more cleare solution vnto, then is in my former Discourse.

ob: If the Court of Assist[ant]s should give an vniust sentence in any Cause, the partye iniured can have no remedye in the generall Court, if the magistr[ate]s (as they are like to doe) shall persist in their former Iudgment.

Answ: 1: If any vniust Judgment be given in the Court of Assist[ant]s, it proceeds more vsually from the error of the Jury, then the corruption of the magistr[ate]s: who will then be competent Judges of it in another Court.

2: If suche Cause be brought into the generall Court vpon newe evidence (which is vsuall and most likely) then shall the magistr[ate]s have good grounde, to change their Judgment.

3: If the magistr[ate]s be godly (as they are like to be while the frame of the Com[mon] w[ealth] remaines suche) then if they erre in Judgment, it must be supposed to be of infirmytye, and want of light: if so, then there is no doubt, but they wilbe readye to attende suche further helpe and light, as the wisdome and counsell of the generall Court may seasonably afforde.

4: If the miscarriage of the magistr[ate]s in their Sentence, should be evident and notorious, either the shame of it would make them change their Judgment: or otherwise they should be made manifest to all the Country, to be such as they are, and then they would be soone removed, and called to Account, and so their vniust Sentence would be reversed in a due Course.

5: Where absolute safetye cannot be provided, (which is and hath been the Case of all Com[mon] w[ealth]s, even that of Gods owne institution) there reasonable and probable meanes of safetye must suffice.

6: If an error in some particular and private Case, should want redresse, for a tyme (which yet is very vnlikely) then we may rest satisfied in this longe approved maxime   It is better for the Com[mon] w[ealth] that a mischeife be tollerated, then an Inconvenience indured, much more, foundations of Goverment overthrowne, as must needs be if this Neg: vo: be layd downe. And it is well proved and concluded by a late Juditious writer, in a book newly come over, intituled an Answ: to Dr. Ferne, that thoughe all Lawes, that are superstructiue, may be altered by the representative bodye of the Com[mon] w[ealth] yet they have not power to alter any thinge which is fundamentall.

Jo: Winthop: Gou[erno]r

(4) 5, 1643

JOHN WINTHROP'S MEMORANDUM OF ARGUMENTS IN SUPPORT OF THE NEGATIVE VOTE[1]

Neg: vote

Ther are 2 sorts of arguments from whence men drawe conclusions: the 1 is Certainty as when David knewe [torn] that the men of Keydon would deliver him up to Sa[ul] he concludes it would not be safe for him to staye the[re]   The other is of probability: as when Ab[raham] considered that the Philistines feared not God, it was probable, if they knewe that Sara was his wife, they would kill him to inioye her, thervpon he concludes, it were best to dissemble it: but it was never knowen that [torn] and godly men have drawne a conclusion into Acte from an Argument of meere possib[il]ity, except where the heart hath been given vp to wickednesse or the conscience scourge with the guilt of some fowll sin. This made Josephs Brethren conclude that he would be revenged of them, being onely possible because it was in his power, but not probable, because he feared God, and had given them longe experience to the contrary. So Dionysius and other Tirants durst not trust their own friends or Children, because being given vp to all licentiousnesse themselves, they durst not trust their life vnder any possible danger.

Charity beleeveth all things and hopeth all things: if this be the Rule of Church towards all our breth[ren] much more towards such as we make

[1] W. 1. 194.

choyse of for their ability and faithfullnesse that our hope and Confidence (vnder God) may rest in them. The hande consisting of two parts: the 4 fingers and the thumbe, have each of them a negative power, so as the fingers cannot effecte any work without the thumbe, nor the thumbe without the fingers.

A windmill may consist of divers wheeles and Rudders hath an vpper wheele or break which hath a neg: power to all the rest, otherwise the mill would make madd work in a tempest.

In an Armye, they are the com[mon] soldiers vpon whom the whole work lyes, yet the Commanders have a neg: power over them as well as direction, otherwise they would soone be in Confusion.

[*Ca.* June 5, 1643]

ROGER WOOD TO JOHN WINTHROP[1]

To his much Honnoured and esteemed frend Mr. John Wenthrop esquire
bee these presented in new England god preserue the vessell

HONNOR[ABLE] SIR, I haue rechud your Lettres and am glad that small present of our fruicts came so seasonably, and wear so acceptable vnto yow which is all I desire, of which wee can make no better vse then by presenting them to our frends, when occasion is offered. they are much desyred in England, but theise Troubles there, prevents vs of shipping to transport them, as also to supply vs. I haue now shipped aboard this vessell 200 of Lymonds, but would haue shipped as many more if the m[aste]r could haue stowed them (as he can informe yow) desyring yow as afore to let Mrs. Ames partake with yow: I feare I presume too much vpon your favour and Trouble in this kinde. my reason is, beeing shipped vnder your protection, they will bee more carefully looked vnto by the seamen, and therefore I pray yow pardon my bouldnesse in this behalfe, and accept this poore present from him whom your noble fame hath endeared to your service, which I shall endeavour to expresse vpon all occasions wherin I may approue my selfe your readie and loving frend to serue yow

ROGER WOOD

DEEPE BAY this 6 June 1643

[*Endorsed by Governor Winthrop:*] mr. Rog: Wood Summers Ilands.

[1] W. 1. 155. For Wood, Governor of Bermuda, 1629–1637, see John H. Lefroy, *Memorials of the*

WILLIAM CODDINGTON TO JOHN WINTHROP[1]

HONNORED SIR, I doe thankefully acknowledge your loue vnto mee in your kind profer to my agent mr. Jer. Clarke to return to me my runn a way servant, Tho. Jonnes in case hee could haue bene found. I shall be redy to bee commaunded by yow in the licke or wherin I may heare. Now deare Sir for soe yow haue bene to mee, as sollomon sayth, ther is a frind that [torn] nearer then a brother! oh, that the nearnes of that relation had never bene vyolated. but wee are men, and so wee shew ourselues, some tymes deifying of men and ordenances, other whyle vylefying of them. the lord hath let mee see the vanetye of my owne spirit, and need of attending of him in all his ordenances, but I cannot inlardge the meassinger staying. my desire is, that that anchent loue which much watters cannot quench, may bee renewed, and in token wherof, that yow would recaiue, at my hands, a smale rememberance therof, in a vessell of beefe, for your winter provishon, which is not yet redy but aginest that tyme by some pinnice that cometh this way, shall be sent vnto yow. though the thing bee not worth the mentioning betweene vs, yet because I remember your loueing excusseing of your nonacceptance (of my profer in this kind att my departuer) so as it did not nore doth not take any Impreshon of vnkindnes with mee, and I hope that which wos then a ground to yow is remoued, yet I desire yow fully to satisefye mee heare in, If it (or rather I) may thus fare fynd acceptance with yow. not other at present, with the rememberance of my loue and my wife to your selfe and yours with all that remember vs I rest, your assuered lo[ving] frind

WM. CODDINGTON

NEWPORT, mo. 4. 12, 1643

EDWARD WINSLOW TO JOHN WINTHROP[2]

SIR, I have deferred writing many times in hope of time to enlarge myselfe to you, but never more streightned then at present, yet ashamed to withhold any longer, but I pray you pardon my brevity. Concerning the Vnion[3] our Majestrates and Deputies approue well of what is done, and two of our townes passed it before the Court; vizt. Plimoth and Marshfield: the rest of

Discovery and Early Settlement of the Bermudas or Somers Islands, 1515–1685, 1 (London, 1877), 297, 492, 531–544.
   [1] W. 2. 129; 4 *Collections*, VI. 318–319.
   [2] Original not located; 4 *Collections*, VI. 173.
   [3] I.e., Articles of Confederation.

the Deputies carried it from the Court to their townes to be confirmed, none doubting of it, and with order to returne their votes this moneth, so that there is no doubt of our thorow close with you therein.

Concerning the cattle, I sent the fiue cowes, a two yeare old heyfer, and a yearling steer, by Roe according to your order, but one of the cows calved two daies before, and he would not take the calfe with him but left it, which was prised at 7*s*, another calfe at 14*s*, and two other calues at 36*s*, and the two yeare old heyfer at 3*li* 15*s*, which in all amounted to 6*li* 12*s*, the just sum which was due to me for the wintering of those seauen beasts: Mr. Bulkley affirming that but to make even money he would not haue yielded to so much. And for the skin of the beast that miscaried at winter I allow 13*s* 4*d* for it, which was due to me upon the former devision. I would haue enlarged but the tide is almost spent, and I haue other letters must needs write, and so hope you will excuse me who saluting you in the Lord Jesus take leave and remaine Yours to his power

EDW: WINSLOW

CARESWELL 13 (4) 43

Mr. Collier and my selfe chosen Commissioners to confirme, and so for the following season.

JOHN ENDECOTT TO JOHN WINTHROP[1]

To the right Wor[shipfu]ll my deare Friend John Winthrop Esq. Gouernour deliver

DEARE SIR, I ame glad that La Tour hath not ayd from vs, and I could wish hee might not haue any from the Shipps. For as longe as La Tour and Dony are opposites they will weaken on another. If La Tour should prevaile against him we shall vndoubtedly haue an ill neighbour. His Father and him-selfe as I ame informed, haue shed the blood of some English already, and tooken away a pinnace and goods from Mr. Allerton. It were (I think) good that that busines were cleared before hee had either ayd or libertie to hire shipps yea or to departe: Sir It is not the manner abroad to suffer strangers to view Forts or Fortifications, as it seems theise French haue done. I must needs say that I feare we shall haue little comfort in hauing any thing to doe with theise Idolatrous French. The Countrie heereabouts is much troubled that they are so intertayned and haue such libertie as they haue to bring their

---

[1] Massachusetts Archives, CCXL; *Hutchinson Papers* (1769), 113; (1865), I. 127. For Winthrop's account of the rivalry between Charles de La Tour and Charles d'Aulnay, in which Massachusetts became involved, see *Journal*, II. 105–116; 127–131.

souldiers ashore and to suffer them to trayne their men. And great Jealousies there are that it is not Dony that is aymed at, seeing such a strength will neither sute such a poore designe, and La Tour a man of weake estate as it is said. Wherefore other mens hands are imployed, and purses to for some other seruice. But I leaue all theise things to your serious considerations, desiring the Lord to guide you therein to his glorie and peace of the Churches heere to whose grace I committ you and humblie rest Yours truelie ever

Jo: ENDECOTT

19. 4. 43

ROBERT CHILD TO JOHN WINTHROP, JR.[1]

To his honoured and much respected freind Mr. John Winthrop Junr. Esq.
at New England

GRAUSEND Jun: the 27th 1643

SIR, I am glad to heare of your safe arrivall at the Wight and hope your voyage to New England hath bin both spedy and prosperous. wee had provided 5 tun of stone at London before wee received letters from you, which you shall receive in this ship. I feare your arrivall will be so late, that you will hardly set the worke forward before Winter, but I know you will doe your indeauour. times here are extreamly distracted god send a good successe to our Armys, who are very nigh there enemys. I haue fully heard Sir Edmund Ploydens Comedy,[2] and the Dutch Tragedy. the Lord preserue your Plantacions from such foolerys and misfortunes: pray remember to send me word concerning the black lead mines, and (if your occasion will permit) send me some Simples, or such like to begin a firme society with John Tredislin, and let me be beholden to you for all sorts of news and passages, and I shall strive to requite you in the same kind. Ile doe my indeauour to get a bloomer, and to get those knaues that ran away punished. [*Illegible*] and these times put me to my wits Ends. Well if our Iron busines goe on, all is well. I cannot further trouble my selfe at this time, but bec[ause] I promised to tell you further concerning it, read in breife Abrege des secrets Fabri. it will give you your desire, but his preparacions are too laborious for any man breathing. I hope to see you next spring then I shall giue you further Satisfaction. Your louing freind

ROBERT CHILD

[1] W. 4. 54; 5 *Collections*, I. 151–152.
[2] For Sir Edmund Plowden and his county palatine of New Albion, see *Narrative and Critical History of America*, Justin Winsor, Editor, III (Boston and New York, 1884), 457–468.

Remember my love to Mr. Downing. I knew not of his going with you else his olive trees should haue bin ready but I shall bring them with me next spring. Remember my seruice to your Father and others who as yet remember me. Yours

R. C.

Some say Colonll Hampden is dead, Wicham plundered.

THOMAS GORGES TO JOHN WINTHROP[1]

PISCATTAQUAKE, 28 June 43

RIGHT WORTHY SIR, I vnderstand by Mr. Parker that you haue written to me by Mr. Shurt, which as yet I haue not rec[eived]. It cannot be vnknown vnto you the fears that we are in since La Tours promise of ayd from you. for my part, I thought fitt to certifye soe much unto you, and I doubt not only these parts which are naked, but all N. E. will finde D'Aulnay a scourge. he hath long wayted (with the expence of neer 800*li* per month) for the apprehendinge of this supply, and if all his hopes shall be frustrated through your ayd, you may conceaue wher he will seeke for satisfaction. if a through worke could be made, that he might vtterly be extirpated, I should like it well, otherwise it cannot be thought but a Souldier and a Gent[leman] will seeke to reuenge himself having 500 men: 2 ships a Galley 3 pinnases well prouided: besides you may please to conceaue in what manner he now beseidges La Tour. his ships lye on the S.W. part of the Iland at the entrance of St. Johns Riuer, in which side is only the entrance for ships. on the N.E. lye his pinnases. it cannot be conceaued but he will fortifye the iland which will debarr the entrance of any of your ships and force them backe, shewinge the will, haueing not the power to hurt him:

I suppose I shall for England in this ship. I am not as yet certayn which makes me forbear to be larger at this tyme, or to desier your commands thither. thus in hast I rest Your honouringe frend and servant

THO. GORGES

---

[1] Massachusetts Archives, CCXL; *Hutchinson Papers* (1769), 114; (1865), I. 128.

SAMUEL WHITING AND THOMAS COBBETT
TO JOHN WINTHROP[1]

RIGHT WORSHIPFULL, May it please you to vnderstand that this present day we spake with mr. ottley and Joseph Armitage about your Arbitration, in which we with other fowre were desired to act this weeke and we desired to know absolutely and fully what they both of them did desire and determine to be done by vs. mr. ottleys Answere was this I desire that all differences betwixt me and Joseph Armitage from the yeare 1638 vnto this present may be fully determined and ended by the Arbitratours. Joseph Armitage his answere is: that he is willinge to putt to arbitration onely such differences which are betweene them since the 16th of August 1642, concerning all debts and the Great action at Boston. soe that we perceiue the former desireth all differences betweene them to be ended which was your worships desire in your letter to vs: the latter desireth not to put all differences to Arbitration but some onely and therefore in as much as they agree not to the termes of the Arbitration, we shall leaue them to that further course that may compell them to agree namely a court triall: hopinge that your worship will excuse vs herein doing our best to drawe them to a more private way of ending theyr differences, but our advise preuayleth not soe Far and soe with our harty desires of the Gracious presence of God with you in that great and weighty worke to which the lord hath called you we take our leaue and rest, yours in all seruice of loue

SA: WHITING
THO: COBBETT

LYNNE this 10th of the 5th m. 1643

RICHARD SALTONSTALL AND OTHERS TO THE GOVERNOR,
DEPUTY GOVERNOR, ASSISTANTS, AND ELDERS[2]

MUCH HONOURED IN THE LORD, Though we doe, and may truly professe, ourselues to be both vnfit, and unwilling to interpose in a matter of such State and weight, as we conceive this French Affaire to bee: yet the Honour we owe to the Religion we professe, the Loyalty we beare to our native

---

[1] W. 4. 118; 5 *Collections*, 1. 328-329.

[2] Massachusetts Archives, CCXL; *Hutchinson Papers* (1769), 115-119; (1865), I. 129-134. The body of the document is in the handwriting of Richard Saltonstall. For Winthrop's account of this letter, see *Journal*, II. 131.

Country, especially in its present condition and the Reference wherein it stands, to the Kingdome of France, our respect to the reputation of our government, and Governours, our tender care of the soules, and lives, of such as are committed to the trust thereof, the eye of care we ought to have upon our freindly Neighbours in the East, our regard to our Christian Con-fœderates, so lately combined with us, in confidence of our piety, and wis-dome, and the religious discharge of our own Consciences and Duties, will not permit us to be silent, so long as there is any roome left for us to speake. We have littel hope to revoke resolutions so farre transacted and ripned, but we presume it shall not be taken amisse, if we labour to wash our hands wholly of this dissigne, and what ill consequences soever it may produce. The Reasons moving us hereto, are our deepe feares that the stated rules of vndertakeing warres, either by proper and direct enterprize, or by lending ayd, haue not beene so duly observed, as we could wish.

1. The grounds of warre ought to be just, and necessary. For the justice of this Warre by la Tore agaynst Daulnay, we conceive that all the light and information, New England hath, or may probably receive, cannot be suffi-cient for us to determine it positively; we vnderstand it hath beene variously judged in the Courts of France, one while for Daulnay, another while for la Tore, and it is not impossible that la Tore hath now rather outfreinded than outpleaded Daulnay; we shall therefore runne into an vnchristian præmunire of presumption if we resolue upon such an enterprize with an irresolved faith, In causâ dubiâ bellum non est suscipiendum. For the necessity of it, it must either be in point of Charity towards de la Tore or upon some en-gageing interest of our owne. For any bond of Charity, we conceive the speech of the prophet to Jehoshaphat, 2 Chron. 19: 2 and of Solomon Prov-erbs 26. 17 not only discharge but strongly prohibite us. 1. For our owne interest, if it be cleare that Daulnay hath offered us such great wrong, as invites us to a warre, (which we much quæstion, for it must be atrox injuria) we suppose it would stand more with the honour of our Religion and Plan-tation, to proceede professedly and orderly agaynst him, then for us English to become but margent notes upon a French text, which to us is as yet but Apocrypha: and to vndertake him upon more certaine grounds, and at a more seasonable time when he doth lesse expect us, and is not so well provided for us as now he is. Warrs are extreame remedies and are not to be enter-prised unlesse their causes will beare out all manner of effects and conse-quences, whether personall or nationall, which may insue. and what may not insue, if either of the nations to whom we belong will comment vpon our action in a State language and how apt a time this is for misconstruc-

tions we cannot be ignorant. The Spirit of warre is Scholastick and Jesuitical, traversing the very Positions and Principles, which peace hath held both Dogmatical and Irrefragable, even to the wonderment of rational men. We are informed that Daulnay desires our Freindship, and we are inclined to beelieve that if it did as well become him to appeale to our judgement as it ill beseemes us to expect it, he would not refuse to cast him self upon our compromise.

2. Warres ought not to be vndertaken without the Counsel and command of the supreame Authority whence expeditions issue. It is not hard to say, the present reference betweene the Kingdomes of England and France considered, that the subjects of the one, ought not to wage warre against the other without a publike Commission of State, vnlesse it be in defence upon a sudden assault: neither do we yet heare that le Tore himself hath any such commission for this his action, though if he had, it were littel to us. It is a rule observed amongst Confœderates, that during any league of peace betweene them, one freind may not ayd another against any part of his province til that part be proscribed by the authority of a general assembly whereof it is a member, and the Confœderates, assured thereof in a state way. The breach of this rule is a breach of league. Publike actions of hostility worke farre and wide haueing their national and confœderal influences and consequences. The Daggers we draw here may happily prove swords in Christendome for ought we know.

But this designe, whatever the cause was, seemed shy even of our new English Counsel to warrant or guide it: how closely it concernes the peace and safety of the whole plantation may easily be conjectured, and how farre it declined the advice thereof in a representative course we are very sorry to consider or mention.

We dare not so much impeach the honour of the advisours as to thinke they would vaile the action with this, that they only permit and give way to volunteirs, for who knowes not this to be a rule of state, that, Not to forbid when there is notice and power, is to bidd.

This were also to proclaime our weaknes in prostrating our Government to nothing, for who is ignorant that To permit volunteirs to issue out in ayd of a freind is never done without an act of state, where any state is?

Daulnay, nor France, are not so feeble in their intellectuals as to deeme it no act of state when upon consultation with some of our cheife persons, our men are suffered, if not incouraged to goe forth with our provision and munition vpon the designe; We doe therefore wonder that our people haueing no warrant from authority will of their owne heads runne such a hazzard of their soules and lives, as can neither looke for any prayers, or thankes for their good successe, nor any succour if it fares ill, and as it may fall out rather call for the curses of their freinds from whom they went, and of posterity yet unborne and yet these poore men presume that if Daulnay should say, as the King of Egypt to Josiah what haue I to doe with thee, thou King of Judah? I come not out agaynst thee this day, but agaynst the house with whome I have warre, or if they should shed innocent bloud or feele their own soules dropping suddenly into hell, they had their warrant from the Counsel and Countenance of those upon whom they might and ought to confide. it were to be wish'd they had beene taught the Germane Proverb, which sayth, He that loseth his life in an vnnecessary quarrel or danger dyes the Devills Martyr had they had the voyces of the people with them it had beene better than nothing but that wind seems to us to blow strong in the Teeth of their voyage. We shall presume to propound these Quæstions. 1: If Daulnay or France shall hereafter demand any of them from us as Enemies, or Murtherers, whether will our Court protect or deliver them? 2: If any of the parents or wives shall require their lives at our hands who shall answer them? 3: If any of their widdowes or children shall require sustenance, or any maimed souldier in this Expedition call for maintenance who shall give it them? or if taken captives and made slaues, who shall rescue or redeeme them?

3: The Ends of warre ought to be religious, what glory is intended hereby to God we see not, and how our peace shall hereby be setled we foresee not, but suspect it will rather be a beginning than an end of our troubles and feares, if we doe not wholly suppresse Daulnay, we may be sure of it. he is alredy very strong, and if our ships and munition fall into his hand, it will deminish from us, and incourage, exasperate and strengthen him.

If La Tore prævaile he is like to cavill with our men for some miscarriages, or we with him for nonpayment. The passage of our Ships to and from England hath hitherto beene quiet and safe in regard of the French, but we cannot so expect it hereafter if they shall meete with any of la Tores or Daulnayes special freinds, or at least with the freinds of such of them as we shall seeme to wrong. Bellum contra hostem non est suscipiendum cum periculo reipublicæ, etc.

4: Vndertakeings of warrs ought to be probably feasable, but this seemes not soe to us. we learn out of the East, by an ey witnesse that Daulnay is very strong, in Artillery, men and munition, at land, and very well provided at sea, insomuch that some of the East haue consulted to repayre to him in his ayd least hee should vpon revenge annoy and ruine them; he is reported to be a valiant, prudent, and experienced souldier and commander, and Defendants haue great advantages of assaylants, soe that we feare, our sheepe haue hastned to their slaughter.

5: Lastly, the manner of enterprising warre calls for many rules, according to scripture and the customes of religious and ingenuous nations, as to summon and give warning before they strike; To heare what the defendant can pleade for the justice of his Cause to offer termes of peace with equal Articles, and to give speciall cautionary Commissions and Commands how farre to persist in ayd, and when to desist, but we neither can send fitt men for such charges, nor can we præscribe such directions without a professed imbarquing ourselves in the action; which it seems is wholly declined on our parts.

We therfore trouble you no further, only we itterate our Protestation that we are and desire to be held cleare and innocent of this vndertakeing, and Your wo[rshi]ps in all Christian affection and services

5th 14to 1643

RICHARD SALTONSTALL
SIMON BRADSTREETE
SAMUEL SYMONDS

NATHL. WARDE
EZ. ROGERS
NATH. ROGERS
JOHN NORTON

THOMAS HOOKER TO JOHN WINTHROP[1]

To his much Honoured freind John Wyntropp Esquier, Governor of the plantations in the Matcheshusets Bay deliver

MUCH HONORED IN OUR BLESSED SAVIOUR, at the returne of our Magistrates when I vnderstood the gratious and desired success of ther indeavor: And by the ioynt relation of them all, not only your christian readines, but enlarged faythfullnes in an especiall manner to promote so good a work:[2] Though the appearance of flattery (If I know my self and be knowne to you) be not only crosse to my conscience but to my disposition, yet my heart would not suffer me, but as vnfeynedly to acknowledge the Lords goodnes, so affectionately to remember your candid, and cordiall cariage in a matter

---

[1] W. 2. 151; 4 *Collections*, VI. 389–390.

[2] I.e., the formation of the New England Confederation, which had been agreed upon by the colonies of Massachusetts, Connecticut, New Haven, and Plymouth on May 19, 1643.

of so great consequence: Laboring by your spetiall prudence to settle a foundation of safety and prosperity in succeeding ages: A work which will be found not only for your comfort, but for your crowne at the great day of your account. Its the greatest good, that can befall a man in this world, to be an instrument vnder God to do a great deale of good: To be the repayrer of the breach, was of ould counted matter of highest prayse and acceptance with God and man: much more to be a meanes not only to mayntayne peace and truth in your dayes, but to leave both, as a Legacy to those that come after, vntill the coming of the Sonne of God in the clouds.

I know my place and I would not abuse your patience or hynder greater imployments, my ayme is nakedly this: To be in the number, and to have my voice with those, that whyle your self and your faythfull Assistants, (as Zerubbabell and his fellow helpers) be laying the first stone of the foundation of this combynation of peace, I may crye grace grace to your indeavors: And by presenting the worth and acceptablenes of the work before you, to strengthen your hands, and encorage your hearts to proceed on with blessing and successe: Goe on therefore (worthy Sir) and be ever enlarged in such worthy services, and the God of truth and peace will ever be with you: which he desires dayly to begg: who desires to be: yours in all due respect

THO: HOOKER

The 15th of the 5th mon: 1642 [1643] SEA-BROOKE

[*Endorsed by Governor Winthrop:*] mr. Hooker Grat[*torn*] Rec: (5) 24, 1643.

JOHN WINTHROP TO RICHARD SALTONSTALL AND OTHERS[1]

GENTLEMEN AND BELOVED BRETHREN, It is not vnknowne to you, that (through the Lords gratious Assistance) I haue thankfully imbraced, and submitted unto the wise and loueing advise and admonitions of any of my brethren: and truly it is still my desire so to doe: And this (I hope) may well stand (vpon this present occasion) with the maintenance of what is good and Righteous in our Cause, about this French busines, and with that faithfulnes that is againe required of me towards yow all whom I loue, honour, and Reverence in the Lord. And though I haue lately written to yow about this matter, yet that which I haue since Receiued from yow,[2] calls vppon me for

---

[1] Massachusetts Archives, CCXL; *Hutchinson Papers* (1769), 121–132; (1865), I. 136–147. All but the last sentence and the signature is in an unidentified handwriting.

[2] See Richard Saltonstall and others to the Governor, Deputy Governor, Assistants, and Elders, July 14, 1643 (pages 397–401, above).

some Addition and Answere also: which I do not with any purpose to contend, but in dischardge of my Conscience and duty of my place, and let the Lord do what seemes good in his eyes.

The protestation which was directed to my selfe first, but came to me through many hands (and so it seemes it was intended by yow, being sent vnsealed) was intertained of me, as proceeding from your zealous care of the publick safety: but considered in it selfe, it is an Act of an exorbitant nature, out of rule, out of season and of dangerous Consequence: Such protestations are publique and Judiciall Acts, and therefore must be warranted by some authority which appears not in this. I knowe no Law, Order, Custome, or etc: that can giue power to 3 Assistants by any such publick Instrument, to contradict the proceedings of a greater number, the Governour also being one of them; and how it will consist with the Obligation of a freeman is also considerable: Suppose now 3 other assistants and so many Elders should protest against your Protestation, it would be of equall force and as warrantable for ought I knowe. Againe it comes not like Solomons apples of Gould in plates of silver: it is Consilium post factum: whereas if you had sent it in season it might perchance haue stopped those proceedings which yow so much complaine against: whereas at present (yow know and all may see) yow do but beate the Ayre, and striue for that, which (yow are sure) yow cannot reach. It is also of dangerous consequence in these respects. 1. It may be a president for others to attempt the like in any Case: for yow take upon yow, the sole Judgment of your owne Act and if others may haue the like Liberty, they may countenance their Opposition to Authority, as well in evill Causes as in good. 2: It blowes a trumpet to division and dissention amongst ourselvs, magistrats protesting against magistrats, Elders against Elders, blameing, condemning, exposeing brethren to the peoples Curses, and casting them downe to hell it selfe: and all this must be indured, while we walk after the light God affords vs from his owne word, and the presidentiall Acts of former times, and of our owne Generall Court (as wilbe expressed hereafter) whereas the way of God and of order, and of peace, had beene to haue referred your grievance to the generall court: and not by such an vnwarranted Protestation, and Outcry against your brethren to incite the people against them: whereof if any evill effect should followe, your Protestation of Innocencie would afford yow little comfort or defence. 3. this is the ready way to hasten vpon vs the evill so much feared: for if D'aulnay vnderstand our divisions to be such, as he is like to haue a party amongst our selvs (as yow declare your Intelligence to be) this may imboulden him to attempt that against vs, which otherwise he dared not have done. It is also against the Rule of justice, your owne plea on D'aulnays behalfe: for yow passe sentence and publish it without calling us to Answer: It may be one or 2 of you haue accidentally heard vs speake somewhat about it: but did yow ever enquire of vs, if we had any more to say for our selvs, why Judgment etc. For yow will find we haue more to say for our selvs than yow formerly heard: and it is a necessary Consequence, If yow had power to be our Judges, yow had the same to require our Answer. I intreate yow to call to mind that beaten rule of equity, *Qui aliquid statuit parte inauditâ alterâ*, etc: We are condemned in Court in Country, by private letters and by publik edict, and never asked why haue yow done this? and all this so carryed on, and vnseasonably dispensed as no man can tell (nor do your selves propound) what yow would haue or how it may tend to any publick good or prevention of that great danger which yow suppose to hang over vs: except it may be conceaued that, either D'aulnay will be pacifyed with a protestation; or the people stirred vp to sacrifice some of vs to make their owne peace: yow say, indeed yow will hereby be innocent of all the evill that may insue etc: Amen say I; but surely wisemen will not believe that such a Protestation will acquit you either before God or men: no more then if one of the magistrates sitting silent in the Court while a man is condemned, and after he is executed shall tender a Protestation of his dissent from the Sentence. And truly (brethren) you might haue dealt a little more tenderly with us, for such faileings as yow had apprehended in our Counsells being the fruite but of a few houres Consultation, seeing your selves, (vppon so many weekes deliberation) could not free your owne Acts from such miscarriage as yow see your Protestation, out of date, and out of Course, doth hould forth.

This I thought needfull to tender to your wise and christian consideration, concerning your Protestation in generall: Somewhat I must say to your Arguments, besids what may concerne them in my former writeinges. But first yow may please to consider, that it cannot be denyed, but that the Governour assisted with some other of the magistrates may take Order for such sudden Affaires of the State as either need not, or may not stay the Assembling of the general court; of which sort, we conceiued this was (the reasons you may see in my former writeing) and when in such Cases, we haue proceeded according to our best skill and Judgment, we are to be excused, and so it was wont to be: And the Generall Court seemes lately to have inlarged this trust, when by the Order of (4) 1641 it giues power out of Court to any 3 magistrates to doe that which may occasion a warre with the Indians as likely as this with the French: For they may giue Commission to any master to right him selfe vppon the Indians, for his fugitiue servant. By like Authority it was that some of vs disarmed the Indians, and imprisoned some of them vpon the late suspicion: and although it was conceiued to be full of danger, and proved troublesome and chargable, yet wee were not reproved for it: Other Instances might be brought, but in those times indeed, when such Protestations were not in vse. Now in this case of the French, wherein the onely doubt was (not whether wee should ingage our selves in a warre with La Toure against D'aulney, or not, for, we know that neither the magistrates, nor the Generall Court it selfe could determine that, but) whether it were safer, and more just and Honourable for vs to stop the Course of Gods Providence, offring vs opportunity to saue a distressed neighbour, to weaken a dangerous enemy without our chardge or engagement, or to suffer it to go on freely in its owne course: Of these 2 we Judged the last to be best, etc: and of this opinion some of vs shall still be vntill we see stronger Arguments against it then as yet we have met with.

Now for your Arguments: (whereof some concerne the Proceedings, others the Consequences) I will passe by that of Jehosaphat as no parallel to our Case; and see if I can free vs from that of Prov. 26. And heere it may be first observed, that he speaks of one that passeth by: viz: that had no calling or invitation to deale in it. But 2, I will shew that this strife betweene La Tore and D'aulnay doth neerely concerne vs: and first in point of duty, in that our distressed neighbour calls to vs for help: a speciall Providence of God and his owne good opinion of our Charitablenes, brought him to vs, for some end, and no other appearing to vs, it was our duty to attend this: nor were we in this case to stand vpon the Justice of the quarrell betweene them, no more than Abraham did when Lot and the Sodomites were in present distresse: nor then any man would doe, if he sawe his neighbour vnder foote and in danger to be killed, he would first rescue him from danger ere he inquire of the Cause. And how we might withhould such helpe from La Tore which that providence which brought him hither, might here offer him in his apparant distresse and danger of vtter ruine, I professe I see no warrant.

For cleareing of this point I desire yow seriously to consider an arg[ume]nt or 2. 1. he is either a neighbour or no neighbour. If he be not a neighbour, then is he in no relation to vs by the 2d table: and then we may Rob, beate, or kill him without breach of any Commandment. But if he be a neighbour then must we do to him in his distresse, as we would haue others do to vs in ours. 2dly. If he be one of those All, to whom by the Rule of the Apostle we must doe good (as he must needs be, if he be either of the houshould of faith, or out of it) then that is the good we must do to him, which he hath most present need of: and that we may not withhould from him, when it is in our hands to giue it him, Prov. 3. 27. I pray yow consider the place. 3dly If my neighbours or mine enemies oxe be in that state as he cannot get to his place without my helpe, I must help him to his place Exod. 23. 4 much rather my neibour himselfe, and therefore La Tour and his Company being now before vs in that Condition, we ought to helpe him home. These are plaine and generall Rules and will not beare Distinctions of Protestant and Papist. For the Morall Law being giuen to man by Nature was giuen to him as man, not as man so and so qualifyed: and therefore when it requires duty from him, it requires it as from a man simply: and when it propounds man as an object of this duty, it propounds him also simply considered without distinction of good or bad, christian or Heathen, etc: and our Saviour inforceth this by propounding the example of our heavenly Father, who causeth the Sun to shine upon the Just and vnjust, etc: and commands vs to followe his example. And the Gospell makes this difference onely, that in question of priority, or necessity of neglect of one, the faithfull must be preferred. Therefore let vs see something of like Authority to dispense with these Rules, or else we must conclude, that this (so farr as we deale in it) is a thing that concernes vs. 2ly. As it concerns vs in point of duty, so doth it also in point of Danger. I haue shewed in my former writeing, how D'aulnay hath dealt with vs and our neighbours, when he was weake, what Principles he is Acted by, and what pretences he hath against vs: and all Histories teach vs that the Ambition and Covetousnes of Conquerours and spoylers, hath always increased with theire power: And shall we not beleeve that D'aulnay onely wilbe more calmed and moderated by accesse of 200 souldiers, and 4 or 5000*li* yearely Revenew? Let the Latin Proverb be attended as well as the Germaine, and that will tell vs that *res nostra agitur, paries cum proximus ardet*. I may strengthen this Concernment by a late Germaine History. When the Bishop of Spiers had begun to raise a strong fortification vppon his owne Territories, the late Palatine of Rhine demolished it by force of Armes in a time of peace, because it might be dangerous to him if warre should arise. And the Lacedemonians being in League with the Athenians (theire owne City being vnwalled) would not suffer the Athenians to wall theires, because it concerned them in point of advantage. And it hath beene vsuall for the States of Europe to interpose in quarrells of theire neighbour States, when they haue concerned them but in point of danger onely. Now for your discourse about our distinction betweene Commanding and not forbidding, let the distinction be rightly stated as it concerns our practise, and not as yow would put vpon us, and we hope it will hould so well, as neither the Advisors nor the Actors shall need to be ashamed to owne it. We disclaime to haue any hand in giueing leaue to any of ours to go make warre vppon D'aulnay, but this we owne and no more, that we gaue leaue to such as could be hyred, etc: to accompany La Tour and to conduct him to his owne place. And such a permission as this (though it were a Commission to this purpose) we stand still to maintaine is no vndertaking of warre, nor Act of hostility, but a meere Liberty of commerce, and if any bloudshed should followe vppon it, it is accidentall and not depending vppon this as any Cause of it. Nor is it any Just provocation of warr, or any breach of peace, nor so accounted among Civil States. I shall cleare it by an Instance or two both private and publ[ic]. If I haue a neighbour within a few miles of mee suspected to be a Robber, if I send my servant to beate him, if he doth so, I am a trespasser, if he kill him, I am a murderer. But if a travellour coms by and tells me that he hath a Chardg about him, and he is afraid to goe alone on his Journey for feare of such a man, and desires me to let my servant go with him to guard him out of danger, in this Case it is my duty to let my servant go with him (if he be willing) though it may be dangerous to his life, and may also procure danger to mee or mine from such Robbers: And if the Traveller be now sett vppon by this Robber and my servant kills him, we may both Justify it. I will giue another instance. A merchant of Spaine being in London, by leaue of the King of England, hires a London ship to transport him and his goods into Spaine; vppon the way a Holland man of warre meetes and fights with him, and men are slaine on both sides, yet without any breach of peace on either side, or any Act of hostility in the King of England, as it would haue beene if he had granted a Commission to Assault the Hollander. So that yow may see there is a wide difference betweene giueing Commission to fight, and giueing leaue to be hyred to guard or transport. So as yow must needs haue beene mistaken in the right stating of the distinction, or else I cannot conceiue what your apprehensions should be of the English and Irish and Scottish who in so greate numbers, for these many yeares, have served the States against the Spaniard, and the Spaniard against the States, the Swede against the emperor and contra without any breach of the peace betweene those nations: But admit such a permission were against a Rule of State, yet if that Rule of State be against the Rule of Charity, it will not be hard to Judge which must giue place. What singular things doe you [*illegible*] I will conclude this point with that Argument which I touched in my former writeinge: That which is lawfull for a priuate person to do in the way of his calling, the magistrate (if he judge it also expedient, or not hurtfull to the Commonwealth) ought to furder or not to hinder him in it. But it is lawfull for the Owners and Masters of Shipps, and is in the way of theire Calling to be hyred by La Tour, to convey him to his rightfull habi-

tation, and we iudge it no way hurtfull but advantageous to this Commonwealth, therefore we did well and according to the duty of our Office, in
giueing leaue to them, and in not hindring them. And it is no sufficient plea
against it, to say that we know not the Justice of his Cause: for that wil not
concerne vs in this Case (and yet we do know it in good measure) but if our
ships shalbe opposed in theire lawfull Course, the Justice of their Cause will
ly in that: As for example: A man travaileing in a wagon in England, and
carrieing his goods with him, his Creditour sets vppon the wagon to take
his debtors goods from him by force, the wagoner may defend him and his
goods being now in his Charge, without any respect to the former ingagement,
for the Justice of his cause ariseth vppon another ground. Neither is there
any need to send to D'aulnay before they goe (no, though they went of purpose to fight with him) for besides divers examples in Scripture to warrant
the forbearance of it, the rule in Deut. 20. 10 giues other direction. When
thou comest *neere to* a City to fight against it, thou shalt send to offer peace,
etc: This point being thus cleared, that we haue not enterprised any warre in
this our proceeding, all your Complaints aginst vs, and all your Arguments
tending that way do fall to the ground: this is not the Case, neither are we
the men and therefore I shall not need to examine your Reasons and Allegations against such: nor am I willing to mention those passadges wherein our
power seemes to be so much slighted. I dare not beleeue that yow intended
all that is held forth in them. I looke at your Quæries also as raised vppon the
same mistaken grounds, which being now cleared to yow, yow will easily resolve yourselves about them. And yet this I will propound to your Consideration: which may be a full answer to them all in the most knotty Construction: viz: If our brethren should erre in there way and thereby bring themselves into distresse, yet (if we must pardon them vppon their Repentance)
sure we may not desert them, nor hide our eyes from theire misery. If any of
our Confederats (through humane infirmity) should against theire Covenant
bring a Just warre upon themselvs, yet if they call to vs for helpe, and tender
themselvs to equall satisfaction, we must not leaue them to destruction. No
relation amongst men could stand or be vsefull, if meere errour (which we
are all and continually subject to) might dissolve it, or obstruct the vitall
Spirits which should breathe in it.

　Whereas yow object that in this permission we make the State as a cypher,
I answer, the State hath the same influence into this which it hath into other
merchants voyages, by a Generall and implicit Consent, which may be sufficient in so free a State as ours is: where there is no restraint vppon persons
or Shipps (but vppon speciall occasion) they goe and come at theire Liberty.

Now for the point of danger. I conceiue, first the Rule of the Apostle Peter will hould even in this case: while we do well we are not to be frighted with any terrour. Againe there is no Course or voyage vndertaken by us, but it may expose the vndertakers to perill, and may occasion displeasure and danger to vs from abroad: but such dangers haue not hitherto deterred vs from any probable way of our safety or advantage: not haue we sustained any harme hitherto, by casting our selvs vppon the Lord and his good providence in such Cases. I will remember yow of some. When we first set up Reformation in our Church way, did not this expose vs to as greate an hazard as we could run both from abroad and at home? Did not our frends in England many of them forewarne vs of it ere we came away? Did not others send letters after vs, to deterre vs from it? Did not some among our selvs (and those no meane ones) inculcate our inevitable dangers at home from no smale Company left out of Church fellowship, and Civill Offices, and freedome hitherto? Yet we trusted in God (though there appeared no meanes of safety) and went on our way: and the Lord hath still preserved vs, and frustrated all Councells and Attempts against vs. Againe when vppon grievous Complaints against vs to the Lords of the Privie Councel, of such Civil innovations amongst vs as we could not Justify by the Lawes of that State, a strict order and Command was sent to vs to deliver vp our patent, or else to expect to haue it fetched by force, what greater danger could be toward vs then appeared in the not obeying of this Command? Yet we had then Courage inough to returne an Answer without our Patent. When we vndertooke a warre against the Pequots, which no necessity put vs vppon, but only in point of Conscience (they had done vs no injury) on others behalfe, there were more objections (in point of dangerous consequences) against that, then against this. our frends of Plimouth complained of it and wrote to vs accordingly, so did our frends of Connecticot, laying forth the dangers we had exposed them vnto by it: wishing we had forborne to a fitter season; but neither of them protesting against it. Yet, in due time, the Lords hand appeared in it to the good of the whole Country, and we felt but little of those great dangers which were justly to be feared. Our intelligence was beleeved, which we heard long since, and hath beene more certainly confirmed of late, that the jesuiticall State haue had an evill eye vppon vs, and not without Cause (as themselvs apprehend) and though we looke at this as the head of all forein enmity, yet the Lord hath still saved vs, and that without any great impression of feare vppon our Spirits. In the treaty about our late Confederacion, the doubtful construction of it in England, the danger from a Generall Governour (especially in regard of our brethren of Plimouth) the necessity of being involved in the quarrel with the Dutch, on the behalfe of our brethren of Hartford, were taken notice of by the Generall Court and many of the Elders: etc: yet neither would the court be deterred hereby from entring into that brotherly league, nor were our Elders or people troubled with feare of those dangers. And now lately when we receiued Pumham and Sawcononoco into our Jurisdiction, the Generall Court considered how offensive it would be to the Naragansets, and so likely to ingage vs in a warre with them: yet, the thing being lawful and expedient for vs, and giueing hope of opening a doore to the Conversion of some of them, they would not let slipp the opportunity of such Advantages, for the feare of doubtfull dangers. More I might add, all amounts to this summe, the Lord hath brought vs hither through the swelling seas, through perills of Pyrats, tempests, leakes, fyres, Rocks, sands, diseases, starvings: and hath here preserved vs these many yeares from the displeasure of Princes, the envy and Rage of Prelats, the malignant Plotts of Jesuits, the mutinous contentions of discontented persons, the open and secret Attempts of barbarous Indians, the seditious and undermineing practises of hereticall false brethren, and is our Confidence and Courage all swallowed vp in the fear of one D'aulnay? Admit we should haue stepped aside out of our way, doth the favour and protection of our God wholely depend vppon our perfect walking? Were we never out of our way before, under all our former mercies and deliverances? Did Abraham, Isaack, Jacob, David, Jehosaphat, the people of Israel, Judah, and others never find protection and deliverance, when by infirmity, they were found to be out of their way? If they did, why may not we still seeke and hope for the like, seeing the Lords mercies indure for ever? For my part (if there were not other sins, which God may haue a controversie with vs for) I should little feare any harme by this. If any breach were made in our Peace, this is not the way to make it vp. We may bring more displeasure and danger vppon ourselvs, by the divisions and breaches of Rule, which may be occasioned by our vnseasonable striveings about that which is now past remedie, then would otherwise arise from any miscarriage in the busines it selfe, in the worst construction that can be made thereof.

The feare of man bringeth a snare; but he that trusteth in the Lord shalbe safe. Prov. 29. 24.

J: W: G[overnor]

[Ca. July 21, 1643]

JOHN ENDECOTT TO JOHN WINTHROP[1]

To the right Wor[shipfu]ll John Winthroppe Esqr. Gouernour at Boston deliver

DEAREST SIR, I finde that your troubles are many and espetiallie about this french busines. The Lord in mercie support you. I ame much grieued to heare what I heare. And I see more of the spiritts of some men then euer I thought I should see. The Lord rebuke Satan: Sir be of good comfort I doubt not, but our God that is in heauen will cary you aboue all the Iniuries of men. For I know you would not permitt any thinge much lesse act in any thinge that might tend to the least dammage of this people, and this I ame assured of, that most of Gods people heere about vs are of the same minde. The rumours of the country you know they rise out of ignorance principallie, and much out of feares, wherefore I pray you let there be satisfaccion giuen as soone as you convenientlie can, in the way you wrote mee of. For I finde the spiritts of men in this Countrie are too quick and forward. I cannot excuse my selfe, Yet I blesse God, not to wronge you but according to the information and light I receaued from you, I acted publiquelie so farre forth as to beate downe all preiudice against yourselfe or the rest that aduized with you. Our prayers heere are publiquely and priuately for a good issue of it and that con[tinually][2] and I hope God will looke upon your sinceritie [in mercie][2] and will heare our requests.

I see no good vse of such protestations as I heare of, but they may proue more dangerous then the french busines by farre if our God hinder not. Howeuer it will be of use (God derectinge) to make a holy vse of it.

Touching my comming to Boston about the Dutch busines, I cannot see how it will be of any vse, for the messenger cannot have a determinate answere till the generall Court, And to morrow we haue appointed many of the Towne for the working of our Fort which vnlesse I be there, there will not anything be done. And I received not your letter till this day after our Lecture.

I conceaue if you doe any thing about Mr. Oatelyes busines, that you also wilbe pleased to apoint some day and graunt some summons to him that hee may bring in his witnesses, That there may not be any Just ground of exceptions giuen: For hee speakes as if hee were much wronged in all the testimonies taken against him, and saith he can disproue them: etc.

[1] William C. Endicott, Jr., MSS., M.H.S.; *Hutchinson Papers* (1769), 120–121; (1865), I. 134–135.

[2] The manuscript has become damaged since the time when Hutchinson used it, and that which is here printed in brackets is now missing.

Touching the note about Bushrode I shall bringe it with mee (God willing) the next Court.

The Lord our Good G[od be with][1] you to vphold you and to continew you amongest vs t[o do yet furt]her[1] service to whose grace I committ you Yours euer truelie to serue

Jo. Endecott

Salem 26 5 mo. 1643

SIMON BRADSTREET TO JOHN WINTHROP[2]

R[igh]t wor[shipfu]ll Sir, I receaved togeather with others two lettres from your selfe concerneing the French affaire, and had I not hoped that yow should have receaved a generall answer from vs all longe before this tyme, I should not have bene soe longe silent, nor shewed soe much seemeing neglect, but being nowe almost out of hope of accomplishing that which was intended, I thought meete to present yow with theis fewe lynes. Howe vn-pleaseing it was to mee, for to expresse my selfe by word or writeing, con-trary to the apprehencion of your selfe, and other Friends, both godly and wise, whome I both love and honour hee that is the searcher of hearts knoweth, and howe farr it was from my will or intent, when I sett my hand to that lettre yow received,[3] to cast any dishonour vpon your selfe or others I hope in tyme yow shall knowe, and be fully perswaded of. the trueth is, our aydeing of Latour was very greivious to many hereabouts, the designe being feared to be vnwarrantable by dyvers, as the case stands with vs, of which number I confesse I was (and soe still remaine) one, and though the busines was soe farr proceeded in when wee writt the lettre, as (for my parte) I had noe hope of stayeing the shipps, yet some of vs thought it might be of good vse to intreate that some cautions might be gyven to those that went, and they strictly required to obserue the same, that soe the vndertakeing myght be preserved from sinne and the comonwealth from danger, soe much as the case was capable of, which cautions if refused, then to signifie vnder our hands, our not consenting to the proceedeing, with our reasons thereof. but for any protestation against your act condemneing it, wee never intended it, but fre-quently fully and expressly declined it, for the sending the lettre without those cautions and after the shipps were gone, concernes those to answer that

---

[1] The manuscript has become damaged since the time when Hutchinson used it, and that which is here printed in brackets is now missing.

[2] Massachusetts Archives, ccxl; *Hutchinson Papers* (1769), 132–134; (1865), I. 147–149.

[3] Cf. Richard Saltonstall and others to the Governor, Deputy Governor, Assistants, and Elders, July 14, 1643 (pages 397–401, above).

did it, for my parte I was much troubled att it soe sone as I heard of it. what errors may be found in our lettre for matter or manner of expressions, (it being intended noe otherwise than I have expressed) I shalbe farr from owneing or iustifyeing when they shall appeare. this I can truely say wee were sollicitously carefull (according to the litle tyme wee had) not to write any thing that might be matter of iust offence, and I hope a favourable interpretacion of words, (our intencions being rightly vnderstoode) may free it from blame. Concerneing the arguments yow alleadge to warrant the designe, I shall forbeare to say any thing att present, not haveing either of your lettres by mee, but rather leave them to be answered by the Elders, whoe it is like will shortly visit yow vpon other occacions, and for my selfe I hope to waite vpon yow att the Court when wee may have opertunity to speake further about the same, and for those many heavy imputacions, which your last lettre chargeth vs with being cheifely grounded vpon the tyme and manner of sending our lettre (of which I had noe knowledge) I hope yow will see cause to ease mee of, as noe wayes diserueing the same, soe humbly praying the god of love and peace to preserue vs in peace and vnity, and this whole plantacion from wayes of sin and provocation, I remaine Your wor[shi]ps vnfeynedly to love and serue yow in the Lord

SIMON BRADSTREET

21th of 6th M. 1643

CLAIMS AGAINST JOHN WINTHROP[1]

	li	s	d
To the Country	100	0	0
To mr. Hill 350 and 150 to him for mr. Mayhew	500	0	0
To mr. Angier of Camb:	180	0	0
To mr. Dummer	100	0	0
To mr. Browne of Tanton	65	0	0
of this 10*li* is paid			
To mr. Fenwick	50	0	0
To Ben: Gillam	90	0	0
wherof paid			
To Capt: Gibbon about	60	0	0
To mr. Russell for mr. Mayhew	50	0	0
To mr. Allen the Teacher of Charlton	70	0	0
To Capt. Sedgwick about	40	0	0

[1] W. 1. 143. This document is in the handwriting of John Winthrop, Jr.

	li	s	d
To mr. Eldred about	47	0	0
To mr. Astwood of Roxbury and mr. Long of Charlton being the executors of Nathaniell Axtell about	60	0	0
To mr. Rich. Parker			
To Capt: Keine			
To Daniell Cole of Plimouth	20	0	0
To Rich. Truesdale			
To Willm. Hudson senr.	18	0	0
To mr. Web			
To mr. Stoddar			
To the Gov[ernou]r of Plimouth or the Government	10	0	0
To Ed: Bendall			
To Jo: Hill of Newhaven	8	0	0
To mr. Cooke of Dedhan	9	18	0
To mr. Hatherly	27	0	0

     this dorchester vndertook to satisfy

[*illegible*] Dexter demandeth 25*li*

[*Ca*. September, 1643]

[*Endorsed by John Winthrop, Jr.:*] The debts for which Tenhills is engaged.[1]

JOHN WHEELWRIGHT TO JOHN WINTHROP[2]

RIGHT WORSHIPFUL, Upon the long and mature consideration of things, I perceive that the main difference between yourselves and some of the reverend elders and me, in point of justification and the evidencing thereof, is not of that nature and consequence as was then presented to me in the false glass of satan's temptations and mine own distempered passions, which makes me unfeignedly sorry that I had such an hand in those sharp and vehement contentions raised thereabouts to the great disturbance of the churches of

---

[1] "John Winthrope Esq: granted vnto Wm. Ting, Thomas Allen Richard Dumme[r] Capt. Gibbons, Capt. Sedgwick, Valentine Hill; Richard Russell, Benjamin Gillom and Edmund Anger, and Richard Parker, his mansion house in Boston together with his Farme called Ten hills (except the neck of land over against the oyster banke) for and in consideration of divers summes of money wherein he stands indebted to them and divers others. And this was by an absolute deed of sale dated the 26⁰ of the 7⁰ month 1643." *Suffolk Deeds,* I. 45.

[2] Original not located; Savage (1826), 162–163; (1853), II. 196; *Journal,* II. 165–166. For Wheelwright, see *John Wheelwright,* Charles H. Bell, Editor (Boston, Prince Society, 1876), 1–78; Morison, *Founding of Harvard College,* 405–406; *D.A.B.*

Christ.[1] It is the grief of my soul that I used such vehement censorious speeches in the application of my sermon, or in any other writing, whereby I reflected any dishonour upon your worships, the reverend elders, or any of contrary judgment to myself. It repents me that I did so much adhere to persons of corrupt judgment, to the countenancing of them in any of their errours or evil practices, though I intended no such thing; and that in the synod I used such unsafe and obscure expressions falling from me as a man dazzled with the buffetings of satan, and that I did appeal from misapprehension of things. I confess that herein I have done very sinfully, and do humbly crave pardon of this honoured state. If it shall appear to me, by scripture light, that in any carriage, word, writing or action, I have walked contrary to rule, I shall be ready, by the grace of God, to give satisfaction: thus hoping that you will pardon my boldness, I humbly take leave of your worship, committing you to the good providence of the Almighty; and ever remain, your worship's in all service to be commended in the Lord

                                                            J. WHEELWRIGHT

WELLS, (7) 10 – 43

JOSHUA FOOTE TO JOHN WINTHROP, JR.[2]

To his louing Frind Mr. John Winttrope at his howse in New En. deliver

                                    LONDON this 20th September 1643

MR. JOHN WINTTROPE, I comend me vnto you etc. I hope you are in a good Forwardnes in your Iron workes   I haue inquired and sought out For to gete a blomrie man and can here of non   I was with Sir John Clattworthie about blomry men   I went in your name and he telles me that times are so in Irland that he thinks thay are kild or ded For he can here of non, and I haue inquird much after some and can here of non and I could never see the ould man sence you went nor here of him so that you must Joyne all your workmans hedes togather and see to breed vpe blomries   a smith aftre a lettell taching will make a blomer man. Mr. Winttrope I lett me intreate you to stand my Frind in New England at your Corte when my kinsman mr. Hewse shall moue my bissnes   my Raquist is and will be Eaquall and Just the bisnes is this   mr. Foxcrafte and I being Formerly and are still of grat acquaintance he hath drawne me in to be bound For him, which my Kinsman will inlarge to you howe I becam bound For him. now mr. Foxcraft is

---

[1] I.e., the Antinomian controversy of 1637.
[2] W. I. 153.

faylled and he hath an estate in New England as he tells me   that which I am bound for him is For 800*li*   now my Requist is that 1600*li* of his estate maye be sequistred there in there hands that his estate is in For me to sequer me tell mr. Foxcraft hath disingaged me here of my bondes and discharg me. when you here by my letter to my kinsman how I becam bound For him you will say tise verry eaquall and Just that I should be sequried by his Estate there   I spare to writ you newse For the passengrs will Ralate to you by word of mouth better then I shall write   for present I rest yours to vse

JOSHUA FOOT

DEED OF JOHN WINTHROP TO JOHN WINTHROP, JR.[1]

This present writinge Testifieth, that I Jo: Winthrop of Boston in Newe England esqr. for and in consideration and satisfaction of one hundred and fifty pounds parte of a greater summe due from me to Jo: Winthrop my eldest sonne, have given granted bargained and sould vnto the said John my sonne All that my farme or parcell of land lying vpon Concorde River about three miles beneath the Towne containinge twelue hundred Acres which was granted me by the Generall Court in (3) mo: 1638 and also one parcell of meadowe adioyning containing about sixty acres more or lesse, granted vnto me allso by the Court in [*blank*] 1639. And allso all that parcell or necke of land now inclosed parte of my farme in Charlton called Tenhills lying ouer against the oyster banck, conteyning about thirty acres more or lesse. To have and to hould all the said lands and premises with their Appurtenances vnto the said Jo: Winthrop my sonne and Eliz: his wife during their liues, the remainder to Fitz John their eldest sonne and his heires forever. Provided allways and Reserved out of this present Grant vnto me the said Jo: Winthrop Marg[are]t my wife for the Terme of our liues and the longer liver of vs one third parte of all such fruit as shalbe yearly growinge vpon the said necke of lande. In witnesse of the premises I have heervnto sett my hand and seale dated this 22 of 7ber 1643

JO: WINTHOP

Sealed and deliuered in the presence of
     JO: ENDECOTT
     THO: FOWLE

[*Endorsed:*] Enrolled the 22° of the 7° Mo. 1643 per me

WILLIAM ASPINWALL *Rec*[*orde*]*r*

---

[1] W. Deeds, 30; *Sketch of John Winthrop the Younger*, 33.

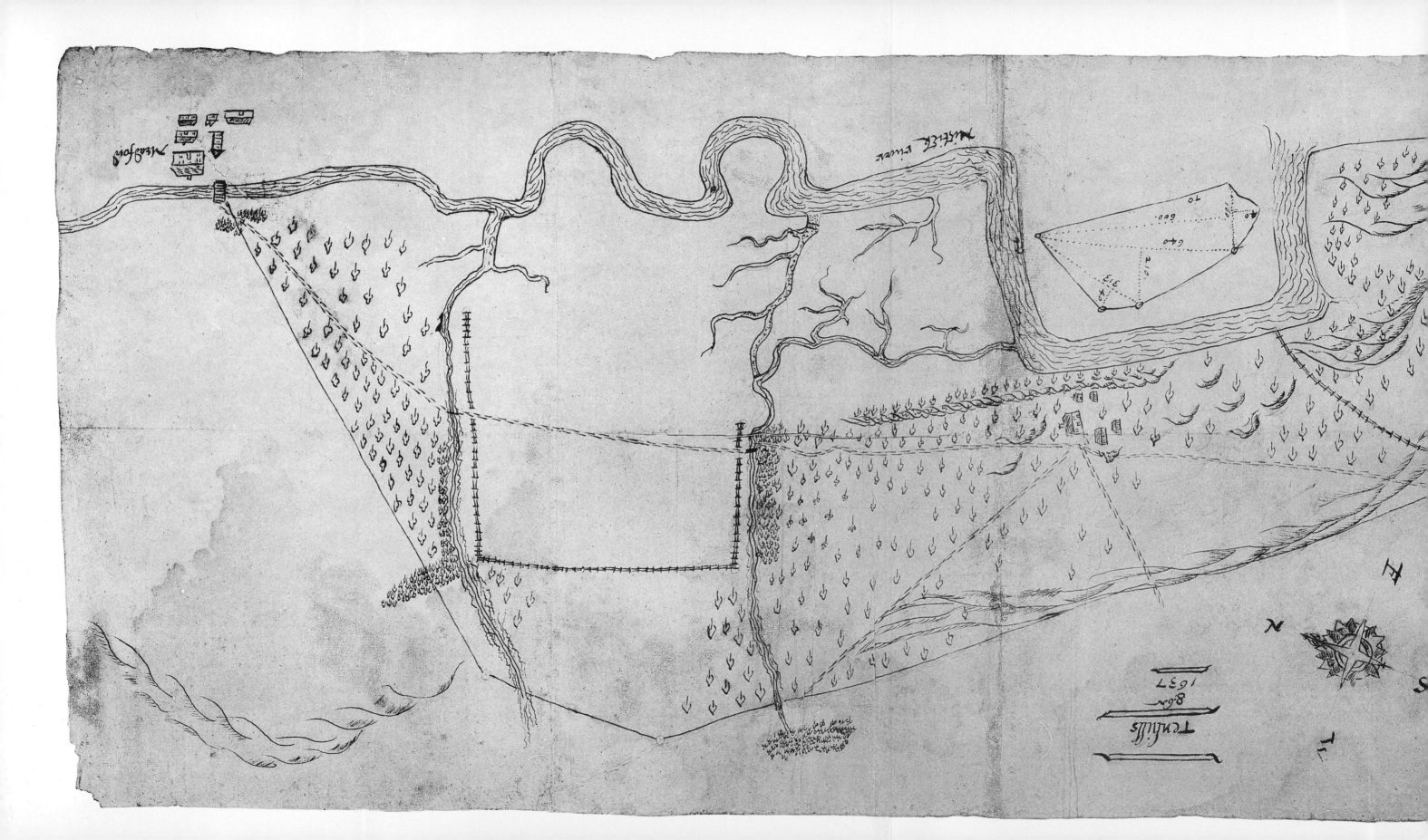

16   48   80   112   144

32   64   96   128   160

Scale of Perches.

JOHN ENDECOTT TO JOHN WINTHROP[1]

DEEREST SIR, I heard nothing further of Glocester busines till the 3d day of this week at euen, when I receaued a letter from Mr. Blinman, together with a complaint of the towne against Griffens companie for severall misdemeanours, And at the foote of the complaint a referrence from your selfe and 3 other Magistrates to mee for the redress of them. I therefore dispatched away a messenger betimes the next morninge with a letter to Mr. Griffen, that hee would send me such of his crew whose names I had vnderwritten his letter, to answere to the misdemeanours of Sabbath breaking swearing and drunkennes: And withall I sent a letter with instructions to Mr. Blinman with a warrant addressed to the constable. That if Mr. Griffen would not send his crew, that the Constable should attach their persons, and bring them before mee: If they did resist or refuse, not to striue with them nor to vse any provoking termes, but to take witnes of their cariadge and to returne mee an answere; which heere I haue sent you inclosed. I would haue proceeded against them according to your former directions (to wit) with force: but I had rather if you see good try first an other way, which is to send a prohibition, vnder your and diuers of the Magistrates hands besides forbidding Mr. Steephens and the rest of the ship carpenters there, or any other within this Jurisdiccion vpon some penaltie, not to worke a stroke of work more vpon Mr. Griffens shippe till they had further order from the governour, etc. I desire therefore to heare from you what you would haue done. In the meane tyme I haue written away another Letter to Mr. Griffen, wishing him to counsell his men (if he cannot commaund them) to submitt to authoritie, seeing they stand out to their owne losse and disaduantage. What the returne will be, You shall heare assoone as I can send it.[2]

I pray you good Sir let mee be excused from comming to this Court, for I am not fitted for Winter Journeyes, and for such bad wayes as we must passe.

I reioyce much to heare of your sonnes Iron and steele   If the Country will not be incouraged by so vsefull a designe, to inlardge themselues for the aduancing of it, I know not what will.

The Lord our good God in mercie keepe you and yours to whose grace I committ you and euer rest Yours truely and vnfeignedly

Jo: ENDECOTT

SALEM, the 1 10 mo. 1643

[1] Massachusetts Archives, CCXL; *Hutchinson Papers* (1769), 134–135; (1865), I. 149–150.
[2] At an Essex County quarterly court held December 27, 1643, Griffin was presented "for swearing by the name of God," and Philip Thorne, Griffin's mate, was presented "for swearing and drink-

I ame glad to heare of your sonne Mr. Steevens safe returne, together with his beloued   I desire to be kindly remembred to them both.

JOHN HAYNES TO JOHN WINTHROP[1]

*To the Right Wor[shipfu]ll Jno. Winthrop Esqr. Gover[nou]r of the Mattatusetts
these present*

WORTHY SIR, The late and last Newes from our native country comparing thinges together, seemes verry sadd and calls for our deepest humiliacion, and serious improovement of our best interest in heaven, by lifting vpp our cryes for the Remnant that is left in these Southerne parts therfor our thoughts are vnanimously to observe A day once every month, to seeke the lord in the behaulfe of his poore Churches ther and elsewher.[2] We should be right glad of your concurrence if it may seeme good to yow, vntill we have further ti-dinges. Ther is lettres come as yow well know from ho[no]rabl[e] persons, to invite Mr. Cotton Mr. Hooker and Mr. Damport   We heare your selves cannot thinke it A meete season for the sending Mr. Cotton, and I suppose, although we have not yett mett for A full determinacion, yett in all proba-bility it will fall ther alsoe with vs, for times being soe hazardous, difficult enough to distinguish frinds from foes, Haven Townes daily taken one each side, and that which is more the maine busines for which they are cheifly called, already sett in such A way, that they being trew to ther owne princi-ples, may rather become A stumble then otherwis   The newes heere of the Indians is and that for certeine that both the Naragansetts and Sequasson have of late sent A quantity of wampham to the Mowhawkes to hire them to fight with the English and Mohegans, and it is said they have preveiled with them to come downe for that purpose, which if it proove soe, they deale not fairely with the English (the Naragansetts I meane) having promised to be peaceable and quiett. if it please yow therfor to acquaint them with what you heare, and to tell them what they doe by ther wampham is as if they did it with ther owne hands and wilbe soe taken, hapily such a messadge in time may prevent A future inconvenience. Ther is A party whose name is Peter Barnefeild that was lately at fisher Iland A carpenter who with the Bartletts heertofor built yow A barne, one knowen to your selfe, hath feloniously

---

ing to excess." *Essex County Quarterly Court Records,* I. 58–59. Other entries in the court records for that date almost certainly relate to other members of Griffin's crew.

[1] W. 2. 142; 4 *Collections,* VI. 356–357.

[2] Cf. *The Public Records of the Colony of Connecticut,* J. Hammond Trumbull, Editor, I (Hartford, 1850), 99.

carryed away and embeseled the goods of Tho: Stanton to the valew of 20*li* and more, who is now at the Bay and purposes to escape away to Engl: It is desired by my selfe and Tho: Stanton that yow would be pleased to cause him to be aprehended, and forthcominge to answear the same.

Thus not doubtinge of your readines out of your love to justice I rest Yours to serve in the lord

JO: HAYNES

HARTF[ORD] the 1st of the 10th mo: 1643

JOHN MASON TO JOHN WINTHROP[1]

To the righte wor[shi]p[fu]ll John Winthroppe Esqr. theis in Boston be Presented with trust

RIGHT WOR[SHI]P[FU]LL, I would not willingly neglect that serv[ice] I owe only in a word there are strong plottings and endevours, not only by Sowquasson and the Indians in our parts but allsoe by the Nannogansetts to procure the Mowhauks to come against vs; haueing sent them such quantities of wampom from all parts as is almost incredible   the Nannogans: haue lately sent three basketts. The men that carryed it retorned last week   the thing certaine beyond scruple, and it is acknowledged by the Indians whoe are frinds to them that theire intendments and resolucons are as well against thenglish as the Monhege only they are not yet resolued how to proceed, viz: whether to fall vpon our plantacions when men are at worke or on the Lords day in time of meeting or to come in a frindly way and cease on our Sachems as they terme them; but for my parte I belieue they will hardly dare to vndertake such an enterprize but that I leaue to god. However it will not thank the Indians in generall; the Dutch are still in straights by reason of the quarrell with the Indians. Captain Pattrick lately invited the Dutch to come with some force against the Indians that liued neare him whoe sent aboue 100 Dutch and Eng: vnder the comand of one Backster an Eng: man. Capt. Pattrick haueing dealt vnder hand with the Indians as is generally conceiued to get wampom deluded the Dutch and whyles they weare wandring with his blynd guide to seeke the Indians he enterteined some of them in his house; on the morrow the Dutch retorned to Capt. Pattricks and findinge the Ind: there weare much trobled   how matters weare carried I know not but one of the Dutch shott Capt. Pattrick in the head with a pistoll that he died

---

[1] W. Au. 106; 4 *Collections*, VII. 411–412. For Mason, see *D.A.B.*

forthwith. The partie was deliuered by their leader to the Eng: at Rippo-
waunce, who was kept as we heare at Capt. vnderhill and being sent for from
Newhauen made escape that night: I haue not time to enlarge, and therfore
I cease comending you to the Lord and rest ever Your wor[shi]ps to comand

JOHN MASON

WINDSOR this 1 (10) 43

I would intreat your wor[shi]p to acquaint Mr. Dudley with these things.

RICHARD VINES TO JOHN WINTHROP[1]

*To the right wor[shipfu]ll his honored Freind John Winthorpe Esqr.
Governour of the Massachusetts Collony These Boston*

RIGHT WOR[SHIPFU]LL, Yours rec[eiued] about Mr. Scott his busines, who
I perceiue is much greived at the late proceedings in our court, in regard we
put his case to a Jury, it being our course to determine such cases by the
bench. Now we may if the parties agree try any accion by a Jury. The
reason why we proceeded soe in this case and others, was to giue a speedy
end to our court, which had held long to the greate charge and trouble of
the country. the busines that held vs were of no validity or consequence, yet
I was fully determined to haue ended Mr. Scotts busines my selfe, before any
tryall, if John Richards had bin present, but he appeared by attourney, as
Mr. Scott did   Two ministers attourneyes, both Plantife and defendant did
soe over value there case in there pleadings, that the bench could not presently determine the case according to mr. Jenners desire who would not stay
for an end of it till the morrow morneing, the tryall being within little of
night, and I had two long myles home and some aboue three, where vpon I
intreated him to referr it till the next court   in the meane tyme it might be
otherwise ended, which he would not consent vnto, but left his papers with
our recorder to see an end of the busines, the next day. now I conceiue it had
bin Mr. Jenners part to haue attended the court till Sentence had bin given
as well as the Comissioners attended for that busines aboue halfe a day. The
truth is the over pleading the case especially by such men, from whose
mouthes all men expected serious truths, (and not lawier like Cavills) which
made the moale hill seeme a mountayne, and we the commissioners and
magistrates, hearing such great damages demanded on both sides thought

[1] W. 3. 94; 4 *Collections*, VII. 343–344.

it fitt to haue some tyme to debate and scan the case before wee did determine it. now our recorder motioned that there might be a Jury empanelled to end this and other triviall accions (as is before specified), to which we all consented and with vs a better attourney then Mr. Jenner, but he was loth to pleade the case, and both the foreman and all the rest of the jury heard the case pleaded. Thus haue you heard the reason of our proceedings, but I must confesse I blamed the Jury for giving such great damages; my iudgement was ever that the Plantife would recover some smale damage, all thought that Whites receipt for all the mouldes would help the defendant at the common law, but the Chauncery would releiue the Plan[ti]ff, for that the def[endant] hath acknowledged that he had some of the mouldes afterward, and made vse of them and our is a mixt court, consisting of chauncery and common law both.

As for a reveiwe of the case, I must desire your Counsell therein, for since I received your letter I heare that exicution is served vpon Mr. Scott his house at Cape Porpus and possession taken for Richards. I proffess, Sir, It was contrary to my knowledge for I never intended but to haue respited iudgement for a while. I confesse I haue bin very bad in my sence of hearing, but in our Court I did dilligently waite vpon all mens lipps, and I canot remember that ever a motion [was] made for exicution by the Plantife. And I may iustly comeplayne of some wrong don me by Mr. Gorges, who left the provinciall Seale with Mr. Gard our recorder. I beinge for the present both Chancellour and Steward Generall; that is the cause that busines passe without my knowledge, and I haue had no opportunity this winter to write to Accominticus to know the carriage of this busines. If you can advise me in any course I shall gladly embrace your advise and be thankefull for it. I know no way but that Mr. Scott must put in his bill of errors which if the court approue of he may haue a new tryall. I am very vnwilling to committ any error against my neighbour, but if any be, I will endevour to amend it, knowing where iustice is equally distributed, the Repub. is happie. Thus craving pardon for my tediousnes with my best service remembred to you and yours, I rest in hast, your vnfeynedly to doe you service

RICH: VINES

SACO first of December 1643

GEORGE SMYTHE TO JOHN WINTHROP[1]

To the Right Wor[shi]p[fu]ll John Wintroope Esquire Governour of the Massetusets at his howse in Boston these deliver

RIGHT WOR[SHIPFU]LL, Whereas yow were pleased to grante Comission vnto Capt. Thomas Wiggin Mr. Francis Williams and myselfe with others, for the executinge the office of magistracie in these partes,[2] now for as much as Mr. Williams hath taken a voyage vnto Virginia, Capt. Wigin and myselfe reste verie doubtfull (we hauinge noe copies of the said Comission) whether we maye call a Courte for tryall of such accions heare dependinge without Mr. Williams or some other Comissioner to ioyne with vs, and therefore I desire that your wor[shi]pp woulde be pleased to certifie either Capt. Wiggin or my selfe, what we may doe concerninge this matter: Thus beinge bolde to trouble you with these few lines I humblie take my leave and reste Your wor[shi]ps to comande to power

GEORGE SMYTHE

DOVER 2 of the xth 1643

post script. In case yf two maye not keep a Courte as is aboue specified I humblie desire that your wor[shi]pp woulde be pleased that one of the Comissioners in the Massetusets maye come hither at the begininge of Aprill nexte, for heare are sundrye pipestaves and Clapboord attached, soe that neither the compl[ainants] nor defend[ant]s can make any vse of the same before the Courte haue taken order therein, and yf noe course be taken about them in Aprill, yt wilbe a preiudice to both complain[an]t and defend[ant].

PETITION OF JOHN WINTHROP, JR., TO THE MASSACHUSETTS GENERAL COURT[3]

TO THE GOVERNOUR MAGISTRATS AND DEPUTIES OF THE HONORED COURT THE HUMBLE PETITION OF JOHN WINTHROP JUNIOR

Humbly sheweth that wheareas these plantacions much abounding with rockie hills the nurceries of mynes and mineralls may probablie conteyne

[1] W. 4. 118; 5 *Collections,* I. 329–330.
[2] Cf. *Records of Massachusetts,* II. 37.
[3] W. I. 153. This document is a contemporary copy in an unidentified handwriting. For the action of the General Court on a later petition, see *Records of Massachusetts,* II. 61.

not only the most necessarie mynes of Iron (which some with much Cost and Difficultyes haue attempted, and in a good measure accomplished to the great benefitt of these plantacions) but alsoe with mynes of lead, tynne, Copper, and other metalls noe lesse profitable to the Countrye, which requires the assistance of manie ingenious heads hands and full purces, minerall matters being slow in growth and heavy in managing, And all necessaries as men skilfull in finding mynes, contriving watercourses stamping mills, ingens for drawing water, refynings, washings etc. being to be procured from farr with much chardge and the vent verie hasardous in all places, espetiellie here where hands require more then ordinarie incouradgement, and the vaynes of these metalls hardly to be found espetiallie in wildernesses, because for the most parte they are imbowelled deepe in their mother earth and often passe through places even impenitrable;

Your peticoner therefore being desirous to promote the publique good in this and to incouradge all men that are willing to spend their tyme and hasard their stockes and labours in these minerall afayres; (the speediest wayes as he supposeth to advance staple Comodityes) he humblie entreates that libertie may be graunted to him and his assignes to search for these mynes in all places within this Jurisdiction, and the same being found, to digg and cary away and dispose thereof for the best advantadge;

And that your peticoner may haue libertie to make wayes and watercourses and to cutt wood for building and coaling, likewise to digg stone, earth, sand etc. in land impropriated giving full satisfaction to the proprietours as three indifferent men shall award, one to be chosen by your peticoner or his assignees the other by the owner of the land the third by the Court; and soe the land to be confirmed to him and his assignes   And that the stock may be free from all publique charges and the labourers freed as in the graunt to the Ironworks with other freedoms, Monopolies only excepted, which he desier not   And lastly if he shall fynde any myne in wast land, that then the same with the land adioyning necessarie for the works be graunted to him his heires and assignees, and when there shalbe a plantation advanced thereon, that then the preveleges of a plantacion may be graunted to them And he shall accept of any person within this Jurisdiction that desires to adventure in this Discovery and prosecuting for these mynes and mineralls soe as he putt in his adventure within six moneths after the grant hereof provided yt be not lesse then fifty poundes in one mans name.

[John Winthrop]

[*Ca.* 1644]

PETITION OF JOHN WINTHROP, JR., TO PARLIAMENT[1]

THE HUMBLE PETITION OF JOHN WINTHROP THE YOUNGER OF NEW ENGLAND TO THE HONORABLE HOUSES OF PARLIAMENT

Sheweth that wheras your petitioner having in Newengland at his great charge searched the country and discovered Iron Ore in divers parts of that country, and made a voyage thence in to England on purpose to procure workemen and materialls for setting vp Iron works in the said place, which might be very beneficiall not only for that plantation, but also to this kingdome, and wheras said petitioner on [*blank*] of may 1643 did at great costs and charges imbarque himself with many workmen servants and materialls for the said setting vp of Iron workes in the said place, in the good ship the An Cleeve of London and the said ship lien with hir goods and passengers many daies at Gravesend to be cleered, was at length, with other ships in company cleered by the officers there apointed, and was on the next day ready with all hir passengers on board to set saile, for hir intended voyage; the said ship was againe when she was setting saile stopped and hindered by one Robinson an officer at Gravesend and wheras the other ships which were cleered at the same tyme did sett saile, and were in the Downes the next day after, your petitioners ship being so stopped, and hindered, was afterward kept in by an Easterly wind, which blew very fresh and continued so long that it might have carried our said ship, by gods assistance cleere of the coast of England and well into the sea onward of hir voyage, (it being the fairest wind could blow for that voyage) your petitioner, having beene vniustly deprived of this oportunity was afterward in the said ship kept above six weekes vpon the coast of England, and by reason thereof was above 14 weekes before he could attaine the port in Newengland, and forced to be at sea all the heat of summer, to the danger of the lives of your petitioner and all his workmen and servants, being all of vs dangerously sick of feavors in the latter part of our voyage, and so weakened that his said servants and workemen were not fitt for any labor or imployment when they came ashore, and it being neere winter before your petitioner arrived, he is hindered from proceeding in the said Iron workes, and is forced to keepe his workmen and servants at great wages and charge without imployment, and thus by this vniust hinderance of your petitioner in his intended voyage at that tyme at Gravesend your

[1] W. 5. 203; 5 *Collections*, VIII. 36–37.

petitioner is damnified in the proceed his intended workes and above 1000*li*
and doth therfore pray for redresse of this his great iniury and losse etc.

[JOHN WINTHROP]

[*Ca.* 1644]

[*Endorsed by John Winthrop, Jr.:*] my petition to Parlament about Robinson
stopping at Gravesend.

REPORT OF JOHN WINTHROP, JR., ON POSSIBLE SITES FOR IRONWORKS[1]

Although this place at Braintre (wherof we have had consultation for the
setting vp of the Ironworke) was principally in my thoughts (in respect of
the Ironston) both before I went into England and since my last arrivall
heere, for the fittest and most convenient place for the first setting vp of an
Iron worke, yet being a worke of consequence, I conceived it necessary to
have other places searched and this place well veiwed, and considered of by
the workemen, both for the vre and the conveniency of waters for furnass
and forge, and woods for supply of coales for both workes.

Therfore after my arrivall heere assoone as it pleased God that I recovered
from that sicknesse which I tooke at sea in some measure and the workmen
also had recovered their health, I tooke them along with me to search in
such parts of the country as by information from others or upon veiw, had
probability of good Ironston. We went first to braintre and so towards Plimoth, and at Greensharbour we found of the same sort of Ironston that was
at Braintre, but could not perceive that it lay in any other but loose stones:
and being among very thick woods in a swa[m]ppy ground; after we re-
tu[rned] thence I went with the miner to Richman Iland, and veiwed all
the parts betweene that and the massachusett, it having beene affirmed confidently that both at Pascataway and Agamenticus there was Ironston and
great store that triall had beene made of it in England by some sent to
Bristol and some to London to Captaine Mason: Also at Sako and at Black-
point it was informed that there was certainly great quantity of very good
mine in those places: In divers of these places we saw some stones that certainly doe conteine Iron in them but in the Judgement of the miner are but
poore of Iron and doubtfull how they will worke none of our workemen
having seene ever such before: in those parts are very few inhabitants, and

[1] W. I. 161; 2 *Proceedings*, VIII. 13–14.

labourers hard to be obteined for their ordinary occasions and at deare rates. there is an other place about 30 miles westward vp in the country which the workmen have likewise viewed and where there is of the same sort of Ironston that is at Braintre but noe appearance of quantity (though great probabilitie) there is yet noe people dwelling though present intention of plantation.

This sort of vre at Braintre is of the same sorte which they call in Ireland the Bogge mine. we have tried of it since we came over from divers places, and the finer hath made good Iron out of it divers tymes, that which we sent into England was made of that from Braintre. there is of the same sort at severall places neere Greensharbour at Nashaway, at Cohasset, at Woburne, and many other places, but the most appearance of hopefull quantity is at Braintre, according to the Judgement of the workmen, who vpon search affirme that it lieth like a veine (which is not in the other places) and that there is likelihood of ynough for a furnasse for 20 yeares: There are 2 places which by the Judgement of the workmen, are convenient for furnasse and forge, but all the ground neere about them is laid out to particular men as also where the mine is, and cannot be obteined but by purchasse. In the common which wilbe above a mile from any of the workes, Boston hath determined to allot 3000 acres to belong to the worke if we sett it vp in that parte that belongeth to their towne and Dorchester etc.

Now heere I desire your serious advice what is to be done for the most advancement of the worke and profitt of the adventurers: whether to goe to some of those remote places where eyther the same sort of Ironston is, or probabilities of other as good or better, where the land may be had next to the workes and as much as may be needfull.

or to beginne heere at Brantre which wilbe in the heart of all the English colonies   if the former be thought best: then there must be a beginning in way of plantation, houses must be first built workmen of all sorts must be carried from these parts and plant themselves there, great store of draft cattle must be provided and the greatest part of our stock expended in such occations before we begin:

If braintre be thought best this helpes   we shall have workmen of all sorts more plenty and neere at hand teemes for carriage may be hired housing for our workmen conveniently neere to be hired and wood ynough for present to be procured neere by purchase, and for future to belong to the works to be fetched further of etc.

Therefore necessity seemes to drive vs to accept of this place.

[*Ca.* 1644]

[*Endorsed by John Winthrop, Jr:*] discourse about the fittest place to begin the Iron workes.

PETITION OF JOHN CHADWICK TO THE COURT OF ASSISTANTS[1]

To the Right Worshipfull the Governour and Maiestrates the humble petition of John Chaddocke

May it plese your Worships fauorably to consider the greate loss by mee lately sustayned[2] the greate charge I am at in settinge oute againe And the large expence of so longe a stay whereby I am mutch disabled to discharge that fine layed vpon mee;[3] And knowing that you ayme at the punishing of vise and not Lucre of gaine I humbly disire your Worships to consider the premises and Remitt, as in your Wisdomes shall bee thoute good; And I shall acknowledge my selfe Your Worships obliged seruant

JOHN CHADDOCKE

[*Ca.* January, 1643/44]

[*Endorsed by Governor Winthrop:*] Capt. Chaddock, Pet[itio]n to the Co: Ass[istan]ts.

EDWARD WINSLOW TO JOHN WINTHROP[4]

To the right w[orshi]pp[fu]ll his much honored Friend Joh. Winthrop Esqr. Gover[nour] of the Mass[achusetts] these be delivered

WORTHY SIR, Another opportunity offering it self I can do no lesse then write, hoping I am not trowblesom therein, for if I be I should be much more if I lived neer you in often discourse. Since the receipt of yours who intimate enlargement if time had permitted, I understand by mr. Prence who had it from an Indian of good esteem amongst them, that the Narr. prepare for war, that the Mowhakes haue promised to aide them with a thowsand men in the spring, that when they come neer they will make a

---

[1] W. 4. 168; 5 *Collections*, I. 492. Chadwick was the son of Captain Thomas Chadwick, who had been Governor of Bermuda, 1637–1640.
[2] I.e., by the blowing up of his ship in Boston Harbor. See *Journal*, II. 153.
[3] Cf. *Journal*, II. 150–151; *Records of the Court of Assistants*, I. 135.
[4] W. 2. 92; 4 *Collections*, VI. 174–176.

stand, that so Vncas may haue notice of it; whereupon they conceiue he will flie to the English; that done they purpose to send a message to the Engl. and demand Vncas; and as they receiue answere so to proceed. Since this we heare from the Dutch that they haue an army of an 120 men Engl. and Dutch ag[ainst] the Indians. These seeke them and haue slaine 20 Indians with the losse of 2 Engl. they haue also taken 4 Indian prisoners whom they make per force to be their guides. That Captain Patrick is slaine by a Dutch man being probably suspected to haue a hand in directing the Indians in their late mischiefe, The manner thus, Patrick having holpen them to an Indian guide to bring them to a Fort, led them amis the whole night, at day knowing where they were, went again to Patricks howse, where a Dutch man called Patrick traytor. he returned the lie and spet in the Dutch mans face whereat he bent his pistoll and shot him in the head so as he fell down dead and never spake more: the delinquent was committed to the safe custody of Capt. Vnderhill but since escaped.

Concerning Morton, our Gover[nor] gaue way that he should winter heer, but begon as soon as winter breaks up. Capt. Standish takes great offence theerat esp[ecially] that he is so neer him at Duxburrow and goeth sometimes a fowling in his ground. he cannot procure the lest respect amongst our people liveth meanely at 4s per week and content to drinke water so he may dyet at that price. But admit he hath a proteccion yet it were worth the while to deale with him till we see it. The truth is I much question his pretended employment: for he hath heer onely shewed the Frame of a Common weale and some old sealed Commissions, but no inside knowne. As for mr. Rigby if he be so honest good and hopefull an Instrument as report passeth on him he hath good hap to light on two of the arrantest known knaues that ever trod on new English shore to be his Agents East and West as Cleves and Morton but I shall be jealous on him till I know him better and hope others will take heed how they trust him who investeth such with power who haue devoted them selues to the ruine of the Countrey, as Morton hath   And for my part (who if my hart deceiue me not can passe by all the evill instrumentally he brought on me) would not haue this serpent stay amongst us who out of doubt in time will gett strength to him if he be suffered who promiseth large porcions of land about Newhaven Narrohigg[anset] etc. to all that will goe with him but hath a promise but of one person who is old weake and decrepid a very athiest and fitt companion for him: but indeed Morton is the odium of our peop[le] at present, and if he be suffered (for we are diversly minded) it will be just with God who hath putt him in our hands and we will foster such an one that afterward we shall suffer for it. But the messenger cals for my letter and I must breake off, and therefore saluting you in the Lord take leaue and remaine Yours ever to be commanded

EDW: WINSLOW

CARESWELL 7 (11) 43[/44]

I pray you Sir in your next write whether ever the message were sent to the Mowhakes, and as you haue occasion salute our Friends at Conect[icott] and New H[aven] from me, and if you judge any of these things materiall impart it.

[*Memorandum by Governor Winthrop:*] Jo: Downam   Wm. Latham his wife at Duxbury.

RICHARD VINES TO JOHN WINTHROP[1]

To the right wor[shipfu]ll his much honored freind John Winthorpe Esqr.
Governour of the Massachusetts Colony These Boston

RIGHT WOR[SHIPFU]LL, I am forced to complayne vnto you of diverse insufferable wrongs don vnto Sir Ferdinando Gorges, his Commissioners and Province, by Mr. Cleiues and his agent, Mr. Tucker, who report that yow protect and countenance there exorbitant practices, which I canot beleiue, for I never yet knew you giue the least encouragement to any sinister practice. Mr. Cleaues having perswaded Mr. Rigby, a worthy gent[leman] (by report) to buy the Plough Patent,[2] which I esteeme no better then a broken tytle, by Mr. Rigby his authority, (and as he sayes by your approbacion,) he hath nominated Comissioners, a Coronell Generall, Provost Marshall, and other officers, extending his goverment from Sackadehock to Cape Porpus, being aboue 13 leagues in lenght, haueing likewise appoynted a Court to be kept in Cascoe bay the 25th of March next, and hath (but this by past weeke) sent his agent Tucker with a paper perswading all such as he findes any way inclyning to innovation, to sett there handes to it, for the better approving of what they haue begun, and allsoe to intreate your wor-[shi]p and the rest of your magistrates to defend them from French, Indians, and other enemyes, which wee construe to be Sir Fard: Gorges Commissioners. neither hath Cleiues, (as he ought) presented any his authority at

---

[1] W. 3. 94; 4 *Collections*, VII. 346–348; *G.S.*, II. 233–237.
[2] For an account of the dispute which ensued between Rigby and Gorges as a result of Rigby's purchase of the Plough Patent, see 4 *Collections*, VII. 90*n.*–91*n.*

our last generall Court but 2 dayes before our Court tooke a vioage into the bay, and all the way as he went from Pascataquack to Boston, he reported he was goeing for ayde against mee, for that I had threatned him, and his authority, to beate him out of this Province. by this false report, and many other the like, I am held an enemy to iustice and piety. Sir, I proffesse vnto you ingeinously I never threatned him directly nor indirectly, neither haue I seene him since he came out of England. I haue suffered him to passe quietly through our plantacion, and to lodge in it, allthought I haue binn informed that he was then plotting against mee. I am troubled at these seditious proceedings; and much more at his most notorius scandalls of Sir Ferdinando Gorges, a man for his age and Integrity worthy of much honor. him he brandes with the foule name of traytor by curcumstance, in reporting that he hath counterfeited the Kings broade Seale, (if he haue any Patent for the Province of Mayne,) For, sayes he I haue serched all the Courtes of Record, and can finde noe such grant. how could he haue giuen that graue knight a deeper wound in his reputacion, the which I know is more deare to him then all the wealth in America. he likewise still maynetaynes his false report of his death, in his Flight into Walles, notwithstanding a letter dated the 25th of 7ber last from a marchant in london of very good credit, and brought in Mr. Payne his Ship, which letter imports Sir Ferd: Gorges his good health, with the restauracion of his possesions agayne. sir, I haue made bould to lay open our grevances, desiring you to take them into your graue Consideracion, hoping if wee be forced to take such courses with Cleiues, as the necessity, and the equity of our cause requires, you will not thinke wee haue don amisse in it. Yett we will (if possibly we may) forbeare till I heare from you. Now for the Patent that Mr. Rigby hath bought, it is not from our kings ma[jes]tie as Cleiues reportes, but from the President and Counsell of New-England, as myne and others are wherein Mr. Rigby hath from there L[ordshi]ps Jura regalia but his ma[jes]tie takes that away by his royall grant to Sir Ferd: Gorges bearing date the third of Aprill in the fifteenth yeare of his highnes raigne. Now I conceiue Mr. Rigby his agent is but to recover soe much land as the grant specifies, and to relinquish there Jura regalia, as you may perceiue in the last Clawse of our grant herewith sent you.[1] I am very confident that Sir Ferd: Gorges hath not as yett disposed of

[1] The extract from the grant to Sir Ferdinando Gorges which Vines sent to Governor Winthrop (W. 3. 95; 4 *Collections*, VII. 348–349) is as follows:

"Neverthelesse our intent and meaninge is, that out of the premisses hereby granted or mencioned to be granted, there shalbe alwayes saved and reserved to all and every such person, and persons as haue or hath any lawfull grant or graunts of landes or Plantacions lawfully setled in the division and premisses aforesaide, the free holding and enioyeing of his and there right, with the libertyes there vnto

his lands here, for without question he would haue given notice of it to his Commissioners, and therefore we ought not vpon the bare reporte of Cleiues to relinquish either his right of possesions or goverment. Yet I did ever, and doe intend, whensoever Mr. Rigby shall send over People to lett them settle peaceably, to ayde and assist them To the best of my power, without questioning of meum et tuum; For this I know, if Sir Ferdinando Gorges and Mr. Rigby meete, all matters wilbe quietly ended, if there be no Incendiaries here. I will endeavour for peace soe far forth as I doe not betray the trust confided in me, by my honored Freind and quondam master. I haue ever found you my worthy freind far beyound my deservings, and haue therefore freely applyed my selfe vnto you, vnto whom I am ever obleiged to remayne your faythfull freind and servant

RICH: VINES

Saco the 9th of January 1643[/44]

Good Sir, present my humble service to your vertuous wife.

[*Endorsed by Governor Winthrop:*] Mr. Vines about mr. Cleves and a Copy of some parte of the prouince Patent. Rec: (1) 8, 1643[/44].

BENEDICT ARNOLD TO JOHN WINTHROP[1]

To his much hounour'd Go[verno]r of Massachusetts Mr. Winthrop at his House these bee delivered In Boston

Much hounoured Sir, vpon occassione of a letter, which, (this mourning) I received by an Indian, From mr. Collucott of Dorchester, I now make bold to send vnto you these few lines; he wrote vnto mee that ther is reports brought by indians, of many thousands of Mow-hoaugs, which (they say) ar come to Nanheaganssitt, and further he wrote that the Counsell willed him to send to mee to inquire concerning the matter, and what they ar com aboute: Now I conceive that such rumors may be preiudiciall to the Country, and therefore although I many times have heard the indians bring many of

appertayning, he and they relinquishing and layeing downe his and ther Jura regalia, (if he, or they haue any,) to the said Sir Ferdinando Gorges his heires and assignes, whome wee haue hereby made proprietour of the province, division and premises aforesaid, and payeing some small acknowledg-ment to the saide Sir Ferdinando Gorges his heires and assignes. In witnes where of wee haue caused thes our letters to be made Patents. witnes our selfe at Westminster, the third day of Aprill in the fifteenth yeare of our raigne, etc. *Copia vera* RICH: VINES"

[1] Trumbull MSS., M.H.S. For Arnold, see 5 *Collections*, i. 330n.

their vssuall reports, which tended to this effect, yett I have not dared to
devulge the same, by word or writting as things worth either declaring or
heareing: for, except I can see, or gather by circumstances that the reports
they bring have reallity in them, I shall be and have bene farre from reporte-
ing it for truith, least for my vnadvised rashnes, the country might suffer many
charges, and distractions, through such reports. It is true that the Indians
have this winter from time to time spoken to mee that within thus or thus
many days the moquaugs would com downe and eat vp and devoure the
Monaheagans, In defence of the Nanhegansitts liveing, and in revenge of
the sachems dead, slaine by Woncas and his men, but when I have gone
about to make them bring forth the authers of the reports, then they would
either say they had it from the Indians of Massachussett, or from Conicticott,
and then if I asked them further, what the Mockquoags would eat by the
way homewards after they had eat vp all the monahegans, then they would
say little or nothing to mee, but when I sayd further that after the Mockquoags had eaten vp the Mownaheagans, they would goe neare to eat the
Nanheagans allsoe, and the rest of the Indians, then they would looke very
slyly, and say that they wer perswaded that the Mockquags would not com
into these parts, and that it hath ben the maner of the Indians in former tims,
to threaten their enemys that live in these parts, that the mockquogs would
com and eat them, but it was never yett seene that the Mockquoags, much
lesse the Mowhaugs, did ever com into these parts to doe as is reported. yett
I suppose that Nanhegansitt sachems have sent to those Indians that live
above mr. Pinchions vpon Conicticot river, to see if they will Joine with them
against Woncas if need bee, yett I canot absolutly say it is soe, but it is as
likly that the Nanheagansitts have rather sent to the sayd Indians to request
them to sitt still and not help Woncas, as they request the English to Doe;
but I canot relate any of certainty but this last is that which I gather most
probibly, For about 4 or 5 days since There came a messenger to mee From
Canonicus, the old sachem of Nanheagansitt, and the somme of his message
was to this effect that Canonicus was in a sadde conditione at present partely
For the distractions of his country, and more particullerly for the death of
his children, which sayd he ar much deminished, for one of them dyed of a
consumtione about 2 years since, and another was slayne this last sommer in
fight by the monaheagans, and a third sonne dyed about tenne days agoe,
and another (sayd he) of his sonns lyeth now ready to give vp the ghoust etc:
Yett, among these distractions the old man (sayd the messenger) willed mee
to certify you, that wheras there ar rumors among the Indianse that the
Mockquoags wer to Joine with the Nanhegansitts against Woncas, yett ther

was noe such agrement, but the Monaheagens doe as much rumor and talke that the Mockquaugs will Joine with them against the Nanheagansitts, and therfore the Nanheagansitt sachems sent to the hithermost people called the mockquoags, living on Conictiquot River above mr. Pinchions Plantations, to know of them how they stood afected in the case and they sayd little to it, but apointed that within a few days there should com downe some 6 or 10 at most of the sayd Indians to Nanheagansitt, and they would com with Deare skins and other furrs to trade with the Nanheagansitts. Further, he named some of the Indians that wer to com downe whom I know, wherof one is he that I spake of to your worship, that had his Fingers cutt of etc: by the Mowhoaugs the last yeare: who was redeemed by the French etc: and further he (the sayd messenger) told mee that they wer to consider with the sachems of nanheagansitt (when they came) of the differences betwene the Nanheagansitts and Monaheagans: And this was the efect of his message, and the Indians ar not yett com, and when they com, I shall write and send a messenger on purpose to declare vnto your Worship, what I can gather from ther coming, if it be of any wieght, and liklie probabillity. Soe desireing your Worships pardon for writeing soe douptfully and Bouldly: I leave this to your worships consideration, what your wisdome may gather of these things by this relation, and rest your worships humble and ready to be comanded

BENEDICT ARNOLD

I thought good to send you this word, to certify your Worship, that mr. greens wife is dead, about a weeke since.

PROVIDENCE: this 19th of the 11th mo. 1643[/44]

[*Endorsed by Governor Winthrop:*] Ben: Arnold about the Mowhakes etc.

GEORGE CLEEVE TO JOHN WINTHROP[1]

To the honered John Wenthrop Esquire Gouernour thes present

CASCO BAY this 27th of the 11 moneth, 1643[/44]

HONERED SIR, With my most humble sarvice I salute you, accnolidging my duty of thankfullnes to you for all formar favors shewed mee, and whereas

[1] W. 3. 98; 4 *Collections*, VII. 363–365; *G.S.*, II. 238–240. For Cleeve, see 4 *Collections*, VII. 363*n*.; James P. Baxter, *George Cleeve of Casco Bay, 1630–1667* (Portland, Maine, Gorges Society, 1885).

you were plesed at my requst to writ to mr. Vines and othars in behalfe of Mr. Rigbies athority of which I informed him in my last lettars assuring my selfe that hee will not be vnmyndfull to requit your love therein. What mr. Vines answered you I know not, but thus can afferme and proue that by his practis he doth slitly regard your advice therein (as may appere by the supplication of the inhabitants of ligonia and othar passeges the truth whereof this bearar can informe you, as allso of there consultations with Mr. Jurdin a ministar of antichrist, there chefe Counsellar,) who doth not only calumniate and slandar the parliament of England with vile reprochfull termes, as Rebellious factias trayteros parssons against the king, But allso Belteth out his blasfemise against the Churches of Christ in this land, charging them with scisme and faction for fasting and praying for the affliction of there Brethren in England; denying yt to be the hand of god vpon the land for Sinn nor the occation of papist or evell Counssellars, but for the rebellion of the parliament and the puritant faction there, with many othar passeges of that vnworthy Ballitte, of which this bearar Mr. Tuckar can informe you, as allso of Vines his dealings with him and of his thretning to send mee pressonar to England in Mr. Trelanies Ship, which inforseth mee once more to Joyne with the inhabitants of ligonia and humbly to desire your assistanc against there vnlawfull practisses and so much the rathar for there wicked oposition of the ways of Christ. They seing vs about to settle ourselues vndar the ministry, and that wee ar in hope that the lord will gathar a Church amoungst vs, this causeth them and there prelatticall Counsellar to raidg the more, which will insite you to assist vs so much the rathar. I nede not here aquaint you what tytle they pretend to haue from the king allthough we nevar sawe any nor know of any they haue, seing you bettar know then my selfe that the king can not lawfully grant what was formarlie granted by that actte of Counsell established at Plymmoth, to whose bettar Judgment I submit, Beseching you to answere the inhabitants petishion and hopefull expectation, committing you to gods holie protextion, Resting evar reddy to sarue your Commands Whilst I am

GEORG CLEEVE

JOHN ENDECOTT TO JOHN WINTHROP[1]

To the Wor[shipfu]ll John Winthrop esqr. Gouvernor deliver

DEAREST SIR, I must needs acknowledge I was somewhat grieued when I heard of Haddock's cariadge to yourselfe, and Mr. Paynes staying abroad that they could not be commanded ashore vpon any occasion. I thought then of Castle Island, that it might be of good vse to controle such Fellowes; But to be any strength to your towne or Countrie I cannot see it. I veriely think that the Countrie will be verie willing that there may be a fort there built at the chardges of the Townes thereabouts:[2] And to vnderstand their willingnes or consent to it, I think it may be done by what is propounded: viz. to send to the Magistrates and Deputies, or if you see good to the magistrates and deputies of the severall shires who may easily come together, without any chardge to the Countrie. We haue heere in Essex appointed a day to meete at Salem viz. the 22th of the next moneth, to consider of some things for the Common Wealth, according to an order of Court. Now then I think it will be soone enough to send in our counsell or consent therein seeing little can be done to the worke in the meane tyme.

I heare you haue great sights upon the water seene betweene the Castle and the Towne: men walking on the water in the night euer since the shippe was blowen vp[3] or fire in the shape of men. There are verie few do beleeue it yet heere is a greate report of it, brought from thence the last day of the weeke.

The maid is now going along with vs to Orchard, where your sonne shall be heartilie welcome.

I ame glad that the Mohaks newes is false. The Lord continew peace unto vs if it be his blessed will to whose grace I committ you, and euer rest Your assured loving Friend and servant.

JO. ENDECOTT

29 of the 11, 1643[/44]

---

[1] William C. Endicott, Jr., MSS., M.H.S.; *Hutchinson Papers* (1769), 135–136; (1865), I. 151.
[2] Cf. *Journal*, II. 155.
[3] I.e., Capt. John Chadwick's ship. Cf. *Journal*, II. 153, 155–156.

RICHARD VINES TO JOHN WINTHROP[1]

To the right wor[shipfu]ll his much honored freind John Wenthorpe Esqr.
Governour of the Massachusetts Colloney These Boston

RIGHT WOR[SHIPFU]LL, I haue formerly sent you two letters, the one in answeare of yours, concer[n]ing the busines of Mr. Scott, the other declaring in part the seditiou[s] and malitious practices of Mr. Cleeues, and Mr. Tucker his agent against the peace and goverment of this Province, and vnder pretence of authority from Mr. Alexander Rigby, a worthy gent[leman] (as I haue bin tould by your Wor[shi]p and others). I presume he will not tollerate any irregular or exorbitant courses either against publique goverment lawfully established, or against perticular persons, for a private revenge. Mr. Cleeues endeavours the ruine of both, as by my former letter to you it is evident. Since which tyme he hath held a court at his house, where were all the refractory men of our Province, and few other. they framed a letter directed to Cleeues and my selfe, telling vs that it was there resolucions (and that they would stand to it) that wee should try our right of goverment before the worthy magistrates of the Massachusetts bay, till it shalbe otherwise made knowne vnto them by a tryall in England, if not, they will stand as newters, and obay neither. this I know to be Cleeues his plott to bring vs all into a distracion, and a mutiny, for he knowes that neither my selfe, nor any other of Sir Ferdinando Gorges Comissioners, haue power to try his title either of land, or power and authority for goverment here, without his authority soe to doe, neither doe I beleiue that your Worship and the rest of your honored Court will medle with any tryall of this nature.

There is likewise by Cleeues a letter of Consosiacion, which I mencioned in my former letter which I haue not seene, but our minister Mr. Jenner, tells mee that the enginere hath soe cunningly contrived it, that all those that have sett there handes to it, for matter of defence against all invasion, haue likewise acknowledged Mr. Rigby to be there governour, being vtterly ignorant of his deceipt therein   Tucker being here 7 dayes since, Mr. Smith our magistrate for Saco, and my selfe examined him vppon the premises; he gaue vs peremtory and abusiue language, wherevpon we asked him for good security for his good abearing, and for his appearance at our next Court. he refusing it, wee comitted him to the marshall   the next day he acknowledged a recognisance of 40*li* for his appearance, and was dismised   he deserved much more, but we forbeare till we heare from your w[orshi]p which I desire

[1] W. 3. 95; 4 *Collections*, VII. 349–351; *G.S.*, II. 240–242.

may be speedily for the preventing of sudden mischeife and mutinous practises. I would haue sent you a copie of there letter to me, but that I heare The
same is comming to you by Tucker, who is goeing for the bay with these
letters seruptitiously gotten, thereby to strenghten there faction, but I hope
your wor[shi]p will seriously in your wisdom consider what I haue written,
and according to the equity of our case, send me your advise. Thus ceasing
furder to trouble you at present, I rest Yours to be commanded to the best of
my power

RICH: VINES

SACO 29th of Jan: 1643[/44]

WILLIAM BRADFORD TO JOHN WINTHROP[1]

*To his much honoured freind Mr. John Winthrop, Gouernour of the Massachusetts,
these deliver*

BELOUED SIR, Hauing so fite an opportunitie, I thought good to salute you
with these few lines. We were much troubled when we heard you kepte
watch in your townes the sharp weather, and so much the reather because
we could not hear the reason therof, nor vnderstand any thing from the
Indeans of our quarters. We haue heard since of some messengers that haue
been sent vnto you; if there be any thing materiall conscerning our comone
saftie, I desire you would be pleased to informe vs in a word or 2 how things
stand aboute the Narigansets or Mowhaks. We allso conceiue that our time
of paimente to you, aboute Mr. Andrews money is expired, and therfore haue
charged a bill on Mr. Hill to make this paymente vnto you. I pray you let
vs hear a word of your acceptance. Sundrie haue been sicke amongst vs this
winter, and some still are. God hath taken away Mr. Atwood, and Mr. Jeney
by death; Mrs. Atwoods state being but low is intangled to Mr. Seawell of
Ipswich, by a bond of 1000*li*. She prayes me on her behalfe to craue your
aduice whether she had best administer or no, her husband haueing made
her exsecutrixe; and if she refuse whether she may not haue her thirds; ther
will be sufficente she conceiues to satisfie any accounte of money due to him,
and some thing for her selfe, but by the bond the title of the land is to be
restored to him, and Mr. Atwood hath sould it to Mr. Sherley, but he tould
me it was only in trust, as he had it, but he tooke no writing vnder his hand

---

[1] Pilgrim Society; 4 *Collections*, VI. 160–161.

that so it is. Thus comending you and all your affairs to the Lord, with salutations, I rest, in hast Your louing friend

WILLIAM BRADFORD

[*Ca.* February, 1643/44]

[*Endorsed by Governor Winthrop:*] Mr. Bradford Rec. (12) 43.

GEORGE CLEEVE TO JOHN WINTHROP AND EDWARD GIBBONS[1]

*To the honered John Wenthrop Esquire and to my loving Frend
Captaine Edward Gibbens of Boston thes present*

HONORED SIR AND LOVING FREND, Whereas the honerable Court of parliament was plesed vpon my petishion presented vnto them, to derect ther honorable ordar vnto you in spetiall, and in Cace of mortality to othars menconed in the said Comishion, to take the answers of partis and wittnesses and the same to returne,[2] the whole prosedings I haue herewith sent, and do humbly desire you to send your warant to cale before you mr. Richard Vines of Sacoe, and Mr. Edward Godfrie of Agamenticous to appere before you at a cartaine day to com, which I conceaue will be most fit, in regard of mens occation of planting to be about the midest of May next, as allso in your warant to requir the apparanc of John Bakar of Pascattaqua, and Frances Robinson of Sacko and Andrew Algar of Strattons Iland as allso John Bonithon, gen. William Royall, and Michell Mitton, and Richard Tucker to proue the artickles, and as I hope you will put in Execution the athority of this honorable Court, so I desire that you will send your warants by this Bearar Mr. Tucker who will with trust deliuar them to the seuarall perssons so sommoned and will make Retorne of there answers that so you may make Retorne of there answers according to the derection of the said ordar, for which as allso for all formar favors I will evar acknowledg my selfe oblidged to be Your humbly Sarvant

GEORG CLEEVE

CASCO BAY the 2th day of the last month 1643[/44]

---

[1] W. 3. 99; 4 *Collections,* VII. 365–366; *G.S.,* II. 243–244.
[2] See *Proceedings and Debates of the British Parliaments Respecting North America,* Leo F. Stock, Editor, I (Washington, 1924), 142–144.

EMMANUEL DOWNING TO JOHN WINTHROP[1]

To his ever honored brother John Winthrop esqr. Governour

Sir, For my Cosen Deanes buisines, I see noe lett nor hindrance but yt may proceede with as much expedition as you please, without any further delay then modesty requireth in such occasions. the portion as I vnderstand is about 200*li* if you be content therewith, I suppose the quality and person of the mayde will not give cause of dislike. I shalbe willing to hasten the dispatch thereof, in hope the sooner to enioye your Company here; I am glad my sister will haue so good an arrand to Groton, for shee is like with Gods blessing to retorne with a modest, quiet and discreet wife for hir sonne and one in whom there is good hope of Grace;

I suppose my Cosen Stephen caryed back the accounts for I cannot yet fynde them. if they come to hand I shall retorne them safe vnto you I feare the lord is offended for sparing the lives of Gorton and his Companions, for if they all be as buisye as this at Salem, there wilbe much evill seed sowne in the Countrye; I hope some of them wilbe brought to tryall next Court for breach of theire order, and if yet you shall spare them, I shall feare a Curse vpon the land.[2] The Good lord direct herein to doe what shalbe pleasing in his sight soe with my love and service to your selfe and all yours I rest your loving brother

Em: Downinge

6. 12. 43[/44]

EDWARD WINSLOW TO JOHN WINTHROP[3]

To the right w[orshi]pp[fu]ll his much honored Friend Joh. Winthrop Esqr. Gov[ernou]r of the Mass[achusetts] these be delivered

Worthy Sir, About a moneth since I wrote to you and now within a few daies it came to my hands againe yet haue I sent it, being glad of the present

---

[1] W. i. 156; 3 *Collections*, i. 15–16.

[2] In October, 1643, Samuel Gorton, who had been charged with being "a blasphemos enemy of the true religion of our Lord Jesus Christ . . . and also of all civill authority among the people of God, and perticulerly in this iurisdiction," had been ordered to be confined in chains at Charlestown during the pleasure of the Court. In the meantime, if he should "either by speach or writing, publish, declare, or maintaine any of the blasphemos or abominable heresies wherewith hee hath bene charged by the Generall Court," he was to be committed to prison, tried before a jury at the next Court of Assistants, and, if convicted, put to death. *Records of Massachusetts*, ii. 51, 52.

[3] Chamberlain Collection, Boston Public Library; 4 *Collections*, vi. 176.

opportunity by mr. Paddy to salute you and all yours in the Lord Jesus   And becawse we would saue your Goverment a labor to send to us for the money due by bond from mr. Bradford my selfe etc. to your Goverment upon Mr. Andrews gift;[1] I haue given mr. Paddy a bill of exchange for the discharge of it, onely becawse I know not the exact sum I haue left a blanck for it, and given him authority to insert it; That so he may take up the bond, upon the delivery of the bill to your selfe.

We heard you were upon your gard but becawse we had no notice from your selfe about it it did not trowble us. We heare you have news from New-haven and Coneetacut. I hope you will impart it to us if there be anithing materiall; however shall be glad to heare of our br[ethre]n there.

Thus with my pr[ayer]s to the Almighty for the continuance and increase of his mercies towards us, humbly take leaue and rest Your assured

EDW. WINSLOW

MARSHFIELD 7 (12) 43[/44]

RICHARD VINES TO JOHN WINTHROP[2]

To the right wor[shipfu]ll his honored freind John Winthope esqr. governour of the Massachusetts Coloney these Boston

RIGHT WOR[SHIPFU]LL, I haue lately written vnto you two letters concern-ing the evell practices of Mr. Cleiues and Mr. Tucker, tending to the ruine of this Province. Now hearing that Tucker is gon to your wor[shi]p with false certificates, at leastwise fraudelently gotten, many haueing sett there handes to they know not what, and besides a greate part of them ar bound over to our Courts for notorious offences, and therefore ar easily perswaded to set there handes to any thing that may be preiudiciall to a peaceable goverment. They reporte that you will ayde them, and Tucker is now gon for that pur-pose, with a letter of consociation, in which Cleiues hath cunningly made all those that haue subscribed to acknowledge Mr. Rigby to be there governour, and yet, in a letter to Cleeues and my selfe from that ignorant route, they will obey neither Sir Ferdinando Gorges, nor Mr. Rigby his authority till there be a tryall for it. this letter is likewise sent to your wor[shi]p with twenty handes to it. You may be pleased to enquire of this bearer Thomas Rogers, what manner of people they ar.

There pretence for ayde is to defend them against the French, but there

---

[1] Cf. Richard Andrews to John Winthrop, July 8, 1639 (pages 129–131, above).
[2] W. 3. 96; 4 *Collections*, VII. 351–352; *G.S.*, II. 244–246.

is no such cause but only to maynetayne there seditious and mutinous practices against Sir Ferdinando Gorges goverment. I shall therefore humbly
intreate your wor[shi]p to consider of my two former letters with this, and
to send me your answear by this bearer and likewise to stop the currant of
Cleeues his illegall proceeding and not to ayde them, till there bee iust cause.
haueing formerly writen at large of this turbulent people vnto you, I cease
farder to trouble at present, resting your assured freind and Servant

RICH: VINES

SACO the 12th of Feb: 1643[/44]

BENEDICT ARNOLD TO JOHN WINTHROP[1]

To the much Hounourd Mr. Winthope Go[vernou]r of Massachusetts Theese deliver

MUCH HONOUR'D SIR, In respect of those Nanheagansitt Indians: which
ar now com to your Worship about their Mohnaheagan emnity and Contentions with Woncas, and I doupt with the English: (if opertunity wer not
wanting) I say in respect of this ocassione, I thought it good: and my duty
to send this Indian with these few lines: to acquaint your Worship of a passage
or two which I have observed concerneing this their Jorney lately: (vizt.)
first: concerneing their Jorney to the Indians called Mock-quaougs: which
live vp the River of quonecticott: I have by Inquiry found that these Nanheagansitts have sent their pressent to them to hire their help against Woncas:
this is talked of among the Indians very frequently: and from this their arose
such a clamor that there wer thousands of Moch-quoags com to Nanheagansitt, etc: which was nothi[n]g soe: for the Mockquoags (for ought I can
gather by what I heare) will have noe hand in the bussinesse: Butt it is strang
to see the vehement shew of desire that the Nanheaganssitts have to reveng
on Woncas: Insoemuch that although I told them (as your worship wrote to
mee in your last letter) that you would send to Quonicticott in the Spring:
concerning the restoreing of the goods and peage that Woncas had (as they
say) taken in pretence of redemtione of Miontonomu: Yett they ar not content to sitt downe vntill then: but now ar solliciting for leave to fight: and to
that end (they tell mee) they ar now come to your worship to buy your leave:
Yett they have ben told that the English will not doe it, nor yett sell the Peace
and lives of such as com for Shelter vnto them: not for any wealth or bribes:
and further I shall Humbly acquaint your Worship that I told these Indians

---

[1] W. 4. 119; 5 *Collections*, I. 330–333.

that your worship would not doe any thing to efect their desires in their errand without advise of a Gen[era]l Court: yett now they would goe, and three days agoe there was a Counseller sent from the Sachems of Nanheagansett to mee to give mee 2 dayes notice that I might lay aside all occassiones to com downe to the bay with these messengers, and to provoke mee to this Journey and to speake in their behalfe: They sent mee 4 Fath[om] of Peage (as a Bribe or Fee or what else it may be termed) I told the sayd counselleur that I did detest to tak their bribes in this or any other ocassiones betwene them and the English: and that he should carry home the beads againe: for I told him it was not the way to buy warre and Contentione by bribes but one good argument would prevayle mor with the English-gentlemen of Massachusetts then a 1000 bribs: and further I told them it was weake Frindship which was bought or sold for money and they might well thinke that if they made the English their freinds only by vertue of Bribs it would bee no other freindship but such as if Woncas would bring a greater Gift would be frustratted againe: soe having had and vsed many passages to this efect to the sayd messinger he then told mee that the peag was sent me as a token of love and Freindship and that he did ill in saying it was to make mee of their Factione: and many other words he vsed with a great deale of Subtlety to the same purpose and that this was but as a peney in respect of what they would give mee hereafter if I would accept to be their Freind: and further that it would bee a great discurtesy offered on my part to send hom the pressentt again: Soe I consented after much discourse, that the Beads should ly in my house, to be returned or kept as I should see the events of things etc.: Soe it is evident what great desires they have of revenge[1] though they first began the quarrell: But I being loath to troble your worship with a long discourse this I vnderstand that the messag sent by captaine harden is not yett deliverd: yett he was at Nanheagansitt the 17th of the 10th Mo., and sint for me: and it being the last day of the weeke when I received his letter, I resolved to sett forward one the 2d day becase I could not reach through in one day: and the weather being very cold and likely to snow which fell out soe that it snowed the 2d day all day and it was the bigest snow we had here this winter: and soe I saw It was a more then ordinary frusterating of the bussnes that time: But now it is tollarable traveling, I shall humbly atend your worships pleasure and apointment in the worke etc.

One thing more I shall make bold to acquaint your worship: that as I was willed last yeare by the Court I have dilligently inquired for your Indian that brake Prisson: I shall intreat your worships further mind (if you pleas)

---

[1] The spelling in the original manuscript is "renenge."

about the takeing of him for this bearer knows where he is and will endevour
to take him and bring him to your worship for which I have promisd him a
Coate: if you please to shew your mind about his being taken. Soe with my
humble Service vnto your worship I remaine Youre Worships humble and
Faithfull Servantt to be comanded

BENEDICT ARNOLD

PROVIDENCE This 14th 12th Mo. 1643[/44]

My father and Mr. Coates remembers their Service vnto your worship.

[*Endorsed by Governor Winthrop:*] Ben. Arnold. (12) 15—1643.

WILLIAM PYNCHON TO JOHN WINTHROP[1]

*To the Right Wor[shi]p[fu]ll Mr. John Wintrop gouernor of the Massachuset
deliver this in Boston*

SPRINGEFEILD this 19 of the 12 month 1643[/44]

MR. GOUERNOR, My respectiue loue remembred vnto you and your wife
and to your son John Wintrop and his wife: I received a letter lately from
you by Nippumsint and another to mr. Haines which I sent him: I blesse god
to heere of your good health and I praise god we are all in good health and
in peace in our plantation and the Lord hath added some 3 or 4 yonge men
out of the Riuer that are godly to us lately: and the Lord has greatly blessed
mr. Moxons ministry to the conversion of many soules that are lately added
to our Church: and hetherto the Lord hath preserued vs in peace from enimies: much talk was of the great actes that the Mowhoaks would do at the
begining of winter but the latest reports are that they will not help Sowa-
quassim and yet they kep his wampum. I doe not certainely heere whether
they will aid the Naricanset Sachim but as far as I can vnderstand they
reiect him also: But wheras you writ that you thought the Naricanset Sachim
would be content to sit still: my intelligence from the Indians of the Riuer
is otherwise: and they haue lately killd a munhegan woman: I conceiue you
vse your best endeuors to hould of the Naricanset, and I suppose they in the
Riuer do also hould of Woncas and in so doinge you doe well: and my advise
is that neather you nor the riuer should do any thing else, but vse delatory
meanes for I perceiue the nature of the Indians is vppon eury litle occasion

QUOTED
"WITCHCRAF
IN NEW
ENGLAND

---

[1] W. Au. 104; 4 *Collections*, VI. 372–373.

to be much prouoked with the desyer of reuenge, but if meanes of delay be vsed but a while the edge of their reuengefull desyer will soone be cooled: I perceiue they are carefull of this not to begin first with the English, but they make account if the English begin first with them to doe great matters: and I veryly beleeue they may soone make lamentable hauock: But I hope the English will neuer put it to the tryall, till they be more then a little prouoked to it:

I had not the news of England, in any large measure till I had first written to mr. Haines, but then he spedily sent me such bookes of records as he had 7 or 8 wherin I blesse god to se that strict and godly couenant betweene England and Scotland: It is the high way of god for their deliuerance. I hope it is now the day of Antichrists great ouerthrow at Armageddon: I greately long to here whether the Scotts be yet come into the aid of the parliment: I hope you will haue newes by the fishing shipps err longe: and so the god of peace be our foregaurd and Reareward all our dayes Amen. Your euer loueinge Frind in the Lord

WILLIAM PYNCHON

LUCY DOWNING TO JOHN WINTHROP[1]

SIR, I was preuented by my cosen dean by wayting for the issue of his farwell with the deputy the morning he went home but he continued his resolution to persist noe further in the busines and his ground of surseas beinge as he tould me apon hir manifestation that she could not set her affections opon him, I did eye it as a thing from prouidence and theerfore durst not be more sollisitus. this I haue obserued and in speciall in mariges it is scarce[2] to be found the approbations of all though godly: but for my owne part in this busines I was principally swayed by the iugdment of some whome I honer much, and doe beleeu it is the senceer disire of theer harts to doe you the best offices they can, and all yours, and not the least discurtisie. But I see it is more acseptable to some others, whome I dare say little less of then of the former, that the busines is at an end, but if it be of the lord he will ease difficulltyes and clear doupts. theerfore I desir aright to commend it to him. some thinge I haue desired longe to speake to you about my poor cosen Feakes. I haue not had opertunity to writ to her since she leeft the bay, nor haue I heard of her but by others, and that only wich was not like to be for her good, or our com-

---

[1] W. 4. 13; 5 *Collections*, I. 34–35.
[2] The spelling in the original manuscript is "scrarce."

fort. and now I hear Patricke is cut of wich makes me hope that by the vse of some good means theer might be more hopes to reduce her.[1] I beceech you to neglect noe opertunity in your power. I speake only in respect of the diffuculty of distance she is in, and the multiplicity of busines you are burthened with, yet euery one is not hir mothers childe, theerfore I am thus far bould, and as far as I can hear hir case is very daungerous in respect she liues whear all good meanes is wanting. somwhat allso I am troubled concerning my sonne georg. I perceiue he is strongly inclined to trauill. Eng. is I fear vnpeacable and other countryes perilous in poynt of religion and maners. besides wee haue not whearwith to acommodate him for such an ocasion: and to goe a seruant I think might not be very fit for him neither, in diuers respects. religious masters or fellowes are not frequent in trauills, nor is he anny scribe. I pray sir be pleased to consider of it, and to giue him your best aduise, for I fear it maye be some present preiudice to him hear, and the liklyest I can perceiue to be his motiue is his littell expectacion, and fears of supplye hear. The good Lord direct him to his owne glory. I pray present all my seruis and euer command yours

L. D.

Fbr. 24, [1643/44]

DOCUMENTS IN THE CASE OF MARY LATHAM AND JAMES BRITTON[2]

To the Constables of Marshfield Situate Hengam Weymouth Braintry Dorcester Roxbury and Boston greeting

Whereas divers and sundry complaints haue commen to me from Weymouth sent and delivered by godly and credible persons against Mary the wife of William Latham late of Marblehead but now at Marshfield for adultery committed upon the body of the said Mary by one James Brittaine of Weymouth, And having apprehended the said Mary and examined her, haue sent her with the examinacion according to my duty to that Government where the fact was committed.

These are therefore in his Ma[jes]ties name to will and command all and every of you the Constables aboue written to receiue and convey her from Constable to Constable till shee come before the Governour of the Massa-

---

[1] For the death of Captain Daniel Patrick, see above, pages 419–420, 428. For the scandals connected at this time and later with the name of Elizabeth Feke, see 2 *Proceedings*, VI. 3–4.

[2] W. I. 157. For Winthrop's account of this case, see *Journal*, II. 161–163.

chusets or some one of his Assistants, together with the letter you shall receiue, And heereof faile not at your perill. Given at Marshfield this pr[ese]nt 24 of Febr. 1643[/44]

per me EDW: WINSLOW

The Constable of Weymouth shall do well the matter being there knowne to carry testimony with him.

[*Memorandum by Governor Winthrop on the verso of the above document:*] Ja: Britten sayth that about 5 or 6 weekes since, by the seaside near his own house he did what he could to commit Adultery with Mary the wife of mr. Latham but he was not then himself, having been drinking all the night till midnight at his own house with 16 of his neighbors wherof 8 had been with him at the [*illegible*] the said Mary came out after them.

That mr. Taylors wife was neer 6 years since she came to his house, and he solic[it]ing her she easyly consented and laye down vpon his bedde (his wife being in another roome) but he was not able to enter her body.

[*Endorsed by Governor Winthrop:*] mr. Winslows warrant for Lathams wife.

STEPHEN BACHILER TO JOHN WINTHROP AND THE ELDERS OF THE CHURCH IN BOSTON[1]

Grace mercy and peace in our L. Jes. Christ

RIGHT WORSHIP[FU]LL AND REUEREND BRETHREN, Myne humble duty and Service in Christ remembred. I had no sooner written and ended this inclosed letter to my brother Cotton, for some satisfaction to certaine cases, waiting for a convenient messenger, but, Casco-messenger came with your Christian and carefull letter of my good and Gods glory (I should haue first said), was deliuerd to me, Which inclosed letter (tho properly belonging to my brother Cotton, yet because it may concerne you all, in respect of a reason or motiue, (which after will appeare in the sequell of this letter) for my furtherance to that work and place, wherto your advice and perswasion seemeth to ayme) I thought good to inclose it and send it to you all (vpon my second thought, as before I intended it to my brother Cotton alone), and this I desire you all to vnderstand to be the true Cause of communicating it vnto you all. Now, as Touching the maine thing it selfe of my calleing to

[1] W. 3. 27; 4 *Collections*, VII. 100–105.

Casco, The reasons and motiues which you vse to further me, were all presented vnto me, and were runing dayly in my consideration of the said calling, In so much, as it caused me to remember a passage of a Sermon of my
brother Cottons (speaking long since vpon thos words in the Acts of Christ
being made the Cornerstone), he vttered words to this effect (and I do think
he will remember and owne the very words themselues) That all the proceedings of the Scribes and Pharisies, and all their adherents together, that
by them all, they did but thrust and shoue at Christ, till they had thrust him
into that very place (vidzt, of being the Corner stone of the fathers building
for the strength and perfecting of the same) to which the father had appoynted
him. so said I to my wife considering what a calling I had, some 14 yeres
agon (by that Company of the ploughe), there to sit downe with them (not
as a Planter only, but as a Pastor also) and considering how the Lord,
(thinking to haue rested at New Towne (then so called) vpon that disaster
which happened to the goods of the Company by the false dealing of thos
entrusted by vs with the ploughe ship, and our goods therin) I say how the
Lord shou'd me thence by an other calling to Sagust, then, from Sagust to
Newbury; then from Newbury to Hampton: and now seems to do the like
from Hampton to the very place it selfe (all the former shoveings and re-
moueings being still directly towards that place, which I thought in my
minde might haue some resemblance to the Pharisies dealing with my Lord
and M[aste]r.) Howebeit, I thought with all, I could not certainely conclude
any such secret Counsayle of the Lorde, seeing the interuenient callings were
also of God, and the last to Hampton, not least certaine to me to be of God,
As (also) that the two last remouealls (N. from Sagust to Newbury, and from
Newbury to our Hampton) not being so proper from god, as from Satan and
some vnjust instruments, and this now from Hampton to Casco to be (after
a sort) forced by like vnjust proceedings, as well (or as much) as by an honorable calling from Casco, and like honorable advice from you etc. I was and
am the more doubtfull in my selfe and is to my speciall frends, whose harts I
haue cause to satisfye, why I should remoue against so many reasons objected
against me. but (I feare) I am too tedious and large, takeing vp too much of
your tyme from imployments of greater moment. I will therfore come to the
very poynt, and to the maine stick of all, which is this. I see not how I can
departe hence, till I haue (or (I meane) God for me) cleered and vindicated
the cause and wronges I haue suffered of the church I liue yet in, that is,
from the Teacher[1] (indeed) who hath don all and ben the cause of all the

[1] I.e., Timothy Dalton. For Winthrop's account of the difficulties in the church at Hampton,
New Hampshire, see *Journal*, II. 179.

dishonour that hath accrew'd to god shame to my selfe, and griefe to all Gods people, by his irregular proceedings, and abuse of the power of the church in his hand, by the maior parte cleaveing to him, being his Countrymen and acquaintance in old Engl. whiles my cause (tho looked sleitly into by diverse Elders and brethren) could neuer come to a judiciall searching forth of things, and an impartiall tryall of my allegations and his defence secundum allegata et probata, which, if (yet) they might, I am confident in God (vpon certaine knowledge and due proufe before your Selues whose hands are subscribed to this letter or calling of advice). The Teachers act of his excomunicateing me, (such as I am, to say no more of my selfe), would proue the foulest matter, both for the cause alleged, of that excom[munication] and the impulsiue cause (even wroth and revenge) and also the manner of all his proceeding thorough out to the very ende: and lastly his keeping me still vnder bonds, and much more then here I may mention, for diverse causes (Christes wrongs and sufferings excepted) that euer was committed against any member of a church. Which (to beare on my shoulder in going hence) is so vncomfortable: tho I can refer it to Gods revenging hand, and wait vpon him (Eccles. 4. 1. 2. and 5. 7 with Psal. 10. 13. 14 verses) yet (then) I am taught againe, that such sinnes, endangering the very state of church and commonwealthe for neglecting of the complaintes of the afflicted in such a state, as wherin both Magistrates, Elders and brethren all are, in the sincerest manner set to finde out Sin, and (with Levie) to search into the complaintes of the poore not knowing father nor mother, Church or Elder. In such a state (I say) in such a wine Seller to finde such a cock-atrice, and not to kill him—to haue such monstrous and fearfull proceedings passed ouer without due justice in proceeding etc. this againe stirs vp my spirit to seek for, and labour to obteine a writ ad melius inquirendum, Towards which the enclosed letter tendeth (as you may perceaue.) Yet (notwithstanding all that I haue said of my burthen and temtations) if your wisedomes shall think it and judg it more safe and reasonable to refer all my wronges (conceaued) to Gods owne judgment, I blesse the Lord for his grace (if I know myne owne hart herein) I can submit my selfe to be over ruled by you. And (here) I give you all more thankes then my pen can expresse, for that aboundant vndeserued care, you plainly shew forthe, in this your letter of advise. Whervpon, I presume, that in case the Lord shall so prevayle with me and vpon me, as (in your w[or-shi]ps short postscript you suppose I will not engage my selfe so fully and sodainly, till I shall haue had good experience, both of place and persons) you will ever haue me in your memories (as occasion shalbe offered) for my gloryfying of God there, and to be ayding and assisting to that whole Province, because I am there, by your encouradgment, that I may still depend vpon you for your Christian Loue and faithfullnes to me and mine. The truth is, I haue sent them of Casco this answer, brieflye. 1. That their necessityes, hunger and thirst after Christ their so free choyse of my selfe (so vnworthy), their offers of Reverence, Credence and subjection to Christes ordinances administred (according vnto God) etc. I purpose (God willing) to come and confer with them about the last week of the next monthe (our first) and that the will of God shall over rule me against all the difficulties of this case (which are many) if that will, or as that will shall cleerlye appeare vnto me: against which I shall not willfully or hypocritically shut myne eyes. This I haue promised, and so far I haue engaged my selfe, and no further. And (indeed) the being of that (my deare brother Jenner) and mr. Wheelwright stablished in thos partes is not a weak motiue to drive, or a cord to drawe me that waye. And now (to conclude) if the Apostles words should be objected, that this is thankes worthy, if a man (for Conscience sake towards god,) shall endure griefe, suffering wrongfully, that (therfore) I ought (in this afforesaid cause of mine to endure the greefe therof, in what soeuer I suffer wrongfully, without seeking for any redresse or justice against the offender) I confesse it was more absolutly necessary so to suffer when the church had no civill power to seek vnto, (then as affore is said) in such a land of righteousness as our new England is. But, I ende, and commending you all to God, with my poore selfe and cause, I rest Your worships at commaund in the Lorde, his moste vnworthy Servant

STEPHEN BACHILER

HAMPTON, this 26 of this last M. 1643[/44]

[*Endorsed by Governor Winthrop:*] Mr. Batchellor Received (1) 8, 43[/44]

JOHN WHEELWRIGHT TO JOHN WINTHROP[1]

To the Right Worship[fu]ll John Winthrope Esq. Govenour of the Massachusets at Boston these present

RIGHT WORSHIP[FU]LL, I haue receiued your letter wherein yow signify vnto me, that yow haue imparted my letter to the H[onored] C[ourt][2] and

---

[1] W. Au. 105; 5 *Collections*, I. 323–324; Savage (1826), 163–164; (1853), II. 197; *Journal*, II. 166–167. The text of Winthrop's copy in the Journal as deciphered by Savage shows some variations from the original. William Hubbard also gives the letter in his *General History of New England* (2 *Collections*, VI. 367, 1st edition) with a text that differs in some respects from both that of the original manuscript and that in Winthrop's Journal.

[2] Cf. John Wheelwright to John Winthrop, September 10, 1643 (pages 414–415, above).

that it finds good acceptance, for which I rejoyce with much thankfullnesse. I am very thankfull to your worships for the letters of Safe Conduct which I formerly receiued,[1] as likwise for the late Act of Court graunting me the same liberty, in case I desire letters to that end.[2] I should very willingly, (vpon letters obtained,) expresse by worde of mouth openly in Court that which I did in writing, might I, (without offence,) explaine my true intent, and meaning more fully to this effect; that notwithstanding my faylings, for which I humbly craue pardon: yet I cannot with a good conscience condemne my selfe for such capitall crimes, dangerous revelations, and grosse errors as haue beene charged vpon me; the concurrence of which, (as I take it,) make vp the very substance of the cause of all my sufferings. I doe not see but in so mixt a cause I am bound to vse, (may it be permitted,) my just defence, so far as I apprehend my selfe to be innocent, as to make my Confession, where I am convinced of any delinquency. Otherwise I shall seemingly and in appearance fall vnder guilt of many haynous offences, from which my conscience doth acquit me. If I seeme to make suit to the H[onored] C[ourt] for relaxation, to be graunted by an act of mercy vpon my sole confession, I must offend my conscience: if by an Act of justice vpon mine Apologie, and lawfull defence, I feare least I shall offend your worships. I leaue all things to your wise, and godly considerations, hoping that yow will pardon my simplicity, and plainnesse, which I am forced vnto by the power of an overruling conscience. I rest your worships in the Lord

JOHN WHELEWRIGHT

W[ELLS] 1 M. d. i. 1643[/44]

[*Endorsed by Governor Winthrop:*] Mr. Wheelwright 2 Lettre.

THE MASSACHUSETTS GENERAL COURT TO THE PROMOTERS OF THE IRONWORKS[3]

1. Answer to the first proposition: They are granted the sole priviledge in our jurisdiction of making of Iron, provided that any shall have liberty to joyne till the end of March next; provided also that within two yeares they make sufficient iron for the use of the country.

---

[1] Cf. *Records of Massachusetts* (under date May 10, 1643), II. 37.

[2] Cf. *Records of Massachusetts* (under date October 17, 1643), II. 50.

[3] Original not located; 2 *Proceedings*, VIII. 15, where it is stated that the document is in the handwriting of John Winthrop, Jr. For the official version of this document, see *Records of Massachusetts*, II. 61–62.

2. To the second proposition they answer: It is not in the Courts power to grant, but they will propound it to the inhabitants of severall townes and doubt not of their consent. In wast lands not granted they consent.

3. To the third they answer as to the former.

4. To the fourth they answer as to the former.

5. To the fifth they answer in proprieties as to the former, that it is not in the Courts power, and in wast lands they grant them leave to looke out six places, only provided that they doe within 10 yeares set up an iron furnace and forge in each of the places and not a bloomery only. And provided that the Court may grant a plantation in any place which the Court thinke fitting, which may not hinder their present proceeding.

6. The sixth is granted.

7. The seventh: There is granted liberty till the next Court.

8. It is referred to the first proposition.

9. It is answered it does not concerne the Court etc.

10. To the 10th it is answered that the undertakers, their agents and associats and servants, shall have such immunities and priviledges as the lawes of the country doe allow, and for 10 yeares shalbe free from publique charges for any stock they imploy in their businesse.

[March 7, 1643/44]

[*Endorsed by John Winthrop, Jr.:*] Answer of the Court to the propositions of the Ironworke.

THOMAS COBBETT TO JOHN WINTHROP[1]

To our honoured Gouernor and his much esteemd freind Mr. Winthop
at his howse in Boston present theise I pray you

WORTHY SIR, I vnderstand that you are by Mr. Humphrey desired to take care of the dispose of his children[2] wherefore I thought meet to acquaint you with a prouidence of God offering an opportunity for the comfortabl disposal of one of them. mr. Daulton of Hampton staying at one of our Brethrens howses lately Inquired after mr. Humphreys children offering to take one of them and to bring it vp as his owne hauing of his owne but one child. his

---

[1] W. 4. 120; 5 *Collections,* I. 333–335.

[2] John Humfrey had returned to England in 1641. For the subsequent misfortunes of his daughters, see *Journal,* II. 83.

Reason he gaue hereof was in that mr. Humphrey had formerly aduentured him self for him in england when in the High Commission Court and was a means of his liberty and therefore he would gladly thus requite that his kindeness, and beeing told hear was none in this towne but Dorcas formerly defiled etc. he replied that was indeed some Blott vppon her but yet he would be content to take her if mr. Humphreis freinds soe pleased. now Sir if you please and that you Judge it meet we shall take some care to send to Mr. Dalton that thear may be further order taken for the conueyance of her to him to Hampton. mr. Ottley is poore, and he cannot helpe her. mr. Walton is for Long Iland shortly there to sitt downe with my Lady Moody from vnder ciuill and church watch among the Dutch and albeit Dorcas be with him at present yet I suppose you will not assent to his carrying of her with him thither if he should desire it and with whome else the child should comfortably be I knowe not vnless some such like prouidence as this is be attended to and Improoued. your worship may please to expresse your minde herein to some of our Brethren that will be at Boston lecture and by them I shall vnderstand your pleasure, and accordingly act in it: beeing willing to doe any freindly office that way out of old resp[ec]ts vnto her Father and Mother. and thus with remembrance of all due respects to yourself and Mrs. Winthrop your wife, commending you and yours to the shadow of the wings of the Almighty I rest Yours to command in him

THO: COBBETT

LYN this 13th of the 1 m. 1643[/44]

　　if your worship please, your self may write to mr. Daulton and it will much aduantage and further the worke propounded.

EDWARD WINSLOW TO JOHN WINTHROP[1]

To the right w[orshi]pp[fu]ll his much honored Friend J. Winthrop Esq.
Governor of the Mass. these be delivered

HONORED SIR, Yours of the 21 (1) 43 I received and haue imparted it to my partner mr. Collier. And perceiue we are like to haue some trowble about the controuersie between Hartfort and the Dutch.[2] The letters from the

---

[1] Original not located; *N. E. Historical and Genealogical Register*, XXIX. 237–240; Nathaniel Morton, *New England's Memorial*, 5th edition, John Davis, Editor (Boston, 1826), 394–396 (extract). The text here printed is, with two exceptions noted below, taken from the *Register*.
[2] Cf. *Journal*, II. 132–134.

Swedes and Dutch[1] I received and haue perused them, and according to your desire haue returned them with such advice as the Lord enableth me for answere. And first for the Dutch I obserue he writeth with great haughtines of spirit, full of confidence (as you say) yet marvell that a gent[leman] so well bread so great a traveller and go[vernor] of so great experience should not be more moderate in writing especially in so publike a way, witnes his uncivill termes towards mr. Hopkins, etc. whom we all know to be a man that makes conscience of his words as well as his actions.[2] To many of the passages by him heer related I can say nothing, onely they agree too well with common Fame and I feare our br[ethre]n of Hartford will be found faulty in them whosoever shall haue the hearing of it. yet am ready to make good every particle of that Relacion which I gaue upon the solemn request first of your gen[eral] Court, and then of the Commissioners, in regard of my experimentall knowledge of the first beginnings of them and us in Coneetacut. to which also I added certaine things which I had from Liuetenant Holmes who was over our people there. For his answer to what I affirme by that generall which he bringeth (if I should grant all he saith) how short it weare you may easily judge who to my best remembrance meddle not at all with any passages between them after they came to clash together. He saith June the 6th 1638 that *I would not defend the Hartford mens cawse for they had hitherto (or thus long) wronged the Dutch.* That I spake somewhat tending thereunto I acknowledge. For mr. Whiting and myselfe being at dinner with him at his table. He flew out upon me (tho' unseasonably being courteous both before and after to me) and charged me to be the man had more wronged the Dutch then any other by giving the first commis[sion] to the Engl[ish] (being then Gov[erno]r of Plym.) to disturbe them at Coneetacutt who were possessed before us etc. But when I had taken off this charge and returned the wrong upon themselues and called Capt. Curlo being one of those fiue at dinner with us to witnes many things. Capt C. replied:

The truth is what mr. Winslow saith Sir is true nor haue we that cawse to complaine of them as of others, nay they haue as much cawse to complaine of Winsor as we haue of Hartford, for looke how the one dealeth with us so doe the other with them, etc. whereupon he turneth againe to me with Violence But will you justefie Hartford men (briefely charging them with many of the things in his letter) nay saith[3] he there sits the man next to you whose howse

---

[1] I.e., from the Director Generals of New Sweden and New Netherland, in reply to letters from the Commissioners of the United Colonies. *Records of the Colony of New Plymouth: Acts of the Commissioners of the United Colonies in New England*, 1 (Boston, 1859), 13.

[2] The word in the *Register* text of this letter is "accounts."

[3] The word in the *Register* text of this letter is "sez."

stands upon our ground and hath thus and thus abused us etc. To which I
replied No Sir I will not justefie Hartford men Tis suffic[ient] I can justefie
our own proceedings. But Mr. Whiting is of age let him speak for himselfe.
And this I added further to it that not onely my selfe but many English did
conceiue the Dutch had hard measure from them in sundry particulars if
things were true that were reported. And this was all I spake to the utmost of
my remembrance. And these were my words the occasion beginning and end
of them. But what is this to answ. that I affirme. That I had a place given
(and the place we after possessed) the yeare before the Dutch began in the
River. That the Dutch came in by way of prevention and stept in between
us and our purpose etc. That this was done without spec[ial] order From
either the States or their m[aste]rs the West India Company and so confessed
by C. Curlo. That the River was not Vacuum domicilium. but inhabited the
yeare before etc. That they bought of Tatobam, whose title to the River was
by conquest. That I brought in Attawanyut and there left him where he lived
and died vpon the ground whom Tatobam the Tyrant had before exspelled
by war. That this Attawanyut by the relacion of Liuetenant Holmes if he
would haue given way to it would haue cut off the Dutch becawse they
entred by Tatobam. I cannot remember all the particulars of that I gaue
under my owne hand writing but one thing more of great consequence I call
to minde That Tatobam for so we termed him after he had chid me for
bringing in his mortall enemy and countenancing him as I did would haue
had me (when indeed hee durst not attempt againe vpon him) to haue given
him but a knife or but an awle blade for his consent to what I had don which
I utterly refused, etc. Now good Sir I pray consider what contradiccion is
heer between my testimony given at your request etc. and either my words
as they were by me spoken, or as he pens them and would haue them. But
the truth is I could say more about their entrance and the unworthines of
it if I would bring our Gov[erno]r on the stage but will not Write it under
hand without his leaue. I perceiue there is no likelihood of Arbiterment
heer bec[ause] he conceiues no Abitracion faire unles it be between some
Royall persons or invested with supreame authority, otherwise I should advise he might haue notice of our meeting next at Coneetacut where they
haue a Fort to receiue him as he terms it. But if the States favor the Parliament, it may easily be either there ended or such Commission procured
either to informe them, there, or heer end the controversie as hee demandeth.
I suppose the late deputed Commissioners notwithstanding their weighty
occasions in Engl. would be brought to do somewhat in it, nay how easie
were it for mr. Peeters to goe furnished with Commission to end it in Holland.

As for the controversie between Mr. Lamberton and them,[1] we heare their yea and his nay. nor doe I know how we can right our Friends of New Haven in any other way then already by the Commission you gaue them, unles he would giue meeting as before which I conceiue he neither can nor will.

The Swedish Letter I haue also perused and conceiue it not the worst way to defer answere till you either heare againe from New Haven or understand what force your Commission hath in those parts. For I suppose its in use ere now.

I thank you for your large and painefull relacion of the State of Engl. at pr[ese]nt. The Lord in mercy look vpon his peop[le] and help forward his owne cawse. Thus saluting your selfe and Mr. Dudley etc. in the L[ord] Jesus with my due respects to both of you and all yours humbly take leaue and remaine Yours till death

EDW: WINSLOW

MARSHFIELD (2) 6. 44

[*Endorsed by Governor Winthrop:*] Mr. Winslow about the Answ: from the Sw: and D[ut]ch.

JOHN ENDECOTT TO JOHN WINTHROP[2]

To the right Wor[shipfu]ll John Winthrop Esqr. Gouer[nour] at Boston deliver

DEAREST SIR, I humblie and heartilie thanck you for your last lettre of newes and for the trees you sent mee. I receaued your lettre lately and the trees I cannot yet heare of, but I hope I shall. I haue sent 2 or 3 tymes about them, and I cannot yet heare of them, The messenger you sent them by being gon to sea. I haue not sent you any trees because I heard not from you. But I haue trees for you, If you please to accept of them whensoeuer you shall send. I thinck it is to late to sett or remoue. I could wish you to remoue in the latter end of the yeare your trees, and I pray you send mee what you want, and I will supply what I can. My Children burnt mee at least 500 trees this spring by setting the ground on fire neere them I cannot send you any newes, but that your Sister is recouering a pace out of her sicknes as Mrs. Gott who kept her told mee yesterday. I shall I hope see her this day my selfe againe. I heard you were not verie well. I desire the Lord to strenghthen you to the worke hee hath called you vnto and to restore you to your health. I

---

[1] Cf. Calder, *The New Haven Colony*, 185–187.
[2] W. 2. 77; 4 *Collections*, VI. 146–147.

vnderstand that Mr. Otely hath a suite with our deacons for some goods that Morecruft left with Mr. Peters which Otely sais Mr. Humfry bought of him, but I thinck it will appeare that Mr. Peters hath bought them and paid for them: If you please therefore to stay the suite till Mr. Peter come ouer, who we hope will be heere this spring, I thinck it will not be amisse, For Mr. Otely is upon going away, and is turning euery stone to get something, For hee is poore and is like to be poorer in the courses hee is in. We haue heere diuers that are taken with Gortons opinions, which is a great griefe vnto vs, and Mr. Norrice is verie much troubled. There is one of them that hath re- viled Mr. Norrice and spoken euill of the Church. I thought good to aduize with you whither it were not best to bynde the partie ouer to Boston Court, to make such a one exemplarie, that others might feare, For assuredly both with you and with vs and in other places, that heresie doeth spread which at length may proue dangerous. The Lord in mercie keepe you to whose grace I commend you and rest Yours euer to be commanded

Jo: Endecott

Salem the 22th of the 2d mo. 1644

Sir, Since I wrot my Lettre, Mr. Norrice came to mee to tell mee, that hee heard that The Lady Moody hath written to you to giue her aduice for her returne. I shall desire that shee may not haue aduice to returne to this Juris- diccion vnlesse shee will acknowledge her euill in opposing the Churches, and leaue her opinions behinde her, For shee is a dangerous woeman. My brother Ludlow writt to mee that by meanes of a booke shee sent to Mrs. Eaton, shee questions her owne baptisme and it is verie doubtefull whither shee will be reclaymed, shee is so farre ingaged.[1] The Lord rebuke Satan the aduersarie of our soules.

[*Memorandum by Governor Winthrop:*] Jo Bibble victualler for Natascut.

---

[1] Cf. *Journal*, II. 126.

STEPHEN BACHILER TO JOHN WINTHROP[1]

To the right Worshipfull Gouernour, John Winthrop Esqr. at his house in Boston,
thes b[e] delivered

Grace, mercy, and peace be multyplied in our Lord Jes. Christ. Amen

RIGHT WORS[HIPFU]LL AND MUCH HONOURED IN THE LORD, vpon the reading of the letters lately receaued from your W[orshi]p and (my speciall frends)
the Elders with you, about your iudgment in the disposeing of me, ether towards Casco, or the people of Exiter: as also vpon the account which our
Messenger (Sam. Greenfield) sent vnto you, made of the judgment of such
other frends (both Magistrates and elders betweene your parts and Exiter,
missing (I suppose) no one in all the waye) to whom your letters referred
him, to enquire of, and my selfe to take counsayle from, to which of the callings I should incline vnto, no one misliking mine inclination to Exiter being
cleerly free from any engagment of promise to Casco, I say, vpon the considera[tion] of the afforsaid premises, as the 1, 2, or 3 opposites had no one word
to oppose further, so were the whole resydue of the planta[tion] (brethren,
and others) thoroughly satisfyed, and encouradged presently to go forward
in the worke, that, vpon my promise to accept of their caling and desire, they
resolued to pich vpon the day of their Constitution and comming into order,
and sending forth their letters for helpe and advice vnto the Churches, whervpon, they pressed me for answer to their calling: which, whiles I desired to
delay for some further short tyme, they answered, that all that tyme would
hinder the work of Christ whervpon, I yet demaunded, whether they all
(who had subscribed their names, and giuen their consents to the afforesaid
calling, and therin their promise of Christian subjection to the work and
gouerment of Christ in me and by me as their Pastor) did yet continue firme
in that their desire and resolution? To which, they all consented with one vote
and voyce whervpon, I could see no sound reason to desire further tyme but
freely consented to their desire and calling, only, earnestly exhorting them,
that as I founde them and tooke them in a state of peace, and earnest desire
to enjoye each other, so we should forever be carefull to liue in Loue and
peace, and so to redeeme whatsoeuer ill opinion the country had conceaued
of them, and wherby the God of peace (and hater of contention) might dwell
amonge vs. Whervpon, they called a meeting, agreed vpon the persons and
materialls of their intended Church, and the day of the helpers meeting which
is the 18 of the 4 and next month succeding, which, if it shall please your

[1] W. 3. 27; 4 *Collections*, VII. 105–108.

W[orshi]p to communicat (with this poore relation to your Reverend Elders, to saue me a little paines in wrighting) I shall stand thankfull to you, and double thankfull to my brother Wilson (as the ablest to travill) in case he would honour vs with his presence, and make it a progresse of recreation to see his ould frend, and so to do me this laste Service, saue to my buryall.[1] And now (Sir) I haue one speciall busynes to communicat vnto you, for advice, which is this, as briefly as I can. I must expect that so soone as I am translated to my new place, the people of Hampton will lay what rates they can vpon my lot and state (which I haue) in Hampton, Whether (now) vpon these true and reasonable considera[tion]s following, I may not obteine fauour from our Goverment, to be favoured and exempted, ether for the short tyme of my life, or for some certaine yeres as shalbe thought fit from any rate. 1. for that I procured the planta[tion] for them, (as your W[orshi]p knowes, I think) and haue ben at great charges many wayes since for the vphoulding and furthering of the same. 2ly. for that I neuer had any maintenance from them hitherto. 3ly. I haue had great losse by fire well knowne to the value of 200*li* with my whole studdy of bookes. 4ly. for the establishment of a church-estate in Exiter, I haue of mine own accord freely consented to allow (out of the wages which they purposed to haue allowed (and I think payd) to Mr. Rashly, yerely) 40*li* to the purchaseing of Mr. Wheelwrights house and accommodations therto, to be mine for my terme only, and so to be lefte (at my ende of terme) to such as shall succeede, without which providence, I cannot see howe they should expect any succession long, if that be not layde for a foundacion to the church, by reason wherof, I haue (in effect) little, or no other meanes or maintenance to depend vpon, but from my lot in Hampton. 5tly. It is considerable, that I voluntaryly remoue for peace sake, and that my remoueing (tho to so neare a place) cannot be but both troublesome and chargable. And lastly, that it can detract but a matter of 3*li* or thervpon (happely a little more, I do not knowe) from the Teachers maintenance or otherwise which yet may be a comfort and benefit to me, if I may be free. This I do propound only to your Consideration, whether I may not lawfully and reasonably desire such a favour of the state? if not, (in your wise and conscionable judgment, and of my brethren yours Elders,) I sit down in silence. If yes, Then I shall beseech you (as a frend and father) to propound my humble suit [to] the Court (as you best know how) with my reasons and considerations, and cast the successe vpon the Lord aboue. And

---

[1] The General Court, on May 29, 1644, ordered that, because of the "divisions and contentions" in Exeter, the proposed gathering of the church of which Bachiler was to be the minister should be indefinitely deferred. *Records of Massachusetts*, II. 67–68.

were it not, that I know your W[orshi]p respecteth no trouble, so you may do any Service for God, or any of his poore servants, I should not be so bowld as I am thus to trouble you with my letters of comp[lain]t and advice. And even so I conclude, with my wiues and my poore service premised to your worsh[i]p and your Christian Consort (myne aunctent frend) with our faithfull prayers for you and my Reverend brethren, I cease, and rest in the Lorde yours to commaunde, his most vnprofitable servant

STEPHEN BACHILER

This 18 or 19 of this 3 M. 1644

Beare with my blotted paper. my maid threw down myne ink glasse vpon it, and I had not resc[r]ibendi tempus.

PETITION OF SOME OF THE INHABITANTS OF HAMPTON, NEW HAMPSHIRE[1]

To the Right Worshipfull the Gournor present these

To the Right Worshipfull the Gournor grace and peace be multiplied

RIGHT WORSHIPFULL AND MUCH HONRED IN THE LORD, wher as our late petition[2] exhibited vnto your worship with the Rest of the worshipfull Genrall Court last houlden at Boston, which p[et]ition not hauing clere suckses[3] one owar b[e]halues against william Howard by Reson that those Comissionars amed at peace Rathar then the Exact Examination of our case wherby the particulars ware not Required nor admited to be proued by oath yet for as much as diuars of the said frends of william Howard doe profes how much thay desiar peace and we knowinge our owne harts doe allso profes the like we thought good to pe[ti]tion to your worship that in case the said Will. Howard shall quitt him selfe and prosede no further in the busnes we likewise for peace sake shall doe the same beinge content Rathar to sufar then make aney further stir to the troble of the peace of this godly gouerment but in case he shall further moue the honred Court in owar absents we do humbly intreat and besech your worships faiuior to signifie to the honred Court that we are willing to proue our said pe[ti]tion before the wisdom of the land in cace your worship will admit vs Judicitor prosecings thearin or if we may finde so much

---

[1] W. 4. 169; 5 *Collections*, I. 493–494. For Swayne and Tuck, signers of this petition, see Savage, *Genealogical Dictionary*, IV. 235, 337.

[2] Massachusetts Archives, LXVII. 33.

[3] Cf. *Records of Massachusetts*, II. 59.

faiuior as to haue our cace Referd vnto the worshipfull the Deputie Gournor mr. Belingham and mr. Bradstret with full Comition In Regard of the pouartie of your worships pe[ti]tionars and we your worships pe[ti]tionars shall not sease to pray for your worships hapines and Rest your worships pour pe-[ti]tionars.[1] We in the behalfe of all the rest dooe set our handes

RICHERD SWAYNE
ROBERT TUCK

HAMPTON this 22th of the 3 mo. (1644)

willyam Howerd haue desyred puplik this last weeke to lay downe his plase which he say he had   we dooe desyre the same.

HENRY WALTON TO JOHN WINTHROP[2]

To the Right Wor[shi]p[fu]ll John Winthrop Esquire Gouernour in Boston

FLATLANDS in New Neatherlands the 4th 4th Mo. 1644

HONNOURED SIR, Haueinge an opertunity I could doe noe lesse than present my humble respects to you and yours desireinge to acquainte your wor-[shi]p with our Condicion which is the worse by reason wee want sufficient strength to carry on our plantacion for present the Indians would haue made peace, and some of them haue but wee dare not trust to them but haue laboured to serue the prouidence of god in A watchfull way and care feareinge the worst for lacke of which Mr. Fowrdams plantacion hath too lately suffered haueinge too much trusted those vnfaithfull heathen. three men haue bene cutt of at their worke and one of goodman Carmans children almost Masachred and An other carryed away and yet to him they pretended greatest friendship. Sir the short of it is that their plott is to cutt of all the christians (as wee call them) in these parts of Ammerica both Dutch English and french, as lately fell out of the backe side of New England betweene the Indians by the Fort Vrania and the french they haueinge now a french man amonge them whome they haue excersised vnheard of Creweltyes vpon to make him tell where the frenches strength did ly. Sir I haue not forgottne the last words your wor[shi]p pleased to vtter to mee as that wee left god and Runne away from ordenances. To which I answer in shorte wee neither doe nor neuer did dispise any ordenance of Jesus christ that did Appeare soe to be, by vertue of any

---

[1] The document to this point and the date line are, to judge from a signature of Richard Swayne in the Massachusetts Archives, in his handwriting. The balance of the document, including the signatures, is in an unidentified handwriting.

[2] W. I. 157.

Rule of his, but shall desire to seale the truth of euery ordenance of his with our bloude as wee doe not know how soone wee may. And this Sir humbly I would speake that our Temptacions our sorrows our hardshipps and hazzards and losse of our liues (I feare) the hostility of New England will one day answer for. might wee haue had our consciences yoake free, wee had not stirred vnto this day. I say litle your wor[shi]p is more wise to consider than I to write, the lord guide you and yours in his way   I shall desire to heare from you my deere [*torn*] and seruice to Mrs. Winthrop. Yours in Christ

HENR. WALTON

JAMES PARKER TO JOHN WINTHROP[1]

For the r[i]ght John Winthropp Dep: Governor theese presente in Bostowne

RIGHT WOR[SHI]PPFULL AND DEARELY RESPECTED, I make bold in theese few lines to open my mind   I have received this inclosed from Mr. Nowell To which I answeare as in gods presence that the business he writes to me off I cann say little off to give it in as matter off Certaintie, that my sayings should be matter off evidence For it is neare 2 yeares or more since that the young woman did make her relation to me, and the young woman is now dead, about $\frac{1}{2}$ a yeare since or more and her brother to whome I suppose she spake as much too as either to my wife or selfe is with you, at Wamouth I meane and her husband that married her and therefore I thinke this Labour might have beene saved, and the greate noise that is about the Country that Mr. Parker, our minister, is sente for by a warrante (and how savorie that will proue to me or to the ghospell I referr it to your selfe for I cannot tell every man the occasion, and a fame is not easily silenced but to soe many as I speake with I cannot but open it). It troubled me when I saw this enclosed for two causes First, in regard the person that I suppose declared it to you I only propounded it too as a matter off secrecie, wherein I desired a little advice And my trust is not answeared. And 2d in regard the thing at the worst is but a heare say from one partie and the Fellow denied it stiffly then, and shee is now dead. And all that I cann say or my wife about it is that he proferd uncleaness to her and this shee complained not off to me but from my wife I hard it accidentally, and examined the mayd, and to my apprehensions found it not worthy off Complaint because there were but hir affirmations some weekes or months after the uncleane passages one his parte And his deniall

---

[1] W. 3. 124; 4 *Collections*, VII. 441–444. For Parker, see 4 *Collections*, VII. 441*n*.

strongly but to avoid the occasion for the time to come, 1 forwarned him off my howse unless occasion cald him thither. And For any Circumstances one one hand or the other I dare not neither my wife speake one oath. Now Good Sir what other jealousies that either you or the Courte should have off me, that either my selfe or wife would countenance sin by concealing this person, I know not only nakedly I have opened what I know or my wife only this warrant implies blame but what ground yet I see it not   I wish I may For I ame off this mind, that I love not to trouble Courte and Country without I see god going before me in some plain testimonie unless it be in case off Bloud or some notorious crime which is unnaturall, And then I desire my evidence to be cleare then for things revealed belong to me to publish (but I will not be too bold). This warrant I heare were followed by wilson with greate violence as some such matter as though it had concerned my life or at Least the welfare off the place where yet I live, and this I were told, they wonderd what the business ment. I had thought that our depositions might haue served in criminall matters, For shee then were a mayd. This is a greater thing is to me then any thing that ever befell me in new England this many yeares considering the employment I ame now vppon And I had thought that I might have beene accounted soe faithfull to god and this state that enquirie might first have beene made before it should have beene positively required off me my personall presence, and wife and Boy: What he cann say I yet know not because I have not yet spoken with him because I were at the Ile off Shoules when the warrant came (and yet ame with my wife) and that late one the 5th or 6th day at night the Last weeke I had this sente over to me as matter off greate Concernement which I conceive not soe much. But pardon my weakness, For my trouble is much about it not soe much For my selfe, if my hearte deceive me not But For the poore people among whome I live, To whome I ame in my spirit deepely Engaged and therefore doe earnestly Beg that For the business betweene Dover and them If it be alterd it might be vppon apparente cleare ground For such is there weakness that they say that they sshall not put much Confidence in the orders off the Generall Courte if it be altered and that chandge mostly argues infirmitie. And make this account off further trouble, For there necessitie cals for it the other certainly doth not But however I could earnestly wish that it might be concluded now if it may be for my parte For it fills the peoples hearts full of trouble that we cann goe one with noe business for ordering off other affairs And For there votes being refused vppon what ground I know not therefore I cannot speake to it Only I ever conceived them to be absolute Free men and to have there votes in the Choise off all officers by the Last order made concerning them, but more I suppose we shall here therefore I leave it For presente   thus with my respect and service to the Governour your selfe Mr. Nowell your Sonn I Leave you and your more serious Affaires to the Lord able to councell you and rest Yours to my utmost in any service For you and the Country

JAMES PARKER

I desire if what we have wrote concer[n]ing Meigs business of suspition off uncleaness satisfie not we may not be compeld to come into the Bay but rather Let vs send our depositions From the hands off some Commissioners here but if we shall be compeld to come we subjecte. We Forgott to write to your Sonn to give him notice that we desierd Mr. Williams to be propounded For a Commissioner.

from the ILE OFF SHOULES, this 10th off the 4th mo[n]th 1644

I could desire to heare From your Wor[shi]pp som word off Answeare and what newes you have with you:

I wrote to your wor[shi]pp about 14 dayes agoe about divers others things but since I received your Letter againe   But this business puts other propositions out off my mind:

[*Endorsed by Governor Winthrop:*] Mr. James Parker Rec: (4) 13 44. Mr. Will[ia]ms to be a Commissioner.

SIR WILLIAM BERKELEY TO JOHN WINTHROP[1]

WORTHY SIR, Hauing received Intelligence and complaint from Mr. John Chew Merchant that certaine of his seruants being run away about May 1643 and are now resident in your Collony of New England I desire you will please to assist this gentleman the Bearer in the regaining of them by all possible meanes that may be, It being but An accustomed fauour reciprocally shewen upon all occassions eyther to other in which at noe tyme we shalbe defectiue as we expect the like from you   he hath made it appear in Court they are his servants   their names are Walter Joy William Woodhead and Henry

---

[1] Massachusetts Archives, CCXL; *Hutchinson Papers* (1769), 136–137; (1865), I. 152. For Berkeley, see *D.A.B.*

King alias Eny soe not doubting of your assistance herein I rest Your Seruant

WILLIAM BERKELEY

VIRGINIA the 12th June 1644

JOHN ENDECOTT TO JOHN WINTHROP[1]

DEAREST SIR, I vnderstand by Mr. Tompson of our Towne the seaman That there is a great partie for the Kinge to the Eastward, and that they are makeing some preparations for some designs. They intertayned twoe of our Towne (fayning themselues to be Caualiers) with much loue and good cheere, and they perceaue that something is in hand: They were plotting to take the plimmoth pinnace, and were sorrie they missed their opportunitie: It is about Richmond Iland that which I speake of, but they haue a partie in all those partes. And hearing that Morton went by sea to Gloster on the sixth day last hoping from thence to get a passage to the Eastward, I sent a warrant to Gloster to apprehend him, if hee be there, For It is probable hee hath endeavored a partie to the Southward and now hee is gon to the Ea[stw]ard to doe the like. It is most likelie that the Jesuites or some that way disposed haue sent him over to doe vs mischiefe to raise vp our enemies round about vs both English and Indean. If you can send mee other speedy adui[ce] what to doe heerein I shall endeauour to put it in execution. If [it be] not to troublesom, I pray you send mee both ours and the Deputies propositions in our last conference touching the differences amongst vs.[2] Thus with my best respects to your selfe and Mrs. Winthrop, with many thancks for your manifold vndeserved kindnesses I rest Yours euer

JO: ENDECOTT

SALEM 23 (4) 1644

JOHN BROWNE TO JOHN WINTHROP[3]

To the Wor[shi]p[fu]ll his Loving Frend mr. John Winthrop these deliver at Boston

TANTON the 26th of the 4 month 1644

SIR, Vppon the last day of this last wek I having notis given by An Indian from Sowames that the Naragansets had Slayne in battell 6 men of the Mon-

---

[1] W. 2. 78; 4 *Collections*, VI. 148–149.
[2] Cf. *Journal*, II. 170–172.
[3] W. 11. 55. For Browne, see Savage, *Genealogical Dictionary*, I. 269–270.

hegens and [*illegible*] and had sent to vssamequam A head and A hande which hee had reseved, the same day I had further newes that vssamequam had sent them to Plimouth, but the Certenty of this I know noe forther for as yet I have hard nothing from plimouth: But vppon these Reports I gave notis to our townsmen that none should depart our town vnder A pretens of working in othor plantakeons, but for the Safty of ther Owne means and the bettor securing of our towne the should make ther Abode in ther own place (for we haue dyuers yong men that vse to wandor) But yestorday one Edward Rew A young man of our town who hath Land Amongst vs, having noe family but himself, did Aduenture to goe, And othor say they do intend to follow if he Rest quiett: my request vnto you therfor is, that you would send your warrant vnto your Cunstable at Brayntrie, that hee may comand the said Rewe to depart that place and to Repayre with Speed to our town of Tanton. this Rewe is to bee Imployed in diging Iron stone at brayntrie as I am Informed. I Intend to see you if god will this somer yet in the menewhyle when your Occasions will permit I could desyre you would wriht mee how you may bee fit for the payment of that which belongeth to mee for I Received Lettors out of England About A yeare sinc that your Sonne did not pay Any of that money for mee theare. my Lettor Imports that his Answar was that hee had noe certayne deractions from you. I haue not bine in the bay this long tyme: one thing more I put to your Consideration, which I pray you thinke on it (namely) that you would not permit that vyle person Morton to pas without some due punishment for he hath in my Judment Abused the Cuntry very much and that In print: But I seace to trouble you further at this tyme but Remayne Your Ever loving frend

JOHN BROWNE

PETITION OF JOHN WINTHROP, JR., TO THE MASSACHUSETTS GENERAL COURT[1]

To the honored Governour and generall court assembled at Boston

THE HUMBLE PETITION OF JOHN WINTHROP IUNR.

Whereas there was a motion formerly by this honored Court for the beginning a plantation about Pequott, and the Court expressed themselves desirous, that some would appear in it, your petitioner being desirous to promote so good a worke (and having formerly discovered some quantity of

[1] W. 2. 171; 4 *Collections*, VI. 517.

the best sort of Iron Ston that hath yet beene discovered lying convenient to be wrought in those parts), doth desire leave to make a plantation in those parts at or neere Pequott, with such fitting workemen, and others, that may present themselves, and to lay out such a convenient place for an Iron-worke as is fitting according to the grant of this court for the incouraging of Iron-workes the last court, and doth desire such liberties as are necessary, and other far remote plantations doe inioy.

28th 4th mo. 1644

The Magistrates desire the consent of the Deputies herein.

JOHN ENDECOT, *governour*

The house of Deputies do consent to this petition, provided, that fit men appeare to carrey on the plantation within three yeares next ensuing.

STEPHEN WINTHROPE *by order of the house*

Vera Copia Witnes INCREASE NOWELL *Secret.*

ORDER OF THE MASSACHUSETTS GENERAL COURT ON THE PETITION OF JOHN WINTHROP, JR.[1]

Vpon the petition of mr. John Winthrop iunr. exhibited to this Courte, for leave to make a plantation att or neere Pequott, it is ordered that the said petition is granted, and that the petitioner shall have liberty to make a plantation in the said Pequott Country, with such others as shall present themselves to joyne in the said plantation, and they shall enioy such liberties as are necessary, and other far remote plantations doe inioy and also to lay out a convenient place for Ironworkes, provided that a convenient number of fitt persons to carry on the said plantation doe appeare to prosecute the same within three yeares.

Dated 28th 4th mo. 1644

Per Curiam INCREASE NOWELL *Secret.*

[*Endorsed by John Winthrop, Jr.:*] order of court about making plantation at Pequot.

---

[1] W. 2. 172; 4 *Collections*, VI. 517–518.

DECLARATION OF THE GOVERNOR, DEPUTY GOVERNOR, AND ASSISTANTS OF MASSACHUSETTS[1]

The Governour Dep: Gov: and [Assi]stants doe hereby declare for the full satisfaction of all men, That as by the patent, and election of the people, they are sett aparte to be the councell of this Common wealth to governe the people in the vacancy of the Generall Courte, and that none can be added vnto them of equall power, but by like election; So they doe hold themselves bound to Governe by law, both fundamentall and positive, and not contrary therevnto, and that the Generall court only hath power to make, and establish, such wholesom lawes orders and ordinances both fundamentall and positive which shall from tyme to tyme be for rules and directions vnto the magistrates to observe, and not to doe contrary therevnto. And further, that the magistrates are bound by God by the trust committed to them, and by their oath to study and endeavour the welfare of this commonwealth and consequently to further the establishing and declaring of all necessary, and wholsome lawes, with certaine penalties where they may be iustly provided for, which they shall conceive of themselves, or shalbe presented to them according to their best Judgement and vnderstanding. lastly that they are in like manner bound to mainteine the liberties of the people in their said elections of their Governours to establish no lawes, nor raise any taxes but by the Generall Court, and if any thing hath passed from them by word or writing that hath or may be misinterpreted contrary heervnto, they doe not approve thereof

[*Ca.* June 28, 1644]

Jo: ENDECOTT *Gou*[*ernou*]*r*
Jo: WINTHOP *D. G.*
THO: DUDLY
JOHN WINTHROP iunr.
INCREAS NOWELL
SYMON BRADSTREET
WI: HIBBINS
THOMAS FLINT
SAMUELL SYMONDS

---

[1] W. 4. 169; 5 *Collections*, I. 494–495. This document, which is a copy in an unidentified handwriting, grew out of a dispute between the assistants and the deputies regarding the powers of the former when the General Court was not in session. For Winthrop's account of the dispute, see *Journal*, II. 170–174.

JOHN WINTHROP'S DISCOURSE ON
ARBITRARY GOVERNMENT[1]

Arbitrary Gouerment described and the Common mistakes about the same (both in the true nature thereof, and in the representation of the Gouerment of the Massachusetts, under such a notion) fully cleared. (5) 1644

Arbitrary Gouerment is, where a people have men sett ouer them without their choyce, or allowance: who haue power, to Gouerne them, and Judge their Causes without a Rule.

God onely hathe this prerogatiue: whose Sovereintye is absolute, and whose will is a perfecte Rule, and Reason it selfe: so as for man, to usurpe such Aut[horit]ye is Tiranye, and impietye.

Where the people have Libertye to admitt, or reiect their Gouernors; and to require the Rule, by which they shalbe governed and Judged, this is not an Arbitrarye Gouerment.

That the Government of the Massachusetts is such, will appeare 1: by the foundation of it: 2: by the positive Lawes therof: 3: by the constant practice, which proves a Custome, then which (when it is for common good) there is no Lawe of man more inviolable.

1: The Foundation of this Gouerment, is the Kinges Lettres Patents: this gaue them their Forme, and beinge, in disposinge a certaine number of persons, into a bodye politike; whereby they became then (in such a politike respecte) as one single person consistinge of severall members: and appointinge to eache, its proper place: it regulates their power and motions, as might best conduce to the preservation, and good of the wholl bodye:

The parties or members of this bodye politike are reduced vnder 2 kinds, Gouernor and Companye, or Freemen: to the Gouernor it adds a Deputye, and 18 Assistants: in these is the power of Aut[horit]ye placed, vnder the name of the Gouernor (not as a person, but as a State) and in the other (which is named the Company) is placed the power of Liberty; which is not a bare passive capacitye of freedome or immunity, but such a Libertye, as hath power to Acte vpon the cheife meanes of its owne wellfare (yet in a waye

---

[1] Boston Public Library; *L. and L.*, II. 440–459. For Winthrop's account of the circumstances which occasioned this Discourse, see *Journal*, II. 217–218, 240–242.

Along with the Discourse itself there have been preserved the following, all in the handwriting of Governor Winthrop: an extract from St. Thomas Aquinas; a copy of the report made by the committee of the deputies which examined the Discourse; Winthrop's answer to the committee's objections; further observations on the subject entitled "The Authors reviewe of his writing"; and certain miscellanea. These latter, hitherto unprinted, have been inserted as footnotes at what appear to be the most pertinent points.

of Libertye, not of Authoritye) and that vnder 2 generall heads, Election, and Counsell: 1: they have Libertye to electe yearly (or oftener if occasion require) all their Gouernors, and other their generall officers, viz: such as should have influence (either Juditiall or ministeriall) into all parts of the Jurisdiction. 2: They haue Libertye of Counsell, in all the generall Assemblyes, so as, without their counsell and consent, no Lawes, decrees, or orders, of any publ[ic] nature or concernment, nor any Taxes, impositions, impresses, or other burdens of what kinde soeuer, can be imposed vpon them, their familyes or estates, by any Authoritye in the Gouernment: which notwithstanding remaines still a distincte member, even in those generall Assemblyes: otherwise our state should be a meer Democratie, if all were Gouernors, or magistrates, and none lefte, to be an obiecte of Gouernment which cant fall out in any kinde of Aristocratie.

To make this cleare, we will sett downe the verye words of the Patent.

1: The words of Constitution of this bodye politike are these A: B: C: and all such others as shall hereafter be admitted and made free of the Company and society hereafter mentioned shalbe etc: one Bodye Politike and Corporate, in fact and name, by the name of the Gouernor and Company of the Mattachusetts Baye in N: E: And that from henceforth, for euer there shalbe one Gouernor, one Deputy Gouernor, and 18 Assistants of the same Company, to be from tyme to tyme, constituted, elected, and chosen, out of the Freemen of the sayd Company for the tyme beinge; In such manner and forme, as heerafter in these presents is expressed, which said officers shall applye themselues to take care for the best disposinge and orderinge of the generall businesse and Affaires of, for, and concerninge the said lands and premises heerby mentioned to be granted, and the plantation thereof, and the Gouernment of the people there.

2: The distribution of power followes, in these words ensueinge That the Gouernor of the said Company for the tyme beinge or in his absence by occasion of sicknesse or otherwise, the Deputie Gou[erno]r for the tyme beinge shall haue Authoritye from tyme to tyme, vpon all occasions, to giue order, for the Assemblinge of the said Company, and calling them together, to Consult and Aduise of the businesses and Affaires of the said Company:

And that the said Gouernor Deputy Gouernor and Assistants of the said Company for the tyme beinge shall or may once euery month or oftener at their pleasures, Assemble and hold and keepe a Court, or Assembly of themselues, for the better orderinge and directing of their Affaires:

And that any 7 or more persons, of the Assistants, togither with the Gouernor or Deputye Gouernor so Assembled shalbe said taken held and reputed to be, and shalbe, a full and sufficient Court or Assembly of the said Company, for the handlinge orderinge and dispatchinge of all such businesses and occurrents, as shall from tyme to tyme happen touching or concerninge the said Company or plantation.

Then follows a Clause, wherby Libertye is granted to hold 4 general Courts in the yeare, wherein (with the Advice and consent of the maior parte of the Freemen) they may admitt others to the Freedome of the Company, they may make all subordinate Officers, and make Lawes and constitutions, for their wellfare and good Gouerment.

Then followeth a Clause for the Annuall Election of all their Officers in these words ensuing.

That yearly once in the yeare foreuer, namely on the last Weddensdaye in Easter Term yearly, the Gouernor Deputy Gou[erno]r and Assistants of the said Company and all other Officers of the said Company shalbe in the generall Court of Assembly, to be held for that day or tyme, newly chosen for the yeare ensueing by such greater parte of the said Company, for the tyme beinge, then and there present as is aforesaid.

Then followes another branch, whereby, in any of their generall Courts, any insufficient or delinquent Officer (of what sorte soeuer) may be removed, and another forthwith putt in place.

The last Clause is for the Gouerning of the Inh[ab]i[ta]nts within the Plantation. For it being the manner for such as procured Patents for Virginia, Bermudas and the Weste Indies, to keep the cheife Gouernment in the hands of the Company residinge in Engl[an]d, (and so this was intended and with much difficulty we gott it abscinded) this clause is incerted in this and all other Patents wherby the Company in Engl[an]d might establish a Gouerment and Officers heer, in any forme vsed in Engl[an]d, as Gouernor and Counsell, Justices of Peace, Maior Baylyfs etc, and accordingly mr. Endicott and others with him, were established a Gou[erno]r and Councell heer, before the Gouernment was transferred hither: and that clause is expressed in these words.

It shall and may be lawfull, to and for the Gouernor etc: and such of the Freemen of the said Company for the tyme beinge, as shalbe assembled in any of their Generall Courts aforesaid, or in any other Courts to be specially summoned and assembled for that purpose, or the greater part of them, whereof the Gouernor or Deputye Gou[erno]r and 6 of the Assistants to be allwayes 7 from tyme to tyme, to make, ordaine, and establish all maner of wholesome and reasonable Orders, Lawes statutes and Ordinances directions and instructions, not contrarye to the Lawes of this our Realme of England:

as well for setling of the formes and Ceremonies of Gouernment and Magistracie, fitt and necessarye for the said Plantation, and Inh[ab]i[t]ants there and for naminge and stilinge of all sorts of Officers, both Superior and inferior, which they shall finde needfull for that Gouernment and Plantation, and the distinguishinge and settinge forth of the seuerall duties, powers and limitts of euery such office etc. for disposinge and orderinge the Elections of such of the said Officers as shalbe annuall, etc: and for settinge downe formes of Oathes and for ministeringe of them etc: and for the directinge Rulinge and disposinge all other matters and thinges, whereby our said people inh[ab]i[t]ants there, may be so religiously peaceably and ciuily governed etc:

Thus it appeares that this Gouernment is not Arbitrary in the foundation of it, but Regulated in all the partes of it.

2: It wilbe yet further found by the positive Lawes thereof: And first by that of (3) 14, 1634, where it is declared, that The generall Court onely may make Freemen: make Lawes: choose Generall Officers, as Gouernor, Deputie, Assistants, Treasurer etc: remove suche: sett out their power and dutye: rayse monyes: dispose of lands in proprietyes: not to be dissolved, but by consent of the maior parte. The Freemen of the severall Townes may sende their Deputyes to everye generall Court who may doe all that the bodye of Freemen might doe, except in Election of magistrates and officers.

And in the 67 Libertye, it is thus described viz. It is the Constant Libertye of the Freemen, to choose yearly at the Court of Election, out of the Freemen, all the generall Officers of this Jurisdiction. If they please to discharge them, at the Court of Elections, by vote, they may doe it without shewing Cause: but if at any other generall Court, we hould it due Justice, that the Reasons thereof be alledged and proved. By Gen[erall] Officers, we meane our Gouernor, Deputye Gou[erno]r Assistants, Treasurer, Generall of our Warres, and our Admirall at Sea; and suche as are or may be heerafter, of like Generall nature.

3: According to these fundamentall Rules, and positiue Lawes, the Course of Gouernment, hathe been carried on in the practice of publ[ic] Administrations to this verye daye, and where any considerable obliquitye hathe been discerned, it hathe been soone brought to the Rule and redressed: for it is not possible in the infancye of a plantation, subiecte to so many and variable occurrents, to holde so exactly to Rules, as when a state is once setled.

By what hathe been allreadye manifested, this Gouernment is freed from any semblance of Arbitrarinesse, either in the forme of it, or the generall officers in it, which is the first branch in the description of Arbitrary Gouernment.

The other Branche (wherin the maine question lyes) is concerninge the Rule: so as if it shall appeare allso, that the Governor and other officers are prescribed suche a Rule, as may be required of them in all their Administrations, then it must needs be granted, that this Government (even in the present state therof) is in no respecte Arbitrarye.

I might shewe a cleare Rule out of the Patent it selfe, but seing it is more particularly, (and as it were membratim) deliniated in later Lawes, I will beginne there (3) 25, 1636. It was Ordered, that vntill a bodye of Fundamentall Lawes (*Agreeable to the word of God*) were established, all causes should be heard and determined, accordinge to the Lawes allreadye in force: and where no Lawe is, there, as neere the Lawe of God as may be To omitt many partic[ular] Lawes enacted vppon occasion, I will sett downe onely the first Aut[horit]ye in the Libertyes: which is as heere followeth. No mans life shalbe taken awaye: no mans honor or good name shalbe stayned: No mans person shalbe arrested, restrained, banished, dismembred, or any wayes punished: No man shalbe depriued of his wife or children: No mans goods or estate shalbe taken away from him: or any waye endamaged, vnder colour of Lawe or Countenance of Aut[horit]ye vnlesse it be by the vertue or equitye, of some expresse Lawe of the Countrye, warrantinge the same, established by a generall Court and sufficiently published: or, in Case of the defecte of a Lawe, in any particular Case, by the worde of God, And in Capitall Cases, or in Cases concerninge dismembringe or Banishment, accordinge to that worde, to be Judged by the Generall Court.

By these it appeares, that the Officers of this Bodye Politick have a Rule to walk by, in all their administrations, which Rule is the *Worde of God*, and such conclusions and deductions, as are, or shalbe regularly drawne from thence.[1]

All Com[mon]wealthes have had some principles, or fundamentalls, from which they have framed deductions to particular Cases, as occasion hathe required. And though no Com[mon]w[ealth] euer had, or can have, a partic[ular] positive Rule, to dispence power, or Justice by in every single Case: yet where the fundamentalls, or generall Rule holde forthe suche direction, as no great damage, or injurye can befall, either the wholl, or any partic[ular] parte, by any vniust Sentence, or disorderly proceedinge, without manifest

[1] The following memorandum appears in the margin: "mr. Dav[enport] that Gods controversye continued still against Engld. etc. because they shaped their Course too much by Politike and nationall prudence, and held not strictly to the Rules of Gods worde and that was a generall error in the worlde and amongst vs: this is not to seek the Lord with all our heart Jer: 29: 13. Isay. 41: 2: God called Abra: to his foote etc: so ought all gouerments to be."

breache of suche generall Rule, there the Rule may be required: and so the Gouernment is Regular and not Arbitrarye.

The Fundamentalls which God gave, to the Com[mon]w[ealth] of Israell, were a sufficient Rule to them, to guide all their Affaires: we havinge the same, with all the Additions, explanations and deductions, which have followed: it is not possible, we should want a Rule in any Case: if God give wisdome to discerne it.

There are some fewe Cases onely (besides the Capitalls) wherein the penalty is prescribed: And the Lord could have doone the like in others, if he had so pleased, but havinge appointed Gov[ernmen]ts vpon earthe, to be his vicegerents, he hathe given them, those fewe, as presidents, to directe them, and to exercise his guifts in them: Deut. 17: 9: 10: 11: In the most difficult Cases, the Judges in Supreme Aut[horit]ye, were to shewe the sentence of the Lawe: whence 3 thinges may be observed: 1: this Sentence was to be declared out of the Lawe established: thoughe not obuious to Comon vnderstandinge 2: this was to be expected in that Ordinance: therefore v: 19: the Kinge was to have a Copye of the Lawe, and to reade them all the dayes of his life: 3: Suche a Sentence was not ordained to be provided before the Case fell out, but pro re nata, when occation required, God promised, to be present in his owne Ordinance, to improue suche gifts as he should please to conferre vpon suche as he should call to place of Goverment. In the Scripture, there are some formes of Prayers and of Sermons sett downe: yet no man will inferre from thence, that ministers should have Sermons and prayers prescribed them for every occasion: for that would destroye the Ordinance of the ministry: and a Readinge Preist might serve in that office, without any learninge or other gifts of the Spirit: So if all penaltyes were prescribed, the Jurye should state the Case, and the booke hold forthe the sentence, and any Schoolboye might pronounce it: and then what need were there of any speciall wisdome, learninge, Courage, zeale or faithfullnesse in a Judge?

This beinge so great a Question now on foote, about prescript penaltyes it wilbe of vse to search as deepe into it, as we may by the light of Scripture, approved patternes and other Rationall Arguments: not tyeinge our discourse to methode, but layinge downe thinges as they come to hande.

England In the right constitution, is not an Arbitrary Gouernment: nor is ours of the Massachusetts: yet Juries, both there and heer, give damages, which (in vulgar sence) are Arbitrary, in most Cases: as in Actions of Slander, Trespasse, Batterye, Breach of Covenant, etc: all which concerne the Peoples Libertyes, no lesse, than Fines and other penaltyes: And if 12 men, who have no callinge to Office, may (in expectation of Gods Assistance) be trusted with

mens estates in a way of distributive Justice, without a prescript Rule etc:
why may not those whose callinge and Office hathe promise of Assistance,
have like trust reposed in them, in vindictive Justice?

In the Libertyes enacted heere of purpose to prevent Arbitrary Goverment,
there are neer 40 Lawes, to the violation whereof no penaltye is prescribed:
nor was ever moved.

God may pronounce Sentence against an Offender, before the offence be
Committed, bothe by his absolute Soveraintye, and allso because he fore-
seethe all Facts, with all their Circumstances: and besides the least degree of
the same Offence deserves more then that full punishment before his Justice:
but man must proceede accordinge to his Commission; by which he canot
sentence another, before he hath offended, and the offence examined, proved,
layd to the Rule, and weighed by all considerable Circumstances, and Libertye given to the partye to Answeare for himselfe, nor is there any thing more
preiudiciall to a subiects Libertye, then to be sentenced before his Cause be
hearde.

England is a State of long standing, yet we have had more positiue and
more holesome Lawes enacted in our shorte tyme then they had in many
hund[re]d yeares. They have indeed some Lawes with prescribed penaltyes
annexed, but they are for the most parte so small, as doe vnder value the least
degree of those offences: they have xij$d$ for an Oathe: 5s for Drunkenesse etc.
but for all great Offences and misdemeanors, as Periurye, Forgerye, Con-
spiracyes, Cousenages, oppressions, Riott, Batteryes, and other breaches of
the Peace etc: there is no penaltye prescribed   how it is in other States in
Europe, I cannot relate (because we knowe not their Lawes) otherwise then
what appeares in their Histories, where we finde some great offences punished, by the discretion of their Judges.

Justice ought to render to every man accordinge to his deservinge, eye for
eye, hand for hande etc: and Luk: 12: 47: the servant, who transgressed against
knowledge was to be beaten with more stripes then he who transgressed of
Ignorance: If we had a Lawe, that every lye should be punished 40s. and 2
offendors should be Convicte at the same tyme: the one a youthe of Honest
Conversation, never known to lye before: and now suddainly surprized, with
feare of some discredit, had tould a lye, wherin was no danger of harme to
any other: The other, an olde notorious lyer: and his lye contrived of purpose,
for a pernitious ende: It were not Juste, to punish both these alike: As 40s
were too little for the one, soe it were too muche for the other. Besides penaltyes (we knowe) comminge of pœna, should cause paine or greife to the offenders. It must be an Affliction: yet not a destruction, except in Capitall, or

other haynous Crimes: but in prescript penaltyes Aut[horit]ye shoots at adventure: if the same penalty hitts a Riche man, it paines him not, it is no Affliction to him, but if it lights vpon a poore man, it breakes his backe.

Everye Lawe must be Just in everye parte of it, but if the penaltye annexed be vniust, how can it be held forthe as a Just Lawe? To prescribe a penaltye, must be by some Rule, otherwise, it is an vsurpation of Gods prerogatiue: but where the Lawe makers, or Declarers canot finde a Rule for prescribinge a penaltye, if it come before the Judges pro re nata, there it is determinable by a certaine Rule, viz: by an ordinance sett vp of God for that purpose, which hathe a sure promise of divine Assistance, Exo: 21: 22, Deut: 16: 18: Judges and Officers shalt thou make etc: and they shall Judge the people with Just Judgment: Deut: 25: 1: 2: and 17: 9: 10: 11. If a Lawe were made that if any man were found drunken he should be punished by the Judges accordinge to the meritt of his offence: this is a iust Lawe, because it is warranted by a Rule: but if a certaine penaltye were prescribed, this would not be iust, because it wants a Rule, but when suche a Case is brought before the Judges, and the qualitye of the person and other circumstances considered, they shall finde a Rule to Judge by; as if Naball, and Uriah, and one of the stronge drunkards of Ephraim were all 3 togither accused before the Judges for drunkennesse, they could so proportion their severall sentences, accordinge to the severall natures and degrees of their offences, as a Just and divine sentence might appeare in them all: for a diuine sentence is in the lipps of the Kinge his mouth transgresseth not in Judgment Pro: 16: but no suche promise was ever made to a paper Sentence of humane Aut[horit]ye or Invention.[1] He who hathe promised his servants to teach them what to Answeare, even in that houer, when they shalbe brought before Judgments seats, etc: will allso teach his ministers the Judges, what sentence to pronounce, if they will allso observe his worde, and trust in him. Care not for the morrowe etc. is a Rule of generall extent, to all Cases where our providence may either crosse with some Rule or Ordinance of his, or may occasion vs to relye more upon our owne strengthe and meanes, then vpon his grace and blessing. In the sentence which Solomon gave betweene the 2 Harlotts: 1: Kings: 3: 28, It is sayd All Israell heard of the Judgment which the Kinge had Judged: and

---

[1] The following paragraphs, written on a separate sheet, give Winthrop's defense of his use of the term "paper sentences":

"4: the Phrase it self is inoffensive, for the App[ostl]e Jo: vseth it when he calls his Ep[ist]les paper writings and it can be no dishonor to vse that in speech, which is not ignominious in printe.

"4: Thus when the Parl[ia]ment call the kings proclamations printed papers they intended not to derogate from his Regall dignity (which they were allwayes tender off,) but onely to shewe forthe the vnwarrantablenesse of suche proclamations, being against the Lawe of the Lande: so all that is held forth heer by paper sentences, is meant such sentences as are not warranted by the worde of God."

they feared the Kinge, for they sawe that the wisedome of God was in him to doe Judgment. see heer, how the wisdome of God was glorified, and the Aut[horit]ye of the Judge strengthned, by this sentence: whereas in mens prescript sentences, neither of these can be attained, but if the Sentence hitt right, all is ascribed to the wisdome of our Ancestors, if otherwise, it is endured as a necessary evill, since it may not be altered.

Prescript penaltyes take away the vse of Admonition, which is allso a divine sentence and an Ordinance of God, warranted by Scripture: as appeares in Solomons Admonition to Adonijah and Nehemiahs to those that brake the Sabbaoth: Eccl: 12: 11: 12: The Words of the wise are as goads, and as nayles fastened by the masters of Assemblys—by these (my sonne) be admonished, Pro: 29: 1: Isay. 11: 4: Pro. 17: 10: A Reproofe entereth more into a wise man, then 100 stripes into a foole.

Judges are Gods vpon earthe: therefore, in their Administrations, they are to holde forthe the wisdome and mercye of God, (which are his Attributes) as well as his Justice: as occasion shall require, either in respecte of the qualitye of the person, or for a more generall good: or evident repentance, in some cases of less publ[ic] consequence, or avoydinge imminent danger to the state, and such like prevalent Considerations. Exo: 22: 8: 9: for thefte and other like Trespasses, double restitution was appointed by the Lawe: but Lev: 6: 2: 5: in such cases, if the partye Confessed his sinne, and brought his offeringe, he should onely restore the principall, and adde a fifthe parte thereto. Adultery and incest deserved deathe, by the Lawe, in Jacobs tyme (as appeares by Juda his sentence, in the case of Thamar): yet Ruben was punished onely with losse of his Birthright, because he was a Patriark. David his life was not taken awaye for his Adulterye and murder, (but he was otherwise punished) in respect of publ[ic] interest and advantage, he was valued at 10000 common men: Bathsheba was not putt to deathe for her Adulterye, because the Kinges desire, had with her, the force of a Lawe. Abiathar was not putt to deathe for his Treason, because of his former good service and faithfullnesse. Shemei was Reprived for a tyme, and had his pardon in his owne power, because of his profession of Repentance in such a season. Those which brake the Sabbaothe in Nehemiah his tyme, were not putt to deathe but first admonished, because the state was not setled etc. Joab was not putt to deathe for his murders, in Davids tyme, for avoydinge imminent publ[ic] danger, the sonnes of Zeruiah had the advantage of David, by their interest in the men of Warre: and the Com[mon] w[ealth] could not yet spare them. But if Judges be tyed to a prescript punishment, and no libertye lefte for dispensation or mitigation in any Case, heer is no place lefte for wisdome or mercye: whereas Sol[omon] saythe Pro: 20: 28: mercy and trueth preserue the Kinge; and his Throne is vpholden by mercye.

I would knowe by what Rule we may take vpon vs, to prescribe penaltyes, where God prescribes none. If it be Answ: from Gods example, I must Re-plye 1: God prescribes none except Capitall, but onely in suche Cases as are betweene party and party, and that is rather in a waye of satisfaction to the partye wronged, then to Justice and intention. 2. Gods examples are not warrants for vs, to goe against Gods Rules; our Rule is to give a Just Sentence, which we cant doe (in most Cases) before the Offence is committed etc. 5s now may be more then 20s heerafter and e contra. if examples in Scripture be warrant for vs to proceed against Rule, then we may passe by Murders, Adulteryes, Idolatryes, etc: without Capitall punishments: then we might putt the Children to deathe for parents offences etc:

If we should enq[uire] allso of the ende of prescribing penaltyes, it can be no other but this, to prevent oppression of the people, by vniust Sentences; and then I am again to seeke of a Rule, to weaken the power and Justice of an Ordinance of God, through distrust of his providence: and promise of Assistance in his owne Ordinance: who must give the Lawe makers wisdome etc. to prescribe sentences? must not God? and may we not then trust him, to give as muche wisdome etc: to suche Judges, as he shall sett vp after vs? it is said when they had Judges by Gods appointment, God was with the Judge. so may we still believe, that if our posterity shall choose Judges accordinge to God, he wilbe with our Judges in tyme to come, as well as with the present.

It may be further demanded, what power we haue over the persons and estates of the succeedinge generations? If we should now prescribe, where our posteritye etc. should dwell, what quantityes of land they should till: what places they should tende vnto: what diet they should use, what Clothes they should weare etc: by what Rule could we challenge this power? yet we have example for some of these in Scripture, as of Jonadab the sonne of Rechab: etc: but no man will take these as warrant for vs to laye suche iniunctions vpon those which come after us, because they are to have the same interest, and freedome in their estates and persons that we have in ours.

And for preventinge of oppression, etc: is there no waye to helpe that, but by breache of Rule? shall we runne into manifest iniustice, for feare of I know not what future danger of it? is there not a cleare waye of helpe in suche cases, by Appeal, or Petition, to the highest Aut[horit]ye? If this will not releiue, in a partic[ular] case, we shall then be in a very ill Case, for all our prescript penaltyes. Besides, there may be such a generall Lawe made (as in magna Charta) that may prevent the overthrowinge of mens estates, or lands, etc:

by Fines, etc: (and I think it as needfull, as any Lawe or Libertye we haue) whereby the Judges may be restrayned, within certaine limitts, which (if occasion should require to exceede) may be referred to the Generall Court. And in Corp[ora]l punishments, a Libertye in suche and suche Cases, to re-deeme them at a certaine rate: This would sufficiently assure the proper per-sons and estates, from any great oppression, if withall, our Courts of Judica-ture, were kept but by 3 or 5 magistrates at most, which may well be ordered, without any deviation from our Patent. and so the greater number of magis-trates should be free from ingagement in any Case, which might come to a reveiw vpon Appeal or Petition.

It is an error so to conceive of Lawes, as if they could not be perfecte with-out penaltyes annexed, for they are as truely distinct as light and darknesse: Lawe was Created with and in man, and so is naturall to him: but penaltye is positiue and accidentall. Lawe is bonum simpliciter, but poena is simplici-ter malum in subiecto: therefore Lawes may be declared and given, without any penaltyes annexed.

Isay. 10: 1: Woe to them that Decree unrighteous Decrees: and write greivousnesse, which they haue prescribed: so that where the penaltye proues greiveous by the vnrighteousnesse of a prescript Decree, it will drawe a woe after it, as well as vnrighteous sentence: Deut: 25: 15: thou shalt have a per-fect and a iust weight and measure: If God be so stricte in Commutative Justice, that every Acte therein must be by a iust and perfecte Rule, what warrant have we, to thinke that we maye dispence distributive or vindictive Justice to our brethren by gesse, when we prescribe a certaine measure to an incertaine meritt.

But it wilbe obiected: volenti non fit iniuria: the people givinge vs power to make lawes to binde them, they doe implicitly give their Consent to them. To this it may be Answeared: that where they putt themselues into our power to binde them to Lawes and penalties, they can intende no other but suche as are iust and righteous: and althoughe their implicit Consent may binde them to outward obedience, yet it neither tyes them to satisfaction, nor frees suche Lawmakers from vnrighteousnesse, nor the Law it self from iniustice; nor will suche a Lawe be a sufficient warrant to the Conscience of the Iudge, to pronounce suche a sentence, as he knowes to be apparently disproportion-able to the offence brought before him.

Althoughe my Arguments conclude against prescript penaltyes indefi-nitely, yet I doe not deny but, they may be lawfull in some Cases: for an vniversall affirmatiue proposition may be true, though it comprehend not euery partic[ular], as when we say All the Country was Rated to such a charge, no man will conceive that everye person and every woman etc, was rated; and when we saye suche an one was cast out by the wholl churche, this is a true speeche (to common intendment) though every partic[ular] member did not consent. Where any penalty may be prescribed by a Rule, so as the Judge may pronounce a Just sentence, I have formerly, and shall still ioyne in it.

We will now Answeare such obiections, as are made, against the libertye required to be lefte to Judges, in their Sentences.

1 ob: Judges are subject to Temptations, if their sentences be not prescribed.

Answ. 1: We may not transgresse Rules, to avoyde Temptations: for God will have his servants exercised with temptations, that the power of his grace may be made manifest in mans Infirmitye: A master will not sende his servant about his businesse in a darke night, to avoyde Temptations of ill companye or the like, which he may possibly meet with in the daye tyme: nor will any Christian man take in his Corne or haye before it be readye, for avoyding a Temptation of takinge it in vpon the Sabbaothe: we doe not forbidd wine to be brought to vs, thought we knowe it is a great occasion of Temptation to sinne.

2: Those, who make Lawes, and prescribe penaltyes, are also men subiecte to Temptations: and may allso miscarrye through Ignorance, heedlessnesse, or sinister respects: and it is not hard, to prove, that the Lawe makers, in all States, have Committed more and more pernitious errors then the Judges: as 40 tymes greater then the law of God [*illegible*] and [*illegible*] as much [*illegible*] to the ruin of a mans estate [*illegible*] and there is good reason for it: 1: they supposinge themselves tyed to no Rule, nor lyable to any accompt, are in the more danger of being misledd: 2: he who prescribes a punishment in a Case, wherein no person stands before him to be iudged, canot be so warye of sheddinge innocent blood, or sparinge a guilty person, or committinge other iniustice, as the Iudge who hathe the person and Cause before him: when Saule prescribed that Capitall sentence against suche as should tast ought before night if Jonathans case had then been before him, he would have Judged otherwise. Dangers more remote are ever lesse heeded. 3: Lawe makers have not so cleare a Callinge, in prescribinge penaltyes, as Judges have in passinge sentences, and therefore, there cannot be expected the like blessinge of Assistance from God. Judges are necessarylye tyed to give sentence in a Cause before them but Lawe makers are not so bounde to prescribe sentences.

3: If a Judge should sometymes erre in his Sentence, through misprision, or Temptation: the error or fault is his owne: and the iniurye or damage extends not farr: but an error in the Lawe, resteth vpon the Ordinance it selfe, and the hurte of it may reache far, even to posterytye. there is more vnrighteousnesse, and dishonor, in one vniust Lawe, then in many vniust Sentences.

2 ob: God prescribed some certaine penaltyes: and that in Cases where offences doe usually vary in their degree and meritt:

Answ: 1: We have shewed before how God might doe it, in regard of his absolute soveraintye.

2: It is no Iniustice in him, because the least degree of the smalest offence, (before his Judgment seate) deserves the highest degree of punishment.

3: In some of thèse (as in Thefte) he variethe the punishment according to the measure and nature of the offence. In others as deathe, perpetuall servitude, etc: beinge the Just Reward of suche offences in their simple nature, they have not a fitt Subiecte, for an increace of punishment to take place vpon: he who is putt to deathe for Adulterye, cannot dye againe for Incest concurringe therewith and he who is adiudged to perpetuall servitude for stealinge 100*li* cannot be capeable of a further sentence for batterye.

4: In all, or most of those Offences, the penaltye was in waye of satisfaction, to such as were damnified thereby and in such cases, Justice will not allowe a Judge any Libertye to alter or remitt any thinge: nor can any circumstance leade to qualification: a Riche man hath the same right to satisfaction for his goods stollen from him, as a poore man: and the poorest mans life is the life of man, as well as a Princes:

5: These Presedents were given to the Judges, not with direction to prescribe penaltyes to other Lawes that had none: but with Commandment to give Judgement in all Cases, by the equitye of these: (there are some formes of prayer and sermons in scripture, but this dothe not prove ergo all etc.)

3 ob: If the determination of the Lawe were lefte to the Judges, that were Arbitrary Goverment: and is it not in reason the same, if the punishment of the Transgression of the Lawe, be committed to them?

Answ: The Reason is not alike in bothe Cases.

1: The determination of Lawe belonges properly to God: he is the onely Lawgiver: but he hathe given power and gifts to men to interprett his Lawes: and this belonges principally to the highest Aut[horit]ye in a Com[mon] W[ealth] and subordinately to other magistrates and Judges according to their severall places.

2: The Lawe is allwayes the same, and not changeable by any circumstances of aggravation, or extenuation, as the penaltye is: and therefore drawes a certaine guilt vpon every Transgressor whither he sinne of Ignorance, or against Knowledge, or presumptuously: and therefore Lawes or the Interpretation of them, may be prescribed, without any danger, because no event can alter the Reason, or Justice of them: as it may of punishments.

3: The Lawe is more generall and lyeth as a burden, vpon all persons and at all tymes: but the penaltye reaches to none, but transgressors and to suche, onely when they are brought vnder sentence, and not before.

4: It is needfull that all men should knowe the Lawes, and their true meaninges, because they are bound to them, and the safety and wellfare of the Com[mon] W[ealth] consists in the observation of them: therefore it is needfull they should be stated and declared, as soone as is possible; but there is not the like necessitye or vse of declaringe their penaltyes before hande, for they who are godly and vertuous, will observe them, for Conscience, and Vertues sake: and for suche as must be helde in by feare of punishment, it is better they should be kept in feare of a greater punishment then to take libertye to transgresse, through the Contempt of a smaller.

4 ob: It is safe for the Com[mon] W[ealth] to have penaltyes prescribed, because we know not what magistrates or Judges we may have heerafter.

Answ: 1: God foresawe, that there would be corrupt Judges in Israell, yet he lefte most penaltyes, to their determination.

2: There is no wisdome of any State can so provide, but that in many thinges of greatest concernment, they must confide in some men: and so it is in all humane Affaires: the wisest merchants, and the most warye, are forced to repose great trust in the wisdome and faithfullnesse of their servants, Factors, masters of their Shipps, etc. All States, in their generalls of warre, Admiralls, Embassadors, Treasurers, etc: and these are Causes of more publ[ic] Consequence, then the Sentence of a Judge in matters of misdemeanor, or other smaler offences.

3: When we have provided against all common, and probable events, we may and ought to trust God for safety from suche dangers, as are onely possible, but not likely, to come vpon vs: especially when our strivinge to prevent suche possible dangers, may hazard the deprivation, or weakninge of a present good; or may drawe those, or other evills, neerer vpon vs.[1]

---

[1] The following, written on a separate sheet, carries the instruction by Governor Winthrop: "I pray ye enter this amonge the obiections."

"It is allso obiected, out of Deut. 22: 28: that 50 shek[els] is a prescribed penaltye for a deflowered virgin, whither poore or riche.

"Answ: 1: there was no suche difference amonge the Israelites then, but that a private man might be a matche without disparragement to a Rulers daughter: and the dignity of any free Israeliteman, was equall and aboue the personall dignity of any woman.

"2: This was not properly a penalty but a Dowrye or recompence of virginity: and so it appeares

This discourse is runne out to more length then was intended: the Conclusion is this: The Goverment of the Massachusetts consists of Magistrates and Freemen: in the one is placed the Aut[horit]ye, in the other the Libertye of the Com[mon] W[ealth] either hath power to Acte, both alone, and both togither, yet by a distinct power, the one of Libertye, the other of Aut[horit]ye: the Freemen Act of them selues in Electinge their magistrates and Officers: the magistrates Acte alone in all occurrences out of Court: and both Acte togither in the Generall Court: yet all limited by certaine Rules, bothe in the greater and smaller affaires: so as the Government is Regular in a mixt Aristocratie, and no waye Arbitrary.

[Extract from St. Thomas Aquinas]¹

Iuditium nihil aliud est, quam quædam diffinitio vel determinatio eius quod iustum est: fit autem aliquid Iustum dupliciter: vel ex natura rei, quod dicitur Ius naturale: vel ex quodam condicto inter homines quod dicitur Ius positivum. Leges autem scribuntur, ad vtriusque Iuris declarationem: aliter, tamen et aliter: nam Legis scriptura, Ius quidem naturale continet, sed non instituit: non enim habet Robur ex Lege, sed ex natura: Ius autem positivum, scripturam Legis et continet, et instituit; dans ei Autoritatis Robur: Ideo necesse est, vt Iuditium fiat, secundum Legis scripturam: alioquin iuditium deficeret, vel a sueto naturali, vel a iusto positivo.

Lex scripta, sicut non dat Robur Iuri naturali, ita nec potest eius Robur minuere, auferre: quia nec voluntas hominis potest immutare naturam: Ideo si scriptura Legis contineat aliquid contra Ius naturale, iniusta est, nec habet vim obligandi: Ibi enim Ius positivum locum habet, vbi, quantum ad Ius naturale, nihil differt, vtrum sic vel aliter fiat, et ideo nec tales scripturæ Leges dicuntur, sed potius Legis corruptiones, et ideo secundum eas non est Iudica[n]dum.

In legibus recte positis, in aliquibus tamen Casibus possunt deficere, ita vt si secundum eas iudicaretur, esse[n]t contra Ius naturale: Et ideo in talibus, non est secundum literam Legis Iudicandum sed recurrendum ad æquitatem,

Exo: 22: 16: 17 and was to be more or lesse according to the Custom, thoughe at that present it was estimated at 50 shek[els] for it was the mores in Israell for men to give a dowry or recompense to the father, for his daughter a virgin: as Jacob offered Laban a price for Rachell and Shekem offers a Dowry for Dinah, and when Dauid alledged his poverty at the tender of Saul his daughter to him: Saul answ: that he would aske no other Dowry but 100 foreskins, whereas Dauid found Saul would have demanded some great portion of mony: wherby it appeares, that Dowry of virgins was not at any certain Rate, but was alterable according to the [*illegible*] quality of the person."

¹ In the arrangement of the several sheets of the original manuscript which was made by Robert C. Winthrop, Sr., when he had them mounted and bound, this extract from St. Thomas Aquinas is placed immediately following the Discourse.

quam intendit Legislator: vnde Iurisperitus dicit: Nulla ratio Iuris, aut æqui-
tatis benignitas patitur, vt quæ salubriter, pro utilitate hominum introdu-
cuntur, ea nos duriore interpretatione contra ipsorum Com[m]odum pro-
ducamus ad seueritatem: et in talibus etiam Legislator aliter Iudicavit et si
considerasset, Lege determinasset. Tho: Aquinas.

*The Returnes of the Committee of the house of Dep: concerning the Book about Arbitrary
Gouernment, in the examination thereof: and the votes of the house past upon each particular viz:*

In the 1 parte thereof

1: Concerninge the Definition, therein made, we conceive it is defectiue.

2: Concerninge the distinction therein made of the bodye Polit[ic], and
the members thereof, in attributinge Aut[horit]ye to the one, and onely Libertye to the other: we finde not any suche distinction in the Patent.

3: Concerninge the Clause recited therin (respecting the generall Court)
which gives onely Libertye to the Freemen, to advise and Counsell, instead
of power and Aut[horit]ye (which the Patent allowes) we conceive it a takinge away of the power and priviledges of the Freemen.

In the 2 parte of the Booke, which concernes the Rule by which a people
should be gouerned, we finde these dangerous positions.

1: That generall Rules are sufficient to cleare a state from Arbitrary
Gouernment.

2: That Judges ought to haue Libertye to varye from suche generall Rules
when they see Cause.

In the followinge of the first of those 2 positions, there are many dangerous
passages, and bitter censurings of all pœnall Lawes. As

1: That they are paper Sentences of humane Aut[horit]ye and invention.

2: That mens prescript Sentences doe denye and exclude bothe the wisdome of God, and the Aut[horit]ye of the Judge.

3: That to prescribe Lawes with certaine penaltyes is an vsurpinge of Gods
Aut[horit]ye.

4: That a Sentence ought not to be provided before the Case fall out, but
immediate Assistance to be expected.

5: That partic[ular] Lawes includinge certaine penaltyes, are not Just
wanting Rule.

The Induction of partic[ular] Instances which are brought to proue this second position, with the Reasons and consequencyes, are pernitious and dangerous.

per ROBT. BRIDGES

By order etc.

[Governor Winthrop's Answer to the Committee's Report]

Answeare, the Committee have been mistaken in most of their objections.

1: The Title shewes that the Author intended not any Definition but a description onely. and to make it the more full and cleare, he layes it downe both Affirmatively and negatively: yet a logitian may frame it into a Definition, thus Arb. Gov. is a Gov. exercised without a Rule, but the description is fals by the Causes and by the effects.

2: There is no suche distinction as is observed, betweene the bodye Politike and the members therof, for that were to distinguish betweene the wholl and the parts: but the distinction betweene the members of that bodye givinge Aut[horit]ye to the one and power of libertye to the other, is warranted by the Patent (as in other places so) partic[ularly] in that clause, which sayth that the Gouernor etc: shall call the Freemen to consult and Advice etc. which is an Acte of Libertye, and not of Aut[horit]ye and for the other part of their power which is matter of Election, the late Order Libertyes *[blank]* sayth it is their constant Libertye, not Aut[horit]ye.

In the 2 parte

1: We finde not any suche position that Generall Rules are sufficient to cleare a state from Arbitrary Gouerment but we finde that the worde of God and the Lawes heer established beinge appointed by order of Court as a Rule for the present, are suche a Rule as may be required of the Judges in all their Administrations, because a Rule may from thence be had (if God give wisdome to discerne it) in any partic[ular] case, which may fall out: otherwise the Lawe of God were not perfect, and from what better grounds shall the Lawe makers drawe all future Lawes and prescribed penaltyes:

But if the Author had expressed himselfe in the verye words of the position, yet it will admitt a safe construction, for all Lawes (not limited to partic[ular] parties or occasions) are generall Rules, and may be so called thoughe they have a certaine penaltye annexed.

2: Nor will the booke owne the 2 position in the words expressed: but this he gathers, bothe from their office, (being Gods vicegerents) and from diverse examples in scripture, which seeme to hold forthe so muche, that some libertye ought to be left to Judges, in some cases, vpon speciall occasions, to hold forth the mercye of God, as well as his Justice: nor doe we conceive, that either in the Com[mon] W[ealth] of Israell, or in any other, the Judges haue been wholly restrayned of such Libertye.

In the followinge Arguments

If the Committee had founde suche dangerous passages, as they intimate, they should have doone well to haue imparted their partic[ular] observations therein vnto vs, that we might have considered of them, for want whereof it cannot be expected, we should deliuer any opinion about them.

The like we may saye for suche bitter censuring as they mention: onely it is vsuall for men to call suche thinges bitter, which themselues disrelishe thoughe they may be harmelesse and whollsome not withstandinge.

For the 5 partic[ular]s mentioned, they are deliuered as Arguments or the Consectaryes thereof so as the Arguments must first be avoyded, before any Judgment can be given about them.[1]

---

[1] The following paragraphs, written on a separate sheet, contain Winthrop's answers to the "5 particulars":

"*1: Paper sentences etc.*

"1: It is not spoken against all pœnall Lawes, but onely such as are of humane Aut[horit]y and invention.

"2: It is true of suche, that no such promise of divine Assistance is made to them, that may be produced.

"3: It is no more offensive, or derogatory to any righteous sentences then if a man should say the like of paper sentences or precepts of humane Aut[horit]y or Invention.

"*2: That mens prescript Sentences doe deny and exclude bothe the wisdome of God, and the Aut[horit]y of the Judge.*

"There is no suche sentence in the booke, but onely a recitall of what followed vpon the Sentence of Solomon between the 2 Harlotts, and an Application of it to the matter in question.

"*3: That to prescribe Lawes with certaine penaltyes is an vsurpinge of Gods Aut[horit]ye.*

"This also is not truely recited, for heer is omitted that which will take awaye all appearance of offence. The words in the book are these: To prescribe a pœnalty must be by some Rule otherwise it is an vsurpation of Gods prærogatiue.

"*4: That a sentence ought not to be provided before the Case fall out, but immediate Assistance is to be expected.*

"This is allso misrecited: The sentence is thus: God will also teach his ministers the Judges what sentence to pronounce, if they will also obserue his words and trust in him.

"*5: That partic[ular] Lawes includinge certaine pœnalties are not Just wantinge Rule.*

"Hunc errorem agnosco, imo amplector etiam viz: that no Lawe penalty or sentence can be iust, if it want a Rule. For the pernitiousnesse and danger of the positions (what they are is not mentioned) what hurt or danger can arise by propoundinge precepts, prouisions, and examples from the worde of God, from our owne practice, and the practice of our Natiue Contrye, and Arguments concurringe therewith, to a Court, which hathe light and wisdome to Judge of them, and Libertye to reiecte what they shall not see Cause to allowe.

"And forasmuche as the most Juditious writings of the best men are not free from all exceptions, through our naturall Ignorance and other human [*illegible*] suche [*illegible*] are not so muche to be

The examples which the Author alledgethe out of Scripture, are onely to shew how God hathe sometymes (in his wisdome and mercye) dispensed with the rigor of his owne Lawe: and that Princes haue sometymes doone the like, vpon publick or other prevalent considerations, which cannot be denyed to be a truethe: and for the warrant they had for it, being (at the most) disputable, it was as free for him to deliuer them in his owne and some other learned and godly mens apprehensions, as it is for others who differ therein: and there canbe no more danger in this, then in other bookes and Sermons, where the same or other passages of Scripture are truely reported, thoughe not applyed to the sence of every godly man, as if one should reason thus: Dauid putt the Amorites to torture, therefore, in some Cases it is lawfull so to doe: this will not be iudged a pernitious doctrine thoughe some godly men doe question the warrantablenesse of the example   the like may be said of all suche examples in scripture, as are controverted amonge godly and learned men: but it is otherwise in such places, as are not questionable, as if a man should reason thus: David sentensed Mephibosheth before he heard him: therefore it is lawfull for a Judge so to doe, this might truly be sayd to be a pernitious doctrine; or if one should argue thus: Saul made a law with a prescript penaltye of deathe to him that should transgresse it, therefore it had been iust, that Jonathan should have bene putt to deathe for transgressinge that Lawe: or therefore it is lawfull for Princes etc: to prescribe penaltyes at their own pleasures, these might be iudged to be pernitious doctrines: because the example is vnquestionable, etc.

The Authors reviewe of his writing

That which gaue me occasion first to enquire after a Rule for prescript penaltyes, was the inequalitye I sawe in some prescribed sentences vpon the breache of diverse morall Lawes: and proceedinge in this enquirye, I kept my intention still vpon that subiect, without respect to suche Lawes as are meerly positiue, hauinge their Aut[horit]ye onely and wholly from humane Institution: therefore you shall find that all my instances are of that kinde, and all my Arguments looke that waye, as in the Instances I bringe of the Lawes of Engl[an]d. If I had intended the positiue and Statute Lawes, it had been a great mistake, for I knowe well that most of the later Statute Lawes haue their penaltyes prescribed, and it must needs be so, for suche as are meerly positiue, for a Judge can haue no Rule for his sentence vpon the

insisted vpon, but rather the scope and Argument of the matter to be intended, which how far the Committee may seeme to have attended in their survey of this booke, I leave to consideration."

breache of suche a Lawe, except he have it from the Lawe it self: as for instance, if the Lawe which forbidds any man to kill an hare or partridge with a gunne, had not allso sett downe the penaltye, the Judge could not have founde out any, which might have been iust because no Lawe of God or nature makes suche an Acte any offence or transgression. But for the Comon Lawes of Engl[an]d (which are the ancient Lawes and of farre more esteem for their wisdome and equity, then the statute Lawes) they had no penaltyes prescribed, and it may be conceived that for suche of them as were grounded vpon the worde of God, and the Light of nature, there must needs be that in the same worde and in the same light of nature (especially where the image of God in man is in parte renewed by Christ) which may lead vs to a iust punishment for the Transgression of such a Lawe. Nor doe I oppose all prescript penaltyes in morall cases but onely such as doe crosse some cleare Rules in the worde of God as will appeare by all my Arguments. And for avoydinge all danger to the subiect for want of prescript penaltyes in some Cases, you may see that I require some suche Lawe to be made, as may limitt Judges within such bounds of moderation, as may prevent suche dangers, and it is one of my expresse conclusions in the first page, that Judges ought to be tyed to a Rule, and suche a Rule, as may be required of them in all their Administrations, and therefore vpon what grounds I should be charged to Assert Arbitrary government, and that Judges should have Libertye to doe what they maye, I leave to your Judgments.

As for Lawes, you shall finde allso, that I conclude the necessitye of declaringe and statinge them, so as all the people may knowe them, for I ever held it vniust, to require of men the obedience to any Lawe, which they may not (by common Intendment) take notice off. Answearable heervnto hathe been my practice: All the vsefull Lawes we have, had my consent, and suche poore helpe as the Lord enabled me, to yeild to them: some of which have prescribed penaltyes, and where I have withhelde my consent to any suche penaltyes, I haue giuen my reasons for it, which have been suche, as in some Cases have satisfied the Court, and heerin I have taken no more libertye then is allowed to every member of the Court. I will not iustifie every passage in my booke: there are 2 or 3 words that offence have been taken at, and althoughe I can give a safe account of them, yet, I must confesse they doe not now please me, but where the matter is good, and the intention of the writer honest, the Lord forbidds vs to make a man an Offender in a word.

Whatsouer is erronious (I saye as I did from the first) I shall leave it to its due censure: but for all that is of God and of the Trueth, or the sincerity of my intentions heerin to the publ[ic] weale, or the Libertye I had by my place to propounde suche considerations to the Court if these be questioned I must stand and fall with them.

Jo: Winthop

JOHN WINTHROP TO WILLEM KIEFT[1]

Sir, Yours of the 28 of the last mo: I received, which I imparted to our gen[era]ll Court being then Assembled: who returne you all respectiue thanks, for that sincerity which they apprehende in you towards vs: and that neighbourly Correspondency, which you hold towards vs and our people, who resorte to you vpon their occasions, and which we see you are willinge still [to] continue: nor do we otherwise beleeve, then as you professe, that you are vnwillingly drawne into this Conversation, with our freinds in those parts: nor can we blame you that in your faithfullnesse to that state which have sett you in place and reposed trust in you you stand strictly to maintain that which you apprehende to be their right, in requiring due recompense for iniuryes: and on the other side we earnestly desire, you would be so perswaded of our integrity and care, to give all humble respecte to the High and mighty Lords the states, as we would not wittingly be countenancers of vnrighteousness, nor give any iust occasion of offense or displeasure to so Potent a state, in respect of whose power and greatnesse so poore and weak a people as we, are of no value: but for so much as you are not ignorant that our brethren of Hartford doe plead the Justice of their Cause as your selfe and your predecessor have also doon in your former lettres to vs of 11 feb. last, [you][2] were pleased to discourse prudently and at large concerning the matters in difference etc: yet in [illegible] what they allso alledge on their parts and the proofes not yet produced on either side, we doe not [know] what Answ: you can expect from vs other then formerly.[3] But wheras the Commissioners of all our Colonyes are to be at Hartford, the last of [August][4] (by the English account) if you would please to send Commissioners thither, to treate with them about the differences It would be very acceptable to vs, and (we are well assured) to all our Confederates, as the most hopefull waye,

---

[1] Massachusetts Archives, ii. 364. For Winthrop's mention of this letter, see *Journal*, ii. 176–177.

[2] Due to the nature of the binding of the volume in which this manuscript is contained, it is not possible to see all the words. In this and in similar succeeding instances where the context is perfectly clear, words have been supplied.

[3] *Acts of the Commissioners of the United Colonies in New England*, i. 13.

[4] This was the date named by Governor Winthrop in a canceled sentence of his draft of this letter. The commissioners actually met on September 5, 1644. *Acts of the Commissioners of the United Colonies in New England*, i. 16.

to bring both your self, and vs all to a right vnderstanding of whatever is in variance either in point of Right, or of Iniury: wherby they might be better prepard for a peaceable and finall issue, in such a Course as to your wisdome may seeme most equall and expedient, according to such offer, as they have formerly made. So desiring you to accept this Tender of our good will to you, with our poore (but faithfull) advice, for hastening soe good ende to all vn-friendly conversations betweene yourself and our deare freinds and brethren: we commend you and your Affaires to the gratious protection and direction of the Allmighty So I take leave and rest at your service in all friendly offices

Jo: W: *D: G:*

by the approval of the Court

Boston N: E: (5) called July: 15, 1644

WILLIAM CODDINGTON TO JOHN WINTHROP[1]

Honered Sir, Yours of the (8) 10–43 I haue receaued filled with exsamples of the Judgments of god of the Duch and English that fell by the Indeans[2] for the English yow mention their forsakeing the fellowship of gods people and ordenances and the vnseasonablenes of seeking of greate things the lord plucking vp what he hath planted, etc. Though I might render some excuses, yet I forbeare and doe acknowledge my neclecte In not writeing vnto yow longe ere this, and returneing a thankefull acknowledgement of your loue in seting before me such graue exhortations [*torn*]lemations. let the righteous smite me it shall not [*torn*] my head noe it shall be a healeing balsome to [*torn*] I haue forsaken yourselfe and others against my own [*torn*] posses in distance of place, yet I hope and liue by his grace never shall in affection till my dyeing day, and the ordenances with yow both in Church and Common wealth are to me the ordenances of the lord Jesus. And the lord hath begunne to let me see by experience that a mans comfort doth not depend in the multetude of those things he doth posese, the lord haueing this last winter taken from me A larg Corne Barne which did cost me aboue, or aboute, 150*li* building, my farme howse 12 Oxen 8 Cowes 6 other beasts in which howses was my Corne for seed and spending and paying my debts, the fyer breaking forth in the night, neither beeding nore howshould stuffe, nore so much as my servants wering Cloth no thing but the shertes of their backes

---

[1] Massachusetts Archives, II. 4–5; Chapin, *Documentary History of Rhode Island*, II. 176–179.
[2] For Winthrop's account of Anne Hutchinson's death at the hands of the Indians, see *Journal*, II. 137–138.

was saued, and liues to the valew of 4 or 500*li*. And yet blessed be his name, he is the portion of my sowle, I shall not wante, he hathe by one providence or other provided for me a considerable suplye so that I haue enough blessed be his name. And being nowe in writeing, I shall make bould to ade a word to 3 or 4 particulers in yours to mr. Brenton and mr. Balstone (my loueing friends) and in them to me yow desire they much consider in what relation they stand to the Church and Common wealth with yow for the Church to answer for itselfe we being not to [*torn*] doe look at that Church meeting at mr. Balstones [*torn*] which I was advised to remaine and commended to the grace of god [*torn*] christ Jesus in so doeing, and the sermon concerneing of it the [*torn*] lord does that wher ther wer not churches to commend ther bretheren vnto ther they might commend them to the grace of god, etc., to carie with it the force of a dismishon which is not my light alone, but of the reverent and larned.[1] I desire that this lynne of devishon was remoued, that I might have such free acsesse to all as to see their faces with comfort, and to partake with yow in the ordenances. 2ly. For the Common wealth the difference arose about mr. Wheelwright banishment of which he is releassed (as I am informed) but if it was a meanes in rayseing any vnquietnes in the Commonwealth I shall vpon information indevor to giue satisefaction, the lord so helping me.

3. For Gorton as he came ther [to] be of the Island before I knew of it, and is here against my mind, soe shall he not be by me protected. I could haue hartely desired for the good I professe of both plantations that we had not bene reiected in alyence with yow aboute the Indeans, which now the generaletie here will be averse from. the trewth is here is a partye which doe adheare vnto Gorton and his Company, in both the plantations, and Judge them so much strength to the place which be neither frinds to yow nore vs. Now the trewth is I desire to haue either such alience with yourselues or Plimouth one or both as might be safe for vs all. I haue my cheefe intrest the Island it being bought to me and my frinds, and how inconvenient it might be if it were possesed by an Enemye lying in the heart of the plantations and convenient for shiping I cannot but see but I want both Counsell and Strength to effecte what I desire. I desire to heare from yow and that you would burye what I write in deepe silence, for what I write I never imparted to any, nor would to yow had I the least doubt of your faythfullnes, that it should be vttered to my preiudice.

for Morton he was insinuateing who was for the king at his first comeing to Portesmouth, and would report to such as he Judged to be of his mynd he

---

[1] See Coddington's earlier reference to this subject, pages 245–246, above.

was glad he meet with so many Caveleres. to Mr. Hart (as I am informed) of Cohannet he discovered some thing in this way, and after doubted he was not trew, and he had lands to dispose of to his followers in each province and from Cape Ann to Cape Codd was one he did and dispossed of some to Lambert Woodward. my Tenant Gould was his host howse, he being much taken with him, and towld me which I will afferme of my oath that he had land to dispose of in each plantation a [*torn*] his son John some Land, and that he had wronge in the bay [to the] valew of 200*li* and mayd bitter Complaints therof but Morton would let it rest as he tould me till the Governour came over to right him and did intimate he knew whose roste his spits and Jackes turned etc., but I feare tediousnes and therefor with the tender of my love to the Go[vernou]r yourselfe mr. Dudlye and who else remember me, I take leaue and rest. yours

WM. CODDINGTON

NEWPORT Aug. 5, 1644

Pesecus nore Canonecus haue not sent vnto me sence I reiected a present of 30 fingers and thumes after their first attempt.

Osemecome was last satterday at my howse and doth say he is all one hart with [*torn*] and sayth that Canonecus sent to him to borrow some peeces he hath to goe agine [*torn*] this next weeke which he refussed to lend. [I] tould him he did well so to doe and to [*torn*] he knew [*torn*] Vale.

JOHN WINTHROP TO THE EARL OF WARWICK[1]

R[IGH]T HON[ORA]BLE AND MY VERY GOOD LORDE, Your Lo[rdshi]pps Lettres by mr. B: I received the 7th of July, which were occasion of Comfort to me, both for your Lo[rdshi]pps wellfare, and for your constant hearty Affection to our Colony and your undeserved favour to my selfe your most vnworthy servant: which shall so farre oblige me to your good Lo[rdshi]pp as my poore prayers and indeavours shalbe euer improved for your honor and wellfare.

Now concerninge that which your Lo[rdshi]pp desires to be satisfied in, I shall truly relate to you the state of the Country and our present Condition therin, so fully and faithfully as you shall not need to inquire any further therabout.

For the Contry it is for the most parte a light soyle black earth aboue and

---

[1] W. 1. 165; *L. and L.*, II. 459–460. For Sir Robert Rich, 2nd Earl of Warwick, see *D.N.B.*

sand beneathe: it is very well watered with rivers, brookes and springs, with faire levels of good meadowe in many places, but much of it is full of hassocks and wett, for want of drayning.

The Timber is oak and pine, with some elme and ashe in the swampes, which are not bogge as in Ireland but in the summer they are dry and fine lande. By the sea Coast there is store of salt marsh which is for 3, 4 or 5 foote a meere Turfe, which will burne well, yet it beares very fine benty grasse, which will maintain Cattle well both in summer and winter.

The grounde is most apt for Rye, and summer wheate which afford some-tymes 30 or 40 bushells of an acre, yet after 2 or 3 Croppes not aboue halfe so much except cost be bestowed upon it. diverse haue founde by experience that 2 or 3 Croppes of Rye will come of one Seedinge, and without any new ploughing. there is also this yeare great store of pease and barly, as good as I haue seen ordinaryly in England.

All sorts of English fruits and garden stuffe prosper very well heere. we have a Croppe of Corne now vpon the grounde that (in the best Judgment) may be sufficient to serve our people for neere 2 years.

Our Cattle thrive and increace as well as in Engld. and are of a large size.

The ayre is pure and healthfull, which makes it the more hott in summer and the sharper in winter.

Our winters are longe, so as we are forced to provide stover for our Cattle for 5 months, yet many tymes the winter is very milde, and the snowe lyes so little tyme as 3 or 4 months provision will suffice our Cattle.

The sea affords great store of Codd and many other sorts of fish, which may be had (some of them) all seasons of the year. Sea Fowle heere is store, but not so easye to be taken now as at our first Comming. heere are allso Partridge and heathe geese, and great multitude of pigeons, and Deare, but the Country is too full of Coverts for hunting or hawking. yet a man may ride all over the Countrye, except the Swamps which are very vaste and hideous.

Many woulves and foxes heere are which doe vs much damage but heere is no wild beast will assault a man.

For our Goverment it is mixed, the freemen (who are all church members) choose the Magistrates and cheife Officers, and deputyes, who make all the Lawes and levye monyes, and minister Justice, without any Appeale to the people. All our magistrates are chosen anewe every yeare. we have in our Jurisdiction 20 townes, and in euery of them a Company gathered into Church fellowshipp. most of them haue 2 ministers and one or 2 ruling Elders: The ministers are sustayned in some Churches by a treasury raised by a weekly contribution, in some others by a voluntary taxation.

Our Courts are of 2 sorts the gen[eral] Courts, which are for making of lawes and levying monyes to which every towne sends one or 2 deputyes, and the other Courts held by the magistrates, which are for Judicature.

The Ministers have great power with the people, wherby throughe the good correspondency between the magistrates and them, they are the more easyly gouerned being of [*illegible*] general sober and religious etc.

JOHN WINTHROP

[*Ca.* September, 1644]

[*Endorsed by Governor Winthrop:*] Resp. d[omi]no Warwick.

ROGER WOOD TO JOHN WINTHROP[1]

To my much Honnoured and much esteemed frend: Jhon Wentrop Esq:
gouernor in new England bee theise presented when god shall please.
god preserue the good shippe and her Company

MY MUCH HONNOURED AND WORTHY FREND, I thanke yow for your Two lettres now rechued by this shippe, and your favour in acquainting mee with such occurrence as came to your knowledge from our miserable distracted cuntrey, which is likely to become to great vassaledge if not vtterly ruinated, the King prevayling against the Parliaments Armies if god in mercie prevent it not. Wee are not free from distractions, and hartburnings amongst vs, by reason of our Ministers setting vp of an Independant Church,[2] from which they will not bee intreated to refraine, vntill wee heare what that Synode in England haue concluded: but having layd downe their ministeriall calling, which they receiued by authoritie of the Church of England, haue preached against the errors and Idolatrie, practised therein, and gathered a congregationall church (as they call it) into which not yet aboue 35 persons men and woemen are entred into covenant who haue called mr. white to bee their Pastor, and the Pastor and Church so gathered, haue chosen mr. Coapland and mr. Goulding to bee ruling elders, and all thus chosen haue elected their deacons and entend to choose wydowes when they fall. The ruling Elders notwithstanding they haue laid downe their ministerie yet exercise their guifts in some places of the Island, but neither baptize the children, nor administer the sacrament of the Lords supper but the pastor only to such are within the pale of their church. here are no papists amongst vs, nor any popistie affected,

---

[1] John Davis MSS., M.H.S.
[2] Cf. Lefroy, *Memorials of the Bermudas*, 1. 585.

but wee think it very strange, that one man having beene so zealous for the Ceremonies of the Church of England, should so suddenly cry them downe, and sett vp a discipline of his owne for hee hath professed not to follow the discipline, either of the Church of old England, or of new England, nor of Scotland, nor of Geneua, but only the rule of Jesus Christ, which I will neuer receiue from the Authoritie of one mans exposition, much doubting of the truth of his revelations in that behalfe. Tis true that by their instigation, wee haue lately had a great change of our publicke officers amongst vs, and I am confident, at the Arryvall of our London shippe, wee shall haue the tide turne, and the winde blowe the contrary way to their expectacion. Wee are assured of a new Governour from England, and of Sir John Hothams and his Ladies comming hither with mr. Waller, an eminent gent[leman] sometimes of the lower house of Parliament who (wee heare) are bannished to theis Islands, for some offences committed of which I am ignorant, but surely they will not come without ministers, if which doe concurre with ours for their Independant Church, I will beleeue that mr. Edwards was ill advised to write against such a Church, and dedicate it to the parliament, who caused it to bee printed and published,[1] which I haue seene, and so well approue of that I will neuer Joyne with an independant church whilst I liue. I will not trouble yow with their vncharitable censures, against all such as Joyne not with them in their Church covenant. but doe patiently awayt the yssue of mr. whites speeches, when hee began this noveltie vizt. That wee should bee patient and see the end, for if it were of god it would stand if not it would fall, which I lyked well and doe awayt the yssue in that kinde. I will not bee further Troublesome at present, but pray you to accept of 100 lymons and so many orenges, which I haue shipped for yow and as many more with yours for my much esteemde frend Mrs. Ames. Intreating that my bouldness with you herein bee not offensiue to yow: so concludes your very loving frend and ready servant in the Lord

RO: WOOD

DEEPE BAY the 3 of Sept. 1644

[*Endorsed by Governor Winthrop:*] mr. Rog. Wood Bermuda 1644.

---

[1] Thomas Edwards, *Antapologia* (London, 1644).

WILLIAM PYNCHON TO STEPHEN DAY[1]

To his Louinge Fre[ind] Steeuen Day tanteuscu [torn] in Nipnett this deliver

SPRINGEFEILD this 8 of the 8 month 1644

STEEUEN DAY, I received a letter from you by an Indian who saith that his name is Ta-mug-gut: whereas you write for butter and cheese it is not to be had in all our plantation. I spend it as fast as I make it, because I haue much resort and many workmen, which eate it as soone as I haue it and as for porke or bacon I haue none. I haue not yet killd any hoggs; only 2 of our neighbors killd some yesterday: but the weomen say with carriage it will putrifie especially seeing Indians will often linger on such a iorney two dayes: only I procured 3 li. of Bacon of a neighbor which is sent you at 6*li* and 2 li. of tobbacco I procured at another place which cost 18*d* per li. I haue no pepper but I haue sent 2 ounces of ginger at 3*d*   also I haue sent 1*d* in a white paper: sault 1 quart sault 1*d* 1 li. sugar, 20*d* 4 loafes 2*s* 5*d*   The whole is 9*s* and the bagg and basket to put the things in 6*d*: so the Lord blesse you in your proceedings. your euer louinge Frind

WILLIAM PYNCHON

if you doe your businesse by Indians you will find it deerer then to send an Englishman:

As for the blew wampam there is 18*s* of it at 3 a peny but I will not take such as this vnder 6 a peny: I had rather haue white wampam then bad blew at 6 a peny: I will kepe it, because you may redeeme it for white if you thinke good   our riuer will vent of any course blew wampam as the Bay doth:

I spake to this Indian in your behalfe: I tould him that the Gouernor sent you to serch for something in the ground, not for Black lead as they suppose but for some other mettell: I tould him that the Hill of Black lead by Quassink, was not so good as that which lay southward of it neere the cornefeild, where one Namoswhat liues. I suppose it is 5 or 6 miles southward of that place by Quassink.

I tould the Indian also that the Gouernor did send you to see what frindship they would shew you: I tould him also that they might safely trust you for venison or Beanes and wished them to let you haue such things vppon

---

[1] W. 2. 149; 4 *Collections*, VI. 376–378. Stephen Day, the printer, was at this time serving as a mining prospector for John Winthrop, Jr. For an account of the graphite or black lead mining enterprise at Tantiusques (Sturbridge), see George H. Haynes, "'The Tale of the Tantiusques,' An Early Mining Venture in Massachusetts," *Proceedings of the American Antiquarian Society*, Second Series, XIV. 471–497.

Trust. I also shewed him how the trust might be made sure on both sides:
by splitting a sticke in the midle and by making notches: euery notch to
stand for 6*d* in wampam: and that the Gouernor (meaning mr. Wintrop)
would pay you at Boston in the Springe of the yeere Though it were 20
fatham.

he Tould me also that they would sell you beanes and corne and deere as
soone as they tak any deere: but I feare they will make you pay well for it. I
giue for a good doe 2 fatham for a fawne of a yeere 1 fatham: though yet I
haue bought none, nor do not expect any this 14 dayes at sonest.

[*Endorsed by John Winthrop, Jr.:*] mr. Pinchen to mr. Day about an other place
of Blacklead.

DEED OF WEBUCKSHAM AND NONMONSHOT
TO JOHN WINTHROP, JR.[1]

This is to testyfi to hom it may concaren that I weboukchen and nonmonshot haf soulled for and in concedocrachoun of souche goods as I haf resayefid
of Mr. John Winthrope ten miles round about the hills where the netwes has
called blak led and for m[r.] wentrouops pesabell ingoymat of it we bind our
sallefs and heyers for ever to the trew pourforemans of the promisis and to
this I sat my hand this prasount day and dat selled and delefoured in the
prasouns of us 8 day of 8 monthe 1644:

the mark X of WEBOKESHEM
the mak X of NONMONSHOT

wetnas the mark X of PUCHDEAT
wetnas THOMAS KING
    STEVEN DAY
    RICHARD SMITH

DEED OF NODAWAHUNT TO JOHN WINTHROP, JR.[2]

These are to testify that I Nodawahunt owner of the land of Tantiusques
where the blacklead hill is doe sell and give vp, and surrender all my right

[1] American Antiquarian Society. This deed was recorded by the Registrar of Deeds for Hampshire County on June 24, 1752. Webucksham was the sachem of the region round about Tantiusques.

[2] American Antiquarian Society. The body of the document is in the handwriting of John Winthrop, Jr. The deed was recorded by the Registrar of Deeds for Hampshire County on June 24, 1752.
Nodawahunt was the uncle of the sachem Webucksham.

in that place for ten miles to John Winthrop the yonger of Mistick, and doe confirme the former sale of the blacklead hill and the land about it at Tantiusques, by Webucksham unto the said John Winthrop, and am fully satisfied for the same   witnesse my hand this 11th of Nov. 1644.

the marke X of Nodawahunt

Stephen Day
Thomas King
gorgis X marek

[*Endorsed by John Winthrop, Jr.:*] Indians grant of Tantiusques the black lead [*and, in another place:*] Nodawahunt Indians sale of Tantiusques.

AGREEMENT BETWEEN THOMAS KING
AND JOHN WINTHROP, JR.[1]

Nov: 27, 1644

It is agreed this 27th of Novemb: betweene John Winthrop iunior and Thomas King, that the said John Winthrop having delivered vnto the said Tho: King twenty pounds in trading cloth, and wampampeage in hand the day above named The said Thomas doth covenant, and agree with him that he will speedily goe vp with other men to be hired by himselfe the said Thomas vnto Tantiusques the blacklead hill and that he will there imploy himselfe, and his men in working vpon the digging vp of Blacklead for the said John Winthrop, for which he is to have after the rate of fourty shillings for every Tunne to be paid him when he hath digged vp twenty Tunnes of good marchantable blacklead, and put it into an house safe from the Indians, of which the summe of twenty pounds delivered him in hand is to be part of the said payment, and he doth promise that he will worke vpon the digging of the said blacklead, in beginning with digging a trench from the lower part of the hill or the descent therof, and carry the same trench into the hill, that the water may be therby Issued from the Vaines of the blacklead, and wheras the Indians have informed the said John Winthrop of another place not farre thence where there is also blacklead, he doth covenant to goe to see that place and to worke the same for the said John Winthrop at the easiest rate that he can, and if he findeth it easier to worke then that at Tantiusques

---

[1] American Antiquarian Society. The body of the document is in the handwriting of John Winthrop, Jr.

then he will certify the same to the said John Winthrop with all the speede he can.

THOMAS KING
JOHN WINTHROP

Witnes JNO. SMYTH

WILLIAM OSBORNE TO JOHN WINTHROP, JR.[1]

Acounts of disbursements at the Furncace to the 7 of december 1644

	li	s	d
paid per me in Wages and Charges	264	8	3
paid per me to the Carpenters	067	12	9
paid per me to the dam maker besides mr. Wintropp notes	062	7	7
	394	8	7

Receapts per me

of mr. Wintropp	189	1	7
of mr. Tinge	054	9	11
of mr. Webb	049	2	5
of mr. Welles of Roxbury	17	8	7
of mr. Huise	23	0	4
	333	2	10
of mager Sedgwick	29	0	0
	362	2	10

SIR, I haue not charged my selfe withe sack that came last home because I haue not spoke with you about it but you may as you please put it on acounts nor all the Iron geres nailes hinges and other thinges that I had out of the Chamber that went to the vse of the furnace but all other things I haue made Received I price as I sold them as you will find in my book the Augares and all those things I haue put downe Receaud 29*li* of Mager Sedgwicks Counte but I cannot perfeckly tell till I haue a note from his book but I suppose I haue put downe full: I could desire that you and I might compare our books together but this at present I haue here gathered it may at farther vew be better perfected.

[1] W. 1. 158. For Osborne, see Savage, *Genealogical Dictionary*, III. 319.

the debts that are owing are as the were last week or more: but the Smith at Dorchester his bill was not mentioned which is allmost 4*li*.

I charg my selfe with 189*li* 1*s* 7*d*, the 3 Casks of sack not counted.

[WILLIAM OSBORNE]

[*Endorsed by John Winthrop, Jr.:*] Willm. Osburnes account Clerk of the Iron Worke.

GEORGE RICHARDSON TO JOHN WINTHROP[1]

To the Worshipfull John Wenthrop delever this

December the 12 day 1644

MR. WINTHROP, WORTHYE SIR, Youe may plese to take notes that I resaved youre later dated the 11 of this present where in youe rit to me about a sarvent of yours: I never se him to my knowledg tell yester day neder did I know that he wase youre worshipes sarvent till I se him   later my Cosen breadkak did tel me that youe disired me if I did se him to send him over   i did anser him I knoe not of him   he tould me that he had brought on of my pasangeres abord   the nixt morneing I inquared of my peopl for him so he came abord in my Cosenes bot   i tould him he must send him to youe   he wase uere unwilling [*torn*] he tould me it wase for being drunk [*torn*] for taking som aples and som bread [*torn*] he wase puneshed and wase forst to flye [*torn*] him if that ware true I wold spare [*torn*] [t]ill i did heare forder   I do onderstand i [*torn*] a thefe and a lyer so I have cased [*torn*] to be put in Irnes and I will send [*torn*] to youre wor[ship] to moro when our bot [*torn*] vp   sir youe may plese to take notis [*torn*] for the love that I have found from youe [*torn*] I will do anye sarves that I can for youe   those that oner god I shall ever oner   I have resaved som loses by som of this Contrye but I shall never blame youre Worship in the leste   if youe have anye sarves for me youe shall find me fathfoll to youe   if I be from under youre Comand yeat I will do for you as if i ware by youe   if I do looke for right of those that hath don me wrong I hop youe will not be ofended with me in so doing   the god of hevene blese youe in helth if it be his will   I take lefe and reste youres in all umell sarves and Cresten afikshon

GEORGE RICHARDSON

[*Endorsed by Governor Winthrop:*] Captain Richardson about Jo: Googe.

[1] W. 1. 159. For Captain Richardson and his experiences in Boston, see *Journal*, II. 199–200.

BOND OF EMMANUEL DOWNING[1]

Whereas John Winthrop Junr. esqr. hath put me into the Ironworke as an adventurour and given me credit for fiftye pounds therein and given me tyme for the payment of the said 50*li* till my retorne next yeare out of England, if therefore I shall not pay him the said 50*li* before the first day of September next, that then the said 50*li* shalbe and remayne to the sole and proper vse of the said John his heires and assignes for euer. Witnes my hand this 16 of December 1644.

EM: DOWNINGE

Wit[ness] ADAM WINTHROP

POWER OF ATTORNEY[2]

I doe heerby give full power to my Loving Brother Mr. Jo: Winthrop to take vpp twentye pownds due to me from Jo: Read of Braintrye also fortye and one pownds doe from James Oliver in Boston vpon all demandes: and Likewise to take what is due to me from Goodman Milam of Boston: and to make vse of such other estate of mine as it shalbe in my Brother Adams hands of the Triall vioag (during my absence or till further Order) as his occations in the Iron Worke shall require   my Brother Adam hath the Accompt and Bill of James Oliver.

STEPH: WINTHROP

18 10mo 44

[*Endorsed by John Winthrop, Jr.:*] Brother Stevens order for receipt of monyes in his absence.

JOSEPH WELD TO JOHN MYLAM[3]

BROTHER MYLAM, I vnderstand that that 15*li* 10*s* which I turnd ouer to be payd to mr. John winthrop is not yet payd   I pray delay not but make speedy payment of it and I shall remaine yours to vse

JOSEPH WELD

BOSTON the 21 of 10 month 1644

[1] W. 2. 47.
[2] W. 1. 158.
[3] W. 1. 158. For Weld, see Savage, *Genealogical Dictionary*, IV. 457–458; for Mylam, see *ibid.*, III. 259.

JOHN WINTHROP, JR., TO LORD FORBES[1]

Boston in New England: Dec: 23, 1644

Right Honorable, I have desired this bearer my vncle Mr. Downing and my brother to repaire to your honour, to give your lordship information concerning the country of Nova Scotia called Arcadie where my lord Starling once possessed a goodly harbour, and a fort in it called Port Royall, but now that and the whole coast adioyning is in the possession of the french which place of Port Royall is sayd to be yet owing for to the heires of my lord Starling, but is in the hands now of Monseir D'Aulney who hath also by violence dis-posessed an other french lord, Monseir de La Tour, a great freind of the lord Starling, who held his possession of Cape Sable from the grant of my lord Sterling, confirmed vnder the broad seale of Scotland, as he hath shewed vnto vs comming lately to request succour against the violence of the said D'Aulney who hath wholy beat him out of Cape Sable, and seeketh by all meane to disposesse him of St. Johns river the place which he and his prede-cessors have long inioyed to which end he had brought commissions out of france: wherof your honor may be pleased to receive their relation   the English colonies heere would be grat[eful] to have their brethren of Scotland to be their neighbours, in enioying that antient right is conceived they had of Nova Scotia or Acadie and therefore I beseech your lordship to informe by this bearer whether the State of Scotland hath wholy deserted that coun-try, and disclaime all right and interest therein, and vpon what ground, whether only vpon my lord Sterlings surrender, and your lordships advice is humbly desired what course may be iustly taken for the succour and protec-tion of Mon[sieur] La Tour, from the iniury an[d] violence of his french ad-versaries, who doe prosecute with all vehemency against him because the thinke him inclining to the protestant religion. not having further to trouble your honor, I humbly take leave and rest Your lordships humble servant

[John Winthrop]

[*Endorsed by John Winthrop, Jr.:*] Coppy of my letter to the Lord Forbes.

[1] W. 2. 172; 4 *Collections,* vi. 518–519. For Lord Forbes, see 4 *Collections,* vi. 518*n.*

ADDENDA

. .

EMMANUEL DOWNING TO JOHN WINTHROP[1]

13. 6, [1639]

SIR, according your direction I haue advised with mr. Endicott and some others about mr. Pester, with whom I am rather encouradged to proceede, then to breake of; but mr. Hathorne tells me from the Elders of the Bay that yt wilbe a scandall to marry my daughter to such a man that hath noe religion   he sayth that I was stayned in poynt of coveteousnes in mr. Cooks buisines, for demaunding my monie before yt was dew; (wherein mr. Sheapheard having the papers I sent may doe me right.) And now in this match, yt wilbe confirmed in theire opinions that I preferr the world above all, which is farr contrarie to my desire and resolution.

Its well knowne how my daughter hath lost fayre opportunityes, and in those tymes when I had monie at will, to haue spared hir, whereof shee is now verie sensible, and feares that if shee should refuse mr. Pester, shee may stay long ere shee meet with a better, vnles I had more monie for hir then now I can spare. I pray afoard me your Councell herein.

Mr. Norris preached here last saboth to the well likeing of most. some few only founde fault with the weaknes of his voyce. I am in some hope to haue him setle with vs.[2] I heare now my Cow is reasonable well. I pray let hir be sold with the Calfe. I could sell hir if shee were here, but I had rather doe yt there to pay you; I doe want 10 bushells of Rye for seede, which I would sowe 3 weeks or a moneth hence at farthest, for which I must entreat you to lett me haue yt   I entend to send sacks or caske for yt. soe for present I rest yours assured

EM: DOWNINGE

---

[1] W. 2. 38; 4 *Collections*, VI. 73–74.
[2] Edward Norris was ordained minister of the church in Salem on March 18, 1639/40. Weis, *Colonial Clergy*, 152.

JAMES LUXFORD TO JOHN WINTHROP[1]

RIGHT WOR[SHIPFUL], Albeit I haue beene soomtime (gently I confesse) rep[*illegible*] for writinge, yet I cannot forbeare my self, but needs I must bee doinge, my hart and harty affections beinge noe lesse toward your wor[ship], but if possible may bee more then formerly, and albeit I am banished from your presence, that I may not see your face, nor heare your voyce, as at other times, yet cannot the remembrance of your wor[ship] be rooted out of my hart, by any other means then death. I know and doe heare that your wor[ship] is dayly incensed agaynst mee, and informed that my hart is not humbled, but I am still proude and lofty; I could desier from my hart and soule that those that thus judge and report of mee, if they doe it out of pitty and tendernesse, as wishinge my euerlastinge good, that as they cannot but know it is not in the power of the most mightyest prince in the world, to breake a hard hart, or to humble a proud hart either by power or policy; but it is the Lord alone that must doe it; that such would joyne with mee in prayer and suplication to the Almighty, that he would take the woorke in hand, for he is able to bringe it to passe; then should I haue great cause to looue them and to pray for them, and to prayse god that should send mee such gratious helpe agaynst that sinn that hath euer beene to mighty for mee; I know ther is none while wee cary this body about with vs that is wholy freed, thought the Lord hath giuen to soome more power to preuayle, not that the stronge should despise the weake, or that he that hath ouercoome should stand affarr of and laugh at him that is yet in hott fight, and like to goe to the woorst: but the Lord who doth it in part, for that end looketh that such should coome forth and helpe the Lord agaynst the mighty, consideringe that if they bee deliuered indeed, that it was not by themselues or by there owne power, but by the power of the Lord; but if they be otherwise minded, and that ther compleynts hearin tend to soome end of ther owne, I say noe more but as Steuen: The good lord pardon them. They know not what they doo. this I am suer of that I find it very hard to bringe downe my hart to that low pitch that I know it must be brought to before the Lord vouchsafe to make his abode with mee. blessed be his name for it, he is not altogether a stranger to my poore soule, but yet as a stranger he giueth mee Coomfort, and an asured expectation of his euerlasting presence with mee, in that hee coomes now and maketh knowen to mee what is the Cause of his absence, and why he is soe strange, and sheweth mee those disorders in my soule which

[1] W. 4. 53; 5 *Collections*, I. 142–147.

I neuer dremed of, which now I see to be such, that while I harbored such
base inmates it was not likely that euer the Lord should coome neare mee in
mercy, and that hee did not coome in euerlastinge Judgment agaynst mee
and giue mee the reward of my doings I cannot but admier exceedingly.
truly, I speke the truth in Christ I ly not; the Lord hath shewed mee such
lothsoome abomynations which I neuer before minded, that haue brought
mee to a secret lothinge of my selfe, and admiration at the bowels of Compassion in the Almighty, that he had not for euer loathed mee: secrets as close
as those, which the Lord shewed to Esekell, when he led him from Chamber
to Chamber; and sayd seest thou these, see yet greter; but because it would be
to tedyous to your wor[ship] to read it I should enter into particulers, and
shew the manner of gods dealinge with mee and any woork of gods grace
on my soule with the manner and seuerall degrees of late times; besides my
person beinge brought into soome Contempt with your wor[ship] I might
be suspected to disemble with you, which thinge farr be it fromm mee:
neither cann it stand with tru grace, for if Dauid would not admitt of a deceitfull person, I am suer dauids god, by whome I looke for saluation will
not; noe vncleane thinge shall dwell with him; but I shall be tedyous; it hath
beene tould mee, that great obiections wear agenst mee in the bay: for that I
liued in an ordinary: but I haue great Cause to feare that they who weare
troubled at that, had rather haue heard of a woorse Condition, that either I
had not liued, or that I had liued amonge the Indyans. I would not willinge
speak soe rashly without soome ground, for soome I know thought I cease to
name them now, did what in them lay to haue hindered my abode heare; for
noe Cause I know that I haue giuen them; but I prayse god I can hartely
pray for them, knowinge that he that is with mee is stronger then he that is
with them while they thus continue thought a member of a Congregation:
perhaps the god whome I hope they serue, doth not allow of it nor good men
when they see it.

these men might a little consider what dauid was putt to in the time of his
strayts, soometime to liue amonge the enemyes of god and his people; soometime in houlds, in woods, with a madd and wiked crud. had they beene then
in Saules Court, or that they might haue coome soe famylyarly to the Kinge,
as they can coome to your wor[ship] and to the Gouerner, how would they
haue incensed the Kings wrath, (as noe question many did as apears by that
of Doegg) against his faithfull and loyall subiect whose hart was vpright with
god, and most true to his prince; thought despised of the Kinge and almost all
his subiects as on not fitt to liue, while yet ther was noe euill found in him why
they should doe this; They know it standeth little otherwise with me and I

haue great Cause to blesse god for that I haue foode; was it not a mercy to Elyah when poore man he fled for his life, was in the wildernesse wher noe succor was to be had; that the Lord commanded the rauens to feed him; Creatures by nature, more like to pray vppon him, and to pick out his eyes, then to feed him, yet when by gods prouidence they brought him meat, he tooke it thankfully, as from the hands of god; and thereby doubtlesse was moore confirmed of gods fatherly Care of him, and faithfulnesse to him that God would not forsake him; I must needs confesse that I haue made this vse of it what euer Construction they make, for when I came hither I found none but did pitty mee, and seemed to be sory for mee, but if this man had not fed me I might haue fed on ther pitty till I dyed; soome which I thought would haue beene helpfull; haue contented themselues, only with this word pitty   fore mr. wislo[1] I thank him, not longe before he came into the Baye, bad mee coome to his house a month or two, and welcoome, for which I gaue him great thanks, rather desiringe that he would if it might be deuise soome way how I might in gods way bee doinge soomthinge, wherby soom glory might coome to god and soome benefitt to soome, rather than to liue like a droone to suck out the hony, which others brought in, protestinge in truth, that rather then I would liue Idly, I would be content to be the town Swinheard, if it would be accepted, but noe man did any way put forth his hand to helpe me, noe not my great frend mr. Padde; saue that the Lord stirred vp mr. Browne whoe did not only pitty mee, but had mee to his house, kept me with him [illegible] dayes, and minded my Condition, by whose meanes, I haue now taken a farme, wheron by the helpe of god I may liue by my labor; my request is now to renue my former sute with your wor[ship] whom I haue euer found redy to helpe mee, that I may haue that liberty to coome into the bay partly to gett a man, partly to try the word of those which haue promised to helpe me if once I setled; for I will asuer your wor[ship] that I beginn now wholy on my portion, which is sufficient   I know that he is able if he will to helpe mee and I haue my Confidence in him that in the lawfull vse of meanes he will not be wantinge; I am else a poore beginner as euer was. I haue neither pott nor pann, spoone nor trencher, bed nor blankett, in a woord nothinge, but the Lord alone; I beseech your wor[ship] to procure me this fauour if it may bee; if I offend the law let mee suffer what you will, this only, which is noe offense, but as nature binds mee, and noe law of god or man doth deny mee, I shall desier in soom place to see my children; but for ther mother, thought I shall while I haue life care for hir as my deare Child, yett

---

[1] Edward Winslow. Cf. his letter to Governor Winthrop, October 10, 1640 (pages 291–292, above).

to see hir, tendeth but to the farther brekinge of my hart neither doe I desier to doe any thinge but what may coomfort hir, and to see mee cannot. pitty my Condition I beeseech you; If your wor[ship] weare suerly perswaded with what hart I write, it may be you would haue pitty on mee, and helpe mee, at lest with your prayers; it is vnknown to your wor[ship] how it is with mee, not in regard of any outward Calamyty I speake in regard that I want meat or drink or the like; but what it is the Lord knoweth. I cease to speake any more. if your wor[ship] be pleased grant me this request; I shall acknowledge my selfe bond to you for it as for all other. Small kindnesse now from your wor[ship] seeme greate and I can prise them; I desier that I may heare from your wor[ship] by this bearer, and how my worthy mystres, with all yours are, willinge to tender life and limm in gods way for you or yours if euer god call me to it   in the meane time I shall remayne in all humble submission Your wor[ship's] to be commanded

JAMES LUXFORD

I would be glad to heare how it is with them at Kambridge; I must needs hearafter if I liue haue on of my children with mee   it would be soom Coomfort to my declininge ould age   It may be soome time it might stopp the streame of tears and cause me to reioyce in gods blessinge.

Ther is noe Condemnation to them that are in Christ Jesus.

[*Endorsed by Governor Winthrop:*] James Luxford, from Plimo[uth] (7) 11 40.

JOHN HAYNES TO JOHN WINTHROP[1]

To the Right Worshipful, his much honoured Friend, John Winthrop, Esq.
Governour of the Jurisdiction of the Mattatusetts these present

WORTHY SIR, I was right glad of any opportunity of hearing from you in this silent time of winter. The messenger you sent by only left your letter at Agawam, or Springfield, from whence it came to my hands; but the party himself was not yet with me, but if he repairs to me, I shall follow your advice in that thing you mentioned concerning Anogamey; for he is not any confederate friend of ours. That the express, that Onkus should take wampham of

[1] Connecticut State Library; 3 *Collections*, I. 229–231. At the time this volume was in preparation, the original manuscript of this letter was, due to the exigencies of wartime, not available for examination. The text is therefore given here as it appears in 3 *Collections*, I.

the Narragansetts for Myantonimo's ransom,[1] (which I have understood also from Mr. Eaton,) I cannot but concur with you, if really it appears so, equity and justice calls for no less; but this I must *needs* say, that this very thing was cast abroad by some Indians of the Narragansett party, and myself coming to understand it somewhat before Myantonimo his death, both myself and Capt. Mason strictly examined Onkus concerning the matter, acquainting him with what we heard. He utterly denied, that he had taken wampham or any other thing upon any such terms. He confessed, indeed, he had wampham and other things given him and his brother freely; and he as freely promised to bring him to the English, which he said he had performed; and this I also know, that the same day that Myantonimo was delivered into our hands and imprisoned, that Onkus and his brother, with many of their men, were at that place where he was committed, myself and Capt. Mason then present also. Onkus desired him to speak before us all; and this Myantonimo did then utter and confess, that the Mohegan sachems had dealt nobly with him in sparing his life, when they took him, and performing their promise in bringing him to the English, (a thing the like he never knew or heard of, that so great a sachem should be so dealt withal,) although he himself pressed it upon them, again and again, (as they all could witness,) to slay him; but they said, No, but you shall be carried to the English; which therefore, if it should prove other upon due trial, I should marvel much; for his own confession, I should think, goes far in the case; but I leave it to further consideration and better judgments. I have not since spoke with him since I received that from you, but I shall by the first opportunity. The Narragansetts, I fear, notwithstanding their fair promises and pretences, will not sit down quiet, as you suppose. (Mr. Pincheon thinks the same also with me,) from whom I lately heard.

The evidence to the contrary are these two, which is manifestly known. First; they have sent a very great present to the Mowhawkes. Secondly; those Pequots, that were under the Niantick and Narragansett sachems, have lately slain a sachem squa that belonged to Onkus. He sent lately a messenger to us to signify the same, desiring he may have the aid of the English against them, as conceiving, by what was read to him, that was agreed upon and sent for that purpose from the commissioners, gave him hope of aid, if the Narragansetts should fall upon him again; which he desired yourself and the rest of the English sachems should be made acquainted withal, that he might understand their pleasure. You may be pleased to return your answer, for I promised to acquaint you with it. There is late news by a vessel that came to the Dutch, and from them to New Haven, by Mr. Allerton. The substance this; that there

---

[1] For Winthrop's account of Miantunnomoh's capture and death, see *Journal*, II. 134–136.

hath been a great battle betwixt the king's and parliament's forces, (since that of Newbery,) at Ailsborow in Buckinghamshire, wherein the parliament forces prevailed, pursuing their victory with very great slaughter of the adverse party. Also, that the fleet is again out under that noble Earl of Warwick, who came lately into the harbour of some great town held by the contrary party full sail with his fleet, both by block-houses and castles, and lands his men, takes the town, sets many prisoners at liberty. (The town's name I heard not.) I leave the truth of the report to be judged of by you, only latest letters give some probable conjectures of the possibility thereof. It was said, there was much sadness in Holland about it; but we received no letters from thence. I am sorry to hear of Mr. Dudley his cause of sorrow and heaviness. I shall add no more, only due respect to yourself; mine with my wife's to Mrs. Winthrop; desiring to be remembered also to Mr. Dudley, Mr. Cotton, Mr. Wilson, I rest yours, to his power

Jo. Haynes

Hartford, the 17th 11, '43[/44]

In the catalogue sent to Mr. Eaton, etc. some of those things Myantonimo confessed he freely gave him; other he took with him, when he apprehended him as due prize. For the remainder, we shall hear what Onkus can say to it, etc.

[CHARLES?] NEWTON TO JOHN WINTHROP[1]

To the Right worshipf[u]l and my most kinde and much honoured good Frende Mr. Winthrope Governor of New Eng. att his house in Boston deliver

Worthy Sir, For my partt, I haue ever acknowledged, ther was iust offence and soe iust cause and call, to the place wher the Lord hath pitched your selfe and many other worthies, and whatt som wold not grant yet now they are convinced and constraynd to confess digitum Dei in your passing from vs. the Lord deliver your Country from that owre of temptation that is com vppon vs; and we know we shall and doe fare the better for your prayers. the Lord recompence them into your and the Bosom of yours for ever.

Sir I have a son[2] I hope alive in your land. he is the nephew of my worthy Brother mr. Edward Allen latly disceasd and I doe most humbly thanke your worship for your Love to him and lovinge wife advice giuen him in his busines

---

[1] W. 15. 123. This is believed to be the Charles Newton who was a woolen draper of Groton, England. *Winthrop Papers,* I. 274*n.*
[2] John Newton.

about his vncles will[1]   I know you are most able to doe it and I know God
hath giuen you a publique spiritt, and therfore most wiling   I know you are
a Just Judge and your selfe and magistrats are famous for doinge rigt to all
with Justice: if it had bine soe in this our Kingdom we had stood to this day
Noble Sir I shall thinke my selfe much bound to you and to your family to
take notice of my poore Boy, and I shall thinke my selfe happy if in any respect, he may be servicable to your selfe or place wher he lives and I thanke
God who gaue me him, and only him, that he gaue me and him a minde and
him a call to that place wher he is, and where he hath receivd so much good
and God hath soe blessd him   I may com to him   I doe not desire he shold
returne to me.

Sir my good Lady Myldmay and her children are in health, her Sonn the
Captane in the North in health and valiant in the Cause   I pray God preserve him. I pray God send yours hom to you in safty   o how much happier
are you then we   the Lord kepe you alsoe still and soe with my most humble
respects to your selfe to good mrs. Winthrope: I committ you to the protection of Almighty God: and rest, your worships assured

NEWTON

Feb: 22, 1643[/44]

---

[1] See *Suffolk Deeds*, I. 34.

INDEX

NOTE

Places are in Massachusetts unless otherwise stated.

Names of ships are grouped under the heading "Ships, shipbuilding, etc."

Names of individual Indians are grouped under the heading "Indians."

Names of Indian tribes are grouped under the heading "Indians, tribes."

INDEX

ACADIA. *See* Nova Scotia.

Adams, Thomas, 204.

Adams, William, navigator, 158.

Agamenticus (Accomenticus). *See* York, Me.

Agawam. *See* Ipswich; Springfield.

Alberts, Jan, shipmaster, 356, 356*n*.

Alchemy, 122; books on, 333, 334–338.

Alexander, Sir William, Earl of Stirling (*d.* 1640), 284*n.*, 501.

Alger (Algar), Andrew, 438.

Allen, ——, 342.

Allen, Rev. John (*d.* 1671), 287.

Allen, John, of Springfield, estate of, 296, 331*n*.

Allen, Richard, deposition, 127.

Allen, Thomas, 413.

Allen, Walter, right to reside in Newbury questioned, 97–98.

Allerton, Isaac, 304, 394, 507.

Alley, ——, 324.

Alleyn (Allen), Edward, 508.

Allyn (Allen), Matthew, 31, 35; bond to John Hill, 255, 255*n.*, 293.

Ames, Joan (Fletcher), 109, 109*n.*, 392, 494.

Ames, Ruth, Hugh Peter's relations with, 109, 109*n.*

Ames, Rev. William, 109*n.*

Andover (Cochichawick, Quichichacke, Quichichchek, Quichichuick, Qutcthicqute), 163, 164, 222, 327–328.

Andrews (Andros), ——, haberdasher, of London, 93.

Andrews (Androwes), Joseph, 91.

Andrews, Richard, merchant, of London, 202; debt of Plymouth Colony to, 129–131, 257, 437; gift for charity in Massachusetts, 129–131, 440; letter to Gov. Winthrop, 129–131.

Angier, Edmund, 413.

Animals, cattle (cows, etc.), 65, 66, 67, 76, 123, 124, 125, 129–130, 141, 147, 148, 149, 161, 173, 202, 209, 215, 232, 233, 236*n.*, 239, 254, 257, 261, 262, 274*n.*, 276, 279, 280, 282, 294, 312, 325, 394, 489, 492, 502; deer, 492, 496; dogs, 281 (beagle); 280; foxes, 492; goats, 147, 215, 236, 295; horses, 67, 161; otters, 155, 204, 206; sheep, 145; swine, 7, 236, 349, 350, 351, 495; wolves, 280, 325, 492.

Anker (Anchor), Thomas, 316.

Antinomian controversy, 8–9, 9*n.*, 14*n.*, 259*n.*, 414–415, 415*n.*; permission to Coddington and others to leave Massachusetts, 14–15; acknowledgment of Samuel Wilbur, remonstrant, 121–122. *See also* Wheelwright, John.

Apothecaries, 55, 189*n. See also* Cooke, Robert.

Apples. *See* Fruit.

Apprentices. *See* Servants.

Aquidneck. *See* Rhode Island.

Arbitration and award, 294–295, 299, 397.

Armitage, Joseph, 397.

Arms and ammunition, 285; gunpowder, 141, 239; shot, 135.

Arnold, Benedict, letters to Gov. Winthrop, 431–433, 441–443.

Arnold, William, 443; charges against, by Roger Williams, 61.

Arresby, Richard, servant, arbitration between, and Mr. Norton, 294–295.

Articles of Confederation. *See* New England Confederation.

Arundel, Earl of. *See* Howard, Thomas.

Aspinwall, William, 17, 416; letter to Gov. Winthrop, 259–260.

Astwood, James, 414.

Atkins, Thomas, M.P., 248.

Atwood, Ann, wife of John, 437.

Atwood, John, 257, 437–438.

Audley, Edmund, appointed administrator of Francis Dent's estate, 95.

Audley, John, 124.

Augers. *See* Tools.

Aulnay (Dony) de Charnisay, Charles de Menou, Sieur d', rivalry between, and La Tour, 394–395, 396, 397–401, 402–410, 501.

Axes. *See* Tools.

Axtell, Nathaniel, 414.

Ayers (Ayres), ——, of Watertown, 97, 98.

Aysheforde, Thomas, 255.

BABB, Thomas, shipmaster, 10, 159, 167, 201, 224.

Bachiler, Rev. Stephen, letters to John Winthrop, Jr., 69–70, Margaret Winthrop, 144–145, Gov. Winthrop and the elders of the Boston Church, 446–449, Gov. Winthrop, 457–459.

Bacon, Francis, of Barham, England, letter to Gov. Winthrop, 228.

Bacon. *See* Food.

Baker, John, 13, 128, 143, 318, 438.

Baker, Walter, 145.

Baker, William, of Plymouth, 7, 15, 31, 35.

Ball, ——, of Newbury, 128.

Ballard, ——, 46.

Ballard, William, 87.

Barley. *See* Grain.

Barnardiston (Bampston, Barnston, Bramstone), Sir Nathaniel, 217, 217*n.*; letters to Gov. Winthrop, 217–218; offers Gov. Winthrop financial assistance, 243, 250.